Health Psychology

Health Psychology

A Textbook

FOURTH EDITION

Jane Ogden

Open University Press

Open University Press
McGraw-Hill Education
McGraw-Hill House
Shoppenhangers Road
Maidenhead
Berkshire
England
SL6 2QL

email: enquiries@openup.co.uk
world wide web: www.openup.co.uk

and Two Penn Plaza, New York, NY 10121-2289, USA

First published 2007

A catalogue record of this book is available from the British Library

ISBN-13: 978 0 335 22263 6 (pb) 978 0 335 22264 3 (hb)
ISBN-10: 0 335 22263 3 (pb) 0 335 22264 1 (hb)

Library of Congress Cataloging-in-Publication Data
CIP data applied for

Typeset by Wearset Ltd, Boldon, Tyne and Wear
Printed and bound in Spain by Mateu Cromo Artes Graficas

The *McGraw·Hill* Companies

Brief table of contents

Detailed table of contents   vi
List of figures and tables   x
List of abbreviations   xii
Preface to the fourth edition   xv
Guided tour   xxv
Technology to enhance learning and teaching   xxix
Acknowledgements   xxxiii

1   An introduction to health psychology   1
2   Health beliefs   13
3   Illness cognitions   47
4   Health professional – patient communication and the role of health
    beliefs   73
5   Smoking and alcohol use   95
6   Eating behaviour   127
7   Exercise   157
8   Sex   173
9   Screening   199
10 Stress   221
11 Stress and illness   239
12 Pain   271
13 Placebos and the interrelationship among beliefs, behaviour and
    health   293
14 HIV and cancer: psychology throughout the course of illness (1)   311
15 Obesity and coronary heart disease: psychology throughout the course
    of illness (2)   333
16 Women's health issues   365
17 Measuring health status: from mortality rates to quality of life   393
18 The assumptions of health psychology   405

Methodology glossary   409
References   411
Index   477

Detailed table of contents

List of figures and tables	x
List of abbreviations	xii
Preface to the fourth edition	xv
Guided tour	xxv
Technology to enhance learning and teaching	xxix
Acknowledgements	xxxiii

1 An introduction to health psychology — 1
Chapter overview — 1
The background to health psychology — 1
What is the biomedical model? — 2
The twentieth century — 2
What are the aims of health psychology? — 5
What is the future of health psychology? — 6
What are the aims of this book? — 7
The contents of this book — 8
The structure of this book — 9
Questions — 10
For discussion — 10
Further reading — 10

2 Health beliefs — 13
Chapter overview — 13
What are health behaviours? — 13
Why study health behaviours? — 14
Lay theories about health — 17
Predicting health behaviours — 17
Some problems with . . . health beliefs research — 23
Cognition models — 23
Focus on research 2.1: Testing a theory – predicting sexual behaviour — 28
Social cognition models — 29
Problems with the models — 34
To conclude — 43
Questions — 43
For discussion — 43
Assumptions in health psychology — 44
Further reading — 44

3 Illness cognitions — 47
Chapter overview — 47
What does it mean to be healthy? — 47
What does it mean to be ill? — 49
What are illness cognitions? — 49
Some problems with . . . illness cognitions research — 52

Leventhal's self-regulatory model of illness cognitions — 52
Why is the model called self-regulatory? — 54
Focus on research 3.1: Testing a theory – illness representations and behavioural outcomes — 55
Stage 1: Interpretation — 56
Stage 2: Coping — 60
The positive interpretation of illness — 67
Using the self-regulatory model to predict outcomes — 67
To conclude — 71
Questions — 71
For discussion — 71
Assumptions in health psychology — 71
Further reading — 72

4 Health professional–patient communication and the role of health beliefs — 73
Chapter overview — 73
What is compliance? — 74
Predicting whether patients are compliant: the work of Ley — 74
How can compliance be improved? — 76
Focus on research 4.1: Testing a theory – patient satisfaction — 77
The wider role of information in illness — 79
Some problems with . . . communication research — 80
The role of knowledge in health professional–patient communication — 81
The problem of doctor variability — 82
To conclude — 92
Questions — 92
For discussion — 92
Assumptions in health psychology — 93
Further reading — 93

5 Smoking and alcohol use — 95
Chapter overview — 95
Who smokes? — 95
Who drinks? — 96
Health implications of smoking and alcohol use — 98
What is an addiction? — 100
Historical changes in attitude and theoretical approach — 100

What is the second disease concept? 102
Problems with a disease model of
addiction 103
What is the social learning
perspective? 104
Some problems with . . . smoking and
alcohol research 106
The stages of substance use 106
Stages 1 and 2: Initiating and
maintaining an addictive behaviour 107
Stage 3: The cessation of an addictive
behaviour 109
Focus on research 5.1: Testing a
theory – stages of smoking cessation 111
Interventions to promote cessation 112
Focus on research 5.2: Putting theory
into practice – worksite smoking ban 118
Stage 4: Relapse in smoking and
drinking 120
A cross-addictive behaviour
perspective 122
To conclude 125
Questions 125
For discussion 125
Assumptions in health psychology 126
Further reading 126

6 Eating behaviour 127
Chapter overview 127
What is a healthy diet? 127
How does diet affect health? 129
Who eats a healthy diet? 129
Developmental models of eating
behaviour 130
Cognitive models of eating behaviour 137
Some problems with . . . eating
research 140
A weight concern model of eating
behaviour 140
The causes of body dissatisfaction 141
Social factors 141
Psychological factors 143
Dieting 145
Focus on research 6.1: Testing a
theory – overeating as a rebellion 153
To conclude 156
Questions 156
For discussion 156
Further reading 156

7 Exercise 157
Chapter overview 157
Developing the contemporary
concern with exercise behaviour 157
What is exercise? 158
Who exercises? 158

Some problems with . . . exercise
research 159
Why exercise? 159
Focus on research 7.1: Testing a
theory – exercise and mood 163
What factors predict exercise? 164
Focus on research 7.2: Testing a
theory – predicting exercise 169
Exercise relapse 170
To conclude 171
Questions 171
For discussion 171
Assumptions in health psychology 171
Further reading 172

8 Sex 173
Chapter overview 173
Developing the contemporary
research perspectives on sex 173
Some problems with . . . sex research 182
Sex as a risk in the context of
STDs/HIV and AIDS 182
Focus on research 8.1: Testing a
theory – the situation and
condom use 189
The broader social context 191
To conclude 196
Questions 196
For discussion 196
Assumptions in health psychology 197
Further reading 197

9 Screening 199
Chapter overview 199
What is screening? 199
The history of the screening ethos 200
Screening as a useful tool 201
Guidelines for screening 202
Psychological predictors of the
uptake of screening 202
Some problems with . . . screening
research 203
Focus on research 9.1: Testing a
theory – predicting screening 206
Screening as problematic 208
To conclude 218
Questions 218
For discussion 218
Assumptions in health psychology 218
Further reading 219

10 Stress 221
Chapter overview 221
What is stress? 221
The development of stress models 222
A role for psychological factors in
stress 225

Some problems with . . . stress
research   228
Stress and changes in physiology   228
Measuring stress   230
Focus on research 10.1: Putting
theory into practice   233
The interaction between psychological
and physiological aspects of stress   234
To conclude   236
Questions   236
For discussion   236
Assumptions in health psychology   236
Further reading   237

11 Stress and illness   239
Chapter overview   239
Does stress cause illness?   239
Stress and changes in behaviour   241
Stress and changes in physiology   244
Individual variability in the
stress–illness link   245
Psychoneuroimmunology   246
Some problems with . . . stress and
illness research   252
The impact of chronic stress   252
Which factors moderate the
stress–illness link?   255
Coping   255
Social support   259
Focus on research 11.1: Testing a
theory – social support and health   261
Personality   262
Control   264
Control and social support in stress
and illness   266
To conclude   268
Questions   268
For discussion   268
Assumptions in health psychology   268
Further reading   269

12 Pain   271
Chapter overview   271
What is pain?   271
Early pain theories – pain as a
sensation   272
Including psychology in theories of
pain   272
The gate control theory of pain   273
Some problems with . . . pain research   275
The role of psychosocial factors in
pain perception   276
Subjective–affective–cognitive
processes   276
Focus on research 12.1: The experience
of pain   281

The role of psychology in pain
treatment   282
Focus on research 12.2: Putting theory
into practice – treating chronic pain   285
The outcome of pain treatment and
management: a role for pain
acceptance?   288
Measuring pain   289
To conclude   290
Questions   290
For discussion   290
Assumptions in health psychology   291
Further reading   291

13 Placebos and the interrelationship
among beliefs, behaviour and health   293
Chapter overview   293
What is a placebo?   294
A history of inert treatments   294
How do placebos work?   295
Some problems with . . . placebo
research   299
The central role of patient
expectations   299
Cognitive dissonance theory   300
Focus on research 13.1: Testing a
theory – 'doing as you're told' as a
placebo   301
The role of placebo effects in health
psychology   306
To conclude   309
Questions   309
For discussion   309
Assumptions in health psychology   310
Further reading   310

14 HIV and cancer: psychology
throughout the course of illness (1)   311
Chapter overview   311
HIV and AIDS   311
The role of psychology in the study
of HIV   313
Some problems with . . . HIV and
cancer research   319
Focus on research 14.1: Testing a
theory – psychology and immune
functioning   320
Cancer   322
Focus on research 14.2: Putting theory
into practice – treating cancer
symptoms   328
To conclude   331
Questions   331
For discussion   331
Assumptions in health psychology   331
Further reading   332

15 Obesity and coronary heart disease: psychology throughout the course of illness (2)   333
Chapter overview   333
Obesity   333
What is obesity?   334
How common is obesity?   336
What are the problems with obesity?   336
What causes obesity?   337
Some problems with . . . obesity and CHD research   345
Obesity treatment   346
Should obesity be treated at all?   348
Conclusion   352
Coronary heart disease (CHD)   353
Focus on research 15.1: Testing a theory – the consequences of disease   356
To conclude   362
Questions   362
For discussion   362
Assumptions in health psychology   362
Further reading   363

16 Women's health issues   365
Chapter overview   365
Miscarriage   365
Termination of pregnancy   369
Some problems with . . . women's health research   376
Pregnancy and birth   377
The transition into motherhood   380
Focus on research 16.1: Exploring experience – the transition into motherhood   382
Problems with research exploring pregnancy and birth   383
The menopause   384

To conclude   391
Questions   391
For discussion   391
Assumptions in health psychology   391
Further reading   392

17 Measuring health status: from mortality rates to quality of life   393
Chapter overview   393
Mortality rates   393
Morbidity rates   394
Measures of functioning   394
Subjective health status   394
What is quality of life?   395
Focus on research 17.1: Putting theory into practice – evaluating hip replacement surgery   398
A shift in perspective   400
Using quality of life in research   400
Some problems with . . . health status research   401
To conclude   403
Questions   403
For discussion   403
Assumptions in health psychology   403
Further reading   404

18 The assumptions of health psychology   405
Chapter overview   405
The assumptions of health psychology   405
Studying a discipline   407
Further reading   408

Methodology glossary   409
References   411
Index   477

List of figures and tables

Figures

1.1 The biopsychosocial model of health and illness   *4*

1.2 Psychology and health: direct and indirect pathways   *5*

2.1 Decline in mortality from tuberculosis   *15*

2.2 The effect of smoking on increase in expectation of life: males, 1838–1970   *16*

2.3 Basics of the health belief model   *24*

2.4 Basics of the protection motivation theory   *27*

2.5 Basics of the theory of reasoned action   *30*

2.6 Basics of the theory of planned behaviour   *31*

2.7 The health action process approach   *32*

3.1 Leventhal's self-regulatory model of illness behaviour   *53*

3.2 Coping with the crisis of illness   *62*

4.1 Ley's model of compliance   *74*

4.2 A simplified model of problem solving   *83*

4.3 Diagnosis as a form of problem solving   *84*

5.1 Changes in smoking, 1974–2004   *96*

5.2 Current smokers, ex-smokers and non-smokers by sex, 1972–92   *97*

5.3 Adults drinking more than the recommended guidelines on at least one day last week, by age and sex, 2004 (GB)   *97*

5.4 Deaths attributable to smoking   *98*

5.5 Alcohol-related deaths in the UK since 1991   *99*

5.6 The stages of substance use   *106*

5.7 Relapse curves for individuals treated for heroin, smoking and alcohol addiction   *120*

5.8 The relapse process   *121*

5.9 Relapse prevention intervention strategies   *122*

6.1 The balance of good health   *128*

6.2 A developmental, cognitive and weight concern model of eating behaviour   *130*

6.3 Social eating   *132*

6.4 Measuring body dissatisfaction   *141*

6.5 Overeating in dieters in the laboratory   *146*

6.6 A boundary model explanation of overeating in dieters   *148*

6.7 A comparison of the boundaries for different types of eaters   *148*

6.8 The 'what the hell' effect as a form of relapse   *151*

6.9 From dieting to overeating   *152*

7.1 Participation in sport in the past 12 months (2003)   *159*

7.2 Mortality and fitness levels in individuals with a BMI > 25.4   *161*

8.1 Percentage using no contraception at first intercourse, by age at first intercourse   *177*

8.2 Contraception use at first intercourse in those aged 16–24   *177*

8.3 Changes in the use of condoms as the usual method of contraception by age, 1983–91   *184*

9.1 Costs per potential cancer prevented for different screening policies   *212*

10.1 Selye's three-stage general adaptation syndrome   222
10.2 The role of appraisal in stress   226
10.3 Stress and changes in physiology   229
10.4 The interaction between psychological and physiological aspects of stress   235
11.1 Chronic/acute model of stress–illness link   240
11.2 Stress-diathesis model   241
11.3 The stress–illness link: physiological moderators   246
11.4 The stress–illness link: psychological moderators   255
11.5 Incidence of CHD by number of children: the role of work stress on illness in women   266
12.1 The gate control theory of pain   273
12.2 Psychosocial aspects of pain   276
12.3 Psychology and pain treatment   283
13.1 The central role of patient expectations in placebo effects   300
13.2 Totman's cognitive dissonance theory of placebo effects   304
13.3 The interrelationship between beliefs, behaviour and health   306
14.1 The potential role of psychology in HIV   314
14.2 The potential role of psychology in cancer   323
15.1 Potential role of psychology in obesity   334
15.2 Grades of obesity by height and weight   335
15.3 Relationship between BMI and mortality   337
15.4 Changes in physical activity and obesity   341
15.5 Changes in food intake from the 1950s to the 1990s   342
15.6 Changes in calorie consumption and obesity   343
15.7 The potential role of psychology in CHD   353
16.1 Rates of miscarriage that require a hospital stay vary by age of mother   368
16.2 Abortion rate in England and Wales by age, 2005   370
16.3 Worldwide abortion rates   371
16.4 Worldwide rates of unsafe abortions   371
16.5 Home birth rates 1961–2004 in the UK   378
16.6 The frequency and severity of menopausal symptoms   385
16.7 The menopause as a biopsychosocial event   386
17.1 A shift in perspective in measuring health   399

Tables

3.1 Adaptive tasks   63
3.2 Coping tasks   64

List of abbreviations

ADL	activity of daily living
AIDS	acquired immune deficiency syndrome
APT	adjuvant psychological therapy
AVE	abstinence violation effect
BDI	Beck depression inventory
BMI	body mass index
BSE	breast self-examination
CAD	coronary artery disease
CAM	complementary and alternative medicines
CBSM	cognitive behavioural stress management
CBT	cognitive behavioural therapy
CFQ	child feeding questionnaire
CHD	coronary heart disease
CIN	cervical intraepithelial neoplasia
CISQ	condom influence strategy questionnaire
CMV	cytomegalovirus
COPD	chronic obstructive pulmonary disease
CR	conditioned response
CS	conditioned stimulus
D&C	dilatation and curettage
DAFNE	dose adjustment for normal eating
DEBQ	Dutch eating behaviour questionnaire
DVT	deep vein thrombosis
ERPC	evacuation of the retained products of conception
FAP	familial adenomatous polyposis
FH	familial hypercholesterolaemia
GAS	general adaptation syndrome
GCT	gate control theory
CHQ	general health questionnaire
GSR	galvanic skin response
HAART	highly active anti-retroviral therapy
HADS	hospital anxiety and depression scale
HAPA	health action process approach
HBM	health belief model
HPA	hypothalamic-pituitary-adrenocorticol
HRT	hormone replacement therapy
IPA	interpretative phenomenological analysis
IPQ	illness perception questionnaire
IPQR	revised version of illness perception questionnaire
LISRES	life stressors and social resources inventory
MAT	medication adherence training
MHLC	multidimensional health locus of control
MI	myocardial infarction

MPQ	McGill pain questionnaire
MACS	Multi Centre AIDS Cohort Study
NHP	Nottingham health profile
NHS	National Health Service
NKCC	natural killer cell cytotoxicity
PDA	personal digital assistant
PFSQ	parental feeding style questionnaire
PMT	protection motivation theory
PSE	present state examination
PSS	perceived stress scale
RCT	random controlled trial
SEIQoL	schedule for the individual quality of life
SES	socio-economic status
SEU	subjective expected utility
SIP	sickness impact profile
SLQ	silver lining questionnaire
SOS	Swedish Obese Subjects study
SRE	schedule of recent experiences
SRRS	social readjustment rating scale
STD	sexually transmitted diseases
TOP	termination of pregnancy
TPB	theory of planned behaviour
TRA	theory of reasoned action
UR	unconditioned response
US	unconditional stimulus
WHO	World Health Organization
WRAP	Women, Risk and AIDS Project

Why I first wrote this book

I first wrote this book in 1995 after several years of teaching my own course in health psychology. The texts I recommended to my students were by US authors and this was reflected in their focus on US research and US health care provision. In addition, they tended to be driven by examples rather than by theories or models which made them difficult to turn into lectures (from my perspective) or to use for essays or revision (from my students' perspective). I decided to write my own book to solve some of these problems. I wanted to supplement US work with that from my colleagues from the UK, the rest of Europe, New Zealand and Australia. I also wanted to emphasize theory and to write the book in a way that would be useful. I hope that the first three editions have succeeded.

Aims of this new fourth edition

The third edition involved a fairly major revision and involved strengthening the book's coverage of the more biological aspects of health psychology, particularly pain, stress and PNI. These are the areas I am personally less involved in and the previous editions had reflected my own research interests with their emphasis on behaviour. This fourth edition has tried to do two things. First, it has updated the book throughout, adding new theories and research studies wherever appropriate. It is surprising how quickly research can look dated to a student in their twenties. In particular I have tried to reflect the increasing use of qualitative methodologies within health psychology by adding qualitative examples when they have been central to the literature being discussed. I have also tried to encourage a more critical and analytical approach to research by highlighting problems where appropriate. Second, this edition includes a new chapter on women's health issues with a focus on miscarriage, termination, pregnancy and birth and the menopause. Some of this reflects my own areas of research interests. More than this, however, it also reflects the interests of my undergraduate and postgraduate students who are predominantly women and are interested in the areas of health that pertain to them. This chapter does not aim to cover all issues relevant to women but those that have been covered in most depth by the research community. Perhaps in the next edition I may even add a chapter on men's health – who knows!

Also in this edition, I have added the following in response to review feedback on the third edition:

- **A new feature called 'Some problems with . . .'** This is a short box that appears in each chapter, asking students to consider some of the issues surrounding research in a particular area of health psychology. For example, Chapter 2 considers some problems with health beliefs research. In this case, how do we know that asking people about health beliefs doesn't change the way they think? Is it possible that beliefs that predict and explain behaviour are different to those that change behaviour? And so on. The aim of including these examples is to encourage students to develop an awareness of some common pitfalls of research in health psychology and to engage them in challenging, evaluating and analysing the integrity of their own research and those of other academics in the field.

- **New research focus examples.** There is some exciting new research under way in health psychology and it is important that students are exposed to new studies and understand that health psychology is a dynamic discipline. Some examples of the new research excerpts include a study to explore the role of coherence in promoting the intentions to quit smoking (2004) in Chapter 3, using the theory of planned behaviour to predict exercise (2005) in Chapter 7, and an abstract about how people experience chronic benign back pain (Smith 2007). There are many other new examples interspersed within the book.

- **New data, references, further reading and review questions.** Finally, as you would expect from a new revision, there is a full update throughout, including new data and figures where appropriate, updated Further Reading sections at the end of each chapter featuring new and recent publications, a comprehensively updated List of References at the end of the text, and new questions at the end of chapters for use either in class as discussion points or as an aid to student learning.

- **An Online Learning Centre website** accompanies this edition with useful materials for students of health psychology and their lecturers, including Powerpoint presentations, artwork and more.

For more information about the new edition's features, see the Guided Tour on pages xix–xxi, which leads you through the textbook chapters from introduction to chapter conclusion and questions.

The structure of the fourth edition

Health psychology is an expanding area in terms of teaching, research and practice. Health psychology *teaching* occurs at both the undergraduate and postgraduate level and is experienced by both mainstream psychology students and those studying other health-related subjects. Health psychology *research* also takes many forms. Undergraduates are often expected to produce research projects as part of their assessment, and academic staff and research teams carry out research to develop and test theories and to explore new areas. Such research often feeds directly into *practice*, with intervention programmes aiming to change the factors identified by research. This book aims to provide a comprehensive introduction to the main topics of health psychology. The book will focus on psychological theory supported by research. In addition, how these theories can be turned into practice will also be described. This book is now supported by a comprehensive website which includes teaching supports such as lectures and assessments.

Health psychology focuses on the indirect pathway between psychology and health which emphasizes the role that *beliefs* and *behaviours* play in health and illness. The contents of the first half of this book reflect this emphasis and illustrate how different sets of beliefs relate to behaviours and how both these factors are associated with illness.

Chapters 2–4 emphasize beliefs. Chapter 2 examines changes in the causes of death over the twentieth century and why this shift suggests an increasing role for beliefs and behaviours. The chapter then assesses theories of health beliefs and the models that have been developed to describe beliefs and predict behaviour. Chapter 3 examines beliefs that individuals have about illness and Chapter 4 examines health professionals' health beliefs in the context of health professional–patient communication.

Chapters 5–9 examine health-related behaviours and illustrate many of the theories and constructs that have been applied to specific behaviours. Chapter 5 describes theories of addictive behaviours and the factors that predict smoking and alcohol consumption. Chapter 6 examines theories of eating behaviour drawing upon developmental models, cognitive theories and the role of weight concern. Chapter 7 describes the literature on exercise behaviour both in terms of its initiation and methods to encourage individuals to continue exercising. Chapter 8 examines sexual behaviour and the factors that predict self-protective behaviour both in terms of pregnancy avoidance and in the context of HIV. Chapter 9 examines screening as a health behaviour and assesses the psychological factors that relate to whether or not someone attends for a health check and the psychological consequences of screening programmes.

Health psychology also focuses on the direct pathway between psychology and health and this is the focus for the second half of the book. Chapter 10 examines research on stress in terms of its definition and measurement and Chapter 11 assesses the links between stress and illness via changes in both physiology and behaviour and the role of moderating variables. Chapter 12 focuses on pain and evaluates the psychological factors in exacerbating pain perception and explores how psychological interventions can be used to reduce pain and encourage pain acceptance. Chapter 13 specifically examines the interrelationships between beliefs, behaviour and health using the example of placebo effects. Chapters 14 and 15 further illustrate this inter-relationship in the context of illness, focusing on HIV and cancer (Chapter 14) and obesity and coronary heart disease (Chapter 15). Chapter 16 examines women's health issues and the role of psychology in understanding women's experiences of miscarriage, termination, pregnancy, birth and the menopause, and highlights how the mode of treatment of intervention can affect these experiences. Chapter 17 explores the problems with measuring health status and the issues surrounding the measurement of quality of life.

Finally, Chapter 18 examines some of the assumptions within health psychology that are described throughout the book.

Essential Readings in Health Psychology edited by Jane Ogden

ISBN: 9780335211388 (Softback) 9780335211395 (Hardback)
Forthcoming in 2007 and available from www.mcgraw-hill.co.uk

Jane Ogden has also produced a new text, a reader in health psychology, containing 29 papers that employ different theories and methods and offer a more in-depth approach to the discipline. Covering the breadth of topics dealt with in this textbook, the reader aims to provide a range of good case examples of health psychology work. By reading them, students of psychology should gain a greater insight into what health psychology research can (and cannot) achieve. **Throughout, the papers are framed by editorial discussions of their context, meaning and contribution to Health Psychology as a whole.**

This textbook has provided the structure for choosing the papers in the reader. The papers have been grouped into five parts, covering the context of health psychology, health behaviours, health care, stress and health, and chronic illness. The reader can therefore be used as an adjunct to this textbook to provide more detail than that covered in a more general introductory text such as this one. In fact some of the papers selected for the reader are referenced in the textbook in brief in the Focus on Research boxes.

However, the structure of the reader also follows the key areas highlighted by the British Psychological Society as central to health psychology and as such would be an ideal resource for any undergraduate or postgraduate course, presenting good examples of key theories, models and methods. It could also provide the starting point for a reading list to accompany an undergraduate or postgraduate course or the papers could be used to focus a seminar discussion or a journal club. In addition, the papers are published in their entirety, including their reference lists, so they can be used to develop reading lists and recommend further reading. Below is the list of papers in *Essential Readings in Health Psychology*:

Section 1: The context of health psychology

Mokdad, A.H., Marks, J.S., Stroup, D.F. and Gerberding, J.L. (2004) Actual causes of death in the United States, 2000, *JAMA*, 10(29): 1238–45.

Kaplan, R.M. (1990) Behaviour as the central outcome in health care, *American Psychologist*, 45: 1211–20.

Section 2: Health behaviours

Sutton, S. (1998) Predicting and explaining intentions and behaviour: how well are we doing? *Journal of Applied Social Psychology*, 28: 1317–38

Ogden, J. (2003) Some problems with social cognition models: a pragmatic and conceptual analysis, *Health Psychology*, 22(4): 424–8.

West, R. (2005) Time for a change: putting the Transtheoretical (Stages of Change) model to rest, *Addiction*, 100: 1036–9.

Armitage, C.J. (2005) Can the Theory of Planned Behaviour predict the maintenance of physical activity? *Health Psychology*, 24(3): 235–45.

Murgraff, V., White, D. and Phillips, K. (1999) An application of protection motivation theory to riskier single occasion drinking, *Psychology and Health*, 14: 339–50.

DiClemente, C.C., Prochaska, J.O., Fairhurst, S.K. et al. (1991) The process of smoking cessation: an analysis of precontemplation, contemplation, and preparation stages of change, *Journal of Consulting and Clinical Psychology*, 59: 295–304.

Wardle, J. and Beales, S. (1988) Control and loss of control over eating: an experimental investigation, *Journal of Abnormal Psychology*, 97: 35–40.

Woodcock, A., Stenner, K. and Ingham, R. (1992) Young people talking about HIV and AIDS: Interpretations of personal risk of infection, *Health Education Research: Theory and Practice*, 7: 229–34.

Aiken, L.S., West, S.G., Woodward, C.K., Reno, R.R. and Reynolds, K.D. (1994) Increasing screening mammography in asymptomatic women: evaluation of a second generation, theory based program, *Health Psychology*, 13: 526–38.

Gollwitzer, P.M. and Sheeran, P. (2006) Implementation intentions and goal achievement: a meta-analysis of effects and processes, *Advances in Experimental Social Psychology*, 38: 69–119.

Section 3: Health care

Roter, D.L., Steward, M., Putnam, S.M. et al. (1997) Communication pattern of primary care physicians, *Journal of the American Medical Association*, 277: 350–6.

Mead, N. and Bower, P. (2000) Patient centredness: a conceptual framework and review of empirical literature, *Social Science and Medicine*, 51: 1087–110.

Marteau, T.M., Senior, V., Humphries, S.E. et al. (2004) Psychological impact of genetic testing for familial hypercholesterolemia within a previously aware population: A randomized controlled trial, *American Journal of Medical Genetics*, 128(A): 285–93.

Horne, R. and Weinman, J. (2002) Self regulation and self management in asthma: exploring the role of illness perceptions and treatment beliefs in explaining non adherence to preventer medication, *Psychology and Health*, 17: 17–32.

Simpson, S.H., Eurich, D.T., Majumdar, S.R., Padwal, R.S., Tsuyuki, R.T., Varney, J. and Johnson, J.A. (2006) A meta-analysis of the association between adherence to drug therapy and mortality, *British Medical Journal*, July 1, 333(7557): 15.

Section 4: Stress and health

Everson, S.A., Lynch, J.W., Chesney, M.A. et al. (1997) Interaction of workplace demands and cardiovascular reactivity in progression of carotid atherosclerosis: population based study, *British Medical Journal*, 314: 553–8.

Pereira, D.B., Antoni, M.H., Danielson, A. et al. (2003) Life stress and cervical squamous intraepithelial lesions in women with human papillomavirus and human immunodeficiency virus, *Psychosomatic Medicine*, 65(1): 1–8.

Ebrecht, M., Hextall, J., Kirtley, L.G., Taylor, A., Dyson, M. and Weinman, J. (2004) Perceived stress and cortisol levels predict speed of wound healing in healthy male adults, *Psychoneuroendocrinology*, 29: 798–809.

Pennebaker, J.W. (1997) Writing about emotional experiences as a therapeutic process, *Psychological Science*, 8(3): 162–6.

Petrie, K.J., Booth, R.J. and Pennebaker, J.W. (1998) The immunological effects of thought suppression, *Journal of Personality and Social Psychology*, 75: 1264–72.

Section 5: Chronic illness

Eccleston, C., Morley, S., Williams, A., Yorke, L. and Mastroyannopoulou, K. (2002) Systematic review of randomised controlled trials of psychological therapy for chronic pain in children and adolescents with a subset meta-analysis of pain relief, *Pain*, 99(1–2): 157–65.

Smith, J.A. (in press) Pain as an assault on the self: an interpretative phenomenological analysis of the psychological impact of chronic benign low back pain, *Psychology and Health*.

Taylor, S.E. (1983) Adjustment to threatening events: a theory of cognitive adaptation, *American Psychologist*, 38: 1161–73.

Petrie, K.J., Cameron, L.D., Ellis, C.J., Buick, D. and Weinman, J. (2002) Changing illness perceptions after myocardial infarction: an early intervention randomized controlled trial. *Psychosomatic Medicine*, 64: 580–6.

Antoni, M.H., Carrico, A.W., Duran, R.E. et al. (2006) Randomized clinical trial of cognitive behavioral stress management on human immunodeficiency virus viral load in gay men treated with highly active anti retroviral therapy, *Psychosomatic Medicine*, 68: 143–51.

Ogden, J., Clementi, C. and Aylwin, S. (2006) The impact of obesity surgery and the paradox of control: a qualitative study, *Psychology and Health*, 21(2): 273–93.

Rapkin, B.D. and Schwartz, C.E. (2004) Towards a theoretical model of quality of life appraisal: Implications of findings from studies of response shift, *Health and quality of life outcomes*, 2: 14.

If you wish to use the reader as a supplementary text alongside this textbook, we have provided a list of chapters of *Health Psychology 4th Edition* alongside the related papers from the reader. Please note that many of the 29 papers appear below more than once because they can be used with several chapters of the textbook:

Chapter in *Health Psychology: A Textbook*, Fourth Edition	Corresponding papers in *A Reader in Health Psychology* (alphabetical by first author)
Chapter 1 An introduction to health psychology	Kaplan, R.M. (1990)
	Mokdad, A.H., Marks, J.S., Stroup, D.F. and Gerberding, J.L. (2004)
Chapter 2 Health beliefs	Aiken, L.S., West, S.G., Woodward, C.K., Reno, R.R. and Reynolds, K.D. (1994)
	Armitage, C.J. (2005)
	DiClemente, C.C., Prochaska, J.O., Fairhurst, S.K. et al. (1991)
	Gollwitzer, P.M. and Sheeran, P. (2006)
	Kaplan, R.M. (1990)
	Mokdad, A.H., Marks, J.S., Stroup, D.F. and Gerberding, J.L. (2004)
	Murgraff, V., White, D. and Phillips, K. (1999)
	Ogden, J. (2003)
	Simpson S.H. et al. (2006)
	Sutton, S. (1998)
	Wardle, J. and Beales, S. (1988)
	West, R. (2005)
	Woodcock, A., Stenner, K. and Ingham, R. (1992)

Chapter 3 Illness cognitions	Antoni, M.H. et al. (2006)
	Horne, R. and Weinman, J. (2002)
	Marteau, T.M. et al. (2004)
	Pennebaker, J.W. (1997)
	Petrie, K.J., Cameron, L.D., Ellis, C.J., Buick, D. and Weinman, J. (2002)
	Simpson S.H. et al. (2006)
	Taylor, S.E. (1983)
Chapter 4 Doctor–patient communication and the role of health professionals' health beliefs	Horne, R. and Weinman, J. (2002)
	Marteau, T.M. et al. (2004)
	Mead, N. and Bower, P. (2000)
	Roter, D.L., Steward, M., Putnam, S.M. et al. (1997)
	Simpson S.H. et al. (2006)
Chapter 5 Smoking and alcohol use	DiClemente, C.C., Prochaska, J.O., Fairhurst, S.K. et al. (1991)
	Murgraff, V., White, D. and Phillips, K. (1999)
	Ogden, J. (2003)
	Sutton, S. (1998)
	West, R. (2005)
Chapter 6 Eating behaviour	Ogden, J. (2003)
	Ogden, J., Clementi, C. and Aylwin, S. (2006)
	Sutton, S. (1998)
	West, R. (2005)
	Wardle, J. and Beales, S. (1988)
Chapter 7 Exercise	Armitage, C.J. (2005)
	Ogden, J. (2003)
	Sutton, S. (1998)
	West, R. (2005)
Chapter 8 Sex	Ogden, J. (2003)
	Sutton, S. (1998)
	West, R. (2005)
	Woodcock, A., Stenner, K. and Ingham, R. (1992)
Chapter 9 Screening	Aiken, L.S., West, S.G., Woodward, C.K., Reno, R.R. and Reynolds, K.D. (1994)
	Marteau, T.M. et al. (2004)
	Ogden, J. (2003)
	Sutton, S. (1998)
	West, R. (2005)
Chapter 10 Stress	Antoni, M.H. et al. (2006)
	Ebrecht, M. et al. (2004)
	Everson, S.A., Lynch, J.W., Chesney, M.A. et al. (1997)
	Pennebaker, J.W. (1997)
	Pereira, D.B. et al. (2003)
	Petrie, K.J., Booth, R.J. and Pennebaker, J.W. (1998)

Chapter 11 Stress and illness	Antoni, M.H. et al. (2006) Ebrecht, M. et al. (2004) Everson, S.A., Lynch, J.W., Chesney, M.A. et al. (1997) Pennebaker, J.W. (1997) Pereira, D.B. et al. (2003) Petrie, K.J., Booth, R.J. and Pennebaker, J.W. (1998)
Chapter 12 Pain	Eccleston, C. et al. (2002) Smith, J.A. (in press)
Chapter 13 Placebos and the interrelationship between beliefs, behaviour and health	Simpson S.H. et al. (2006) Taylor, S.E. (1983)
Chapter 14 HIV and cancer: psychology throughout the course of illness (1)	Antoni, M.H. et al. (2006) Pereira, D.B. et al. (2003) Petrie, K.J., Booth, R.J. and Pennebaker, J.W. (1998) Taylor, S.E. (1983) Woodcock, A., Stenner, K. and Ingham, R. (1992)
Chapter 15 Obesity and coronary heart disease: psychology throughout the course of illness (2)	Everson, S.A., Lynch, J.W., Chesney, M.A. et al. (1997) Ogden, J., Clementi, C. and Aylwin, S. (2006) Petrie, K.J., Cameron, L.D., Ellis, C.J., Buick, D. and Weinman, J. (2002)
Chapter 16 Women's health issues	No specific paper included, although many themes elsewhere are related to women's health issues.
Chapter 17 Measuring health status: from mortality rates to quality of life	Rapkin, B.D. and Schwartz, C.E. (2004)
Chapter 18 The assumptions of health psychology	NB All the papers related to this issue to some degree.

Chapter overview

Chapter overview

This chapter examines the background against which health (1) the traditional biomedical model of health and illness century, and (2) changes in perspectives of health and illness chapter highlights differences between health psychology an ines the kinds of questions asked by health psychologists. psychology in terms of both clinical health psychology and b chologist is discussed. Finally, this chapter outlines the aims the book is structured.

This chapter covers

- The background to health psychology
- What is the biomedical model?
- What are the aims of health psychology?
- What is the future of health psychology?
- How is this book structured?

The background to health psychology

During the nineteenth century, modern medicine was es century term) was studied using dissection, physical investi Darwin's thesis, *The Origin of Species*, was published in 1856

Chapter overview

An introduction to the main themes, issues and topics to be covered in that chapter, including a list of contents for quick reference.

Figures and tables

Clear and well-represented tables and figures throughout the book provide up-to-date information and data in a clear and easy-to-read format.

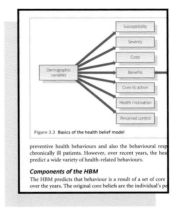

Figure 2.3 **Basics of the health belief model**

preventive health behaviours and also the behavioural resp chronically ill patients. However, over recent years, the hea predict a wide variety of health-related behaviours.

Components of the HBM

The HBM predicts that behaviour is a result of a set of core over the years. The original core beliefs are the individual's pe

Focus on research 2.1

Testing a theory – pre

A study to predict sexual behavio Velde and van der Pligt 1991).

This study integrates the PMT with context of HIV. It highlights the po a specific behaviour. This study is models of health behaviour.

Background

Since the identification of the HIV promote safer sexual behaviour. T appraisal of the threat and an app these factors elicit a state called 'pr with the threat. This study examine addition examines the effect of exp social norms and previous behaviou

Methodology

Subjects

Focus on research

Boxes that include both recent and classic research studies in health psychology, explaining the background, methodology, results and conclusion of the work.

Box 2.1 Some problems with . . . he

Below are some problems with research in this area

1. Asking people about their health beliefs may way they think.
2. We study health beliefs as a means to under beliefs that predict and explain behaviour are d
3. Much research in this field relies upon self-rep accurate. However, objective measures may no
4. Much research in this area relies upon cross-se the same time. Conclusions are then made ab possible, however, that behaviours predict or c get around this problem. Only experimental d be made.
5. There are many factors that may influence ho individual model (e.g. what happened on the happened to them in the pub as they were in that remains unexplained.
6. Trying to explain as much variance as possi removed from the interesting psychological c

Problems with . . .

A new feature in this edition which encourages you to pause for thought and reflect on health psychology research. Each box highlights some concerns with collecting, evaluating and validating research and includes three or more potential problems to consider.

To conclude

The role of health beliefs in predicting health-related be
salient with the recent changes in causes of mortality. Some
emphasized lay theories, which present individuals as having
their health which influence their behaviour. This persp
rational and examines lay theories in a relatively unstru
approach. Other studies have taken a more quantitative appr
such as attributions, health locus of control, unrealistic optir
change. Psychologists have also developed structured model
and to predict health behaviours such as the health belief
theory, the theory of planned behaviour and the health actio
consider individuals to be processors of information and
address the individual's cognitions about their social world.
health behaviours quantitatively and have implications for
change.

Questions

1 Recent changes in mortality rates can be explained in te
  Discuss.
2 Discuss the contribution of attribution theory to unders
3 Health beliefs predict health behaviours. Discuss with re

Conclusion

A wrap-up of the main themes to emerge from
the chapter and a useful revision tool to recap
the material in a topic area.

Questions

Short questions to test your understanding
and encourage you to consider some of the
issues raised in the chapter. A useful means
of assessing your comprehension and
progress.

Questions

1 Recent changes in mortality rates car
  Discuss.
2 Discuss the contribution of attributio
3 Health beliefs predict health behaviou
4 Discuss the role of the social world in
5 Human beings are rational informatio
6 Discuss the argument that changing a
7 Discuss some of the problems with th
8 To what extent can social cognition n
9 Design a research project to promo
  models of health beliefs.

For discussion

Consider a recent change in your healt
changed diet, aimed to get more sleep,
change.

2 Discuss the contribution of attribution theo
3 Health beliefs predict health behaviours. Di
4 Discuss the role of the social world in under
5 Human beings are rational information pro
6 Discuss the argument that changing an indi
7 Discuss some of the problems with the struc
8 To what extent can social cognition models
9 Design a research project to promote no
  models of health beliefs.

For discussion

Consider a recent change in your health-relat
changed diet, aimed to get more sleep, etc.).
change.

For discussion

A discussion point for a seminar or group work,
or to form the basis of an essay.

Assumptions in health psy

Research into health beliefs highlights some of

1 *Human beings as rational information*
  assume that behaviour is a consequenc
  measured. For example, it is assumed tha
  of a behaviour, assesses the seriousness
  decides how to act. This may not be the c
  the social cognition models include past
  assume some degree of rationality.
2 *Cognitions as separate from each other.*
  ferent cognitions (perceptions of severity
  tions) as if they are discrete and separate
  be an artefact of asking questions relating
  an individual may not perceive susceptib
  rate to self-efficacy (e.g. 'I am confident
  avoid HIV') until they are asked specific
3 *Cognitions as separate from methodolog*
  cognitions are separate from each other,

Assumptions in health psychology

A section that explains some of the basic
assumptions made in health psychology of
which you should be aware when reading the
material.

Further reading

Aboud, F.E. (1998) *Health Psychology in Global P*
    This book emphasizes the cross-cultural aspe
    beliefs within the cultural context.
Kaplan, R.M. (1990) Behaviour as the central
    1211–20.
    This paper provides an interesting discussion
    that rather than focusing on biological o
    researchers should aim to change behaviour
    interventions on the basis of whether this aim
Kaptein, A. and Weinman, J. (eds) (2004). *Health*
    This edited collection provides further detaile
    to health psychology.
Michie, S. and Abraham, C. (2004) *Health Psycho*
    This edited collection provides a detailed acco
    chartered health psychologist in the UK. Hov
    ally to anyone interested in pursuing a career
Ogden, J. (2007) *Essential Readings in Health Psy*
    This is my new reader which consists of 29
    theory, research, methodology or debate. The

Further reading

A list of useful essays, articles, books and research which can take your study further. A good starting point for your research for essays or assignments.

Glossary

At the end of the text there is a brief glossary of the commonly used terms in health psychology methodology.

Methodology glos

E
Experimental design: this involves a controlled study in which variables are manipulated in order to specifically examine the relationship between the independent variable (the cause) and the dependent variable (the effect); for example, does experimentally induced anxiety change pain perception?

I
Independent variable: the characteristic that appears to cause a change in the dependent variable; for example, smoking

interviews in orde
data from subject
data is a way of d
variety of beliefs,
interpretations ar
from a heterogen
group without m
generalizations to
population as a w
believed that qual
studies are more
access the subject
without contamin
data with the rese
own expectations.
Qualitative data a
in terms of theme
categories.
Quantitative study:

Online Learning Centre (OLC)

After completing each chapter, log on to the supporting Online Learning Centre website. Take advantage of the study tools offered to reinforce the material you have read in the text, and to develop your knowledge in a fun and effective way.

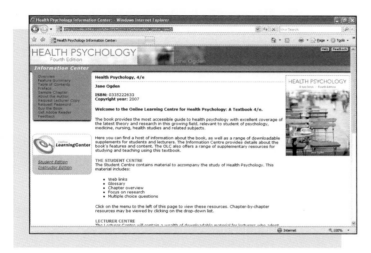

Resources for students include:

- *New chapter-by-chapter multiple choice quizzes*
- *Useful weblinks to extra health psychology resources online*
- *Searchable online glossary*
- *Chapter overviews*

Also available for lecturers:

- *Teaching tips to assist lecturers in preparing their module*
- *PowerPoint presentations for use in class or as handouts*
- *Artwork from the text*
- *Suggested essay questions to help prepare assessments and exams*

Visit **www.mcgraw-hill.co.uk/textbooks/ogden** today

Custom Publishing Solutions: Let us help make our **content** your **solution**

At McGraw-Hill Education our aim is to help the lecturer find the most suitable content for their needs and the most appropriate way to deliver the content for their students. Our **custom publishing solutions** offer the ideal combination of content delivered in the way which suits lecturer and students the best.

The idea behind our custom publishing programme is that via a database of over two million pages called Primis, www.primisonline.com the lecturer can select just the material they wish to deliver to their students:

Lecturers can select chapters from:

- textbooks
- professional books
- case books – Harvard Articles, Insead, Ivey, Darden, Thunderbird and BusinessWeek
- Taking Sides – debate materials

Across the following imprints:

- McGraw-Hill Education
- Open University Press
- Harvard Business School Press
- US and European material

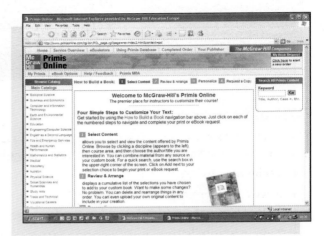

There is also the option to include material authored by lecturers in the custom product – this does not necessarily have to be in English.

We will take care of everything from start to finish in the process of developing and delivering a custom product to ensure that lecturers and students receive exactly the material needed in the most suitable way.

With a Custom Publishing Solution, students enjoy the best selection of material deemed to be the most suitable for learning everything they need for their courses – something of real value to support their learning. Teachers are able to use exactly the material they want, in the way they want, to support their teaching on the course.

Please contact your local McGraw-Hill representative with any questions or alternatively contact Warren Eels **e:** warren_eels@mcgraw-hill.com.

Acknowledgements

My thanks again go to my students and research assistants and to my colleagues over the years for their comments, feedback and research input. I am also grateful to David Armstrong for being (and staying) there and for conversation and cooking, and to Harry and Ellie for giving me that work–life balance and for going to bed on time.

The publishers would also like to thank the reviewers who commented on the previous edition and gave their time and expertise to provide helpful and constructive feedback. Their advice and suggestions were extremely helpful in shaping the new fourth edition. The reviewers were:

Deborah Biggerstaff, University of Warwick
Sheila Bonas, University of Leicester
Heather Buchanan, University of Derby
Orla Dunn, Coventry University
Peter La Cour, Copenhagen University, Denmark
Omer van der Bergh, University of Leuven, Belgium

Finally, every effort has been made to contact copyright holders to secure permission to republish material in this textbook, and to include correct acknowledgements where required. The publishers would be happy to hear from any copyright holders whom it has not been possible for us to contact.

Chapter 1

An introduction to health psychology

Chapter overview

This chapter examines the background against which health psychology developed in terms of (1) the traditional biomedical model of health and illness that emerged in the nineteenth century, and (2) changes in perspectives of health and illness over the twentieth century. The chapter highlights differences between health psychology and the biomedical model and examines the kinds of questions asked by health psychologists. Then the possible future of health psychology in terms of both clinical health psychology and becoming a professional health psychologist is discussed. Finally, this chapter outlines the aims of the textbook and describes how the book is structured.

This chapter covers

- The background to health psychology
- What is the biomedical model?
- What are the aims of health psychology?
- What is the future of health psychology?
- How is this book structured?

The background to health psychology

During the nineteenth century, modern medicine was established. 'Man' (the nineteenth-century term) was studied using dissection, physical investigations and medical examinations. Darwin's thesis, *The Origin of Species*, was published in 1856 and described the theory of evolution. This revolutionary theory identified a place for man within nature and suggested that we were part of nature, that we developed from nature and that we were biological beings. This was in accord with the biomedical model of medicine, which studied man in the same way that other members of the natural world had been studied in earlier years. This model described human beings as having a biological identity in common with all other biological beings.

What is the biomedical model?

The biomedical model of medicine can be understood in terms of its answers to the following questions:

- *What causes illness?* According to the biomedical model of medicine, diseases either come from outside the body, invade the body and cause physical changes within the body, or originate as internal involuntary physical changes. Such diseases may be caused by several factors such as chemical imbalances, bacteria, viruses and genetic predisposition.

- *Who is responsible for illness?* Because illness is seen as arising from biological changes beyond their control, individuals are not seen as responsible for their illness. They are regarded as victims of some external force causing internal changes.

- *How should illness be treated?* The biomedical model regards treatment in terms of vaccination, surgery, chemotherapy and radiotherapy, all of which aim to change the physical state of the body.

- *Who is responsible for treatment?* The responsibility for treatment rests with the medical profession.

- *What is the relationship between health and illness?* Within the biomedical model, health and illness are seen as qualitatively different – you are either healthy or ill, there is no continuum between the two.

- *What is the relationship between the mind and the body?* According to the biomedical model of medicine, the mind and body function independently of each other. This is comparable to a traditional dualistic model of the mind–body split. From this perspective, the mind is incapable of influencing physical matter and the mind and body are defined as separate entities. The mind is seen as abstract and relating to feelings and thoughts, and the body is seen in terms of physical matter such as skin, muscles, bones, brain and organs. Changes in the physical matter are regarded as independent of changes in state of mind.

- *What is the role of psychology in health and illness?* Within traditional biomedicine, illness may have psychological consequences, but not psychological causes. For example, cancer may cause unhappiness but mood is not seen as related to either the onset or progression of the cancer.

The twentieth century

Throughout the twentieth century, there were challenges to some of the underlying assumptions of biomedicine. These developments included the emergence of psychosomatic medicine, behavioural health, behavioural medicine and, most recently, health psychology. These different areas of study illustrate an increasing role for psychology in health and a changing model of the relationship between the mind and body.

Psychosomatic medicine

The earliest challenge to the biomedical model was psychosomatic medicine. This was developed at the beginning of the twentieth century in response to Freud's analysis of the relationship between the mind and physical illness. At the turn of the century, Freud described a condition called 'hysterical paralysis', whereby patients presented with paralysed limbs with no obvious physical cause and in a pattern that did not reflect the organization of nerves. Freud argued that this condition was an indication of the individual's state of mind and that repressed experiences and feelings were expressed in terms of a physical problem. This explanation indicated an interaction between mind and body and suggested that psychological factors may not only be consequences of illness but may contribute to its cause.

Behavioural health

Behavioural health again challenged the biomedical assumptions of a separation of mind and body. Behavioural health was described as being concerned with the maintenance of health and prevention of illness in currently healthy individuals through the use of educational inputs to change behaviour and lifestyle. The role of behaviour in determining the individual's health status indicates an integration of the mind and body.

Behavioural medicine

A further discipline that challenged the biomedical model of health was behavioural medicine, which has been described by Schwartz and Weiss (1977) as being an amalgam of elements from the behavioural science disciplines (psychology, sociology, health education) and which focuses on health care, treatment and illness prevention. Behavioural medicine was also described by Pomerleau and Brady (1979) as consisting of methods derived from the experimental analysis of behaviour, such as behaviour therapy and behaviour modification, and involved in the evaluation, treatment and prevention of physical disease or physiological dysfunction (e.g. essential hypertension, addictive behaviours and obesity). It has also been emphasized that psychological problems such as neurosis and psychosis are not within behavioural medicine unless they contribute to the development of illness. Behavioural medicine therefore included psychology in the study of health and departed from traditional biomedical views of health by not only focusing on treatment, but also focusing on prevention and intervention. In addition, behavioural medicine challenged the traditional separation of the mind and the body.

Health psychology

Health psychology is probably the most recent development in this process of including psychology in an understanding of health. It was described by Matarazzo as 'the aggregate of the specific educational, scientific and professional contribution of the discipline of psychology to the promotion and maintenance of health, the promotion and treatment of illness and related dysfunction' (Matarazzo 1980: 815). Health psychology again challenges the mind–body split by suggesting a role for the mind in both the cause and treatment of illness but differs from psychosomatic medicine, behavioural health and behavioural medicine in that research within health psychology is more specific to the discipline of psychology.

Health psychology can be understood in terms of the same questions that were asked of the biomedical model:

- *What causes illness?* Health psychology suggests that human beings should be seen as complex systems and that illness is caused by a multitude of factors and not by a single causal factor. Health psychology therefore attempts to move away from a simple linear model of health and claims that illness can be caused by a combination of biological (e.g. a virus), psychological (e.g. behaviours, beliefs) and social (e.g. employment) factors. This approach reflects the *biopsychosocial model of health and illness*, which was developed by Engel (1977, 1980) and is illustrated in Figure 1.1. The biopsychosocial model represented

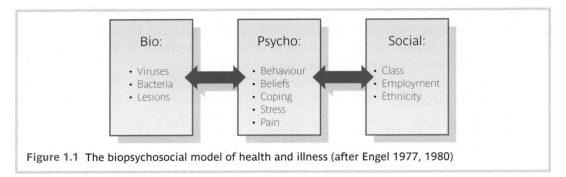

Figure 1.1 The biopsychosocial model of health and illness (after Engel 1977, 1980)

an attempt to integrate the psychological (the 'psycho') and the environmental (the 'social') into the traditional biomedical (the 'bio') model of health as follows: (1) the *bio* contributing factors included genetics, viruses, bacteria and structural defects; (2) the *psycho* aspects of health and illness were described in terms of cognitions (e.g. expectations of health), emotions (e.g. fear of treatment) and behaviours (e.g. smoking, diet, exercise or alcohol consumption); (3) the *social* aspects of health were described in terms of social norms of behaviour (e.g. the social norm of smoking or not smoking), pressures to change behaviour (e.g. peer group expectations, parental pressure), social values on health (e.g. whether health was regarded as a good or a bad thing), social class and ethnicity.

- *Who is responsible for illness?* Because illness is regarded as a result of a combination of factors, the individual is no longer simply seen as a passive victim. For example, the recognition of a role for behaviour in the cause of illness means that the individual may be held responsible for their health and illness.

- *How should illness be treated?* According to health psychology, the whole person should be treated, not just the physical changes that have taken place. This can take the form of behaviour change, encouraging changes in beliefs and coping strategies and compliance with medical recommendations.

- *Who is responsible for treatment?* Because the whole person is treated, not just their physical illness, the patient is therefore in part responsible for their treatment. This may take the form of responsibility to take medication, responsibility to change beliefs and behaviour. They are not seen as a victim.

- *What is the relationship between health and illness?* From this perspective, health and illness are not qualitatively different, but exist on a continuum. Rather than being either healthy or ill, individuals progress along this continuum from healthiness to illness and back again.

- *What is the relationship between the mind and body?* The twentieth century has seen a challenge to the traditional separation of mind and body suggested by a dualistic model of health and illness, with an increasing focus on an interaction between the mind and the body. This shift in perspective is reflected in the development of a holistic or a whole-person approach to health. Health psychology therefore maintains that the mind and body interact. However, although this represents a departure from the traditional medical perspective, in that these two entities are seen as influencing each other, they are still categorized as separate – the existence of two different terms (the mind/the body) suggests a degree of separation and 'interaction' can only occur between distinct structures.

- *What is the role of psychology in health and illness?* Health psychology regards psychological factors not only as possible consequences of illness but as contributing to its aetiology. Health psychologists consider both a direct and indirect association between psychology and health. The direct pathway is reflected in the physiological literature and is illustrated by research exploring the impact of stress on illnesses such as coronary heart disease and cancer. From this perspective, the way a person experiences their life ('I am feeling stressed') has a direct impact upon their body which can change their health status. The indirect pathway is reflected more in the behavioural literature and is illustrated by research exploring smoking, diet, exercise and sexual behaviour. From this perspective, the ways a person thinks ('I am feeling stressed') influences their behaviour ('I will have a cigarette') which in turn can impact upon their health. The direct and indirect pathways are illustrated in Figure 1.2.

What are the aims of health psychology?

Health psychology emphasizes the role of psychological factors in the cause, progression and consequences of health and illness. The aims of health psychology can be divided into (1) understanding, explaining, developing and testing theory, and (2) putting this theory into practice.

1 *Health psychology aims to understand, explain, develop and test theory by:*
   a Evaluating the role of behaviour in the aetiology of illness. For example:
      ○ Coronary heart disease is related to behaviours such as smoking, food intake and lack of exercise.
      ○ Many cancers are related to behaviours such as diet, smoking, alcohol and failure to attend for screening or health check-ups.
      ○ A stroke is related to smoking, cholesterol and high blood pressure.
      ○ An often overlooked cause of death is accidents. These may be related to alcohol consumption, drugs and careless driving.
   b Predicting unhealthy behaviours. For example:
      ○ Smoking, alcohol consumption and high fat diets are related to beliefs.
      ○ Beliefs about health and illness can be used to predict behaviour.

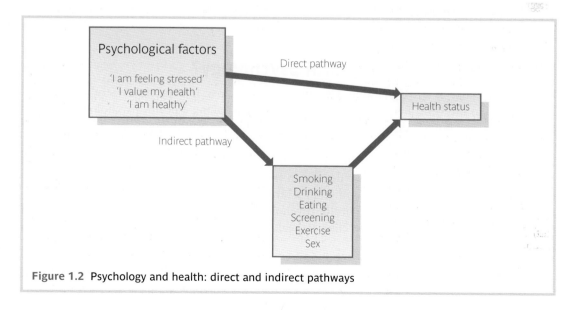

Figure 1.2 Psychology and health: direct and indirect pathways

    c Evaluating the interaction between psychology and physiology. For example:
- The experience of stress relates to appraisal, coping and social support.
- Stress leads to physiological changes which can trigger or exacerbate illness.
- Pain perception can be exacerbated by anxiety and reduced by distraction.

    d Understanding the role of psychology in the experience of illness. For example:
- Understanding the psychological consequences of illness could help to alleviate symptoms such as pain, nausea and vomiting.
- Understanding the psychological consequences of illness could help alleviate psychological symptoms such as anxiety and depression.

    e Evaluating the role of psychology in the treatment of illness. For example:
- If psychological factors are important in the cause of illness they may also have a role in its treatment.
- Changing behaviour and reducing stress could reduce the chances of a further heart attack.
- Treatment of the psychological consequences of illness may have an impact on longevity.

2 *Health psychology also aims to put theory into practice. This can be implemented by:*

    a Promoting healthy behaviour. For example:
- Understanding the role of behaviour in illness can allow unhealthy behaviours to be targeted.
- Understanding the beliefs that predict behaviours can allow these beliefs to be targeted.
- Understanding beliefs can help these beliefs to be changed.

    b Preventing illness. For example:
- Changing beliefs and behaviour could prevent illness onset.
- Modifying stress could reduce the risk of a heart attack.
- Behavioural interventions during illness (e.g. stopping smoking after a heart attack) may prevent further illness.
- Training health professionals to improve their communication skills and to carry out interventions may help to prevent illness.

What is the future of health psychology?

Health psychology is an expanding area in the UK, across Europe, in Australia and New Zealand and in the USA. For many students this involves taking a health psychology course as part of their psychology degree. For some students health psychology plays a part of their studies for other allied disciplines, such as medicine, nursing, health studies and dentistry. However, in addition to studying health psychology at this preliminary level, an increasing number of students carry out higher degrees in health psychology as a means to develop their careers within this field. This has resulted in a range of debates about the future of health psychology and the possible roles for a health psychologist. To date these debates have highlighted two possible career pathways: the clinical health psychologist and the professional health psychologist.

The clinical health psychologist

A clinical health psychologist has been defined as someone who merges 'clinical psychology with its focus on the assessment and treatment of individuals in distress … and the content field of health psychology' (Belar and Deardorff 1995). In order to practise as a clinical health psychologist, it is generally accepted that someone would first gain training as a clinical psychologist and then later acquire an expertise in health psychology, which would involve an understanding of the theories and methods of health psychology and their application to the health care setting (Johnston and Kennedy 1998). A trained clinical health psychologist would tend to work within the field of physical health, including stress and pain management, rehabilitation for patients with chronic illnesses (e.g. cancer, HIV or cardiovascular disease) or the development of interventions for problems such as spinal cord injury and disfiguring surgery.

A professional health psychologist

A professional health psychologist is someone who is trained to an acceptable standard in health psychology and works as a health psychologist. Within the UK, the British Psychological Society has recently sanctioned the term 'Chartered Health Psychologist'. Across Europe, Australasia and the USA, the term 'professional health psychologist' or simply 'health psychologist' is used (Marks et al. 1998). Although still being considered by a range of committees, it is now generally agreed that a professional health psychologist should have competence in three areas: research, teaching and consultancy. In addition, they should be able to show a suitable knowledge base of academic health psychology normally by completing a higher degree in health psychology. Having demonstrated that they meet the required standards, a professional/chartered health psychologist could work as an academic within the higher education system, within the health promotion setting, within schools or industry, and/or work within the health service. The work could include research, teaching and the development and evaluation of interventions to reduce risk-related behaviour.

What are the aims of this book?

Health psychology is an expanding area in terms of teaching, research and practice. Health psychology *teaching* occurs at both the undergraduate and postgraduate level and is experienced by both mainstream psychology students and those studying other health-related subjects. Health psychology *research* also takes many forms. Undergraduates are often expected to produce research projects as part of their assessment, and academic staff and research teams carry out research to develop and test theories and to explore new areas. Such research often feeds directly into *practice*, with intervention programmes aiming to change the factors identified by research. This book aims to provide a comprehensive introduction to the main topics of health psychology. The book will focus on psychological theory supported by research. In addition, how these theories can be turned into practice will also be described. This book is now supported by a comprehensive website which includes teaching supports such as lectures and assessments.

A note on theory and health psychology

Health psychology draws upon a range of psychological perspectives for its theories. For example, it uses learning theory with its emphasis on associations and modelling, social cognition theories with their emphasis on beliefs and attitudes, stage theories with their focus on change and progression, decision-making theory highlighting a cost–benefit analysis and the role of hypothesis testing and physiological theories with their interest in biological processes and their links with health. Further, it utilizes many key psychological concepts such as stereotyping, self-identity, risk perception, self-efficacy and addiction. This book describes many of these theories and explores how they have been used to explain health status and health-related behaviours. Some of these theories have been used across all aspects of health psychology such as social cognition models and stage theories. These theories are therefore described in detail in Chapter 2. In contrast, other theories and constructs have tended to be used to study specific behaviours. These are therefore described within each specific chapter. However, as cross-fertilization is often the making of good research, many of these theories could also be applied to other areas.

A note on methodology and health psychology

Health psychology also uses a range of methodologies. It uses quantitative methods in the form of surveys, randomized control trials, experiments and case control studies. It also uses qualitative methods such as interviews and focus groups and researchers analyse their data using approaches such as discourse analysis, interpretative phenomenological analysis (IPA) and grounded theory. A separate chapter on methodology has not been included as there are many comprehensive texts that cover methods in detail (see Further Reading at the end of this chapter). The aim of this book is to illustrate this range of methods and approaches to data analysis through the choice of examples described throughout each chapter.

The contents of this book

Health psychology focuses on the indirect pathway between psychology and health, and emphasizes the role that *beliefs* and *behaviours* play in health and illness. The contents of the first half of this book reflect this emphasis and illustrate how different sets of beliefs relate to behaviours and how both these factors are associated with illness.

Chapters 2–4 emphasize beliefs. Chapter 2 examines changes in the causes of death over the twentieth century and why this shift suggests an increasing role for beliefs and behaviours. The chapter then assesses theories of health beliefs and the models that have been developed to describe beliefs and predict behaviour. Chapter 3 examines beliefs that individuals have about illness and Chapter 4 examines health beliefs in the context of health professionals–patient communication.

Chapters 5–9 examine health-related behaviours and illustrate many of the theories and constructs that have been applied to specific behaviours. Chapter 5 describes theories of addictive behaviours and the factors that predict smoking and alcohol consumption. Chapter 6 examines theories of eating behaviour drawing upon developmental models, cognitive theories and the role of weight concern. Chapter 7 describes the literature on exercise behaviour both in terms of its initiation and methods to encourage individuals to continue exercising. Chapter 8 examines sexual behaviour and the factors that predict self-protective behaviour both in terms of pregnancy avoidance and in the context of HIV. Chapter 9 examines screening as a health behaviour and assesses the psychological factors that relate to whether or not someone attends for a health check and the psychological consequences of screening programmes.

Health psychology also focuses on the direct pathway between psychology and health and this is the focus of the second half of the book. Chapter 10 examines research on stress in terms of its definition and measurement and Chapter 11 assesses the links between stress and illness via changes in both physiology and behaviour and the role of moderating variables. Chapter 12 focuses on pain and evaluates the psychological factors in exacerbating pain perception and explores how psychological interventions can be used to reduce pain and encourage pain acceptance. Chapter 13 specifically examines the interrelationships between beliefs, behaviour and health using the example of placebo effects. Chapters 14 and 15 further illustrate this interrelationship in the context of illness, focusing on HIV and cancer (Chapter 14) and obesity and coronary heart disease (Chapter 15). Chapter 16 focuses specifically on aspects of women's health and Chapter 17 explores the problems with measuring health status and the issues surrounding the measurement of quality of life.

Finally, Chapter 18 examines some of the assumptions within health psychology that are described throughout the book.

The structure of this book

This book takes the format of a complete course in health psychology. Each chapter could be used as the basis for a lecture and/or reading for a lecture and consists of the following features:

- A chapter overview, which outlines the content and aims of the chapter.
- A set of questions for seminar discussion or essay titles.
- Recommendations for further reading.
- Diagrams to illustrate the models and theories discussed within the text.
- A 'focus on research' section, which aims to illustrate three aspects of health psychology: (1) 'testing a theory', which examines how a theory can be turned into a research project with a description of the background, methods used (including details of measures), results and conclusions for each paper chosen; (2) 'putting theory into practice', which examines how a theory can be used to develop an intervention; and (3) 'the experience of . . .', which presents studies addressing the patients' experience. Each 'focus on research' section takes one specific paper that has been chosen as a good illustration of either theory testing or practical implications.
- A 'some problems with . . .' section which describes some of the main methodological and conceptual problems for each area of research.
- An 'assumptions in health psychology' section, which examines some of the assumptions that underlie both the research and practice in health psychology, such as the role of methodology and the relationship between the mind and body. These assumptions are addressed together in Chapter 18.

In addition, there is a glossary at the end of the book, which describes terms within health psychology relating to methodology.

❓ Questions

1 To what extent does health psychology challenge the assumptions of the biomedical model of health and illness?

2 Discuss the processes involved in the indirect pathway to health and illness.

3 What problems are there with dividing up the pathways into indirect and direct pathways?

4 To what extent does health psychology enable the whole person to be studied?

5 Design a research study to illustrate the impact of the bio, psycho and social processes in an illness of your choice.

For discussion

Consider the last time you were ill (e.g. flu, headache, cold, etc.). Discuss the extent to which factors other than biological ones may have contributed to your illness.

Further reading

Aboud, F.E. (1998) *Health Psychology in Global Perspective*. London: Sage.

This book emphasizes the cross-cultural aspects of health psychology and locates behaviour and beliefs within the cultural context.

Kaplan, R.M. (1990) Behaviour as the central outcome in health care, *American Psychologist*, 45: 1211–20.

This paper provides an interesting discussion about the aims of health psychology and suggests that rather than focusing on biological outcomes, such as longevity and cell pathology, researchers should aim to change behaviour and should therefore evaluate the success of any interventions on the basis of whether this aim has been achieved.

Kaptein, A. and Weinman, J. (eds) (2004). *Health Psychology*. Oxford: BPS Blackwell.

This edited collection provides further detailed description and analysis of a range of areas central to health psychology.

Michie, S. and Abraham, C. (2004) *Health Psychology in Practice*. Oxford: Blackwell.

This edited collection provides a detailed account of the competencies and skills required to be a chartered health psychologist in the UK. However, the information is also relevant internationally to anyone interested in pursuing a career in health psychology.

Ogden, J. (2007) *Essential Readings in Health Psychology*. Maidenhead: Open University Press.

This is my new reader which consists of 29 papers that I have selected as good illustrations of theory, research, methodology or debate. The book also contains a discussion of each paper and a justification for its inclusion.

For reading on research methods

Bowling, A. and Ebrahim, S. (2005) *Handbook of Health Research Methods: Investigation, Measurement and Analysis*. Buckingham: Open University Press.

This provides an excellent overview of quantitative and qualitative methods including systematic reviews, surveys, questionnaire design, modeling and trials. Its focus is on health research.

Breakwell, G., Hammond, S., Fife-Schaw, C. and Smith, J.A. (eds) (2006) *Research Methods in Psychology* (3rd edn). London: Sage.

This edited book provides a thorough and accessible overview of a range of different qualitative and quantitative research methods specific to psychology.

Jenkinson, C. (2002) *Assessment and Evaluation of Health and Medical Care.* Buckingham: Open University Press.

This is an accessible and detailed account of a range of quantitative research designs including cohort studies, trials and case control studies.

Lyons, E. and Coyle, A. (eds) (2007) *Analyzing Qualitative Data in Psychology.* London: Sage.

This book provides an excellent overview of four different qualitative approaches (IPA, grounded theory, narrative analysis, discourse analysis) and then explores how they can be used and the extent to which they produce different or similar accounts of the data.

Smith, J.A. (2003) *Qualitative Psychology: A Practical Guide to Research Methods.* London: Sage.

This offers a very clear hands-on guide to the different qualitative approaches and is extremely good at showing how to carry out qualitative research in practice.

Willig, C. (2001) *Introducing Qualitative Research in Psychology: Adventures in Theory and Method.* Buckingham: Open University Press.

This is an extremely well-written and clear guide to the different qualitative approaches and offers an accessible overview of their similarities and differences in terms of epistemology and method.

Health beliefs

Chapter overview

Changes in causes of death throughout the twentieth century can in part be explained in terms of changes in behaviour-related illnesses, such as coronary heart disease, cancers and HIV. This chapter first examines lay theories of health and then explores theories of health behaviours and the extent to which health behaviours can be predicted by health beliefs such as the attributions about causes of health and behaviour, perceptions of risk and the stages-of-change model. In particular, the chapter describes the integration of these different types of health belief in the form of models (health belief model, protection motivation theory, theory of reasoned action, theory of planned behaviour, health action process approach). It explores problems with these models and describes studies that address the gap between behavioural intentions and actual behaviour. The chapter then explores how these theories can be used for developing interventions designed to change behaviour and finally describes research examining the longer-term maintenance of behaviour change.

This chapter covers

- What are health behaviours?
- Why study health behaviours?
- Lay theories about health
- What factors predict health behaviours?
- Social cognition models
- Problems with social cognition models
- The intention–behaviour gap
- Developing theory-based interventions
- Understanding maintenance of behaviour change

What are health behaviours?

Kasl and Cobb (1966) defined three types of health-related behaviours. They suggested that:

- a *health behaviour* was a behaviour aimed to prevent disease (e.g. eating a healthy diet)
- an *illness behaviour* was a behaviour aimed to seek remedy (e.g. going to the doctor)

■ a *sick role behaviour* was any activity aimed to get well (e.g. taking prescribed medication, resting).

Health behaviours were further defined by Matarazzo (1984) in terms of either:

■ *health-impairing habits*, which he called 'behavioural pathogens' (e.g. smoking, eating a high fat diet), or

■ *health protective behaviours*, which he defined as 'behavioural immunogens' (e.g. attending a health check).

In short, Matarazzo distinguished between those behaviours that have a negative effect (the behavioural pathogens, such as smoking, eating foods high in fat, drinking large amounts of alcohol) and those behaviours that may have a positive effect (the behavioural immunogens, such as tooth brushing, wearing seat belts, seeking health information, having regular check-ups, sleeping an adequate number of hours per night).

Generally health behaviours are regarded as behaviours that are related to the health status of the individual.

Why study health behaviours?

Over the past century health behaviours have played an increasingly important role in health and illness. This relationship has been highlighted by McKeown (1979).

McKeown's thesis
The decline of infectious diseases

In his book *The Role of Medicine*, Thomas McKeown (1979) examined the impact of medicine on health since the seventeenth century. In particular, he evaluated the widely held assumptions about medicine's achievements and the role of medicine in reducing the prevalence and incidence of infectious illnesses, such as tuberculosis, pneumonia, measles, influenza, diphtheria, smallpox and whooping cough. McKeown argued that the commonly held view was that the decline in illnesses, such as tuberculosis, measles, smallpox and whooping cough, was related to medical interventions such as chemotherapy and vaccinations; for example, that antibiotics were responsible for the decline in illnesses such as pneumonia and influenza. He showed, however, that the reduction in such illnesses was already under way before the development of the relevant medical interventions. This is illustrated in Figure 2.1 for tuberculosis.

McKeown therefore claimed that the decline in infectious diseases seen throughout the past three centuries is best understood not in terms of medical intervention, but in terms of social and environmental factors. He argued that:

> The influences which led to [the] predominance [of infectious diseases] from the time of the first agricultural revolution 10,000 years ago were insufficient food, environmental hazards and excessive numbers and the measures which led to their decline from the time of the modern Agricultural and Industrial revolutions were predictably improved nutrition, better hygiene and contraception. (McKeown 1979: 117)

The role of behaviour

McKeown also examined health and illness throughout the twentieth century. He argued that contemporary illness is caused by 'influences ... which the individual determines by his own

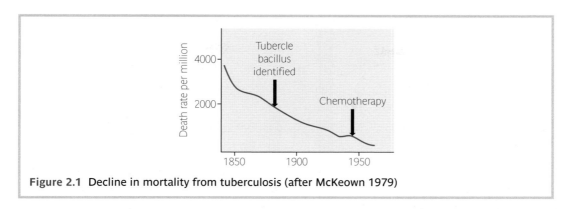

Figure 2.1 Decline in mortality from tuberculosis (after McKeown 1979)

behaviour (smoking, eating, exercise, and the like)' (McKeown 1979: 118) and claimed that 'it is on modification of personal habits such as smoking and sedentary living that health primarily depends' (McKeown 1979: 124). To support this thesis, McKeown examined the main causes of death in affluent societies and observed that most dominant illnesses, such as lung cancer, coronary heart disease and cirrhosis of the liver, are caused by behaviours.

Behaviour and mortality

It has been suggested that 50 per cent of mortality from the ten leading causes of death is due to behaviour. This indicates that behaviour and lifestyle have a potentially major effect on longevity. For example, Doll and Peto (1981) reported estimates of the role of different factors as causes for all cancer deaths. They estimated that tobacco consumption accounts for 30 per cent of all cancer deaths, alcohol for 3 per cent, diet for 35 per cent, and reproductive and sexual behaviour for 7 per cent. Accordingly, approximately 75 per cent of all deaths due to cancer are related to behaviour. More specifically, lung cancer, which is the most common form of cancer, accounts for 36 per cent of all cancer deaths in men and 15 per cent in women in the UK. It has been calculated that 90 per cent of all lung cancer mortality is attributable to cigarette smoking, which is also linked to other illnesses such as cancers of the bladder, pancreas, mouth, larynx and oesophagus and coronary heart disease. Similarly, in 2004 Mokdad et al. concluded that health behaviours such as smoking, poor diet and a sedentary lifestyle can cause serious health problems and are associated with a range of cancers, diabetes, heart disease and mortality. The impact of smoking on mortality was shown by McKeown when he examined changes in life expectancies in males from 1838 to 1970. His data are shown in Figure 2.2, which indicates that the increase in life expectancy shown in non-smokers is much reduced in smokers. The relationship between mortality and behaviour is also illustrated by bowel cancer, which accounts for 11 per cent of all cancer deaths in men and 14 per cent in women. Research suggests that bowel cancer is linked to behaviours such as a diet high in total fat, high in meat and low in fibre.

Longevity: cross-cultural differences

The relationship between behaviour and mortality can also be illustrated by the longevity of people in different countries. For example, in the USA and the UK, only 3 people out of every 100,000 live to be over 100. However, in Georgia, among the Abkhazians, 400 out of every 100,000 live to be over 100, and the oldest recorded Abkhazian is 170 (although this is obviously problematic in terms of the validity of any written records in the early 1800s). Weg (1983) examined the longevity of the Abkhazians and suggested that their longevity relative to that in other countries was due to a combination of biological, lifestyle and social factors including:

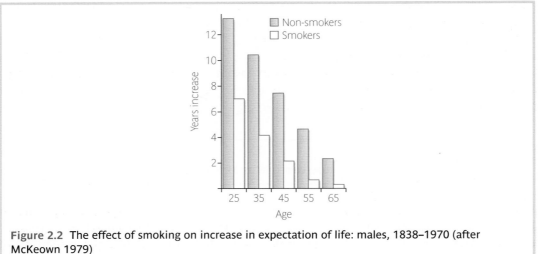

Figure 2.2 The effect of smoking on increase in expectation of life: males, 1838–1970 (after McKeown 1979)

- genetics
- maintaining vigorous work roles and habits
- a diet low in saturated fat and meat and high in fruit and vegetables
- no alcohol or nicotine
- high levels of social support
- low reported stress levels.

Analysis of this group of people suggests that health behaviours may be related to longevity and are therefore worthy of study. However, such cross-sectional studies are problematic to interpret, particularly in terms of the direction of causality: does the lifestyle of the Abkhazians cause their longevity or is it a product of it?

Longevity: the work of Belloc and Breslow

Belloc and Breslow (1972), Belloc (1973) and Breslow and Enstrom (1980) examined the relationship between mortality rates and behaviour among 7000 people. They concluded from this correlational analysis that seven behaviours were related to health status. These behaviours were:

1 Sleeping 7–8 hours a day.
2 Having breakfast every day.
3 Not smoking.
4 Rarely eating between meals.
5 Being near or at prescribed weight.
6 Having moderate or no use of alcohol.
7 Taking regular exercise.

The sample was followed up over five-and-a-half and ten years in a prospective study and the authors reported that these seven behaviours were related to mortality. In addition, they suggested that for people aged over 75 who carried out all of these health behaviours, health was comparable to those aged 35–44 who followed less than three.

Health behaviours seem to be important in predicting mortality and the longevity of individuals. Health psychologists have therefore attempted to understand and predict health-related behaviours. Some of this research has used qualitative methods to explore and understand 'lay theories' and the ways in which people make sense of their health. Other research has used quantitative methods in order to describe and predict health behaviours.

Lay theories about health

Such research has examined lay theories about health and has tended to use a qualitative methodology rather than a quantitative one.

In particular medical sociologists and social anthropologists have examined beliefs about health in terms of lay theories or lay representations. Using in-depth interviews to encourage subjects to talk freely, studies have explored the complex and elaborate beliefs that individuals have. Research in this area has shown that these lay theories are at least as elaborate and sophisticated as medicine's own explanatory models, even though they may be different. For example, medicine describes upper respiratory tract infections such as the common cold as self-limiting illnesses caused by viruses. However, Helman (1978) in his paper, 'Feed a cold, starve a fever', explored how individuals make sense of the common cold and other associated problems and reported that such illnesses were analysed in terms of the dimensions hot–cold, wet–dry with respect to their aetiology and possible treatment. In one study, Pill and Stott (1982) reported that working-class mothers were more likely to see illness as uncontrollable and to take a more fatalistic view of their health. In one study, Graham (1987) reported that, although women who smoke are aware of all the health risks of smoking, they report that smoking is necessary to their well-being and an essential means for coping with stress (see Chapter 3 for a further discussion of what people think health is). Lay theories have obvious implications for interventions by health professionals; communication between health professional and patient would be impossible if the patient held beliefs about their health that were in conflict with those held by the professional (see Chapter 4 for a discussion of communication).

Predicting health behaviours

Much research has used quantitative methods to explore and predict health behaviours. For example, Kristiansen (1985) carried out a correlational study looking at the seven health behaviours defined by Belloc and Breslow (1972) and their relationship to a set of beliefs. She reported that these seven health behaviours were correlated with (1) a high value on health; (2) a belief in world peace; and (3) a low value on an exciting life. Obviously there are problems with defining these different beliefs, but the study suggested that it is perhaps possible to predict health behaviours.

Leventhal et al. (1985) described factors that they believed predicted health behaviours:

- social factors, such as learning, reinforcement, modelling and social norms
- genetics, suggesting that perhaps there was some evidence for a genetic basis for alcohol use
- emotional factors, such as anxiety, stress, tension and fear
- perceived symptoms, such as pain, breathlessness and fatigue

- the beliefs of the patient
- the beliefs of the health professionals.

Leventhal et al. suggested that a combination of these factors could be used to predict and promote health-related behaviour.

In fact, most of the research that has aimed to predict health behaviours has emphasized beliefs. Approaches to health beliefs include attribution theory, the health locus of control, unrealistic optimism, self-affirmation theory and the stages-of-change model.

Attribution theory
The development of attribution theory

The origins of attribution theory can be found in the work of Heider (1944, 1958), who argued that individuals are motivated to see their social world as predictable and controllable – that is, a need to understand causality. Kelley (1967, 1971) developed these original ideas and proposed a clearly defined attribution theory suggesting that attributions about causality were structured according to causal schemata made up of the following criteria:

- *Distinctiveness*: the attribution about the cause of a behaviour is specific to the individual carrying out the behaviour.
- *Consensus*: the attribution about the cause of a behaviour would be shared by others.
- *Consistency over time*: the same attribution about causality would be made at any other time.
- *Consistency over modality*: the same attribution would be made in a different situation.

Kelley argued that attributions are made according to these different criteria and that the type of attribution made (e.g. high distinctiveness, low consensus, low consistency over time, low consistency over modality) determines the extent to which the cause of a behaviour is regarded as a product of a characteristic internal to the individual or external (i.e. the environment or situation).

Since its original formulation, attribution theory has been developed extensively and differentiations have been made between self-attributions (i.e. attributions about one's own behaviour) and other attributions (i.e. attributions made about the behaviour of others). In addition, the dimensions of attribution have been redefined as follows:

- *internal versus external* (e.g. my failure to get a job is due to my poor performance in the interview versus the interviewer's prejudice)
- *stable versus unstable* (e.g. the cause of my failure to get a job will always be around versus was specific to that one event)
- *global versus specific* (e.g. the cause of my failure to get the job influences other areas of my life versus only influenced this specific job interview)
- *controllable versus uncontrollable* (e.g. the cause of my failure to get a job was controllable by me versus was uncontrollable by me).

Brickman et al. (1982) have also distinguished between attributions made about the causes of a problem and attributions made about the possible solution. For example, they claimed that whereas an alcoholic may believe that he is responsible for becoming an alcoholic due to his lack of willpower (an attribution for the cause), he may believe that the medical profession is responsible for making him well again (an attribution for the solution).

Attributions for health-related behaviours

Attribution theory has been applied to the study of health and health-related behaviour. Her-zlich (1973) interviewed 80 people about the general causes of health and illness and found that health is regarded as internal to the individual and illness is seen as something that comes into the body from the external world.

More specifically, attributions about illness may be related to behaviours. For example, Bradley (1985) examined patients' attributions for responsibility for their diabetes and reported that perceived control over illness ('is the diabetes controllable by me or a powerful other?') influenced the choice of treatment by these patients. Patients could choose (1) an insulin pump (a small mechanical device attached to the skin, which provides a continuous flow of insulin), (2) intense conventional treatment, or (3) a continuation of daily injections. The results indi-cated that the patients who chose an insulin pump showed decreased control over their diabetes and increased control attributed to powerful doctors. Therefore, if an individual attributed their illness externally and felt that they personally were not responsible for it, they were more likely to choose the insulin pump and were more likely to hand over responsibility to the doctors. A further study by King (1982) examined the relationship between attributions for an illness and attendance at a screening clinic for hypertension. The results demonstrated that if the hyperten-sion was seen as external but controllable by the individual then they were more likely to attend the screening clinic ('I am not responsible for my hypertension but I can control it').

Health locus of control

The internal versus external dimension of attribution theory has been specifically applied to health in terms of the concept of a health locus of control. Individuals differ as to whether they tend to regard events as controllable by them (an internal locus of control) or uncontrollable by them (an external locus of control). Wallston and Wallston (1982) developed a measure of the health locus of control which evaluates whether an individual regards their health as control-lable by them (e.g. 'I am directly responsible for my health'), whether they believe their health is not controllable by them and in the hands of fate (e.g. 'whether I am well or not is a matter of luck'), or whether they regard their health as under the control of powerful others (e.g. 'I can only do what my doctor tells me to do'). Health locus of control has been shown to be related to whether an individual changes their behaviour (e.g. gives up smoking) and to the kind of com-munication style they require from health professionals. For example, if a doctor encourages an individual who is generally external to change their lifestyle, the individual is unlikely to comply if they do not deem themselves responsible for their health. The health locus of control is illus-trated in **Focus on Research 9.1** (p. 206).

Although the concept of a health locus of control is intuitively interesting, there are several problems with it:

- Is the health locus of control a state or a trait? (Am I always internal?)
- Is it possible to be both external and internal?
- Is going to the doctor for help external (the doctor is a powerful other who can make me well) or internal (I am determining my health status by searching out appropriate intervention)?

Unrealistic optimism

Weinstein (1983, 1984) suggested that one of the reasons that people continue to practise unhealthy behaviours is due to inaccurate perceptions of risk and susceptibility – their unrealistic optimism. He asked subjects to examine a list of health problems and to state 'compared to other people of your age and sex, what are your chances of getting [the problem] – greater than, about the same, or less than theirs?' The results of the study showed that most subjects believed that they were less likely to get the health problem. Weinstein called this phenomenon *unrealistic optimism* as he argued that not everyone can be less likely to contract an illness. Weinstein (1987) described four cognitive factors that contribute to unrealistic optimism: (1) lack of personal experience with the problem; (2) the belief that the problem is preventable by individual action; (3) the belief that if the problem has not yet appeared, it will not appear in the future; and (4) the belief that the problem is infrequent. These factors suggest that perception of own risk is not a rational process.

In an attempt to explain why individuals' assessment of their risk may go wrong, and why people are unrealistically optimistic, Weinstein (1983) argued that individuals show selective focus. He claimed that individuals ignore their own risk-increasing behaviour ('I may not always practise safe sex but that's not important') and focus primarily on their risk-reducing behaviour ('but at least I don't inject drugs'). He also argues that this selectivity is compounded by egocentrism: individuals tend to ignore others' risk-decreasing behaviour ('my friends all practise safe sex but that's irrelevant'). Therefore an individual may be unrealistically optimistic if they focus on the times they use condoms when assessing their own risk and ignore the times they do not and, in addition, focus on the times that others around them do not practise safe sex and ignore the times that they do.

In one study, subjects were required to focus on either their risk-increasing ('unsafe sex') or their risk-decreasing behaviour ('safe sex'). The effect of this on their unrealistic optimism for risk of HIV was examined (Hoppe and Ogden 1996). Heterosexual subjects were asked to complete a questionnaire concerning their beliefs about HIV and their sexual behaviour. Subjects were allocated to either the risk-increasing or risk-decreasing condition. Subjects in the risk-increasing condition were asked to complete questions such as 'since being sexually active how often have you asked about your partners' HIV status?' It was assumed that only a few subjects would be able to answer that they had done this frequently, thus making them feel more at risk. Subjects in the risk-decreasing condition were asked questions such as 'since being sexually active how often have you tried to select your partners carefully?' It was believed that most subjects would answer that they did this, making them feel less at risk. The results showed that focusing on risk-decreasing factors increased optimism by increasing perceptions of others' risk. Therefore, by encouraging the subjects to focus on their own healthy behaviour ('I select my partners carefully'), they felt more unrealistically optimistic and rated themselves as less at risk compared with those who they perceived as being more at risk.

Self-affirmation theory

Central to unrealistic optimism is the notion of risk perception and the proposal that individuals can process risk information in ways that enables them to continue their unhealthy behaviour. In fact research suggests that those least persuaded by risk data are often those most at risk (Sherman et al. 2000). An example of this is smokers' ability to continue to smoke even when the words 'smoking kills' are written on their packet of cigarettes. Recently, however, it has been suggested that self-affirmation may help reduce the tendency to resist threat information. Self-affirmation theory suggests that people are motivated to protect their sense of self-integrity and their sense of themselves as being 'adaptively and morally adequate' (Steele 1988). Therefore if presented with information that threatens their sense of self, they behave defensively. However, if given the opportunity to self-affirm in another domain of their lives, then their need to become defensive is reduced. For example, if a smoker thinks that they are a sensible person, when confronted with a message that says that smoking is not sensible their integrity is threatened and they behave defensively by blocking the information. If given the chance, however, to think about another area in which they are sensible then they are less likely to become defensive about the anti-smoking message. A couple of recent studies have tested the impact of self-affirmation on the processing of information about the link between alcohol and breast cancer in young women and smoking in young smokers (Harris and Napper 2005; Harris et al. 2006). In the first study, young women who were drinking above the recommended limit were randomized either to the self-affirmation condition or the control condition (Harris and Napper 2005). Those in the self-affirmation condition were asked to write about their most important value and why it was important to them. All were then given a health message about the links between excessive alcohol intake and breast cancer. The results showed that those who had self-affirmed were more accepting of the health message. In a similar study, smokers were asked to study four images depicting the dangers of smoking and half underwent a self-affirmation task. These results also showed that those who had self-affirmed rated the images as more threatening and reported higher levels of self-efficacy and intentions to stop smoking (Harris et al. 2006). Therefore it would seem that although people can deny and block the risks associated with their behaviour, this defensive process is reduced if they are encouraged to self-affirm. This approach has implications for a wide range of health-related behaviours and the development of more effective interventions to change behaviour.

The stages-of-change model

The transtheoretical model of behaviour change was originally developed by Prochaska and DiClemente (1982) as a synthesis of 18 therapies describing the processes involved in eliciting and maintaining change. It is now more commonly known as the stages-of-change model. Prochaska and DiClemente examined these different therapeutic approaches for common processes and suggested a new model of behaviour change based on the following stages:

1 *Pre-contemplation:* not intending to make any changes.
2 *Contemplation:* considering a change.
3 *Preparation:* making small changes.
4 *Action:* actively engaging in a new behaviour.
5 *Maintenance:* sustaining the change over time.

These stages, however, do not always occur in a linear fashion (simply moving from 1 to 5) but the theory describes behaviour change as dynamic and not 'all or nothing'. For example, an individual may move to the preparation stage and then back to the contemplation stage several times before progressing to the action stage. Furthermore, even when an individual has reached the maintenance stage, they may slip back to the contemplation stage over time.

The model also examines how the individual weighs up the costs and benefits of a particular behaviour. In particular, its authors argue that individuals at different stages of change will differentially focus on either the costs of a behaviour (e.g. stopping smoking will make me anxious in company) or the benefits of the behaviour (e.g. stopping smoking will improve my health). For example, a smoker at the action (I have stopped smoking) and the maintenance (for four months) stages tend to focus on the favourable and positive feature of their behaviour (I feel healthier because I have stopped smoking), whereas smokers in the pre-contemplation stage tend to focus on the negative features of the behaviour (it will make me anxious).

The stages-of-change model has been applied to several health-related behaviours, such as smoking, alcohol use, exercise and screening behaviour (e.g. DiClemente et al. 1991; Marcus et al. 1992). If applied to smoking cessation, the model would suggest the following set of beliefs and behaviours at the different stages:

1 *Pre-contemplation:* 'I am happy being a smoker and intend to continue smoking'.
2 *Contemplation:* 'I have been coughing a lot recently, perhaps I should think about stopping smoking'.
3 *Preparation:* 'I will stop going to the pub and will buy lower tar cigarettes'.
4 *Action:* 'I have stopped smoking'.
5 *Maintenance:* 'I have stopped smoking for four months now'.

This individual, however, may well move back at times to believing that they will continue to smoke and may relapse (called the revolving door schema). The stages-of-change model is illustrated in **Focus on Research 5.1** (p. 111).

The stages-of-change model is increasingly used both in research and as a basis to develop interventions that are tailored to the particular stage of the specific person concerned. For example, a smoker who has been identified as being at the preparation stage would receive a different intervention to one who was at the contemplation stage. However, the model has recently been criticized for the following reasons (Weinstein et al. 1998; Sutton 2000, 2002a; West 2006):

■ It is difficult to determine whether behaviour change occurs according to stages or along a continuum. Researchers describe the difference between linear patterns between stages which are not consistent with a stage model and discontinuity patterns which are consistent.

■ However, the absence of qualitative differences between stages could either be due to the absence of stages or because the stages have not been correctly assessed and identified.

■ Changes between stages may happen so quickly as to make the stages unimportant.

■ Interventions that have been based on the stages-of-change model may work because the individual believes that they are receiving special attention, rather than because of the effectiveness of the model *per se.*

■ Most studies based on the stages-of-change model use cross-sectional designs to examine differences between different people at different stages of change. Such designs do not allow conclusions to be drawn about the role of different causal factors at the different stages (i.e. people at the preparation stage are driven forward by different factors than those at the contemplation stage). Experimental and longitudinal studies are needed for any conclusions about causality to be valid.

■ The concept of a 'stage' is not a simple one as it includes many variables: current behaviour, quit attempts, intention to change and time since quitting. Perhaps these variables should be measured separately.

■ The model focuses on conscious decision-making and planning processes. Further it assumes that people make coherent and stable plans.

■ Using the model may be no better than simply asking people, 'Do you have any plans to try to...?' or 'Do you want to...?'.

Integrating these different health beliefs: developing models

In summary, attribution theory and the health locus of control emphasize attributions for causality and control; unrealistic optimism and self-affirmation theory focus on perceptions of susceptibility and risk; and the stages-of-change model emphasizes the dynamic nature of beliefs, time and costs and benefits. These different aspects of health beliefs have been integrated into structured models of health beliefs and behaviour. For simplicity, these models are often all called *social cognition models* as they regard cognitions as being shared by individuals within the same society. However, for the purpose of this chapter these models will be divided into *cognition models* and *social cognition models* in order to illustrate the varying extent to which the models specifically place cognitions within a social context.

Box 2.1 **Some problems with . . . health beliefs research**

Below are some problems with research in this area that you may wish to consider.

1 Asking people about their health beliefs may not be a benign process; it may actually change the way they think.

2 We study health beliefs as a means to understand and change behaviour. It is possible that the beliefs that predict and explain behaviour are different to those that change behaviour.

3 Much research in this field relies upon self-report measures of behaviour. These may not always be accurate. However, objective measures may not always be possible to obtain.

4 Much research in this area relies upon cross-sectional designs which assess beliefs and behaviours at the same time. Conclusions are then made about the ways in which beliefs predict behaviour. It is possible, however, that behaviours predict or cause beliefs. Even longitudinal design cannot entirely get around this problem. Only experimental designs can really allow conclusions about causality to be made.

5 There are many factors that may influence how a person behaves which cannot be captured by any individual model (e.g. what happened on the bus as they were intending to go to the doctor; what happened to them in the pub as they were intending not to smoke). There will always be variance that remains unexplained.

6 Trying to explain as much variance as possible can make the research too focused and too far removed from the interesting psychological questions (i.e. I can predict quite well what you are about to do in one minute's time in a specified place but am I really interested in that?).

Cognition models

Cognition models examine the predictors and precursors to health behaviours. They are derived from subjective expected utility (SEU) theory (Edwards 1954), which suggested that behaviours result from a rational weighing-up of the potential costs and benefits of that behaviour. Cognition models describe behaviour as a result of rational information processing and emphasize individual cognitions, not the social context of those cognitions. This section examines the health belief model and the protection motivation theory.

The health belief model

The health belief model (HBM) (see Figure 2.3) was developed initially by Rosenstock (1966) and further by Becker and colleagues throughout the 1970s and 1980s in order to predict

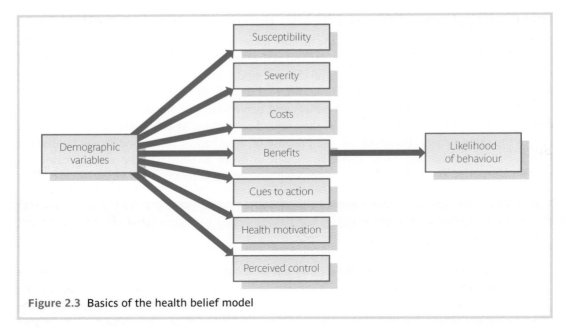

Figure 2.3 Basics of the health belief model

preventive health behaviours and also the behavioural response to treatment in acutely and chronically ill patients. However, over recent years, the health belief model has been used to predict a wide variety of health-related behaviours.

Components of the HBM

The HBM predicts that behaviour is a result of a set of core beliefs, which have been redefined over the years. The original core beliefs are the individual's perception of:

- susceptibility to illness (e.g. 'my chances of getting lung cancer are high')
- the severity of the illness (e.g. 'lung cancer is a serious illness')
- the costs involved in carrying out the behaviour (e.g. 'stopping smoking will make me irritable')
- the benefits involved in carrying out the behaviour (e.g. 'stopping smoking will save me money')
- cues to action, which may be internal (e.g. the symptom of breathlessness), or external (e.g. information in the form of health education leaflets).

The HBM suggests that these core beliefs should be used to predict *the likelihood that a behaviour will occur*. In response to criticisms the HBM has been revised originally to add the construct 'health motivation' to reflect an individual's readiness to be concerned about health matters (e.g. 'I am concerned that smoking might damage my health'). More recently, Becker and Rosenstock (1987) have also suggested that perceived control (e.g. 'I am confident that I can stop smoking') should be added to the model.

Using the HBM

If applied to a health-related behaviour such as screening for cervical cancer, the HBM predicts regular screening for cervical cancer if an individual perceives that she is highly susceptible to cancer of the cervix, that cervical cancer is a severe health threat, that the benefits of regular screening are high, and that the costs of such action are comparatively low. This will also be true if she is subjected to cues to action that are external, such as a leaflet in the doctor's waiting room, or internal, such as a symptom perceived to be related to cervical cancer (whether correct or not), such as pain or irritation. When using the new amended HBM, the model would also predict that a woman would attend for screening if she is confident that she can do so and if she is motivated to maintain her health. Using the HBM to predict screening behaviour is described in **Focus on Research 9.1** (p. 206).

Support for the HBM

Several studies support the predictions of the HBM. Research indicates that dietary compliance, safe sex, having vaccinations, making regular dental visits and taking part in regular exercise programmes are related to the individual's perception of susceptibility to the related health problem, to their belief that the problem is severe and their perception that the benefits of preventive action outweigh the costs (e.g. Becker 1974; Becker et al. 1977; Becker and Rosenstock 1984).

Research also provides support for individual components of the model. Norman and Fitter (1989) examined health screening behaviour and found that perceived barriers are the greatest predictors of clinic attendance. Several studies have examined breast self-examination behaviour and report that barriers (Lashley 1987; Wyper 1990) and perceived susceptibility (Wyper 1990) are the best predictors of healthy behaviour.

Research has also provided support for the role of cues to action in predicting health behaviours, in particular external cues such as informational input. In fact, health promotion uses such informational input to change beliefs and consequently promote future healthy behaviour. Information in the form of fear-arousing warnings may change attitudes and health behaviour in such areas as dental health, safe driving and smoking (e.g. Sutton 1982; Sutton and Hallett 1989). General information regarding the negative consequences of a behaviour is also used both in the prevention and cessation of smoking behaviour (e.g. Sutton 1982; Flay 1985). Health information aims to increase knowledge and several studies report a significant relationship between illness knowledge and preventive health behaviour. Rimer et al. (1991) report that knowledge about breast cancer is related to having regular mammograms. Several studies have also indicated a positive correlation between knowledge about breast self-examination (BSE) and breast cancer and performing BSE (Alagna and Reddy 1984; Lashley 1987; Champion 1990). One study manipulated knowledge about pap tests for cervical cancer by showing subjects an informative videotape and reported that the resulting increased knowledge was related to future healthy behaviour (O'Brien and Lee 1990).

Conflicting findings

However, several studies have reported conflicting findings. Janz and Becker (1984) found that healthy behavioural intentions are related to low perceived severity, not high as predicted, and several studies have suggested an association between low susceptibility (not high) and healthy behaviour (Becker et al. 1975; Langlie 1977). Hill et al. (1985) applied the HBM to cervical cancer, to examine which factors predicted cervical screening behaviour. The results suggested that barriers to action was the best predictor of behavioural intentions and that perceived susceptibility to cervical cancer was also significantly related to screening behaviour. However, benefits and perceived severity were not related. Janz and Becker (1984) carried out a study using the HBM and found that the best predictors of health behaviour are perceived barriers and perceived susceptibility to illness. However, Becker and Rosenstock (1984), in a review of

19 studies using a meta-analysis that included measures of the HBM to predict compliance, calculated that the best predictors of compliance are the costs and benefits and the perceived severity.

Criticisms of the HBM

The HBM has been criticized for these conflicting results. It has also been criticized for several other weaknesses, including the following:

- its focus on the conscious processing of information (for example, is tooth-brushing really determined by weighing up the pros and cons?)
- its emphasis on the individual (for example, what role does the social and economic environment play?)
- the interrelationship between the different core beliefs (for example, how should these be measured and how should they be related to each other? Is the model linear or multifactorial?)
- the absence of a role for emotional factors such as fear and denial
- it has been suggested that alternative factors may predict health behaviour, such as outcome expectancy and self-efficacy (Seydel et al. 1990; Schwarzer 1992)
- Schwarzer (1992) has further criticized the HBM for its static approach to health beliefs and suggests that within the HBM, beliefs are described as occurring simultaneously with no room for change, development or process
- Leventhal et al. (1985) have argued that health-related behaviour is due to the perception of symptoms rather than to the individual factors as suggested by the HBM.

Although there is much contradiction in the literature surrounding the HBM, research has used aspects of this model to predict screening for hypertension, screening for cervical cancer, genetic screening, exercise behaviour, decreased alcohol use, changes in diet and smoking cessation.

The protection motivation theory

Rogers (1975, 1983, 1985) developed the protection motivation theory (PMT) (see Figure 2.4), which expanded the HBM to include additional factors.

Components of the PMT

The original PMT claimed that health-related behaviours are a product of four components:

1 Severity (e.g. 'Bowel cancer is a serious illness').
2 Susceptibility (e.g. 'My chances of getting bowel cancer are high').
3 Response effectiveness (e.g. 'Changing my diet would improve my health').
4 Self-efficacy (e.g. 'I am confident that I can change my diet').

These components predict *behavioural intentions* (e.g. 'I intend to change my behaviour'), which are related to behaviour. Rogers (1985) has also suggested a role for a fifth component, fear (e.g. an emotional response), in response to education or information. The PMT describes severity, susceptibility and fear as relating to *threat appraisal* (i.e. appraising to outside threat) and response effectiveness and self-efficacy as relating to *coping appraisal* (i.e. appraising the individual themselves). According to the PMT, there are two types of sources of information,

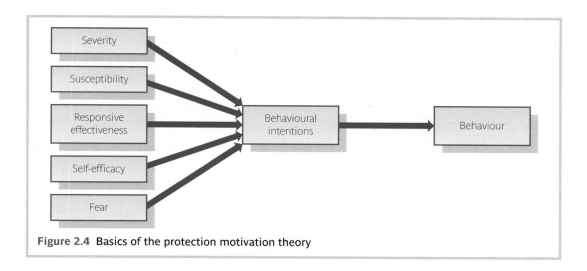

Figure 2.4 Basics of the protection motivation theory

environmental (e.g. verbal persuasion, observational learning) and intrapersonal (e.g. prior experience). This information influences the five components of the PMT (self-efficacy, response effectiveness, severity, susceptibility, fear), which then elicit either an 'adaptive' coping response (i.e. behavioural intention) or a 'maladaptive' coping response (e.g. avoidance, denial).

Using the PMT

If applied to dietary change, the PMT would make the following predictions: information about the role of a high fat diet in coronary heart disease would increase fear, increase the individual's perception of how serious coronary heart disease was (perceived severity), and increase their belief that they were likely to have a heart attack (perceived susceptibility/susceptibility). If the individual also felt confident that they could change their diet (self-efficacy) and that this change would have beneficial consequences (response effectiveness), they would report high intentions to change their behaviour (behavioural intentions). This would be seen as an adaptive coping response to the information. The PMT is illustrated in **Focus on Research 2.1** (p. 28).

Support for the PMT

Rippetoe and Rogers (1987) gave women information about breast cancer and examined the effect of this information on the components of the PMT and their relationship to the women's intentions to practise BSE. The results showed that the best predictors of intentions to practise BSE were response effectiveness, severity and self-efficacy. In a further study, the effects of persuasive appeals for increasing exercise on intentions to exercise were evaluated using the components of the PMT. The results showed that susceptibility and self-efficacy predicted exercise intentions but that none of the variables was related to self-reports of actual behaviour. In another study, Beck and Lund (1981) manipulated dental students' beliefs about tooth decay using persuasive communication. The results showed that the information increased fear, and that severity and self-efficacy were related to behavioural intentions. Norman et al. (2003) also used the PMT to predict children's adherence to wearing an eye patch. Parents of children diagnosed with eye problems completed a baseline questionnaire concerning their beliefs and a follow-up questionnaire after two months describing the child's level of adherence. The results showed that perceived susceptibility and response costs were significant predictors of adherence.

Testing a theory – predicting sexual behaviour

A study to predict sexual behaviour and behavioural intentions using the PMT (van der Velde and van der Pligt 1991).

This study integrates the PMT with other cognitions in order to predict sexual behaviour in the context of HIV. It highlights the possibility of adapting models to the specific factors related to a specific behaviour. This study is interesting as it represents an attempt to integrate different models of health behaviour.

Background

Since the identification of the HIV virus, research has developed means to predict and therefore promote safer sexual behaviour. The PMT suggests that behaviour is a consequence of an appraisal of the threat and an appraisal of the individual's coping resources. It suggests that these factors elicit a state called 'protection motivation', which maintains any activity to cope with the threat. This study examines the role of the PMT in predicting sexual behaviour and in addition examines the effect of expanding the PMT to include variables such as coping styles, social norms and previous behaviour.

Methodology

Subjects

A total of 147 homosexual and 84 heterosexual subjects with multiple partners in the past six months took part in the study. They were recruited from Amsterdam through a variety of sources including informants, advertisements and a housing service.

Design

Subjects completed a questionnaire (either postal or delivered).

Questionnaire

The questionnaire consisted of items on the following areas rated on a 5-point Likert scale:

1 **Sexual behaviour and behavioural intentions:** the subjects were asked about their sexual behaviour during the previous six months, including the number and type of partners, frequencies of various sexual techniques, condom use and future intentions.

2 **Protection motivation variables:** (a) perceived severity, (b) perceived susceptibility, (c) response efficacy, (d) self-efficacy, (e) fear.

3 **Additional beliefs:** (a) social norms, (b) costs, (c) benefits, (d) knowledge, (e) situational constraints.

4 In addition, the authors included variables from Janis and Mann's (1977) conflict theory: (a) vigilance, (b) hypervigilance, (c) defensive avoidance.

Results

The results were analysed to examine the best predictors of sexual behaviour in both homosexual and heterosexual subjects. It was found that although the variables of the PMT were predictive of behaviour and behavioural intentions in both populations, the results were improved with the additional variables. For example, when social norms and previous behaviour were also considered, there was improved association with future behaviour. In addition, the results suggested that although there was a relationship between fear and behavioural intentions, high levels of fear detracted from this relationship. The authors suggested that when experiencing excess fear, attention may be directed towards reducing anxiety, rather than actually avoiding danger through changing behaviour.

Conclusion

The results from this study support the use of the PMT to predict sexual behaviour in the context of HIV. Further, the model is improved by adding additional variables. Perhaps, rather than developing models that can be applied to a whole range of behaviours, individual models should be adapted for each specific behaviour. Furthermore, the results have implications for developing interventions, and indicate that the health education campaigns which promote fear may have negative effects, with individuals having to deal with the fear rather than changing their behaviour.

Criticisms of the PMT

The PMT has been less widely criticized than the HBM; however, many of the criticisms of the HBM also relate to the PMT. For example, the PMT assumes that individuals are conscious information processors; it does not account for habitual behaviours, nor does it include a role for social and environmental factors.

Social cognition models

Social cognition models examine factors that predict behaviour and/or behavioural intentions and in addition examine why individuals fail to maintain a behaviour to which they are committed. Social cognition theory was developed by Bandura (1977, 1986) and suggests that behaviour is governed by expectancies, incentives and social cognitions. Expectancies include:

- *situation outcome expectancies*: the expectancy that a behaviour may be dangerous (e.g. 'smoking can cause lung cancer')
- *outcome expectancies*: the expectancy that a behaviour can reduce the harm to health (e.g. 'stopping smoking can reduce the chances of lung cancer')
- *self-efficacy expectancies*: the expectancy that the individual is capable of carrying out the desired behaviour (e.g. 'I can stop smoking if I want to').

The concept of *incentives* suggests that a behaviour is governed by its consequences. For example, smoking behaviour may be reinforced by the experience of reduced anxiety, having a cervical smear may be reinforced by a feeling of reassurance after a negative result.

Social cognitions are a central component of social cognition models. Although (as with cognition models) social cognition models regard individuals as information processors, there is an important difference between cognition models and social cognition models – social cognition models include measures of the *individual's representations of their social world*. Accordingly, social cognition models attempt to place the individual within the context both of other people and the broader social world. This is measured in terms of their normative beliefs (e.g. 'people who are important to me want me to stop smoking').

Several models have been developed using this perspective. This section examines the theory of planned behaviour (derived from the theory of reasoned action) and the health action process approach.

The theories of reasoned action and planned behaviour

The theory of reasoned action (TRA) (see Figure 2.5) was extensively used to examine predictors of behaviours and was central to the debate within social psychology concerning the relationship between attitudes and behaviour (Fishbein 1967; Ajzen and Fishbein 1970; Fishbein and Ajzen 1975). The theory of reasoned action emphasized a central role for social cognitions in the form of subjective norms (the individual's beliefs about their social world) and included both beliefs and evaluations of these beliefs (both factors constituting the individual's attitudes). The TRA was therefore an important model as it placed the individual within the social context and in addition suggested a role for value which was in contrast to the traditional more rational approach to behaviour. The theory of planned behaviour (TPB) (see Figure 2.6) was developed by Ajzen and colleagues (Ajzen 1985; Ajzen and Madden 1986; Ajzen 1988) and represented a progression from the TRA.

Components of the TPB

The TPB emphasizes *behavioural intentions* as the outcome of a combination of several beliefs. The theory proposes that intentions should be conceptualized as 'plans of action in pursuit of behavioural goals' (Ajzen and Madden 1986) and are a result of the following beliefs:

■ Attitude towards a behaviour, which is composed of either a positive or negative evaluation of a particular behaviour and beliefs about the outcome of the behaviour (e.g. 'exercising is fun and will improve my health').

■ Subjective norm, which is composed of the perception of social norms and pressures to perform a behaviour and an evaluation of whether the individual is motivated to comply with this pressure (e.g. 'people who are important to me will approve if I lose weight and I want their approval').

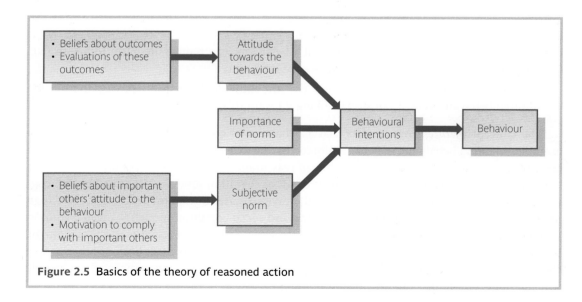

Figure 2.5 Basics of the theory of reasoned action

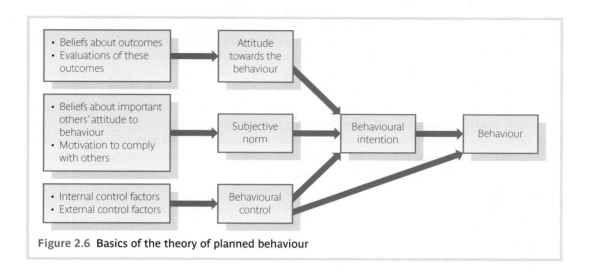

Figure 2.6 Basics of the theory of planned behaviour

■ Perceived behavioural control, which is composed of a belief that the individual can carry out a particular behaviour based upon a consideration of internal control factors (e.g. skills, abilities, information) and external control factors (e.g. obstacles, opportunities), both of which relate to past behaviour.

According to the TPB, these three factors predict behavioural intentions, which are then linked to behaviour. The TPB also states that perceived behavioural control can have a direct effect on behaviour without the mediating effect of behavioural intentions.

Using the TPB

If applied to alcohol consumption, the TPB would make the following predictions: if an individual believed that reducing their alcohol intake would make their life more productive and be beneficial to their health (attitude to the behaviour) and believed that the important people in their life wanted them to cut down (subjective norm), and in addition believed that they were capable of drinking less alcohol due to their past behaviour and evaluation of internal and external control factors (high behavioural control), then this would predict high intentions to reduce alcohol intake (behavioural intentions). The model also predicts that perceived behavioural control can predict behaviour without the influence of intentions. For example, if perceived behavioural control reflects actual control, a belief that the individual would not be able to exercise because they are physically incapable of exercising would be a better predictor of their exercising behaviour than their high intentions to exercise. Using the TPB to predict exercise is described in **Focus on Research 7.2** (p. 169).

Support for the TPB

The TPB has been used to assess a variety of health-related behaviours. For example, Brubaker and Wickersham (1990) examined the role of the theory's different components in predicting testicular self-examination and reported that attitude towards the behaviour, subjective norm and behavioural control (measured as self-efficacy) correlated with the intention to perform the behaviour. A further study evaluated the TPB in relation to weight loss (Schifter and Ajzen 1985). The results showed that weight loss was predicted by the components of the model; in particular, goal attainment (weight loss) was linked to perceived behavioural control. Similarly,

Conner, Lawton et al. (2006) used the TPB to predict speeding behaviour using a driving simulator and an on-road speed camera and showed a significant role for most of the TPB variables in predicting both intentions and actual behaviour. Recently, O'Connor et al. (2006) also used the TPB to predict deliberate self-harm and suicidality at three months' follow-up as a means to explore whether the TPB was relevant to more extreme behaviour and whether social cognitive variables were better predictors than clinical variables. The results showed a strong role for variables such as self-efficacy, attitude and descriptive norm and that these were better predictors than depression. There have now been several reviews and meta-analyses of the TPB which describe the extent to which this model can predict a range of health behaviours (Sheeran and Taylor 1999; Armitage and Conner 2001; Trafimow et al. 2002).

Criticisms of the TPB

Schwarzer (1992) has criticized the TPB for its omission of a temporal element and argues that the TPB does not describe either the order of the different beliefs or any direction of causality. However, in contrast to the HBM and the PMT, the model attempts to address the problem of social and environmental factors (in the form of normative beliefs). In addition, it includes a role for past behaviour within the measure of perceived behavioural control.

The health action process approach

The health action process approach (HAPA) (see Figure 2.7) was developed by Schwarzer (1992) following his review of the literature, which highlighted the need to include a temporal element in the understanding of beliefs and behaviour. In addition, it emphasized the importance of self-efficacy as a determinant of both behavioural intentions and self-reports of behaviour. The HAPA includes several elements from all previous theories and attempts to predict both behavioural intentions and actual behaviour.

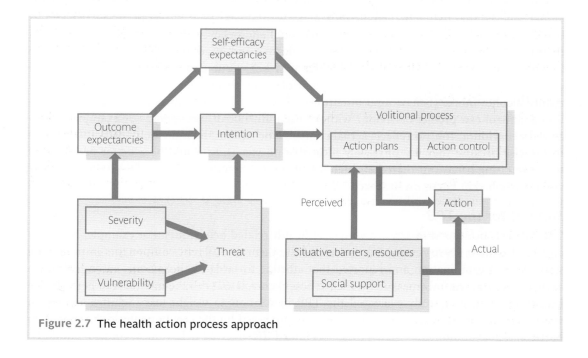

Figure 2.7 The health action process approach

Components of the HAPA

The main addition made by the HAPA to the existing theories is the distinction between a decision-making/motivational stage and an action/maintenance stage. Therefore the model adds a temporal and process factor to understanding the relationship between beliefs and behaviour and suggests that individuals initially decide whether or not to carry out a behaviour (the *motivation* stage), and then make plans to initiate and maintain this behaviour (the *action* phase).

According to the HAPA, the motivation stage is made up of the following components:

- *self-efficacy* (e.g. 'I am confident that I can stop smoking')
- *outcome expectancies* (e.g. 'stopping smoking will improve my health'), which has a subset of *social outcome expectancies* (e.g. 'other people want me to stop smoking and if I stop smoking I will gain their approval')
- *threat appraisal*, which is composed of beliefs about the severity of an illness and perceptions of individual vulnerability.

According to the HAPA the end result of the HAPA is an intention to act.

The action stage is composed of cognitive (volitional), situational and behavioural factors. The integration of these factors determines the extent to which a behaviour is initiated and maintained via these self-regulatory processes. The cognitive factor is made up of action plans (e.g. 'if offered a cigarette when I am trying not to smoke I will imagine what the tar would do to my lungs') and action control (e.g. 'I can survive being offered a cigarette by reminding myself that I am a non-smoker'). These two cognitive factors determine the individual's determination of will. The situational factor consists of social support (e.g. the existence of friends who encourage non-smoking) and the absence of situational barriers (e.g. financial support to join an exercise club).

Schwarzer (1992) argued that the HAPA bridges the gap between intentions and behaviour and emphasizes self-efficacy, both in terms of developing the intention to act and also implicitly in terms of the cognitive stage of the action stage, whereby self-efficacy promotes and maintains action plans and action control, therefore contributing to the maintenance of the action. He maintained that the HAPA enables specific predictions to be made about causality and also describes a process of beliefs whereby behaviour is the result of a series of processes.

Support for the HAPA

The individual components of the HAPA have been tested providing some support for the model. In particular, Schwarzer (1992) claimed that self-efficacy was consistently the best predictor of behavioural intentions and behaviour change for a variety of behaviours such as the intention to use dental floss, frequency of flossing, effective use of contraception, breast self-examination, drug addicts' intentions to use clean needles, intentions to quit smoking, and intentions to adhere to weight loss programmes and exercise (e.g. Beck and Lund 1981; Seydel et al. 1990).

Criticisms of the HAPA

Again, as with the other cognition and social cognition models, the following questions arise when assessing the value of the HAPA in predicting health behaviours: are individuals conscious processors of information? And what role do social and environmental factors play? The social cognition models attempt to address the problem of the social world in their measures of normative beliefs. However, such measures only access the individual's cognitions about their social world.

Problems with the models

Cognition and social cognition models provide a structured approach to understanding health beliefs and predicting health behaviours and provide a framework for designing questionnaires and developing interventions. Over recent years, however, several papers have been published criticizing these models. These problems can be categorized as conceptual, methodological and predictive.

Conceptual problems

Some researchers have pointed to some conceptual problems with the models in terms of their variables and their ability to inform us about the world. These problems are as follows:

- Each model is made up of different concepts such as perceived behavioural control, behavioural intentions, perceived vulnerability and attitudes. Norman and Conner (1996) have argued that there is some overlap between these variables and Armitage and Conner (2000) have argued for a 'consensus' approach to studying health behaviour, whereby key constructs are integrated across models.

- The models describe associations between variables which assume causality. For example, the TPB describes attitude as causing behavioural intention. Sutton (2002a) argues that these associations are causally ambiguous and cannot be concluded unless experimental methods are used. Similarly, Smedlund (2000) criticized the models for their logical construction and said that assumptions about association are flawed.

- A theory should enable the collection of data which can either lead to theory being supported or rejected. Ogden (2003) carried out an analysis of studies using the HBM, TRA, PMT and TPB over a four-year period and concluded that the models cannot be rejected as caveats can always be offered to perpetuate the belief that the model has been supported.

- Research should generate truths which are true by observation and require an empirical test (e.g. smoking causes heart disease) rather than by definition (i.e. heart disease causes narrowing of the arteries). Ogden (2003) concluded from her analysis than much research using the models produces statements that are true by definition (i.e. I am certain that I will use a condom therefore I intend to use a condom). She argues that the findings are therefore tautological.

- Research should inform us about the world rather than create the world. Ogden (2003) argues that questionnaires that ask people questions such as 'Do you think the female condom decreases sexual pleasure for a man?' may change the way in which people think rather than just describe their thoughts. This is similar to changes in mood following mood check lists, and the ability of diaries to change behaviour.

Methodological problems

Much research using models such as the TPB, TRA and HBM use cross-sectional designs involving questionnaires which are analysed using multiple regression analysis. Researchers have highlighted some problems with this approach.

- Cross-sectional research can only show associations rather than causality. To solve this, prospective studies are used which separate the independent and dependent variables by time. Sutton (2002a) argues that both these designs are problematic and do not allow inferences about causality to be made. He suggests that randomized experimental designs are the best solution to this problem.

- Hankins et al. (2000a) provide some detailed guidelines on how data using the TRA and TPB should be analysed and state that much research uses inappropriate analysis. They state that if multiple regression analysis is used adjusted R_2 should be the measure of explained variance, that residuals should be assessed and that semi-partial correlations should be used to assess the unique contribution of each variable. They also state that 'Structural Equation Modelling' might be a better approach as this makes explicit the assumptions of the models.

- Much psychological research does not involve a sample size calculation or a consideration of the power of the study. Hankins et al. (2000) argue that research using social cognition models should do this if the results are to be meaningful.

- The TRA involves a generalized measure of attitude which is reflected in the interaction between 'expectancy beliefs' about the likelihood of the given behaviour leading to particular consequences and evaluations about the desirability of these consequences. For example, an attitude to smoking is made up of the belief 'smoking will lead to lung cancer' and the belief 'lung cancer is unpleasant'. This is calculated by multiplying one belief with the other to create a 'multiplicative composite'. This is called the 'expectancy value' belief. In subsequent analysis this new variable is simply correlated with other variables. French and Hankins (2003) argue that this is problematic as the correlation between a multiplicative composite and other variables requires a ratio scale with a true zero. As with other psychological constructs, the 'expectancy value belief has no true zero, only an arbitrary was chosen by the researcher'. Therefore they argue that the expectancy value belief should not be used.

Predictive problems

Models such as the TRA, TPB, HBM and PMT are designed to predict behavioural intentions and actual behaviour. However, two main observations have been made. First, it has been suggested that these models are not that successful at predicting behavioural intentions and that they should be expanded to incorporate new cognitions. Second, it has been argued that they are even less successful in predicting actual behaviour. This second criticism has resulted in research exploring the intention–behaviour gap.

Predicting intentions: the need to incorporate new cognitions

Sutton (1998a) argued that studies using models of health beliefs only manage to predict between 40 and 50 per cent of the variance in behavioural intentions. Therefore, up to 50 per cent of the variance remains unexplained. Some new variables have been developed to improve the effectiveness of the models.

Expanded norms

The theory of reasoned action and the theory of planned behaviour include measures of social pressures to behave in a particular way – the subjective norms variable. However, it has been suggested that they should also assess other forms of norms. For example, the intention to carry out behaviours that have an ethical or moral dimension such as donating blood, donating organs for transplant, committing driving offences or eating genetically produced food may result from not only general social norms but also moral norms. Some research has shown the usefulness of including a moral norms variable (e.g. Sparks 1994; Parker et al. 1995; Légaré et al. 2003). For example, Godin et al. (2005) analysed six data sets relating to smoking, driving over the speed limit, exercising and applying precautions when taking blood. The results showed that people were more likely to carry out the behaviour if their intentions to perform the behaviour were in line with their moral norms. In addition, however, this role for moral norms was only present when people construed the behaviour in moral terms. This is in line with Norman and Conner's (1996) suggestion that moral norms may only be relevant to a limited range of behaviours. The concept of social norms has also been further expanded to include 'descriptive norms' which reflect the person's perception of whether other people carry out the behaviour (i.e. 'Do you think doctors eat healthily?') and 'injunctive norms' which reflect that other people might approve or disapprove of the behaviour (e.g. Povey et al. 2000).

Anticipated regret

The protection motivation theory explicitly includes a role for emotion in the form of fear. Researchers have argued that behavioural intentions may be related to anticipated emotions. For example, the intention to practise safer sex – 'I intend to use a condom' – may be predicted by the anticipated feeling 'if I do not use a condom I will feel guilty'. Some research has shown that anticipated regret is important for predicting behavioural intentions (Richard and van der Pligt 1991). Similarly, Conner, Sandberg et al. (2006) reported that anticipated regret was significantly related both to the intentions to start smoking and actual smoking in a group of adolescents.

Self-identity

Another variable which has been presented as a means to improve the model's ability to predict behavioural intentions is self-identity. It has been argued that individuals will only intend to carry out a behaviour if that behaviour fits with their own image of themselves. For example, the identity 'I am a healthy eater' should relate to the intention to eat healthily. Further, the identity 'I am a fit person' should relate to the intention to carry out exercise. Some research has supported the usefulness of this variable (Sparks and Shepherd 1992). However, Norman and Conner (1996) suggested that this variable may also only have limited relevance.

Ambivalence

Most models contain a measure of attitude towards the behaviour which conceptualizes individuals as holding either positive or negative views towards a given object. Recent studies, however, have also explored the role of ambivalence in predicting behaviour (Thompson et al. 1995) which has been defined in a variety of different ways. For example, Breckler (1994) defined it as 'a conflict aroused by competing evaluative predispositions' and Emmons (1996) defined it as 'an approach – avoidance conflict – wanting but at the same time not wanting the same goal object'. Sparks et al. (2001) incorporated the concept of ambivalence into the theory of planned behaviour and assessed whether it predicted meat or chocolate consumption. A total of 325 volunteers completed a questionnaire including a measure of ambivalence assessed in terms of the mean of both positive and negative evaluations (e.g. 'how positive is chocolate' and 'how negative is chocolate') and then subtracting this mean from the absolute difference between the two evaluations (i.e. 'total positive minus total negative'). This computation provides a score that reflects the balance between positive and negative feelings. The results showed that the relationship between attitude and intention was weaker in those participants with higher ambivalence. This implies that holding both positive and negative attitudes to a food makes it less likely that the overall attitude will be translated into an intention to eat it.

Affective beliefs

One of the central criticisms of social cognition models is that they do not adequately account for the role of affect (Manstead and Parker 1995; van der Pligt et al. 1998). To address this, some researchers have argued for the inclusion of affect into the models. Because of the ways in which the beliefs are elicited and measured for social cognition research, researchers have addressed this problem by including affective beliefs. For example, while beliefs that a behaviour is healthy, harmful, safe or useful can be considered instrumental beliefs, those that describe a behaviour as enjoyable, pleasurable, worrying or depressing reflect affective beliefs (Manstead and Parker 1995). Lawton et al. (2006) recently explored the relative contribution of instrumental and affective beliefs in predicting driving above the speed limit and smoking in adolescents. The results showed that negative affective beliefs were the best predictors of observed speeding and that positive and negative affective beliefs were the best predictors of smoking.

Personality

There is much research in psychology that emphasizes the role of personality in predicting health and health-related behaviours (Vollrath and Toergersen 2002). In the main personality research reflects a more stable, trait-like approach to the individual than much cognitive work and covers a range of personality traits such as the 'big five' which are agreeableness, conscientiousness, emotional stability, extraversion and intellect. These aspects of personality have been shown to be associated with a range of health behaviours such as smoking and diet (Bogg and Roberts 2004). Ingledew and Ferguson (2006) explored the role of personality alongside motivation in predicting safer sex in university students and concluded that the traits of agreeableness and conscientiousness predicted safer sex and this effect occurred due to the impact of these personality traits upon an individual's motivation.

Predicting behaviour: exploring the intention–behaviour gap

Social cognition research assesses behavioural intentions as a means to predict behaviour. The link between intentions and behaviour, however, is not always that straightforward. Sutton (1998a) argued that, although structured models are not that effective at predicting behavioural intentions, they are even less effective at predicting actual behaviour. In fact, he suggested that studies using these models only predict 19–38 per cent of the variance in behaviour. Similar analyses of the links between intention and behaviour have also been carried out by Armitage and Conner (2001) and Milne et al. (2002). Some of this failure to predict behaviour may be due to the behaviour being beyond the control of the individual concerned. For example, 'I intend to study at university' may not be translated into 'I am studying at university' due to economic or educational factors. Further, 'I intend to eat healthily' may not be translated into 'I am eating healthily' due to the absence of healthy food. In such instances, the correlation between intentions and behaviour would be zero. However, for most behaviours the correlation between intentions and behaviour is not zero but small, suggesting that the individual does have some control over the behaviour. Psychologists have addressed the problem of predicting actual behaviour in three ways: (1) the concept of behavioural intentions has been expanded; (2) past behaviour has been used as a direct predictor of behaviour; and (3) variables that bridge the intention–behaviour gap have been studied.

Expanding behavioural intentions

Much of the research that uses models to predict health behaviours focuses on behavioural intentions as the best predictor of actual behaviour. However, recent researchers have called for additional variables to be added which expand behavioural intentions. These include the following:

- *Self-predictions* – Sheppard et al. (1988) argued that, rather than just measuring behavioural intentions (i.e. 'I intend to start swimming next week'), it is also important to assess an individual's own prediction that this intention is likely to be fulfilled (e.g. 'it is likely that I will start swimming next week'). They suggested that such self-predictions are more likely to reflect the individual's consideration of those factors that may help or hinder the behaviour itself. To date, some research supports the usefulness of this new variable (Sheppard et al. 1988) while some suggests that the correlation between intentions and self-predictions is too high for self-predictions to add anything extra to a model of health behaviour (Norman and Smith 1995).

- *Behavioural willingness* – Along similar lines to the introduction of self-predictions, researchers have called for the use of behavioural willingness. For example, an individual may not only intend to carry out a behaviour (e.g. 'I intend to eat more fruit') but is also willing to do so (e.g. 'I am willing to eat more fruit'). Gibbons et al. (1998) explored the usefulness of both intentions and willingness, and suggested that willingness may be of particular importance when exploring adolescent behaviour, as adolescents may behave in a less reasoned way, and be unwilling to carry out behaviour that is unpleasant ('I intend to stop smoking').

- *Perceived need* – It may not only be intentions to behave, or self-predictions or even willingness that are important. Paisley and Sparks (1998) argued that it is the perception by an individual that they need to change their behaviour that is critical. For example, an intention – 'I intend to stop smoking' – may be less influential than a perceived need to stop smoking – 'I need to stop smoking'. These authors examined the role of perceived need in predicting expectations of reducing dietary fat and argued for the use of this variable in future research.

- *Temporal stability of intentions* – Intentions may not always predict behaviour because intentions change over time and by the time the new behaviour occurs the old intentions no longer matter. Conner and Godin (2006) explored this possibility and reported that more stable intentions (that did not change over time) were associated with a better intention–behaviour link than those intentions that did change over time.

- *Intention type* – Some behavioural intentions describe what people intend not to do, as in 'I will not smoke'. Other behavioural intentions describe what they intend to do, as in 'I will eat more healthily'. Ogden, Karim et al. (2006) explored the relative effect of these different types of intentions and concluded that successfully reducing calories was related to greater positive rather negative intentions.

Therefore, by expanding behavioural intentions to include self-predictions, behavioural willingness and/or perceived need and by recognizing that intentions change and may be either positive or negative, it is argued that the models will be become better predictors of actual behaviour.

The role of past behaviour

Most research assumes that cognitions predict behavioural intentions, which in turn predict behaviour. This is in line with the shift from 'I think, therefore I intend to do, therefore I do'. It is possible, however, that behaviour is not predicted by cognitions but by behaviour. From this perspective, individuals are more likely to eat healthily tomorrow if they ate healthily today. They are also more likely to go to the doctor for a cervical smear if they have done so in the past. Behaviour has been measured in terms of both past behaviour and habit. In terms of past behaviour, research suggests that it predicts behaviours such as cycle helmet use (Quine et al. 1998), breast self-examination (Hodgkins and Orbell 1998), bringing up condom use (Yzer et al. 2001), wearing an eye patch (Norman et al. 2003) and attendance at health checks (Norman and Conner 1993). In addition, past behaviour may itself predict cognitions that then predict behaviour (Gerrard et al. 1996). In terms of habit, research indicates a role in explaining condom use (Trafimow 2000) and that habit reduces people's use of information (Aarts et al. 1998).

Bridging the intention–behaviour gap

The third approach to address the limited way in which research has predicted behaviour has been to suggest variables that may bridge the gap between intentions to behave and actual behaviour. In particular, some research has highlighted the role of plans for action, health goals commitment and trying as a means to tap into the kinds of cognitions that may be responsible for the translation of intentions into behaviour (Bagozzi and Warshaw 1990; Schwarzer 1992; Bagozzi 1993; Luszczynska and Schwarzer 2003). Most research, however, has focused on Gollwitzer's (1993) notion of implementation intentions. According to Gollwitzer, carrying out an intention involves the development of specific plans as to what an individual will do given a specific set of environmental factors. Therefore implementation intentions describe the 'what' and the 'when' of a particular behaviour. For example, the intention 'I intend to stop smoking' will be more likely to be translated into 'I have stopped smoking' if the individual makes the implementation intention 'I intend to stop smoking tomorrow at 12.00 when I have finished my last packet'. Further, 'I intend to eat healthily' is more likely to be translated into 'I am eating healthily' if the implementation intention 'I will start to eat healthily by having an apple tomorrow lunchtime' is made. Some experimental research has shown that encouraging individuals to make implementation intentions can actually increase the correlation between intentions and behaviour for behaviours such as taking a vitamin C pill (Sheeran and Orbell 1998), performing breast self-examination (Orbell et al. 1997), writing a report (Gollwitzer and Brandstatter 1997) and reducing dietary fat (Armitage 2004). Gollwitzer and Sheeran (2006) carried out a meta-analysis of 94 independent tests of the impact of implementation intentions on a range of behavioural goals including eating a low fat diet, using public transport, exercise and a range of personal goals. The results from this analysis indicated that implementation intentions had a medium to large effect on goal attainment and the analysis provides some insights into the processes involved in this approach. The use of implementation intentions is also supported by the goal-setting approach of cognitive behavioural therapy. Therefore by tapping into variables such as implementation intentions it is argued that the models may become better predictors of actual behaviour.

Developing theory-based interventions

The cognition and social cognition models have been developed to describe and predict health behaviours such as smoking, screening, eating and exercise. Over recent years there has been a call towards using these models to inform and develop health behaviour interventions. This has been based upon two observations. First, it was observed that many interventions designed to change behaviour were only minimally effective. For example, reviews of early interventions to change sexual behaviour concluded that these interventions had only small effects (e.g. Oakley et al. 1995) and dietary interventions for weight loss may result in weight loss in the short term but the majority show a return to baseline by follow-up (e.g. NHS Centre for Reviews and Dissemination 1997). Second, it was observed that many interventions were not based upon any theoretical framework, nor were they drawing upon research that had identified which factors were correlated with the particular behaviour (e.g. Fisher and Fisher 1992). One interesting illustration of this involved the content analysis of health promotion leaflets to assess their theoretical basis. Abraham et al. (2002) collected sexual health leaflets from general practitioners' surgeries and clinics for the treatment of sexually transmitted diseases (STDs) across Germany (37 leaflets) and the UK (74 leaflets). They included those that promoted the use of condoms and/or prevention of STDs including HIV and AIDS and were available widely. They excluded those that were aimed at lesbians due to their focus on protective measures other than condoms and those that targeted a limited audience such as HIV-positive men. The authors then identified the best cognitive and behavioural correlates of condom use based upon a meta-analysis by Sheeran et al. (1999), defined 20 correlate representative categories to reflect these correlates and then rated the leaflets according to the inclusion and frequency of these factors. The results showed very little association between theory and this form of behavioural intervention. Specifically, only 25 per cent of the leaflets referred to ten or more of the correlates and two-thirds of the leaflets failed to frequently target more than two of the correlates. Although research is often aimed at informing practice, it would seem that this is not often the case. How theory can be used to inform practice will now be explored.

Putting theory into practice

Given the call for more theory-based interventions, some researchers have outlined how this can be done. In particular, Sutton (2002b) draws upon the work of Fishbein and Middlestadt (1989) and describes a series of steps that can be followed to develop an intervention based upon the TRA, although he argued that the steps could also be applied to other models.

Step 1: Identify target behaviour and target population.
Step 2: Identify the most salient beliefs about the target behaviour in the target population using open-ended questions.
Step 3: Conduct a study involving closed questions to determine which beliefs are the best predictors of behavioural intention. Choose the best belief as the target belief.
Step 4: Analyse the data to determine the beliefs that best discriminate between intenders and non-intenders. These are further target beliefs.
Step 5: Develop an intervention to change these target beliefs.

However, as Sutton (2002b) points out, this process provides clear details about the preliminary work before the intervention. But the intervention itself remains unclear. Hardeman et al. (2002) carried out a systematic review of 30 papers which used the TPB as part of an intervention and described a range of frameworks that had been used. These included persuasion, information, increasing skills, goal setting and rehearsal of skills. These have recently been developed and integrated into a causal modelling approach for the development of behaviour change programmes (Hardeman et al. 2005). Sutton (2002b) indicates that two additional frameworks could also be useful. These are guided mastery experiences which involve getting people to focus on specific beliefs (e.g. Bandura 1997) and the 'Elaboration Likelihood' model (Petty and Cacioppo 1986) involving the presentation of 'strong arguments' and time for the recipient to think about and elaborate upon these arguments. Studies have also used a range of methods for their interventions including leaflets, videos, lectures and discussions. However, to date although there has been a call for interventions based upon social cognition models, clear guidelines concerning how theory could translate into practice have yet to be developed.

Existing theory-based interventions

Over recent years an increasing number of behavioural interventions have drawn upon a theory of behaviour change (Rutter and Quine 2002). Those based upon social cognition models have attempted to change a range of behaviours. For example, Quine et al. (2001) followed the steps outlined earlier to identify salient beliefs about safety helmet wearing for children. They then developed an intervention based upon persuasion to change these salient beliefs. The results showed that after the intervention the participants showed more positive beliefs about safety helmet wearing than the control group and were more likely to wear a helmet at five months' follow-up. Similarly, McClendon and Prentice-Dunn (2001) targeted suntanning and developed an intervention based upon the PMT. PMT variables were measured at baseline and one month follow-up and those in the intervention group were subjected to lectures, videos, an essay and discussions. The results showed that the intervention was associated with an increase in PMT variables and lighter skin as judged by independent raters. Other theory-based interventions have targeted behaviours such as condom use (Conner et al. 1999b), sun cream use (Castle et al. 1999) and cervical cancer screening (Sheeran and Orbell 2000). However, as Hardeman et al. (2002) found from their systematic review, although many interventions are based upon theory, this is often used for the design of process and outcome measures and to predict intention and behaviour rather than to design the intervention itself. Further, although there is some evidence that theory-based interventions are successful, whether the use of theory relates to the success of the intervention remains unclear. For example, Hardeman et al. (2002) reported that the use of the TPB to develop the intervention was not predictive of the success of the intervention.

Understanding sustained behaviour change

Even though there has been much research and a multitude of interventions, many people continue to behave in unhealthy ways. For example, although smoking in the UK has declined from 45 per cent in 1970 to 26 per cent in 2004, a substantial minority of the population still continue to smoke (National Statistics 2005). Similarly, the prevalence of diet- and exercise-related problems, particularly obesity and overweight, rising (Obesity in the United Kingdom 2005; Ogden et al. 2006a). Further, even though many people show initial changes in their health-related behaviours, rates of sustained behaviour change are poor, with many people reverting to their old habits. For example, although obesity treatments in the last 20 years have improved rates of initial weight loss, there has been very little success in weight loss maintenance in the longer term with up to 95 per cent of people returning to baseline weights by five years (NHS Centre for Reviews and Dissemination 1997; Jeffery et al. 2000; see Chapter 15). Similarly, nearly half of those smokers who make a quit attempt return to smoking within the year (National Statistics 2005; see Chapter 5). If real changes are to be made to people's health status then research needs to address the issue of behaviour change in the longer term. To date, however, most research has focused on the onset of new behaviours or changes in behaviour in the short term due to the use of quantitative methods, with prospective designs that have follow-ups varying from a few weeks only to a year, as longer-term follow-ups require greater investment of time and cost. Some research, however, has addressed the issue of longer-term behaviour change maintenance, particularly for weight loss, smoking cessation and exercise.

- *Weight loss maintenance* – Research indicates that although the majority of the obese regain the weight they lose, a small minority show weight loss maintenance. The factors that predict this are described in detail in Chapter 15; they illustrate a role for profile characteristics such as baseline body mass index (BMI), gender and employment status, historical factors such as previous attempts at weight loss, the type and amount of help received and psychological factors including motivations and individuals' beliefs about the causes of their weight problem. In particular, research suggests that longer-term weight loss maintenance is associated with a behavioural model of obesity whereby behaviour is seen as central to both its cause and solution (Ogden 2000). This is in line with much research on adherence and illness representations and is discussed in detail in Chapter 3.

- *Smoking cessation* – In terms of smoking cessation, much research has drawn upon a stage model approach and suggests that smoking cessation relates to factors such as action plans, goal setting and the transition through stages (e.g. Prochaska and Velicer 1997, see Chapter 5). In contrast, however, West and Sohal (2006) asked almost 2000 smokers and ex-smokers about their quit attempts and reported that nearly half had made quit attempts that were unplanned and that unplanned attempts were more likely to succeed than planned ones. They argue that longer-term smoking cessation may not always be the result of plans and the transition through stages and is often the result of 'catastrophies' which suddenly motivate change.

- *Exercise* – As with changes in diet and smoking, much research exploring exercise uptake has focused on short-term changes. From this perspective most research shows that exercise is related to social factors and enjoyment rather than any longer-term consideration of health goals (see Chapter 7). Armitage (2005) aimed to explore the problem of exercise maintenance and explored the predictors of stable exercise habits over a 12-week period. This study used the standard TPB measures and indicated that perceived behavioural control predicted behaviour in terms of both initiation and maintenance.

In general it would seem that there is a role for a range of demographic, psychological and structural factors in understanding longer-term changes in behaviour and that, while some changes in behaviour may result from the 'drip drip' effect illustrated by stages and plans, other forms of change are the result of more sudden shifts in an individual's motivation. To date, however, there remains very little research on longer-term changes in behaviour. Further, the existing research tends to focus on behaviour-specific changes rather than factors that may generalize across behaviours.

To conclude

The role of health beliefs in predicting health-related behaviours has become increasingly salient with the recent changes in causes of mortality. Some studies exploring health beliefs have emphasized lay theories, which present individuals as having complex views and theories about their health which influence their behaviour. This perspective regards individuals as less rational and examines lay theories in a relatively unstructured format using a qualitative approach. Other studies have taken a more quantitative approach and have explored constructs such as attributions, health locus of control, unrealistic optimism, self-affirmation and stages of change. Psychologists have also developed structured models to integrate these different beliefs and to predict health behaviours such as the health belief model, the protection motivation theory, the theory of planned behaviour and the health action process approach. These models consider individuals to be processors of information and vary in the extent to which they address the individual's cognitions about their social world. The models can be used to predict health behaviours quantitatively and have implications for developing methods to promote change.

❓ Questions

1 Recent changes in mortality rates can be explained in terms of behaviour-related illnesses. Discuss.

2 Discuss the contribution of attribution theory to understanding health behaviours.

3 Health beliefs predict health behaviours. Discuss with reference to two models.

4 Discuss the role of the social world in understanding health behaviours.

5 Human beings are rational information processors. Discuss.

6 Discuss the argument that changing an individual's beliefs would improve their health.

7 Discuss some of the problems with the structured models of health beliefs.

8 To what extent can social cognition models be used to change health behaviours?

9 Design a research project to promote non-smoking in a group of smokers using two models of health beliefs.

For discussion

Consider a recent change in your health-related behaviours (e.g. stopped/started smoking, changed diet, aimed to get more sleep, etc.). Discuss your health beliefs that relate to this change.

Assumptions in health psychology

Research into health beliefs highlights some of the assumptions in health psychology:

1 *Human beings as rational information processors.* Many models of health beliefs assume that behaviour is a consequence of a series of rational stages that can be measured. For example, it is assumed that the individual weighs up the pros and cons of a behaviour, assesses the seriousness of a potentially dangerous illness and then decides how to act. This may not be the case for all behaviours. Even though some of the social cognition models include past behaviour (as a measure of habit), they still assume some degree of rationality.

2 *Cognitions as separate from each other.* The different models compartmentalize different cognitions (perceptions of severity, susceptibility, outcome expectancy, intentions) as if they are discrete and separate entities. However, this separation may only be an artefact of asking questions relating to these different cognitions. For example, an individual may not perceive susceptibility (e.g. 'I am at risk from HIV') as separate to self-efficacy (e.g. 'I am confident that I can control my sexual behaviour and avoid HIV') until they are asked specific questions about these factors.

3 *Cognitions as separate from methodology.* In the same way that models assume that cognitions are separate from each other, they also assume that they exist independent of methodology. However, interview and questionnaire questions may actually create these cognitions.

4 *Cognitions without a context.* Models of health beliefs and health behaviours tend to examine an individual's cognitions out of context. This context could either be the context of another individual or the wider social context. Some of the models incorporate measures of the individuals' representations of their social context (e.g. social norms, peer group norms), but this context is always accessed via the individuals' cognitions.

Further reading

Conner, M. and Norman, P. (eds) (1998) Special issue: social cognition models in health psychology, *Psychology and Health*, 13: 179–85.
This special issue presents research in the area of social cognition models. The editorial provides an overview of the field.

Conner, M. and Norman, P. (2005) *Predicting Health Behaviour* (2nd edn) Buckingham: Open University Press.
This book provides an excellent overview of the different models, the studies that have been carried out using them and the new developments in this area.

Gollwitzer, P.M. and Sheeran, P. (2006). Implementation intentions and goal achievement: a meta-analysis of effects and processes, *Advances in Experimental Social Psychology*, 38: 69–119.
This paper provides a detailed account of the research using implementation intentions. It is also an excellent example of a meta-analysis and how this approach can be used effectively.

Rutter, D. and Quine, L. (eds) (2003) *Changing Health Behaviour: Intervention and Research with Social Cognition Models.* Buckingham: Open University Press.

This edited book provides an excellent review of the intervention literature including an analysis of the problems with designing interventions and with their evaluation.

Webb, T.L. and Sheeran, P. (2006) Does changing behavioural intentions engender behaviour change? A meta-analysis of the experimental evidence, *Psychological Bulletin*, 132: 249–68.

This paper presents a meta-analysis of the research exploring the links between intentions and behaviour. It is a useful paper in itself but also provides an excellent source of references.

Woodcock, A., Stenner, K. and Ingham, R. (1992) Young people talking about HIV and AIDS: interpretations of personal risk of infection, *Health Education Research: Theory and Practice*, 7: 229–47.

This paper illustrates a qualitative approach to health beliefs and is a good example of how to present qualitative data.

Chapter 3

Illness cognitions

Chapter overview

Chapter 2 described health beliefs and the models that have been developed to evaluate these beliefs and their relationship to health behaviours. Individuals, however, also have beliefs about illness. This chapter examines what it means to be 'healthy' and what it means to be 'sick' and reviews these meanings in the context of how individuals cognitively represent illness (their illness cognitions/illness beliefs). The chapter then assesses how illness beliefs can be measured and places these beliefs within Leventhal's self-regulatory model. It then discusses the relationship between illness cognitions, symptom perception and coping behaviour. Finally, the chapter examines the relationship between illness cognitions and health outcomes and the role of coherence.

This chapter covers

- What does it mean to be healthy?
- What does it mean to be ill?
- What are illness cognitions?
- Measuring illness cognitions
- Leventhal's self-regulatory model of illness cognitions
- Symptom perception
- Coping
- Illness cognitions and health outcomes

What does it mean to be healthy?

For the majority of people living in the western world, being healthy is the norm – most people are healthy for most of the time. Therefore, beliefs about being ill exist in the context of beliefs about being healthy (e.g. illness means not being healthy, illness means feeling different to usual, etc.). The World Health Organization (1947) defined good health as 'a state of complete physical, mental and social well being'. This definition presents a broad multidimensional view of health that departs from the traditional medical emphasis on physical health only.

Over recent years this multidimensional model has emerged throughout the results of several qualitative studies that have asked lay people the question 'what does it mean to be healthy?' For example, from a social anthropological perspective, Helman (1978) explored the extent to which beliefs inherent within the eighteenth-century's humoral theory have survived alongside those of conventional medicine. In particular, he focused on the saying 'feed a cold and starve a fever', and argued that lay constructs of health could be conceptualized according to the dimensions 'hot/cold' and 'wet/dry'. For example, problems with the chest were considered either 'hot and wet' (e.g. fever and productive cough) or 'cold and wet' (e.g. cold and non-productive cough). Likewise, problems could be considered 'hot and dry' (e.g. fever, dry skin, flushed face, dry throat, non-productive cough) or 'cold and dry' (e.g. cold, shivering, rigour, malaise, vague muscular aches). In a similar vein, medical sociologists have also explored lay conceptions of health. For example, Herzlich (1973) interviewed 80 French subjects and categorized their models of health into three dimensions: 'health in a vacuum', implying the absence of illness; 'the reserve of health', relating to physical strength and resistance to illness; and 'equilibrium' indicating a full realization of the individual's reserve of health. Likewise, Blaxter (1990) asked 9000 individuals to describe someone whom they thought was healthy and to consider, 'What makes you call them healthy?' and, 'What is it like when you are healthy?' A qualitative analysis was then carried out on a sub-sample of these individuals. For some, health simply meant not being ill. However, for many health was seen in terms of a reserve, a healthy life filled with health behaviours, physical fitness, having energy and vitality, social relationships with others, being able to function effectively and an expression of psychosocial well-being. Blaxter also examined how a concept of health varied over the life course and investigated any sex differences. Furthermore, Calnan (1987) explored the health beliefs of women in England and argued that their models of health could be conceptualized in two sets of definitions: positive definitions including feeling energetic, plenty of exercise, feeling fit, eating the right things, being the correct weight, having a positive outlook and having a good life/marriage; and negative definitions including not getting coughs and colds, only in bed once, rarely go to the doctor and have check-ups – nothing wrong.

The issue of 'what is health?' has also been explored from a psychological perspective with a particular focus on health and illness cognitions. For example, Lau (1995) found that when young healthy adults were asked to describe in their own words 'what being healthy means to you', their beliefs about health could be understood within the following dimensions:

- *physiological/physical*, for example, good condition, have energy
- *psychological*, for example, happy, energetic, feel good psychologically
- *behavioural*, for example, eat, sleep properly
- *future consequences*, for example, live longer
- *the absence of illness*, for example, not sick, no disease, no symptoms.

Lau (1995) argued that most people show a positive definition of health (not just the absence of illness), which also includes more than just physical and psychological factors. He suggested that healthiness is most people's normal state and represents the backdrop to their beliefs about being ill. Psychological studies of the beliefs of the elderly (Hall et al. 1989), those suffering from a chronic illness (Hays and Stewart 1990) and children (Normandeau et al. 1998; Schmidt and Frohling 2000) have reported that these individuals also conceptualize health as being multidimensional. This indicates some overlap between professional (WHO) and lay views of health (i.e. a multidimensional perspective involving physical and psychological factors).

What does it mean to be ill?

In his study of the beliefs of young healthy adults, Lau (1995) also asked participants 'what does it mean to be sick?' Their answers indicated the dimensions they use to conceptualize illness:

- *not feeling normal*, for example, 'I don't feel right'
- *specific symptoms*, for example, physiological/psychological
- *specific illnesses*, for example, cancer, cold, depression
- *consequences of illness*, for example, 'I can't do what I usually do'
- *time line*, for example, how long the symptoms last
- *the absence of health*, for example, not being healthy.

These dimensions of 'what it means to be ill' have been described within the context of illness cognitions (also called illness beliefs or illness representations).

What are illness cognitions?

Leventhal and his colleagues (Leventhal et al. 1980, 1997; Leventhal and Nerenz 1985) defined illness cognitions as 'a patient's own implicit common sense beliefs about their illness'. They proposed that these cognitions provide patients with a framework or a schema for *coping with* and *understanding their illness*, and *telling them what to look out for if they are becoming ill.* Using interviews with patients suffering from a variety of different illnesses, Leventhal and his colleagues identified five cognitive dimensions of these beliefs:

1 *Identity*: This refers to the label given to the illness (the medical diagnosis) and the symptoms experienced (e.g. I have a cold – 'the diagnosis', with a runny nose – 'the symptoms').

2 *The perceived cause of the illness*: These causes may be biological, such as a virus or a lesion, or psychosocial, such as stress- or health-related behaviour. In addition, patients may hold representations of illness that reflect a variety of different causal models (e.g. 'My cold was caused by a virus', 'My cold was caused by being run down').

3 *Time line*: This refers to the patients' beliefs about how long the illness will last, whether it is acute (short term) or chronic (long term) (e.g. 'My cold will be over in a few days').

4 *Consequences*: This refers to the patient's perceptions of the possible effects of the illness on their life. Such consequences may be physical (e.g. pain, lack of mobility), emotional (e.g. loss of social contact, loneliness) or a combination of factors (e.g. 'My cold will prevent me from playing football, which will prevent me from seeing my friends').

5 *Curability and controllability*: Patients also represent illnesses in terms of whether they believe that the illness can be treated and cured and the extent to which the outcome of their illness is controllable either by themselves or by powerful others (e.g. 'If I rest, my cold will go away', 'If I get medicine from my doctor my cold will go away').

Evidence for these dimensions of illness cognitions

The extent to which beliefs about illness are constituted by these different dimensions has been studied using two main methodologies – qualitative and quantitative research.

Qualitative research

Leventhal and his colleagues carried out interviews with individuals who were chronically ill, had been recently diagnosed as having cancer, and with healthy adults. The resulting descriptions of illness suggest underlying beliefs that are made up of the aforementioned dimensions. Leventhal and colleagues argued that interviews are the best way to access illness cognitions as this methodology avoids the possibility of priming the subjects. For example, asking a subject 'to what extent do you think about your illness in terms of its possible consequences?' will obviously encourage them to regard consequences as an important dimension. However, according to Leventhal, interviews encourage subjects to express their own beliefs, not those expected by the interviewer.

Quantitative research

Other studies have used more artificial and controlled methodologies, and these too have provided support for the dimensions of illness cognitions. Lau et al. (1989) used a card-sorting technique to evaluate how subjects conceptualized illness. They asked 20 subjects to sort 65 statements into piles that 'made sense to them'. These statements had been made previously in response to descriptions of 'your most recent illness'. They reported that the subjects' piles of categories reflected the dimensions of identity (diagnosis/symptoms), consequences (the possible effects), time line (how long it will last), cause (what caused the illness) and cure/control (how and whether it can be treated).

A series of experimental studies by Bishop and colleagues also provided support for these dimensions. For example, Bishop and Converse (1986) presented subjects with brief descriptions of patients who were experiencing six different symptoms. Subjects were randomly allocated to one of two sets of descriptions: high prototype in which all six symptoms had been previously rated as associated with the same disease, or low prototype in which only two of the six symptoms had been previously rated as associated with the same disease. The results showed that subjects in the high prototype condition labelled the disease more easily and accurately than subjects in the low prototype condition. The authors argued that this provides support for the role of the identity dimension (diagnosis and symptoms) of illness representations and also suggested that there is some consistency in people's concept of the identity of illnesses. In addition, subjects were asked to describe in their own words 'what else do you think may be associated with this person's situation?'. They reported that 91 per cent of the given associations fell into the dimensions of illness representations as described by Leventhal and his colleagues. However, they also reported that the dimensions consequences (the possible effects) and time line (how long it will last) were the least frequently mentioned.

There is also some evidence for a similar structure of illness representations in other cultures. Weller (1984) examined models of illness in English-speaking Americans and Spanish-speaking Guatemalans. The results indicated that illness was predominantly conceptualized in terms of contagion and severity. Lau (1995) argued that contagion is a version of the cause dimension (i.e. the illness is caused by a virus) and severity is a combination of the magnitude of the perceived consequences and beliefs about time line (i.e. how will the illness affect my life and how long will it last) – dimensions that support those described by Leventhal and his colleagues. Hagger and Orbell (2003) carried out a meta-analysis of 45 empirical studies which used Leventhal's model of illness cognitions. They concluded from their analysis that there was consistent support for the different illness cognition dimensions and that the different cognitions showed a logical pattern across different illness types.

Measuring illness cognitions

Leventhal and colleagues originally used qualitative methods to assess people's illness cognitions. Since this time other forms of measurement have been used. These will be described in terms of questionnaires that have been developed and methodological issues surrounding measurement.

The use of questionnaires

Although it has been argued that the preferred method to access illness cognitions is through interview, interviews are time consuming and can only involve a limited number of subjects. In order to research further into individuals' beliefs about illness, researchers in New Zealand and the UK have developed the 'illness perception questionnaire' (IPQ) (Weinman et al. 1996). This questionnaire asks subjects to rate a series of statements about their illness. These statements reflect the dimensions of identity (e.g. a set of symptoms such as pain, tiredness), consequences (e.g. 'My illness has had major consequences on my life'), time line (e.g. 'My illness will last a short time'), cause (e.g. 'Stress was a major factor in causing my illness') and cure/control (e.g. 'There is a lot I can do to control my symptoms'). This questionnaire has been used to examine beliefs about illnesses such as chronic fatigue syndrome, diabetes and arthritis and provides further support for the dimensions of illness cognitions (Weinman and Petrie 1997). Recently a revised version of the IPQ has been published – IPQR (Moss-Morris et al. 2002) – which had better psychometric properties than the original IPQ and included three additional subscales: cyclical time-line perceptions, illness coherence and emotional representations. People have beliefs not only about their illness but also about their treatment, whether it is medication, surgery or behaviour change. In line with this, Horne (1997; Horne et al. 1999) developed a questionnaire to assess beliefs about medicine which was conceptualized along four dimensions. Two of these are specific to the medication being taken: 'specific necessity' (to reflect whether their medicine is seen as important) and 'specific concerns' (to reflect whether the individual is concerned about side effects); and two of these are general beliefs about all medicines: 'general overuse' (to reflect doctors' overuse of medicines) and 'general harm' (to reflect the damage that medicines can do). These two core dimensions of necessity and concerns have been shown to describe people's beliefs about anti-retroviral therapy for HIV/AIDS (Cooper et al. 2002b; Horne et al. 2004a) and to be relevant to a range of beliefs about medicines for illnesses such as asthma, renal disease, cancer, HIV and cardiac failure (e.g. Horne and Weinman 1999). Research also shows that although individuals may report a consistent pattern of beliefs, this pattern varies according to cultural background (Horne et al. 2004a).

Measurement issues

Beliefs about illness can be assessed using a range of measures. Some research has used interviews (e.g. Leventhal et al. 1980; Leventhal and Nerenz 1985; Schmidt and Frohling 2000), some has used formal questionnaires (e.g. Horne and Weinman 2002; Llewellyn et al. 2003), some have used vignette studies (e.g. French, Senior et al. 2002) and others have used a repertory grid method (e.g. Walton and Eves 2001). French and colleagues asked whether the form of method used to elicit beliefs about illness influenced the types of beliefs reported. In one study French, Senior et al. (2002) compared the impact of eliciting beliefs using either a questionnaire or a vignette. Participants were asked either simply to rate a series of causes for heart attack (the questionnaire) or to read a vignette about a man and to estimate his chances of having a heart attack. The results showed that the two different methods resulted in different beliefs about the causes of heart attack and different importance placed upon these causes. Specifically, when using the questionnaire, smoking and stress came out as more important causes than family history, whereas when using the vignette, smoking and family history came out as more important causes than stress. In a similar vein French et al. (2001) carried out a systematic review of studies involving attributions for causes of heart attack and compared these causes according to method used. The results showed that stressors, fate or luck were more common beliefs about causes when using interval rating scales (i.e. 1–5) than when studies used dichotomous answers (i.e. yes/no). French, Marteau et al. (2005) also asked whether causal beliefs should be subjected to a factor analysis as a means to combine different sets of beliefs into individual constructs (e.g. external causes, lifestyle causes, etc.) and concluded that although many researchers use this approach to combine their data it is unlikely to result in very valid groups of causal beliefs.

In summary, it appears that individuals may show consistent beliefs about illness that can be used to make sense of their illness and help their understanding of any developing symptoms. These illness cognitions have been incorporated into a model of illness behaviour to examine the relationship between an individual's cognitive representation of their illness and their subsequent coping behaviour. This model is known as the 'self-regulatory model of illness behaviour'.

Box 3.1 **Some problems with . . . illness cognitions research**

Below are some problems with research in this area that you may wish to consider.

1 Research often explores how people feel about their symptoms or illness by using existing questionnaires. It is possible that such measures change beliefs rather than simply access them (i.e. do I really have a belief about what has caused my headache until I am asked about it?).

2 Models of illness behaviour describe how the different constructs relate to each other (i.e. illness representations are associated with coping). It is not always clear, however, whether these two constructs are really discrete (e.g. 'I believe my illness is not going to last a long time' could either be an illness cognition or a coping mechanism).

3 Many of the constructs measured as part of research on illness behaviour are then used to predict health outcomes such as illness beliefs and coping. It is not clear how stable these constructs are and whether they should be considered states or traits. As a self-regulatory model, the changing nature of these constructs is central. However, it presents a real methodological problem in terms of when to measure what and whether variables are causes or consequences of each other.

Leventhal's self-regulatory model of illness cognitions

Leventhal incorporated his description of illness cognitions into his self-regulatory model of illness behaviour. This model is based on approaches to problem solving and suggests that illness/symptoms are dealt with by individuals in the same way as other problems (see Chapter 4 for details of other models of problem solving). It is assumed that, given a problem or a change in the *status quo*, the individual will be motivated to solve the problem and re-establish their state of normality. Traditional models describe problem solving in three stages: (1) interpretation (making sense of the problem); (2) coping (dealing with the problem in order to regain a state of equilibrium); and (3) appraisal (assessing how successful the coping stage has been). According to models of problem solving these three stages will continue until the coping strategies are deemed to be successful and a state of equilibrium has been attained. In terms of health and illness, if healthiness is an individual's normal state, then any onset of illness will be interpreted as a problem and the individual will be motivated to re-establish their state of health (i.e. illness is not the normal state).

These stages have been applied to health using the self-regulatory model of illness behaviour (see Figure 3.1) and are described briefly here and in more detail later on page 56.

Stage 1: Interpretation

An individual may be confronted with the problem of a potential illness through two channels: *symptom perception* ('I have a pain in my chest') or *social messages* ('the doctor has diagnosed this pain as angina').

Once the individual has received information about the possibility of illness through these channels, according to theories of problem solving, the individual is then motivated to return to a state of 'problem-free' normality. This involves assigning meaning to the problem. According to Leventhal, the problem can be given meaning by accessing the individual's illness cognitions. Therefore the symptoms and social messages will contribute towards the development of illness cognitions, which will be constructed according to the following dimensions: identity, cause, consequences, time line, cure/control. These cognitive representations of the 'problem' will give the problem meaning and will enable the individual to develop and consider suitable coping strategies.

However, a cognitive representation is not the only consequence of symptom perception and social messages. The identification of the problem of illness will also result in changes in emotional state. For example, perceiving the symptom of pain and receiving the social message that this pain may be related to coronary heart disease may result in anxiety. Therefore, any coping strategies have to relate to both the illness cognitions and the emotional state of the individual.

Stage 2: Coping

The next stage in the self-regulatory model is the development and identification of suitable coping strategies. Coping can take many forms, which will be discussed in detail later in this

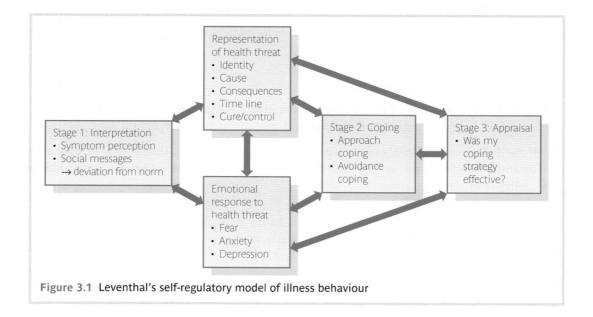

Figure 3.1 Leventhal's self-regulatory model of illness behaviour

chapter and in Chapter 11. However, two broad categories of coping have been defined that incorporate the multitude of other coping strategies: approach coping (e.g. taking pills, going to the doctor, resting, talking to friends about emotions) and avoidance coping (e.g. denial, wishful thinking). When faced with the problem of illness, the individual will therefore develop coping strategies in an attempt to return to a state of healthy normality.

Stage 3: Appraisal

The third stage of the self-regulatory model is appraisal. This involves individuals evaluating the effectiveness of the coping strategy and determining whether to continue with this strategy or whether to opt for an alternative one.

Why is the model called self-regulatory?

This process is regarded as self-regulatory because the three components of the model (interpretation, coping, appraisal) interrelate in order to maintain the *status quo* (i.e. they regulate the self). Therefore, if the individual's normal state (health) is disrupted (by illness), the model proposes that the individual is motivated to return the balance back to normality. This self-regulation involves the three processes interrelating in an ongoing and dynamic fashion. Therefore, interactions occur between the different stages. For example:

- Symptom perception may result in an emotional shift, which may exacerbate the perception of symptoms (e.g. 'I can feel a pain in my chest. Now I feel anxious. Now I can feel more pain as all my attention is focused on it').

- If the individual opts to use denial as their coping strategy, this may result in a reduction in symptom perception, a decrease in any negative emotions and a shift in their illness cognition (e.g. 'This pain is not very bad' (denial); 'Now I feel less anxious' (emotions); 'This pain will not last for long' (time line); 'This illness will not have any serious consequences for my lifestyle' (consequences)).

- A positive appraisal of the effectiveness of the coping strategy may itself be a coping strategy (e.g. 'My symptoms appear to have been reduced by doing relaxation exercises' may be a form of denial).

Problems with assessment

This dynamic, self-regulatory process suggests a model of cognitions that is complex and intuitively sensible, but poses problems for attempts at assessment and intervention. For example:

1 If the different components of the self-regulatory model interact, should they be measured separately? For example, is the belief that an illness has no serious consequences an illness cognition or a coping strategy?

2 If the different components of the self-regulatory model interact, can individual components be used to predict outcome or should the individual components be seen as co-occurring? For example, is the appraisal that symptoms have been reduced a successful outcome or is it a form of denial (a coping strategy)?

Testing a theory – illness representations and behavioural outcomes

A study to explore the role of coherence in promoting the intentions to quit smoking (Hall et al. 2004).

This paper presents the results from two studies to examine the relationship between women's beliefs about cervical cancer and their intentions to quit smoking. In particular the study explored whether, by making beliefs about threat and behaviour more coherent with each other, people are more likely to be motivated to change their behaviour.

Background

Research shows that women who smoke have twice the chance of developing cervical cancer than those who do not. Most women, however, are unaware of this association and, when told that smoking can increase the risk of cervical cancer, report finding this information confusing and nonsensical ('how [can] smoking a cigarette in your mouth cause you problems down-stairs?'). Leventhal's self-regulatory model illustrates that people represent their illness in the form of illness representations. He also argues that if people are to act on threats to their health they need to have a coherent model whereby their beliefs about the nature of the threat are coherent with their beliefs about any action that could be taken. The relationship between smoking and cervical cancer does not immediately make sense, suggesting that most people do not have a coherent model about the link between these factors. The present study used an experimental design to present women with a coherent model of how smoking is linked to cervical cancer and to explore whether a more coherent model was associated with a greater intention to quit smoking.

Study 1
Methodology
Design
The study used an experimental design with women receiving either a detailed leaflet about cervical cancer and smoking, a less detailed leaflet or no leaflet.

Sample
The sample consisted of female smokers aged between 20 and 64 years who were recruited from two general practices in the UK.

Procedure
Women who received a leaflet in the post were then asked to complete a questionnaire a week later. Those who did not receive a leaflet were just sent the questionnaire.

Measures
Women completed measures of response efficacy (the extent to which stopping smoking would reduce vulnerability to cervical cancer), self-efficacy for smoking cessation, severity, coherence (the extent to which they believed they had a coherent explanation for the link between smoking and cervical cancer) and intentions to quit smoking in the next month. In addition, measures of smoking behaviour were taken.

Data analysis

The results were analysed to assess the impact of the leaflets on women's level of coherence, beliefs and intentions. The results were then analysed to assess the relationship between level of coherence, beliefs and intentions.

Results

The results showed that the detailed and less detailed leaflet were equally as effective at producing a coherent model of the relationship between smoking and cervical cancer and were both more effective than receiving no leaflet. The results also showed that those who received a leaflet (regardless of level of detail) reported higher vulnerability to cervical cancer, greater response efficacy and higher intentions to quit smoking. Finally, in terms of the relationship between coherence, beliefs and intentions the results showed that greater intentions, to quit smoking were predicted by greater coherence, greater perceptions of severity, higher response efficacy and higher self-efficacy. Furthermore, greater perceptions of vulnerability to cervical cancer only predicted intentions to quit smoking in those women who showed a coherent model of the link between smoking and cervical cancer.

Conclusion

The results therefore show the importance of a coherent model in creating a link between beliefs and intentions. The results also show that coherence can be changed by a simple leaflet intervention.

Study 2

Because of the weakness of some of the measures in Study 1, the authors replicated their study with a further 178 women smokers and included an improved measure of vulnerability.

The results directly replicated the findings of Study 1.

Conclusion

This study illustrates a role for coherence between beliefs about threat and subsequent action and supports Leventhal's model. Therefore people would seem more likely to intend to change their behaviour if they have a coherent model as to how this behaviour may impact upon their health status.

The individual processes involved in the self-regulatory model will now be examined in greater detail.

Stage 1: interpretation

Symptom perception

Individual differences in symptom perception

Symptoms such as a temperature, pain, a runny nose or the detection of a lump may indicate to the individual the possibility of illness. However, symptom perception is not a straightforward process (see Chapter 12 for details of pain perception and Chapter 16 for details of menopausal symptoms). For example, what might be a sore throat to one person could be another's tonsillitis, and whereas a retired person might consider a cough a serious problem, a working person might be too busy to think about it. Pennebaker (1983) has argued that there are individual differences in the amount of attention people pay to their internal states. Whereas some individuals may sometimes be internally focused and more sensitive to symptoms, others may be more externally focused and less sensitive to any internal changes. However, this difference is not always consistent with differences in accuracy. Some research suggests that internal focus is related to overestimation. For example, Pennebaker (1983) reported that individuals who were more focused on their internal states tended to overestimate changes in their heart rate compared with subjects who were externally focused. In contrast Kohlmann et al. (2001) examined the relationship between cardiac vigilance and heart-beat detection in the laboratory and reported a negative correlation; those who stated they were more aware of their heart underestimated their heart rate. Being internally focused has also been shown to relate to a perception of slower recovery from illness (Miller et al. 1987) and to more health-protective behaviour (Kohlmann et al. 2001). Being internally focused may result in a different perception of symptom change, not a more accurate one.

Mood, cognitions, environment and symptom perception

Skelton and Pennebaker (1982) suggested that symptom perception is influenced by factors such as mood, cognitions and the social environment.

Mood

The role of mood in symptom perception is particularly apparent in pain perception with anxiety increasing self-reports of the pain experience (see Chapter 12 for a discussion of anxiety and pain). In addition, anxiety has been proposed as an explanation for placebo pain reduction as taking any form of medication (even a sugar pill) may reduce the individual's anxiety, increase their sense of control and result in pain reduction (see Chapter 13 for a discussion of anxiety and placebos and Chapter 16 for a discussion of anxiety and birth and menopausal symptoms). Cropley and Steptoe (2005) directly explored the relationship between recent life stress and general symptom reporting and found that higher stress was associated with an increased frequency of a range of symptoms. Stegen et al. (2000) explored the impact of negative affectivity on both the experience of symptoms and attributions for these symptoms. In an experimental study, participants were exposed to low intensity somatic sensations induced by breathing air high in carbon dioxide. They were then told that the sensation would be either positive, negative or somewhere between and were asked to rate both the pleasantness and intensity of their symptoms. The results showed that what the participants were told about the sensation influenced their ratings of its pleasantness. The results also showed that although people who rated high on negative affectivity, showed similar ratings of pleasantness to those low on negative affectivity they did report more negative meanings and worries about their symptoms. This indicates that expectations about the nature of a symptom can alter the experience of that symptom and that negative mood can influence the attributions made about a symptom. Similarly, Mora et al. (in press) explored the role of negative affect on symptom perception and the processes underlying this relationship. Their study involved both a cross-sectional and longitudinal design and assessed trait and state negative affect in adults with moderate and severe asthma. The results showed that higher trait negative affect was related to higher reports of all symptoms whether or not they were related to asthma. In addition, the results showed that only those who were worried about their asthma attributed their asthma symptoms to asthma. This suggests that negative affect increases symptom perception; and further, that worrying about asthma enables the individual to associate their symptoms with their illness. In line with this relationship between mood and symptoms, a recent study explored the impact of manipulating psychological stress on symptom perception (Wright et al. 2005). Using an experimental design, 42 patients with heartburn and reflux were exposed either to a psychological stressor or a no-stress control condition. They then rated their state anxiety and symptom perception. In addition, objective ratings of reflux symptoms were taken. The results showed that the stressor resulted in increased subjective ratings of symptoms. The stressor, however, did not result in any increase in actual reflux. Therefore the stressor resulted in a greater dissociation between subjective and objective symptoms. This study is important as it not only illustrates the impact of stress on symptom perception but also illustrates that gap between objective and subjective accounts of symptoms.

Cognition

An individual's cognitive state may also influence their symptom perception. This is illustrated by the placebo effect with the individual's expectations of recovery resulting in reduced symptom perception (see Chapter 13). It is also illustrated by Stegen et al.'s (2000) study of breathing symptoms with expectations changing symptom perception. Ruble (1977) carried out a study in which she manipulated women's expectations about when they were due to start menstruating. She gave subjects an 'accurate physiological test' and told women either that their period was due very shortly or that it was at least a week away. The women were then asked to report any premenstrual symptoms. The results showed that believing that they were about to start menstruating (even though they were not) increased the number of reported premenstrual symptoms. This indicates an association between cognitive state and symptom perception. Pennebaker also reported that symptom perception is related to an individual's attentional state and that boredom and the absence of environmental stimuli may result in over-reporting, whereas distraction and attention diversion may lead to under-reporting (Pennebaker 1983). One study provides support for Pennebaker's theory. Sixty-one women who had been hospitalized during pre-term labour were randomized to receive either information, distraction or nothing (van Zuuren 1998). The results showed that distraction had the most beneficial effect on measures of both physical and psychological symptoms, suggesting that symptom perception is sensitive to attention. Symptom perception can also be influenced by the ways in which symptoms are elicited. For example, Eiser (2000) carried out an experimental study whereby students were asked to indicate their symptoms, from a list of 30 symptoms, over the past month and the past year and also to rate their health status. However, whereas half were asked to endorse their symptoms (i.e. mark those they had had), half were asked to exclude their symptoms (i.e. mark those they had not had). The results showed that those in the 'exclude' condition reported 70 per cent more symptoms than those in the 'endorse' condition. In addition, those who had endorsed the symptoms rated their health more negatively than those who had excluded symptoms. This suggests that it is not only focus and attention that can influence symptom perception but also the ways in which this focus is directed.

Environment

Symptom perception is therefore influenced by mood and cognition. It is also influenced by an individual's social context. Cross-cultural research consistently shows variation in the presentation of psychiatric symptoms such as anxiety, psychosis and depression. For example, Minsky et al. (2003) explored diagnostic patterns in Latino, African American and European American psychiatric patients and reported that not only did the diagnoses of major depression and schizophrenic disorders vary by ethnic group, but so did symptom presentation, with Latinos reporting a higher frequency of psychotic symptoms than the other groups. Similarly, a consensus statement by the International Consensus Group of Depression and Anxiety (Ballenger et al. 2001) concluded that there was wide cultural variation not only in the diagnosis and responsiveness to treatment for depression and anxiety but also significant variation in symptom presentation. A similar pattern of variation can also be found for somatic symptoms such as headaches, fatigue, constipation and back pain although research in this area is less extensive. For example, epidemiological studies indicate that while headache is a common symptom in the USA and Western Europe, its prevalence remains much lower in China and in African and Asian populations (e.g. Ziegler 1990; Stewart et al. 1996; Wang et al. 1997). Similarly, large surveys of primary care attenders report that those from less developed countries and from Latin America tend to report more somatic symptoms in general (Gureje et al. 1997; Piccinelli and Simon 1997). One study explored cataract patients' reports of visual function and the extent to which they were bothered by their cataract and explored differences by culture (Alonso et al. 1998). The results showed that after controlling for clinical and sociodemographic characteristics, patients from Canada and Barcelona reported less trouble with their vision than patients from Denmark or the USA, suggesting cultural variation in the perception of visual symptoms. Symptom perception and diagnosis are therefore highly influenced by the individual's context and cultural background.

Mood, cognition and environment therefore influence symptom perception. These different factors are illustrated by a condition known as 'medical students' disease', which has been described by Mechanic (1962). A large component of the medical curriculum involves learning about the symptoms associated with a multitude of different illnesses. More than two-thirds of medical students incorrectly report that at some time they have had the symptoms they are being taught about. Perhaps this phenomenon can be understood in terms of the following:

- *Mood*: Medical students become quite anxious due to their workload. This anxiety may heighten their awareness of any physiological changes, making them more internally focused.
- *Cognition*: Medical students are thinking about symptoms as part of their course, which may result in a focus on their own internal states.
- *Social*: Once one student starts to perceive symptoms, others may model themselves on this behaviour.

Therefore, symptom perception influences how an individual interprets the problem of illness.

Social messages

Information about illness also comes from other people. This may come in the form of a formal diagnosis from a health professional or a positive test result from a routine health check. Such messages may or may not be a consequence of symptom perception. For example, a formal diagnosis may occur after symptoms have been perceived; when the individual has subsequently been motivated to go to the doctor and has been given a diagnosis. However, screening and health checks may detect illness at an asymptomatic stage of development and therefore attendance for such a test may not have been motivated by symptom perception. Information about illness may also come from other lay individuals who are not health professionals. Before (and after) consulting a health professional, people often access their social network, which has been called their 'lay referral system' by Freidson (1970). This can take the form of colleagues, friends or family and involves seeking information and advice from multiple sources. For example, coughing in front of one friend may result in the advice to speak to another friend who had a similar cough, or a suggestion to take a favoured home remedy. Alternatively, it may result in a lay diagnosis or a suggestion to seek professional help from the doctor. In fact, Scambler et al. (1981) reported that three-quarters of those taking part in their study of primary care attenders had sought advice from family or friends before seeking professional help. Such social messages will influence how the individual interprets the 'problem' of illness. The language used by the doctor is also an important source of information. Some research has explored how the language used by the doctor can influence how the patient feels about their problem. For example, Ogden et al. (2003) explored the relative effect of calling a problem by its lay term (i.e. sore throat/stomach upset) or by its medical term (i.e. tonsillitis/gastroenteritis) and showed that whereas the medical terms made the patient feel that their symptoms were being taken seriously and reported greater confidence in the doctor, the lay terms made the patient feel more ownership of the problem which could be associated with unwanted responsibility and blame. In a similar vein, Tayler and Ogden (2005) explored the relative effect of describing a problem as either 'heart failure' or the doctors' preferred euphemism for the symptoms that are considered as heart failure – 'fluid on your lungs as your heart is not pumping hard enough'. The results showed that manipulating the name of the problem in this way resulted in significant shifts in people's beliefs about the problem. In particular, the term 'heart failure' resulted in people believing that the problem would have more serious consequences, would be more variable over time, would last for longer and made them feel more anxious and depressed about their problem compared to the euphemism. People therefore receive social messages about the nature of their problem which influence how they represent this problem and subsequently how they then behave.

Stage 2: coping

There is a vast literature on how people cope with a range of problems including stress, pain and illness. Coping with stress and pain is covered in Chapters 11 and 12. This section will examine three approaches to coping with illness: (1) coping with a diagnosis; (2) coping with the crisis of illness; and (3) adjustment to physical illness and the theory of cognitive adaptation. These different theoretical approaches have implications for understanding the differences between adaptive and maladaptive coping, and the role of reality and illusions in the coping process. They therefore have different implications for understanding the outcome of the coping process.

Coping with a diagnosis

Shontz (1975) described the following stages of coping that individuals often go through after a diagnosis of a chronic illness:

- *Shock*: Initially, according to Shontz, most people go into a state of shock following a diagnosis of a serious illness. Being in shock is characterized by being stunned and bewildered, behaving in an automatic fashion and having feelings of detachment from the situation.
- *Encounter reaction*: Following shock, Shontz argued that the next stage is an encounter reaction. This is characterized by disorganized thinking and feelings of loss, grief, helplessness and despair.
- *Retreat*: Retreat is the third stage in the process of coping with a diagnosis. Shontz argued that this stage is characterized by denial of the problem and its implications and a retreat into the self.

Implications for the outcome of the coping process

Shontz developed these stages from observations of individuals in hospital and suggested that, once at the retreat stage, individuals with a diagnosis of a serious illness can gradually deal with the reality of their diagnosis. According to Shontz, retreat is only a temporary stage and denial of reality cannot last forever. Therefore the retreat stage acts as a launch pad for a gradual reorientation towards the reality of the situation, and as reality intrudes, the individual begins to face up to their illness. Therefore this model of coping focuses on the immediate changes following a diagnosis, suggesting that the desired outcome of any coping process is to face up to reality and that reality orientation is an adaptive coping mechanism.

Coping with the crisis of illness

In an alternative approach to coping with illness, Moos and Schaefer (1984) have applied 'crisis theory' to the crisis of physical illness.

What is crisis theory?

Crisis theory has been generally used to examine how people cope with major life crises and transitions and has traditionally provided a framework for understanding the impact of illness or injury. The theory was developed from work done on grief and mourning and a model of developmental crises at transition points in the life cycle. In general, crisis theory examines the impact of any form of disruption on an individual's established personal and social identity. It suggests that psychological systems are driven towards maintaining homeostasis and equilibrium in the same way as physical systems. Within this framework any crisis is self-limiting as the individual will find a way of returning to a stable state; individuals are therefore regarded as self-regulators.

Physical illness as a crisis

Moos and Schaefer (1984) argued that physical illness can be considered a crisis as it represents a turning point in an individual's life. They suggest that physical illness causes the following changes, which can be conceptualized as a crisis:

- *Changes in identity*: Illness can create a shift in identity, such as from carer to patient, or from breadwinner to person with an illness.
- *Changes in location*: Illness may result in a move to a new environment such as becoming bed-ridden or hospitalized.
- *Changes in role*: A change from independent adult to passive dependant may occur following illness, resulting in a changed role.
- *Changes in social support*: Illness may produce isolation from friends and family, effecting changes in social support.
- *Changes in the future*: A future involving children, career or travel can become uncertain.

In addition, the crisis nature of illness may be exacerbated by factors that are often specific to illness such as:

- *Illness is often unpredicted*: If an illness is not expected then the individual will not have had the opportunity to consider possible coping strategies.
- *Information about the illness is unclear*: Much of the information about illness is ambiguous and unclear, particularly in terms of causality and outcome.

- *A decision is needed quickly*: Illness frequently requires decisions about action to be made quickly (e.g. should we operate, should we take medicines, should we take time off from work, should we tell our friends).

- *Ambiguous meaning*: Because of uncertainties about causality and outcome, the meaning of the illness for an individual will often be ambiguous (e.g. is it serious? how long will it affect me?).

- *Limited prior experience*: Most individuals are healthy most of the time. Therefore illness is infrequent and may occur to individuals with limited prior experience. This lack of experience has implications for the development of coping strategies and efficacy based on other similar situations (e.g. 'I've never had cancer before, what should I do next?').

Many other crises may be easier to predict, have clearer meanings and occur to individuals with a greater degree of relevant previous experience. Within this framework, Moos and Schaefer considered illness a particular kind of crisis, and applied crisis theory to illness in an attempt to examine how individuals cope with this crisis.

The coping process

Once confronted with the crisis of physical illness, Moos and Schaefer (1984) described three processes that constitute the coping process: (1) cognitive appraisal; (2) adaptive tasks; and (3) coping skills. These processes are illustrated in Figure 3.2.

Process 1: Cognitive appraisal

At the stage of disequilibrium triggered by the illness, an individual initially appraises the seriousness and significance of the illness (e.g. is my cancer serious? How will my cancer influence my life in the long run?). Factors such as knowledge, previous experience and social support may influence this appraisal process. In addition, it is possible to integrate Leventhal's illness cognitions at this stage in the coping process as such illness beliefs are related to how an illness will be appraised.

Process 2: Adaptive tasks

Following cognitive appraisal, Moos and Schaefer describe seven adaptive tasks that are used as part of the coping process. These can be divided into three illness-specific tasks and four general tasks. These are illustrated in Table 3.1.

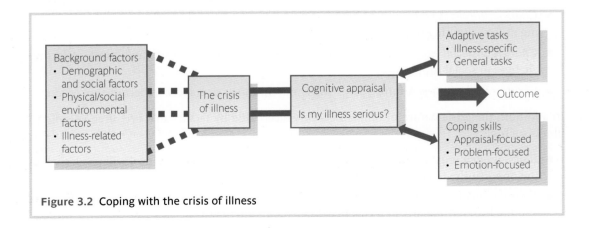

Figure 3.2 Coping with the crisis of illness

Illness-related tasks

- Dealing with pain and other symptoms
- Dealing with the hospital environment and treatment procedures
- Developing and maintaining relationships with health professionals

General tasks

- Preserving an emotional balance
- Preserving self-image, competence and mastery
- Sustaining relationships with family and friends
- Preparing for an uncertain future

Table 3.1 Adaptive tasks

The three illness-specific tasks can be described as:

1 *Dealing with pain, incapacitation and other symptoms.* This task involves dealing with symptoms such as pain, dizziness, loss of control and the recognition of changes in the severity of the symptoms.

2 *Dealing with the hospital environment and special treatment procedures.* This task involves dealing with medical interventions such as mastectomy, chemotherapy and any related side effects.

3 *Developing and maintaining adequate relationships with health care staff.* Becoming ill requires a new set of relationships with a multitude of health professionals. This task describes the development of those relationships.

The four general tasks can be described as:

1 *Preserving a reasonable emotional balance.* This involves compensating for the negative emotions aroused by illness with sufficient positive ones.

2 *Preserving a satisfactory self-image and maintaining a sense of competence and mastery.* This involves dealing with changes in appearance following illness (e.g. disfigurement) and adapting to a reliance on technology (e.g. pacemaker).

3 *Sustaining relationships with family and friends.* This involves maintaining social support networks even when communication can become problematic due to changes in location and mobility.

4 *Preparing for an uncertain future.* Illness can often result in loss (e.g. of sight, lifestyle, mobility, life). This task involves coming to terms with such losses and redefining the future.

Process 3: Coping skills

Following both appraisal and the use of adaptive tasks, Moos and Schaefer described a series of coping skills that are accessed to deal with the crisis of physical illness. These coping skills can be categorized into three forms: (1) appraisal-focused coping; (2) problem-focused coping; and (3) emotion-focused coping (see Table 3.2).

Appraisal-focused coping involves attempts to understand the illness and represents a search for meaning. Three sets of appraisal-focused coping skills have been defined:

Appraisal-focused
- Logical analysis and mental preparation
- Cognitive redefinition
- Cognitive avoidance or denial

Problem-focused
- Seeking information and support
- Taking problem-solving action
- Identifying rewards

Emotion-focused
- Affective regulation
- Emotional discharge
- Resigned acceptance

Table 3.2 Coping tasks

1 Logical analysis and mental preparation, involving turning an apparently unmanageable event into a series of manageable ones.

2 Cognitive redefinition, involving accepting the reality of the situation and redefining it in a positive and acceptable way.

3 Cognitive avoidance and denial, involving minimizing the seriousness of the illness.

Problem-focused coping involves confronting the problem and reconstructing it as manageable. Three types of problem-focused coping skills have been defined:

1 Seeking information and support, involving building a knowledge base by accessing any available information.

2 Taking problem-solving action, involving learning specific procedures and behaviours (e.g. insulin injections).

3 Identifying alternative rewards, involving the development and planning of events and goals that can provide short-term satisfaction.

Emotion-focused coping involves managing emotions and maintaining emotional equilibrium. Three types of emotion-focused coping skills have been defined:

1 Affective, involving efforts to maintain hope when dealing with a stressful situation.

2 Emotional discharge, involving venting feelings of anger or despair.

3 Resigned acceptance, involving coming to terms with the inevitable outcome of an illness.

Therefore, according to this theory of coping with the crisis of a physical illness, individuals appraise the illness and then use a variety of adaptive tasks and coping skills which in turn determine the outcome.

However, not all individuals respond to illness in the same way and Moos and Schaefer (1984) argued that the use of these tasks and skills is determined by three factors:

1 Demographic and personal factors, such as age, sex, class, religion.

2 Physical and social/environmental factors, such as the accessibility of social support networks and the acceptability of the physical environment (e.g. hospitals can be dull and
depressing).

3 Illness-related factors, such as any resulting pain, disfigurement or stigma.

Implications for the outcome of the coping process

Within this model, individuals attempt to deal with the crisis of physical illness via the stages of
appraisal, the use of adaptive tasks and the employment of coping skills. The types of tasks and
skills used may determine the outcome of this process and such outcome may be psychological
adjustment or well-being, or may be related to longevity or quality of life (see Chapter 17).
According to crisis theory, individuals are motivated to re-establish a state of equilibrium and
normality. This desire can be satisfied by either short-term or long-term solutions. Crisis theory
differentiates between two types of new equilibrium: *healthy adaptation*, which can result in
maturation, and a *maladaptive response* resulting in deterioration. Within this perspective,
healthy adaptation involves reality orientation and adaptive tasks and constructive coping skills.
Therefore, according to this model of coping the desired outcome of the coping process is
reality orientation.

Adjustment to physical illness and the theory of cognitive adaptation

In an alternative model of coping, Taylor and colleagues (e.g. Taylor 1983; Taylor et al. 1984)
examined ways in which individuals adjust to threatening events. Based on a series of interviews
with rape victims and cardiac and cancer patients, they suggested that coping with threatening
events (including illness) consists of three processes: (1) a search for meaning; (2) a search for
mastery; and (3) a process of self-enhancement. They argued that these three processes are
central to developing and maintaining illusions and that these illusions constitute a process of
cognitive adaptation. Again, this model describes the individual as self-regulatory and as motivated to maintain the *status quo*. In addition, many of the model's components parallel those
described earlier in terms of illness cognitions (e.g. the dimensions of cause and consequence).
This theoretical perspective will be described in the context of their results from women who
had recently had breast cancer (Taylor et al. 1984).

A search for meaning

A search for meaning is reflected in questions such as 'Why did it happen?', 'What impact has it
had?', 'What does my life mean now?' A search for meaning can be understood in terms of a
search for causality and a search to understand the implications.

A search for causality (Why did it happen?)

Attribution theory suggests that individuals need to understand, predict and control their
environment (e.g. Weiner 1986). Taylor et al. (1984) reported that 95 per cent of the women
they interviewed offered an explanation of the cause of their breast cancer. For example, 41 per
cent explained their cancer in terms of stress, 32 per cent held carcinogens such as the birth
control pill, chemical dumps or nuclear waste as responsible, 26 per cent saw hereditary factors
as the cause, 17 per cent blamed diet and 10 per cent considered a blow to the breast to blame.
Several women reported multiple causes. Taylor (1983) suggested that no one perception of
cause is better than any other, but that what is important for the process of cognitive adaptation
is the search for any cause. People need to ask 'Why did it happen?'

Understanding the implications (what effect has it had on my life?)

Taylor (1983) also argued that it is important for the women to understand the implications of the cancer for their life now. Accordingly, over 50 per cent of the women stated that the cancer had resulted in them reappraising their life, and others mentioned improved self-knowledge, self-change and a process of reprioritization.

Understanding the cause of the illness and developing an insight into the implications of the illness gives the illness meaning. According to this model of coping, a sense of meaning contributes to the process of coping and cognitive adaptation.

A search for mastery

A search for mastery is reflected in questions such as 'How can I prevent a similar event reoccurring?', 'What can I do to manage the event now?' Taylor et al. (1984) reported that a sense of mastery can be achieved by believing that the illness is controllable. In accordance with this, 66 per cent of the women in the study believed that they could influence the course or reoccurrence of the cancer. The remainder of the women believed that the cancer could be controlled by health professionals. Taylor reported that a sense of mastery is achieved either through psychological techniques such as developing a positive attitude, meditation, self-hypnosis or a type of causal attribution, or by behavioural techniques such as changing diet, changing medications, accessing information or controlling any side effects.

These processes contribute towards a state of mastery, which is central to the progression towards a state of cognitive adaptation.

The process of self-enhancement

Following illness, some individuals may suffer a decrease in their self-esteem. The theory of cognitive adaptation suggests that, following illness, individuals attempt to build their self-esteem through a process of self-enhancement. Taylor et al. (1984) reported that only 17 per cent of the women in their study reported only negative changes following their illness, whereas 53 per cent reported only positive changes. To explain this result, Taylor and colleagues developed social comparison theory (Festinger 1957). This theory suggests that individuals make sense of their world by comparing themselves with others. Such comparisons may either be downward comparisons (e.g. a comparison with others who are worse off: 'At least I've only had cancer once'), or upward (e.g. a comparison with others who are better off: 'Why was my lump malignant when hers was only a cyst?'). In terms of their study of women with breast cancer, Taylor et al. (1984) reported that, although many of the women in their study had undergone disfiguring surgery and had been diagnosed as having a life-threatening illness, most of them showed downward comparisons. This indicates that nearly all the women were comparing themselves with others worse off than themselves in order to improve their self-esteem. For example, women who had had a lumpectomy compared themselves with women who had had a mastectomy. Those who had had a mastectomy compared themselves with those who had a possibility of having generalized cancer. Older women compared themselves favourably with younger women, and younger women compared themselves favourably with older women. Taylor and her colleagues suggested that the women selected criteria for comparison that would enable them to improve their self-esteem as part of the process of self-enhancement.

The role of illusions

According to the theory of cognitive adaptation, following a threatening event individuals are motivated to search for meaning, search for mastery and improve their sense of self-esteem. It is suggested that these processes involve developing illusions. Such illusions are not necessarily in contradiction to reality but are positive interpretations of this reality. For example, although there may be little evidence for the real causes of cancer, or for the ability of individuals to control the course of their illness, those who have suffered cancer wish to hold their own illusions about these factors (e.g. 'I understand what caused my cancer and believe that I can control whether it comes back'). Taylor and her colleagues argued that these illusions are a necessary and essential component of cognitive adaptation and that reality orientation (as suggested by other coping models) may actually be detrimental to adjustment.

The need for illusions raises the problem of disconfirmation of the illusions (what happens when the reoccurrence of cancer cannot be controlled?). Taylor argued that the need for illusions is sufficient to enable individuals to shift the goals and foci of their illusions so that the illusions can be maintained and adjustment persist.

Implications for the outcome of the coping process

According to this model of coping, the individual copes with illness by achieving cognitive adaptation. This involves searching for meaning ('I know what caused my illness'), mastery ('I can control my illness') and developing self-esteem ('I am better off than a lot of people'). These beliefs may not be accurate but they are essential to maintaining illusions that promote adjustment to the illness. Therefore, within this perspective the desired outcome of the coping process is the development of illusions, not reality orientation.

The positive interpretation of illness

Most theories of coping emphasize a desire to re-establish equilibrium and a return to the *status quo*. Therefore, effective coping would be seen as that which enables adjustment to the illness and a return to normality. Some research, however, indicates that some people perceive benefits from being ill and see themselves as being better off because they have been ill. This approach is in line with positive psychology and its emphasis on positive rather than negative affect (see stress and positive psychology, Chapters 10–11). For example, Laerum et al. (1988) interviewed 84 men who had had a heart attack and found that although the men reported some negative consequences for their lifestyle and quality of life, 33 per cent of them considered their life to be somewhat or considerably improved. Similarly, Collins et al. (1990) interviewed 55 cancer patients and also reported some positive shifts following illness. Sodergren and colleagues have explored positivity following illness and have developed a structured questionnaire called the Silver Lining Questionnaire (SLQ) (Sodergren and Hyland 2000; Sodergren et al. 2002). They concluded from their studies that the positive consequences of illness are varied and more common than often realized. They also suggest that positivity can be improved by rehabilitation.

Using the self-regulatory model to predict outcomes

The self-regulatory model describes a transition from interpretation, through illness cognitions, emotional response and coping to appraisal. This model has primarily been used in research to ask the questions 'How do different people make sense of different illnesses?' and 'How do illness cognitions relate to coping?' Research, however, has also explored the impact of illness cognitions on psychological and physical health outcomes. Some research has addressed the links between illness cognitions and adherence to treatment. Other research has examined their impact on recovery from illnesses including stroke and myocardial infarction (MI – heart attack).

Predicting adherence to treatment

Beliefs about illness in terms of the dimensions described by Leventhal et al. (1980, 1997) have been shown to relate to coping. They have also been associated with whether or not a person takes their medication and/or adheres to other suggested treatments. Some research shows that symptom perception is directly linked to adherence to medication. For example, Halm et al. (2006) explored asthmatics' beliefs about their problem, their perception of symptoms and their adherence to medication. The study involved 198 adults who had been hospitalized for their asthma over a 12-month period and identified a 'no symptoms, no asthma' belief whereby people only believed they had asthma when they had symptoms, rather than seeing it as a chronic illness that is ongoing regardless of the level of symptomatology. Further, the results showed that those who held the 'acute asthma belief' were also less likely to take their medication. In a similar vein, Brewer et al. (2002) examined the relationship between illness cognitions and both adherence to medication and cholesterol control in patients with hypercholesterolaemia (involving very high cholesterol). The results showed that a belief that the illness has serious consequences was related to medication adherence. In addition, actual cholesterol control was related to the belief that the illness was stable, asymptomatic with serious consequences. Some research has also included a role for treatment beliefs. For example, Horne and Weinman (2002) explored the links between beliefs about both illness and treatment and adherence to taking medication for asthma in 100 community-based patients. The results showed that non-adherers reported more doubts about the necessity of their medication, greater concerns about the consequences of the medication and more negative beliefs about the consequences of their illness. Overall, the analysis indicated that illness and treatment beliefs were better predictors of adherence than both clinical and demographic factors. In a similar study, Llewellyn et al. (2003) explored the interrelationships between illness beliefs, treatment beliefs and adherence to home treatment in patients with severe haemophilia. The results showed that poor adherence was related to beliefs about the necessity of the treatment, concerns about the consequences of treatment and beliefs about illness identity. Further, Senior and Marteau (2006) showed that greater beliefs about perceived effectiveness of medication was related to better adherence in people with familial hypercholesterolaemia (FH).

Predicting recovery from stroke

Research has also explored links between illness cognitions and recovery from stroke. For example, Partridge and Johnston (1989) used a prospective study and reported that individuals' beliefs about their perceived control over their problem predicted recovery from residual disability in stroke patients at follow-up. The results showed that this relationship persisted even when baseline levels of disability were taken into account. In line with this, Johnston, Morrison et al. (1999) also explored the relationship between perceived control and recovery from stroke and followed up 71 stroke patients one and six months after discharge from hospital. In addition, they examined the possible mediating effects of coping, exercise and mood. Therefore they asked the questions 'Does recovery from stroke relate to illness cognitions?' and 'If so, is this relationship dependent upon other factors?' The results showed no support for the mediating effects of coping, exercise and mood but supported earlier work to indicate a predictive relationship between control beliefs and recovery. This was also supported by a further study which explored the role of a range of clinical and demographic and psychological factors to predict functional recovery three years following a stroke. The results showed that perceptions of control at baseline added to the variance accounted for by both clinical and demographic variables (Johnston et al. 2004). To further assess the factors that may relate to recovery from stroke, Johnston, Bonetti et al. (2006) developed a workbook-based intervention which was designed to change cognitions about control in patients who had just had a stroke. In particular the intervention focused on coping skills, encouraged self-management and offered encouragement. The results showed that at six months' follow-up, those receiving the intervention showed better disability recovery than those in the control group. However, it was unclear how the intervention had worked as the intervention group showed no significant changes in any psychological process variables apart from confidence in recovery which did not itself relate to actual disability recovery. Research therefore indicates that control cognitions may relate to recovery from stroke. Further, an intervention to change such cognitions seems to improve recovery. It is not clear, however, what processes are involved in this change as the intervention did not actually change stroke patients' beliefs about control.

Predicting recovery from MI

Research has also explored the relationship between illness cognitions and recovery from MI. From a broad perspective, research suggests that beliefs about factors such as the individual's work capacity (Maeland and Havik 1987), helplessness towards future MIs (called 'cardiac invalidism') (Riegel 1993) and general psychological factors (Diederiks et al. 1991) relate to recovery from MI as measured by return to work and general social and occupational functioning. Using a self-regulatory approach, research has also indicated that illness cognitions relate to recovery – in particular, the Heart Attack Recovery Project, which was carried out in New Zealand and followed 143 first-time heart attack patients aged 65 or under for 12 months following admission to hospital. All subjects completed follow-up measures at 3, 6 and 12 months after admission. The results showed that those patients who believed that their illness had less serious consequences and would last a shorter time at baseline, were more likely to have returned to work by six weeks (Petrie et al. 1996). Furthermore, those with beliefs that the illness could be controlled or cured at baseline predicted attendance at rehabilitation classes (Petrie et al. 1996). In a recent study authors did not only explore the patients' beliefs about MI but also the beliefs of their spouse to ask whether congruence between spouse and patient's beliefs was related to recovery from MI (Figueiras and Weinman 2003). Seventy couples in which the man had had an MI completed a baseline measure of the illness cognitions which were correlated with follow-up measures of recovery taken at 3, 6 and 12 months. The results showed that in couples who had similar positive beliefs about the identity and consequences of the illness, the patients showed improved recovery in terms of better psychological and physical functioning, better sexual functioning and lower impact of the MI on social and recreational activities. In addition, similar beliefs about time line were related to lower levels of disability and similar cure/control beliefs were associated with greater dietary changes. In a novel approach to assessing patients' beliefs about their MI, Broadbent et al. (in press) asked 69 patients who had just had an MI to draw their heart and how they felt it looked just after their heart attack. They also completed a series of questionnaires and repeated these drawings and measures at three and six months. The results showed that increases in the size of heart between baseline and three months was related to slower return to work, activity restriction and anxiety about having another MI as measured by a range of factors. The authors conclude that the increased size of the heart in the drawings may reflect the 'extent to which their heart condition plays on their mind'. Beliefs about illness therefore seem to be associated with recovery. Further, congruence in beliefs also seems to influence outcomes. This is further discussed in Chapter 15.

A self-regulatory approach may be useful for describing illness cognitions and for exploring the relationship between such cognitions and coping, and also for understanding and predicting other health outcomes.

The central role of coherence

Central to much research on illness beliefs and their relationship to outcome is the importance of a coherent model whereby beliefs about the illness are consistent with beliefs about treatment (Leventhal et al. 1997). For example, Horne and Weinman (2002) report that adherence is more likely to occur when illness beliefs and treatment beliefs are coherent with each other. Similarly, Llewellyn et al. (2003) reported that adherence to medication for patients with haemophilia was also greater when beliefs about illness and treatment were matched. Examples of such coherence include the following: a belief that breathlessness is caused by smoking would relate to a decision to stop smoking, and a belief that asthma symptoms were caused by bronchial constriction would relate to adherence to a medication that caused bronchial dilation. Most research addressing the issue of coherence has focused on cross-sectional associations between the different sets of beliefs. Recently, however, several studies have explored whether or not beliefs can be changed to be more in line with each other. For example, Hall et al. (2004) examined whether giving people a leaflet containing information about the link between smoking and cervical cancer, which provided them with a coherent model of this association, could change intentions to quit smoking. The results showed that the leaflet did increase women's coherent model of the association between smoking and cervical cancer. Further, the results showed that perceptions of vulnerability to cervical cancer were associated with intentions to quit smoking but only in those with a coherent model. Similarly, Ogden and Sidhu (2006) report how taking medication for obesity, which produces highly visual side effects, can result in both adherence and behaviour change if the side effects act as an education and bring people's beliefs about the causes of their obesity in line with a behavioural solution (see Chapter 15 for further details). Both these studies illustrate the importance of coherence and the benefits of changing beliefs. In contrast, however, Wright et al. (2003) explored the impact of informing smokers about their genetic predisposition towards nicotine dependence on their choice of method for stopping smoking. In line with the studies described earlier, giving information did change beliefs. However, while those who believed that they were genetically prone to dependency were more likely to choose a medical form of cessation (a drug to reduce cravings), they were likely to endorse relying upon their own willpower. Changing beliefs towards a more medical cause meant that smokers were less able to change their behaviour on their own and more in need of medical support. These results illustrate the importance of a coherent model. But they also illustrate that changing beliefs may not always be beneficial to subsequent changes in behaviour.

To conclude

In the same way that people have beliefs about health, they also have beliefs about illness. Such beliefs are often called 'illness cognitions' or 'illness representations'. Beliefs about illness appear to follow a pattern and are made up of: (1) identity (e.g. a diagnosis and symptoms); (2) consequences (e.g. beliefs about seriousness); (3) time line (e.g. how long it will last); (4) cause (e.g. caused by smoking, caused by a virus); and (5) cure/control (e.g. requires medical intervention). This chapter examined these dimensions of illness cognitions and assessed how they relate to the way in which an individual responds to illness via their coping and their appraisal of the illness. Further, it has described the self-regulatory model, its implications for understanding and predicting health outcomes and the central role for coherence.

❓ Questions

1 How do people make sense of health and illness?

2 Discuss the relationship between illness cognitions and coping.

3 Why is Leventhal's model 'self-regulatory'?

4 Symptoms are more than just a sensation. Discuss.

5 Discuss the role of symptom perception in adjusting to illness.

6 Discuss the role of coherence in illness representations.

7 Illness cognitions predict health outcomes. Discuss.

8 Design a research project to assess the extent to which illness severity predicts patient adjustment and highlight the role that illness cognitions may have in explaining this relationship.

For discussion

Think about the last time you were ill (e.g. headache, flu, broken limb, etc.). Consider the ways in which you made sense of your illness and how they related to your coping strategies and how you recovered.

Assumptions in health psychology

The literature examining illness cognitions highlights some of the assumptions in health psychology:

1 *Humans as information processors.* The literature describing the structure of illness cognitions assumes that individuals deal with their illness by processing the different forms of information. In addition, it assumes that the resulting cognitions are clearly defined and consistent across different people. However, perhaps the information is not always processed rationally and perhaps some cognitions are made up of only some of the components (e.g. just time line and cause), or made up of other components not included in the models.

▶

2 *Methodology as separate to theory.* The literature also assumes that the structure of cognitions exists prior to questions about these cognitions. Therefore it is assumed that the data collected are separate from the methodology used (i.e. the different components of the illness cognitions pre-date questions about time line, causality, cure, etc.). However, it is possible that the structure of these cognitions is in part an artefact of the types of questions asked. In fact, Leventhal originally argued that interviews should be used to access illness cognitions as this methodology avoided 'contaminating' the data. However, even interviews involve the interviewer's own preconceived ideas which may be expressed through the structure of their questions, through their responses to the interviewee, or through their analysis of the transcripts.

Further reading

Cameron, L. and Leventhal, H. (eds) (2003) *The Self-regulation of Health and Illness Behaviour.* London: Routledge.
    This is a good book which presents a comprehensive coverage of a good selection of illness representations research and broader self-regulation approaches.

de Ridder, D. (1997) What is wrong with coping assessment? A review of conceptual and methodological issues, *Psychology and Health*, 12: 417–31.
    This paper explores the complex and ever-growing area of coping and focuses on the issues surrounding the questions 'What is coping?' and 'How should it be measured?'

Ogden, J. and Sidhu, S. (2006) Adherence, behaviour change and visualisation: a qualitative study of patients' experiences of obesity medication, *The Journal of Psychosomatic Research*, 62: 545–52.
    Although this is one of my papers (!) I think it provides an example of how beliefs about a problem can be changed through experience and how coherence is a essential part of illness representations. It also illustrates a qualitative approach to illness representations.

Petrie, K.J. and Weinman, J.A. (eds) (1997) *Perceptions of Health and Illness.* Amsterdam: Harwood.
    This is an edited collection of projects using the self-regulatory model as their theoretical framework.

Taylor, S.E. (1983) Adjustment to threatening events: a theory of cognitive adaptation, *American Psychologist*, 38: 1161–73.
    This is an excellent example of an interview-based study. It describes and analyses the cognitive adaptation theory of coping with illness and emphasizes the central role of illusions in making sense of the imbalance created by the absence of health.

Chapter 4

Health professional–patient communication and the role of health beliefs

Chapter overview

This chapter first examines the problem of compliance and then describes Ley's (1981, 1989) cognitive hypothesis model of communication, which emphasizes patient understanding, recall and satisfaction. This educational perspective explains communication in terms of the transfer of knowledge from medical expert to layperson. Such models of the transfer of expert knowledge assume that the health professionals behave according to their education and training, not their subjective beliefs. The chapter then looks at the role of information in terms of determining compliance and also in terms of the effect on recovery, and then reviews the adherence model, which was an attempt to go beyond the traditional model of doctor–patient communication. Next, the chapter focuses on the problem of variability and suggests that variability in health professionals' behaviour is not only related to levels of knowledge but also to the processes involved in clinical decision making and the health beliefs of the health professional. This suggests that many of the health beliefs described in Chapter 2 are also relevant to health professionals. Finally, the chapter examines health professional–patient communication as an interaction and the role of agreement, shared models, patient centredness and informed choice.

This chapter covers

- What is compliance?
- The work of Ley
- How can compliance be improved?
- The role of knowledge in health professional–patient communication
- The problem of doctor variability
- Explaining variability – the role of clinical decision making
- Explaining variability – the role of health beliefs
- Health professional–patient communication as an interaction
- Patient centredness
- Informed choice

What is compliance?

Haynes et al. (1979) defined compliance as 'the extent to which the patient's behaviour (in terms of taking medications, following diets or other lifestyle changes) coincides with medical or health advice'. Compliance has excited an enormous amount of clinical and academic interest over the past few decades and it has been calculated that 3200 articles on compliance in English were listed between 1979 and 1985 (Trostle 1988). Compliance is regarded as important primarily because following the recommendations of health professionals is considered essential to patient recovery. However, studies estimate that about half of the patients with chronic illnesses, such as diabetes and hypertension, are non-compliant with their medication regimens and that even compliance for a behaviour as apparently simple as using an inhaler for asthma is poor (e.g. Dekker et al. 1992). Further, compliance also has financial implications as money is wasted when drugs are prescribed, prescriptions are cashed, but the drugs not taken.

Predicting whether patients are compliant: the work of Ley

Ley (1981, 1989) developed the cognitive hypothesis model of compliance. This claimed that compliance can be predicted by a combination of patient satisfaction with the process of the consultation, understanding of the information given and recall of this information. Several studies have been done to examine each element of the cognitive hypothesis model. This model is illustrated in Figure 4.1.

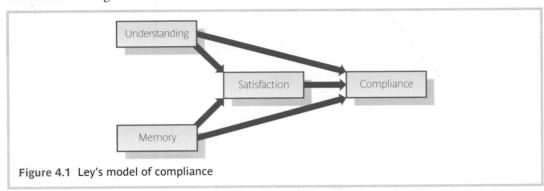

Figure 4.1 Ley's model of compliance

Patient satisfaction

Ley (1988) examined the extent of patient satisfaction with the consultation. He reviewed 21 studies of hospital patients and found that 41 per cent of patients were dissatisfied with their treatment and that 28 per cent of general practice patients were dissatisfied. Studies by Haynes et al. (1979) and Ley (1988) found that levels of patient satisfaction stem from various components of the consultation, in particular the affective aspects (e.g. emotional support and understanding), the behavioural aspects (e.g. prescribing, adequate explanation) and the competence (e.g. appropriateness of referral, diagnosis) of the health professional. Ley (1989) also reported that satisfaction is determined by the content of the consultation and that patients want to know as much information as possible, even if this is bad news. For example, in studies looking at cancer diagnosis, patients showed improved satisfaction if they were given a diagnosis of cancer rather than if they were protected from this information.

Berry et al. (2003) explored the impact of making information more personal to the patient on satisfaction. Participants were asked to read some information about medication and then to rate their satisfaction. Some were given personalized information, such as 'If you take this medicine, there is a substantial chance of you getting one or more of its side effects', whereas some were given non-personalized information, such as 'A substantial proportion of people who take this medication get one or more of its side effects'. The results showed that a more personalized style was related to greater satisfaction, lower ratings of the risks of side effects and lower ratings of the risk to health.

Sala et al. (2002) explored the relationship between humour in consultation and patient satisfaction. The authors coded recorded consultations for their humour content and for the type of humour used. They then looked for differences between high and low satisfaction-rated consultations. The results showed that high satisfaction was related to the use of more light humour, more humour that relieved tension, more self-effacing humour and more positive-function humour. Some research has also explored whether patient satisfaction can be improved. For example, in a large-scale randomized control trial in Denmark, Frostholm et al. (2005) randomly allocated GPs into an educational programme to improve their communication with patients presenting with a new problem which was considered to be a medically unexplained symptom (e.g. headaches, tiredness, etc.). The educational programme focused on aspects of assessment, treatment and management and used a cognitive-orientated approach. In addition, measures were taken of patients' beliefs about their problem using the illness perception questionnaire (IPQ) (see Chapter 3). The results showed that the training did improve patients' satisfaction with the consultation. The results also showed that those patients who felt uncertain about the nature of their problem and felt more worried and upset about their problem were less satisfied, particularly if they had visited a GP who had not been trained. Patient satisfaction therefore relates to a range of professional and patient variables and is increasingly used in health care assessment as an indirect measure of health outcome based on the assumption that a satisfied patient will be a more healthy patient. This has resulted in the development of a multitude of patient satisfaction measures and a lack of agreement as to what patient satisfaction actually is (see Fitzpatrick 1993). However, even though there are problems with patient satisfaction, some studies suggest that aspects of patient satisfaction may correlate with compliance with the advice given during the consultation.

Patient understanding

Several studies have also examined the extent to which patients understand the content of the consultation. Boyle (1970) examined patients' definitions of different illnesses and reported that, when given a checklist, only 85 per cent correctly defined arthritis, 77 per cent correctly defined jaundice, 52 per cent correctly defined palpitations and 80 per cent correctly defined bronchitis. Boyle further examined patients' perceptions of the location of organs and found that only 42 per cent correctly located the heart, 20 per cent located the stomach and 49 per cent located the liver. This suggests that understanding of the content of the consultation may well be low. Further studies have examined the understanding of illness in terms of causality and seriousness. Roth (1979) asked patients what they thought peptic ulcers were caused by and found a variety of responses, such as problems with teeth and gums, food, digestive problems or excessive stomach acid. He also asked individuals what they thought caused lung cancer, and found that although the understanding of the causality of lung cancer was high in terms of smoking behaviour, 50 per cent of individuals thought that lung cancer caused by smoking had a good prognosis. Roth also reported that 30 per cent of patients believed that hypertension could be cured by treatment.

If the doctor gives advice to the patient or suggests that they follow a particular treatment programme and the patient does not understand the causes of their illness, the correct location of the relevant organ or the processes involved in the treatment, then this lack of understanding is likely to affect their compliance with this advice.

Patient's recall

Researchers also examined the process of recall of the information given during the consultation. Bain (1977) examined the recall from a sample of patients who had attended a GP consultation and found that 37 per cent could not recall the name of the drug, 23 per cent could not recall the frequency of the dose and 25 per cent could not recall the duration of the treatment. A further study by Crichton et al. (1978) found that 22 per cent of patients had forgotten the treatment regime recommended by their doctors. In a meta-analysis of the research into recall of consultation information, Ley (1981, 1989) found that recall is influenced by a multitude of factors. For example, Ley argued that anxiety, medical knowledge, intellectual level, the importance of the statement, primacy effect and the number of statements increase recall. However, he concluded that recall is not influenced by the age of the patient, which is contrary to some predictions of the effect of ageing on memory and some of the myths and counter-myths of the ageing process. Recalling information after the consultation may be related to compliance.

How can compliance be improved?

Compliance is considered to be essential to patient well-being. Therefore studies have been carried out to examine which factors can be used in order to improve compliance.

The role of information

Researchers have examined the role of information and the type of information on improving patient compliance with recommendations made during the consultation by health professionals. Using meta-analysis, Mullen et al. (1985) looked at the effects of instructional and educational information on compliance and found that 64 per cent of patients were more compliant when using such information. Haynes (1982) took a baseline of 52 per cent compliance with

Testing a theory – patient satisfaction

A study to examine the effects of a general practitioner's consulting style on patient satisfaction (Savage and Armstrong 1990).

This study examined the effect of an expert, directive consulting style and a sharing, patient-centred consulting style on patient satisfaction. This paper is interesting for both methodological and theoretical reasons. Methodologically, it uses a random control design in a naturalistic setting. This means that it is possible to compare the effects of the two types of consulting style without the problem of identifying individual differences (these are controlled for by the design) and without the problem of an artificial experiment (the study took place in a natural environment). Theoretically, the study examines the prediction that the educational model of doctor–patient communication is problematic (i.e. is the expert approach a suitable one?) and examines patient preferences for the method of doctor–patient communication.

Background

A traditional model of doctor–patient communication regards the doctor as an expert who communicates their 'knowledge' to the naïve patient. Within this framework, the doctor is regarded as an authority figure who instructs and directs the patient. However, recent research has suggested that the communication process may be improved if a sharing, patient-centred consulting style is adopted. This approach emphasizes an interaction between the doctor and the patient and suggests that this style may result in greater patient commitment to any advice given, potentially higher levels of compliance and greater patient satisfaction. Savage and Armstrong (1990) aimed to examine patients' responses to receiving either a 'directive/doctor-centred consulting style' or a 'sharing/patient-centred consulting style'.

Methodology
Subjects

The study was undertaken in a group practice in an inner city area of London. Four patients from each surgery for one doctor, over four months, were randomly selected for the study. Patients were selected if they were aged 16–75, did not have a life-threatening condition, if they were not attending for administrative/preventive reasons, and if the GP involved considered that they would not be upset by the project. Overall, 359 patients were invited to take part in the study and a total of 200 patients completed all assessments and were included in the data analysis.

Design

The study involved a randomized controlled design with two conditions: (1) sharing consulting style and (2) directive consulting style. Patients were randomly allocated to one condition and received a consultation with the GP involving the appropriate consulting style.

Procedure

A set of cards was designed to randomly allocate each patient to a condition. When a patient entered the consulting room they were greeted and asked to describe their problem. When this was completed, the GP turned over a card to determine the appropriate style of consultation. Advice and treatment were then given by the GP in that style. For example, the doctor's

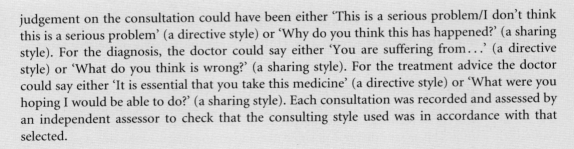

judgement on the consultation could have been either 'This is a serious problem/I don't think this is a serious problem' (a directive style) or 'Why do you think this has happened?' (a sharing style). For the diagnosis, the doctor could say either 'You are suffering from...' (a directive style) or 'What do you think is wrong?' (a sharing style). For the treatment advice the doctor could say either 'It is essential that you take this medicine' (a directive style) or 'What were you hoping I would be able to do?' (a sharing style). Each consultation was recorded and assessed by an independent assessor to check that the consulting style used was in accordance with that selected.

Measures

All subjects were asked to complete a questionnaire immediately after each consultation and one week later. This contained questions about the patient's satisfaction with the consultation in terms of the following factors:

- *The doctor's understanding of the problem.* This was measured by items such as 'I perceived the general practitioner to have a complete understanding'.
- *The adequacy of the explanation of the problem.* This was measured by items such as 'I received an excellent explanation'.
- *Feeling helped.* This was measured by the statements 'I felt greatly helped' and 'I felt much better'.

Results

The results were analysed to evaluate differences in aspects of patient satisfaction between those patients who had received a directive versus a sharing consulting style. In addition, this difference was also examined in relation to patient characteristics (whether the patient had a physical problem, whether they received a prescription, had any tests and were infrequent attenders).

The results showed that although all subjects reported high levels of satisfaction immediately after the consultation in terms of doctor's understanding, explanation and being helped, this was higher in those subjects who had received a directive style in their consultation. In addition, this difference was also found after one week. When the results were analysed to examine the role of patient characteristics on satisfaction, the results indicated that the directive style produced higher levels of satisfaction in those patients who rarely attended the surgery, had a physical problem, did not receive tests and received a prescription.

Conclusion

The results suggest that a directive consulting style was associated with higher levels of patient satisfaction than a sharing consulting style. This provides support for the educational model of doctor–patient communication with the doctor as the 'expert' and the patient as the 'layperson'. In addition, it suggests that patients in the present study preferred an authority figure who offered a formal diagnosis rather than a sharing doctor who asked for the patient's views. Therefore, although recent research has criticized the traditional educational model of doctor–patient communication, the results from this study suggest that some patients may prefer this approach.

recommendations made during a consultation, and found that information generally only improved compliance to a level of 66 per cent. However, Haynes reported that behavioural and individualized instruction improved compliance to 75 per cent. Information giving may therefore be a means of improving compliance.

Recommendations for improving compliance

Several recommendations have been made in order to improve communication and therefore improve compliance.

Oral information

Ley (1989) suggested that one way of improving compliance is to improve communication in terms of the content of an oral communication. He believes the following factors are important:

- primacy effect – patients have a tendency to remember the first thing they are told
- to stress the importance of compliance
- to simplify the information
- to use repetition
- to be specific
- to follow up the consultation with additional interviews.

Written information

Researchers also looked at the use of written information in improving compliance. Ley and Morris (1984) examined the effect of written information about medication and found that it increased knowledge in 90 per cent of the studies, increased compliance in 60 per cent of the studies, and improved outcome in 57 per cent of the studies.

Ley's cognitive hypothesis model, and its emphasis on patient satisfaction, understanding and recall, has been influential in terms of promoting research into the communication between health professionals and patients. In addition, the model has prompted the examination of using information to improve the communication process. As a result of this, the role of information has been explored further in terms of its effect on recovery and outcome.

The wider role of information in illness

Information and recovery from surgery

Information may also be related to recovery and outcome following illness and surgery. On the basis that the stress caused by surgery may be related to later recovery, Janis (1958) interviewed patients before and after surgery to examine the effects of pre-operative fear on post-operative recovery. Janis examined the differences between pre-operative extreme fear, moderate fear and little or no fear on outcome. Extreme fear was reflected in patients' constant concern, anxiety and reports of vulnerability; moderate fear was reflected in reality orientation with the individual seeking out information; and little or no fear was reflected by a state of denial. The results were that moderate pre-operative fear (i.e. a reality orientation and information seeking) was related to a decrease in post-operative distress. Janis suggested that moderate fear results in the individual developing a defence mechanism, developing coping strategies, seeking out relevant information, and rehearsing the outcome of the surgery. This approach may lead to increased confidence in the outcome, which is reflected in the decreased post-operative distress. However, there is conflicting evidence regarding this 'U'-shaped relationship between anxiety and outcome (see Johnston and Vogele 1993).

Using information to improve recovery

If stress is related to recovery from surgery, then obviously information could be an important way of reducing this stress. There are different types of information that could be used to affect the outcome of recovery from a medical intervention. These have been described as: (1) *sensory information*, which can be used to help individuals deal with their feelings or to reflect on these feelings; (2) *procedural information*, which enables individuals to learn how the process or the intervention will actually be done; (3) *coping skills information*, which can educate the individual about possible coping strategies; and (4) *behavioural instructions*, which teach the individual how to behave in terms of factors such as coughing and relaxing.

Researchers have evaluated the relative roles of these different types of information in promoting recovery and reducing distress. Johnson and Leventhal (1974) gave sensory information (i.e. information about feelings) to patients before an endoscopic examination and noted a reduction in the level of distress experienced by these patients. Egbert et al. (1964) gave sensory information (i.e. about feelings), and coping skills information (i.e. about what coping skills could be used), to patients in hospital undergoing abdominal surgery. They reported that sensory and coping information reduced the need for pain killers and in addition reduced the hospital stay by three days. Young and Humphrey (1985) gave information to patients going into hospital, and found that information specific to how they could survive hospital reduced the distress and their length of stay in the hospital. Research has also specifically examined the role of pre-operative information. Johnston (1980) found that pre-operative information can

Box 4.1 Some problems with . . . communication research

Below are some problems with research in this area that you may wish to consider.

1 Research exploring the communication process highlights how health professionals' beliefs relate to their behaviour in terms of diagnosis, management or referral. It is possible, however, that their behaviour also influences their beliefs and that beliefs and behaviour exist in a dynamic relationship.

2 The current emphasis within clinical care is on patient centredness, shared decision making and informed decisions. This emphasizes respecting the patient's perspective and understanding the patient's beliefs. However, health professionals also have training and expertise which encourages them to feel they know what is the correct mode of management and the correct way forward. At times these two perspectives can clash. For example, an epileptic patient may believe that they can manage their problem through self-care and the use of alternative medicines. The doctor may disagree and feel that anti-epileptic drugs are the safest option. How these two perspectives can sit alongside each other while enabling the doctor to be both patient centred and safe is unclear. Sometimes the literature appears to be trying to have it all ways.

3 Research exploring the interaction between health professional and patient uses a variety of methods. Some studies ask each party about the interaction, some record the interaction, some code the interaction and some observe the interaction. All these methods involve a level of interpretation (by the researcher, the health professional or the patient). Trying to access what 'really' goes on in a consulting room is not really possible.

influence recovery and reduce anxiety, pain rating, length of hospitalization and analgesic intake. Further, in a detailed meta-analysis of the published and unpublished literature on preparation for surgery, Johnston and Vogele (1993) concluded that preparation for surgery in the form of both procedural information (i.e. what will happen) and behavioural instructions (i.e. how to behave afterwards) resulted in significant benefits on all outcome variables explored, including mood, pain, recovery, physiological indices and satisfaction. Although the reasons that pre-operative information is so successful remain unclear, it is possible that pre-operative information may be beneficial to the individual in terms of the reduction of anxiety by enabling the patient to mentally rehearse their anticipated worries, fears and changes following the operation; thus any changes become predictable. These results therefore suggest that information communicated correctly by the doctor or the health professional may be an important part of reducing the distress following hospitalization or a hospital intervention.

The role of knowledge in health professional–patient communication

Ley's approach to health professional–patient communication can be understood within the framework of an educational model involving the transfer of medical knowledge from expert to layperson (Marteau and Johnston 1990). This traditional approach has motivated research into health professionals' medical knowledge, which is seen as a product of their training and education. Accordingly, the communication process is seen as originating from the health professional's knowledge base.

Boyle (1970), although emphasizing patients' knowledge, also provided some insights into doctors' knowledge of the location of organs and the causes of a variety of illnesses. The results showed that although the doctors' knowledge was superior to that of the patients', some doctors wrongly located organs such as the heart and wrongly defined problems such as 'constipation' and 'diarrhoea'. It has also been found that health professionals show inaccurate knowledge about diabetes (Etzwiler 1967; Scheiderich et al. 1983) and asthma (Anderson et al. 1983). Over recent years, due to government documents such as *Health for All* and *The Health of the Nation*, primary care team members are spending more time on health promotion practices, which often involve making recommendations about changing behaviours such as smoking, drinking and diet. Research has consequently examined health professionals' knowledge about these practices. Murray et al. (1993) examined the dietary knowledge of primary care professionals in Scotland. GPs, community nurses and practice nurses completed a questionnaire consisting of a series of commonly heard statements about diet and were asked to state whether they agreed or disagreed with them. The results showed high levels of correct knowledge for statements such as 'most people should eat less sugar' and 'most people should eat more fibre', and relatively poor accuracy for statements such as 'cholesterol in food is the most important dietary factor in controlling blood lipid levels'. The authors concluded that primary health care professionals show generally good dietary knowledge but that 'there is clearly an urgent need to develop better teaching and training in the dietary aspects of coronary heart disease'.

Problems with the traditional approach to health professional – patient communication

Traditional models of the communication between health professionals and patients have emphasized the transfer of knowledge from expert to layperson. Ley's cognitive hypothesis model of communication includes a role for the patient and emphasizes patient factors in the communication process as well as health professional factors such as the provision of relevant information. This approach has encouraged research into the wider role of information in health and illness. However, there are several problems with this educational approach, which can be summarized as follows:

- It assumes that the communication from the health professional is from an expert whose knowledge base is one of objective knowledge and does not involve the health beliefs of that individual health professional.
- Patient compliance is seen as positive and unproblematic.
- Improved knowledge is predicted to improve the communication process.
- It does not include a role for patient health beliefs.

The adherence model of communication

In an attempt to further our understanding of the communication process, Stanton (1987) developed the model of adherence. The shift in terminology from 'compliance' to 'adherence' illustrates the attempt of the model to depart from the traditional view of doctor as an expert who gives advice to a compliant patient. The adherence model suggested that communication from the health professional results in enhanced patient knowledge and patient satisfaction and an adherence to the recommended medical regime. This aspect of the adherence model is similar to Ley's model. In addition, however, it suggested that patients' beliefs are important and the model emphasized the patient's locus of control, perceived social support and the disruption of lifestyle involved in adherence. Therefore the model progresses from Ley's model, in that it includes aspects of the patients and emphasizes the interaction between the health professionals and the patients.

However, yet again this model of communication assumes that the health professionals' information is based on objective knowledge and is not influenced by their own health beliefs. Patients are regarded as laypeople who have their own varying beliefs and perspectives that need to be dealt with by the doctors and addressed in terms of the language and content of the communication. In contrast, doctors are regarded as objective and holding only professional views.

The problem of doctor variability

Traditionally, doctors are regarded as having an objective knowledge set that comes from their extensive medical education. If this were the case then it could be predicted that doctors with similar levels of knowledge and training would behave in similar ways. In addition, if doctors' behaviour was objective then their behaviour would be consistent. However, considerable variability among doctors in terms of different aspects of their practice has been found. For example, Anderson et al. (1983) reported that doctors differ in their diagnosis of asthma. Mapes (1980) suggested that they vary in terms of their prescribing behaviour, with a variation of 15–90 per cent of patients receiving drugs. Bucknall et al. (1986) reported variation in the methods used by doctors to measure blood pressure, and Marteau and Baum (1984) also reported that doctors vary in their treatment of diabetes.

According to a traditional educational model of doctor–patient communication, this variability could be understood in terms of differing levels of knowledge and expertise. However, this variability can also be understood by examining the other factors involved in the clinical decision-making process.

Explaining variability – clinical decision making as problem solving

A model of problem solving

Clinical decision-making processes are a specialized form of problem solving and have been studied within the context of problem solving and theories of information processing. It is often assumed that clinical decisions are made by the process of *inductive reasoning*, which involves collecting evidence and data and using these data to develop a conclusion and a hypothesis. For example, within this framework, a general practitioner would start a consultation with a patient without any prior model of their problem. The GP would then ask the appropriate questions regarding the patient's history and symptoms and develop a hypothesis about the presenting problem. However, doctors' decision-making processes are generally considered within the framework of the *hypothetico-deductive* model of decision making. This perspective emphasizes the development of hypotheses early on in the consultation and is illustrated by Newell and Simon's (1972) model of problem solving, which emphasizes hypothesis testing. Newell and Simon suggested that problem solving involves a number of stages that result in a solution to any given problem. This model has been applied to many different forms of problem solving and is a useful framework for examining clinical decisions (see Figure 4.2).

The stages involved are as follows:

1 *Understand the nature of the problem and develop an internal representation.* At this stage, the individual needs to formulate an internal representation of the problem. This process involves understanding the goal of the problem, evaluating any given conditions and assessing the nature of the available data.

2 *Develop a plan of action for solving the problem.* Newell and Simon differentiated between two types of plans: heuristics and algorithms. An algorithm is a set of rules that

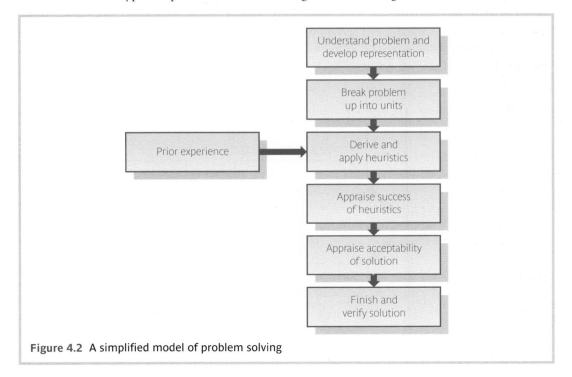

Figure 4.2 A simplified model of problem solving

will provide a correct solution if applied correctly (e.g. addition, multiplication, etc. involve algorithms). However, most human problem solving involves heuristics, which are rules of thumb. Heuristics are less definite and specific but provide guidance and direction for the problem solver. Heuristics may involve developing parallels between the present problem and previous similar ones.

3 *Apply heuristics.* Once developed, the plans are then applied to the given situation.

4 *Determine whether heuristics have been fruitful.* The individual then decides whether the heuristics have been successful in the attempt to solve the given problem. If they are considered unsuccessful, the individual may need to develop a new approach to the problem.

5 *Determine whether an acceptable solution has been obtained.*

6 *Finish and verify the solution.* The end-point of the problem-solving process involves the individual deciding that an acceptable solution to the problem has been reached and that this solution provides a suitable outcome.

According to Newell and Simon's model of problem solving, hypotheses about the causes and solutions to the problem are developed very early on in the process. They regarded this process as dynamic and ever-changing and suggested that at each stage of the process the individual applies a 'means end analysis', whereby they assess the value of the hypothesis, which is either accepted or rejected according to the evidence. This type of model involves information processing whereby the individual develops hypotheses to convert an open problem, which may be unmanageable with no obvious end-point, to one that can be closed and tested by a series of hypotheses.

Clinical decisions as problem solving

Clinical decisions can be conceptualized as a form of problem solving and involve the development of hypotheses early on in the consultation process. These hypotheses are subsequently tested by the doctor's selection of questions. Models of problem solving have been applied to clinical decision making by several authors (e.g. MacWhinney 1973; Weinman 1987), who have argued that the process of formulating a clinical decision involves the following stages (see Figure 4.3):

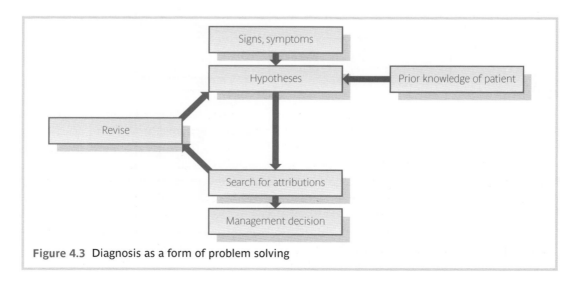

Figure 4.3 Diagnosis as a form of problem solving

1 *Accessing information about the patient's symptoms.* The initial questions in any consultation from health professional to the patient will enable the health professional to understand the nature of the problem and to form an internal representation of the type of problem.

2 *Developing hypotheses.* Early on in the problem-solving process, the health professional develops hypotheses about the possible causes and solutions to the problem.

3 *Search for attributes.* The health professional then proceeds to test the hypotheses by searching for factors either to confirm or to refute their hypotheses. Research into the hypothesis-testing process has indicated that although doctors aim to either confirm or refute their hypothesis by asking balanced questions, most of their questioning is biased towards confirmation of their original hypothesis. Therefore an initial hypothesis that a patient has a psychological problem may cause the doctor to focus on the patient's psychological state and ignore the patient's attempt to talk about their physical symptoms. Studies have shown that doctors' clinical information collected subsequent to the development of a hypothesis may be systematically distorted to support the original hypothesis (Wallsten 1978). Furthermore, the type of hypothesis has been shown to bias the collection and interpretation of any information received during the consultation (Wason 1974).

4 *Making a management decision.* The outcome of the clinical decision-making process involves the health professional deciding on the way forward. Weinman (1987) suggested that it is important to realize that the outcome of a consultation and a diagnosis is not an absolute entity, but is itself a hypothesis and an informed guess that will be either confirmed or refuted by future events.

Explaining variability

Variability in the behaviour of health professionals can therefore be understood in terms of the processes involved in clinical decisions. For example, health professionals may:

- access different information about the patient's symptoms
- develop different hypotheses
- access different attributes either to confirm or to refute their hypotheses
- have differing degrees of a bias towards confirmation
- consequently reach different management decisions.

Explaining variability – the role of health professionals' health beliefs

The hypothesis testing model of clinical decision making provides some understanding of the possible causes of variability in health professional behaviour. Perhaps the most important stage in the model that may lead to variability is the development of the original hypothesis. Patients are described as having lay beliefs, which are individual and variable. Health professionals are usually described as having professional beliefs, which are often assumed to be consistent and predictable. However, the development of the original hypothesis involves the health professional's own health beliefs, which may vary as much as those of the patient. Components of models such as the health belief model, the protection motivation theory and attribution theory have been developed to examine health professionals' beliefs. The beliefs involved in making the original hypothesis can be categorized as follows:

1 *The health professional's own beliefs about the nature of clinical problems.* Health professionals have their own beliefs about health and illness. This pre-existing factor will influence their choice of hypothesis. For example, if a health professional believes that health and illness are determined by biomedical factors (e.g. lesions, bacteria, viruses) then they will develop a hypothesis about the patient's problem that reflects this perspective (e.g. a patient who reports feeling tired all the time may be anaemic). However, a health professional who views health and illness as relating to psychosocial factors may develop hypotheses reflecting this perspective (e.g. a patient who reports feeling tired all the time may be under stress).

2 *The health professional's estimate of the probability of the hypothesis and disease.* Health professionals will have pre-existing beliefs about the prevalence and incidence of any given health problem that will influence the process of developing a hypothesis. For example, some doctors may regard childhood asthma as a common complaint and hypothesize that a child presenting with a cough has asthma, whereas others may believe that childhood asthma is rare and so will not consider this hypothesis.

3 *The seriousness and treatability of the disease.* Weinman (1987) argued that health professionals are motivated to consider the 'pay-off' involved in reaching a correct diagnosis and that this will influence their choice of hypothesis. He suggested that this pay-off is related to their beliefs about the seriousness and treatability of an illness. For example, a child presenting with abdominal pain may result in an original hypothesis of appendicitis as this is both a serious and treatable condition, and the benefits of arriving at the correct diagnosis for this condition far outweigh the costs involved (such as time-wasting) if this hypothesis is refuted. Marteau and Baum (1984) have argued that health professionals vary in their perceptions of the seriousness of diabetes and that these beliefs will influence their recommendations for treatment. Brewin (1984) carried out a study looking at the relationship between medical students' perceptions of the controllability of a patient's life events and the hypothetical prescription of antidepressants. The results showed that the students reported variability in their beliefs about the controllability of life events; if the patient was seen not to be in control (i.e. the patient was seen as a victim), the students were more likely to prescribe antidepressants than if the patient was seen to be in control. This suggests that not only do health professionals report inconsistency and variability in their beliefs, this variability may be translated into variability in their behaviour.

4 *Personal knowledge of the patient.* The original hypothesis will also be related to the health professional's existing knowledge of the patient. Such factors may include the patient's medical history, knowledge about their psychological state, an understanding of their psychosocial environment and a belief about why the patient uses the medical services.

5 *The health professional's stereotypes.* Stereotypes are sometimes seen as problematic and as confounding the decision-making process. However, most meetings between health professionals and patients are time-limited and consequently stereotypes play a central role in developing and testing a hypothesis and reaching a management decision. Stereotypes reflect the process of 'cognitive economy' and may be developed according to a multitude of factors such as how the patient looks/talks/walks or whether they remind the health professional of previous patients. Without stereotypes, consultations between health professionals and patients would be extremely time-consuming.

Other factors that may influence the development of the original hypothesis include the following:

1 ***The health professional's mood.*** The health professional's mood may influence the choice of hypotheses and the subsequent process of testing this hypothesis. Isen et al. (1991) manipulated mood in a group of medical students and evaluated the effect of induced positive affect on their decision-making processes. Positive affect was induced by informing subjects in this group that they had performed in the top 3 per cent of all graduate students nationwide in an anagram task. All subjects were then given a set of hypothetical patients and asked to decide which one was most likely to have lung cancer. The results showed that those subjects in the positive affect group spent less time to reach the correct decision and showed greater interest in the case histories by going beyond the assigned task. The authors therefore concluded that mood influenced the subjects' decision-making processes.

2 ***The profile characteristics of the health professional.*** Factors such as age, sex, weight, geographical location, previous experience and the health professional's own behaviour may also affect the decision-making process. For example, smoking doctors have been shown to spend more time counselling about smoking than their non-smoking counterparts (Stokes and Rigotti 1988). Further, thinner practice nurses have been shown to have different beliefs about obesity and offer different advice to obese patients than overweight practice nurses (Hoppe and Ogden 1997).

In summary, variability in health professionals' behaviour can be understood in terms of the factors involved in the decision-making process. In particular, many factors pre-dating the development of the original hypothesis such as the health professional's own beliefs may contribute to this variability.

Communicating beliefs to patients

If health professionals hold their own health-related beliefs, these may be communicated to the patients. This has particularly been studied in the domain of risk communication. A study by McNeil et al. (1982) examined the effects of health professionals' language on the patients' choice of hypothetical treatment. They assessed the effect of offering surgery either if it would 'increase the probability of survival' or would 'decrease the probability of death'. The results showed that patients are more likely to choose surgery if they believed it increased the probability of survival rather than if it decreased the probability of death. The phrasing of such a question would very much reflect the individual beliefs of the doctor, which in turn influenced the choices of the patients. Similarly, Senior et al. (2000) explored the impact of framing risk for heart disease or arthritis as either genetic or unspecified using hypothetical scenarios. The results showed that how risk was presented influenced both the participants' ratings of how preventable the illness was and their beliefs about causes. In a similar vein, Misselbrook and Armstrong (2000) asked patients whether they would accept treatment to prevent stroke and presented the effectiveness of this treatment in four different ways. The results showed that although all the forms of presentation were actually the same, 92 per cent of the patients said they would accept the treatment if it reduced their chances of stroke by 45 per cent (relative risk); 75 per cent said they would accept the treatment if it reduced their risk from 1 in 400 to 1 in 700 (absolute risk); 71 per cent said they would accept it if the doctor had to treat 35 patients for 25 years to prevent one stroke (number needed to treat); and only 44 per cent said they would accept it if the treatment had a 3 per cent chance of doing them good and a 97 per cent chance of doing no good or not being needed (personal probability of benefit). Therefore, although the actual risk of the treatment was the same in all four conditions, the ways of presenting this risk varied and this resulted in a variation in patient uptake. Harris and Smith (2005) carried out a similar study but compared absolute risk (high versus low risk) with comparative risk (above average versus below average). They asked participants to read information about deep vein thrombosis (DVT) and to rate a range of beliefs. Participants were then told to imagine their risk of DVT in either absolute or comparative terms. The results showed that the US sample were more disturbed by absolute risk. A detailed analysis of risk communication can be found in Berry (2004). However, doctors not only have beliefs about risk but also about illness which could be communicated to patients. Ogden et al. (2003) used an experimental design to explore the impact of type of diagnosis on patients' beliefs about common problems. Patients were asked to read a vignette in which a person was told either that they had a problem using a medical diagnostic term (tonsillitis/gastroenteritis) or using a lay term (sore throat/stomach upset). The results showed that, although doctors are often being told to use lay language when speaking to patients, patients actually preferred the medical labels as it made the symptoms seem more legitimate and gave the patient more confidence in the doctor. In contrast the lay terms made the patients feel more to blame for the problem. Therefore, if a doctor holds particular beliefs about risk or the nature of an illness, and chooses language that reflects these beliefs, then these beliefs may be communicated to the patient in a way that may then influence the patient's own beliefs and their subsequent behaviour.

Explaining variability – an interaction between health professional and patient

The explanations of variability in health professionals' behaviour presented so far have focused on the health professional in isolation. The educational model emphasizes the knowledge of the health professional and ignores the factors involved in the clinical decision-making process and their health beliefs. This perspective accepts the traditional divide between lay beliefs and professional beliefs. Emphasizing the clinical decision-making processes and health beliefs represents a shift from this perspective and attempts to see the divide between these two types of belief as problematic; health professionals have their own individualized 'lay beliefs' similar to patients. However, this explanation of variability ignores another important factor, namely the patient. Any variability in health professionals' behaviour exists in the context of both the health professional and the patient. Therefore, in order to understand the processes involved in health professional–patient communication, the resulting management decisions and any variability in the outcome of the consultation, both the patient and health professional should be considered as a dyad. The consultation involves two individuals and a communication process that exists between these individuals. This shift from an expert model towards an interaction is reflected in the emphasis on patient centredness, agreement between the health professional and patient and recent concerns about informed choice.

Patient centredness

First developed by Byrne and Long in 1976, the concept of patient centredness has become increasingly in vogue over recent years. The prescriptive literature has recommended patient centredness as the preferred style of doctor–patient communication as a means to improve patient outcomes (Pendleton et al. 1984; Neighbour 1987; McWhinney 1995). Further, empirical research has explored both the extent to which consultations can be deemed to be patient centred. For example, in one classic study Tuckett et al. (1985) analysed recorded consultations and described the interaction between doctor and patient as a 'meeting between experts'. Research has also addressed whether patient centredness is predictive of outcomes such as patient satisfaction, compliance and patient health status (Henbest and Stewart 1990; Savage and Armstrong 1990). Such research has raised questions concerning both the definition of patient centredness and its assessment which has resulted in a range of methodological approaches. For example, some studies have used coding frames such as the Stiles verbal response mode system (Stiles 1978) or the Roter index (Roter et al. 1997) as a means to code whether a particular doctor is behaving in a patient-centred fashion. In contrast, other studies have used interviews with patients and doctors (Henbest and Stewart 1990) while some have used behavioural checklists (Byrne and Long 1976). Complicating the matter further, research studies exploring the doctor–patient interaction and the literature proposing a particular form of interaction have used a wide range of different but related terms such as shared decision making (Elwyn et al. 1999), patient participation (Guadagnoli and Ward 1998) and patient partnership (Coulter 1999). However, although varying in their operationalization of patient centredness, in general the construct is considered to consist of three central components, namely: (1) a receptiveness by the doctor to the patient's opinions and expectations, and an effort to see the illness through the patient's eyes; (2) patient involvement in the decision making and planning of treatment; and (3) an attention to the affective content of the consultation in terms of the emotions of both the patient and the doctor. This framework is comparable to the six interactive components described by Levenstein et al. (1986) and is apparent in the five key dimensions described by Mead and Bower (2000) in their comprehensive review of the patient-centred literature. Finally, it is explicitly described by Winefield et al. (1996) in their work comparing the effectiveness of different measures. Patient centredness is now the way in which consultations are supposed to be managed. It emphasizes negotiation between doctor and patient and places the interaction between the two as central. In line with this approach, research has explored the relationship between health professional and patient with an emphasis not on either the health professional or the patient but on the interaction between the two in the following ways: the level of agreement between health professional and patient and the impact of this agreement on patient outcome.

Agreement between health professional and patient

If health professional–patient communication is seen as an interaction between two individuals then it is important to understand the extent to which these two individuals speak the same language, share the same beliefs and agree as to the desired content and outcome of any consultation. This is of particular relevance to general practice consultations where patient and health professional perspectives are most likely to coincide. For example, Pendleton et al. (1984) argued that the central tasks of a general practice consultation involved agreement with the patient about the nature of the problem, the action to be taken and subsequent management. Tuckett et al. (1985) likewise argued that the consultation should be conceptualized as a 'meeting between experts' and emphasized the importance of the patient's and doctor's potentially different views of the problem.

Recent research has examined levels of agreement between GPs' and patients' beliefs about different health problems. Ogden et al. (1999) explored GPs' and patients' models of depression in terms of symptoms (mood and somatic), causes (psychological, medical, external) and treatments (medical and non-medical). The results showed that GPs and patients agreed about the importance of mood-related symptoms, psychological causes and non-medical treatments. However, the GPs reported greater support for somatic symptoms, medical causes and medical treatments. Therefore the results indicated that GPs hold a more medical model of depression than patients. From similar perspective, Ogden, Bandara et al. (2001) explored GPs' and patients' beliefs about obesity. The results showed that the GPs and patients reported similar beliefs for most psychological, behavioural and social causes of obesity. However, they differed consistently in their beliefs about medical causes. In particular, the patients rated a gland/hormone problem, slow metabolism and overall medical causes more highly than did the GPs. For the treatment of obesity, a similar pattern emerged with the two groups reporting similar beliefs for a range of methods, but showing different beliefs about who was most helpful. Whereas the patients rated the GP as more helpful, the GPs rated the obese patients themselves more highly. Therefore, although GPs seem to have a more medical model of depression, they have a less medical model of obesity. Research has also shown that doctors and patients differ in their beliefs about the role of the doctor (Ogden et al. 1997), about the value of patient-centred consultations (Ogden et al. 2002), about the very nature of health (Ogden, Baig et al. 2001), about chronic disease and the role of stress (Heijmans et al. 2001) and in terms of what is important to know about medicines (Berry et al. 1997). If the health professional–patient communication is seen as an interaction, then these studies suggest that it may well be an interaction between two individuals with very different perspectives. Do these different perspectives influence patient outcomes?

The role of agreement in patient outcomes

If doctors and patients have different beliefs about illness, different beliefs about the role of the doctor and about medicines, does this lack of agreement relate to patient outcomes? It is possible that such disagreement may result in poor compliance to medication ('why should I take antidepressants if I am not depressed?'), poor compliance to any recommended changes in behaviour ('why should I eat less if obesity is caused by hormones?') or low satisfaction with the consultation ('I wanted emotional support and the GP gave me a prescription'). To date little research has explored these possibilities. One study did, however, examine the extent to which a patient's expectations of a GP consultation were met by the GP and whether this predicted patient satisfaction. Williams et al. (1995) asked 504 general practice patients to complete a measure of their expectations of the consultation with their GP prior to it taking place and a measure of whether their expectations were actually met afterwards. The results showed that having more expectations met was related to a higher level of satisfaction with the consultation. However, this study did not explore compliance, nor did it examine whether the GP and patient had a shared belief about the nature of the consultation. Therefore, further research is needed to develop methodological and theoretical approaches to the consultation as an interaction. In addition, research is needed to explore whether the nature of the interaction and the level of the agreement between health professional and patient predicts patient outcomes.

Informed choice

Gaining informed consent has become a central requirement for any research study or clinical intervention and aims to ensure that the participants have understood what they are about to take part in and any side effects that it might have. Informed consent can be either written or verbal depending on the nature of the study and is an essential requirement for gaining ethical approval, and medical councils across the world stipulate that patients must be given sufficient information to enable them to consent to any procedure in an informed way. Informed consent therefore relates to a formal process prior to research or clinical work. Within health psychology, researchers have also focused on informed choice and informed decision making, although defining the differences between these is often difficult. It is generally agreed that an informed decision is one that is made effectively but whether effectiveness relates to evaluations of the final choice (i.e. the outcome) or the way in which the decision is made (i.e. the process) is unclear. Bekker (2003) provides a clear analysis of these two different perspectives and highlights the theoretical positions that inform the emphasis on either outcome or process.

Outcome

Bekker (2003) describes how the emphasis on outcome reflects classical decision or rational choice theory which suggests that a choice can be deemed effective if it conforms to expected utility theory. This means that a choice is effective if the individual has surveyed all the decision options, evaluated the consequences of each option in terms of likelihood (i.e. the expected probability of the consequences occurring), assessed the attractiveness of the outcome of each option (utility) and then created an 'expected utility' value for each option by combining the likelihood of consequence (expected probability) and attractiveness (utility) and then choosing the option that has the greatest expected utility. This approach therefore emphasizes the outcome of a decision. The problem with this approach is that most decisions are not made in this rational way and so would be judged to be ineffective decisions. Further, it is possible that even if the individual were to be so rational, they may be basing it upon inaccurate information. If this were to occur, the decision would be deemed effective but the final decision would be incomplete.

Process

In contrast to this approach is one that emphasizes process. Bekker (2003) argues that this approach is informed by reasoned choice models which suggest that an effective decision is one that has met three criteria in terms of the process used to make the decision. These criteria are: the decision is based on information about the alternatives and their consequences; the likelihood and desirability of the consequences are evaluated accurately; a trade-off between these factors is evident. Further, central to this approach is a role for the individual's own beliefs as the evaluation of the consequences and desirability of the options takes place in the context of any existing values or beliefs.

Adding behaviour

O'Connor and O'Brien-Pallas (1989) take a process approach to informed choice but also add in the individual's behaviour. They describe an effective decision as one that is informed, consistent with the decision maker's values and then behaviourally implemented.

Measuring informed choice

As a means to assess informed choice Marteau et al. (2001) developed a new measure of informed choice which was based upon O'Connor and O'Brien-Pallas's definition and included measures of knowledge, attitudes and behaviour. They argue that when these three components are consistent with each other, then the person can be deemed to have made an informed choice.

There are therefore different ways of defining informed choice and informed decision making. To date, however, there remains no consensus as to the nature of informed choice or decision making although these terms are still widely used and regarded as essential to the research and clinical process.

To conclude

Traditional educational models of doctor–patient communication emphasized patient factors and considered non-compliance to be the result of patient variability. The relationship between health professionals and patients was seen as the communication of expert medical knowledge from an objective professional to a subjective layperson. Within this framework, Ley's model explained failures in communication in the context of the failure to comply in terms of patient factors, including patient's satisfaction, lack of understanding, or lack of recall. In addition, methods to improve communication focused on the health professional's ability to communicate this factual knowledge to the patient. However, recent research has highlighted variability in the behaviours of health professionals that cannot simply be explained in terms of differences in knowledge. This variability can be examined in terms of the processes involved in clinical decision making by the health professional and in particular the factors that influence the development of hypotheses. This variability has also been examined within the context of health beliefs, and it is argued that the division between professional and lay beliefs may be a simplification, with health professionals holding both professional and lay beliefs; health professionals have beliefs that are individual to them in the way that patients have their own individual beliefs. However, perhaps to further conceptualize the communication process, it is important to understand not only the health professional's preconceived ideas/prejudices/stereotypes/lay beliefs/professional beliefs or the patient's beliefs, but to consider the processes involved in any communication between health professional and patient as an interaction that occurs in the context of these beliefs.

❓ Questions

1 To what extent is a medical diagnosis based upon knowledge and expertise?
2 What are the problems with the hypothetico-deductive model of decision making?
3 Discuss the role of health professionals' beliefs in the communication process.
4 To what extent is non-compliance the responsibility of the patient?
5 Consider the problems inherent in determining whether someone has made an informed choice.
6 Health professionals should attempt to respect and share the beliefs of their patients. Discuss.
7 Design a research project to assess the role of affect in influencing health professionals' decision making.

For discussion

Consider the last time you had contact with a health professional (e.g. doctor, dentist, nurse, etc.). Discuss the content of the consultation and think about how the health professional's health beliefs may have influenced this.

Assumptions in health psychology

Some of the research cited in this chapter illustrates the kinds of assumptions that under-lie the study of health professionals and also provides insights into the assumptions of health psychology.

1 *The mind–body split.* Health psychology attempts to challenge the biomedical model of health and illness. This involves challenging biomedical assumptions such as the mind–body split. However, perhaps by emphasizing the mind (attitudes, cognitions, beliefs) as a separate entity, the mind–body split is not challenged but reinforced.

2 *Biomedical outcomes.* Challenging the biomedical model also involves questioning some of the outcomes used by medicine. For example, compliance with recommen-dations for drug taking, accuracy of recall, changing health behaviours following advice are all established desired outcomes. Health psychology accepts these out-comes by examining ways in which communication can be improved, variability can be understood and reduced, and compliance promoted. However, again, accepting these outcomes as legitimate is also a way of supporting biomedicine. Perhaps vari-ability is acceptable. Perhaps inaccuracy of recall sums up what happens in commu-nication (psychologists who study memory would argue that memory is the only process that is defined by its failures – memory is about reconstruction). Even though psychology adds to a biomedical model, by accepting the same outcomes it does not challenge it.

3 *Adding the social context.* Individuals exist within a social world and yet health psy-chology often misses out this world. An emphasis on the interaction between health professionals and patients represents an attempt to examine the cognitions of both these groups in the context of each other (the relationship context). However, this interaction is still accessed through an individual's beliefs. Is asking someone about the interaction actually examining the interaction or is it examining their cognitions about this interaction?

Further reading

Berry, D. (2004) *Risk, Communication and Health Psychology.* Maidenhead: Open University Press.
    The communication of risk is a central part of many consultations. This book provides a compre-hensive overview of research on risk communication.

Boyle, C.M. (1970) Differences between patients' and doctors' interpretations of common medical terms, *British Medical Journal,* 2: 286–9.
    This is a classic paper illustrating differences between doctors' and patients' knowledge and inter-pretation. At the time it was written it was central to the contemporary emphasis on a need to acknowledge how uninformed patients were. However, it also illustrates some variability in doctors' knowledge.

Marteau, T.M. and Johnston, M. (1990) Health professionals: a source of variance in health out-comes, *Psychology and Health,* 5: 47–58.
    This paper examines the different models of health professionals' behaviour and emphasizes the role of health professionals' health beliefs.

Roter, D.L., Stewart, M., Putnam, S.M., Lipkin, M., Stiles, W. and Inui, T.S. (1997) Communication pattern of primary care physicians, *Journal of the American Medical Association*, 277: 350–6.
This presents the classic paper describing the Roter index which is frequently used to assess communication.

Trostle, J.A. (1988) Medical compliance as an ideology, *Social Science and Medicine*, 27: 1299–308.
This theoretical paper examines the background to the recent interest in compliance and discusses the relationship between compliance and physician control.

Tuckett, D., Boulton, M., Olson, C. and Williams, A. (1985) *Meetings Between Experts*. London: Tavistock.
This is a classic book which describes a study involving consultation analysis. It set the scene for much subsequent research and shifted the emphasis from doctor as expert to seeing the consultation as an interaction.

Chapter 5

Smoking and alcohol use

Chapter overview

This chapter examines the prevalence of smoking and alcohol consumption and evaluates the health consequences of these behaviours. The history of theories of addictive behaviours and the shift from a disease model of addictions to the social learning theory perspective is then described. The chapter also examines the four stages of substance use from initiation and maintenance to cessation and relapse, and discusses these stages in the context of the different models of addictive behaviours. The chapter concludes with an examination of a cross-behavioural perspective on addictive behaviours and an assessment of the similarities and differences between smoking and drinking and their relationship to other behaviours.

This chapter covers

- The prevalence of smoking and alcohol consumption
- What is an addiction?
- What is the second disease concept?
- What is the social learning perspective?
- The stages of substance use
- Initiating and maintaining an addictive behaviour
- The cessation of an addictive behaviour
- Relapse in smoking and drinking
- A cross-addictive behaviour perspective

Who smokes?

Worldwide data show that in developed countries about 35 per cent of men and 22 per cent of women smoke whereas in developing countries about 50 per cent of men and 9 per cent of women smoke (National Statistics 2005). China has the highest percentage of male smokers, about 300 million men. This is equivalent to the entire US population. In the UK the overall prevalence of smoking has decreased in men from 52 per cent in 1974, to 30 per cent in 1990 to 26 per cent in 2004. In women it has decreased from 41 per cent in 1970, to 29 per cent in 1990 to 23 per cent in 2004. The highest prevalence of smoking is in those aged between 20 and 34, and whereas 32 per cent of those with routine or manual occupations smoke in the UK, only 16 per cent of those in professional occupations smoke. This decrease in smoking behaviour follows a trend for an overall decline and is shown in Figure 5.1. However, the data also showed that, although women smoke fewer cigarettes than men, fewer women than men are giving up.

Smokers can also be categorized in terms of whether they are 'ex-smokers', 'current smokers' or whether they have 'never smoked'. The trends in smoking behaviour according to these categories are shown in Figure 5.2. Again, sex differences can be seen for these types of smoking behaviour with men showing an increase in the numbers of 'never smoked' and 'ex-smokers', and a decrease in 'current smokers', while women show the same profile of change for both 'current smokers' and 'ex-smokers' but show a consistently high level of individuals who have 'never smoked'.

In general, data about smoking behaviour (*General Household Survey* 2004) suggest the following about smokers:

- Smoking behaviour is on the decline, but this decrease is greater in men than in women.
- Smokers tend to be in the unskilled manual group.
- There has been a dramatic reduction in the number of smokers smoking middle-tar cigarettes.
- Two-thirds of smokers report wanting to give up smoking.
- The majority of smokers (58 per cent) say that it would be fairly/very difficult to go without smoking for a whole day.

Who drinks?

According to the *General Household Survey* men on average drank 15.9 units a week (about eight pints of beer) and women drank about 5.4 units (about two and a half pints of beer). For

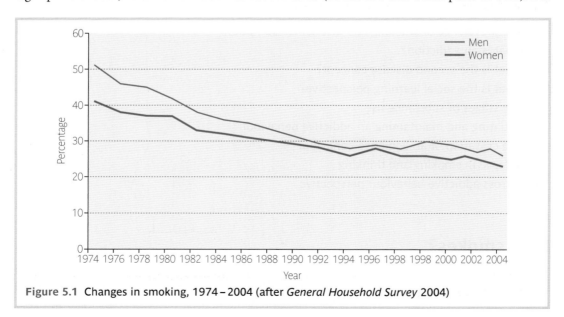

Figure 5.1 Changes in smoking, 1974–2004 (after *General Household Survey* 2004)

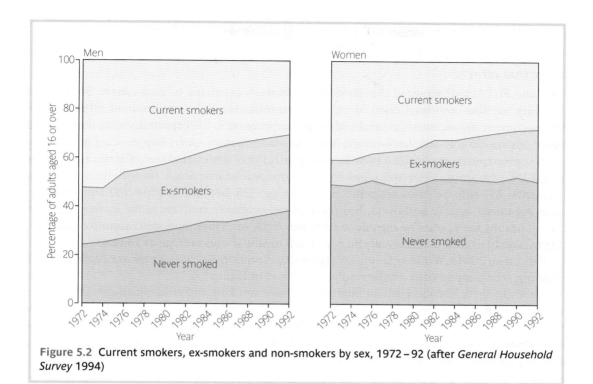

Figure 5.2 Current smokers, ex-smokers and non-smokers by sex, 1972–92 (after *General Household Survey* 1994)

2003, when asked about alcohol excessive consumption 'last week', 40 per cent of men drank more than four units on one day and 23 per cent of men drank more than eight units on one day, whereas 23 per cent of women drank more than three units in one day and 9 per cent drank more than six units on one day. Twenty-six per cent of men and 41 per cent of women drank no alcohol in the last week. Sex differences in drinking more than the recommended intake of alcohol by sex are shown in Figure 5.3.

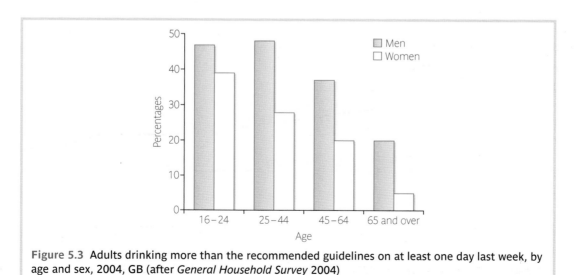

Figure 5.3 Adults drinking more than the recommended guidelines on at least one day last week, by age and sex, 2004, GB (after *General Household Survey* 2004)

Health implications of smoking and alcohol use

Is smoking bad for health?

Negative effects

Doll and Hill (1954) reported that smoking cigarettes was related to lung cancer. Since then, smoking has also been implicated in coronary heart disease and a multitude of other cancers such as throat, stomach and bowel. In addition, the increase in life expectancy over the past 150 years is considerably less for smokers than for non-smokers (see Chapter 2). The risks of smoking were made explicit in a book by Peto et al. (1994), who stated that of 1000 20 year olds in the UK who smoke cigarettes regularly about one will be murdered, six will die from traffic accidents, 250 will die from cigarettes in middle age (35–69) and another 250 will die from smoking in old age (70 and over). In industrialized countries smoking is the leading cause of loss of healthy life years. The average smoker dies eight years early and starts to suffer disability 12 years early while a quarter of smokers who fail to stop die an average of 23 years early (West and Shiffman 2004). Worldwide it is estimated that 4 million deaths per year are attributable to smoking. The number of deaths by smoking is shown in Figure 5.4.

Recently, there has also been an interest in passive smoking and research suggests an association between passive smoking and lung cancer in adults and respiratory ill health in children (US Environmental Protection Agency 1992). In addition, a recent review of the literature concluded that smoking may interfere with recovery following surgery and that a longer period of smoking cessation prior to having an operation is associated with a reduction in the number of complications following surgery (Theadom and Cropley 2006; see Chapter 11 for a discussion of wound healing and psychoneuroimmunology).

Positive effects

There are very few positive health effects of cigarette smoking. It has been suggested that smokers report positive mood effects from smoking and that smoking can help individuals to cope with difficult circumstances (Graham 1987).

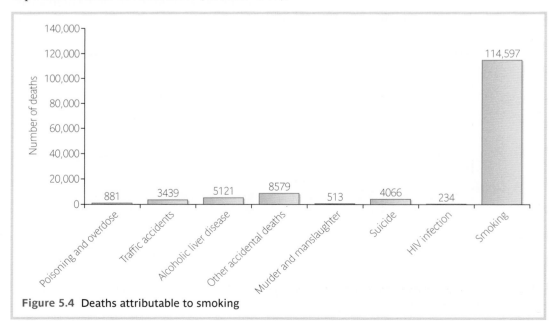

Figure 5.4 Deaths attributable to smoking

Is alcohol consumption bad for health?

Negative effects

Alcohol consumption has several negative effects on health. For example, alcoholism increases the chance of disorders such as liver cirrhosis, cancers (e.g. pancreas and liver), hypertension and memory deficits (Smith and Kraus 1988). Alcohol also increases the chances of self-harm through accidents. In terms of its impact on mortality, data from the UK show that the number of alcohol-related deaths has increased from 6.9 per 100,000 in 1991 to 13.0 in 2004 and that the number of deaths has more than doubled from 4144 in 1991 to 8380 in 2004. Data also show that death rates are higher for men than for women and that this gap has widened over recent years. These data are shown in Figure 5.5.

Positive effects

Alcohol may also have a positive effect on health. In a longitudinal study, Friedman and Kimball (1986) reported that light and moderate drinkers had lower morbidity and mortality rates than both non-drinkers and heavy drinkers. They argued that alcohol consumption reduces coronary heart disease via the following mechanisms: (1) a reduction in the production of catecholamines when stressed; (2) the protection of blood vessels from cholesterol; (3) a reduction in blood pressure; (4) self-therapy; and (5) a short-term coping strategy. The results from the *General Household Survey* (1992) also showed some benefits of alcohol consumption with the reported prevalence of ill health being higher among non-drinkers than among drinkers. However, it has been suggested that the apparent positive effects of alcohol on health may be an artefact of poor health in the non-drinkers who have stopped drinking due to health problems.

In an attempt to understand why people smoke and drink, much health psychology research has drawn upon the social cognition models described in Chapter 2. However, there is a vast addiction literature which has also been applied to smoking and drinking. Addiction theories will now be explored.

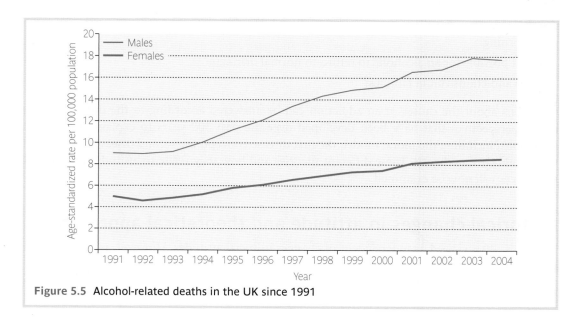

Figure 5.5 Alcohol-related deaths in the UK since 1991

What is an addiction?

Many theories have been developed to explain addictions and addictive behaviours, including moral models, which regard an addiction as the result of weakness and a lack of moral fibre; biomedical models, which see an addiction as a disease; and social learning theories, which regard addictive behaviours as behaviours that are learned according to the rules of learning theory. The multitude of terms that exist and are used with respect to behaviours such as smoking and alcohol are indicative of these different theoretical perspectives and in addition illustrate the tautological nature of the definitions. For example:

- *An addict*: someone who 'has no control over their behaviour', 'lacks moral fibre', 'uses a maladaptive coping mechanism', 'has an addictive behaviour'.
- *An addiction*: 'a need for a drug', 'the use of a substance that is psychologically and physiologically addictive', 'showing tolerance and withdrawal'.
- *Dependency*: 'showing psychological and physiological withdrawal'.
- *Drug*: 'an addictive substance', 'a substance that causes dependency', 'any medical substance'.

These different definitions indicate the relationship between terminology and theory. For example, concepts of 'control', 'withdrawal' and 'tolerance' are indicative of a biomedical view of addictions. Concepts such as 'lacking moral fibre' suggest a moral model of addictions, and 'maladaptive coping mechanism' suggests a social learning perspective. In addition, the terms illustrate how difficult it is to use one term without using another with the risk that the definitions become tautologies.

Many questions have been asked about different addictive behaviours, including the following:

- What causes someone to start smoking?
- What causes drinking behaviour to become a problem?
- Why can some people just smoke socially while others need to smoke first thing in the morning?
- Is it possible for an alcoholic to return to normal drinking?
- Do addictions run in families?

Questions about the causes of an addiction can be answered according to the different theoretical perspectives that have been developed over the past 300 years to explain and predict addictions, including the moral model, the first disease concept, the second disease concept and the social learning theory. These different theories and how they relate to attitudes to different substances will now be examined.

Historical changes in attitude and theoretical approach

Theory is often viewed as independent of changes in social attitudes. However, parallels can be seen between changes in theoretical perspective over the past 300 years and contemporary attitudes. These parallels will be discussed in terms of alcohol use.

The seventeenth century and the moral model of addictions

During the seventeenth century, alcohol was generally held in high esteem by society. It was regarded as safer than water, nutritious, and the innkeeper was valued as a central figure in the community. In addition, at this time humans were considered to be separate from Nature, in terms of possessing a soul and a will and being responsible for their own behaviour. Animals' behaviour was seen as resulting from biological drives, whereas the behaviour of humans was seen to be a result of their own free choice. Accordingly, alcohol consumption was considered an acceptable behaviour, but excessive alcohol use was regarded as a result of free choice and personal responsibility. Alcoholism was therefore seen as a behaviour that deserved punishment, not treatment; alcoholics were regarded as choosing to behave excessively. This model of addiction was called the *moral model*. This perspective is similar to the arguments espoused by Thomas Szasz in the 1960s concerning the treatment versus punishment of mentally ill individuals and his distinction between being 'mad' or 'bad'. Szasz (1961) suggested that to label someone 'mad' and to treat them, removed the central facet of humanity, namely personal responsibility. He suggested that holding individuals responsible for their behaviour gave them back their sense of responsibility even if this resulted in them being seen as 'bad'. Similarly, the moral model of addictions considered alcoholics to have chosen to behave excessively and therefore deserving of punishment (acknowledging their responsibility), not treatment (denying them their responsibility). In effect, contemporary social attitudes were reflected in contemporary theory.

The nineteenth century and the first disease concept

During the nineteenth century, attitudes towards addictions, and in particular alcohol, changed. The temperance movement was developed and spread the word about the evils of drink. Alcohol was regarded as a powerful and destructive substance and alcoholics were regarded as its victims. This perspective is also reflected in prohibition and the banning of alcohol consumption in the USA. During this time, the *first disease concept* of addiction was developed. This was the earliest form of a biomedical approach to addiction and regarded alcoholism as an illness. Within this model, the focus for the illness was the substance. Alcohol was seen as an addictive substance, and alcoholics were viewed as passively succumbing to its influence. The first disease concept regarded the substance as the problem and called for the treatment of excessive drinkers. Again, social attitudes to addiction were reflected in the development of theory.

The twentieth century and the second disease concept

Attitudes towards addiction changed again at the beginning of the twentieth century. The USA learned quickly that banning alcohol consumption was more problematic than expected, and governments across the western world realized that they could financially benefit from alcohol sales. In parallel, attitudes towards human behaviour were changing and a more liberal, *laissez-faire* attitude became dominant. Likewise, theories of addiction reflected these shifts. The *second disease model* of addiction was developed, which no longer saw the substance as the problem but pointed the finger at those individuals who became addicted. Within this perspective, the small minority of those who consumed alcohol to excess were seen as having a problem, but for the rest of society alcohol consumption returned to a position of an acceptable social habit. This perspective legitimized the sale of alcohol, recognized the resulting government benefits and emphasized the treatment of addicted individuals. Alcoholism was regarded as an illness developed by certain individuals who therefore needed support and treatment.

The 1970s and onwards – social learning theory

Over the past few years attitudes towards addictions have changed again. With the development of behaviourism, learning theory and a belief that behaviour was shaped by an interaction with both the environment and other individuals, the belief that excessive behaviour and addictions were illnesses began to be challenged. Since the 1970s, behaviours such as smoking, drinking and drug taking have been increasingly described within the context of all other behaviours. In the same way that theories of aggression shifted from a biological cause (aggression as an instinct) to social causes (aggression as a response to the environment/upbringing), addictions were also seen as learned behaviours. Within this perspective, the term 'addictive behaviour' replaced 'addictions' and such behaviours were regarded as a consequence of learning processes. This shift challenged the concepts of addictions, addict, illness and disease; however, the theories still emphasized treatment.

Therefore over the past 300 years there have been shifts in attitudes towards addictions and addictive behaviours that are reflected by the changing theoretical perspectives. Although the development of social learning theory highlighted some of the problems with the second disease concept of addictions, both these perspectives still remain, and will now be examined in greater detail.

What is the second disease concept?

The three perspectives in this category represent: (1) pre-existing physical abnormalities; (2) pre-existing psychological abnormalities; and (3) acquired dependency theory. All of these have a similar model of addiction in that they:

- regard addictions as discrete entities (you are either an addict or not an addict)
- regard an addiction as an illness
- focus on the individual as the problem
- regard the addiction as irreversible
- emphasize treatment
- emphasize treatment through total abstinence.

A pre-existing physical abnormality

There are a number of perspectives that suggest that an addiction is the result of a pre-existing physical abnormality. For example, Alcoholics Anonymous argue that some individuals may have an allergy to alcohol and therefore become addicted once exposed to the substance. From this perspective comes the belief 'one drink – a drunk', 'once a drunk, always a drunk' and stories of abstaining alcoholics relapsing after drinking sherry in a sherry trifle. In terms of smoking, this perspective would suggest that certain individuals are more sensitive to the effects of nicotine.

Nutritional/endocrinological theories suggest that some individuals may metabolize alcohol differently to others, that they become drunk quicker and may not experience any of the early symptoms of drunkenness. Similarly, this perspective would suggest that some individuals may process nicotine differently to others.

Genetic theories suggest that there may be a genetic predisposition to becoming an alcoholic or a smoker. To examine the influences of genetics, researchers have examined either identical twins reared apart or the relationship between adoptees and their biological parents. These methodologies tease apart the separate effects of environment and genetics. In an early study on genetics and smoking, Sheilds (1962) reported that out of 42 twins reared apart, only 9 were discordant (showed different smoking behaviour). He reported that 18 pairs were both non-smokers and 15 pairs were both smokers. This is a much higher rate of concordance than predicted by chance. Evidence for a genetic factor in smoking has also been reported by Eysenck (1990) and in an Australian study examining the role of genetics in both the uptake of smoking (initiation) and committed smoking (maintenance) (Hannah et al. 1985). Research into the role of genetics in alcoholism has been more extensive and reviews of this literature can be found elsewhere (Peele 1984; Schuckit 1985). However, it has been estimated that a male child may be up to four times more likely to develop alcoholism if they have a biological parent who is an alcoholic.

A pre-existing psychological abnormality

Some theories suggest that certain individuals may become addicts due to a pre-existing psychological problem. For example, Freud argued that an addiction may be the result of either latent homosexuality, or a need for oral gratification. It has also been suggested that alcoholism may be related to a self-destructive personality or a need for power (e.g. McClelland et al. 1972). This perspective emphasizes a psychological abnormality that is irreversible and pre-dates the onset of the addictive behaviour.

Acquired dependency

Models within the second disease perspective have also viewed addiction as the result of excess. For example, Jellinek in the 1960s developed a theory of species of alcoholism and phases of alcoholism (Jellinek 1960). This suggested that there were different types of addiction (alpha, gamma, delta) and that increased consumption of alcohol caused the individual to progress through different stages of the illness. He suggested that addiction stemmed from exposure to the addictive substance and resulted in: (1) acquired tissue tolerance; (2) adaptive cell metabolism; (3) withdrawal and craving; and (4) loss of control. In a similar vein, Edwards and Gross's (1976) theory of alcohol dependence syndrome argued that consistent alcohol use resulted in cell changes and subsequent dependency. Applied to smoking, this perspective suggests that nicotine causes addiction through its constant use. Although this perspective is classified as a second disease concept, it is reminiscent of the first disease concept as the emphasis is on the substance rather than on the individual.

Problems with a disease model of addiction

Although many researchers still emphasize a disease model of addictions, there are several problems with this perspective:

- The disease model encourages treatment through lifelong abstinence. However, lifelong abstinence is very rare and may be difficult to achieve.
- The disease model does not incorporate relapse into its model of treatment. However, this 'all or nothing' perspective may actually promote relapse through encouraging individuals to set unreasonable targets of abstinence and by establishing the self-fulfilling prophecy of 'once a drunk, always a drunk'.

■ The description of controlled drinking, which suggested that alcoholics can return to 'normal drinking' patterns (Davies 1962; Sobel and Sobel 1976, 1978), challenged the central ideas of the disease model. The phenomenon of controlled drinking indicated that perhaps an addiction was not irreversible and that abstinence may not be the only treatment goal.

What is the social learning perspective?

The social learning perspective differs from the disease model of addiction in several ways:

■ Addictive behaviours are seen as acquired habits, which are learned according to the rules of social learning theory.

■ Addictive behaviours can be unlearned; they are not irreversible.

■ Addictive behaviours lie along a continuum; they are not discrete entities.

■ Addictive behaviours are no different from other behaviours.

■ Treatment approaches involve either total abstinence or relearning 'normal' behaviour patterns.

The processes involved in learning an addictive behaviour

To a social learning perspective, addictive behaviours are learned according to the following processes: (1) classical conditioning; (2) operant conditioning; (3) observational learning; and (4) cognitive processes.

Classical conditioning

The rules of classical conditioning state that behaviours are acquired through the processes of associative learning. For example, an unconditioned stimulus (US, e.g. going to the pub) may elicit an unconditioned response (UR, e.g. feeling relaxed). If the unconditioned stimulus is associated with a conditioned stimulus (CS, e.g. a drink), then eventually this will elicit the conditioned response (CR, e.g. feeling relaxed). This will happen as follows:

The unconditioned stimulus and the unconditioned response:
going to the pub + feeling relaxed
(US) + (UR)

Pairing the unconditioned stimulus and the conditioned stimulus:
going to the pub + a drink
(US) + (CS)

The conditioned stimulus and the conditioned response:
a drink + feeling relaxed
(CS) + (CR)

Therefore the conditioned stimulus now elicits the conditioned response.

What factors can pair with the conditioned stimulus?

Two types of factor can pair with the conditioned stimulus: *external* (e.g. the pub) and *internal* (e.g. mood) cues. In terms of a potentially addictive behaviour, smoking cigarettes may be associated with external cues (e.g. seeing someone else smoking, being with particular friends), or with internal cues (e.g. anxiety, depression or happiness). It has been argued that a pairing with an internal cue is more problematic because these cues cannot be avoided. In addition, internal cues also raise the problem of *generalization*. Generalization occurs when the withdrawal symptoms from a period of abstinence from an addictive behaviour act as cues for further behaviour. For example, if an individual has paired feeling anxious with smoking, their withdrawal symptoms may be interpreted as anxiety and therefore elicit further smoking behaviour; the behaviour provides relief from its own withdrawal symptoms.

Operant conditioning

The rules of operant conditioning state that the probability of behaviour occurring is increased if it is either *positively reinforced* by the presence of a positive event, or *negatively reinforced* by the absence or removal of a negative event. In terms of an addictive behaviour such as smoking, the probability of smoking will be increased by feelings of social acceptance, confidence and control (the positive reinforcer) and removal of withdrawal symptoms (the negative reinforcer).

Observational learning/modelling

Behaviours are also learned by observing significant others carrying them out. For example, parental smoking, an association between smoking and attractiveness/thinness, and the observation of alcohol consumption as a risk-taking behaviour may contribute to the acquisition of the behaviour.

Cognitive factors

Factors such as self-image, problem-solving behaviour, coping mechanisms and attributions also contribute to the acquisition of an addictive behaviour.

Integrating a disease and social learning perspective

Researchers often polarize a disease and a social learning perspective of addiction. For example, while some researchers argue that smoking is entirely due to the addictive properties of nicotine, others argue that it is a learned behaviour. However, implicit within each approach is the alternative explanation. For example, while a disease model may emphasize acquired tolerance following smoking or drinking behaviour and therefore draws upon a disease perspective, it implicitly uses a social learning approach to explain why some people start smoking/drinking in the first place and why only some continue to the extent that they develop acquired tolerance. People need exposure and reinforcement to make the smoke or drink enough to develop tolerance. The concept of tolerance may be a disease model concept but it relies upon some degree of social learning theory for it to operate. Likewise, people might smoke an increasing number of cigarettes because they have learned that smoking relieves withdrawal symptoms. However, while this form of association is derived from a social learning perspective it implicitly uses a disease perspective in that it requires the existence of physical withdrawal symptoms. Therefore most researchers draw upon both disease and social learning perspectives. Sometimes this interaction between the two forms of model is made explicit and the researchers acknowledge that they believe both sources of influence are important. However, at times this interaction is only implicit. West (2006) offers a new synthetic model of addiction that brings together a range of medical and psychological constructs including compulsion, self-control, habit and motivational states as a means to understand why people become addicted in the first place and how and why they sometimes manage to change their behaviour.

> ### Box 5.1 **Some problems with . . . smoking and alcohol research**
>
> Below are some problems with research in this area that you may wish to consider.
>
> 1 There are very different theoretical perspectives on addictive behaviours which colour research in terms of theory, methods and interpretation. For example, those from a medical perspective emphasize the addictive nature of the drug while those from a behavioural perspective emphasize the behaviour. At times these two perspectives contradict each other but mostly these two camps publish in different journals and do not really communicate. This can lead to polarizing our understanding of these behaviours.
>
> 2 Most measures of smoking and alcohol are self-report. This can be problematic as people may under-report their behaviour in order to seem healthier than they are. There are some more objective measures available such as cotinine levels. However, these involve more commitment by both the researcher and the subject. In addition, measuring these behaviours may change them as any form of measurement can make people more aware of their behaviours.
>
> 3 The factors that explain smoking and alcohol use are many and complex. Theories to explain them are therefore complex and often difficult to operationalize. More simple theories are easier to operationalize but may miss many of the variables that predict these behaviours. There therefore always needs to be a trade-off between comprehensiveness and usefulness.

The stages of substance use

Research into addictive behaviours has defined four stages of substance use: (1) initiation; (2) maintenance; (3) cessation; and (4) relapse. These four stages will now be examined in detail for smoking and alcohol use and are illustrated in Figure 5.6.

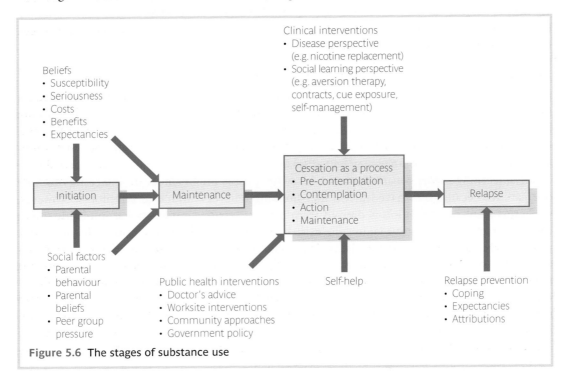

Figure 5.6 The stages of substance use

Stages 1 and 2: initiating and maintaining an addictive behaviour

Smoking initiation and maintenance

In 1954, Doll and Hill indicated that smoking was predictive of lung cancer. Fifty years later, approximately 30 per cent of the adult population still smoke even though most of them are aware of the related health risks. In fact, research exploring whether smokers appreciate the risks of smoking in comparison with the risks of murder and traffic accidents showed that smokers were accurate in their perception of the risks of smoking and showed similar ratings of risk to both ex-smokers and those who had never smoked (Sutton 1998b). The early health promotion campaigns focused mainly on the determinants of smoking in adult men, but over recent years there has been an increasing interest in smoking in children. Most children/adolescents try a puff of a cigarette. It is therefore difficult to distinguish between actual initiation and maintenance of smoking behaviour. Accordingly, these stages will be considered together.

Smoking in children

Doll and Peto (1981) reported that people whose smoking is initiated in childhood have an increased chance of lung cancer compared with those who start smoking later on in life. This is particularly significant as most adult smokers start the habit in childhood and very few people start smoking regularly after the age of 19 or 20 (Charlton 1992). Lader and Matheson (1991) reviewed the data from national surveys between 1982 and 1990 and indicated that smoking behaviour in 11- to 15-year-old school boys – including those boys who have just tried a cigarette – had fallen from 55 to 44 per cent and that smoking in school girls of a comparable age had fallen from 51 to 42 per cent. Although this showed a decrease, it was less than the decrease shown in adult smoking, and the data showed that in 1990 nearly a half of the school children had at least tried one cigarette. In fact, many children try their first cigarette while at primary school (Murray et al. 1984; Swan et al. 1991).

Psychological predictors of smoking initiation

In an attempt to understand smoking initiation and maintenance, researchers have searched for the psychological and social processes that may promote smoking behaviour. Models of health behaviour such as the health belief model, the protection motivation theory, the theory of reasoned action and the health action process approach (see Chapter 2) have been used to examine the cognitive factors that contribute to smoking initiation (e.g. Sherman et al. 1982; Sutton 1982). Additional cognitions that predict smoking behaviour include associating smoking with fun and pleasure, smoking as a means of calming nerves and smoking as being sociable and building confidence, all of which have been reported by young smokers (Charlton 1984; Charlton and Blair 1989; see also Chapter 11 for a discussion of smoking and stress reduction). In a recent study Conner, Sandberg et al. (2006) explored the role of theory of planned behaviour variables (see Chapter 2) as well as anticipated regret and intention stability in predicting smoking initiation in adolescents aged between 11 and 12 years old: 675 non-smoking adolescents completed measures at baseline and then were followed up after nine months to see if they had tried smoking which was assessed using a carbon monoxide breath monitor. The results showed that smoking initiation was predicted by baseline intentions. This association between intentions and behaviour was only present, however, in those who did not express regret about starting smoking at baseline and who showed stable intentions.

Social predictors of smoking initiation and maintenance

Much research focuses on the individual and takes the individual out of their social context. Individual cognitions may predict smoking behaviour but they are a product of the individual's socialization. Interactions within the individual's social world help to create and develop a child's beliefs and behaviour. In Britain, there have been five longitudinal studies that have identified elements of the child's social world that are predictive of smoking behaviour (Murray et al. 1984; McNeil et al. 1988; Charlton and Blair 1989; Gillies and Galt 1990; Goddard 1990). The main factor that predicts smoking is parental smoking, with reports that children are twice as likely to smoke if their parents smoke (Lader and Matheson 1991). In addition, parents' attitudes to smoking also influence their offspring's behaviour. For example, if a child perceives the parents as being strongly against smoking, he or she is up to seven times less likely to be a smoker (Murray et al. 1984). The next most important influence on smoking is peer group pressure. Studies in the USA have examined the relationship between peer group identity and tobacco use. The results showed that individuals who are identified by themselves and others as being problem-prone, doing poorly at school, rarely involved in school sports, high in risk-taking behaviour such as alcohol and drug use, and with low self-esteem were more likely to have smoked (Mosbach and Leventhal 1988; Sussman et al. 1990). On the other hand, research has also found that high rates of smoking can also be found in children who are seen as leaders of academic and social activities, have high self-esteem and are regarded as popular by their peers (Mosbach and Leventhal 1988). Another factor that influences whether children smoke is the attitude of their school to smoking behaviour. A Cancer Research Campaign study (1991) found that smoking prevalence was lower in schools that had a 'no smoking' policy, particularly if this policy included staff as well as students. In summary, social factors such as the behaviour and beliefs of parents, peers and schools influence the beliefs and behaviours of children. Using an entirely different methodology, Graham used interviews with low-income women with pre-school children to explore the contextual factors that may maintain smoking behaviour. She argued that although smoking is seen by researchers as unhealthy and something to be prevented, the women in her study regarded smoking as central to their attempts to 'reconcile health keeping and housekeeping when their reserves of emotional and physical energy may be seriously depleted' (Graham 1987: 55). She stated that smoking works to promote these women's sense of well-being and to help them cope with caring. She reports that smoking can be seen as 'the only activity they do, just for themselves'. Smoking is therefore a product not only of beliefs but also an individual's social world.

Alcohol initiation and maintenance

Most people try alcohol at some time in their lives. However, one survey showed that about a quarter of those questioned (men and women) described themselves as lifelong abstainers (*General Household Survey* 1994). The most common reasons for never drinking alcohol were religion and not liking it. Therefore, rather than examining predictors of drinking 'ever' or 'occasionally', this section examines what factors predict developing a problem with drinking.

Psychological predictors of alcohol initiation and maintenance

The tension-reduction hypothesis (Cappell and Greeley 1987) suggests that individuals may develop a drink problem because alcohol reduces tension and anxiety. Tension creates a heightened state of arousal and alcohol reduces this state, which perpetuates further drinking behaviour. However, it has been suggested that it is not the actual effects of alcohol use that promote drinking but the expected effects (George and Marlatt 1983). Therefore, because a small amount of alcohol may have positive effects, people assume that these positive effects will continue with increased use. This perspective is in line with the social learning model of addictive behaviours and emphasizes the role of reinforcement and cognitions.

Social predictors of alcohol initiation and maintenance

Many of the social factors that relate to smoking behaviour are also predictive of alcohol consumption. For example, parental drinking is predictive of problem drinking in children. According to a disease model of addictions, it could be argued that this reflects the genetic predisposition to develop an addictive behaviour. However, parental drinking may be influential through 'social hereditary factors', with children being exposed to drinking behaviour and learning this behaviour from their parents (Orford and Velleman 1991). In addition, peer group alcohol use and abuse also predicts drinking behaviour, as does being someone who is sensation seeking, with a tendency to be aggressive and having a history of getting into trouble with authority. Johnston and White (2003) used the theory of planned behaviour (see Chapter 2) to predict binge drinking in students. However, given the social nature of binge drinking, they focused on the role of norms. Using a longitudinal design, 289 undergraduate students completed a questionnaire concerning their beliefs with follow-up collected about reported binge drinking. The results showed an important role for norms, particularly if the norms were of a behaviourally relevant reference group with which the student strongly identified.

Stage 3: the cessation of an addictive behaviour

Because of the potential health consequences of both smoking and alcohol consumption, research has examined different means to help smokers and drinkers quit their behaviour. Cessation of an addictive behaviour can be examined in terms of the *processes* involved in cessation and the *interventions* designed to motivate individuals to quit their behaviour.

The process of cessation

Most research to date has conceptualized cessation as the result of a slow process of cognitive shifts. In contrast recent research has emphasized a more unplanned approach to cessation. These two approaches will now be considered.

Cessation as a slow process

Much research emphasizes the 'drip, drip' approach to cessation and the development and implementation of behavioural intentions or plans. For example, the TPB (Ajzen and Madden 1986), conceptualizes behavioural intentions as a prerequisite for behaviour change, implementation intention research highlights the development of plans (Gollwitzer 1993) and the stages-of-change model focuses on the gradual progression through a series of stages (Prochaska and DiClemente 1982). In particular, Prochaska and DiClemente (1984; see Chapter 2) adapted their stages-of-change model to examine cessation of addictive behaviours. This model highlighted the processes involved in the transition from a smoker to a non-smoker and from a drinker to a non-drinker. They argued that cessation involves a shift across five basic stages:

1 *pre-contemplation*: defined as not seriously considering quitting

2 *contemplation*: having some thoughts about quitting

3 *preparation*: seriously considering quitting

4 *action*: initial behaviour change

5 *maintenance*: maintaining behaviour change for a period of time.

Prochaska and DiClemente maintain that individuals do not progress through these stages in a straightforward and linear fashion but may switch backwards and forwards (e.g. from pre-contemplation to contemplation and back to pre-contemplation again). They call this 'the revolving door' schema and emphasize the dynamic nature of cessation. This model of change has been tested to provide evidence for the different stages for smokers and outpatient alcoholics (DiClemente and Prochaska 1982, 1985; DiClemente and Hughes 1990), and for the relationship between stage of change for smoking cessation and self-efficacy (DiClemente 1986). In addition, DiClemente et al. (1991) examined the relationship between stage of change and attempts to quit smoking and actual cessation at one- and six-month follow-ups. The authors categorized smokers into either pre-contemplators or contemplators and examined their smoking behaviour at follow-up. They further classified the contemplators into either contemplators (those who were smoking, seriously considering quitting within the next six months, but not within the next 30 days) or those in the preparation stage (those who were seriously considering quitting smoking within the next 30 days). The results showed that those in the preparation stage of change were more likely to have made a quit attempt at both one and six months, that they had made more quit attempts, and were more likely to be not smoking at the follow-ups. This study is described in detail in **Focus on research 5.1** (p. 111).

Research has also used the health beliefs and structured models outlined in Chapter 2 to examine the predictors of both intentions to stop smoking and successful smoking cessation. For example, individual cognitions such as perceptions of susceptibility, past cessation attempts and perceived behavioural control have been shown to relate to reductions in smoking behaviour (Giannetti et al. 1985; Cummings et al. 1988; Godin et al. 1992). In addition, the theory of planned behaviour (TPB) has been used as a framework to explore smoking cessation in a range of populations, including those following a worksite ban (Borland et al. 1991), pregnant women and the general population (Godin et al. 1992).

Along these lines, one study examined the usefulness of the TPB at predicting intention to quit smoking and making a quit attempt in a group of smokers attending health promotion clinics in primary care (Norman et al. 1999). The results showed that the best predictors of intentions to quit were perceived behavioural control (i.e. 'How much control do you feel you have over not smoking over the next six months?') and perceived susceptibility (i.e. 'How likely do you think it might be that you will develop any of the following problems in the future if you continue to smoke?'). At follow-up, the best predictors of making a quit attempt were intentions at baseline (i.e. 'How likely is it that you will not smoke during the next six months?') and the number of previous quit attempts. Therefore the process of smoking cessation can be explored using either a stages-of-change perspective, individual cognitions or structured models such as the TPB.

Cessation as unplanned

In contrast to this 'drip, drip' approach to cessation West (2006; West and Sohal 2006) has argued that sometimes cessation of an addictive behaviour can be unplanned. In a large-scale cross-sectional survey of smokers who had made at least one quit attempt ($n = 918$) and ex-smokers ($n = 996$) they asked participants to describe whether they had made a serious quit attempt ('By serious attempt I mean you decided that you would try to make sure you never smoked another cigarette'). Those who had tried were then asked to describe the extent to which their attempt had been planned (ranging from 'I did not plan the quit attempt in advance' to 'I planned the quit attempt a few months beforehand') (West and Sohal 2006). The results showed that almost half (48.6 per cent) of the attempts had been made without planning. In addition the results showed that unplanned attempts were more likely to last for at least six months (65.4 per cent) compared to planned attempts (42.3 per cent). These results remained even when age, sex and social class were controlled for. These findings are in contrast to much of the research described earlier which emphasizes the role of plans and stages.

Testing a theory – stages of smoking cessation

A study to examine the stages of change in predicting smoking cessation (DiClemente et al. 1991). Traditionally addictive behaviours were viewed as 'either/or' behaviours. Therefore smokers were considered either smokers, ex-smokers or non-smokers. However, DiClemente and Prochaska (1982) developed their trans-theoretical model of change to examine the stages of change in addictive behaviours. This is a classic study which examined the validity of the stages-of-change model and assessed the relationship between stage of change and smoking cessation.

Background

The original stages-of-change model describes the following stages:

- *Pre-contemplation*: not seriously considering quitting in the next six months.
- *Contemplation*: considering quitting in the next six months.
- *Action*: making behavioural changes.
- *Maintenance*: maintaining these changes.

The model is described as dynamic, not linear, with individuals moving backwards and forwards across the stages. In this study, the authors categorized those in the contemplation stage as either contemplators (not considering quitting in the next 30 days) and those in the preparation stage (planning to quit in the next 30 days).

Methodology
Subjects

A total of 1466 subjects were recruited for a minimum-intervention smoking-cessation programme from Texas and Rhode Island. The majority of the subjects were white, female, had started smoking at about 16 and smoked on average 29 cigarettes a day.

Design

The subjects completed a set of measures at baseline and were followed up at one and six months.

Measures

The subjects completed the following set of measures:

- *Smoking abstinence self-efficacy* (DiClemente et al. 1985), which measures the smokers' confidence that they would not smoke in 20 challenging situations.

focus on research 5.1

- *Perceived stress scale* (Cohen et al. 1985), which measures how much perceived stress the individual has experienced in the last month.
- *Fagerstrom Tolerance Questionnaire* which measures physical tolerance to nicotine.
- *Smoking decisional balance scale* (Velicer et al. 1985), which measures the perceived pros and cons of smoking.
- *Smoking processes-of-change scale* (DiClemente and Prochaska 1985), which measures the individual's stage of change. According to this scale, subjects were defined as pre-contemplators ($n = 166$), contemplators ($n = 794$) and those in the preparation stage ($n = 506$).
- *Demographic data*, including age, gender, education and smoking history.

Results

The results were first analysed to examine baseline difference between the three subject groups. They showed that those in the preparation stage smoked less, were less addicted, had higher self-efficacy, rated the pros of smoking as less and the costs of smoking as more, and had made more prior quitting attempts than the other two groups. The results were then analysed to examine the relationship between stage of change and smoking cessation. At both one and six months, the subjects in the preparation stage had made more quit attempts and were more likely to not be smoking.

Conclusion

The results provide support for the stages-of-change model of smoking cessation and suggest that it is a useful tool for predicting successful outcome of any smoking-cessation intervention.

Interventions to promote cessation

Interventions to promote cessation can be described as: (1) clinical interventions, which are aimed at the individual; (2) self-help movements; or (3) public health interventions, which are aimed at populations.

Clinical interventions: promoting individual change

Clinical interventions often take the form of group or individual treatment programmes based in hospitals or universities requiring regular attendance over a 6- or 12-week period. These interventions use a combination of approaches that reflect the different disease and social learning theory models of addiction and are provided for those individuals who seek help.

Disease perspectives on cessation

Within the most recent disease models of addiction, nicotine and alcohol are seen as addictive and the individual who is addicted is seen as having acquired tolerance and dependency to the substance. Accordingly, cessation programmes offer ways for the individual to reduce this dependency. For example, *nicotine fading* procedures encourage smokers to gradually switch to brands of low nicotine cigarettes and gradually to smoke fewer cigarettes. It is believed that when the smoker is ready to quit completely, their addiction to nicotine will be small enough to minimize any withdrawal symptoms. Although there is no evidence to support the effectiveness of nicotine fading on its own, it has been shown to be useful alongside other methods such as relapse prevention (for example, Brown et al. 1984).

Nicotine replacement procedures also emphasize an individual's addiction and dependency on nicotine. For example, nicotine chewing gum is available over the counter and is used as a way of reducing the withdrawal symptoms experienced following sudden cessation. The chewing gum has been shown to be a useful addition to other behavioural methods, particularly in preventing short-term relapse (Killen et al. 1990). However, it tastes unpleasant and takes time to be absorbed into the bloodstream. More recently, nicotine patches have become available, which only need to be applied once a day in order to provide a steady supply of nicotine into the bloodstream. They do not need to be tasted, although it could be argued that chewing gum satisfies the oral component of smoking. However, whether nicotine replacement procedures are actually compensating for a physiological addiction or whether they are offering a placebo effect via expecting not to need cigarettes is unclear. Treating excessive drinking from a disease perspective involves aiming for total abstinence as there is no suitable substitute for alcohol.

Social learning perspectives on cessation

Social learning theory emphasizes learning an addictive behaviour through processes such as operant conditioning (rewards and punishments), classical conditioning (associations with internal/external cues), observational learning and cognitions. Therefore cessation procedures emphasize these processes in attempts to help smokers and excessive drinkers stop their behaviour. These cessation procedures include: aversion therapies, contingency contracting, cue exposure, self-management techniques and multi-perspective cessation clinics:

1 *Aversion therapies* aim to punish smoking and drinking rather than rewarding it. Early methodologies used crude techniques such as electric shocks whereby each time the individual smoked a puff of a cigarette or drank some alcohol they would receive a mild electric shock. However, this approach was found to be ineffective for both smoking and drinking (e.g. Wilson 1978), the main reason being that it is difficult to transfer behaviours that have been learnt in the laboratory to the real world. In an attempt to transfer this approach to the real world, alcoholics are sometimes given a drug called Antabuse, which induces vomiting whenever alcohol is consumed. This therefore encourages the alcoholic to associate drinking with being sick. This has been shown to be more effective than electric shocks (Lang and Marlatt 1982) but requires the individual to take the drug and also ignores the multitude of reasons behind their drink problem. Imaginal aversion techniques have been used for smokers and encourage the smoker to imagine the negative consequence of smoking, such as being sick (rather than actually experiencing them). However, imaginal techniques seem to add nothing to other behavioural treatments (Lichtenstein and Brown 1983). Rapid smoking is a more successful form of aversion therapy (Danaher 1977) and aims to make the actual process of smoking unpleasant. Smokers are required to sit in a closed room and take a puff every six seconds until it becomes so unpleasant they cannot smoke any more. Although there is some evidence to support rapid smoking as a smoking-cessation technique, it has obvious side effects, including increased blood carbon monoxide levels and heart rates. Other aversion therapies include focused smoking, which involves smokers concentrating on all the negative experiences of smoking, and smoke-holding, which involves smokers holding smoke in

their mouths for a period of time and again thinking about the unpleasant sensations. Smoke-holding has been shown to be more successful at promoting cessation than focused smoking and it does not have the side effects of rapid smoking (Walker and Franzini 1985).

2 *Contingency contracting* procedures also aim to punish smoking and drinking and to reward abstinence. Smokers and drinkers are asked to make a contract with either a therapist, a friend or partner and to establish a set of rewards/punishments, which are contingent on their smoking/drinking cessation. For example, money may be deposited with the therapist and only returned when they have stopped smoking/drinking for a given period of time. They are therefore rewarding abstinence. Schwartz (1987) analysed a series of contingency contracting studies for smoking cessation from 1967 to 1985 and concluded that this procedure seems to be successful in promoting initial cessation but once the contract was finished, or the money returned, relapse was high. In a study of alcoholics, 20 severe alcoholics who had been arrested for drunkenness were offered employment, health care, counselling, food and clothing if they remained sober (Miller 1975). The results showed that those with the contracts were arrested less, employed more, and were more often sober according to unannounced blood alcohol checks than those who were given these 'rewards' non-contingently. However, whether such changes in behaviour would persist over time is unclear. In addition, this perspective is reminiscent of a more punitive moral model of addictions.

3 *Cue exposure procedures* focus on the environmental factors that have become associated with smoking and drinking. For example, if an individual always smokes when they drink alcohol, alcohol will become a strong external cue to smoke and vice versa. Cue exposure techniques gradually expose the individual to different cues and encourage them to develop coping strategies to deal with them. This procedure aims to extinguish the response to the cues over time and is opposite to cue avoidance procedures, which encourage individuals not to go to the places where they may feel the urge to smoke or drink. Cue exposure highlights some of the problem with inpatient detoxification approaches to alcoholism whereby the alcoholic is hospitalized for a length of time until they have reduced the alcohol from their system. Such an approach aims to reduce the alcoholic's physiological need for alcohol by keeping them away from alcohol during their withdrawal symptoms. However, being in hospital does not teach the alcoholic how to deal with the cues to drink. It means that they avoid these cues, rather than being exposed to them.

4 *Self-management procedures* use a variety of behavioural techniques to promote smoking and drinking cessation in individuals and may be carried out under professional guidance. Such procedures involve self-monitoring (keeping a record of own smoking/drinking behaviour), becoming aware of the causes of smoking/drinking (What makes me smoke? Where do I smoke? Where do I drink?), and becoming aware of the consequences of smoking/drinking (Does it make me feel better? What do I expect from smoking/drinking?). However, used on their own, self-management techniques do not appear to be more successful than other interventions (Hall et al. 1990).

5 *Multi-perspective cessation clinics* represent an integration of all the above clinical approaches to smoking and drinking cessation and use a combination of aversion therapies, contingency contracting, cue exposure and self-management. In addition, for smoking cessation this multi-perspective approach often incorporates disease model-based interventions such as nicotine replacement. Lando (1977) developed an integrated model of smoking cessation, which has served as a model for subsequent clinics. His approach included the following procedures:

- six sessions of rapid smoking for 25 minutes for one week
- doubled daily smoking rate outside the clinic for one week
- onset of smoking cessation
- identifying problems encountered when attempting to stop smoking
- developing ways to deal with these problems
- self-reward contracts for cessation success (e.g. buying something new)
- self-punishment contracts for smoking (e.g. give money to a friend/therapist).

Lando's model has been evaluated and research suggested a 76 per cent abstinence rate at 6 months (Lando 1977) and 46 per cent at 12 months (Lando and McGovern 1982), which was higher than the control group's abstinence rates. Killen et al. (1984) developed Lando's approach but used smoke-holding rather than rapid smoking, and added nicotine chewing gum into the programme. Their results showed similarly high abstinence rates to the study by Lando.

Multi-perspective approaches have also been developed for the treatment of alcohol use. These include an integration of the aforementioned approaches and also an emphasis on drinking as a coping strategy. Drinking is therefore not simply seen as an unwanted behaviour that should stop but as a behaviour that serves a function in the alcoholic's life. Such approaches include the following:

- Assessing the drinking behaviour both in terms of the degree of the problem (e.g. frequency and amount drunk) and the factors that determine the drinking (e.g. What function does the drinking serve? When does the urge to drink increase/decrease? What is the motivation to change? Do the individual's family/friends support their desire to change?).
- Self-monitoring (e.g. When do I drink?).
- Developing new coping strategies (e.g. relaxation, stress management).
- Cue exposure (e.g. learning to cope with high-risk situations).

Multi-perspective approaches are often regarded as skills training approaches as they encourage individuals to develop the relevant skills needed to change their behaviour.

Self-help movements

Although clinical and public health interventions have proliferated over the past few decades, up to 90 per cent of ex-smokers report having stopped without any formal help (Fiore et al. 1990). Lichtenstein and Glasgow (1992) reviewed the literature on self-help quitting and reported that success rates tend to be about 10–20 per cent at one-year follow-up and 3–5 per cent for continued cessation. The literature suggests that lighter smokers are more likely to be successful at self-quitting than heavy smokers and that minimal interventions, such as follow-up telephone calls, can improve this success. Research also suggests that smokers are more likely to quit if they receive support from their partners and if their partners also stop smoking (Cohen and Lichtenstein 1990) and that partner support is particularly relevant for women trying to give up smoking during pregnancy (e.g. Appleton and Pharoah 1998). However, although many ex-smokers report that 'I did it on my own', it is important not to discount their exposure to the multitude of health education messages received via television, radio or leaflets.

Public health interventions: promoting cessation in populations

Public health interventions aim to promote behaviour change in populations and have become increasingly popular over recent years. Such interventions are aimed at all individuals, not just those who seek help. For smoking cessation, they take the form of doctor's advice, worksite interventions, community-wide approaches and government interventions. For drinking behaviour, most public health interventions take the form of government interventions.

1 *Doctor's advice.* Approximately 70 per cent of smokers will visit a doctor at some time each year. Research suggests that the recommendation from a doctor, who is considered a credible source of information, can be quite successful in promoting smoking cessation. In a classic study carried out in five general practices in London (Russell et al. 1979), smokers visiting their GP over a four-week period were allocated to one of four groups: (1) follow-up only; (2) questionnaire about their smoking behaviour and follow-up; (3) doctor's advice to stop smoking, questionnaire about their smoking behaviour and follow-up; and (4) doctor's advice to stop smoking, leaflet giving tips on how to stop and follow-up. All subjects were followed up at 1 and 12 months. The results showed at one-year follow-up that 3.3 per cent of those who had simply been told to stop smoking were still abstinent, and 5.1 per cent of those who were told to stop and had received a leaflet showed successful cessation. This was in comparison to 0.3 per cent in the group that had received follow-up only and 1.6 per cent in the group that had received the questionnaire and follow-up. Although these changes are quite small, if all GPs recommended that their smokers stopped smoking, this would produce half a million ex-smokers within a year in the UK. Research also suggests that the effectiveness of doctors' advice may be increased if they are trained in patient-centred counselling techniques (Wilson et al. 1988). Minimum interventions for smoking cessation by health professionals are also illustrated by the results of the OXCHECK and Family Heart Study results (Muir et al. 1994; Wood et al. 1994), which are described in Chapter 9.

2 *Worksite interventions.* Over the past decade there has been an increasing interest in developing worksite-based smoking-cessation interventions. These take the form of either a company adopting a no-smoking policy and/or establishing work-based health promotion programmes. Worksite interventions have the benefit of reaching many individuals who would not consider attending a hospital or a university-based clinic. In addition, the large number of people involved presents the opportunity for group motivation and social support. Furthermore, they may have implications for reducing passive smoking at work, which may be a risk factor for coronary heart disease (He et al. 1994). Research into the effectiveness of no-smoking policies has produced conflicting results, with some studies reporting an overall reduction in the number of cigarettes smoked for up to 12 months (e.g. Biener et al. 1989) and others suggesting that smoking outside work hours compensates for any reduced smoking at the workplace (e.g. Gomel et al. 1993) (see **Focus on Research 5.2**, p. 118). In two Australian studies, public service workers were surveyed following smoking bans in 44 government office buildings about their attitudes to the ban immediately after the ban and after six months. The results suggested that although immediately after the ban many smokers felt inconvenienced, these attitudes improved at six months with both smokers and non-smokers recognizing the benefits of the ban. However, only 2 per cent stopped smoking during this period (Borland et al. 1990). Although worksite interventions may be a successful means to access many smokers, this potential does not yet appear to have been fully realized.

3 **Community-based programmes.** Large community-based programmes have been established as a means of promoting smoking cessation within large groups of individuals. Such programmes aim to reach those who would not attend clinics and to use the group motivation and social support in a similar way to worksite interventions. Early community-based programmes were part of the drive to reduce coronary heart disease. In the Stanford Five City Project, the experimental groups received intensive face-to-face instruction on how to stop smoking and in addition were exposed to media information regarding smoking cessation. The results showed a 13 per cent reduction in smoking rates compared with the control group (Farquhar et al. 1990). In the North Karelia Project, individuals in the target community received an intensive educational campaign and were compared with those in a neighbouring community who were not exposed to the campaign. The results from this programme showed a 10 per cent reduction in smoking in men in North Karelia compared with men in the control region. In addition, the results also showed a 24 per cent decline in cardiovascular deaths, a rate twice that of the rest of the country (Puska et al. 1985). Other community-based programmes include the Australia North Coast Study, which resulted in a 15 per cent reduction in smoking over three years, and the Swiss National Research Programme, which resulted in an 8 per cent reduction over three years (Egger et al. 1983; Autorengruppe Nationales Forschungsprogramm 1984).

4 **Government interventions.** An additional means to promote both smoking cessation and healthy drinking is to encourage governments to intervene. Such interventions can take several forms:

■ *Restricting/banning advertising.* According to social learning theory, we learn to smoke and drink by associating smoking and drinking with attractive characteristics, such as 'It will help me relax', 'It makes me look sophisticated', 'It makes me look sexy', 'It is risky'. Advertising aims to access and promote these beliefs in order to encourage smoking and drinking. Implementing a ban/restriction on advertising would remove this source of beliefs. In the UK, cigarette advertising was banned in 2003.

■ *Increasing the cost.* Research indicates a relationship between the cost of cigarettes and alcohol and their consumption. Increasing the price of cigarettes and alcohol could promote smoking and drinking cessation and deter the initiation of these behaviours, particularly among children. According to models of health beliefs, this would contribute to the perceived costs of the behaviours and the perceived benefits of behaviour change.

■ *Banning smoking in public places.* Smoking is already restricted to specific places in many countries (e.g. in the UK most public transport is no smoking). A wider ban on smoking may promote smoking cessation. According to social learning theory, this would result in the cues to smoking (e.g. restaurants, bars) becoming eventually disassociated from smoking. However, it is possible that this would simply result in compensatory smoking in other places as illustrated by some of the research on worksite no-smoking policies. To date, smoking has been banned in public places in Ireland, Scotland, several states in the US, much of Italy and will be banned in England from July 2007.

■ *Banning cigarette smoking and alcohol drinking.* Governments could opt to ban cigarettes and alcohol completely (although they would forego the large revenues they currently receive from advertising and sales). Such a move might result in a reduction in these behaviours. In fact the smoking bans in Ireland and in some states in the USA have resulted in a range of positive outcomes such as a reduction in smoking per se and even a decline in patients admitted to hospital for heart attacks.

Putting theory into practice – worksite smoking ban

A pilot study to examine the effects of a workplace smoking ban on smoking, craving, stress and other behaviours (Gomel et al. 1993).

Over the past few years many organizations have set up workplace bans. These offer an opportunity to examine the effects of policy on behaviour change and to assess the effectiveness of public health interventions in promoting smoking cessation.

Background

Workplace bans provide an opportunity to use group motivation and group social support to promote smoking cessation. In addition, they can access individuals who would not be interested in attending clinics based in hospitals or universities. The present study examined the effect of worksite ban on smoking behaviour (both at work and outside) and also examined the interrelationship between smoking and other behaviours. The ban was introduced on 1 August 1989 at the New South Wales Ambulance Service in Australia. This study is interesting because it included physiological measures of smoking to identify any compensatory smoking.

Methodology
Subjects

A screening question showed that 60 per cent of the employees were current smokers ($n = 47$). Twenty-four subjects (15 males and 9 females) completed all measures. They had an average age of 34 years, had smoked on average for 11 years and smoked an average of 26 cigarettes a day.

Design

The subjects completed a set of measures one week before the ban (time 1), one week after (time 2), and six weeks after (time 3).

Measures

At times 1, 2 and 3, the subjects were evaluated for cigarette and alcohol consumption, demographic information (e.g. age), exhaled carbon monoxide and blood cotinine. The subjects also completed daily record cards for five working days and two non-working days, including measures of smoking, alcohol consumption, snack intake and ratings of subjective discomfort.

Results

The results showed a reduction in self-reports of smoking in terms of number of cigarettes smoked during a working day and the number smoked during working hours at both the one-week and six-week follow-ups compared with baseline, indicating that the smokers were smoking less following the ban. However, the cotinine levels suggested that although there was an initial decrease at week one, by six weeks blood cotinine was almost back to baseline levels, suggesting that the smokers may have been compensating for the ban by smoking more outside work. The results also showed increases in craving and stress following the ban; these lower levels of stress were maintained, whereas craving gradually returned to baseline (supporting compensatory smoking). The results showed no increases in snack intake or alcohol consumption.

Conclusion

The self-report data from the study suggest that worksite bans may be an effective form of public health intervention for decreasing smoking behaviour. However, the physiological data suggest that simply introducing a no-smoking policy may not be sufficient as smokers may show compensatory smoking.

Methodological problems evaluating clinical and public health interventions

Although researchers and health educators are motivated to find the best means of promoting smoking cessation and healthy drinking, evaluating the effectiveness of any intervention is fraught with methodological problems. For smoking cessation these problems include the following:

- *Who has become a non-smoker?* Someone who has not smoked in the last month/week/day? Someone who regards themselves as a non-smoker? (Smokers are notorious for under-reporting their smoking.) Does a puff of a cigarette count as smoking? Do cigars count as smoking? These questions need to be answered to assess success rates.

- *Who is still counted as a smoker?* Someone who has attended all clinic sessions and still smokes? Someone who dropped out of the sessions half-way through and has not been seen since? Someone who was asked to attend but never turned up? These questions need to be answered to derive a baseline number for the success rate.

- *Should the non-smokers be believed when they say they have not smoked?* Methods other than self-report exist to assess smoking behaviour, such as carbon monoxide in the breath and cotinine in the saliva. These are more accurate, but time-consuming and expensive.

- *How should smokers be assigned to different interventions?* In order for success rates to be calculated, comparisons need to be made between different types of intervention (e.g. aversion therapy versus cue exposure). These groups should obviously be matched for age, gender, ethnicity and smoking behaviour. What about stage of change (contemplation versus pre-contemplation versus preparation)? What about other health beliefs such as self-efficacy, costs and benefits of smoking? The list could be endless.

For interventions aimed at changing drinking behaviour, these problems include the following:

- *What is the desired outcome of any intervention?* Being totally abstinent (for the last month/week)? Drinking a normal amount? (What is normal?) Coping with life? (What constitutes acceptable coping?) Drinking that is not detrimental to work? (Should work be a priority?) Drinking that is no longer detrimental to family life? (Should family life be a priority?) In his autobiography, John Healy (1991) describes his transition from an alcoholic living on the 'Grass Arena' in London to becoming addicted to chess. Is this success? Should the experts impose their view of success on a drinker, or should success be determined by them?

- *How should drinking behaviour be measured?* Should intrusive measures such as blood taking be used? Should self-reports be relied on?

Stage 4: relapse in smoking and drinking

Although many people are successful at initially stopping smoking and changing their drinking behaviour, relapse rates are high. For example, nearly half of those smokers who make a quit attempt return to smoking within the year (National Statistics 2005). Interestingly, the pattern for relapse is consistent across a number of different addictive behaviours, with high rates initially tapering off over a year. This relapse pattern is shown in Figure 5.7.

Marlatt and Gordon (1985) developed a relapse prevention model of addictions, which specifically examined the processes involved in successful and unsuccessful cessation attempts. The relapse prevention model was based on the following concept of addictive behaviours:

- Addictive behaviours are learned and therefore can be unlearned; they are reversible.
- Addictions are not 'all or nothing' but exist on a continuum.
- Lapses from abstinence are likely and acceptable.
- Believing that 'one drink – a drunk' is a self-fulfilling prophecy.

They distinguished between a lapse, which entails a minor slip (e.g. a cigarette, a couple of drinks), and a relapse, which entails a return to former behaviour (e.g. smoking 20 cigarettes, getting drunk). Marlatt and Gordon examined the processes involved in the progression from abstinence to relapse and in particular assessed the mechanisms that may explain the transition from lapse to relapse (see Figure 5.8). These processes are described below.

Baseline state

Abstinence. If an individual sets total abstinence as the goal, then this stage represents the target behaviour and indicates a state of behavioural control.

Pre-lapse state

High-risk situation. A high-risk situation is any situation that may motivate the individual to carry out the behaviour. Such situations may be either external cues, such as someone else

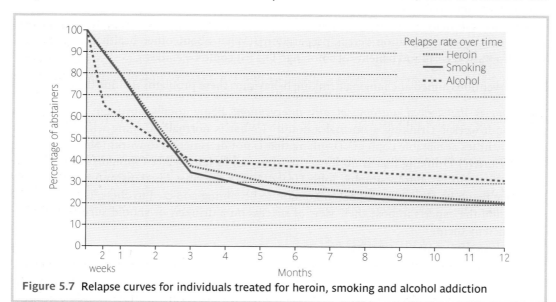

Figure 5.7 Relapse curves for individuals treated for heroin, smoking and alcohol addiction

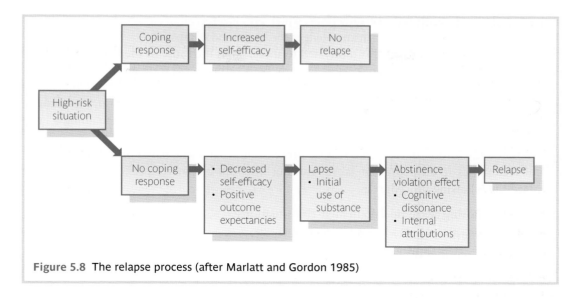

Figure 5.8 The relapse process (after Marlatt and Gordon 1985)

smoking or the availability of alcohol, or internal cues, such as anxiety. Research indicates that the most commonly reported high-risk situations are negative emotions, interpersonal conflict and social pressure. This is in line with social learning theories, which predict that internal cues are more problematic than external cues.

Coping behaviour. Once exposed to a high-risk situation the individual engages the coping strategies. Such strategies may be behavioural, such as avoiding the situation or using a substitute behaviour (e.g. eating), or cognitive, such as remembering why they are attempting to abstain.

Positive outcome expectancies. According to previous experience the individual will either have positive outcome expectancies if the behaviour is carried out (e.g. smoking will make me feel less anxious) or negative outcome expectancies (e.g. getting drunk will make me feel sick).

No lapse or lapse?

Marlatt and Gordon (1985) argue that when exposed to a high-risk situation, if an individual can engage good coping mechanisms and also develop negative outcome expectancies, the chances of a lapse will be reduced and the individual's self-efficacy will be increased. However, if the individual engages poor coping strategies and has positive outcome expectancies, the chances of a lapse will be high and the individual's self-efficacy will be reduced.

- *No lapse*: good coping strategies and negative outcome expectancies will raise self-efficacy, causing the period of abstinence to be maintained.
- *Lapse*: poor or no coping strategies and positive outcome expectancies will lower self-efficacy, causing an initial use of the substance (the cigarette, a drink). This lapse will either remain an isolated event and the individual will return to abstinence, or will become a full-blown relapse. Marlatt and Gordon describe this transition as the abstinence violation effect (AVE).

The abstinence violation effect

The transition from initial lapse to full-blown relapse is determined by dissonance conflict and self-attribution. Dissonance is created by a conflict between a self-image as someone who no longer smokes/drinks and the current behaviour (e.g. smoking/drinking). This conflict is exacerbated by a disease model of addictions, which emphasizes 'all or nothing', and minimized by a social learning model, which acknowledges the likelihood of lapses.

Having lapsed, the individual is motivated to understand the cause of the lapse. If this lapse is attributed to the self (e.g. 'I am useless, it's my fault'), this may create guilt and self-blame. This internal attribution may lower self-efficacy, thereby increasing the chances of a full-blown relapse. However, if the lapse is attributed to the external world (e.g. the situation, the presence of others), guilt and self-blame will be reduced and the chances of the lapse remaining a lapse will be increased.

Marlatt and Gordon developed a relapse prevention programme based on cognitive behavioural techniques to help prevent lapses turning into full-blown relapses. This programme involved the following procedures:

- self-monitoring (what do I do in high-risk situations?)
- relapse fantasies (what would it be like to relapse?)
- relaxation training/stress management
- skills training
- contingency contracts
- cognitive restructuring (learning not to make internal attributions for lapses).

How these procedures relate to the different stages of relapse is illustrated in Figure 5.9.

A cross-addictive behaviour perspective

According to the disease models of addiction, each behaviour is examined separately. Therefore an addiction to cigarettes is seen as separate and different to an addiction to alcohol. However,

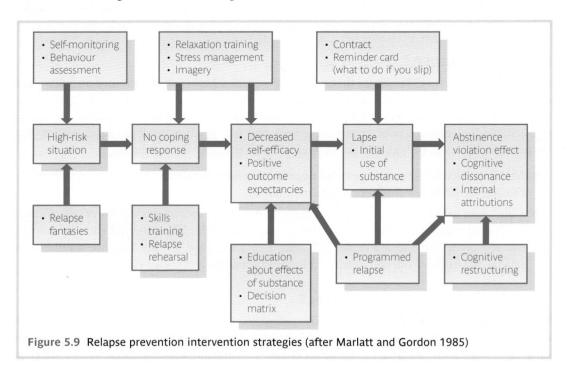

Figure 5.9 Relapse prevention intervention strategies (after Marlatt and Gordon 1985)

from a social learning perspective, it is possible to examine similarities between behaviours and to apply similar processes to the initiation, maintenance, cessation and relapse of behaviours such as exercise, sex, gambling and eating (e.g. Orford 1985). Research has examined these behaviours independently of each other and, in addition, has also assessed the associations between them. In particular, recent research has examined the interrelationship between smoking and eating behaviour.

Smoking and eating behaviour

Research into the interrelationship between smoking and eating has examined: (1) gender differences in smoking; (2) smoking cessation and changes in food intake; and (3) substitution between substances.

Gender differences in smoking

Research has highlighted gender differences in tobacco use (Grunberg et al. 1991) with the suggestion being that, while male smoking has remained stable, or even declined over the past 20 years in the USA and UK, female smoking has increased. This increase is reflected by reports of gender differences in cancer, with lung cancer now being the leading cause of death in American women. To explain increases in female smoking, research has focused on the perceived benefits of smoking, suggesting that smokers of both genders continue to smoke for fear of weight gain. Consequently, the present cultural obsession with thinness in women may account for increased female smoking. Smokers generally weigh about 7 lb less than comparably aged non-smokers, and abstinent smokers tend to show weight gains of about 6 lb (US Department of Health and Human Services 1990). As a result, research suggests that female dieters may use cigarette smoking as a weight loss/maintenance strategy (Klesges and Klesges 1988; Ogden and Fox 1994). For example, in a recent study dieters showed greater agreement with statements relating to smoking initiation and smoking maintenance for weight control, the role of weight gain in previous experiences of smoking relapse, intentions to quit following weight loss and intentions to quit in five years (Ogden and Fox 1994).

Smoking and changes in food intake

How cigarette smoking influences weight is unclear, with different possible mechanisms predicting either a change or no change in food intake. For example, it has been proposed that weight gain could be a result of decreased energy use due to withdrawal or fatigue, or that nicotine may increase metabolic rate; both mechanisms suggest no post-cessation changes in eating behaviour. However, Grunberg (1986) suggests that nicotine may increase blood sugar levels and that post-cessation weight gain could be explained by an increase in sweet food consumption, which has been supported by both animal and human research. Further research suggests that smoking cessation may result in increases in consumption of calories, increases in sucrose, fats and carbohydrate intake (see Ogden 1994 for an overview). Theories to explain the changes in food intake following smoking cessation have focused on physiological factors such as a release of brain serotonin following nicotine withdrawal (Benwell et al. 1988), which may be compensated for by carbohydrates. However, an alternative explanation of the relationship focuses on the subjective experience of craving for a substance.

The subjective experience of craving

The desire to eat and the response to food deprivation are characterized by the experience of 'emptiness', 'tension', 'agitation', 'light-headedness' as well as more specific feelings such as a 'rumbling stomach'. Smoking abstainers also describe their desire for a cigarette in similar ways, again using language such as 'emptiness', 'agitation' and 'light-headedness'. A possible explanation of the interaction between smoking and eating is that sensations of deprivation may be interchangeable. Alcohol research suggests that craving for alcohol may be a form of misattribution of internal states, with the alcoholic labelling internal states as a desire for alcohol (Ludwig and Stark 1974; Marlatt 1978). With reference to eating and smoking, the desire to smoke may be labelled as hunger and therefore satiated by food intake. In an experimental study, smokers were asked either to abstain for 24 hours or to continue smoking as usual, and their craving for food and cigarettes and food intake was compared with each other and with a group of non-smokers (Ogden 1994). The results showed that smoking abstinence resulted in an increased craving for food and increased food intake. In addition, the results showed that an increased craving for cigarettes resulted in increased food intake. Furthermore, the results showed that this association between craving for cigarettes and food was greater in women than men, and particularly apparent in dieting women.

These studies support a cross-behavioural perspective of addictions and suggest an interrelationship between different behaviours. It is possible that because women dieters may use smoking as a means to reduce their eating they develop an association between these behaviours. It is also possible that the substitution between addictive behaviours may also exist between other behaviours such as alcohol and smoking (stopping smoking increases drinking), or gambling and eating (stopping gambling increases eating). One study in 2001 used an experimental design to explore the relationship between smoking and exercise (Ussher et al. 2001). Seventy-eight smokers abstained from smoking for about 12 hours and then either exercised for 10 minutes on an exercise bicycle or took part in a control condition which involved waiting or watching a video. The results showed that 10 minutes of exercise significantly reduced desire to smoke and withdrawal symptoms.

To conclude

Smoking and alcohol consumption both have negative effects on health and yet are common behaviours. There are many different theories to explain why people smoke or drink and how they can be encouraged to adopt healthy behaviours. This chapter examined the different models of addiction, including the moral model, the disease models and the social learning perspective. It then examined the stages of substance use from initiation and maintenance (involving psychological factors, such as beliefs and expectancies, and social factors, such as parental and peer group behaviour), to cessation (involving clinical perspectives, self-help methods and public health interventions) or relapse. Finally, this chapter examined the interrelationship between different behaviours, in particular smoking and eating, to examine the validity of a cross-behavioural perspective.

Questions

1 Could we become addicted to anything?

2 Discuss the role of learning in the initiation and maintenance of an addictive behaviour.

3 Smoking is an addiction to nicotine. Discuss.

4 Discuss the role of health beliefs in the initiation of smoking behaviour.

5 It is the government's responsibility to stop smoking. Discuss.

6 Lung cancer from smoking is a self-inflicted disease. Discuss.

7 To what extent are addictions governed by similar processes?

8 We have known for a half a century that smoking causes lung cancer. Why do people still continue to smoke?

9 Smoking varies by gender. Outline a research project designed to evaluate why men and women smoke in different ways.

For discussion

Have you ever tried a puff of a cigarette? If so, consider the reasons that you did or did not become a smoker. If you have never even tried a cigarette, discuss the possible reasons for this.

Assumptions in health psychology

The research on smoking and alcohol highlights some of the assumptions in health psychology:

1 *Mind–body dualism.* Theories of addictions and addictive behaviour emphasize either the psychological or physiological processes. This separation is reflected in the differences between the disease models and the social learning perspectives. Therefore, although some of the treatment perspectives emphasize both mind (e.g. cue exposure) and body (e.g. nicotine replacement), they are still seen as distinct components of the individual.

2 *Changes in theory represent improvement.* It is often assumed that the most recent theoretical perspective is an improvement on previous theories. In terms of addictive behaviours, the moral model is seen as more naïve than the disease model, which is more naïve than a social learning theory perspective. However, perhaps these different models also illustrate different (and not necessarily better) ways of explaining behaviour and of describing the individual. Therefore, to see an individual who drinks a great deal as to blame and as being responsible for his or her behaviour (the moral model) reflects a different model of the individual than an explanation that describes a physiological predisposition (the second disease model) or learning the behaviour via reinforcement.

Further reading

Heather, N. and Robertson, D. (1989) *Problem Drinking.* Oxford: Oxford University Press.
   This book examines the different theories of addictive behaviours and in particular outlines the contribution of social learning theory.

Marlatt, G.A. and Gordon, J.R. (1985) *Relapse Prevention.* New York: Guilford Press.
   This book provides a detailed analysis and background to relapse prevention and applies this approach to a variety of addictive behaviours. Chapter 1 is a particularly useful overview.

Orford, J. (2002) *Excessive Appetites: A Psychological View of Addictions* (2nd edn). Chichester: John Wiley.
   This book illustrates the extent to which different addictive behaviours share common variables in both their initiation and maintenance and discusses the interrelationship between physiological and psychological factors.

West, R. (2005) Time for a change: putting the transtheoretical (stages of change) model to rest, *Addiction,* 100, 1036–9.
   This paper presents a critique of the SOC model and suggests that there are better ways of understanding addictive behaviours. It is accompanied by a series of papers which join in the debate including a response by the authors of the SOC.

West, R. (2006) *Theory of Addiction.* Oxford: Blackwell.
   This is an interesting and comprehensive book which describes existing theories of addiction and offers a new synthetic model of addiction which combines a range of psychological processes.

West, R. and Shiffman, S. (2003) *Smoking Cessation.* Oxford: Health Press.
   This is a very clearly written, accessible book which describes physiological and psychosocial reasons for smoking and provides an excellent account of smoking-cessation strategies.

Chapter 6

Eating behaviour

Chapter overview

This chapter first examines what constitutes a healthy diet, the links between diet and health and who does and does not eat healthily. Three main psychological perspectives which have been used to study food intake are then described. First, the chapter describes developmental models of eating behaviour with their focus on exposure, social learning and associative learning. Second, it examines cognitive theories with their emphasis on motivation and social cognition models. Third, it explores the emphasis on weight concern and the role of body dissatisfaction and restrained eating.

This chapter covers

- What is a healthy diet?
- How does diet influence health?
- Who eats a healthy diet?
- Developmental models of eating behaviour
- Cognitive models of eating behaviour
- Weight concern and the role of body dissatisfaction and dieting

What is a healthy diet?

The nature of a good diet has changed dramatically over the years. In 1824 *The Family Oracle of Good Health* published in the UK recommended that young ladies should eat the following at breakfast: 'plain biscuit (not bread), broiled beef steaks or mutton chops, under done without any fat and half a pint of bottled ale, the genuine Scots ale is the best' or if this was too strong it suggested 'one small breakfast cup . . . of good strong tea or of coffee – weak tea or coffee is always bad for the nerves as well as the complexion'. Dinner is later described as similar to breakfast with 'no vegetables, boiled meat, no made dishes being permitted much less fruit, sweet things or pastry . . . the steaks and chops must always be the chief part of your food'. Similarly in the 1840s Dr Kitchener recommended in his diet book a lunch of 'a bit of roasted poultry, a basin of good beef tea, eggs poached . . . a sandwich – stale bread – and half a pint of good home brewed beer' (cited in Burnett 1989: 69). Nowadays, there is, however, a consensus among nutritionists as to what constitutes a healthy diet (DoH 1991a). Food can be considered in terms of its basic constituents: carbohydrate, protein and fat. Descriptions of healthy eating tend to describe food in terms of broader food groups and make recommendations as to the relative consumption of each of these groups. Current recommendations are as follows and illustrated in Figure 6.1.

- *Fruit and vegetables:* A wide variety of fruit and vegetables should be eaten and preferably five or more servings should be eaten per day.
- *Bread, pasta, other cereals and potatoes:* Plenty of complex carbohydrate foods should be eaten, preferably those high in fibre.
- *Meat, fish and alternatives:* Moderate amounts of meat, fish and alternatives should be eaten and it is recommended that the low-fat varieties are chosen.
- *Milk and dairy products:* These should be eaten in moderation and the low-fat alternatives should be chosen where possible.
- *Fatty and sugary foods:* Food such as crisps, sweets and sugary drinks should be eaten infrequently and in small amounts.

Other recommendations for a healthy diet include a moderate intake of alcohol (a maximum of 3–4 units per day for men and 2–3 units per day for women), the consumption of fluoridated water where possible, a limited salt intake of 6g per day, eating unsaturated fats from olive oil and oily fish rather than saturated fats from butter and margarine, and consuming complex carbohydrates (e.g. bread and pasta) rather than simple carbohydrates (e.g. sugar). It is also recommended that men aged between 19 and 59 require 2550 calories per day and that similarly aged women require 1920 calories per day although this depends upon body size and degree of physical activity (DoH 1995).

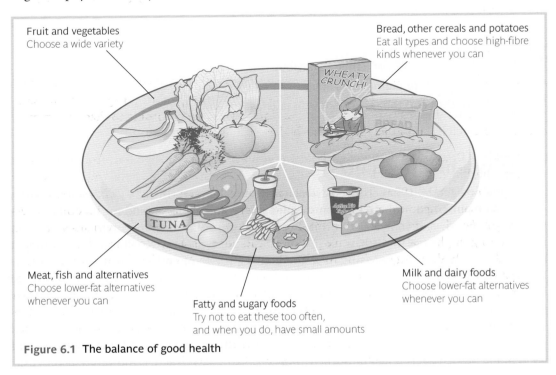

Fruit and vegetables
Choose a wide variety

Bread, other cereals and potatoes
Eat all types and choose high-fibre
kinds whenever you can

Meat, fish and alternatives
Choose lower-fat alternatives
whenever you can

Fatty and sugary foods
Try not to eat these too often,
and when you do, have small amounts

Milk and dairy foods
Choose lower-fat alternatives
whenever you can

Figure 6.1 **The balance of good health**

How does diet affect health?

Diet is linked to health in two ways: by influencing the onset of illness and as part of treatment and management once illness has been diagnosed.

Diet and illness onset

Diet affects health through an individual's weight in terms of the development of eating disorders or obesity. Eating disorders are linked to physical problems such as heart irregularities, heart attacks, stunted growth, osteoporosis and reproduction. Obesity is linked to diabetes, heart disease and some forms of cancer (see Chapter 15). In addition, some research suggests a direct link between diet and illnesses such as heart disease, cancer and diabetes (see Chapters 14 and 15). Much research has addressed the role of diet in health and, although at times controversial, studies suggest that foods such as fruits and vegetables, oily fish and oat fibre can be protective while salt and saturated fats can facilitate poor health.

Diet and treating illness

Diet also has a role to play in treating illness once diagnosed. Obese patients are mainly managed through dietary-based interventions (see Chapter 15). Patients diagnosed with angina, heart disease or following a heart attack are also recommended to change their lifestyle with particular emphasis on stopping smoking, increasing their physical activity and adopting a healthy diet (see Chapter 15). Dietary change is also central to the management of both Type 1 and Type 2 diabetes. At times this aims to produce weight loss as a 10 per cent decrease in weight has been shown to result in improved glucose metabolism (Blackburn and Kanders 1987; Wing et al. 1987). Dietary interventions are also used to improve the self-management of diabetes and aim to encourage diabetic patients to adhere to a more healthy diet.

Who eats a healthy diet?

A healthy diet therefore consists of high carbohydrate and low fat intake and links have been found between diet and both the onset of illnesses and their effective management. However, research indicates that many people across the world do not eat according to these recommendations. Research has explored the diets of children, adults and the elderly.

- *Children:* Data on children's diets in the western world do not match the recommendations for a healthy diet, and children have been shown to eat too much fat and too few fruit and vegetables (USDA 1999). Therefore dietary recommendations aimed at the western world in the main emphasize a reduction in food intake and the avoidance of becoming overweight. For the majority of the developing world, however, undereating remains a problem resulting in physical and cognitive problems and poor resistance to illness due to lowered intakes of both energy and micronutrients. Recent data from the World Health Organization indicate that 174 million children under the age of 5 in the developing world are malnourished and show low weight for age and that 230 million are stunted in their growth. Further, the WHO estimates that 54 per cent of childhood mortality is caused by malnutrition, particularly related to a deficit of protein and energy consumption. Such malnutrition is the highest in South Asia which is estimated to be five times higher than in the western hemisphere, followed by Africa then Latin America.

■ *Adults:* Research also explored the diets of young adults. One large-scale study carried out between 1989–90 and 1991–92 examined the eating behaviour of 16,000 male and female students aged between 18 and 24 from 21 European countries (Wardle et al. 1997). The results suggest that the prevalence of these fairly basic healthy eating practices was low in this large sample of young adults. In terms of gender differences, the results showed that the women in this sample reported more healthy eating practices than the men. The results also provided insights into the different dietary practices across the different European countries. Overall, there was most variability between countries in terms of eating fibre, red meat, fruit and salt. Fat consumption seemed to vary the least. Countries such as Sweden, Norway, The Netherlands and Denmark ate the most fibre, while Italy, Hungary, Poland and Belgium ate the least. Mediterranean countries such as Italy, Portugal and Spain ate the most fruit and England and Scotland ate the least. Further, Belgium and Portugal made least attempts to limit red meat while Greece, Austria, Norway and Iceland made more attempts. Finally, salt consumption was highest in Poland and Portugal and lowest in Sweden, Finland and Iceland.

■ *The elderly:* Research exploring the diets of the elderly indicates that although many younger and non-institutionalized members of this group have satisfactory diets, many elderly people, particularly the older elderly, report diets that are deficient in vitamins, too low in energy and have poor nutrient content.

Research indicates that many people do not eat according to current recommendations. Much research has explored why people eat what they do. This chapter will describe developmental models, cognitive models and the role of weight concern in understanding eating behaviour (see Figure 6.2).

Developmental models of eating behaviour

A developmental approach to eating behaviour emphasizes the importance of learning and experience and focuses on the development of food preferences in childhood. An early pioneer

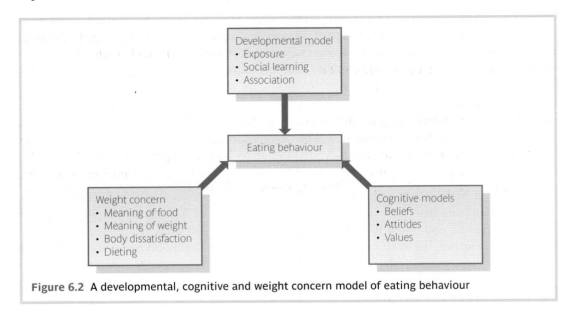

Figure 6.2 A developmental, cognitive and weight concern model of eating behaviour

of this research was Davis (1928, 1939), who carried out studies of infants and young children living in a paediatrics ward in the USA for several months. The work was conducted at a time when current feeding policies endorsed a very restricted feeding regime and Davis was interested to examine infants' responses to a self-selected diet. She explored whether there was an 'instinctive means of handling . . . the problem of optimal nutrition' (Davis 1928). The children were offered a variety of 10 to 12 healthy foods prepared without sugar, salt or seasoning and were free to eat whatever they chose. Her detailed reports from this study showed that the children were able to select a diet consistent with growth and health and were free from any feeding problems. The results from this study generated a theory of 'the wisdom of the body' which emphasized the body's innate food preferences. In line with this, Davis concluded from her data that children have an innate regulatory mechanism and are able to select a healthy diet. She also, however, emphasized that they could only do so as long as healthy food was available and argued that the children's food preferences changed over time and were modified by experience. Birch, who has extensively studied the developmental aspects of eating behaviour, interpreted Davis's data to suggest that what was innate was the 'ability to learn about the consequences of eating [and] to learn to associate food cues with the consequences of ingestion in order to control food intake' (Birch 1989). Birch therefore emphasized the role of learning and described a developmental systems perspective (e.g. Birch 1999). In line with this analysis, the development of food preferences can be understood in terms of exposure, social learning and associative learning.

Exposure

Human beings need to consume a variety of foods in order to have a balanced diet and yet show fear and avoidance of novel foodstuffs called neophobia. This has been called the 'omnivore's paradox' (Rozin 1976). Young children will therefore show neophobic responses to food but must come to accept and eat foods that may originally appear as threatening. Research has shown that mere exposure to novel foods can change children's preferences. For example, Birch and Marlin (1982) gave 2-year-old children novel foods over a six-week period. One food was presented 20 times, one 10 times, one 5 times while one remained novel. The results showed a direct relationship between exposure and food preference and indicated that a minimum of about 8 to 10 exposures was necessary before preferences began to shift significantly. Neophobia has been shown to be greater in males than females (both adults and children), to run in families (Hursti and Sjoden 1997), to be minimal in infants who are being weaned onto solid foods but greater in toddlers, pre-school children and adults (Birch et al. 1998).

One hypothesized explanation for the impact of exposure is the 'learned safety' view (Kalat and Rozin 1973) which suggests that preference increases because eating the food has not resulted in any negative consequences. This suggestion has been supported by studies that exposed children either to just the sight of food or to both the sight and taste of food. The results showed that looking at novel foods was not sufficient to increase preference and that tasting was necessary (Birch et al. 1987). It would seem, however, that these negative consequences must occur within a short period of time after tasting the food as telling children that a novel food is 'good for you' has no impact on neophobia whereas telling them that it will taste good does (Pliner and Loewen 1997). The exposure hypothesis is also supported by evidence indicating that neophobia reduces with age (Birch 1989).

Social learning

Social learning describes the impact of observing other people's behaviour on one's own behaviour and is sometimes referred to as 'modelling' or 'observational learning'. An early study explored the impact of 'social suggestion' on children's eating behaviours and arranged to have children observe a series of role models making eating behaviours different to their own (Duncker 1938). The models chosen were other children, an unknown adult and a fictional hero. The results showed a greater change in the child's food preference if the model was an older child, a friend or the fictional hero. The unknown adult had no impact on food preferences. In another study peer modelling was used to change children's preference for vegetables (Birch 1980). The target children were placed at lunch for four consecutive days next to other children who preferred a different vegetable to themselves (peas versus carrots). By the end of the study the children showed a shift in their vegetable preference which persisted at a follow-up assessment several weeks later. The impact of social learning has also been shown in an intervention study designed to change children's eating behaviour using video-based peer modelling (Lowe et al. 1998). This series of studies used video material of 'food dudes' who were older children enthusiastically consuming refused food which was shown to children with a history of food refusal. The results showed that exposure to the 'food dudes' significantly changed the children's food preferences and specifically increased their consumption of fruit and vegetables. Food preferences therefore change through watching others eat (see Figure 6.3).

Parental attitudes to food and eating behaviours are also central to the process of social learning. In line with this, Wardle (1995) contended that 'Parental attitudes must certainly

Figure 6.3 Social eating

affect their children indirectly through the foods purchased for and served in the household, . . . influencing the children's exposure and . . . their habits and preferences'. Some evidence indicates that parents do influence their children's eating behaviour. For example, Klesges et al. (1991) showed that children selected different foods when they were being watched by their parents compared to when they were not. Olivera et al. (1992) reported a correlation between mothers' and children's food intakes for most nutrients in pre-school children, and suggested targeting parents to try to improve children's diets. Likewise, Contento et al. (1993) found a relationship between mothers' health motivation and the quality of children's diets, and Brown and Ogden (2004) reported consistent correlations between parents and their children in terms of reported snack food intake, eating motivations and body dissatisfaction. Parental behaviour and attitudes are therefore central to the process of social learning with research highlighting a positive association between parents' and children's diets.

There is, however, some evidence that mothers and children are not always in line with each other. For example, Wardle (1995) reported that mothers rated health as more important for their children than for themselves. Alderson and Ogden (1999) similarly reported that whereas mothers were more motivated by calories, cost, time and availability for themselves, they rated nutrition and long-term health as more important for their children. In addition, mothers may also differentiate between themselves and their children in their choices of food. For example, Alderson and Ogden (1999) indicated that mothers fed their children more of the less healthy dairy products, breads, cereals and potatoes and fewer of the healthy equivalents to these foods than they ate themselves. Furthermore, this differentiation was greater in dieting mothers, suggesting that mothers who restrain their own food intake may feed their children more of the foods that they are denying themselves. A relationship between maternal dieting and eating behaviour is also supported by a study of 197 families with pre-pubescent girls by Birch and Fisher (2000). This study concluded that the best predictors of the daughter's eating behaviour were the mother's level of dietary restraint and the mother's perceptions of the risk of her daughter becoming overweight. In sum, parental behaviours and attitudes may influence those of their children through the mechanisms of social learning. This association, however, may not always be straightforward with parents differentiating between themselves and their children both in terms of food-related motivations and eating behaviour.

The role of social learning is also shown by the impact of television and food advertising. For example, after Eyton's *The F Plan Diet* was launched by the media in 1982 which recommended a high-fibre diet, sales of bran-based cereals rose by 30 per cent, whole-wheat bread rose by 10 per cent, whole-wheat pasta rose by 70 per cent and baked beans rose by 8 per cent. Similarly, in December 1988 Edwina Curry, the then Junior Health Minister in the UK, said on television, 'most of the egg production in this country sadly is now infected with salmonella' (ITN 1988). Egg sales then fell by 50 per cent and by 1989 were still only at 75 per cent of their previous levels (Mintel 1990). Similarly, massive publicity about the health risks of beef in the UK between May and August 1990 resulted in a 20 per cent reduction in beef sales. One study examined the public's reactions to media coverage of 'food scares' such as salmonella, listeria and BSE and compared it to their reactions to coverage of the impact of food on coronary heart disease. The study used interviews, focus groups and an analysis of the content and style of media presentations (MacIntyre et al. 1998). The authors concluded that the media have a major impact upon what people eat and how they think about foods. They also argued that the media can set the agenda for public discussion. The authors stated, however, that the public do not just passively respond to the media 'but that they exercise judgement and discretion in how much they incorporate media messages about health and safety into their diets' (MacIntyre

1998: 249). Further, they argued that eating behaviours are limited by personal circumstances such as age, gender, income and family structure and that people actively negotiate their understanding of food within both the micro context (such as their immediate social networks) and the macro social contexts (such as the food production and information production systems). The media are therefore an important source for social learning. This study suggests, however, that the individuals learn from the media by placing the information being provided within the broader context of their lives.

In summary, social learning factors are central to choices about food. This includes significant others in the immediate environment, particularly parents and the media which offer new information, present role models and illustrate behaviour and attitudes that can be observed and incorporated into the individual's own behavioural repertoire.

Associative learning

Associative learning refers to the impact of contingent factors on behaviour. At times these contingent factors can be considered reinforcers in line with operant conditioning. In terms of eating behaviour, research has explored the impact of pairing food cues with aspects of the environment. In particular, food has been paired with a reward, used as the reward and paired with physiological consequences. Research has also explored the relationship between control and food.

Rewarding eating behaviour

Some research has examined the effect of rewarding eating behaviour as in 'if you eat your vegetables I will be pleased with you'. For example, Birch et al. (1980) gave children food in association with positive adult attention compared with more neutral situations. This was shown to increase food preference. Similarly a recent intervention study using videos to change eating behaviour reported that rewarding vegetable consumption increased that behaviour (Lowe et al. 1998). Rewarding eating behaviour seems to improve food preferences.

Food as the reward

Other research has explored the impact of using food as a reward. For these studies gaining access to the food is contingent upon another behaviour as in 'if you are well behaved you can have a biscuit'. Birch et al. (1980) presented children with foods either as a reward, as a snack or in a non-social situation (the control). The results showed that food acceptance increased if the foods were presented as a reward but that the more neutral conditions had no effect. This suggests that using food as a reward increases the preference for that food.

The relationship between food and rewards, however, appears to be more complicated than this. In one study, children were offered their preferred fruit juice as a means to be allowed to play in an attractive play area (Birch et al. 1982). The results showed that using the juice as a means to get the reward reduced the preference for the juice. Similarly, Lepper et al. (1982) told children stories about children eating imaginary foods called 'hupe' and 'hule' in which the child in the story could only eat one if he/she had finished the other. The results showed that the food that was used as the reward became the least preferred one which has been supported by similar studies (Birch et al. 1984; Newman and Taylor 1992). These examples are analogous to saying, 'if you eat your vegetables you can eat your pudding'. Although parents use this approach to encourage their children to eat vegetables the evidence indicates that this may be increasing their children's preference for pudding even further as pairing two foods results in the 'reward' food being seen as more positive than the 'access' food. As concluded by Birch, 'although these practices can induce children to eat more vegetables in the short run, evidence from our research suggests that in the long run parental control attempts may have negative effects on the quality of children's diets by reducing their preferences for those foods' (1999: 10).

Not all researchers, however, agree with this conclusion. Dowey (1996) reviewed the literature examining food and rewards and argued that the conflicting evidence may relate to methodological differences between studies and that studies designed to change food preference should be conducted in real-life situations, should measure outcomes over time and not just at one time point, should involve clear instructions to the children and should measure actual food intake, not just the child's stated preference. The recent intervention study described earlier incorporated these methodological considerations into its design (Lowe et al. 1998) and concluded that food preferences could be improved by offering rewards for food consumption as long as the 'symbolic context' of reward delivery was positive and did not indicate that 'eating the target foods was a low value activity' (Lowe et al. 1998: 78). As long as the child cannot think that 'I am being offered a reward to eat my vegetables, therefore vegetables must be an intrinsically negative thing', then rewards may work.

Food and control

The associations between food and rewards highlight a role for parental control over eating behaviour. Some research has addressed the impact of control as studies indicate that parents often believe that restricting access to food and forbidding them to eat food are good strategies to improve food preferences (Casey and Rozin 1989). Birch (1999) reviewed the evidence for the impact of imposing any form of parental control over food intake and argued that it is not only the use of foods as rewards that can have a negative effect on children's food preferences but also attempts to limit a child's access to foods. She concluded from her review that 'child feeding strategies that restrict children's access to snack foods actually make the restricted foods more attractive' (1999: 11). For example, when food is made freely available, children will choose more of the restricted than the unrestricted foods, particularly when the mother is not present (Fisher and Birch 1999; Fisher et al. 2000). From this perspective parental control would seem to have a detrimental impact upon a child's eating behaviour. In contrast, however, some studies suggest that parental control may actually reduce weight and improve eating behaviour. For example, Wardle et al. (2002: 453) suggested that 'lack of control of food intake [rather than higher control] might contribute to the emergence of differences in weight'. Similarly, Brown and Ogden (2004) reported that greater parental control was associated with higher intakes of healthy snack foods. Furthermore, other studies indicate that parental control may have no impact in some populations (Constanzo and Woody 1985). There are several possible explanations for these conflicting results. First, the studies have been carried out using different populations in different countries. Second, the studies have used different measures, with Birch et al. (2001) using the child feeding questionnaire which operationalizes control in terms of monitoring, restriction and pressure to eat, and Wardle et al. (2002) using the parental feeding style questionnaire (PFSQ) which operationalizes control in terms of restriction and items such as 'I control how many snacks my child should have'. Third, and related to the above, these contradictory results may reflect the contradictory nature of parental control, with parental control being a more complex construct than acknowledged by any of the existing measures. Ogden, Reynolds et al. (2006) explored this third possibility and examined the effect of differentiating between 'overt control' which can be detected by the child (e.g. being firm about how much your child should eat) and 'covert control' which cannot be detected by the child (e.g. not buying unhealthy foods and bringing them into the house). The results showed that these different forms of control differently predicted snack food intake and that, while higher covert control was related to decreased intake of unhealthy snacks, higher overt control predicted an increased intake of healthy snacks.

Food and physiological consequences

Studies have also explored the association between food cues and physiological responses to food intake. There is a wealth of literature illustrating the acquisition of food aversions following negative gastrointestinal consequences (e.g. Garcia et al. 1974). For example, an aversion to shellfish can be triggered after one case of stomach upset following the consumption of mussels. Research has also explored pairing food cues with the sense of satiety which follows their consumption. One early study of infants showed that by about 40 days of age infants adjusted their consumption of milk depending upon the calorific density of the drink they were given (Formon 1974). Similarly children can adjust their food intake according to the flavour of foods if certain flavours have been consistently paired with a given calorific density (Birch and Deysher 1986).

Problems with a developmental model

A developmental approach to eating behaviour provides detailed evidence on how food preferences are learned in childhood. This perspective emphasizes the role of learning and places the individual within an environment that is rich in cues and reinforcers. Such an analysis also allows for a moderate interaction between learning and physiology. However, there are some problems with this perspective as follows:

- Much of the research carried out within this perspective has taken place within the laboratory as a means to provide a controlled environment. Although this methodology enables alternative explanations to be excluded, the extent to which the results would generalize to a more naturalistic setting remains unclear.

- A developmental model explores the meaning of food in terms of food as a reward, food as a means to gain a reward, food as status, food as pleasant and food as aversive. However, food has a much more diverse set of meanings which are not incorporated into this model. For example, food can mean power, sexuality, religion and culture. Such complex meanings are not incorporated into a developmental perspective.

- Once eaten, food is incorporated into the body and can change body size. This is also loaded with a complex set of meanings such as attractiveness, control, lethargy and success. A developmental model does not address the meanings of the body.

- A developmental model includes a role for cognitions as some of the meanings of food including reward and aversion are considered to motivate behaviour. These cognitions remain implicit, however, and are not explicitly described.

In sum, developmental models of eating behaviour highlight a central role for learning. From this perspective, eating behaviour is influenced by exposure which can reduce neophobia, social learning through the observation of important others and associative learning as food cues can be paired with aspects of the environment and the physiological consequences of eating.

Cognitive models of eating behaviour

A cognitive approach to eating behaviour focuses on an individual's cognitions and has explored the extent to which cognitions predict and explain behaviour. Some research has highlighted a weak link between health locus of control and dietary behaviour (e.g. Bennett et al. 1995). Similarly, one large-scale study of dietary practice across Europe reported an association between beliefs about the importance of specific dietary practices and the implementation of these practices (Wardle et al. 1997). Most research using cognitive approach has, however, drawn upon social cognition models. These models have been applied to eating behaviour both as a means to predict eating behaviour and as central to interventions to change eating behaviour. This chapter will focus on research using the TRA and TPB as these have most commonly been applied to aspects of eating behaviour (see Chapter 2 for details).

Using the TRA and TPB

Some research using a social cognitive approach to eating behaviour has focused on predicting the intentions to consume specific foods. For example, research has explored the extent to which cognitions relate to the intentions to eat biscuits and wholemeal bread (Sparks et al. 1992), skimmed milk (Raats et al. 1995) and organic vegetables (Sparks and Shepherd 1992). Much research suggests that behavioural intentions are not particularly good predictors of behaviour *per se* which has generated work exploring the intention behaviour gap (Sutton 1998a; Gollwitzer 1993). Therefore studies have also used the TRA and the TPB to explore the cognitive predictors of actual behaviour. For example, Shepherd and Stockley (1985) used the TRA to predict fat intake and reported that attitude was a better predictor than subjective norms. Similarly, attitudes have also been found to be the best predictor of table salt use (Shepherd and Farleigh 1986), eating in fast food restaurants (Axelson et al. 1983), the frequency of consuming low-fat milk (Shepherd 1988) and healthy eating conceptualized as high levels of fibre and fruit and vegetables and low levels of fat (Povey et al. 2000). Research has also pointed to the role of perceived behavioural control in predicting behaviour particularly in relation to weight loss (Schifter and Ajzen 1985) and healthy eating (Povey et al. 2000). The social norms component of these models has consistently failed to predict eating behaviour.

Adding extra variables

Some studies have explored the impact of adding extra variables to the standard framework described within the social cognition models. For example, Shepherd and Stockley (1987) examined the predictors of fat intake and included a measure of nutritional knowledge but found that this was not associated with either their measure of attitudes or their participants' behaviour. Povey et al. (2000) included additional measures of descriptive norms (e.g. 'To what extent do you think the following groups eat a healthy diet?') and perceived social support (e.g. 'To what extent do you think the following groups would be supportive if you tried to eat a healthy diet?') but found that these variables did not add anything to the core cognitions of the TPB. Research has also examined the impact of accessing the individual's hedonic responses to food with a focus on beliefs about the sensory properties of the food concerned. The results, however, in this area have been contradictory. For example, Tuorila-Ollikainen et al. (1986) asked participants to rate their beliefs about low-salt bread both before and after tasting some bread and reported that the post-tasting hedonic ratings predicted eating behaviour above their measure of attitudes. In contrast, Tuorila (1987) asked participants to rate milk, which varied in its fat content, for its hedonic properties and reported that these ratings of the sensory aspects of the food did not add anything to the basic cognitive model. Shepherd (1989) provided a review of these studies and suggested that the hedonic responses to food may be more important if the food is novel than if it is familiar.

The attitudinal research described so far conceptualizes individuals as holding either positive or negative views towards a given object. In terms of eating behaviour it is assumed that people either like or dislike certain foods and that this value-laden attitude predicts food intake. Recent studies, however, have also explored the role of ambivalence in predicting behaviour (Thompson et al. 1995) and this has been applied to eating behaviour (Sparks et al. 2001). Ambivalence has been defined in a variety of different ways. For example, Breckler (1994) defined it as 'a conflict aroused by competing evaluative predispositions' and Emmons (1996) defined it as 'an approach – avoidance conflict – wanting but at the same time not wanting the same goal object'. Central to all definitions of ambivalence is the simultaneous presence of both positive and negative values which seems particularly pertinent to eating behaviour as individuals may hold contradictory attitudes towards foods in terms of 'tasty', 'healthy', 'fattening' and 'a treat'. Sparks et al. (2001) incorporated the concept of ambivalence into the theory of planned behaviour and assessed whether it predicted meat or chocolate consumption. Participants were 325 volunteers who completed a questionnaire including a measure of ambivalence assessed in terms of the mean of both positive and negative evaluations (e.g. 'how positive is chocolate' and 'how negative is chocolate') and then subtracting this mean from the absolute difference between the two evaluations (i.e. 'total positive minus total negative'). This computation provides a score which reflects the balance between positive and negative feelings. In line with previous TPB studies, the results showed that attitudes *per se* were the best predictor of the intention to consume both meat and chocolate. The results also showed that the relationship between attitude and intention was weaker in those participants with higher ambivalence. This implies that holding both positive and negative attitudes to a food makes it less likely that the overall attitude will be translated into an intention to eat it.

In line with other research using social cognition models (see Chapter 2), research in this area has also added implementation intentions as a means to predict and change dietary behaviour. For example, Armitage (2004) asked 264 participants from a company in northern England to rate their motivation to eat a low-fat diet before being randomly allocated to either the implementation condition or the control condition. Those in the implementation condition were asked to describe a plan to eat a low-fat diet for the next month and to formulate their plans in as much detail as possible. Their food intake was measured using a food frequency questionnaire after one month. The results showed that this simple intervention resulted in a significant decrease in the proportion of energy derived from fat which could not be explained by baseline differences in motivations, indicating that implementation intentions had changed subsequent behaviour.

A cognitive approach to eating behaviour, however, has been criticized for its focus on individual level variables only and for the assumption that the same set of cognitions are relevant to all individuals. For example, Resnicow et al. (1997) carried out a large-scale study involving 1398 school children as a means to predict their fruit and vegetable intake. The study measured social cognitive variables including self-efficacy, social norms and added additional cognitive variables including preferences and outcome expectations. The results showed that only preferences and outcome expectations predicted actual eating behaviour but that 90 per cent of the variance in eating behaviour remained unaccounted for. The authors concluded from this study that 'SCT (social cognition theory) may not be a robust framework for explaining dietary behaviour in children' (Resnicow et al. 1997: 275) and suggested that a broader model, which included factors such as self-esteem, parental and family dietary habits and the availability of fruit and vegetables, may be more effective.

Problems with a cognitive model of eating behaviour

A cognitive model of eating behaviour highlights the role of cognitions that makes explicit the cognitions which remain only implicit within a developmental perspective. It provides a useful framework for studying these cognitions and highlights their impact upon behaviour. However, there are some problems with this approach as follows:

- Most research carried out within a cognitive perspective uses quantitative methods and devises questionnaires based upon existing models. This approach means that the cognitions being examined are chosen by the researcher rather than offered by the person being researched. It is possible that many important cognitions are missed which are central to understanding eating behaviour.

- Although focusing on cognitions, those incorporated by the models are limited and ignore the wealth of meanings associated with food and body size.

- Research from a cognitive perspective assumes that behaviour is a consequence of rational thought and ignores the role of affect. Emotions such as fear (of weight gain, of illness), pleasure (over a success which deserves a treat) and guilt (about overeating) might contribute towards eating behaviour.

- Some cognitive models incorporate the views of others in the form of the construct 'subjective norm'. This does not adequately address the central role that others play in a behaviour as social as eating.

- At times the cognitive models appear tautological in that the independent variables do not seem conceptually separate from the dependent variables they are being used to predict. For example, is the cognition 'I am confident I can eat fruit and vegetables' really distinct from the cognition 'I intend to eat fruit and vegetables'?

- Although the cognitive models have been applied extensively to behaviour, their ability to predict actual behaviour remains poor, leaving a large amount of variance to be explained by undefined factors.

In sum, from a social cognitive perspective, eating behaviour can be understood and predicted by measuring an individual's cognitions about food. The research in this area points to a consistently important role for attitudes towards a food (e.g. 'I think eating a healthy meal is enjoyable') and a role for an individual's beliefs about behavioural control (e.g. 'How confident are you that you could eat a healthy diet?'). There is also some evidence that ambivalence may moderate the association between attitude and intention and that implementation intentions can change behaviour. However, there is no evidence for either social norms or other hypothesized variables. Such an approach ignores the role of a range of other cognitions, particularly those relating to the meaning of food and the meaning of size and at times the associations between variables is weak, leaving much of the variance in eating behaviour unexplained.

Box 6.1 **Some problems with . . . eating research**

Below are some problems with research in this area that you may wish to pause to consider.

1 Measuring behaviour is always difficult. Measuring eating behaviour is particularly difficult as it is made up of many different components, happens at many different times and in different places. Further, measuring it either by self-report, observation or in the laboratory can both be inaccurate and can actually change the ways in which people eat.

2 Much research uses healthy eating as the outcome variable by trying to predict healthy eating or promote a better diet. However, trying to define what is a healthy diet and what foods are either 'good' or 'bad' is very problematic.

3 There are very different models and theories of eating behaviour which take different perspectives and emphasize different variables. How these fit together or can be integrated is unclear.

A weight concern model of eating behaviour
The meaning of food and weight

So far this chapter has explored developmental and cognitive models of eating behaviour. Developmental models emphasize the role of learning and association and cognitive models emphasize the role of attitudes and beliefs. However, food is associated with many meanings such as a treat, a celebration, the forbidden fruit, a family get-together, being a good mother and being a good child (Ogden 2003). Furthermore, once eaten, food can change the body's weight and shape, which is also associated with meanings such as attractiveness, control and success (Ogden 2003). As a result of these meanings many women, in particular, show weight concern in the form of body dissatisfaction, which often results in dieting. Weight concern and its impact on eating behaviour will now be described.

What is body dissatisfaction?

Body dissatisfaction comes in many forms. Some research has conceptualized body dissatisfaction in terms of a *distorted body size estimation* and a perception that the body is larger than it really is. For example, Slade and Russell (1973) asked anorexics to adjust the distance between two lights on a beam in a darkened room until the lights represented the width of aspects of their body such as their hips, waist and shoulders. The results showed that anorexics consistently overestimated their size compared with control subjects. Other studies coming from the same perspective have asked subjects to mark either two ends of a life-size piece of paper (Gleghorn et al. 1987), to adjust the horizontal dimensions on either a television or video image of themselves (Freeman et al. 1984; Gardner et al. 1987), or to change the dimensions on a distorting mirror (Brodie et al. 1989). This research has consistently shown that individuals with clinically defined eating disorders show greater perceptual distortion than non-clinical subjects. However, the research has also shown that the vast majority of women, with or without an eating disorder, think that they are fatter than they actually are.

Some research has emphasized a discrepancy between *perceptions of reality versus those of an ideal* without a comparison to the individual's actual size as objectively measured by the researcher. This research has tended to use whole-body silhouette pictures of varying sizes whereby the subject is asked to state which one is closest to how they look now and which one best illustrates how they would like to look. For example, Stunkard et al. (1983) used this approach with normal male and female students; Counts and Adams (1985) used it with bulimics, dieters and ex-obese females; and Collins (1991) used it with pre-adolescent children. It has consistently been shown that most girls and women would like to be thinner than they are and most males would like to be either the same or larger (see Figure 6.4).

The final and most frequent way in which body dissatisfaction is understood is simply in terms of *negative feelings* and cognitions towards the body. This has been assessed using questionnaires such as the body shape questionnaire (Cooper et al. 1987), the body areas satisfaction scale (Brown et al. 1990) and the body dissatisfaction subscale of the eating disorders inventory (Garner 1991). These questionnaires ask questions such as 'Do you worry about parts of your body being too big?', 'Do you worry about your thighs spreading out when you sit down?' and 'Does being with thin women make you feel conscious of your weight?' The research has shown that, although individuals with eating disorders show greater body dissatisfaction than those without, dieters show greater body dissatisfaction than non-dieters and women in general show greater body dissatisfaction than men.

Therefore body dissatisfaction can be conceptualized as either a discrepancy between individuals' perception of their body size and their real body size, a discrepancy between their perception of their actual size and their ideal size, or simply as feelings of discontent with the body's size and shape. However, whichever conceptualization is used and whichever measurement tool is chosen to operationalize body dissatisfaction, it seems clear that it is a common phenomenon and certainly not one that is limited to those few individuals with clinically defined eating disorders. So what causes this problem?

The causes of body dissatisfaction

Much research has looked at the role of social factors in causing body dissatisfaction in terms of the media, ethnicity, social class and the family environment. In addition, research has explored the role of psychological factors that may translate the social factors into actual body dissatisfaction.

Social factors
The role of the media

The most commonly held belief in both the lay and academic communities is probably that body dissatisfaction is a response to representations of thin women in the media. Magazines, newspapers, television, films and even novels predominantly use images of thin women. These women may be advertising body size-related items, such as food and clothes, or neutral items,

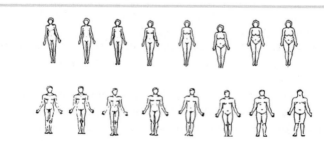

Figure 6.4 Measuring body dissatisfaction

such as vacuum cleaners and wallpaper, but they are always thin. Alternatively they may be characters in a story or simply passers-by who illustrate the real world, but this real world is always represented by thinness. Whatever their role and wherever their existence, women used by the media are generally thin and we are therefore led to believe that thinness is not only the desired norm but also the actual norm. On those rare occasions when a fatter woman appears, she is usually there making a statement about being fat (fat comedians make jokes about choco- late cake and fat actresses are either evil or unhappy), not simply as a normal woman. Do these representations then make women dissatisfied with their bodies? Some research suggests that this is the case. For example, Ogden and Mundray (1996) asked men and women to rate their body dissatisfaction both before and after studying pictures of either fat or thin men or women (the pictures were matched in gender to the participant). The results showed that all particip- ants, regardless of sex, felt more body satisfied after studying the fatter pictures and more body dissatisfied after studying the thinner pictures. It was also shown that this response was greater in the women than the men. Similar results have been found for anorexics, bulimics and preg- nant women (Waller et al. 1992; Hamilton and Waller 1993; Sumner et al. 1993). If such changes in body dissatisfaction can occur after only acute exposure to these images, then it is possible that longer-term exposure might be more serious. However, is the media the only explanation of body dissatisfaction? Are women (and sometimes men) simply passive victims of the whims of the media? Perhaps body dissatisfaction also comes from a range of additional sources.

Ethnicity

Although body dissatisfaction has predominantly been seen as a problem for white women, the literature examining the relationship between body dissatisfaction and ethnic group is contra- dictory. For example, higher rates of a range of behaviours associated with body dissatisfaction have been found in white women when compared with black and/or Asian women in terms of bulimic behaviours (Gray et al. 1987), generalized disordered eating (Abrams et al. 1992; Akan and Grilo 1995) and body dissatisfaction and eating concerns (Rucker and Cash 1992; Powell and Khan 1995). However, in direct contrast, other studies report the reverse relationship between ethnicity and weight concern. For example, Mumford et al. (1991) reported results from a school in the north of England that indicated that the prevalence of bulimia nervosa was higher among Asian schoolgirls than their white counterparts. In parallel, Striegel-Moore et al. (1995) reported higher levels of drive for thinness in black girls, and Hill and Bhatti (1995) reported higher levels of dietary restraint in 9-year-old Asian girls when both these samples were compared with white girls. Furthermore, additional studies have suggested that equally high levels of weight concern can be found in women and girls regardless of their ethnicity (Dolan et al. 1990; Ahmed et al. 1994). Therefore some research indicates that whites are more body dissatisfied than Asians and blacks, other research shows that whites are less dissatisfied and some research even shows that there is no difference by ethnic group.

Social class

Body dissatisfaction is also generally believed to be a problem for the higher classes. However, the literature on social class is also contradictory. Several studies in this area indicate that factors ranging from body dissatisfaction, body distortion and dieting behaviour to eating dis- orders are more prevalent in higher-class individuals. For example, Dornbusch et al. (1984) examined social class and the desire to be thin in a representative sample of 7000 American adolescents and concluded that higher-class females wanted to be thinner when compared with their lower-class counterparts. In parallel, Drenowski et al. (1994) reported that the higher-class subjects in their sample showed increased prevalence of dieting, bingeing and vigorous exercise for weight loss, and Wardle and Marsland (1990) reported that, although their higher-class school children were thinner, they showed greater levels of weight concern. Similar results have also been reported for the prevalence of anorexia nervosa (Crisp et al. 1976).

However, research also suggests that the relationship between social class and weight concern is not straightforward. For example, in direct contrast to the above studies, Story et al. (1995) reported the results from a sample of 36,320 American students and suggested that higher social class was related to greater weight satisfaction and lower rates of pathological weight control behaviours such as vomiting. Similar results were reported by Eisler and Szmukler (1985), who examined abnormal eating attitudes. Furthermore, additional studies reported that social class is unrelated to factors such as body dissatisfaction, the desire for thinness, the desire for weight loss and symptoms indicative of eating disorders (Cole and Edelmann 1988; Whitaker et al. 1989). Therefore, although social class is believed to be a cause of body dissatisfaction, the results remain unclear.

The family

Research has also focused on the impact of the family on predicting body dissatisfaction. In particular, it has highlighted a role for the mother and suggested that mothers who are dissatisfied with their own bodies communicate this to their daughters which results in the daughters' own body dissatisfaction. For example, Hall and Brown (1982) reported that mothers of girls with anorexia show greater body dissatisfaction than mothers of non-disordered girls. Likewise, Steiger et al. (1994) found a direct correspondence between mothers' and daughters' levels of weight concern, and Hill et al. (1990) reported a link between mothers' and daughters' degree of dietary restraint. However, research examining concordance between mothers and daughters has not always produced consistent results. For example, Attie and Brooks-Gunn (1989) reported that mothers' levels of compulsive eating and body image could not predict these factors in their daughters. Likewise, Ogden and Elder (1998) reported discordance between mothers' and daughters' weight concern in both Asian and white families.

Therefore research exploring the role of social factors has highlighted a role for the media, ethnicity, social class and the mother's own body dissatisfaction. However, there are problems with the literature. First, much of the evidence is contradictory and therefore straightforward conclusions are problematic. Second, even if there was a relationship between social factors and body dissatisfaction, simply looking for group differences (i.e. white versus Asian, lower class versus higher class, mother versus daughter) does not explain how body dissatisfaction may come about. Therefore research has also looked for psychological explanations.

Psychological factors

The research suggests that body dissatisfaction may be related to class, ethnicity and the family environment but that this relationship is not a consistent one. Perhaps simply looking for group differences hides the effect of other psychological causes. From this perspective, ethnicity may relate to body dissatisfaction, but only when ethnicity is also accompanied by a particular set of beliefs. Similarly, it may not be class *per se* that is important but whether class reflects the way an individual thinks. Further, a mother's body dissatisfaction may only be important if it occurs within a particular kind of relationship. So what might these psychological factors be? Research has explored the role of beliefs, the mother–daughter relationship and the central role of control.

Beliefs

Some research has examined the beliefs held by the individuals themselves and their family members. For example, when attempting to understand ethnicity, studies have highlighted a role for beliefs about competitiveness, the value of achievement, material success and a parental belief that the child is their future (Ogden and Chanana 1998). In addition, the literature has also emphasized beliefs about a woman's role within society. For example, Mumford et al. (1991) concluded that eating disorders in Asian girls may be related to a family background that believes in a traditional role for women. Such conclusions were also made by Hill and Bhatti (1995).

In a similar vein, when attempting to explain the role of social class, research has highlighted a role for beliefs about achievement and it has been suggested that eating disorders may be a response to such pressures (Bruch 1974; Kalucy et al. 1977; Selvini 1988). Lower-class individuals, in contrast, may aspire more in terms of family life and having children, which may be protective against weight concern. Cole and Edelmann (1988) empirically tested this possibility and assessed the relationship between the need to achieve and eating behaviour. However, although the need to achieve was associated with class, it was not predictive of weight concern. It has also been suggested that class may be associated with a greater value placed on physical appearance and attitudes towards obesity (Wardle et al. 1995). Further, Dornbusch et al. (1984) commented that 'there are higher standards for thinness in higher social classes', which may contribute to higher levels of weight concern. In addition, Striegel-Moore et al. (1986) argued that higher-class women are more likely to emulate trend-setters of beauty and fashion, again predisposing them to feelings of dissatisfaction with their appearance.

Therefore beliefs about competitiveness, achievement, material success, the role of women, stereotypes of beauty and the child–parent relationship have been highlighted as the kinds of beliefs that may predict body dissatisfaction. Ogden and Chanana (1998) explored the role of these beliefs in Asian and white teenage girls and Ogden and Thomas (1999) focused on lower- and higher-class individuals, both studies concluding that, although social factors such as class and ethnicity may be related to body dissatisfaction, it is likely that their influence is mediated through the role of such beliefs held by both the individual who is dissatisfied with their body and their family members.

Mother–daughter relationship

Some research has also explored the nature of the mother–daughter relationship. For example, Crisp et al. (1980) argued that undefined boundaries within the family and the existence of an enmeshed relationship between mother and daughter may be important factors. Likewise, Smith et al. (1995) suggested that a close relationship between mother and daughter may result in an enmeshed relationship and problems with separation in adolescence. Further, Minuchin et al. (1978) argued that although optimum autonomy does not mean breaking all bonds between mother and daughter, mother–daughter relationships that permit poor autonomy for both parties may be predictive of future psychopathology. Further, Bruch (1974) argued that anorexia may be a result of a child's struggle to develop her own self-identity within a mother–daughter dynamic that limits the daughter's autonomy. Some authors have also examined the relationship between autonomy, enmeshment and intimacy. For example, Smith et al.

(1995) argued that an increased recognition of autonomy within the mother–daughter relationship corresponds with a decrease in enmeshment and a resulting increase in intimacy. Further, it is suggested that such intimacy may be reflected in a reduction in conflict and subsequent psychological problems (Smith et al. 1995). One study directly explored whether the mother–daughter relationship was important in terms of a 'modelling hypothesis' (i.e. the mother is body dissatisfied and therefore so is the daughter) or an 'interactive hypothesis' (i.e. it is the relationship itself between mother and daughter that is important). Therefore it examined both the mothers' and the daughters' own levels of body dissatisfaction and the nature of the relationship between mother and daughter (Ogden and Steward 2000). The results showed no support for the modelling hypothesis but suggested that a relationship in which mothers did not believe in either their own or their daughter's autonomy and rated projection as important was more likely to result in daughters who were dissatisfied with their bodies.

It would seem that body dissatisfaction may come from the media. Further, it may be related to social factors such as ethnicity, social class and the mother's own body dissatisfaction. In addition, it is possible that the impact of such social factors is mediated through psychological factors such as beliefs and the nature of relationships. Research has suggested that all these factors illustrate a central role for the need for control.

The role of control

Beliefs relating to materialism, competitiveness, achievement, autonomy, the role of women and a projected relationship between mother and daughter all have one thing in common. They are based on the assumption that the object of these beliefs (i.e. the daughter) has control over her destiny. It is being assumed that she can achieve, she can compete and she can fulfil the desires of others if only she were to put her mind to it; anything can be achieved if the effort is right. This is quite a lot of pressure to place on anyone. It is particularly a lot of pressure to place upon a woman who may well feel that the world is still designed for men. And it is even more pressure to place upon a young woman who may feel that the world is designed for adults. Such expectations may result in feelings of being out of control: 'how can I achieve all these things?', 'what do I have to do?', 'I can never fulfil everyone's demands', 'my world is simply not that open to change', 'things are not that controllable'. However, the one thing that we are led to believe can be changed is our body. A family's beliefs may make us want to control and change a whole range of factors. But the only factor that may seem controllable may simply be the way we look. In fact the media constantly tell us that this is so. Therefore feelings of being out of control need to be expressed. Body dissatisfaction may well be an expression of this lack of control (Orbach 1978; Ogden 1999).

Dieting

Body dissatisfaction is consistently related to dieting and attempting to eat less. Restraint theory (e.g. Herman and Mack 1975; Herman and Polivy 1984) was developed to evaluate the causes and consequences of dieting (referred to as restrained eating) and suggests that dieters show signs of both undereating and overeating.

Dieting and undereating

Restrained eating aims to reduce food intake and several studies have found that at times this aim is successful. Thompson et al. (1988) used a preload/taste test methodology to examine restrained eaters' eating behaviour. This experimental method involves giving subjects either a high calorie preload (e.g. a high calorie milk shake, a chocolate bar) or a low calorie preload (e.g. a cracker). After eating/drinking the preload, subjects are asked to take part in a taste test. This involves asking subjects to rate a series of different foods (e.g. biscuits, snacks, ice cream) for a variety of different qualities, including saltiness, preference and sweetness. The subjects are left alone for a set amount of time to rate the foods and then the amount they have eaten is weighed (the subjects do not know that this will happen). The aim of the preload/taste test method is to measure food intake in a controlled environment (the laboratory) and to examine the effect of preloading on their eating behaviour. Thompson and colleagues reported that in this experimental situation the restrained eaters consumed fewer calories than the unrestrained eaters after both the low and high preloads. This suggests that their attempts at eating less were successful. Kirkley et al. (1988) assessed the eating style of 50 women using four-day dietary self-monitoring forms and also reported that the restrained eaters consumed fewer calories than the unrestrained eaters. Laessle et al. (1989) also used food diaries and found that the restrained eaters consumed around 400 calories less than the unrestrained eaters, with the restrained eaters specifically avoiding food items of high carbohydrate and fat content. Therefore restrained eaters aim to eat less and are sometimes successful.

Dieting and overeating

In opposition to these findings, several studies have suggested that higher levels of restrained eating are related to increased food intake. For example, Ruderman and Wilson (1979) used a preload/taste test procedure and reported that restrained eaters consumed significantly more food than the unrestrained eaters, irrespective of preload size. In particular, restraint theory has identified the disinhibition of restraint as characteristic of overeating in restrained eaters (Herman and Mack 1975; Spencer and Fremouw 1979; Herman et al. 1987). The original study illustrating disinhibition (Herman and Mack 1975) used a preload/taste test paradigm, and involved giving groups of dieters and non-dieters either a high calorie preload or a low calorie preload.

The results are illustrated in Figure 6.5 and indicate that, whereas the non-dieters showed compensatory regulatory behaviour, and ate less at the taste test after the high calorie preload,

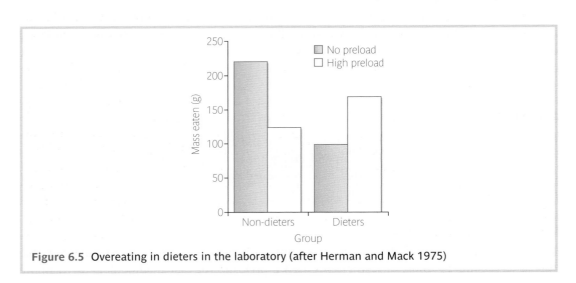

Figure 6.5 Overeating in dieters in the laboratory (after Herman and Mack 1975)

the dieters consumed more in the taste test if they had had the high calorie preload than the low calorie preload.

This form of disinhibition or the 'what the hell' effect illustrates overeating in response to a high calorie preload. Disinhibition in general has been defined as 'eating more as a result of the loosening restraints in response to emotional distress, intoxication or preloading' (Herman and Polivy 1989: 342), and its definition paved the way for a wealth of research examining the role of restraint in predicting overeating behaviour.

The causes of overeating

Research has explored possible mechanisms for the overeating shown by restrained eaters. These are described below and include the causal model of overeating, the boundary model of overeating, cognitive shifts, mood modification, denial, escape theory, overeating as relapse and the central role for control.

The causal analysis of overeating

The causal analysis of eating behaviour was first described by Herman and Polivy (Herman and Mack 1975; Herman and Polivy 1980, 1988; Polivy and Herman 1983, 1985). They suggested that dieting and bingeing were causally linked and that 'restraint not only precedes overeating but contributes to it causally' (Polivy and Herman 1983). This suggests that attempting not to eat, paradoxically increases the probability of overeating – the specific behaviour that dieters are attempting to avoid. The causal analysis of restraint represented a new approach to eating behaviour and the prediction that restraint actually caused overeating was an interesting reappraisal of the situation. Wardle (1980) further developed this analysis and Wardle and Beales (1988) experimentally tested the causal analysis of overeating. They randomly assigned 27 obese women to either a diet group, an exercise group or a no-treatment control group for seven weeks. At weeks four and six all subjects took part in a laboratory session designed to assess their food intake. The results showed that subjects in the diet condition ate more than both the exercise and the control group, supporting a causal link between dieting and overeating. From this analysis the overeating shown by dieters is actually caused by attempts at dieting.

The boundary model of overeating

In an attempt to explain how dieting causes overeating, Herman and Polivy (1984) developed the 'boundary model', which represented an integration of physiological and cognitive perspectives on food intake. The boundary model is illustrated in Figure 6.6.

According to the model, food intake is motivated by a physiologically determined hunger boundary and deterred by a physiologically determined satiety boundary. In addition, the boundary model suggests that the food intake of restrained eaters is regulated by a cognitively determined 'diet boundary'. It indicates that dieters attempt to replace physiological control with cognitive control which represents 'the dieter's selected imposed quota for consumption on a given occasion' (Herman and Polivy 1984: 149). Herman and Polivy (1984) described how, after a low calorie preload, the dieter can maintain her diet goal for the immediate future since food intake remains within the limits set by the 'diet boundary'. However, after the dieter has crossed the diet boundary (i.e. eaten something 'not allowed'), they will consume food ad lib until the pressures of the satiety boundary are activated. The boundary model proposes a form of dual regulation, with food intake limited either by the diet boundary or the satiety boundary. The boundary model has also been used to examine differences between dieters, binge eaters, anorexics and normal eaters. This comparison is shown in Figure 6.7.

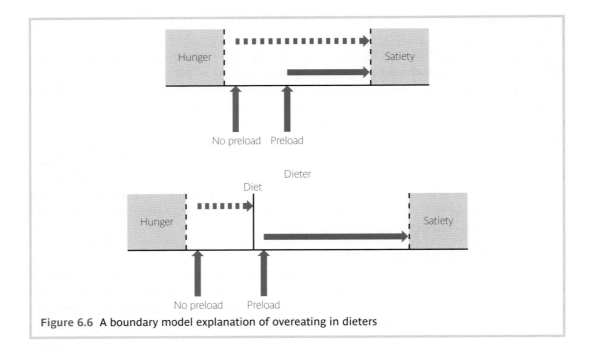

Figure 6.6 A boundary model explanation of overeating in dieters

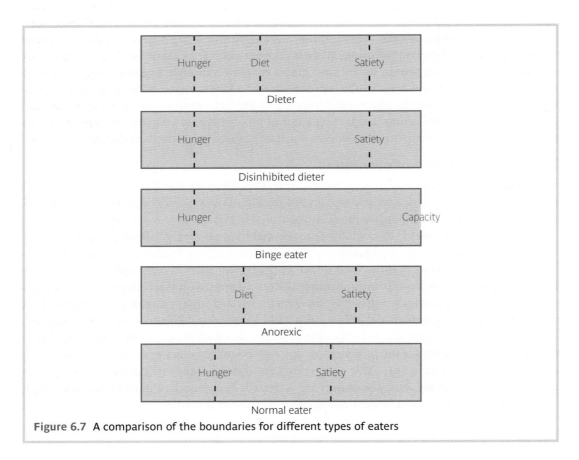

Figure 6.7 A comparison of the boundaries for different types of eaters

Cognitive shifts

The overeating found in dieters has also been understood in terms of shifts in the individual's cognitive set. Primarily this has been described in terms of a breakdown in the dieter's self-control reflecting a 'motivational collapse' and a state of giving in to the overpowering drives to eat (Polivy and Herman 1983). Ogden and Wardle (1991) analysed the cognitive set of the dis-inhibited dieter and suggested that such a collapse in self-control reflected a passive model of overeating and that the 'what the hell' effect as described by Herman and Polivy (1984) con-tained elements of passivity in terms of factors such as 'giving in', 'resignation' and 'passivity'. In particular, interviews with restrained and unrestrained eaters revealed that many restrained eaters reported passive cognitions after a high calorie preload, including thoughts such as 'I'm going to give in to any urges I've got' and 'I can't be bothered, it's too much effort to stop eating' (Ogden and Wardle 1991). In line with this model of overeating, Glynn and Ruderman (1986) developed the eating self-efficacy questionnaire as a measure of the tendency to overeat. This also emphasized motivational collapse and suggested that overeating was a consequence of the failure of this self-control.

An alternative model of overeating contended that overeating reflected an active decision to overeat, and Ogden and Wardle (1991) argued that implicit within the 'what the hell' effect was an active reaction against the diet. This hypothesis was tested using a preload/taste test para-digm and cognitions were assessed using rating scales, interviews and the Stroop task which is a cognitive test of selective attention. The results from two studies indicated that dieters responded to high calorie foods with an increase in an active state of mind characterized by cog-nitions such as 'rebellious', 'challenging' and 'defiant' and thoughts such as 'I don't care now, I'm just going to stuff my face' (Ogden and Wardle 1991; Ogden and Greville 1993; see **Focus on Research 6.1**, p. 153). It was argued that, rather than simply passively giving in to an over-whelming desire to eat, as suggested by other models, the overeater may actively decide to overeat as a form of rebellion against self-imposed food restrictions. This rebellious state of mind has also been described by obese binge eaters who report bingeing as 'a way to unleash resentment' (Loro and Orleans 1981). Eating as an active decision may at times also indicate a rebellion against the deprivation of other substances such as cigarettes (Ogden 1994) and against the deprivation of emotional support (Bruch 1974).

Mood modification

Dieters overeat in response to lowered mood and researchers have argued that disinhibitory behaviour enables the individual to mask their negative mood with the temporary heightened mood caused by eating. This has been called the 'masking hypothesis' and has been tested by empirical studies. For example, Polivy and Herman (1999) told female subjects that they had either passed or failed a cognitive task and then gave them food either *ad libitum* or in small controlled amounts. The results in part supported the masking hypothesis as the dieters who ate *ad libitum* attributed more of their distress to their eating behaviour than to the task failure. The authors argued that dieters may overeat as a way of shifting responsibility for their negative mood from uncontrollable aspects of their lives to their eating behaviour. This mood modifica-tion theory of overeating has been further supported by research indicating that dieters eat more than non-dieters when anxious, regardless of the palatability of the food (Polivy et al. 1994). Overeating is therefore functional for dieters as it masks dysphoria and this function is not influenced by the sensory aspects of eating.

The role of denial

Cognitive research illustrates that thought suppression and thought control can have the paradoxical effect of making the thoughts that the individual is trying to suppress more salient (Wenzlaff and Wegner 2000). This has been called the 'theory of ironic processes of mental control' (Wegner 1994). For example, in an early study participants were asked to try not to think of a white bear but to ring a bell if they did (Wegner et al. 1987). The results showed that those who were trying not to think about the bear thought about the bear more frequently than those who were told to think about it. Similar results have been found for thinking about sex (Wegner et al. 1999), thinking about mood (Wegner et al. 1993) and thinking about a stigma (Smart and Wegner 1999). A decision not to eat specific foods or to eat less is central to the dieter's cognitive set. This results in a similar state of denial and attempted thought suppression and dieters have been shown to see food in terms of 'forbiddenness' (e.g. King et al. 1987) and to show a preoccupation with the food that they are trying to deny themselves (Grilo et al. 1989; Ogden 1995a). Therefore, as soon as food is denied it simultaneously becomes forbidden which translates into eating which undermines any attempts at weight loss. Boon et al. (2002) directly applied the theory of ironic processes of thought control to dieting and overeating. They used a factorial design and a standard preload taste test paradigm. Restrained and unrestrained eaters were given a preload that they were told was either high or low in calories and then were either distracted or not distracted. Their food intake was then measured in a taste test. The results showed that the restrained eaters ate particularly more than the unrestrained eaters in the high calorie condition if they were distracted. The authors argued that this lends support to the theory of ironic processes as the restrained eaters have a limited cognitive capacity, and when this capacity is 'filled' up by the distraction their preoccupation with food can be translated into eating. In a similar vein Soetens et al. (2006) used an experimental design to explore the impact of trying to suppress eating-related thoughts on subsequent thoughts about eating. The sample was divided into restrained and unrestrained eaters; the restrained eaters were then divided into those who were either high or low on disinhibition. The results showed that the disinhibited restrained eaters (i.e. those who try to eat less but often overeat) used more thought suppression than the other groups. The results also showed that this group also showed a rebound effect following the thought suppression task. This means that restrained eaters who tend to overeat try to suppress thoughts about food more often, but if they do, they think about food more often afterwards.

Escape theory

Researchers have also used escape theory to explain overeating (Heatherton and Baumeister 1991; Heatherton et al. 1991, 1993). This perspective has been applied to both the overeating characteristic of dieters and the more extreme form of binge eating found in bulimics, and describes overeating as a consequence of 'a motivated shift to low levels of self-awareness' (Heatherton and Baumeister 1991). It is argued that individuals prone to overeating show comparisons with 'high standards and demanding ideals' (Heatherton and Baumeister 1991: 89) and that this results in low self-esteem, self-dislike and lowered mood. It is also argued that inhibitions exist at high levels of awareness when the individual is aware of the meanings associated with certain behaviours. In terms of the overeater, a state of high self-awareness can become unpleasant as it results in self-criticism and low mood. However, such a state is accompanied by the existence of inhibitions. The individual is therefore motivated to escape from self-awareness to avoid the accompanying unpleasantness, but although such a shift in self-awareness may provide relief from self-criticism, it results in a reduction in inhibitions thereby causing overeating. Within this analysis disinhibitory overeating is indicative of a shift from high to low self-awareness and a subsequent reduction in inhibitions.

Overeating as a relapse

Parallels exist between the undereating and overeating of the restrained eater and the behaviour of the relapsing smoker or alcoholic. The traditional biomedical perspective of addictive behaviours viewed addictions as being irreversible and out of the individual's control (see Chapter 5). It has been argued that this perspective encourages the belief that the behaviour is either 'all or nothing', and that this belief is responsible for the high relapse rate shown by both alcoholics and smokers (Marlatt and Gordon 1985). Thus the abstaining alcoholic believes in either total abstention or relapse, which itself may promote the progression from lapse to full-blown relapse. In the case of the restrained eater, it is possible that they too believe in the 'all or nothing' theory of excess which promotes the shift from a high calorie lapse to the 'what the hell' characterized by disinhibition. This transition from lapse to relapse and the associated changes in mood and cognitions is illustrated in Figure 6.8.

These parallels have been supported by research suggesting that both excessive eating and alcohol use can be triggered by high risk situations and low mood (Brownell et al. 1986b; Grilo et al. 1989). In addition, the transition from lapse to relapse in both alcohol and eating behaviour has been found to be related to the internal attributions (e.g. 'I am to blame') for the original lapse (e.g. Ogden and Wardle 1990). In particular, researchers exploring relapses in addictive behaviours describe the 'abstinence violation effect' which describes the transition from a lapse (one drink) to a relapse (becoming drunk) as involving cognitive dissonance (e.g. 'I am trying not to drink but I have just had a drink'), internal attributions (e.g. 'It is my fault') and guilt (e.g. 'I am a useless person') (Marlatt and Gordon 1985). These factors find reflection in the overeating shown by dieters (Ogden and Wardle 1990).

The role of control

The interview data from a study of 25 women who were attempting to lose weight provide further insights into the mechanisms behind overeating (Ogden 1992). The results from this study indicated that the women described their dieting behaviour in terms of the impact on their family life, a preoccupation with food and weight and changes in mood. However, the concept of self-control transcended these themes. For example, when describing how she had prepared a meal for her family, one woman said, 'I did not want to give in, but I felt that after preparing a three-course meal for everyone else, the least I could do was enjoy my efforts'.

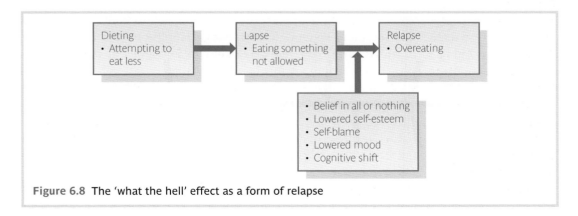

Figure 6.8 The 'what the hell' effect as a form of relapse

The sense of not giving in suggests an attempt to impose control over her eating. In terms of the preoccupation with food, one woman said, 'Why should I deprive myself of nice food?' and another said, 'Now that I've eaten that I might as well give in to all the drives to eat'. Such statements again illustrate a sense of self-control and a feeling that eating reflects a breakdown in this control. In terms of mood, one woman said that she was 'depressed that something as simple as eating cannot be controlled'. Likewise this role of self-control was also apparent in the women's negative descriptions of themselves, with one woman saying, 'I'm just totally hopeless and weak, and though I hate being fat I just don't have the willpower to do anything about it'.

In summary, restraint theory indicates that dieting is linked with overeating and research inspired by this perspective has explored the processes involved in triggering this behaviour. Studies have used experimental and descriptive designs and suggest a role for physiological boundaries, cognitive shifts, mood modification, denial, a shift in self-awareness and control. These are illustrated in Figure 6.9.

Dieting and weight loss

Dieting is therefore associated with periods of overeating. Research indicates that this is sometimes translated into weight fluctuations. Although dieters aim to lose weight by attempting to restrict their food intake, this aim is only sometimes achieved. Heatherton et al. (1991) reported that restrained eaters show both under- and overeating and that this behaviour results in weight fluctuations but not actual weight loss. Thus actual weight loss is limited by compensatory overeating. Heatherton et al. (1988: 20) argued that 'the restrained eater who is exclusively restrained . . . is not representative of restrained eaters in general, whereas the restrained eater who occasionally splurges is'. Ogden (1993) examined the concept of restraint as assessed by a variety of measures and found that high scorers on measures of restraint were characterized by both successful and failed restriction, suggesting that restrained eating is best characterized as an intention which is only sporadically realized. Therefore 'to diet' is probably best understood as 'attempting to lose weight but not doing so' and 'attempting to eat less which often results in eating more'.

The role of dieting in mood and cognitive changes

A classic study by Keys et al. (1950) suggested that overeating is not the only possible consequence of restricting food intake. The study involved 36 healthy non-dieting men who were conscientious objectors from the Korean War. They received a carefully controlled daily food

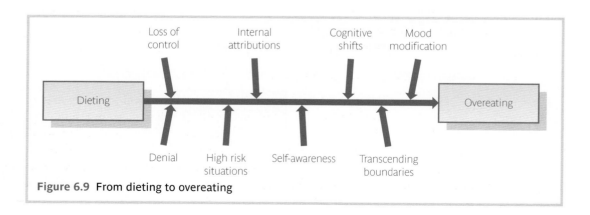

Figure 6.9 From dieting to overeating

Testing a theory – overeating as a rebellion

A study to examine the cognitive changes to preloading using self-report and the Stroop task (Ogden and Greville 1993).

The aim of this study was to examine changes in cognitive state in dieters and non-dieters following the consumption of a 'forbidden food'. The study used both self-report measures and the Stroop task to examine these changes. Self-report measures provide some insights into an individual's state of mind, but are open to factors such as denial and expectancy effects. The Stroop task, however, also aims to access an individual's cognitions but without these problems. The Stroop task is a useful cognitive tool which can be applied to study a range of behaviours and beliefs other than eating.

Background

Dieters have been shown to overeat following a high calorie preload. This behaviour has been called disinhibition or the 'what the hell' effect. The boundary model of overeating suggests that the preload forces the dieters to cross their diet boundary and consequently overeat. It has been suggested that this overeating may be related to lowered mood (either as a result of the preload or independently) and/or changes in their cognitive state. This study aimed to examine shifts in cognitive state following the consumption of a 'forbidden food' using self-report measures and the Stroop task.

Methodology

Subjects

A total of 56 female subjects from a London university took part in the study and were categorized as either restrained eaters or unrestrained eaters according to their scores on the restrained eating section of the Dutch eating behaviour questionnaire (DEBQ) (van Strien et al. 1986). They ranged in age from 19 to 25 years and were of average weight.

Design

The subjects were randomly allocated to one of two conditions (low calorie preload versus high calorie preload) and completed a set of rating scales and the Stroop tasks before and after the preload.

Procedure

After completing the rating scales and the Stroop tasks, the subjects were given either a high calorie preload (a chocolate bar) or a low calorie preload (a cream cracker). Subjects then completed the ratings scales and Stroop tasks again.

Measures

The following measures were completed before and after the preload:

1 *Stroop tasks.* The original Stroop task (Stroop 1935) involved a repeated set of colour names (e.g. 'green', 'red', 'blue', 'black') written on a card in different colour inks (e.g. green, red, blue, black). Subjects were asked to name the colour of the ink (not the word itself). For example, if the word 'green' was written in blue ink, the subject should say 'blue'. The time to complete the task was recorded and it was argued that a longer time indicated greater interference of the meaning of the word. Research has used the Stroop

task to examine anxiety, phobias and post-traumatic stress disorder using words such as 'fear', 'anxiety' and 'panic' instead of names of colours. Subjects are still asked to name the colour of the ink and it has been suggested that longer times infer that the words are more relevant to the individual's concerns. For example, an anxious subject would take longer to colour name anxiety-related words than a non-anxious one. The present study used an adaptation of the Stroop task to examine: (1) 'food' words; (2) 'body shape' words and words relating to the individual; and (3) cognitive state, in order to assess the effect of pre-loading on the subjects' processing of these words.

- Food Stroop: the subjects were asked to colour name a set of food-related words (e.g. dinner, cake, sugar), which were compared with a set of neutral words matched for word length and frequency (e.g. record, powder, boot).
- Body shape Stroop: the subjects colour named body shape words (e.g. chest, fat, thigh) and matched neutral words (e.g. crowd, grass, rust).
- Cognitive state: items were included to examine two types of cognitive state, which were hypothesized to trigger overeating. These were a 'passive cognitive state' (e.g. submit, quit, abandon) representing 'giving in to the overpowering drive to eat' and an 'active cognitive state' (e.g. rebellious, defiant, challenge) representing overeating as an active decision to rebel against self-imposed restraint.

2 *Rating scales.* The subjects also completed the following set of rating scales:

- Motivational state: the subjects completed ratings of their hunger and fullness using visual analogue scales ('not at all hungry/full' to 'as hungry/full as I've ever been').
- Mood: anxiety and depression were measured using the profile of mood state checklist (McNair et al. 1971).
- Cognitive state: the active and passive cognitive states were measured using a checklist of relevant items.

Results

The results for the Stroop tasks were analysed by creating a pure reaction time (experimental words – matched control words) and then by assessing the effect of condition (low preload versus high preload) on the change in the reaction time from before the preload to after the preload. The results showed that the dieters responded to the high calorie preload with increases in 'rebelliousness', as measured by the active cognitive state Stroop, increases in pre-occupation with body shape and increases in the preoccupation with food, as indicated by retarded reaction times on these tasks compared with the non-dieters, and the dieters' responses to the low calorie preload. The results also suggested that the dieters showed an increase in rebelliousness as measured by the rating scales.

Conclusion

The results suggest that overeating in dieters in response to preloading may be related to increased feelings of rebelliousness ('what the hell, I'm going to eat whatever I want'), increased concern with body shape and increased preoccupation with food. These results indicate that diet-breaking behaviour shown by normal-weight dieters, the obese on weight-reduction pro-grammes and bulimics may relate to an active decision to overeat and suggest that perhaps self-imposed limits ('I'm going to eat less') may activate a desire to rebel against these limits.

intake of approximately half their normal intake for a period of 12 weeks, and consequently lost 25 per cent of their original body weight. Keys stated that they developed a preoccupation with food, often resulting in hoarding or stealing it. They showed an inability to concentrate and mood changes, with depression and apathy being common. At the end of the period of dieting, the men were allowed to eat freely. They often ate continuously and reported loss of control over their eating behaviour, sometimes resulting in binge eating. The authors concluded that these effects were probably due to the restriction of their diet. To examine the effects of dieting without extreme weight loss, Warren and Cooper (1988) carried out a controlled study for a two-week period and found that food restriction resulted in increased preoccupation with food. In a further study, Ogden (1995a) monitored the effects of self-imposed dieting over a six-week period and reported increased depression and preoccupation with food. These results suggest that dieting can have several negative consequences and that these changes are possibly involved in causing overeating.

Restraint theory therefore suggests that:

- Dieters aim to eat less as a means to lose weight and change their body shape. At times this aim is achieved and they successfully manage to restrict their food intake. Dieters therefore sometimes show undereating. Sometimes they eat the same as non-dieters.

- Dieters, however, also show episodes of overeating, particularly in response to triggers such as high calorie preloads, anxiety or smoking abstinence.

- This overeating can be understood in terms of the transgression of boundaries, shifts in cognitive set, mood modification, a response to denial, an escape from awareness, a lapse or changes in self-control. Increasing or promoting dieting can result in an increased pre-occupation with food, increased depression and, paradoxically, increased eating behaviour.

The dieter's aim to eat less and consequently to lose weight is rarely achieved and this failure may be a product of changes that occur as a direct response to imposing a cognitive structure upon eating behaviour. Dieting is also related to changes in weight in terms of weight variability, the development of eating disorders and the onset and progression of obesity.

Problems with a weight concern model of eating behaviour

Although a weight concern model of eating and restraint theory has generated a wealth of research and provided an insight into overeating behaviour, there are several problems with this theory:

- Central to the boundary model is the traditional dualistic division between mind and body. The concept of separate biological and psychological boundaries suggests that the physical and psychological are separate entities which interact.

- Restraint theory relies on a belief in the association between food restriction and overeating. However, although dieters, bulimics and bingeing anorexics report episodes of overeating, restricting anorexics cannot be accounted for by restraint theory. If attempting not to eat results in overeating, how do anorexics manage to starve themselves?

- If attempting not to eat something results in eating it, how do vegetarians manage never to eat meat?

To conclude

Although notions of what constitutes a healthy diet have changed over time, currently the consensus states that a healthy diet should be high in carbohydrate and low in fat. Diet is related to health in terms of promoting good health and managing illness. This chapter has explored three core approaches which have been used to understand eating behaviour. Developmental models emphasize the importance of learning by association and reward, cognitive models emphasize the role of beliefs and attitudes, and weight concern research highlights the impact of body dissatisfaction and dieting on food intake.

❓ Questions

1 How might parents influence their children's eating behaviour?

2 How do our beliefs about food influence what we eat?

3 What are the problems with the developmental and cognitive models of eating behaviour?

4 Dieting causes overeating. Discuss.

5 How could a parent limit their child's intake of unhealthy foods without making those foods 'forbidden fruit'?

6 To what extent is our food intake governed by taste?

For discussion

Think of someone you know who has successfully changed their eating behaviour (e.g. become a vegetarian, eaten less, cut out chocolate). What factors contributed towards their success?

Further reading

Connor, M. and Armitage, C. (2003) *The Social Psychology of Eating*. Maidenhead: Open University Press.

This book provides a good overview of the more social perspectives on why we eat what we eat.

Ogden, J. (2003) *The Psychology of Eating: From Healthy to Disordered Behaviour*. Oxford: Blackwell.

This book provides a detailed map of research relating to eating behaviour, obesity and eating disorders and addresses questions such as 'Why do so many people not eat a healthy diet?', 'Why do women feel unhappy with their body shape?', 'What are the causes of obesity?', 'Why do people develop eating disorders?'. It is written in a similar style to this textbook.

Szmukler, G., Dare, C. and Treasure, J. (eds) (1995) *Handbook of Eating Disorders: Theory Research and Treatment*. London: Wiley.

Eating disorders are not usually covered within health psychology. For those interested, this book provides a detailed account of current theory and research.

Chapter 7

Exercise

Chapter overview

Over the past few decades, there has been an increasing interest in the role of exercise in promoting health. This chapter examines the development of the contemporary interest in exercise and describes definitions of exercise and fitness. The chapter then examines the physical and psychological benefits of exercise, describes programmes designed to increase exercise uptake and evaluates social/political and individual predictors of exercise behaviour.

This chapter covers

- What is exercise?
- Why exercise?
- What factors predict exercise?
- Exercise relapse

Developing the contemporary concern with exercise behaviour

Until the 1960s exercise was done by the young and talented and the emphasis was on excellence. The Olympics, Wimbledon tennis and football leagues were for those individuals who were the best at their game and who strove to win. At this time, the focus was on high levels of physical fitness for the élite. However, at the beginning of the 1960s there was a shift in perspective. The 'Sport for All' initiative developed by the Council of Europe, the creation of a Minister for Sport and the launching of the Sports Council suggested a shift towards exercise for everyone. Local councils were encouraged to build swimming pools, sports centres and golf courses. However, although these initiatives included everyone, the emphasis was still on high levels of fitness and the recommended levels of exercise were intensive. The 'no pain, no gain' philosophy abounded. More recently, however, there has been an additional shift. Exercise is no longer for the élite, nor does it have to be at intensive and often impossible levels. Government initiatives such as 'Look After Yourself', 'Feeling Great' and 'Fun Runs' encourage everyone to be involved at a manageable level. In addition, the emphasis is no longer on fitness, but on both physical and psychological health. Contemporary messages about exercise promote moderate exercise for everyone to improve general (physical and psychological) well-being. In addition, there is also an increasing recognition that exercise that can be included in a person's daily life may be the way to create maximum health benefits. The most sedentary members of the population are more likely to make and sustain smaller changes in lifestyle such as walking, cycling and stair use rather than the more dramatic changes required by the uptake of rigorous exercise programmes. This shift in perspective is illustrated by contemporary research on the benefits of exercise.

What is exercise?

Aspects of exercise have been defined in different ways according to intention, outcome and location.

1 *Intention.* Some researchers have differentiated between different types of behaviours in terms of the individual's intentions. For example, Caspersen et al. (1985) distinguished between physical activity and exercise. *Physical activity* has been defined as 'any bodily movement produced by skeletal muscles which results in energy expenditure'. This perspective emphasizes the physical and biological changes that happen both automatically and through intention. *Exercise* has been defined as 'planned, structured and repetitive bodily movement done to improve or maintain one or more components of physical fitness'. This perspective emphasizes the physical and biological changes that happen as a result of intentional movements.

2 *Outcome.* Distinctions have also been made in terms of the outcome of the behaviour. For example, Blair et al. (1992) differentiated between physical exercise that improves fitness and physical exercise that improves health. This distinction illustrates a shift in emphasis from intensive exercise resulting in cardiovascular fitness to moderate exercise resulting in mild changes in health status. It also illustrates a shift towards using a definition of health that includes both biological and psychological changes.

3 *Location.* Distinctions have also been made in terms of location. For example, Paffenbarger and Hale (1975) differentiated between *occupational activity*, which was performed as part of an individual's daily work, and *leisure activity*, which was carried out in the individual's leisure time.

These definitions are not mutually exclusive and illustrate the different ways that exercise has been conceptualized.

Who exercises?

The Healthy People 2000 programmes in the USA show that only 23 per cent of adults engage in light to moderate physical activity five times per week and up to a third remain completely sedentary across all industrialized countries (Allied Dunbar National Fitness Survey 1992; United States National Center for Health Statistics 1996). The results of a survey in 2003 in which men and women in the UK were asked about their exercise behaviour over the past 12 months are shown in Figure 7.1. They suggest that the five most common forms of exercise are walking (46 per cent), swimming (35 per cent), keep fit/yoga (22 per cent), cycling (19 per cent) and snooker/pool/billiards (17 per cent). Overall, 75 per cent of adults had taken part in some sport/game/physical activity in the past 12 months but men were generally more likely to have done so than women and activity generally decreased with age.

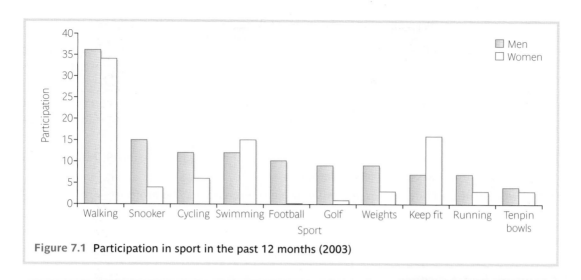

Figure 7.1 Participation in sport in the past 12 months (2003)

Box 7.1 **Some problems with . . . exercise research**

Below are some problems with research in this area that you may wish to consider.

1 Measuring exercise behaviour is difficult as some exercise takes the form of structured organized activity such as sport, whereas some takes the form of behaviour which is integrated in a person's daily life such as walking and stair climbing. Self-report measures may be inaccurate and more objective measures (e.g. monitors) may actually change behaviour.

2 Exercise can promote both psychological (e.g. well-being) and physiological (e.g. heart rate) changes. Working out how these changes interact is complicated. Further, combining research is made difficult as some studies focus on psychological outcomes while others rely upon physiological outcomes.

3 Exercise is mostly studied as a behaviour that is under the control of the individual, that is, we explore whether a person's beliefs, emotions or motivations determine whether or not they exercise. However, it is also a behaviour that is very much determined by the environment which may not be controllable. For example, structural factors such as safe paths, street lighting, free access to sport centres, and town planning may have an enormous impact upon activity levels. Research needs to incorporate such factors into the models used.

Why exercise?

Research has examined the possible physical and psychological benefits of exercise.

The physical benefits of exercise

Longevity

Paffenbarger et al. (1986) examined the relationship between weekly energy expenditure and longevity for a group of 16,936 Harvard alumni aged 35 to 70. They reported the results from a longitudinal study which suggested that individuals with a weekly energy expenditure of more than 2000 kcals on exercise reported as walking, stair climbing and sports, lived for 2.5 years longer on average than those with an energy expenditure of less than 500 kcal per week on these activities.

The possible reasons for the effects of exercise on longevity are as follows:

1 *Reduction in blood pressure:* physical activity has an inverse relationship to both diastolic and systolic blood pressure. Therefore increased exercise decreases blood pressure. This effect is particularly apparent in those who have mild or moderately raised blood pressure.

2 *Reduction in weight and obesity:* overweight and obesity are related to certain cancers, hypertension and coronary heart disease. Exercise may help promote weight loss/maintenance (see Chapter 15 for details of exercise and obesity).

3 *Reduction in diabetes:* exercise may be related to improved glucose control, resulting in a reduction in the possible effects of diabetes.

4 *Protection against osteoporosis and thinning bones:* exercise may be protective against osteoporosis, which is common among older women.

5 *Reduction in coronary heart disease:* the main effect of exercise is on the occurrence of coronary heart disease and rehabilitation following a heart attack.

Coronary heart disease

The effects of exercise on coronary heart disease have been examined by assessing the consequences of both occupational activity and leisure activity. Regarding *occupational activity*, Paffenbarger and Hale (1975) followed up 3975 longshoremen for 22 years. Longshoremen have occupations that involve a range of energy expenditure. The results showed that at the end of this period, 11 per cent had died from coronary heart disease and that those longshoremen who expended more than 8500 kcal per week had a significantly lower risk of coronary heart disease than those in jobs requiring less energy. This difference remained when other risk factors such as smoking and blood pressure were controlled. This relationship between occupational activity and coronary heart disease has also been shown in samples of both men and women (Salonen et al. 1982).

Research has also evaluated the relationship between *leisure-time activity* and coronary heart disease. Morris et al. (1980) followed up a group of middle-aged sedentary office workers over 8.5 years and compared those who engaged in sport with those who reported no leisure-time activity. The results showed that those who attempted to keep fit showed less than half the incidence of coronary heart disease at follow-up compared with the other subjects. This association has also been reported in students in the USA (Paffenbarger et al. 1978, 1983, 1986).

Regardless of the location of the activity, research indicates an association between physical fitness and health status. Blair (1993) has carried out much research in this area and has argued that increases in fitness and physical activity can result in significant reductions in the relative risk of disease and mortality (see also Blair et al. 1989, 1995, 1996). For example, Blair et al. (1989) examined the role of generalized physical fitness and health status in 10,224 men and 3120 women for eight years and reported that physical fitness was related to a decrease in both mortality rates (all cause) and coronary heart disease. Blair has also explored the relationship between fatness and fitness. The data from one study are shown in Figure 7.2.

This study indicated that overweight men and women who showed low fitness scores had a high risk of all-cause mortality. Those overweight individuals, however, who showed either medium fitness scores or high fitness scores showed a substantial reduction in this risk. Fitness was therefore protective against the effects of fatness.

Exercise may influence coronary heart disease in the following ways:

1 Increased muscular activity may protect the cardiovascular system by stimulating the muscles that support the heart.

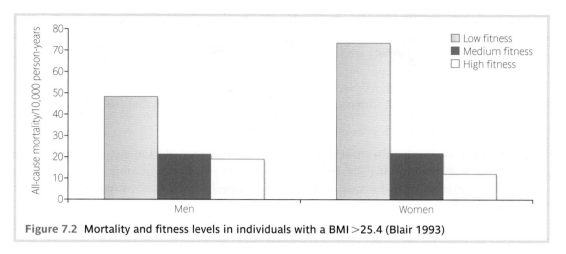

Figure 7.2 Mortality and fitness levels in individuals with a BMI >25.4 (Blair 1993)

2 Increased exercise may increase the electrical activity of the heart.

3 Increased exercise may increase an individual's resistance to ventricular fibrillation.

4 Exercise may be protective against other risk factors for coronary heart disease (e.g. obesity, hypertension).

The physical benefits of exercise have been summarized by Smith and Jacobson (1989) as: (1) improved cardiovascular function; (2) increased muscle size and strength and ligament strength for maintaining posture, preventing joint instability and decreasing back pain; (3) improved work effort; and (4) changing body composition.

The psychological benefits of exercise

Research also indicates that exercise may improve psychological well-being. These effects are outlined below.

Depression

Research using correlational designs suggests an association between the amount of exercise carried out by an individual and their level of depression. Many of the reviews into this association have stressed the correlational nature of the research and the inherent problems in determining causality (e.g. Morgan and O'Connor 1988). However, McDonald and Hodgdon (1991) carried out a meta-analysis of both the correlational and experimental research into the association between depression and exercise. They concluded that aerobic exercise was related to a decrease in depression and that this effect was greatest in those with higher levels of initial depressive symptoms. In an attempt to clarify the problem of causality, McCann and Holmes (1984) carried out an experimental study to evaluate the effect of manipulating exercise levels on depression. Forty-three female students who scored higher than the cut-off point on the Beck depression inventory (BDI) were randomly allocated to one of three groups: (1) aerobic exercise group (one hour of exercise, twice a week for ten weeks); (2) placebo group (relaxation); (3) no treatment. After five weeks, the results showed a significant reduction in depressive symptomatology in the exercise group compared with the other two subject groups, supporting the relationship between exercise and depression and suggesting a causal link between these two variables, that is, increased exercise resulted in a reduction in depression. However, the authors report that subsequent exercise had no further effects. Hall et al. (2002)

also used an experimental design to explore the relationship between exercise and affect with 30 volunteers rating their affective state every minute as they ran on a treadmill. The results showed improvements in affect from baseline to follow-up which supports previous research suggesting that exercise is beneficial. However, the results also showed a brief deterioration in mood mid-exercise. The authors suggest that although prolonged exercise may improve mood, this dip in mood may explain why people fail to adhere to exercise programmes.

Anxiety

Research has also indicated that exercise may be linked to a reduction in anxiety. Again, there are problems with determining the direction of causality in this relationship, but it has been suggested that exercise may decrease anxiety by diverting the individual's attention away from the source of anxiety.

Response to stress

Exercise has been presented as a mediating factor for the stress response (see Chapters 10 and 11). Exercise may influence stress either by changing an individual's appraisal of a potentially stressful event by distraction or diversion (e.g. 'This situation could be stressful but if I exercise I will not have to think about it') or may act as a potential coping strategy to be activated once an event has been appraised as stressful (e.g. 'Although the situation is stressful, I shall now exercise to take my mind off things').

Self-esteem and self-confidence

It has also been suggested that exercise may enhance an individual's psychological well-being by improving self-esteem and self-confidence. King et al. (1992) report that the psychological consequences of exercise may be related to improved body satisfaction, which may correlate to general self-esteem and confidence. In addition, exercise may result in an improved sense of achievement and self-efficacy.

Exercise and smoking withdrawal

Many people experience withdrawal symptoms such as agitation, craving and the desire to smoke, irritability and restlessness when they have stopped smoking, even for just a few hours. Some research has explored the effectiveness of exercise at reducing withdrawal symptoms following smoking cessation. For example, Ussher et al. (2001) explored the impact of a 10-minute period of exercise of moderate intensity on withdrawal symptoms caused by an overnight period of smoking cessation. The results showed that those who had exercised reported a significant reduction in withdrawal symptoms while exercising which lasted up to 15 mins post-exercise. In a similar vein Daniel et al. (2004) examined the impact of either light intensity or moderate intensity exercise and reported that only moderate intensity exercise reduced withdrawal symptoms. As a means to explore why exercise might have this effect, Daniel et al. (2006) compared exercise with a cognitive distraction task to see whether the benefits of exercise were due to exercise *per se* or just the process of doing something to take one's mind off smoking. The results showed that exercise was still more effective when compared to the distraction task. In addition, this effect was not just due to the impact of exercise on mood.

How does exercise influence psychological well-being?

Many theories have been developed to explain the factors that mediate the link between exercise and psychological state. These reflect both the *physiological* and *psychological* approaches to the study of exercise. For example, it has been argued that exercise results in the release of endorphins, the brain's natural opioids (Steinberg and Sykes 1985), and increases in the levels of brain norepinephrine, reductions of which can cause depression. It has also been suggested that improved psychological state is related to the social activity often associated with exercise and the resulting increased confidence and self-esteem. Any reduction in levels of depression may be related to greater social contact, improved social support and increased self-efficacy.

Testing a theory – exercise and mood

A study to examine the effects of exercise on mood (Steptoe et al. 1993).

This study examined the relationship between exercise and mood. Because of the experimental design, the results allow some conclusions to be made about the direction of causality.

Background

Exercise is believed to be important for a healthy life. However, as with many health-related behaviours, adherence to health promotion recommendations may be more motivated by short-term immediate effects (e.g. feeling good) than the potential changes in the long term (e.g. living longer). Therefore understanding the immediate effects of exercise on mood has obvious implications for encouraging individuals to take regular exercise. Steptoe et al. (1993) examined changes in mood, mental vigour and exhilaration in sportsmen and inactive men following maximal, moderate and minimal exercise.

Methodology
Subjects

The subjects were 36 male amateur athletes who were regularly involved in a variety of sports and exercised for more than 30 minutes at least three times per week, and 36 inactive men who exercised for less than 30 minutes per week.

Design

All subjects took part in two exercise sessions and completed measures of mood before and after each exercise session. This study was therefore experimental in design and involved repeated measures.

Procedure

At session 1, all subjects completed a set of profile questionnaires (background physical and psychological measures) and took part in a maximal exercise session on a cycle ergometer. Maximal exercise was determined by oxygen uptake. At session 2, subjects were randomly allocated to 20 minutes of either maximal, moderate or minimal exercise. All subjects completed ratings of mood before exercise, 2 minutes after exercise and after 30 minutes of recovery.

Measures

The subjects rated items relating to tension/anxiety, mental vigour, depression/dejection, exhilaration and perceived exertion before and after each exercise session. In addition, all subjects completed measures of (1) personality and (2) trait anxiety once only at the beginning of the first session.

▶ **Results**

The results were analysed to examine the effect of the differing degrees of exercise on changes in mood in the sportsmen and the inactive men. The results showed that only the sportsmen reported decreases in tension/anxiety after the maximal exercise. However, *all* subjects reported increased exhilaration and increased mental vigour two minutes after both the maximal and moderate exercise compared with the minimal condition, and in addition, the increase in exhilaration was maintained after the 30 minutes of recovery.

Conclusion

The authors conclude that both maximal and moderate exercise results in beneficial changes in both mental vigour and exhilaration in both sportsmen and inactive men and suggest that 'exercise leads to positive mood changes even among people who are unaccustomed to physical exertion'. They also suggest that greater attention to the immediate effects of exercise may improve adherence to exercise programmes.

What factors predict exercise?

Because of the potential benefits of exercise, research has evaluated which factors are related to exercise behaviour. The determinants of exercise can be categorized as either social/political or individual.

Social/political predictors of exercise

An increased reliance on technology and reduced daily activity in paid and domestic work may have resulted in an increase in the number of people having relatively sedentary lifestyles. In addition, a shift towards a belief that exercise is good for an individual's well-being and is relevant for everyone has set the scene for social and political changes in terms of emphasizing exercise. Therefore, since the late 1960s many government initiatives have aimed to promote sport and exercise. Factors such as the availability of facilities and cultural attitudes towards exercise may be related to individual participation. Consequently the Sports Council launched an official campaign in 1972 in an attempt to create a suitable climate for increasing exercise behaviour. Initiatives such as 'Sport for All', 'Fun Runs' and targets for council facilities, such as swimming pools and sports centres, were part of this initiative. In collaboration with the Sports Council, McIntosh and Charlton (1985) reported that the provision of council services had exceeded the Sports Council's targets by 100 per cent. This evaluation concluded that:

- central government funding for sport and specific local authority allocations have helped participation in sport
- despite small improvements, the Sport for All objective is far from being realized and inequalities persist
- inequalities in the provision of sport facilities have diminished – especially for indoor sport
- the recognition of the Sports Council's earlier emphasis on élite sports has been slow and disproportionately large amounts of the Council's funds are still being spent on élite sport.

One recent approach to increasing exercise uptake is the exercise prescription scheme whereby GPs refer targeted patients for exercise. Therefore, in the same way that an overweight or depressed patient would be referred to see a counsellor, or a patient with a suspected skin cancer would be referred to a hospital specialist, a GP can now also refer a patient for exercise. This could take the form of vouchers for free access to the local leisure centre, an exercise routine with a health and fitness adviser at the leisure centre, or recommendations from the health and fitness adviser to follow a home-based exercise programme, such as walking.

An alternative and simpler approach involves the promotion of stair rather than escalator or lift use. Interventions to promote stair use are cheap and can target a large population. In addition, they can target the most sedentary members of the population who are least likely to adopt more structured forms of exercise. This is in line with calls to promote changes in exercise behaviour which can be incorporated into everyday life (Dunn et al. 1998). Research also indicates that stair climbing can lead to weight loss, improved fitness and energy expenditure and reduced risk of osteoporosis in women (e.g. Brownell et al. 1980; Boreham et al. 2000). Some research has therefore attempted to increase stair use. For example, some research has explored the impact of motivational posters between stairs and escalators or lifts and has shown that such a simple intervention can increase stair walking (e.g. Andersen et al. 1998; Russell et al. 1999; Kerr et al. 2001). In a more detailed study, Kerr et al. (2001) explored what characteristics of poster prompts was most effective and explored whether this varied according to message, gender and setting. The results showed that larger posters were more effective at promoting stair use, that effectiveness was not related overall to whether the message emphasized time and health (i.e. 'stay healthy, save time, use the stairs') or just health (i.e. 'stay healthy, use the stairs'), but that whereas the message including time was more effective for women in the train station, it was more effective for men when presented at a shopping centre.

Therefore these initiatives have aimed to develop a suitable climate for promoting exercise. In addition, as a result of government emphasis on exercise, specific exercise programmes have been established in an attempt to assess the best means of encouraging participation. In particular it is possible to differentiate between individual and supervised exercise programmes.

Individual versus supervised exercise programmes

King et al. (1991) carried out a study in the USA to examine the relative value of individual versus supervised exercise programmes. Using random telephone numbers they identified 357 adults, aged 50–65, who led relatively sedentary lifestyles. These subjects were then randomly allocated to one of four groups:

- Group 1: the subjects were encouraged to attend a one-hour vigorous exercise session at a local community centre at least three times a week.
- Group 2: the subjects were instructed to do some intensive exercise on their own and were encouraged and monitored with periodic phone calls.
- Group 3: the subjects were instructed to do lower intensity exercise on their own.
- Group 4: the control subjects were not instructed to do any exercise.

The results showed greater adherence in the unsupervised home-based programmes than in the supervised programme. However, all subjects who had been instructed to do some exercise showed an increase in cardiovascular fitness compared with the control group. The authors suggested that the results from this study provide insights into the development of successful national campaigns to promote exercise behaviour that involve a minimal and cheap intervention and argued for an emphasis on unsupervised individual exercising.

Other factors that appear to play a role in developing successful exercise programmes are the use of behavioural contracts, whereby the individual signs a contract with an instructor agreeing to participate in a programme for a set period of time (e.g. Oldridge and Jones 1983) and the use of instructor praise and feedback and flexible goal-setting by the subject (e.g. Martin et al. 1984). These factors involve supervised exercise and suggest that individualized exercise programmes may not be the only form of intervention.

The social/political climate therefore has implications for predicting and promoting exercise. However, even if councils provide the facilities and government programmes are established, individuals have to make decisions about whether or not to participate. Research has therefore also examined the individual predictors of exercise behaviour.

Individual predictors of exercise

Dishman and colleagues (Dishman 1982; Dishman and Gettman 1980) carried out a series of studies to examine the best individual predictors of exercise and suggested that these factors can be defined as either non-modifiable or modifiable.

Non-modifiable predictors of exercise

Dishman (1982) reported that non-modifiable factors such as age, education, smoking, ease of access to facilities, body fat/weight and self-motivation were good predictors of exercise. The results of a prospective study indicated that the best predictors of exercise behaviour were low body fat, low weight and high self-motivation (Dishman and Gettman 1980). However, whether factors such as access to facilities and self-motivation should be regarded as non-modifiable is problematic. King et al. (1992) reported the results of a study that evaluated the factors predicting being active in leisure time. They described the profile of an active individual as younger, better educated, more affluent and more likely to be male. However, it is possible that other individuals (less affluent/less educated) may be more active at work. Research has also examined ethnic differences in predicting exercise behaviour. Several studies indicate that blacks are less active than whites, that black women are especially less active and that these differences persist even when income and education are controlled (e.g. Shea et al. 1992).

Modifiable predictors of exercise

Dishman et al. (1985) summarized the following variables as modifiable predictors:

- *Childhood exercise*: individuals who exercise as children are more likely to exercise as adults.
- *Positive self-image*: research also indicates that a positive self-image and confidence in one's ability influence future activity levels.
- *No role for knowledge*: interestingly the research suggests that good knowledge about the benefits of exercise does not predict exercise behaviour.

The role of attitudes and beliefs

Research has examined the role of attitudes and beliefs in predicting exercise. Research into beliefs has used either a cross-sectional or a prospective design. Cross-sectional research examines the relationships between variables that co-occur, whereas prospective research attempts to predict future behaviour.

Cross-sectional research

This type of research indicates a role for the following beliefs and attitudes:

■ *Perceived social benefits of exercise.* Research examining the predictors of exercise behaviour consistently suggests that the main factors motivating exercise are the beliefs that it is enjoyable and provides social contact. In a cross-sectional study examining the differences in attitude between joggers and non-joggers, the non-joggers reported beliefs that exercise required too much discipline, too much time, they did not believe in the positive effects of jogging and reported a lower belief that significant others valued regular jogging (Riddle 1980).

■ *Value on health.* Although many individuals exercise for reasons other than health, a MORI poll in 1984 suggested that the second main correlate of exercising is a belief that health and fitness are important (MORI 1984). In support of this, the non-joggers in the study by Riddle (1980) also reported a lower value on good health than the joggers.

■ *Benefits of exercise.* Exercisers have also been shown to differ from non-exercisers in their beliefs about the benefits of exercise. For example, a study of older women (aged 60–89 years) indicated that exercisers reported a higher rating for the health value of exercise, reported greater enjoyment of exercise, rated their discomfort from exercise as lower and perceived exercise programmes to be more easily available than non-exercisers (Paxton et al. 1997).

■ *Barriers to exercise.* Hausenblas et al. (2001) argued that it is not only the benefits of exercise that promote exercise but also the barriers to exercise that prevent exercise uptake. They developed a questionnaire entitled the 'Temptation to Not Exercise Scale' which measured two forms of barriers: 'affect' and 'competing demands'. Subjects are asked to rate a series of answers following the statement 'Please indicate how tempted you are not to exercise in the following situations . . .'. The answers include 'when I am angry' and 'when I am satisfied' to reflect 'affect' and 'when I feel lazy' and 'when I am busy' to reflect competing interests. The authors argue that such temptations are central to understanding exercise uptake and should be used alongside the stages-of-change model.

Prospective research

This has examined which factors predict the uptake of exercise. It has often been carried out in the context of the development of exercise programmes and studies of adherence to these programmes. Sallis et al. (1986) examined which factors predicted initiation and maintenance of vigorous/moderate exercise for one year. The results indicated that exercise self-efficacy, attitudes to exercise and health knowledge were the best predictors. In a further study, Jonas et al. (1993) followed up 100 men and women and reported the best predictors of intentions to participate in the exercise programmes and actual participation were attitudes to continued participation, perceived social norms and perceived behavioural control. Jones et al. (1998) also examined the predictors of uptake and adherence, and used repertory grids to explore the personal constructs of those individuals who had been referred to exercise as part of an exercise prescription scheme. They concluded that having realistic aims and an understanding of the possible outcomes of a brief exercise programme were predictive of adherence to the programme.

To further understand the predictors of exercise adherence, social cognition models have been used. Riddle (1980) examined predictors of exercise using the theory of reasoned action (Fishbein and Ajzen 1975; see Chapter 2) and reported that attitudes to exercise and the normative components of the model predicted intentions to exercise and that these intentions were related to self-reports of behaviour. The theory of planned behaviour (TPB) has also been developed to assess exercise behaviour. Valois et al. (1988) incorporated a measure of past exercising behaviour (a central variable in the TPB) and reported that attitudes, intentions and past behaviour were the best predictors of exercise. Similarly, Hagger et al. (2001) used the TPB to predict exercise in children and concluded that most variables of the TPB were good predictors of behavioural intentions and actual behaviour at follow-up, and Norman and Smith (1995) found that, although most of the TPB variables were related to exercise, the best predictor of future behaviour was past behaviour. The use of TPB to predict exercise is discussed further in **Focus on Research 7.2** (p. 169). Research has also used the health belief model (Sonstroem 1988) and models emphasizing exercise self-efficacy (e.g. Schwarzer 1992), task self-efficacy and scheduling self-efficacy (Rodgers et al. 2002).

Research has also applied the stages-of-change model to exercise behaviour (see Chapters 2 and 5). This model describes behaviour change in five stages: pre-contemplation, contemplation, preparation, action and maintenance (e.g. DiClemente and Prochaska 1982) and suggests that transitions between changes is facilitated by a cost–benefit analysis and by different cognitions. Marcus et al. (1992) examined the relationship between the pros and cons of exercise and stage of change in 778 men and women. The pros and cons of exercise and decisional balance (pros versus cons) were related to exercise adoption and higher ratings of pros were found in those individuals closer to the maintenance stage of behaviour. This suggests that encouraging individuals to focus on the pros of exercise may increase the transition from thinking about exercising to actually doing it. In a similar vein, Couneya et al. (2001) used the stages-of-change model in conjunction with the TPB to assess which cognitions predicted the transitions between different stages of exercise behaviour. The study included a large sample of adults who completed measures by telephone at baseline and then recorded their exercise stage by mail after one year. The results showed that baseline attitude, intention and subjective norm predicted the transition from pre-contemplation to contemplation, that progression from contemplation to preparation was predicted by intention, perceived behavioural control, attitudes and social support, that progression from preparation to action was predicted by intention and attitude and that transition from action to maintenance was predicted by intention, attitude and social support. Cropley et al. (2003) explored people's beliefs about the costs and benefits of exercise within the framework of the stages-of-change model. They used a reasoning task to assess beliefs about the pros and cons of exercise and asked people to list 'as many advantages/disadvantages of taking part in exercise'. They then explored how accessible these beliefs were by timing how long it took for people to think of their first pro or con and then assessed how many pros and cons could be generated in 60 seconds. Participants were then divided according to whether they were pre-contemplators or maintainers. The results showed that pre-contemplators could think of more cons than pros and that maintainers could think of more pros than cons. In addition, the pre-contemplators were quicker to think of their first pro reason. The authors concluded that while maintainers can think of lots of benefits of exercise, the pre-contemplators may not exercise because they can't think of any reason to exercise.

Testing a theory – predicting exercise

A study using the theory of planned behaviour to predict exercise (Armitage 2005).

This study used a prospective design to explore the role of TPB variables in predicting actual participation in physical activity over a 12-week period. This is an interesting study as it tracks behaviour change over time and uses an objective measure of actual behaviour as its outcome variable.

Background

Research shows that, although exercise is linked with improved psychological and physical health, many people remain inactive. Furthermore, although some people may start an exercise routine, maintenance of this routine remains poor. The present study focused on the development of exercise habits over a 12-week period and explored whether the TPB variables predicted behavioural intentions and actual behaviour and also assessed the time at which habits were established and when relapse rates started to diminish.

Methodology

Design

The study used a prospective design with measures taken at baseline and after 12 weeks. Behaviour was measured objectively throughout the study.

Sample

Ninety-four participants were recruited through a private gym in the south of England. They were aged between 16 and 65, split in terms of men and women and had never attended this particular gym before the onset of the study.

Measures

At baseline all participants completed measures of the following variables: attitudes, subjective norm, perceived behavioural control, behavioural intentions. These were all assessed using 7-point Likert scales. Self-reported behaviour was measured using the question 'How often have you participated in regular physical activity in the last three months?' Actual attendance at the gym was monitored on a weekly basis by using the computer records of membership swipe cards.

Data analysis

The data were analysed in the following ways:

- *The role of TPB variable in predicting behaviour.* Because of the repeated measures nature of the data (i.e. baseline and follow-up and all the intervening assessments of actual behaviour), the data were analysed using repeatable events survival analysis. This enabled the results to be analysed to assess the role of the TPB variables in predicting lapses in exercise behaviour.

- *The development of habits.* The results were also analysed to explore the impact of past behaviour on future behaviour as a means to assess the development of habits. This was done using Helmert contrasts and repeated measures analysis. This enabled the association between past behaviour and actual behaviour to be determined and enabled an assessment of when past behaviour stopped influencing future behaviour. This second form of analysis was done so that the formation of habits could be assessed in terms of when the habit was created and when the habit was stopped.

Results

The results showed that baseline levels of perceived behavioural control predicted both behavioural intentions and actual behaviour. The results also showed that stable exercise habits developed in the first five weeks of the study. This meant that those who had not developed these habits tended to stop exercising by this time point, whereas those who had developed these habits were very unlikely to stop exercising by the end of the 12-week period. Further, the results showed that successful exercising behaviour in the past enhanced participants' perceptions of behavioural control.

Conclusions

The author concludes that the perceived behavioural control component of the TPB predicts exercise behaviour in the longer term. Further, the results show that once exercise habits have been established (i.e. past behaviour reliably predicts actual present behaviour), then they are less likely to extinguish and that the establishment of habits enhances perceptions of control over behaviour.

Exercise relapse

Research has also examined which variables predict relapse and drop-out rates from exercise programmes. Dishman et al. (1985) examined factors that predicted relapse rates and indicated that relapse was highest among blue-collar workers, smokers, those who believed that exercise was an effort, and lowest in those who reported a history of past participation, those with high self-motivation, those who had the support of a spouse, those who reported having the available time, those who had access to exercise facilities, and those who reported a belief in the value of good health. Further, using a stages-of-change approach, Ingledew et al. (1998) explored which factors were important for the transition between the earlier stages of adoption and the later stages of continued behaviour and concluded that continued exercise was predicted by intrinsic motives, specifically enjoyment. These factors are very similar to those that relate to both the initiation and maintenance of exercise behaviour and reflect the role of both non-modifiable and modifiable factors.

To conclude

Exercise is regarded as central to promoting good health both in terms of physical and psychological well-being. Research has therefore examined factors that correlate and predict exercise behaviour. Such factors include the social and political climate and the individual's beliefs. Although interventions aimed to promote exercise do so because of the health benefits, an interest in these benefits does not appear to be the best predictor of initiation or maintenance of exercise behaviour. The recognition of this is reflected in recent recommendations for exercise, which emphasize the encouragement of small changes in lifestyle, not major increases in exercise through vigorous and intensive exercise campaigns.

❓ Questions

1 Exercise has both psychological and physical benefits. Discuss.

2 To what extent can we predict exercise behaviour?

3 How does the exercise research contribute to our understanding of the mind–body problem?

4 How can psychological models be used to promote exercise behaviour?

5 Making people more active is easier than getting them to exercise. Discuss.

6 Exercise behaviour has to be an integrated part of people's lives. Discuss.

7 Describe a possible research project designed to predict attendance at an exercise class.

For discussion

Consider your own exercise behaviour and discuss the extent to which your health beliefs are contributing factors.

Assumptions in health psychology

The exercise literature illustrates some of the assumptions central to health psychology:

1 *The mind–body problem.* Research into exercise maintains the mind–body split. This is illustrated in the discussion of the benefits of exercise (physical and psychological) and the reasons for exercising (e.g. health and fitness versus enjoyment).

2 *Data exist independently of the methodology used.* If different sets of cognitions are measured according to the different models, do these beliefs exist prior to the subject being asked about them (e.g. the question 'Do you think health is important?' primes the subject to think about health as having a value)? Methodology is seen as objective, and not interacting with the 'data'.

Further reading

American College of Sports Medicine (2000) *ACSM's Guidelines for Exercise Testing and Prescription*, 6th edn. Baltimore, MD: Lippincott Williams & Wilkins.

This book is considered the 'gold standard' of advice on how to measure, test and prescribe exercise.

Biddle, S.J.H., Fox, K.R. and Boutcher, S.H. (eds) (2000) *Physical Activity and Psychological Well-being*. London: Routledge.

This book provides a description of the research exploring the links between exercise and aspects of mental health including emotion, mood, self-esteem, self-perception, depression, stress and cognitive performance.

Dishman, R.K. (1982) Compliance/adherence in health-related exercise, *Health Psychology*, 1: 237–67.

This is an early classic paper that examines the literature on factors predicting exercise behaviour.

Faulkner, G.E.J. and Taylor, A.H. (eds) (2005) *Exercise, Health and Mental Health*. London: Routledge.

This is a comprehensive edited collection of chapters that cover the impact of exercise on a range of physical health problems including cancer, heart failure, HIV and schizophrenia. It provides a good summary of the existing research and provides a useful summary chapter at the end.

Marcus, B.H., Rakowski, W. and Rossi, J.S. (1992) Assessing motivational readiness and decision-making for exercise, *Health Psychology*, 22: 3–16.

This paper applies the trans-theoretical approach to exercise behaviour and illustrates the extent to which research can be used to change behaviour.

Chapter 8

Sex

Chapter overview

This chapter first examines the literature on sex, including early discussions of reproduction and the debate about sexual pleasure. It then focuses on the more recent literature, which has examined the risks of sexual behaviour initially in the context of pregnancy avoidance and subsequently in the light of sexually transmitted diseases (STDs)/HIV and AIDS. This literature includes a variety of psychological perspectives from the use of social cognition models, which highlight the role of individual cognitions, to an emphasis on an interaction between individuals in terms of the relationship context. Finally the chapter outlines literature that examines the broader social context in terms of educational influences, the gay community, gendered power relations and theories about sex, HIV and illness.

This chapter covers

- Developing the contemporary perspectives on sex
- Sex as a risk and pregnancy avoidance
- Sex as a risk in the context of STDs/HIV and AIDS
- Sex as an interaction between individuals – adding the relationship context
- The broader social context

Developing the contemporary research perspectives on sex
Sex as biological, for reproduction

Prior to the nineteenth century, sexual behaviour was regarded as a religious or spiritual concern. However, from the beginning of the 1800s sexuality and sexual behaviour became a focus for scientific study. Doctors and scientists took over the responsibility for teaching about sex and it was subsequently studied within medicine and biological sciences. Sex was viewed as a biological function alongside eating and drinking.

During the nineteenth century, much was written about sexual behaviour. Attempts were made to develop criteria to describe sexual normality and abnormality. Generally behaviours linked to reproduction were seen as normal and those such as masturbation and homosexuality as abnormal. This is illustrated by the Victorian concern with sexual morality, movements proclaiming sexual puritanism and attempts to control prostitution. Sex was seen as a biological drive that needed to be expressed but which should be expressed within the limitations of its function: reproduction.

Sex as biological, for pleasure

From the beginning of the twentieth century, there was a shift in perspective. Although sex was still seen as biological, the emphasis was now on sexual behaviour rather than on outcome (reproduction). This involved a study of sexual desire, sexual pleasure and orgasms. It resulted in a burgeoning literature on sex therapy and manuals on how to develop a good sex life. This emphasis is illustrated by the classic survey carried out by Kinsey in the 1940s and 1950s, the research programmes developed by Masters and Johnson in the 1960s and the Hite reports on sexuality in the 1970s and 1980s.

The Kinsey Report

Kinsey interviewed and analysed data from 12,000 white Americans and his attempts to challenge some of the contemporary concerns with deviance were credited with causing 'a wave of sexual hysteria' (e.g. Kinsey et al. 1948). He developed his analysis of sexual behaviour within models of biological reductionism and argued that sex was natural and therefore healthy. Kinsey argued that the sexual drive was a biological force and the expression of this drive to attain pleasure was not only acceptable but desirable. He challenged some of the contemporary concerns with premarital sex and argued that as animals do not get married, there could be no difference between marital and premarital sex. He emphasized similarities between the sexual behaviour of men and women and argued that if scientific study could promote healthy sex lives then this could improve the quality of marriages and reduce the divorce rates. His research suggested that a variety of sexual outlets were acceptable and emphasized the role of sexual pleasure involving both sexual intercourse and masturbation for men and women.

Masters and Johnson

This emphasis on the activity of sex is also illustrated by the work of Masters and Johnson in the 1960s. Masters and Johnson used a variety of experimental laboratory techniques to examine over 10,000 male and female orgasms in 694 white middle-class heterosexuals (e.g. Masters and Johnson 1966). They recorded bodily contractions, secretions, pulse rates and tissue colour changes and described the sexual response cycle in terms of the following phases: (1) excitement; (2) plateau; (3) orgasm; and (4) resolution. They emphasized similarities between men and women (although it has been argued that their data suggest more difference than they acknowledged; Segal 1994) and emphasized that stable marriages depended on satisfactory sex. According to Masters and Johnson, sexual pleasure could be improved by education and sex therapy and again their research suggested that masturbation was an essential component of sexuality – sex was for pleasure, not for reproduction.

The Hite Reports

Shere Hite (1976, 1981, 1987) published the results from her 20 years of research in her reports on female and male sexuality. Her research also illustrates the shift from the outcome of sex to sex as an activity. Hite's main claim is that 'most women (70 per cent) do not orgasm as a result of intercourse' but she suggests that they can learn to increase clitoral stimulation during intercourse to improve their sexual enjoyment. She describes her data in terms of women's dislike of penetrative sex ('Perhaps it could be said that many women might be rather indifferent to intercourse if it were not for feelings towards a particular man') and discusses sex within the context of pleasure, not reproduction. Segal (1994) has criticized Hite's interpretation of the data and argues that the women in Hite's studies appear to enjoy penetration (with or without orgasm). Although this is in contradiction to Hite's own conclusion, the emphasis is still on sex as an activity.

In summary

From the start of the twentieth century, therefore, sex was no longer described as a biological means to an end (reproduction) but as an activity in itself. Discussions of 'good sex', orgasms and sexual pleasure emphasized sex as action; however, even as an activity sex remained predominantly biological. Kinsey regarded sex as a drive that was natural and healthy, Masters and Johnson developed means to measure and improve the sexual experience by examining physiological changes and Hite explained pleasure with descriptions of physical stimulation.

Sex as a risk to health

Recently there has been an additional shift in the literature on sex. Although research still emphasizes sex as an activity, this activity has been viewed as increasingly risky and dangerous. As a consequence, sex is discussed in terms of health promotion, health education and self-protection. This shift has resulted in a psychological literature on sex as a risk both in terms of pregnancy avoidance and in the context of STDs/HIV preventive behaviour. However, studying sexual behaviour is not straightforward from a psychological perspective as it presents a problem for psychologists – a problem of interaction.

Sex as interaction

Social psychologists have spent decades emphasizing the context within which behaviour occurs. This is reflected in the extensive literature on areas such as conformity to majority and minority influence, group behaviour and decision making, and obedience to authority. Such a perspective emphasizes that an individual's behaviour occurs as an interaction both with other individuals and with the broader social context. Sex highlights this interaction as it is inherently an interactive behaviour. However, health psychology draws on many other areas of psychology (e.g. physiological, cognitive, behavioural), which have tended to examine individuals on their own. In addition, psychological methodologies such as questionnaires and interviews involve an individual's experience (e.g. I felt, I believe, I think, I did). Even if individuals discuss their interactions with other individuals (e.g. we felt, we believe, we think, we did), or place their experiences in the context of others (e.g. I felt happy because she made me feel relaxed), only their own individual experiences are accessed using the psychological tools available. Therefore sex provides an interesting problem for psychologists. Sex is intrinsically an interaction between individuals, yet many areas of psychology traditionally study individuals on their own. Furthermore, the recent emphasis on sex as a risk to health and resulting attempts to examine individuals' competence at protecting themselves from danger, may have resulted in a more individualistic model of behaviour. This problem of interaction is exacerbated by the psychological methodologies available (unless the researcher simply observes two people having sex!). The following theories of sexual behaviour both in the context of pregnancy avoidance and STD/HIV preventive behaviour illustrate the different ways in which psychologists have attempted to deal with the problem of the interaction. They highlight the problem with adding both the relationship context (e.g. the interaction between individuals) and the wider social context (e.g. social meanings, social norms) onto the individual (e.g. their beliefs and knowledge). They also raise the following question: how much can and should psychologists be concerned with the context of individual behaviour?

Sex as a risk and pregnancy avoidance

A focus on sex for pleasure and an emphasis on sex as a risk has resulted in a literature on contraception use and pregnancy avoidance. Research on the termination of pregnancy is described in Chapter 16. Psychologists have developed models in order to describe and predict this behaviour.

What is contraceptive use?

Researchers have used several different classifications of contraception in an attempt to predict contraceptive use. For example, contraception has been characterized as:

- coitus independent (the pill) or coitus dependent (the condom)
- reliable (the pill, condom) or unreliable (rhythm method)
- female controlled (the pill, IUD) or male controlled (the condom)
- prescription based (the pill, IUD) or prescription independent (the condom).

In addition, different measures of actual behaviour have been used when predicting contraception use:

- at first ever intercourse
- at most recent intercourse
- at last serious intercourse
- at last casual intercourse.

Who uses contraception?

The National Survey of Sexual Attitudes and Lifestyles (Wellings et al. 1994) examined the sexual behaviour of nearly 20,000 men and women across Britain. This produced a wealth of data about factors such as age of first intercourse, homosexuality, attitudes to sexual behaviours and contraception use. For example, Figure 8.1 shows the proportion of respondents who used no contraception at first intercourse. These results suggest that the younger someone is when they first have sex (either male or female), the less likely they are to use contraception.

The results from this survey also show what kinds of contraception people use at first intercourse. The data for men and women aged 16–24 years are shown in Figure 8.2 and suggest that the condom is the most popular form of contraception; however, many respondents in this age group reported using no contraception, or unreliable methods, such as withdrawal or the safe period.

The different measures of contraception use have implications for interpreting findings on contraception. Sheeran et al. (1991) discussed these problems and analysed the literature on contraceptive use in 'never married' individuals aged 13–25 years, and suggested that models used to examine contraceptive use for pregnancy avoidance can be described as either *developmental models* or *decision-making models*. The focus on sex as risky resulted in a need to understand risk-taking behaviour. Developmental models are more descriptive, whereas decision-making models examine the predictors and precursors to this behaviour.

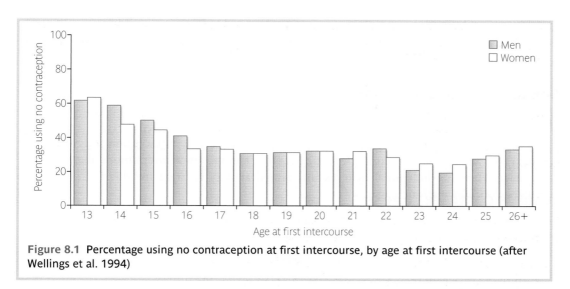

Figure 8.1 Percentage using no contraception at first intercourse, by age at first intercourse (after Wellings et al. 1994)

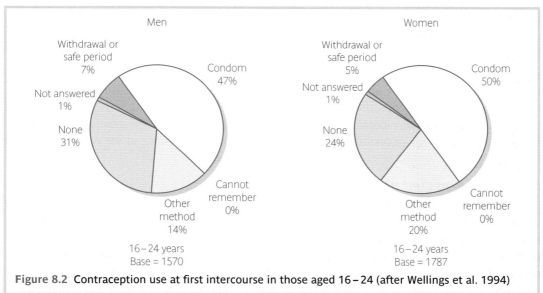

Figure 8.2 Contraception use at first intercourse in those aged 16–24 (after Wellings et al. 1994)

Developmental models

Developmental models emphasize contraception use as involving a series of stages. They suggest that the progress through these stages is related to sexual experience and an increasing role for sexuality in the individual's self-concept. Therefore they describe the transition through the different stages but do not attempt to analyse the cognitions that may promote this transition.

Lindemann's three-stage theory

Lindemann (1977) developed the three-stage theory of contraception use, which suggests that the likelihood of an individual using contraception increases as they progress through the three stages:

1 *Natural stage:* at this stage intercourse is relatively unplanned, and the individual does not regard themselves as sexual. Therefore contraception use is unlikely.

2 *Peer prescription stage:* at this stage the individual seeks contraceptive advice from friends, sexual intercourse is more frequent and most contraception involves less effective methods.

3 *Expert stage:* at this stage, the individual has incorporated sexuality into their self-concept and will seek professional advice and plan contraceptive use.

Rains's model

This model was developed by Rains (1971) and again places contraception use within the context of sexuality and self-concept. It suggests that contraception use is more likely to occur at a stage when the individual believes that sexual activity is 'right for them'. This process involves the following four stages:

1 Falling in love: this provides a rationale for sex.

2 Having an exclusive, long-term relationship.

3 Sexual intercourse becomes an acceptable behaviour.

4 Individuals accept themselves as sexual and plan sex for the future.

According to this model, reaching stage 4 predicts reliable contraception use.

Decision-making models

Decision-making models examine the psychological factors that predict and are the precursors to contraception use. There are several different decision-making models and they vary in their emphasis on individual cognitions (e.g. costs and benefits of contraception use) and the extent to which they place these cognitions within the specific context of the relationship (e.g. the interaction, seriousness of relationship, frequency of sexual intercourse in the relationship) and the broader social context (e.g. peer norms, social attitudes).

Subjective expected utility theory

Most decision-making models of behaviour are based on the subjective expected utility theory (SEU) (Edwards 1954). The SEU predicts that individuals make subjective estimates of the possible costs and benefits of any particular behaviour and, based on this assessment, make a decision as to which behaviour results in the least costs and the most benefits (material, social and psychological). It therefore characterizes behaviour as rational. Luker (1975) examined the SEU in the context of contraceptive use and argued that individuals weigh up the costs and benefits of pregnancy against the costs and benefits of contraception. Sheeran et al. (1991) argued that this approach was important as it undermined the belief that contraception has no costs for women and pregnancy had no benefits. The SEU is predominantly individualistic and the role of both the relationship and social context is minimal.

The five-component model

This model was developed by Reiss et al. (1975) and, although it still regards contraceptive use as resulting from a rational appraisal of the situation, it includes measures of more general attitudes. The components of the model are: (1) endorsement of sexual choices (e.g. permissiveness, religiosity); (2) self-assurance; (3) early information on sex and contraception; and (4) congruity between premarital sexual standards and behaviour and commitment. Reiss et al. tested the model and reported support for the first three of the variables as predictive of contraception use. This model is still predominantly concerned with individual cognitions.

The health belief model

This model was developed by Rosenstock and Becker (e.g. Rosenstock 1966; Becker and Rosenstock 1987) and is described in detail in Chapter 2. The original HBM emphasized individual cognitions and ignores the problem of interaction. Lowe and Radius (1982) developed the HBM specifically to predict contraception and aimed to examine individual cognitions within both the context of the relationship and broader social norms. They added the following variables:

- self-esteem
- interpersonal skills
- knowledge about sex and contraception
- attitudes to sex and contraception
- previous sexual, contraceptive and pregnancy experiences
- peer norms
- relationship status
- substance use prior to sex.

Therefore, although this model still examines cognitions, it includes measures of the individuals' cognitions about their social world.

The theory of reasoned action

This theory was developed by Fishbein and Ajzen (1975) and is described in detail in Chapter 2. The TRA was the first cognition model to include measures of individuals' cognitions about their social world in the form of subjective norms. It therefore represents an attempt to add the social context to individual cognitive variables and consequently addresses the problem of interaction. The TRA has been used to predict contraceptive use and research has indicated a correlation between the components of the model and intentions to use the oral contraceptive (Cohen et al. 1978). In addition, research by Werner and Middlestadt (1979) reported correlations between attitudes to contraception and subjective norms and actual use of oral contraception.

Sexual behaviour sequence model

This model was developed by Byrne et al. (1977) and adds sexual arousal and emotional responses to sex to the factors included in the TRA. Sexual arousal refers to how aroused an individual is at the time of making a decision about contraception. Emotional responses to sex describes a personality trait that Byrne et al. defined as either erotophilia (finding sexual cues pleasurable) or erotophobia (finding sexual cues aversive). According to the sexual behaviour sequence model, decisions about contraception are made in the context of both rational information processing and emotions. This model attempts to add a degree of emotions and social norms (from the TRA) to the individual's cognitions.

Herold and McNamee's (1982) model

This model is made up of the following variables: (1) parental and peer group norms for acceptance of premarital intercourse; (2) number of lifetime sexual partners; (3) guilt about intercourse and attitudes to contraception; (4) involvement with current partner; (5) partner's influence to use contraception; and (6) frequency of intercourse. This model differs from other models of contraception use as it includes details of the relationship. It places contraception use both within the general context of social norms and also within the context of the relationship.

In summary

These decision-making models regard contraceptive use as resulting from an analysis of the relevant variables. However, they vary in the extent to which they attempt to place the individual's cognitive state within a broader context, both of the relationship and the social world.

Integrating developmental and decision-making approaches to contraception use

Developmental models emphasize behaviour and describe reliable contraception use as the end product of a transition through a series of stages. These models do not examine the psychological factors, which may speed up or delay this transition. In contrast, decision-making models emphasize an individual's cognitions and, to a varying degree, place these cognitions within the context of the relationship and social norms. Perhaps these cognitions could be used to explain the behavioural stages described by the developmental models. Sheeran et al. (1991) argued that these perspectives could be combined and that the best means to examine contraceptive use is as a product of (1) background, (2) intrapersonal, (3) interpersonal, and (4) situational factors. They defined these factors as follows.

Background factors

1 *Age:* evidence suggests that young women's contraceptive use increases with age (e.g. Herold 1981).

2 *Gender:* women appear to be more likely to use contraception than men (e.g. Whitley and Schofield 1986).

3 *Ethnicity:* some evidence suggests that whites are more likely to use contraception than blacks (e.g. Whitley and Schofield 1986).

4 *Socio-economic status:* there is conflicting evidence concerning the relationship between socio-economic status (SES) and contraceptive use with some research indicating a relationship (e.g. Hornick et al. 1979) and others indicating no relationship (e.g. Herold 1981).

5 *Education:* evidence indicates that higher school performance and higher educational aspirations may be linked with contraception use (e.g. Herold and Samson 1980; Furstenburg et al. 1983).

Although these background factors may influence contraceptive use, whether this effect is direct or through the effect of other factors such as knowledge and attitudes is unclear.

Intrapersonal factors

1 *Knowledge:* Whitley and Schofield (1986) analysed the results of 25 studies of contraceptive use and reported a correlation of 0.17 between objective knowledge and contraceptive use in both men and women, suggesting that knowledge is poorly linked to behaviour. Ignorance about contraception has also been shown by several studies. For example, Cvetkovich and Grote (1981) reported that, of their sample, 10 per cent did not believe that they could become pregnant the first time they had sex, and 52 per cent of men and 37 per cent of women could not identify the periods of highest risk in the menstrual cycle. In addition, Lowe and Radius (1982) reported that 40 per cent of their sample did not know how long sperm remained viable.

2 *Attitudes:* Fisher (1984) reported that positive attitudes towards contraception parallel actual use. Negative attitudes included beliefs that 'it kills spontaneity', 'it's too much trouble to use' and that there are possible side effects. In addition, carrying contraceptives around is often believed to be associated with being promiscuous (e.g. Lowe and Radius 1982).

3 *Personality:* many different personality types have been related to contraceptive use. This research assumes that certain aspects of individuals are consistent over time and research has reported associations between the following types of personality:

- *Conservatism and sex role* have been shown to be negatively related to contraceptive use (e.g. Geis and Gerrard 1984; McCormick et al. 1985).

- *An internal locus of control* appears to correlate with contraceptive use but not with choice of type of contraception (Morrison 1985).

- *Sex guilt and sex anxiety* positively relate to use and consistency of use of contraception (Herold and McNamee 1982).

- Personality is often measured using the big-five factors (Goldberg 1999). These are *agreeableness, conscientiousness, emotional stability, extraversion* and *intellect.* Ingledew and Ferguson (2006) explored the role of personality in predicting riskier sexual behaviour. The results showed that agreeableness and conscientiousness reduced riskier behaviour. The results also showed that this effect was related to different forms of motivation.

Interpersonal factors

Research highlights a role for characteristics of the following significant others:

1 *Partner:* facets of the relationship may influence contraception use including duration of relationship, intimacy, type of relationship (e.g. casual versus steady), exclusivity, and ability to have overt discussions about contraception (e.g. DeLamater and MacCorquodale 1978, 1979).

2 *Parents:* there is some evidence to suggest that increased parental permissiveness and explicit communication between mothers and daughters about contraception is related to contraception use (e.g. Herold and McNamee 1982).

3 *Peers:* increased contraceptive use relates to peer permissiveness and peers' own contraceptive behaviour (e.g. Herold 1981).

Situational factors

Sheeran et al. (1991) have also argued that situational factors contribute to contraceptive use, including the following:

1 *The spontaneity of sex:* spontaneity is often given as a reason for not using contraception (e.g. Holland et al. 1990b).

2 *Substance use prior to sex:* taking substances such as drugs or alcohol prior to sex may relate to risky sex.

3 *The accessibility of contraception:* research has also examined whether easy access to contraception both in general (i.e. the provision of condom machines in pubs) and at the time of contemplating sex predicts contraception use (e.g. Gold et al. 1991).

Sheeran et al. (1991) argued that these different variables interact in order to predict contraception use. They included interpersonal and situational factors as a means to place the individual's cognitions within the context of the relationship and the broader social world. These variables can be applied individually or alternatively incorporated into models. In particular, social cognition models emphasize cognitions about the individual's social world, particularly their normative beliefs. However, whether asking an individual about the relationship really accesses the interaction between two people is questionable. For example, is the belief that 'I decided to go on the pill because I had talked it over with my partner' a statement describing the interaction between two individuals, or is it one individual's cognitions about that interaction?

Since the beginnings of the HIV/AIDS epidemic, sex as a risk has taken on a new dimension – the dimension of chronic illness and death. Research into HIV and AIDS preventive behaviour also illustrates the different ways of dealing with sex as an interaction. Although sometimes ignored, this research is also relevant to other sexually transmitted diseases.

Box 8.1 Some problems with . . . sex research

Below are some problems with research in this area that you may wish to consider.

1   Sexual behaviour involves two people and therefore results out of an interaction between two sets of beliefs, emotions and behaviours. Although ultimately all behaviour is located in its social context, sexual behaviour explicitly illustrates this and therefore results in specific problems in terms of understanding and measuring what factors relate to whether someone has sex or not and whether they engage in risky behaviours.

2   Sexual behaviour can generate embarrassment and is considered a sensitive and personal area of research. This can lead to problems gaining ethical approval and in encouraging people to speak opening and honestly.

3   Most sexual behaviour research focuses on the problems associated with sex such as STDs and HIV. To date little research in health psychology has highlighted sex as a healthy and pleasurable activity. In part this is due to issues of embarrassment and in part is due to funders' emphasis on health problems.

4   Sexual behaviour research can be loaded with ideological perspectives in terms of whether people believe abstinence is the way forward, whether they are judgemental of homosexual behaviour, whether they believe in monogamy and whether they are critical of 'promiscuity'. Research may therefore be biased in terms of the areas of research selected, the data collected and funded and ways in which the research is interpreted and presented.

Sex as a risk in the context of STDs/HIV and AIDS

The HIV virus was identified in 1982 (see Chapter 14 for a discussion of HIV and AIDS). Since then, health education programmes have changed in their approach to preventing the spread of the virus. For example, early campaigns emphasized monogamy or at least cutting down on the number of sexual partners. Campaigns also promoted non-penetrative sex and suggested alternative ways to enjoy a sexual relationship. However, more recent campaigns emphasize safe sex and using a condom. In fact, Reiss and Leik (1989) argued that increased condom use and not abstinence or non-penetrative sex or a reduction in the number of partners is likely to be the best approach to HIV. As a result, research has examined the prerequisites to safer sex and condom use in an attempt to develop successful health promotion campaigns.

Do people use condoms?

Young people

Some researchers have suggested that the mass media campaigns have not changed teenagers' sexual behaviour (Sherr 1987) and that there has even been an increase in sexually transmitted diseases (STDs) among this age group in the USA (Boyer and Kegles 1991). In the UK, data indicate that there has been an increase in chlamydia and that the dramatic reduction in gonorrhoea seen in the older population is not evident among younger people. Richard and van der Pligt (1991) examined condom use among a group of Dutch teenagers and report that 50 per cent of those with multiple partners were consistent condom users. In an American study, 30 per cent of adolescent women were judged to be at risk from STDs, of whom 16 per cent used condoms consistently (Weisman et al. 1991). The Women, Risk and AIDS Project (WRAP) (e.g. Holland et al. 1990b) interviewed and collected questionnaires from heterosexual women aged 16–19 years. It reported that 16 per cent of these used condoms on their own, 13 per cent had used condoms while on the pill, 2 per cent had used condoms in combination with spermicide and 3 per cent had used condoms together with a diaphragm. Overall only 30 per cent of their sample had ever used condoms, while 70 per cent had not. Fife-Schaw and Breakwell (1992) undertook an overview of the literature on condom use among young people and found that between 24 per cent and 58 per cent of 16- to 24-year-olds had used a condom during their most recent sexual encounter. Recently, Hatherall et al. (2006) also explored condom use in young people and reported that 62 per cent said that they had used a condom on their most recent sexual experience. However, of these 31 per cent described putting on the condom after penetration at least once in the previous six months and 9 per cent reported having penetration after the condom had been removed. This suggests that even when condoms are used they are not always used in the most effective way. Furthermore, Stone et al. (2006) explored the use of condoms during oral sex as this is recommended for the prevention of STD transmission and the results showed that, of those that had had oral sex, only 17 per cent reported ever using a condom and only 2 per cent reported consistent condom use. Reasons for non-use included reduced pleasure and lack of motivation and reasons for use included hygiene and avoidance of the 'spit/swallow dilemma'.

Homosexuals

Research has also examined condom use among homosexually active men. Weatherburn et al. (1991) interviewed 930 homosexually active men in England and Wales and reported that 270 of them had had insertive anal intercourse in the preceding month, with 38.9 per cent reporting always using a condom, 49.6 per cent never using a condom and 11.5 per cent sometimes using a condom. Of the 254 who reported having receptive anal sex in the preceding month, 42.5 per cent had always used a condom, 45.7 per cent had never used a condom and 11.8 per cent had sometimes used a condom. Weatherburn et al. (1991) reported that condom use was associated with casual, not regular sexual partners and was more common in open and not monogamous relationships. Therefore, within this high-risk group, condom use is low.

Bisexuals

In one study, Boulton et al. (1991) asked 60 bisexual men about their sexual behaviour and their condom use. Over the previous 12 months, 80 per cent had had male partners, 73 per cent had had female partners and 60 per cent had had at least one male and one female partner. In terms of their condom use with their current partner, 25 per cent reported always using a condom with their current male partner, 12 per cent reported always using a condom with their current female partner, 27 per cent reported sometimes/never using a condom with their male partner and 38 per cent reported sometimes/never using a condom with their female partner.

In terms of their non-current partner, 30 per cent had had unprotected sex with a man and 34 per cent had had unprotected sex with a woman. Bisexuals are believed to present a bridge between the homosexual and heterosexual populations and these data suggest that their frequency of condom use is low. This highlights a need to identify possible reasons for this behaviour.

Changes in condom use

In an attempt to examine the effects of HIV prevention educational campaigns in The Netherlands, Hooykaas et al. (1991) examined changes in sexual behaviour in 340 heterosexual men and women and prostitutes. They reported that over the one-year follow-up, condom use during vaginal intercourse with prostitutes/clients was high and remained high, condom use with private partners was low and remained low, but that both men and women reduced their number of sexual partners by 50 per cent.

The results from the *General Household Survey* (1993) provided some further insights into changes in condom use in Britain from 1983 to 1991 (see Figure 8.3). These data indicate an overall increase in condom use as the usual form of contraception, which is particularly apparent in the younger age groups. However, not all research indicates such an increase. Early data from San Francisco, which had one of the highest homosexual incidences of HIV, showed that by the late 1980s the incidence of new HIV infections had fallen dramatically and that by the late 1990s had become essentially stable (Katz 1997; Schwarcz et al. 2001). However, since this time there has been an increase in rectal gonorrhoea, and clinical experience, cross-sectional and longitudinal studies suggest that unprotected anal sex is resurfacing as an increasing problem. This suggests that the substantial increase in condom use which occurred after the initial AIDS prevention efforts may be beginning to reverse.

Condom use is recommended as the main means to prevent the spread of the HIV virus. These data suggest that many individuals do report using condoms, although not always on a regular basis. In addition, many individuals say that they do not use condoms. Therefore, although the health promotion messages may be reaching many individuals, many others are not complying with their recommendations.

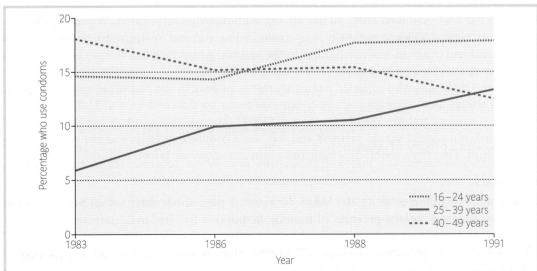

Figure 8.3 Changes in the use of condoms as the usual method of contraception by age, 1983–91 (after *General Household Survey* 1993)

Predicting condom use

Simple models using knowledge only have been used to examine condom use. However, these models ignore the individual's beliefs and assume that simply increasing knowledge about HIV will promote safe sex. In order to incorporate an individual's cognitive state, social cognition models have been applied to condom use in the context of HIV and AIDS (see Chapter 2 for a discussion of these models). These models are similar to those used to predict other health-related behaviours, including contraceptive use for pregnancy avoidance, and illustrate varying attempts to understand cognitions in the context of the relationship and the broader social context.

Social cognition models

The health belief model (HBM)

The HBM was developed by Rosenstock and Becker (e.g. Rosenstock 1966; Becker and Rosenstock 1987) (see Chapter 2) and has been used to predict condom use. McCusker et al. (1989) adapted the HBM to predict condom use in homosexual men over a 12-month period. They reported that the components of the model were not good predictors and only perceived susceptibility was related to condom use. In addition, they reported that the best predictor was previous risk behaviour. This suggests that condom use is a habitual behaviour and that placing current condom use into the context of time and habits may be the way to assess this behaviour.

The reasons that the HBM fails to predict condom use have been examined by Abraham and Sheeran (1994). They suggest the following explanations:

- *Consensus of severity*: everyone knows that HIV is a very serious disease. This presents the problem of a ceiling effect with only small differences in ratings of this variable.
- *Failure to acknowledge personal susceptibility*: although people appear to know about HIV, its causes and how it is transmitted, feelings of immunity and low susceptibility ('it won't happen to me') are extremely common. This presents the problem of a floor effect with little individual variability. Therefore these two central components of the HBM are unlikely to distinguish between condom users and non-users.
- *Safer sex requires long-term maintenance of behaviour*: the HBM may be a good predictor of short-term changes in behaviour (e.g. taking up an exercise class, stopping smoking in the short term), but safer sex is an ongoing behaviour, which requires an ongoing determination to adopt condom use as a habit.
- *Sex is emotional and involves a level of high arousal*: these factors may make the rational information-processing approach of the HBM redundant.
- *Sex is interactive and involves negotiation*: condom use takes place between two people, it involves a process of negotiation and occurs within the context of a relationship. Assessing individual cognitions does not access this negotiation process. Abraham and Sheeran (1993) suggest that social skills may be better predictors of safe sex.
- *From beliefs to behaviour*: the HBM does not clarify how beliefs (e.g. 'I feel at risk') are translated into behaviour (e.g. 'I am using a condom').

The theory of reasoned action (TRA) and the theory of planned behaviour (TPB)

In an attempt to resolve some of the problems with the HBM, the TRA and TPB have been used to predict condom use. These models address the problem of how beliefs are turned into action using the 'behavioural intentions' component. In addition, they attempt to address the problem of placing beliefs within a context by an emphasis on social cognitions (the normative beliefs component). Research suggests that the TRA has had some degree of success at predicting condom use with behavioural intentions predicting condom use at one, three and four months (Fisher 1984; Boyd and Wandersman 1991; van der Velde et al. 1992). In addition, attitudes to condoms predict behavioural intentions (Boldero et al. 1992), and perceived partner support (partner norms) appears to be a good predictor of condom use by women (Weisman et al. 1991).

Research has also explored the relative usefulness of the TRA compared with the TPB at predicting intentions to use condoms (Sutton et al. 1999). The results from this study indicated that the TPB was not more effective than the TRA (in contrast to the authors' predictions) and that past behaviour was the most powerful predictor. In a recent study of condom use, the best predictors appeared to be a combination of normative beliefs involving peers, friends, siblings, previous partners, parents and the general public. This suggests that although cognitions may play a role in predicting condom use, this essentially interactive behaviour is probably best understood within the context of both the relationship and the broader social world, highlighting the important role of social cognitions in the form of normative beliefs. Therefore, although the TRA and the TPB address some of the problems with the HBM, they still do not address some of the others.

The role of self-efficacy

The concept of self-efficacy (Bandura 1977) has been incorporated into many models of behaviour. In terms of condom use, self-efficacy can refer to factors such as confidence in buying condoms, confidence in using condoms or confidence in suggesting that condoms are used. Research has highlighted an association between perceived self-efficacy and reported condom use (Richard and van der Pligt 1991), and a denial of HIV risk during the contemplation of sex (Abraham et al. 1994). Schwarzer (1992) developed the health action process approach (HAPA, see Chapter 2), which places self-efficacy in a central role for predicting behaviour. In addition, this model may be particularly relevant to condom use as it emphasizes time and habit.

Problems with social cognition models

Many of the problems highlighted by the HBM are also characteristic of other social cognition models (see Chapter 2 for a detailed discussion). These problems can be summarized as follows:

1 *Inconsistent findings.* The research examining condom use has not produced consistent results. For example, whereas Fisher (1984) reported an association between intentions and actual behaviour, Abraham et al. (1991) did not. Joseph et al. (1987) suggested that condom use is predicted by peer norms, whereas Catania et al. (1989) found that it is not. Furthermore, Catania et al. (1989) reported that condom use relates to perceived severity and self-efficacy, but Hingson et al. (1990) said that it does not relate to these factors. However, such studies have used very different populations (homosexual, heterosexual, adolescents, adults). Perhaps models of condom use should be constructed to fit the cognitive sets of different populations; attempts to develop one model for everyone may ignore the multitude of different cognitions held by different individuals within different groups.

2 *Sex as a result of individual cognitions.* Models that emphasize cognitions and information processing intrinsically regard behaviour as the result of information processing – an individualistic approach to behaviour. In particular, early models tended to focus on represen-

tations of an individual's risks without taking into account their interactions with the outside world. Furthermore, models such as the HBM emphasized this process as rational. However, recent social cognition models have attempted to remedy this situation by emphasizing cognitions about the individual's social world (the normative beliefs) and by including elements of emotion (the behaviour becomes less rational).

3 *Perception of susceptibility.* In addition, these models predict that, because people appear to know that HIV is an extremely serious disease, and they know how it is transmitted, they will feel vulnerable (e.g. 'HIV is transmitted by unprotected sex, I have unprotected sex, therefore I am at risk from HIV'). This does not appear to be the case. Furthermore, the models predict that high levels of susceptibility will relate to less risk-taking behaviour (e.g. 'I am at risk, therefore I will use condoms'). Again this association is problematic.

4 *Sex as an interaction between individuals – the relationship context.* Models of condom use focus on cognitions. In attempts to include an analysis of the place of this behaviour (the relationship), variables such as peer norms, partner norms and partner support have been added. However, these variables are still accessed by asking one individual about their beliefs about the relationship. Perhaps this is still only accessing a cognition, not the interaction.

5 *Sex in a social context.* Sex also takes place within a broader social context, involving norms about sexual practices, gender roles and stereotypes, the role of illness and theories of sexual behaviour. Cognitive models cannot address this broader context.

Perceptions of susceptibility, sex as an interaction between individuals and the broader social context will now be dealt with in more detail.

Perceptions of susceptibility – are you at risk?

Having a sexual career today involves a relationship to risk that is different to that seen previously. However, one of the most consistent findings to emerge from the research is the perception of personal invulnerability in heterosexual and homosexual populations. These feelings of invulnerability to HIV are shown by quantitative studies that have examined ratings of perceived susceptibility and unrealistic optimism (see Chapters 2 and 13). For example, Abrams et al. (1990: 49) concluded from their survey in 1988 that young people 'have a strong sense of AIDS invulnerability which seems to involve a perception that they have control over the risk at which they place themselves'. In a study of beliefs in a population of young people in Scotland from 1988 to 1989, the authors reported an increased sense of complacency and invulnerability over this time period.

In addition, qualitative methods have been used to further examine whether individuals feel that they are at risk from HIV. Woodcock et al. (1992) interviewed 125 young people aged 16–25 years about their sexual behaviour and examined how these individuals evaluated their own risk factors. The authors reported that many of the interviewees endorsed risky behaviour and gave reasons both acknowledging their own risk and denying that they had put themselves at risk. These ways of coping with risk were as follows:

1 *Acknowledging risk.* One subject acknowledged that their behaviour had been risky, saying, 'I'm a chancer and I know I'm a chancer . . . with this AIDS thing, I know that I should use a condom'. However, most subjects, even though they acknowledged some degree of risk, managed to dismiss it in terms of 'it would show by now', 'it was in the past' or 'AIDS wasn't around in those days' (from a 21-year-old interviewee).

2 *Denying risk.* Most commonly, people denied that they had ever put themselves at risk and the complex ways in which their sexual behaviour was rationalized illustrates how complicated the concept of susceptibility and 'being at risk' is. Woodcock et al. (1992) presented many ways of rationalizing risky behaviour. These include believing 'it's been blown out of proportion', that 'AIDS is a risk you take in living' and the authors report that 'the theme of being run over, particularly by buses' was common and believing that 'it doesn't affect me' was also apparent. In addition, the interviewees evaluated their own risk in the context of the kinds of people with whom they had sex. For example, 'I don't go with people who go around a lot', 'He said I've only slept with you in the last six months', and 'I do not have sex in risky geographical areas' – one interviewee said, 'London is the capital: has to be more AIDS'.

Most cognitive models emphasizing rational information processing suggest that condom use is related to feelings of susceptibility and being at risk from HIV. However, many people do not appear to believe that they themselves are at risk, which is perhaps why they do not engage in self-protective behaviour, and even when some acknowledgement of risk is made, this is often dismissed and does not appear to relate to behaviour change.

Sex as an interaction between individuals

Because sex is intrinsically an interactive behaviour, psychologists have attempted to add an interactive component to the understanding of condom use. In an attempt to access the interaction between individuals, Abraham and Sheeran (1993) argued that social cognition models should be expanded to include the interpersonal and situational variables described by the literature on contraception use. In particular, they have argued that relationship factors such as duration, intimacy, quality of communication, status (casual versus steady) should be added to intrapersonal factors such as knowledge and beliefs and situational factors such as substance use and spontaneity. Wilkinson et al. (2002) also emphasized sex as an interaction and highlighted a role for partner cooperation. They asked 398 unmarried students to rate both their sexual behaviour and their perception of how cooperative their partner had been to practise safer sex. The results showed that partner cooperation was linked to safer sexual behaviour.

To further the understanding of the process of interaction, some research has used qualitative methods and has focused on negotiation between people. The Women's Risk and AIDS Project (WRAP) interviewed 150 women from London and Manchester about their sexual histories and sexual behaviour and described the factors that related to the negotiation of condom use. Holland et al. (1990b: 4) stated that during sex 'words are likely to be the most difficult things to exchange' and suggest that the negotiation of condom use is far more complex than 'a simple, practical question about dealing rationally with risk, it is the outcome of negotiation between potentially unequal partners'. They suggested that although the process of negotiation may be hindered by embarrassment as suggested by some of the health promotion campaigns, this 'embarrassment over using condoms is not simply a question of bad timing but indicates a very complex process of negotiation'. Therefore they place condom use within the context of the relationship and, rather than see the interaction between individuals as only one component of the process of condom use, they place this interaction centrally.

The results from the WRAP study provide some insights into the process of negotiation and the interaction between individuals. Some of the interviewees reported no difficulties in demanding safe sex, with one woman saying, 'if they don't want to wear a condom, then tough, you know, go and find someone else'. Another woman said, 'he really hates using them, so I

Testing a theory – the situation and condom use

A study to examine situational factors and cognitions associated with condom use in gay men (Gold et al. 1991).

Background

Homosexual men are at greatest risk from HIV in the western world. Therefore understanding safer sex in this group has obvious implications for health promotion. The aim of this study was to examine which situational factors (e.g. physical location, type of partner) and cognitions (e.g. desires, intentions to use drugs/alcohol) and mood are related to either protected or unprotected sex. This study by Gold et al. (1991) illustrates an attempt to place individual cognitions within both the relationship context and the broader social context. In addition, the mood measurements reflect an attempt to examine the less rational aspects of sex.

Methodology

Subjects

A total of 219 Australian gay men completed a questionnaire containing questions about two sexual encounters in the preceding year. They were recruited from a range of gay venues (e.g. gay bar/disco, sex-on-premises venue, established gay group, AIDS council premises a medical practice known to have a large gay clientele).

Design

The study involved a cross-sectional design with all subjects completing a self-administered questionnaire.

Questionnaire

The subjects were asked to think about two sexual encounters in the preceding year, one involving safe sex and one involving unsafe sex. They were asked to complete the following ratings/questions about each of these encounters:

1 *Details of the encounters.* The subjects were asked questions about their encounters, including: (i) how long ago it had taken place; (ii) whether the respondent had known about AIDS at the time of the encounter; and (iii) what form of sexual activity had occurred (e.g. intercourse, ejaculation into the rectum). The encounter was then divided into four temporal stages: (i) start of the 'evening'; (ii) time of meeting the potential partner; (iii) start of sex; and (iv) during sex. The subjects were then asked to answer questions about each stage of the encounter for both the safe and unsafe encounter.

2 *Start of the evening.* The subjects were asked to rate: (i) the type of desires that had been in their mind (e.g. to have sex without intercourse, to have intercourse without a condom, to have exciting sex, to have a drink or get mildly stoned); and (ii) to rate their mood at this time (e.g. happy, relaxed, under stress) and how intoxicated they were.

3 *Meeting the partner.* The subjects were asked: (i) where they met their partner (e.g. at my place, at his place); (ii) which of the above various desires had been on his mind; (iii) how sexually attracted he was to his partner; and (iv) how intoxicated he was.

▶

4 *Start of sex.* The subjects were asked: (i) how much time there was between meeting the partner and the start of sex; (ii) details of the sex (e.g. place, time of day); (iii) kinds of desires; (iv) how sexually aroused he was; (v) how intoxicated he was; and (iv) whether he/his partner had communicated a desire for safe sex.

5 *During sex.* The subject was asked: (i) how intoxicated he was; and (ii) whether he/his partner communicated about safe sex.

6 *Additional questions for unsafe encounter.* Subjects were also asked to rate a series of statements for the unsafe encounter. They related to: (i) ways in which the subjects may have engaged in unsafe sex without really wanting to (e.g. physically forced, tricked); and (ii) self-justifications for not using a condom (e.g. 'I thought to myself something like … condoms are such horrible things and to put one on destroys the magic of sex. Here we are on cloud nine: how can we suddenly interrupt everything just to get a bit of rubber out and roll it on', 'Other guys fuck without a condom much more often than I do. I'm less at risk than most guys').

Results

The results were analysed to examine the characteristics of both the safe and unsafe encounter and to evaluate any differences. The results showed that type of partner, desires, sexual attraction, mood, knowledge of condom availability and communication about safe sex differentiated between the two encounters. For example, unsafe sex was more likely to occur if the partner was a regular lover, if the subject reported a greater desire to have sex without a condom, to be more interested in having exciting sex, to be more attracted to their partner, to be in a better mood, to have less communication about safe sex, and to be less knowledgeable about the availability of a condom. However, level of intoxication was not related to the type of resulting encounter. The results were also analysed to examine the frequency of self-justifications used. The most common justification was a belief that they could have sex without ejaculation ('It'll be safe to fuck without a condom, so long as we don't cum up the arse. So we'll just fuck without cumming'), followed by beliefs about faithfulness.

Conclusion

This study is interesting because it integrates cognitions with situational factors. Therefore it attempts to place safe and unsafe sex in a context. The authors discuss the results in terms of developing educational interventions to promote safe sex. In addition, the authors emphasize that it is the thoughts and beliefs that occur during sexual encounters that are perhaps more relevant than those described in the cold light of day.

used to say to him, look, right, look, I have no intention of getting pregnant again and you have no intention to become a father so you put one of these on'. However, other women described how difficult it was to suggest safe sex to their partner with reasons for this relating to not wanting to hurt their boyfriend's feelings, not wanting to 'ruin the whole thing', and not being able to approach the subject. One woman said, 'When I got pregnant I thought to myself, "I'm not using a condom here, I'm not using anything" but I just couldn't say, just couldn't force myself to say, "look you know"'. Holland et al. (1990b) argued that safe sex campaigns present condoms as neutral objects, which can be easily negotiated prior to sex and that this did not appear to be the case with the women they interviewed. The qualitative data from the WRAP study provide some insights into the process of negotiation; they also emphasize sex as an interaction. In addition, these data provide a relationship context for individual beliefs and cognitions. In line with the WRAP study, Debro et al. (1994) examined the strategies use by 393 heterosexual college students to negotiate condom use and concluded that they used reward, emotional coercion, risk information, deception, seduction and withholding sex. Noar et al. (2002) built upon Debro et al.'s work and developed and validated a measure to quantify negotiation strategies called the condom influence strategy questionnaire (CISQ). They conceptualized negotiation in terms of six strategies: withholding sex, direct request, education, relationship conceptualizing, risk information and deception, and indicated that these factors account to variance in a range of safer sex variable such as behavioural intentions and actual condom use. Stone and Ingham (2002) also explored partner communication in the context of predicting the use of contraception at first intercourse. The study involved a survey of 963 students aged between 16 and 18 and explored the role of a range of individual, contextual and background factors. The results showed that communication with partner was a significant predictor of contraception use for both men and women. In particular, young men's contraception use was predicted by discussing contraception beforehand, giving an intimate reason for having sex the first time (e.g. they loved their partner as opposed to losing their virginity) and having parents who portrayed sexuality positively. For young women, contraception use was predicted by discussing contraception beforehand, being older, expecting to have sex, comfort and ease of interacting with boys and not having visited a service provider prior to having sex (this last result was in contrast to much previous work).

Therefore qualitative and quantitative research has emphasized the importance of negotiation which seems to have been taken on board by health education campaigns with advertisements highlighting the problem of raising the issue of safer sex (e.g. when would you mention condoms?). However, do interviews really access the interaction? Can the interaction be accessed using the available (and ethical) methodologies? (It would obviously be problematic to observe the interaction!) Are qualitative methods actually accessing something different from quantitative methods? Are interviews simply another method of finding out about people's cognitions and beliefs? Debates about methodology (quantitative versus qualitative) and the problem of behaviour as an interaction are relevant to all forms of behaviour but are particularly apparent when discussing sex.

The broader social context

Beliefs, attitudes and cognitions about sex, risk and condom use do not just exist within individuals, or within the context of an interaction between two individuals; they exist within a much broader social context. This social context takes many forms such as the form and influence of sex education, the social meanings, expectations and social norms developed and presented through the multiple forms of media, and created and perpetuated by individual communities and the wider world of gender and inequality. Psychological theory predominantly studies the individual. However, it is important to have some acknowledgement and understanding of this broader world. The final part of this chapter will examine this context in terms of sex education, sexual health services, power relations between men and women, social norms of the gay community and discourses about sex, HIV and illness.

Sex education

Education about sex, pregnancy, HIV and contraception comes from a variety of different sources, including government health education campaigns, school sex education programmes and from an individual's social world. These three sources of information will now be examined further.

Sexual health services

Specialist family planning clinics, genito-urinary clinics, general practitioner, the chemist and nurse practitioners all provide sexual health services offering access to contraception and sexual health information and advice. Even condom machines in public toilets and free condoms in youth clubs act as a form of sexual health service. Research shows that, to be effective, sexual health services must be user friendly, non-judgemental, accessible, approachable and confidential (Allen 1991; Scalley and Hadley 1995; Stone and Ingham 2000). For example, Allen evaluated three new family planning and pregnancy counselling projects for young people set up in 1987 and subsequently monitored their use over an 18-month period (Allen 1991). This evaluation identified a range of factors that made contraception services more or less acceptable to young people, including inconvenient opening times, embarrassment from being seen by other people while seeking sexual health advice, not feeling comfortable with the staff, judgemental or unhelpful staff, fear of the services not being confidential and having to give personal details. In a similar vein, Harden and Ogden (1999b) asked 967 16–19-year-olds about their beliefs and use of contraception services and reported that the chemist and the condom machine had been used by the largest number of respondents, with men favouring the condom machine and women favouring the GP or family planning clinic. In terms of beliefs, the condom machine was regarded as the easiest and most comfortable to use but the least confidential, with men reporting higher ratings for ease of use than women. Much research shows that young people in particular do not use sexual health services and often report finding contraceptives difficult (Stone and Ingham 2000). Stone and Ingham (2003) gave a questionnaire to 747 attendees at a youth-targeted sexual health service to investigate why they use the service. The results showed that 29 per cent had used a service before having ever had sex 'to be prepared' but that the remainder had only used a service after having sex. The most common reasons for non-use of service were being embarrassed or scared, concerned about confidentiality or not knowing about where the services were.

Government health education campaigns

Ingham et al. (1991) examined UK campaigns that promoted safe sex and suggested that slogans such as 'Unless you're completely sure about your partner, always use a condom', 'Nowadays is it really wise to have sex with a stranger?', and 'Sex with a lot of partners, especially with people you don't know, can be dangerous' emphasize knowing your partner. They interviewed a group of young people in the south of England to examine how they interpreted 'knowing their partners'. The results suggest that 27 per cent of the interviewees had had sex within 24 hours of becoming a couple, that 10 per cent of the sample reported having sex on the first ever occasion on which they met their partner, and that over 50 per cent reported having sex within two weeks of beginning a relationship. In terms of 'knowing their partner', 31 per cent of males and 35 per cent of females reported knowing nothing of their partner's sexual history, and knowing was often explained in terms of 'she came from a nice family and stuff', and having 'seen them around'. The results from this study indicate that promoting 'knowing your partner' may not be the best way to promote safe sex as knowledge can be interpreted in a multitude of different ways. In addition, safer sex campaigns emphasize personal responsibility and choice in the use of condoms, and condoms are presented as a simple way to prevent contraction of the HIV virus. This presentation is epitomized by government health advertisement slogans such as 'You know the risks: the decision is yours'. This view of sex and condom use is in contradiction with the research suggesting that people believe that they are not at risk from HIV and that condom use involves a complex process of negotiation.

School sex-education programmes

Information about sex also comes from sex-education programmes at school. Holland et al. (1990a) interviewed young women about their experiences of sex education and concluded that sex education in schools is impersonal, mechanistic and concerned with biology. The women in their study made comments such as 'It was all from the book. It wasn't really personal' and 'Nobody ever talks to you about the problems and the entanglements, and what it means to a relationship when you start having sex'. It has been argued that this impersonal and objective approach to sex education is counterproductive (Aggleton 1989) and several alternatives have been suggested. Aggleton and Homans (1988) argued for a 'socially transformatory model' for AIDS education, which would involve discussions of: (1) ideas about sex; (2) social relations; (3) political processes involved; and (4) the problem of resource allocation. This approach would attempt to shift the emphasis from didactic teachings of facts and knowledge to a discussion of sex within a context of relationships and the broader social context. An additional solution to the problem of sex education is a skills training approach recommended by Abraham and Sheeran (1993). They argued that individuals could be taught a variety of skills, including buying condoms, negotiation of condom use and using condoms. These skills could be taught using tuition, role-play, feedback, modelling and practice. They are aimed at changing cognitions, preparing individuals for action and encouraging people to practise different aspects of the sequences involved in translating beliefs into behaviour. Ingham (2005) provides a detailed analysis of sex and relationship education. He explores how sex education is currently evaluated and highlights what is missing from current ideas about the nature of 'good education'. Further, he then provides an analysis of how sex education could be improved. Central to Ingham's argument (2005) is the importance of teaching young people about desire and pleasure and how these are important both to physical and mental health. In particular, Ingham suggests that by learning about their bodies and how to achieve sexual pleasure, young people may feel more empowered to have healthier and happier sexual relationships. He argues that 'if young people are enabled to feel more relaxed about their own bodies, and about bodily pleasures then they may be less affected by the pressures to engage in sexual activity against their wishes or in ways that they do not feel comfortable about ' (2005: 385). Ingham then suggests that the use of small group teaching, organized around friendship groups with people at similar stages of sexual development and experience, could enable a deeper and more focused discussion of both the 'factual' and pleasure aspects of sex. These problems with school sex education reflect the debates about using psychological models to examine sexual behaviour and emphasize a need to place an individual's beliefs within the context of an interaction between individuals. In addition, the discussions about sex education in schools highlight the social context in which sex occurs.

An individual's social world

Information about sex also comes from an individual's social world in terms of one's peers, parents and siblings. Holland et al. (1990a) argued that sex education and the process of learning about sex occurs in the context of a multitude of different sources of information. They redefined the 'problem of sex education' as something that is broader than acquiring facts. They also argued that the resulting knowledge not only influences an individual's own knowledge and beliefs but also creates their sexuality. They identified the following five sources: school, peers, parents, magazines, and partners and relationships. Holland et al. argued that through these different sources, individuals learn about sex and their sexuality and suggested that 'the constructions which are presented are of women as passive, as potential victims of male sexuality or at best reproductive' (1990a: 43). However, they also argued that women do not simply passively accept this version of sexuality but are in a 'constant process of negotiating and re-negotiating the meaning which others give to their behaviour' (1990a: 43). Therefore, perhaps any understanding of sexual behaviour should take place within an understanding of the social context of sex education in the broadest sense.

Power relations between men and women

Sex has also been studied within the context of power relations between men and women. Holland et al. (1990b) argued that condom use 'must be understood in the context of the contradictions and tensions of heterosexual relationships' and the 'gendered power relations which construct and constrain choices and decisions'. They presented examples of power inequalities between men and women and the range of ways in which this can express itself, from coercion to rape. For example, one woman in their study said, 'I wasn't forced to do it but I didn't want to do it' and another explained her ambivalence to sex as 'like do you want a coffee? Okay, fine you drink the coffee, because you don't really like drinking coffee but you drink it anyway'. In fact, empirical research suggests that men's intentions to use condoms may be more likely to correlate with actual behaviour than women's, perhaps because women's intentions may be inhibited by the sexual context (Abraham et al. 1996). Sex should also be understood within the context of gender and power.

Social norms of the gay community

Sex also occurs between two individuals of the same gender and within gay communities, which have their own sets of norms and values. A study by Flowers et al. (1997, 1998) explored 'the transformation of men who come to find themselves within a specific gay culture, one in which there are clear values which structure their new social world, shaping their relationships and their sexual behaviour'. Therefore, Flowers et al. asked the question 'How do the social norms and values of the gay community influence gay men's sexual practices?' They interviewed 20 gay men from a small town in northern England about their experiences of becoming gay within a gay community. The results provided some interesting insights into the norms of gay culture and the impact of this social context on an individual's behaviour. First, the study describes how men gain access to the gay community: 'through sex and socialising they come to recognise the presence of other gay men where once . . . they only felt isolation'; second, the study illustrates how simply having a gay identity is not enough to prepare them for their new community and that they have 'to learn a gay specific knowledge and a gay language'; and third, the study describes how this new culture influences their sexual behaviour. For example, the interviewees described how feelings of romance, trust, love, commitment, inequality within the relationship, lack of experience and desperation resulted in having anal sex without a condom even though they had the knowledge that their behaviour was risky (Flowers et al. 1997, 1998). Therefore sexual behaviour also occurs within the context of specific communities with their own sets of norms and values.

Discourses about sex, HIV and illness

Sex also takes place within the broader context of theories and discussions about sex, HIV and illness. This literature is beyond the scope of this book but includes discussions about HIV as a metaphor for concerns about sexuality and death in the late twentieth century (Sontag 1988), the social response to HIV as a moral panic (Weeks 1985) and the social construction of sex through theory and practice (Foucault 1979). Many of these discussions about sex challenge the traditional biological reductionist approach to sex and argue for an understanding of sex within a context of social meanings and discourses.

To conclude

Since the beginning of the twentieth century sex has been studied as an activity rather than in terms of its biological outcome. Recently sex has also been examined in terms of it being a risk to health. Psychologists have contributed to this literature in terms of an examination of sexual behaviour both in the context of pregnancy avoidance and HIV/AIDS. These behaviours have been predominantly understood using cognitive models, which emphasize individual differences and individual cognitions. However, sex presents a problem for psychologists as it is intrinsically an interactive behaviour involving more than one person. Therefore cognitive models have been expanded in an attempt to emphasize cognitions about the individual's social world, particularly in terms of the relationship. To further the understanding of sex as an interaction, qualitative methods have been used to examine the process of negotiation. However, sex also occurs within a broader social context. Social cognition models have also been developed in an attempt to address individuals' representations of this world – their normative beliefs. However, perhaps an understanding of sexual behaviour can only take place within the wider context of educational influences, service provision, power relations, community norms and theories about sexuality.

❓ Questions

1 To what extent do decision-making models predict contraceptive use?

2 Is contraceptive use a rational process?

3 Can social cognition models be expanded to understand contraceptive use as an interaction?

4 Why do people use condoms?

5 How can qualitative research contribute to an understanding of condom use?

6 To what extent can psychology incorporate the context of a behaviour?

7 To what extent do the problems highlighted by the sex literature relate to other health behaviours?

8 Describe a possible research study aimed at predicting condom use in adolescents.

For discussion

Health education campaigns frequently use billboards and magazines to promote safe sex. Consider a recent advertisement and discuss whether or not this would encourage you to use condoms.

Assumptions in health psychology

The research into sex and contraceptive use highlights some of the assumptions that are central to psychology as follows:

1 *Methodology accesses information, it does not create it.* It is believed that questionnaires/interviews provide us with insights into what people think and believe. However, does the method of asking questions influence the results? For example, do people have beliefs about risk until they are asked about risk? Do people have behavioural intentions prior to being asked whether they intend to behave in a particular way?

2 *Individuals can be studied separately from their social context.* Social psychologists have studied processes such as conformity, group dynamics, obedience to authority and diffusion of responsibility, all of which suggest that individuals behave differently when on their own than when in the presence of others and also indicate the extent to which an individual's behaviour is determined by their context. However, much psychological research continues to examine behaviour and beliefs out of context. To what extent can psychological research incorporate the context? To what extent should it attempt to incorporate the environment?

3 *Theories are derived from data.* Theories are not data themselves. It is assumed that eventually we will develop the best way to study sex, which will enable us to understand and predict sexual behaviour. However, perhaps the different approaches to sex can tell us something about the way we see individuals. For example, attempting to incorporate interactions between individuals into an understanding of sex may be a better way of understanding sex, and it may also suggest that we now see individuals as being interactive. In addition, examining the social context may also suggest that our model of individuals is changing and we see individuals as being social products.

Further reading

Gallois, C., Terry, D., Timmins, P., Kashima, Y. and McCamish, M. (1994) Safe sex intentions and behaviour among heterosexuals and homosexual men: testing the theory of reasoned action, *Psychology and Health*, 10: 1–16.
This study uses the TRA to examine condom use and in particular focuses on the relationship between intentions and actual behaviour.

Holland, J., Ramazanoglu, C. and Scott, S. (1990) Managing risk and experiencing danger: tensions between government AIDS health education policy and young women's sexuality, *Gender and Education*, 2: 125–46.
This paper presents some of the results from the WRAP studies and examines how young women feel about their sexuality in the context of HIV.

Ingham, R. and Aggleton, P. (eds) (2005) *Promoting Young People's Sexual Health*. London: Routledge.
This book provides an excellent analysis of the practical and ideological barriers to enhancing sexual health in young people and offers a detailed account of cross-cultural differences and the problems faced in developing countries.

Lee, E., Clements, S., Ingham, R. and Stone, N. (2004) *A Matter of Choice? Explaining National Variations in Teenage Abortion and Motherhood*. York: Joseph Rowntree Foundation.
This book provides a detailed analysis of young people's sexual behaviour and their decisions about becoming a parent.

Chapter 9

Screening

Chapter overview

This chapter examines definitions of screening and describes the history of the screening of populations both in general practice and in hospital-based medical centres. It outlines the guidelines for developing screening programmes and assesses the patient, health professional and organizational predictors of screening uptake. The chapter then examines recent research which has emphasized the negative consequences of screening in terms of ethical principles, the cost effectiveness and the possible psychological consequences.

This chapter covers

- What is screening?
- Guidelines for screening
- Predictors of screening uptake
- Screening as problematic
- Is screening ethical?
- Is screening cost-effective?
- What are the psychological consequences of screening?

What is screening?

There are three forms of prevention aimed at improving a nation's health:

1 *Primary prevention* refers to the modification of risk factors (such as smoking, diet, alcohol intake) before illness onset. The recently developed health promotion campaigns are a form of primary prevention.

2 *Secondary prevention* refers to interventions aimed at detecting illness at an asymptomatic stage of development so that its progression can be halted or retarded. *Screening* is a form of secondary prevention.

3 *Tertiary prevention* refers to the rehabilitation of patients or treatment interventions once an illness has manifested itself.

Screening programmes (secondary prevention) take the form of health checks, such as measuring weight, blood pressure, height (particularly in children), urine, carrying out cervical smears and mammograms and offering genetic tests for illnesses such as Huntington's disease, some forms of breast cancer and cystic fibrosis. Until recently, two broad types of screening were defined: *opportunistic screening*, which involves using the time when a patient is involved with the medical services to measure aspects of their health. For example, when seeing a patient for a sore throat the GP may decide to also check their blood pressure, and *population screening*, which involves setting up services specifically aimed at identifying problems. For example, current programmes involve cervical screening and breast screening. Recently a new form of screening has emerged in the form of *self-screening*. For example, people are encouraged to practise breast and testicular self-examination and it is now possible to buy over-the-counter kits to measure blood pressure, cholesterol and blood sugar levels.

The aim of all screening programmes is to detect a problem at the asymptomatic stage. This results in two outcomes. First, screening can discover a risk of the disease. This is called primary screening. For example, cervical screening may detect pre-cancerous cells which place the individual at risk of cervical cancer; genetic screening for cystic fibrosis would give the person an estimate of risk of producing children with cystic fibrosis; and cholesterol screening could place an individual at high risk of developing coronary heart disease. Second, screening can detect the illness itself. This is called secondary screening. For example, a mammogram may discover breast cancer, genetic testing may discover the gene for Huntington's disease and blood pressure assessment may discover hypertension.

The history of the screening ethos
Early screening programmes

Screening has increasingly become an important facet of biomedicine throughout the twentieth century. The drive to detect an illness at an asymptomatic stage of its development (secondary prevention) can be seen throughout both secondary and primary care across the western world. In 1900, Gould introduced the regular health examination in the USA, which stimulated interest in the concept of population screening. In Britain, the inter-war years saw the development of the Pioneer Health Centre in Peckham, south London, which provided both a social and health nucleus for the community and enabled the health of the local community to be surveyed and monitored with ease (Williamson and Pearse 1938; Pearse and Crocker 1943). The ethos of screening received impetus from multiphasic screening, which became popular in the USA in the late 1940s, and in 1951 the Kaiser Permanente organization incorporated screening methods into its health examinations. Sweden mounted a large-scale multiphasic screening programme that was completed in 1969 and similar programmes were set up in the former West Germany and Japan in 1970. In London, in 1973, the Medical Centre at King's Cross organized a computerized automated unit that could screen 15,000 individuals a year. General practice also promoted the use of screening to evaluate what Last (1963) called the 'iceberg of disease'. In the 1960s and 1970s, primary care developed screening programmes for disorders such as anaemia (Ashworth 1963), diabetes (Redhead 1960), bronchitis (Gregg 1966), cervical cancer (Freeling 1965) and breast cancer (Holleb et al. 1960).

Recent screening programmes

Enthusiasm for screening has continued into recent years. Forrest chaired a working party in 1985 to consider the validity of a breast screening programme in the UK. The report (Forrest 1986) concluded that the evidence of the efficacy of screening was sufficient to establish a screening programme with three-year intervals. Furthermore, in the late 1980s, Family Practitioner Committees began computer-assisted calls of patients for cervical screening, and in 1993 a report from the Professional Advisory Committee for the British Diabetic Association suggested implementing a national screening programme for non-insulin-dependent diabetes for individuals aged 40–75 years (Patterson 1993). In addition, the new contracts for GPs include mandatory tasks such as assessments of patients over 75, and financial incentives for achieving set levels of immunizations, cervical screening and health checks for pre-school children (Department of Health and Welsh Office 1989). Likewise, practice nurses routinely measure weight and blood pressure to screen for obesity and hypertension. Recent screening programmes have also focused on self-screening in terms of breast and testicular self-examination and over-the-counter tests to measure blood sugar levels, blood pressure and blood cholesterol.

Genetic testing

Advancements in ultrasound technology has meant that pregnant mothers can now undergo screening for genetic or developmental problems such as Down's syndrome, spina bifida, congenital heart defects and gross anatomical deformities such as anencephaly (a child with a seriously deformed head), missing limbs or underdeveloped organs. In addition, genetic testing and genetic counselling are now offered for genetic disorders such as cystic fibrosis; Alzheimer's disease; Huntington's disease; forms of muscular dystrophy; breast, ovarian or colon cancer; and familial hypercholesterolaemia which is a predisposition for raised cholesterol and is linked with coronary heart disease. There are different types of genetic tests depending upon the condition involved. Carrier testing refers to genetic tests that identify people who have a mutation for a recessive condition, who will not develop the condition themselves but may have children who have the condition if the other parent is also a carrier. In contrast, predictive testing is concerned with identifying people who are at risk of developing the disease in the future. A few conditions can be definitely predicted by predictive testing. For example, a person who tests positive for Huntington's disease will definitely develop it in the future. However, for most conditions such as cancer, Alzheimer's and heart disease a positive test only illustrates a high risk of developing the disease. Furthermore, even though people may develop the disease in the future, the severity of the disease can show great variability. A good example of this is sickle cell anaemia which has a clear genetic basis but can express itself and is experienced by the sufferer in very different ways.

Screening as a useful tool

The proliferation of screening programmes was at first welcomed as an invaluable and productive means of improving the health of a country's population. It was seen as a cost-effective method of preventing disease as well as providing statistics on the prevalence and incidence of a wide variety of disorders and illnesses. Morris, in his book *Uses of Epidemiology* (1964), stressed the importance of penetrating to the 'early minor stages', then back to the precursors of disease and then back to its predispositions. In 1968, Butterfield, in a Rock Carling Lecture on priorities in medicine, advocated a new emphasis on screening in health-care delivery. This enthusiasm is reflected in a statement by Edward VII that is often repeated: 'If preventable, why not prevented?'

Guidelines for screening

As a result of the enthusiasm for screening, sets of criteria have been established. Wilson (1965) outlined the following set of screening criteria:

- *The disease*
  - an important problem
  - recognizable at the latent or early symptomatic stage
  - natural history must be understood (including development from latent to symptomatic stage)
- *The screen*
  - suitable test or examination (of reasonable sensitivity and specificity)
  - test should be acceptable by the population being screened
  - screening must be a continuous process
- *Follow-up*
  - facilities must exist for assessment and treatment
  - accepted form of effective treatment
  - agreed policy on whom to treat
- *Economy*
  - cost must be economically balanced in relation to possible expenditure on medical care as a whole.

More recently, the criteria have been developed as follows:

- The disease must be sufficiently prevalent and/or sufficiently serious to make early detection appropriate.
- The disease must be sufficiently well defined to permit accurate diagnosis.
- There must be a possibility (or probability) that the disease exists undiagnosed in many cases (i.e. that the disease is not so manifest by symptoms as to make rapid diagnosis almost inevitable).
- There must be a beneficial outcome from early diagnosis in terms of disease treatment or prevention of complications.
- There must be a screening test that has good sensitivity and specificity and a reasonably positive predictive value in the population to be screened.

Psychological predictors of the uptake of screening

The numbers of individuals who attend different screening programmes vary enormously according to factors such as the country, the illness being screened and time of the screening programme. For example, uptake for neonatal screening for phenylketonuria is almost 100 per cent. However, whereas up to 99 per cent of pregnant women in Sweden and France undertake HIV testing (Larsson et al. 1990; Moatti et al. 1990), in the UK and North America only a small

---

Box 9.1 Some problems with . . . screening research

Below are some problems with research in this area that you may wish to consider.

1 The ability of medicine to screen reflects new and ever advancing medical technology. Because of this it is often seen by the health profession as a positive development. However, just because something can be done does not mean that it should be done. At times the research on screening can seem polarized between those that promote screening and the use of technology and those that seem wary of it. This can lead to contradictory findings or research that simply supports the ideological position of those involved.

2 Evaluating the impact of screening can involve measuring both psychological (e.g. fear, anxiety) and medical outcomes (e.g. health status, detection). Sometimes these outcomes occur in opposite directions (it may make a person anxious but benefit their health status). Combining these contradictory outcomes and deciding upon the right way forward can be a complex and difficult process.

3 Screening may detect an illness at an early stage. Some people, however, may not wish to know that they have something wrong with them. This can present researchers and clinicians with a dilemma as medicine also emphasizes truth telling, openness and patient autonomy. Balancing the different ethical positions and perspectives of medicine can prove difficult.

---

minority elect to take the test. Marteau (1993) suggested that there are three main factors that influence uptake of screening: patient factors, health professional factors and organizational factors.

Patient factors

Several studies have been carried out to examine which factors predict the uptake of screening. These have included demographic factors, beliefs, emotional factors and contextual factors.

Demographic factors

MacLean et al. (1984) reported that women who attended for breast screening were more likely to be of high socio-economic status, and Owens et al. (1987) reported that older women were more likely to attend for breast screening than younger women. Similarly, Simpson et al. (1997) concluded that older women were more likely to attend a worksite screening programme for cardiovascular disease than either younger women or men. In addition, Waller et al. (1990) suggested that those individuals who are the most healthy are more likely to attend for an HIV test, and Sutton et al. (2000) reported that men, home-owners, non-smokers, those who have regular check-ups at the dentist and those with better subjective health were more likely to attend for flexible sigmoidoscopy which screens for colorectal cancer.

Health beliefs

Health beliefs have also been linked to uptake and have been measured using models (see Chapter 2). For example, Bish et al. (2000) used the health belief model (HBM) and the theory of planned behaviour (TPB) to predict uptake of a routine cervical smear test. The results showed that the TPB was a better predictor of behavioural intentions but that neither model successfully predicted actual uptake at follow-up. Pakenham et al. (2000) also used the HBM in conjunction with knowledge and sociodemographic variables to predict re-attendance for mammography screening. The results showed that although the re-attenders were older and more likely to be married, the HBM variable of perceived benefits of the mammography were a better predictor overall of re-attendance than sociodemographic variables. Similarly, Sutton et al. (2000) also included measures of beliefs and reported that a perception of fewer barriers and more benefits predicted attendance for sigmoidoscopy screening.

Emotional factors

Emotional factors such as anxiety, stress, fear, uncertainty and feeling indecent have also been shown to relate to uptake. For example, Simpson et al. (1997) indicated that non-attenders at a worksite screening programme reported more fear of the results and MacLean et al. (1984) reported that women who attended for breast screening had suffered less anxiety following the invitation to attend. Negative emotions would therefore seem to be linked to no uptake. In contrast, however, Lerman et al. (1997) explored what factors determined whether someone requested the results from genetic testing for breast and ovarian cancer susceptibility. The results showed that, after controlling for sociodemographic factors and objective risk, those with higher levels of cancer-specific distress were three times more likely to request the results. Shiloh et al. (1997) examined the predictors of uptake for four screening programmes (a dental check-up, blood pressure measurement and cholesterol testing, a cervical smear, mammography) and suggested that both the cognitions derived from a range of models and emotional factors such as reassurance predicted uptake. However, they also argued that although beliefs and emotions predict screening uptake, the nature of these beliefs and emotions is very much dependent upon the screening programme being considered. Research, however, also shows that declining a test can result in elevated stress. For example, Almqvist et al. (2003) explored the longer-term consequences of either having or not having a genetic test for Huntington's disease and reported that those who declined the test were the most distressed over a period of 12 months. Some research has also focused on patients' need to reduce their uncertainty and to find 'cognitive closure'. For example, Eiser and Cole (2002) used a quantitative method based upon the stages-of-change model and explored differences between individuals at different stages of attending for a cervical smear in terms of 'cognitive closure' and barriers to screening. The results showed that the pre-contemplators reported most barriers and the least need for closure and to reduce uncertainty. One qualitative study further highlighted the role of emotional factors in the form of feeling indecent. Borrayo and Jenkins (2001) interviewed 34 women of Mexican descent in five focus groups about their beliefs about breast cancer screening and their decision whether or not to take part. The analyses showed that the women reported a fundamental problem with breast screening as it violates a basic cultural standard. Breast screening requires women to touch their own breasts and to expose their breasts to health professionals. Within the cultural norms of respectable female behaviour for these women, this was seen as 'indecent'.

Contextual factors

Finally contextual factors have also been shown to predict uptake. For example, Smith et al. (2002) interviewed women who had been offered genetic testing for Huntington's disease. The results showed that the women often showed complex and sometimes contradictory beliefs about their risk status for the disease which related to factors such as prevalence in the family, family size, attempts to make the numbers 'add up' and beliefs about transmission. The results also showed that uptake of the test related not only to the individual's risk perception but also to contextual factors such as family discussion or a key triggering event. For example, one woman described how she had shouted at the cats for going onto the new stair carpet which had been paid for from her father's insurance money after he had died from Huntington's disease. This had made her resolve to have the test.

Health professional factors

Marteau and Johnston (1990) argued that it is important to assess health professionals' beliefs and behaviour alongside those of the patients. In a study of general practitioners' attitudes and screening behaviour, a belief in the effectiveness of screening was associated with an organized approach to screening and time spent on screening (Havelock et al. 1988). Such factors may influence patient uptake. In addition, the means of presenting a test may also influence patient uptake. For example, uptake rates for HIV testing at antenatal clinics are reported to vary from 3 to 82 per cent (Meadows et al. 1990). These rates may well be related to the way in which these tests were offered by the health professional, which in turn may reflect the health professional's own beliefs about the test. Some research has used qualitative methods to further analyse health professional factors. For example, Michie et al. (1999) used structured interviews to explore how clinical geneticists and genetic counsellors view the function of a genetic consultation in terms of its aims, the skills involved and patient expectations. The analyses showed that the interviewees described the consultations in terms of four main themes which were often contradictory. These were providing information that is both objective and full and tailored to the needs of the individual; dealing with emotion by both eliciting it and containing it; communicating both directively and non-directively; and performing sophisticated skills while having only minimal training. These themes and their contradictions suggest that consultations would vary enormously between patients and between clinicians. For example, while a clinician may offer full information for one patient, the same clinician might limit the information for another. Similarly, while one clinician might tend to be more directive, another might be less so. Such variation in health professional beliefs about the consultation and their subsequent behaviour could influence the patient's decision about whether or not to have a particular test (see Chapter 4 for more details on communication).

Organizational factors

Many organizational factors may also influence the uptake of screening. Research has examined the effects of the means of invitation on the uptake rate and indicates that if the invitation is issued in person, and if the individual is expected to opt out, not in, the rates of uptake are higher (Mann et al. 1988; Smith et al. 1990). The place of the screening programme may also be influential, with more accessible settings promoting high uptake. In addition, making attendance at a screening programme mandatory rather than voluntary will also obviously have an effect (Marteau 1993). Uptake may also be influenced by education and media campaigns. For example, Fernbach (2002) evaluated the impact of a large media campaign designed to influence women's self-efficacy and uptake of cervical screening. The media campaign was called the 'Papscreen Victoria' campaign and took place in Australia. It was evaluated by face-to-face interviews with 1571 women at baseline and two follow-ups. The results showed that women reported an increase in awareness of cervical screening and rated this as a greater health priority than before the campaign. However, the results were not all positive. The women also stated after the campaign that they would find it more difficult to ring up for test results and reported lowered self-efficacy.

Testing a theory – predicting screening

A study to examine the role of the health belief model, health locus of control and emotional control in predicting women's cancer screening behaviour (Murray and McMillan 1993).

This study examines the role of three social psychological models in predicting breast self-examination and cervical screening behaviour. The study illustrates how theories can be empirically tested and how research results can be used to develop interventions to promote screening behaviour.

Background

It is generally believed that early detection of both breast and cervical cancer may reduce mortality from these illnesses. Therefore screening programmes aim to help the detection of these diseases at the earliest possible stages. However, even when invited to attend for cervical screening, or when encouraged to practise breast self-examination, many women still do not carry out these health protective behaviours. Social psychology models have been used to predict cancer screening behaviour. This study examined the HBM and health locus of control (see Chapter 2) in the context of cancer screening. In addition, the authors included a measure of emotional control (sometimes described as expressed emotion, repression and defensiveness). Individuals with high emotional control are sometimes described as having a cancer-prone personality (see Chapter 13), which has been linked to cancer onset.

Methodology
Subjects

A letter informing residents about a regional health survey was sent to 1530 randomly selected addresses in Northern Ireland. An interviewer then visited each address and contacted a 'responsible adult' in order to record details of all of those in the household aged over 16. One person from each household was then randomly selected and left a questionnaire. After follow-up letters and visits to the household, 65.1 per cent of the eligible sample completed the questionnaire. This paper reports the results from 391 women who completed questions about breast and cervical screening behaviour.

Design

The study involved a cross-sectional design with subjects completing a questionnaire once.

Measures

The questionnaire consisted of the following measures:

1 *Screening behaviour (the dependent variables).* The subjects were asked about their breast and cervical screening behaviour.

   - Breast screening behaviour: the subjects were asked, 'If you examine your breasts for lumps how often do you do this?' (rated from 'once a month' to less than 'once every six months').

   - Cervical screening behaviour: the subjects were asked, (i) 'Have you had a cervical smear test?' (rated 'once', 'several times', 'never'), (ii) 'Did you have a smear test because . . .

(a) you asked for it, (b) your doctor suggested it, (c) it was taken routinely at a post-natal check-up, (d) because of some other reason?'. From these responses the women were classified as non-attenders, passive attenders (following advice from someone else) or active attenders (asked for the test).

2 *Health beliefs (the independent variables).* The subjects rated 22 items for how much they agreed with them. These items reflected the dimensions of the HBM as follows:

- Susceptibility: the subjects rated items such as 'my chances of getting cancer are great' and 'my physical health makes it more likely that I will get cancer'.

- Seriousness: the subjects rated items such as 'the thought of cancer scares me' and 'I am afraid to even think about cancer'.

- Benefits: the subjects rated items such as 'if cancer is detected early it can be successfully treated' and 'there has been much progress in the treatment of cancer in the past ten years'.

- Barriers: the subjects rated items such as 'I just don't like doctors or hospitals' and 'I would be afraid that I might need to have an operation'.

- Costs: the subjects rated items such as 'I would have trouble because of the distance or time to get to the doctor or clinic' and 'I would have to wait a long time at the doctor's office or clinic'.

In addition, the questionnaire included measures of the following health beliefs:

- Health motivation: the subjects were asked whether they engaged in a list of five health-related activities (e.g. take physical exercise, reduce alcohol consumption).

- Cancer knowledge: the subjects were asked open-ended questions about their knowledge of the early warning signs of breast and cervical cancer.

- Confidence: the subjects were asked to rate their confidence in performing breast self-examination as a measure of their self-efficacy.

- Contact with cancer: the subjects were asked whether or not a member of their family had ever had cancer.

3 *Health locus of control (the independent variables).* The subjects completed the 18-item multidimensional health locus of control scale (MHLC) (Wallston et al. 1978). The questionnaire was used to provide a measure of internal control (e.g. 'If I get sick it is my own behaviour that determines how soon I get well again'), external control/powerful others (e.g. 'Whenever I don't feel well I should consult my doctor') and external control/chance (e.g. 'Good health is largely a matter of good luck').

4 *Emotional control (the independent variables).* The subjects completed the 21-item Courtauld emotional control scale developed by Watson and Greer (1983). This consists of three subscales to measure the extent to which someone expresses or controls (i) anger, (ii) depressed mood and (iii) anxiety.

Demographic characteristics

In addition, subjects completed questions about their age, social class, marital status and religion.

Results

The results were analysed to assess the role of the different social psychological models in predicting screening behaviour for both breast and cervical cancer. Originally, individual correlations were evaluated between the dependent variables (breast cancer and cervical cancer screening behaviour) and the subjects' demographic characteristics, their health beliefs, health locus of control and their emotional control.

Breast self-examination

The results showed that breast self-examination was more frequent among those who attended for smear tests; negatively related to age and social class, a high belief in the costs of attendance for treatment, a high belief in the role of powerful others; and positively related to marital status, benefits of treatment, health motivation, knowledge of breast and cervical cancer.

Cervical screening behaviour

The results indicated that attending for cervical smears was positively related to religion, marital status, perceived benefits of treatment, health motivation, knowledge of breast and cervical cancer; and negatively associated with social class, perceived barriers and costs and a belief in the role of chance.

The results were then analysed to assess the overall best predictors of screening behaviour using multiple-regression analysis. This type of analysis puts a multitude of variables into the equation to see which combination of the independent variables is the best predictor of the dependent variable. The results suggest that the best predictor of breast self-examination was confidence in carrying out the examination (self-efficacy) and the best predictor of attending for cervical smears was having a lower fear of the consequences of the investigation (barriers).

Conclusion

The results from this study provide some support for the individual components of the health belief model and health locus of control in predicting screening behaviour for both cervical and breast cancer. In particular, the results suggest that self-efficacy (added to the recent version of the HBM, see Chapter 2) and barriers are the most powerful predictors of behaviour. However, the results provide no support for a role of emotional control in screening behaviour. The authors conclude that health promotion aimed at increasing breast self-examination 'must consider how to improve women's confidence in how to practise it' and education aimed at promoting attendance for cervical smears should 'reduce the anxiety felt among many women about the possible consequences of the investigation'. This paper therefore illustrates how a theory can be tested, and how the results from such a study could be turned into practice.

Screening as problematic

Over the past decade a new dimension has emerged in the screening literature, namely the negative elements of screening. There are now debates about the following aspects of screening: (1) *ethics*, in terms of the relevance of the four main ethical principles (beneficence, non-maleficence, autonomy and justice); (2) *the cost-effectiveness* of screening programmes; and (3) the possible *psychological side effects* of screening on the individual. These criticisms constitute what can be seen as a backlash against the screening of populations.

Is screening ethical?

Debates about the ethical issues surrounding screening have traditionally been polarized between what Sackett and Holland (1975) referred to as 'the evangelists and snails'. These debates are best understood within the context of the four major ethical principles relating to decision-making principles in medicine: beneficence, non-maleficence, autonomy and justice.

Beneficence – screening as beneficial to the patient

Beneficence refers to the likelihood that any benefits to the patient will outweigh any burdens. Screening should therefore bring about benefits to the patient in terms of detecting a treatable disease or abnormality and enabling the individual's life to be prolonged or enhanced. There is evidence both in favour and against screening as a benefit to the patient.

Evidence for beneficence

In terms of screening for hypertension, Hart (1987) has argued 'we are surely under a moral if not legal obligation to record blood pressure at least once in every five year span for every registered adult in our practice'. In terms of cervical screening it has been estimated that for every 40,000 smears, one life has been saved (*Lancet* 1985). In terms of breast cancer, reports from the Health Insurance Plan Study (Shapiro et al. 1972; Shapiro 1977) suggested that early detection of breast cancer through screening reduced mortality in the study group compared with the control group by 30 per cent. Results at follow-up indicated that the study group were still benefiting after 12 years (Shapiro et al. 1982). Further results concerning the benefits of breast screening have been reported following a large random controlled trial in Sweden (Lundgren 1981). Hinton (1992: 231) concluded from his review of the literature that 'lives may be saved by annual mammographic screening'. Jones (1992) argued that screening for colorectal cancer may also be beneficial. He suggested that the 'evidence and arguments . . . are becoming compelling' and noted that the death rate due to colorectal cancer was ten times that due to cervical cancer, for which there is an existing screening programme. In addition, the identification of the absence of illness through screening may also benefit the patient in that a negative result may 'give health back to the patient' (Grimes 1988). Therefore, according to the ethical principle of beneficence, screening may have some positive effects on those individuals being screened.

Evidence against beneficence

Electronic foetal monitoring was introduced as a way of improving obstetric outcomes. However, the results from two well-controlled trials indicated that such monitoring may increase the rate of Caesarean section without any benefit to the babies both immediately after birth (MacDonald et al. 1985) and at 4 years of age (Grant and Elbourne 1989). In addition, electronic foetal monitoring appeared to increase the rate of cerebral palsy measured at 18 months of age (Shy et al. 1990). In a recent review of the effects of antenatal blood pressure screening on the incidence of pre-eclampsia (high blood pressure in pregnancy, which threatens the mother's life), the authors concluded that the introduction of antenatal screening has had no significant effect on pre-eclampsia, suggesting that this screening process does not benefit the individual. Recent papers have also questioned the efficacy of screening for congenital dislocation of the hip in neonates (Leck 1986), hypertension, breast cancer and cervical cancer in terms of the relative effectiveness of early (rather than later) medical interventions and the effects of simply increasing the lead time (the period of time between detection and symptoms).

Non-maleficence – screening must do no harm

Skrabanek (1988) suggested that screening should be subjected to the same rigours as any experimental procedure, that the possible risks should be evaluated and that the precept of 'first do no harm' should be remembered. Therefore, for screening to be ethical, it must not only benefit the patient, but it must also have no negative consequences either to the individual or to society as a whole. The psychological and financial consequences of screening will be dealt with under later headings. However, screening may cause personal harm in terms of biological consequences and false-negative results (receiving a negative result when the problem is actually present) or false-positive results (receiving a positive result when the problem is actually absent); it may also cause social harm in terms of the medicalization of populations and the exacerbation of the existing stigmatization of certain groups of individuals.

Personal harm

Some of the techniques used to monitor an individual's health may have a detrimental effect on their biological state. This is of particular concern for the frequent use of mammography for the detection of breast cancer. Evidence for the harmful effects of the irradiation of breast tissue and the links to cancer can be found in reports of breast cancer in women who have been treated for benign conditions using radiation therapy (Metler et al. 1969; Simon 1977), in survivors of the bombings of Hiroshima and Nagasaki (Wanebo et al. 1968) and in women who have been given fluoroscopy for tuberculosis (MacKenzie 1965). It has been argued that there is a threshold below which radiation could be considered totally safe, and that the above examples of an association between irradiation and breast cancer are due to the unusually high levels of radiation (Perquin et al. 1976). However, there is some disagreement with this view. In particular, Upton et al. (1977) suggested that exposure to 1 rad would increase the risk of breast cancer by 1 per cent. Furthermore, Strax (1978) suggested that if 40 million women were screened for 20 years, 120 would die from radiation-induced breast cancer. However, since these concerns were raised, the dose of radiation used in mammography has been reduced, although some concerns still remain.

All tests are fallible and none can promise 100 per cent accuracy. Therefore there is always the chance of false positives and false negatives. A false-positive result may lead to unnecessary treatment interventions and the associated anxiety and uncertainty. A false-negative result may lead to an illness remaining undetected, untreated and consequently progressing without medical intervention. In addition, a false-negative result may lead to subsequent signs of illness (e.g. a breast lump, vaginal discharge) being ignored by the patient.

Social harm

Zola (1972) has argued that medicine is a means of social control and suggested that there is a danger if individuals become too reliant on experts. In terms of screening, monitoring and surveillance of populations could be seen as a forum for not only examining individuals but controlling them. This argument is also made by Illich in his book *Medical Nemesis* (1974), where he argued that medicine is taking over the responsibility for people's health and creating a society of medical addicts. Screening epitomizes this shift towards social control in that not only are the ill seen by the medical profession but also the healthy as all individuals are now 'at risk' from illness (Armstrong 1995). Skrabanek (1988: 1155) argued that screening and the medicalization of health 'serves as a justification for State intrusion into people's private lives, and for stigmatising those who do not conform'.

The possibility that screening may exacerbate existing stigma of particular social groups is particularly relevant to the screening for genetic disorders. At present, society is constituted of a variety of individuals, some of whom have genetic deficits such as Down's syndrome, cystic fibrosis and sickle-cell anaemia. Although these individuals may be subjected to stereotyping and stigma, society provides treatment and support and attempts to integrate them into the rest of the population. It is possible, however, that screening for such disorders would lead to terminations of pregnancy and a reduction in this stigmatized population. Although this would lead to fewer individuals with these disorders (this may be a positive consequence, as no one wants to suffer from sickle-cell anaemia) the individuals who are born with these problems may face increased stigma as they would be part of a greatly reduced minority existing in a world with reduced social provisions for support and treatment.

Autonomy – the patient has a right to choose

The third ethical principle is that of autonomy. This is based on the view that 'mentally competent and mature individuals should make decisions about their own future, subject to the constraints required to ensure social order' (Burke 1992). Proponents of screening argue that screening is central to promoting autonomy in that the individual has a right to have access to information about their health status. According to this model of screening, the doctor is the patient's gatekeeper to relevant information. However, screening may also undermine an individual's autonomy if it is construed as a form of social control and doctors are seen as 'lifestyle police'.

Justice – the equal distribution of resources

The fourth ethical principle of justice refers to the need for an equal distribution of resources. This principle is relevant because screening programmes may be costly and involve shifting funds from other services. In addition, the 'inverse care law' (Hart 1971), which suggests that those who seek out tests most frequently are often those who need them the least, when applied to screening, highlights a shifting of finances to the most healthy individuals in society.

Is screening cost-effective?

The second problem with screening concerns its cost-effectiveness. A cost-effectiveness analysis involves assessing either how to achieve a set objective at minimum cost or how to use a fixed resource to produce the best output. In terms of screening, this raises issues about the objectives of screening (to detect asymptomatic illness, which can be treated) and the degree of resources required to achieve these objectives (minimum interventions such as opportunistic weighing versus expensive interventions such as breast screening clinics). The economic considerations of screening have been analysed for different policies for cervical screening (Smith and Chamberlain 1987). The different policies include: (1) opportunistic screening (offer a smear test when an individual presents at the surgery); (2) offer a smear test every five years; (3) offer a smear test every three years; and (4) offer a smear test annually. The results from this analysis are shown in Figure 9.1. These different policies have been offered as possible solutions to the problem of screening for cervical cancer. The results suggest that annual screening in England and Wales would cost £165 million and would potentially prevent 4300 cancers, whereas smears every five years would cost £34 million and would potentially prevent 3900 cancers.

The problem of cost-effectiveness is also highlighted by a discussion of the OXCHECK and Family Heart Study results (Muir et al. 1994; Wood et al. 1994). Both studies indicated that intensive screening, counselling and health checks have only a moderate effect on risk factors and the authors discuss these results in terms of the implications for government policies for health promotion through doctor-based interventions.

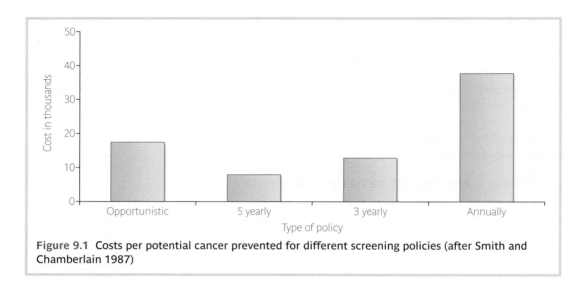

Figure 9.1 Costs per potential cancer prevented for different screening policies (after Smith and Chamberlain 1987)

The Family Heart Study

The Family Heart Study (Wood et al. 1994) examined the effects of screening and lifestyle interventions on cardiovascular risk factors in families over a one-year period. The study involved 26 general practices in 13 towns in Britain and recruited 12,472 individuals aged 40–59 years. The total sample consisted of 7460 men and 5012 women. The practices within each town were paired according to sociodemographic characteristics and were randomly designated as either the intervention or the comparison practice. Intervention practices were then randomly allocated either to a further comparison group or to an intervention group. This provided both an internal and external comparison with the subjects receiving the intervention. All intervention practices received screening, but only the intervention group of these practices received lifestyle counselling and follow-up within the one-year period. All subjects from all practices were followed up at one year. The screening process involved an appointment with a trained research nurse, who asked about demographic, lifestyle and medical factors and measured height, weight, carbon monoxide, blood pressure, blood glucose and blood cholesterol. The subjects in the intervention group also received lifestyle counselling and repeated follow-up. The counselling used a client-centred family approach and involved an assessment of the patients' risk status, educational input and a booklet for the subject to document their personally negotiated lifestyle changes. All subjects were then offered follow-up every 1, 2, 3, 4, 6 or 12 months, depending on their risk status. Outcome was measured at the follow-up in terms of changes in the main risk factors for coronary heart disease and the Dundee risk score, which is dependent on serum cholesterol concentration, systolic blood pressure, and previous and current smoking behaviour. Outcome was compared within the intervention practices, between the intervention practice and the internal comparison practice, and between the intervention practice and practices in the external comparison group. The results showed a 16 per cent reduction in overall risk score in the intervention practices at one year, a 4 per cent reduction in smoking, a small reduction in systolic (7 mmHg) and diastolic (3 mmHg) blood pressure and marginal reductions in weight (1 kg) and cholesterol concentrations (0.1 m). The results showed no changes in blood glucose levels. In addition, the greatest changes in risk status were reported in subjects with the highest risk levels. Although this intensive screening and intervention did result in changes in risk for coronary heart disease in the correct direction, Wood et al. (1994: 319) concluded that 'whether these small reductions can be sustained long term is not known, but even if they were they would correspond only to a 12 per cent lower risk of coronary heart disease events'. The authors also concluded that the government-sponsored health promotion clinics 'would probably have achieved considerably less and possibly no change at all' (Wood et al. 1994: 319) and that 'the government's screening policy cannot be justified by these results' (1994: 313).

The OXCHECK study

The results from the OXCHECK study also produced similarly pessimistic conclusions (Muir et al. 1994). This study involved 6124 patients recruited from five urban practices in Bedfordshire and aimed to evaluate the effectiveness of health checks by nurses in general practice in reducing risk factors for cardiovascular disease. All subjects received an initial health check and the intervention group received an additional follow-up health check after one year (further results were also collected for subjects over a four-year period). The health checks involved the nurse recording information about personal and family history of heart disease, stroke, hypertension, diabetes and cancer. Information about smoking history, alcohol consumption and habitual diet, height, weight, serum cholesterol concentration and blood pressure was also recorded. The nurses were also instructed to counsel patients about risk factors and to negotiate priorities and targets for risk reduction. The re-examination was briefer than the original health check but it involved re-measurement of the same profile and lifestyle factors. The results showed a lower cholesterol level (by 2.3 per cent) in the intervention group than the control group, lower systolic (2.5 per cent) and diastolic (2.4 per cent) blood pressure, and no differences in body mass index, or smoking prevalence or quit rates. The authors concluded that using health checks to reduce smoking may be ineffective as the effectiveness of health information may be diluted if the health check attempts to change too many risk factors at once. They suggested that the reduction in blood pressure was probably due to an accommodation effect, suggesting that the health checks were ineffective. Muir et al. (1994: 312) also concluded that, although the health checks did appear to reduce serum cholesterol concentration, 'it is disappointing that the difference ... was smaller in men than in women in view of the greater effect of cholesterol concentration on absolute risk in men' and they questioned whether such a shift in concentration could be sustained in the long term in the light of a previous trial in Oxfordshire. Therefore, although the results of the OXCHECK study suggested some reduction in risk factors for cardiovascular disease, the authors were fairly pessimistic in their presentation of these reductions.

Both of the above studies suggested that screening and minimal interventions are not cost-effective, as the possible benefits are not worthy of the amount of time and money needed to implement the programmes.

The effects of screening on the psychological state of the individual

The third problem with screening concerns its impact on the individual's psychological state.

The debates

Early evaluations of screening included an assessment of screening outcome in terms of the patients' understanding and recall of their diagnosis, not in terms of possible negative consequences (Sibinga and Friedman 1971; Reynolds et al. 1974). Recent discussions of the effects of screening, however, have increasingly emphasized negative consequences. McCormick (1989), in a discussion of the consequences of screening, suggested that 'false positive smears in healthy women cause distress and anxiety that may never be fully allayed' (McCormick 1989: 208). Grimes (1988) stated that 'promotion of health inevitably results in the awareness of sickness' and suggested that screening results in introspection. Skrabanek (1988: 1156) specifically expressed an awareness of the negative consequences of screening in his statement that 'the hazards of screening are undisputed: they include false positives leading to unnecessary investigations and treatments, with resulting iatrogenic morbidity both physical and psychological'. He was supported by Marteau (1989), who commented that 'a positive result in any screening test is invariably received with negative feelings'.

The research: the psychological impact of screening

The negative sequelae of screening have been described as 'the intangible costs' (Kinlay 1988) but research suggests that they are indeed experienced by the individuals involved. These psychological sequelae can be a result of the various different stages of the screening process:

1 *The receipt of a screening invitation.* Research indicates that sending out invitations to enter into a screening programme may not only influence an individual's behaviour, but also their psychological state. Fallowfield et al. (1990) carried out a retrospective study of women's responses to receiving a request to attend a breast screening session. Their results showed that 55 per cent reported feeling worried although 93 per cent were pleased. Dean et al. (1984) sent a measure of psychological morbidity to women awaiting breast screening and then followed them up six months later. The results showed no significant increases in psychological morbidity. However, when asked in retrospect 30 per cent said that they had become anxious after receiving the letter of invitation. Therefore receiving a screening invitation may increase anxiety. However, some research suggests that this is not always the case (Cockburn et al. 1994).

2 *The receipt of a negative result.* It may be assumed that receiving a negative result (i.e. not having the condition being tested for) would only decrease an individual's anxiety. Most research suggests that this is the case and that a negative result may create a sense of reassurance (Orton et al. 1991) or no change in anxiety (Dean et al. 1984; Sutton et al. 1995). Further, Sutton (1999), in his review of the literature on receiving a negative result following breast cancer screening, concluded that 'anxiety is not a significant problem among women who receive a negative screening result'. However, some research points towards a relationship between a negative result and an increased level of anxiety (Stoate 1989) or residual levels of anxiety which do not return to baseline (Baillie et al. 2000). Further, research indicates that, even following negative results, some people attend for further tests even though these tests have not been clinically recommended (e.g. Lerman et al. 2000; Michie et al. 2002). Michie et al. (2003) used qualitative methods to explore why negative genetic results can fail to reassure. They interviewed nine people who had received a negative result for familial adenomatous polyposis (FAP) which is a genetic condition and results in polyps in the bowel which can become cancerous if not detected and removed by surgery. They argued that people may not be reassured by a negative result for two reasons. First, they may hold a belief about the cause of the illness that does not directly map onto the cause being tested for. In the case of FAP, people described how they believed that it was caused by genetics but that genetics could change. Therefore, although the test indicated that they did not have the relevant genes, this may not be the case in the future. Second, they may show a lack of faith in the test itself. For FAP, people were sceptical about the ability of a blood test to inform about a disease that occurred in the bowel. Some

research has also explored the ways in which a negative result is presented. In the UK in 1997 the policy recommendation for cervical smear results stated that the term 'negative result' could be confusing as women would feel 'positive' to such a 'negative' result and that the term 'normal' smear result should be used instead. Marteau et al. (2006) explored the impact of receiving a result that was either presented as 'normal', or normal and a series of statements of risk, that is, 'you are at low risk of having or developing cervical cancer in the next five years' and a range of numerical presentations of risk. Participants were then asked to describe their levels of perceived risk. The results showed that, when only told that their smear result was 'normal' without any description of risk, women described feeling less at risk than when they received 'normal' and the description of risk. Marteau et al. argue that a negative smear result still implies a low risk of getting cervical cancer and that the term 'normal' makes people underestimate this risk.

3   *The receipt of a positive result.* As expected, the receipt of a positive result can be associated with a variety of negative emotions ranging from worry to anxiety and shock. In 1978, Haynes et al. pointed to increased absenteeism following a diagnosis of hypertension and suggested that the diagnosis may have caused distress. Moreover, an abnormal cervical smear may generate anxiety, morbidity and even terror (Campion et al. 1988; Nathoo 1988; Wilkinson et al. 1990). Psychological costs have also been reported after screening for coronary heart disease (Stoate 1989), breast cancer (Fallowfield et al. 1990) and genetic diseases (Marteau et al. 1992). In addition, levels of depression have been found to be higher in those labelled as hypertensive (Bloom and Monterossa 1981). However, some research suggests that these psychological changes may only be maintained in the short term (Reelick et al. 1984) and shortly return to baseline levels (Broadstock et al. 2000). This decay in the psychological consequences has been particularly shown with the termination of pregnancy following the detection of foetal abnormalities (Black 1989) and following the receipt of a positive genetic test result (Broadstock et al. 2000). Some research has also explored the impact of receiving a positive genetic test result upon individuals' beliefs about their condition and subsequent behaviour. Such an approach is in line with a self-regulatory model (see Chapter 3). For example, Marteau et al. (2004) explored the impact of telling people that they had tested positive for familial hypercholesterolaemia on their beliefs about the nature of their condition and their behaviour. The results showed that those who were told that they had a genetic mutation reported a lower belief that their cholesterol could be managed by diet. Therefore being given a medical model of their problem made them less likely to endorse a behavioural solution No effect was found, however, for perceptions of control, adherence to medication or risk-reducing behaviours. This is in line with research exploring people's matched models (see Chapter 3 for a discussion of matched models). It also finds reflection in a recent analysis of the use of a self-regulatory approach to understand reactions of risk information and the importance of a 'fit' between existing cognitive representations and new risk information (Marteau and Weinman 2006).

4   *The receipt of an inadequate test result.* Although many tests produce either positive or negative results, some produce inadequate results which neither confirm nor disconfirm the presence of the condition. An example of this is cervical screening whereby the test can be 'ruined' due to the presence of pus or the absence of sufficient number of cervical cells. French et al. (2004, 2006) explored the immediate and longer-term psychological consequences of receiving either an inadequate test result ($n = 180$) or a normal test result

($n = 226$). The results showed that women with an inadequate result reported more anxiety and more concern about their result, perceived themselves to be more at risk of cervical cancer and were less satisfied with the information they had received immediately following the result. By three months' follow-up, the women who had the inadequate results were no longer more anxious. They were, however, more concerned about their test results and less satisfied with the information they had received even after having normal results from subsequent tests.

5 *The psychological effects of subsequent interventions.* Although screening is aimed at detecting illness at an asymptomatic stage of development and subsequently delaying or averting its development, not all individuals identified as being 'at risk' receive treatment. In addition, not all of those identified as being 'at risk' will develop the illness. The literature concerning cervical cancer has debated the efficacy of treating those individuals identified by cervical screening as 'at risk' and has addressed the possible consequence of this treatment. Duncan (1992) produced a report on NHS guidelines concerning the management of positive cervical smears. This suggested that all women with more severe cytological abnormalities should be referred for colposcopy, while others with milder abnormalities should be monitored by repeat cervical smears. Shafi (1994) suggests that it is important to consider the psychological impact of referral and treatment and that this impact may be greater than the risk of serious disease. However, Soutter and Fletcher (1994) suggest that there is evidence of a progression from mild abnormalities to invasive cervical cancer and that these women should also be directly referred for a colposcopy. This suggestion has been further supported by the results of a prospective study of 902 women presenting with mild or moderate abnormalities for the first time (Flannelly et al. 1994). A study carried out in 1993 examined the effects of a diagnosis of pre-cancerous changes of the cervix on the psychological state of a group of women and further assessed the additional impact of treatment (Palmer et al. 1993). The results showed that, following the diagnosis, the women experienced high levels of intrusive thoughts, avoidance and high levels of anger. In addition, the diagnosis influenced their body image and sexuality. However, the authors reported that there was no additional impact of treatment on their psychological state. Perhaps the diagnosis following screening is the factor that creates distress and the subsequent treatment is regarded as a constructive and useful intervention. Further research is needed to assess this aspect of screening.

6 *The existence of a screening programme.* Marteau (1993) suggested that the existence of screening programmes may influence social beliefs about what is healthy and may change society's attitude towards a screened condition. In a study by Marteau and Riordan (1992), health professionals were asked to rate their attitudes towards two hypothetical patients, one of whom had attended a screening programme and one who had not. Both patients were described as having developed cervical cancer. The results showed that the health professionals held more negative attitudes towards the patient who had not attended. In a further study, community nurses were given descriptions of either a heart attack patient who had changed their health-related behaviour following a routine health check (healthy behaviour condition) or a patient who had not (unhealthy behaviour condition) (Ogden and Knight 1995). The results indicated that the nurses rated the patient in the unhealthy behaviour condition as less likely to follow advice, more responsible for their condition and rated the heart attack as more preventable. In terms of the wider effects of screening programmes, it is possible that the existence of such programmes encourages society to see

illnesses as preventable and the responsibility of the individual, which may lead to victim blaming of those individuals who still develop these illnesses. This may be relevant to illnesses such as coronary heart disease, cervical cancer and breast cancer, which have established screening programmes. In the future, it may also be relevant to genetic disorders, which could have been eradicated by terminations.

Why has this backlash happened?

Screening in the form of secondary prevention involves the professional in both detection and intervention and places the responsibility for change with the doctor. The backlash against screening could, therefore, be analysed as a protest against professional power and paternalistic intervention. Recent emphasis on the psychological consequences of screening could be seen as ammunition for this movement, and the negative consequences of population surveillance as a useful tool to burst the 'screening bubble'. Within this framework, the backlash is a statement of individualism and personal power.

The backlash may reflect, however, a shift in medical perspective – a shift from 'doctor help' to 'self-help'. In 1991, the British government published the *Health of the Nation* document, which set targets for the reduction of preventable causes of mortality and morbidity (DoH 1991b). This document no longer emphasized the process of secondary prevention – and therefore implicitly that of professional intervention – but illustrated a shift towards primary prevention, health promotion and 'self-help'. General practitioners are still encouraged to promote good health – no longer by identifying diseases at an asymptomatic stage, but by encouraging patients to change their behaviour. During recent years there has been a shift towards self-help and health promotion, reflected by the preoccupation with diet, smoking, exercise and self-examination. Prevention and cure are no longer the result of professional intervention but come from the individual – patients are becoming their own doctors.

To conclude

Screening (secondary prevention) has been developed throughout the twentieth century as an important means to detect illness at an asymptomatic stage. Specific criteria have been developed to facilitate the screening process and research has been carried out to evaluate means to increase patient uptake of screening programmes. Recently, however, there have been debates about the problems with screening. These have concerned the ethics of screening, its cost-effectiveness and its possible psychological consequences. Although screening programmes are still being developed and regarded as an important facet of health, there has been a recent shift from a system of 'doctor help' to 'self-help', which is reflected in the growing interest in health beliefs and health behaviour and the process of health promotion.

❓ Questions

1 Screening is an essential aspect of health promotion. Discuss.

2 Discuss why people turn up for screening.

3 Screening is unethical. Discuss.

4 What are the possible psychological side effects of screening for illness?

5 How might screening do harm?

6 Develop a research protocol designed to improve attendance for breast cancer screening.

For discussion

Consider which factors (e.g. beliefs, environmental) relate to whether you do or do not practise cervical screening (for women) or testicular self-examination (for men).

Assumptions in health psychology

The literature on screening highlights some of the assumptions in health psychology:

1 *Challenging the biomedical model.* Health psychology aims to challenge the biomedical model. However, it often does not challenge some of the biomedical approaches to 'a successful outcome'. For example, although by examining the psychological consequences of screening it is suggested that screening for its own sake is not necessarily a good idea, there is still an emphasis on methods to improve uptake of screening. Perhaps promoting uptake implicitly accepts the biomedical belief that screening is beneficial.

2 *Changes in theory reflect progression.* It is often assumed that changes in theoretical perspective reflect greater knowledge about how individuals work and an improved understanding of health and illness. Therefore, within this perspective, a shift in focus towards an examination of the potential negative consequences of screening can be understood as a better understanding of ways to promote health. However, perhaps the 'backlash' against screening also reflects a different (not necessarily better) way of seeing individuals – a shift from individuals who require expert help from professionals towards a belief that individuals should help themselves.

Further reading

Marteau, T.M. and Weinman, J. (2006) Self-regulation and the behavioural response to DNA risk information: a theoretical analysis and framework for future research, *Social Science and Medicine*, 62: 1360–8.

This is an interesting theoretical paper which describes existing research on reactions to DNA risk information and illustrates how these reactions can be understood within a self-regulatory model. In particular it highlights the importance of a 'fit' between existing cognitive representations of the problem and any new information.

Norman, P. (1993) Predicting uptake of health checks in general practice: invitation methods and patients' health beliefs, *Social Science and Medicine*, 37: 53–9.

This paper illustrates how to use the HBM and how theory can be translated into practice.

Orbell, S. and Sheeran, P. (1993) Health psychology and uptake of preventive health services: a review of 30 years' research on cervical screening, *Psychology and Health*, 8: 417–33.

This paper provides a comprehensive overview of the literature on screening and examines the contribution of psychological, service provision and demographic factors.

Shaw, C., Abrams, K. and Marteau, T.M. (1999) Psychological impact of predicting individuals' risk of illness: a systematic review, *Social Science and Medicine*, 49: 1571–98.

This comprehensive review examines the research to date on the impact of receiving either a positive or negative test result in terms of cognitive, emotional and behavioural outcomes.

Chapter **10**

Stress

Chapter overview

This chapter examines definitions of stress and looks at the early models of stress in terms of the fight/flight response, the general adaptation syndrome and life events theory. It then describes the concept of appraisal and Lazarus's transactional model of stress which emphasizes psychology as central to eliciting a stress response. The chapter then describes the physiological model of stress and explores the impact of stress on changes in physiological factors such as arousal and cortisol production. Finally, it describes how stress has been measured both in the laboratory and in a more naturalistic setting and compares physiological and self-report measurement approaches.

This chapter covers

- What is stress?
- The development of stress theories
- The transactional model of stress
- Stress and appraisal
- Stress and changes in physiology
- Measuring stress

What is stress?

The term 'stress' means many things to many different people. A layperson may define stress in terms of pressure, tension, unpleasant external forces or an emotional response. Psychologists have defined stress in a variety of different ways. Contemporary definitions of stress regard the external environmental stress as a stressor (e.g. problems at work), the response to the stressor as stress or distress (e.g. the feeling of tension), and the concept of stress as something that involves biochemical, physiological, behavioural and psychological changes. Researchers have also differentiated between stress that is harmful and damaging (distress) and stress that is positive and beneficial (eustress). In addition, researchers differentiate between acute stress, such as an exam or having to give a public talk, and chronic stress, such as job stress and poverty. The most commonly used definition of stress was developed by Lazarus and Launier

(1978), who regarded stress as a transaction between people and the environment and described stress in terms of 'person–environment fit'. If a person is faced with a potentially difficult stressor such as an exam or having to give a public talk, the degree of stress they experience is determined first by their appraisal of the event ('is it stressful?') and second by their appraisal of their own personal resources ('will I cope?). A good person–environment fit results in no or low stress and a poor fit results in higher stress.

The development of stress models

Over the past few decades, models of stress have varied in terms of their definition of stress, their differing emphasis on physiological and psychological factors, and their description of the relationship between individuals and their environment.

Cannon's fight-or-flight model

One of the earliest models of stress was developed by Cannon (1932). This was called the fight-or-flight model of stress, which suggested that external threats elicited the fight-or-flight response involving an increased activity rate and increased arousal. He suggested that these physiological changes enabled the individual to either escape from the source of stress or fight. Within Cannon's model, stress was defined as a response to external stressors, which was predominantly seen as physiological. Cannon considered stress to be an adaptive response as it enabled the individual to manage a stressful event. However, he also recognized that prolonged stress could result in medical problems.

Selye's general adaptation syndrome

Selye's general adaptation syndrome (GAS) was developed in 1956 and described three stages in the stress process (Selye 1956). The initial stage was called the 'alarm' stage, which described an increase in activity, and occurred as soon as the individual was exposed to a stressful situation. The second stage was called 'resistance', which involved coping and attempts to reverse the effects of the alarm stage. The third stage was called 'exhaustion', which was reached when the individual had been repeatedly exposed to the stressful situation and was incapable of showing further resistance. This model is shown in Figure 10.1.

Problems with Cannon's and Selye's models

Cannon's early fight/flight model and Selye's GAS laid important foundations for stress research. However, there are problems with them:

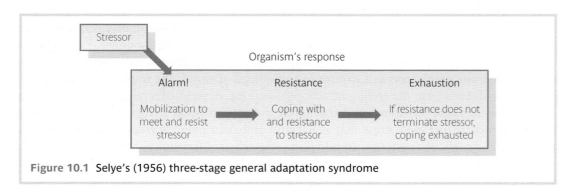

Figure 10.1 Selye's (1956) three-stage general adaptation syndrome

1 Both regarded the individual as automatically responding to an external stressor and described stress within a straightforward stimulus–response framework. They therefore did not address the issue of individual variability and psychological factors were given only a minimal role. For example, while an exam could be seen as stressful for one person, it might be seen as an opportunity to shine to another.

2 Both also described the physiological response to stress as consistent. This response is seen as non-specific in that the changes in physiology are the same regardless of the nature of the stressor. This is reflected in the use of the term 'arousal' which has been criticized by more recent researchers. Therefore these two models described individuals as passive and as responding automatically to their external world.

Life events theory

In an attempt to depart from both Selye's and Cannon's models of stress, which emphasized physiological changes, the life events theory was developed to examine stress and stress-related changes as a response to life experiences. Holmes and Rahe (1967) developed the schedule of recent experiences (SRE), which provided respondents with an extensive list of possible life changes or life events. These ranged in supposed objective severity from events such as 'death of a spouse', 'death of a close family member' and 'jail term' to more moderate events such as 'son or daughter leaving home' and 'pregnancy' to minor events such as 'vacation', 'change in eating habits', 'change in sleeping habits' and 'change in number of family get-togethers'. Originally the SRE was scored by simply counting the number of actual recent experiences. For example, someone who had experienced both the death of a spouse and the death of a close family member would receive the same score as someone who had recently had two holidays. It was assumed that this score reflected an indication of their level of stress. Early research using the SRE in this way showed some links between individuals' SRE score and their health status. However, this obviously crude method of measurement was later replaced by a variety of others, including a weighting system whereby each potential life event was weighted by a panel, creating a degree of differentiation between the different life experiences.

Problems with life events theory

The use of the SRE and similar measures of life experiences have been criticized for the following reasons:

1 *The individual's own rating of the event is important.* It has been argued by many researchers that life experiences should not be seen as either objectively stressful or benign, but that this interpretation of the event should be left to the individual. For example, a divorce for one individual may be regarded as extremely upsetting, whereas for another it may be a relief from an unpleasant situation. Pilkonis et al. (1985) gave checklists of life events to a group of subjects to complete and also interviewed them about these experiences. They reported that a useful means of assessing the potential impact of life events is to evaluate the individual's own ratings of the life experience in terms of: (1) the desirability of the event (was the event regarded as positive or negative?); (2) how much control they had over the event (was the outcome of the event determined by the individual or others?); and (3) the degree of required adjustment following the event. This methodology would enable the individual's own evaluation of the events to be taken into consideration.

2 *The problem of retrospective assessment.* Most ratings of life experiences or life events are completed retrospectively, at the time when the individual has become ill or has come into contact with the health profession. This has obvious implications for understanding the causal link between life events and subsequent stress and stress-related illnesses. For example, if an individual has developed cancer and is asked to rate their life experiences over the last year, their present state of mind will influence their recollection of that year. This effect may result in the individual over-reporting negative events and under-reporting positive events if they are searching for a psychosocial cause of their illness ('I have developed cancer because my husband divorced me and I was sacked at work'). Alternatively, if they are searching for a more medical cause of their illness they may under-report negative life events ('I developed cancer because it is a family weakness; my lifestyle and experiences are unrelated as I have had an uneventful year'). The relationship between self-reports of life events and causal models of illness is an interesting area of research. Research projects could select to use this problem of selective recall as a focus for analysis. However, this influence of an individual's present state of health on their retrospective ratings undermines attempts at causally relating life events to illness onset.

3 *Life experiences may interact with each other.* When individuals are asked to complete a checklist of their recent life experiences, these experiences are regarded as independent of each other. For example, a divorce, a change of jobs and a marriage would be regarded as an accumulation of life events that together would contribute to a stressful period of time. However, one event may counter the effects of another and cancel out any negative stressful consequences. Evaluating the potential effects of life experiences should include an assessment of any interactions between events.

4 *What is the outcome of a series of life experiences?* Originally, the SRE was developed to assess the relationship between stressful life experiences and health status. Accordingly, it was assumed that if the life experiences were indeed stressful then the appropriate outcome measure was one of health status. The most straightforward measure of health status would be a diagnosis of illness such as cancer, heart attack or hypertension. Within this framework, a simple correlational analysis could be carried out to evaluate whether a greater number of life experiences correlated with a medical diagnosis. Apart from the problems with retrospective recall and so on, this would allow some measure of causality – subjects with higher numbers of life events would be more likely to get a medical diagnosis. However, such an outcome measure is restrictive, as it ignores lesser 'illnesses' and relies on an intervention by the medical profession to provide the diagnosis. In addition, it also ignores the role of the diagnosis as a life event in itself. An alternative outcome measure would be to evaluate symptoms. Therefore the individual could be asked to rate not only their life experiences but also their health-related symptoms (e.g. pain, tiredness, loss of appetite, etc.). Within this framework, correlational analysis could examine the relationship between life events and symptoms. However, this outcome measure has its own problems: is 'a change in eating habits' a life event or a symptom of a life event? I s 'a change in sleeping habits' a stressor or a consequence of stress? Choosing the appropriate outcome measure for assessing the effects of life events on health is therefore problematic.

5 *Stressors may be short term or ongoing.* Traditionally, assessments of life experiences have conceptualized such life events as short-term experiences. However, many events may be ongoing and chronic. Moos and Swindle (1990) identified domains of ongoing stressors, which they suggested reflect chronic forms of life experiences:

- physical health stressors (e.g. medical conditions)
- home and neighbourhood stressors (e.g. safety, cleanliness)
- financial stressors
- work stressors (e.g. interpersonal problems, high pressure)
- spouse/partner stressors (e.g. emotional problems with partner)
- child stressors
- extended family stressors
- friend stressors.

They incorporated these factors into their measure – the life stressors and social resources inventory (LISRES) – which represented an attempt to emphasize the chronic nature of life experiences and to place them within the context of the individual's coping resources. Moos and Swindle (1990) argued that life events should not be evaluated in isolation but should be integrated into two facets of an individual's life: their ongoing social resources (e.g. social support networks, financial resources) and their ongoing stressors.

A role for psychological factors in stress

Both Cannon's and Selye's early models of stress conceptualized stress as an automatic response to an external stressor. This perspective is also reflected in versions of life events theory, which suggests that individuals respond to life experiences with a stress response that is therefore related to their health status. However, the above criticisms of the life events theory suggest a different approach to stress, an approach that includes an individual who no longer simply passively responds to stressors but actively interacts with them. This approach to stress provides a role for an individual's psychological state and is epitomized by Lazarus's transactional model of stress and his theory of appraisal.

The transactional model of stress
The role of appraisal

In the 1970s, Lazarus's work on stress introduced psychology to understanding the stress response (Lazarus and Cohen 1973, 1977; Lazarus 1975; Lazarus and Folkman 1987). This role for psychology took the form of his concept of appraisal. Lazarus argued that stress involved a transaction between the individual and their external world, and that a stress response was elicited if the individual appraised a potentially stressful event as actually being stressful. Lazarus's model of appraisal therefore described individuals as psychological beings who appraised the outside world, not simply passively responding to it. Lazarus defined two forms of appraisal: primary and secondary. According to Lazarus, the individual initially appraises the event itself – defined as *primary appraisal*. There are four possible ways that the event can be appraised: (1) irrelevant; (2) benign and positive; (3) harmful and a threat; (4) harmful and a challenge. Lazarus then described *secondary appraisal*, which involves the individual evaluating the pros and cons of their different coping strategies. Therefore primary appraisal involves an appraisal of the outside world and secondary appraisal involves an appraisal of the individual themselves. This model is shown in Figure 10.2. The form of the primary and secondary appraisals determines whether the individual shows a stress response or not. According to Lazarus's model this stress response can take different forms: (1) direct action; (2) seeking

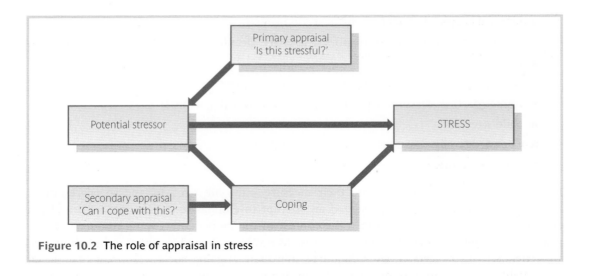

Figure 10.2 The role of appraisal in stress

information; (3) doing nothing; or (4) developing a means of coping with the stress in terms of relaxation or defence mechanisms.

Lazarus's model of appraisal and the transaction between the individual and the environment indicated a novel way of looking at the stress response – the individual no longer passively responded to their external world, but interacted with it.

Does appraisal influence the stress response?

Several studies have examined the effect of appraisal on stress and have evaluated the role of the psychological state of the individual on their stress response. In an early study by Speisman et al. (1964), subjects were shown a film depicting an initiation ceremony involving unpleasant genital surgery. The film was shown with three different soundtracks. In condition 1, the trauma condition, the soundtrack emphasized the pain and the mutilation. In condition 2, the denial condition, the soundtrack showed the participants as being willing and happy. In condition 3, the intellectualization condition, the soundtrack gave an anthropological interpretation of the ceremony. The study therefore manipulated the subjects' appraisal of the situation and evaluated the effect of the type of appraisal on their stress response. The results showed that subjects reported that the trauma condition was most stressful. This suggests that it is not the events themselves that elicit stress, but the individuals' interpretation or appraisal of those events. Similarly, Mason (1975) argued that the stress response needed a degree of awareness of the stressful situation and reported that dying patients who were unconscious showed less signs of physiological stress than those who were conscious. He suggested that the conscious patients were able to appraise their situation whereas the unconscious ones were not. These studies therefore suggest that appraisal is related to the stress response. However, in contrast to these studies some research indicates that appraisal may not always be necessary. For example, Repetti (1993) assessed the objective stressors (e.g. weather conditions, congestion) and subjective stressors (e.g. perceived stress) experienced by air traffic controllers and reported that both objective and subjective stressors independently predicted both minor illnesses and psychological distress.

This could indicate that either appraisal is not always necessary or that at times individuals do not acknowledge their level of subjective stress. In line with this possibility some researchers have identified 'repressors' as a group of individuals who use selective inattention and forgetting to avoid stressful information (Roth and Cohen 1986). Such people show incongruence between their physiological state and their level of reported anxiety. For example, when confronted with a stressor they say, 'I am fine' but their body is showing arousal. This suggests that although appraisal may be central to the stress response there may be some people in some situations who deny or repress their emotional response to a stressor.

What events are appraised as stressful?

Lazarus has argued that an event needs to be appraised as stressful before it can elicit a stress response. It could be concluded from this that the nature of the event itself is irrelevant – it is all down to the individual's own perception. However, research shows that some types of event are more likely to result in a stress response than others.

- *Salient events*. People often function in many different domains such as work, family and friends. For one person, work might be more salient, while for another their family life might be more important. Swindle and Moos (1992) argued that stressors in salient domains of life are more stressful than those in more peripheral domains.

- *Overload*. Multitasking seems to result in more stress than the chance to focus on fewer tasks at any one time. Therefore a single stressor which adds to a background of other stressors will be appraised as more stressful than when the same stressor occurs in isolation – commonly known as the straw that broke the camel's back.

- *Ambiguous events*. If an event is clearly defined then the person can efficiently develop a coping strategy. If, however, the event is ambiguous and unclear then the person first has to spend time and energy considering what coping strategy is best. This is reflected in the work stress literature which illustrates that poor job control and role ambiguity in the workplace often result in a stress response.

- *Uncontrollable events*. If a stressor can be predicted and controlled then it is usually appraised as less stressful than a more random uncontrollable event. For example, experimental studies show that unpredictable loud bursts of noise are more stressful than predictable ones (Glass and Singer 1972). The issue of control is dealt with in more depth later on.

Self-control and stress

Recently theories of stress have emphasized forms of self-control as important in understanding stress. This is illustrated in theories of self-efficacy, hardiness and feelings of mastery.

1 *Self-efficacy*. In 1987, Lazarus and Folkman suggested that self-efficacy was a powerful factor for mediating the stress response. Self-efficacy refers to an individual's feeling of confidence that they can perform a desired action. Research indicates that self-efficacy may have a role in mediating stress-induced immunosuppression and physiological changes such as blood pressure, heart rate and stress hormones (e.g. Bandura et al. 1982, 1988; Wiedenfeld et al. 1990). For example, the belief 'I am confident that I can succeed in this exam' may result in physiological changes that reduce the stress response. Therefore a belief in the ability to control one's behaviour may relate to whether or not a potentially stressful event results in a stress response (see later for a discussion of PNI).

2 *Hardiness.* This shift towards emphasizing self-control is also illustrated by Kobasa's concept of 'hardiness' (Kobasa et al. 1982; Maddi and Kobasa 1984). Hardiness was described as reflecting: (a) personal feelings of control; (b) a desire to accept challenges; and (c) commitment. It has been argued that the degree of hardiness influences an individual's appraisal of potential stressors and the resulting stress response. Accordingly, a feeling of being in control may contribute to the process of primary appraisal.

3 *Mastery.* Karasek and Theorell (1990) defined the term 'feelings of mastery', which reflected an individual's control over their stress response. They argued that the degree of mastery may be related to the stress response.

In summary, most current stress as researchers consider stress as the result of a person–environment fit and emphasize the role of primary appraisal ('is the event stressful?') and secondary appraisal ('can I cope?'). Psychological factors are seen as a central component to the stress response. However, they are always regarded as co-occurring with physiological changes.

Box 10.1 **Some problems with . . . stress research**

Below are some problems with research in this area that you may wish to consider.

1 Defining stress can be difficult as it can be assessed using self-report or physiological changes which have their problems. Self-report can be open to bias and a desire to appear more or less stressed depending upon the person and the situation. Physiological measures may be intrusive and actually create stress and may change the way in which a person responds to their environment.

2 The appraisal model suggests that people appraise the stressor and then appraise their coping mechanisms. This conceptualizes these two processes as separate and discrete. However, it is likely that they are completely interdependent as a stressor is only really stressful in the context of whether the individual feels they can or cannot cope with it.

3 Stress is considered to be made up of both psychological and physiological changes. However, how these two sets of processes interact is unclear as it is possible to perceive stress without showing physiological changes or to show a physiological reaction without labelling it as stress.

Stress and changes in physiology

The physiological consequences of stress have been studied extensively, mostly in the laboratory using the acute stress paradigm which involves bringing individuals into a controlled environment, putting them into a stressful situation such as counting backwards, completing an intelligence task or giving an unprepared speech, and then recording any changes. This research has highlighted two main groups of physiological changes (see Figure 10.3):

1 *Sympathetic activation.* When an event has been appraised as stressful it triggers responses in the sympathetic nervous system. This results in the production of catecholamines (adrenalin and noradrenalin, also known as epinephrine and norepinephrine) which cause changes in factors such as blood pressure, heart rate, sweating and pupil dilation and is experienced as a feeling of arousal. This process is similar to the fight-or-flight response described by Cannon (1932). Catecholamines also have an effect on a range of the body's tissues and can lead to changes in immune function.

2 *Hypothalamic-pituitary-adrenocortical (HPA) activation.* In addition to the aforementioned sympathetic activation, stress also triggers changes in the HPA system. This results in the production of increased levels of corticosteroids, the most important of which is cortisol, which results in more diffuse changes such as the management of carbohydrate stores and inflammation. These changes constitute the background effect of stress and cannot be detected by the individual. They are similar to the alarm, resistance and exhaustion stages of stress described by Selye (1956). In addition, raised levels of the brain opioids beta endorphin and enkephalin have been found following stress which are involved in immune-related problems.

The physiological aspects of the stress response are linked to stress reactivity, stress recovery, the allostatic load and stress resistance.

Stress reactivity

Changes in physiology are known as 'stress reactivity' and vary enormously between people. For example, some individuals respond to stressful events with high levels of sweating, raised blood pressure and heart rate while others show only a minimal response. This, in part, is due to whether the stressor is appraised as stressful (primary appraisal) and how the individual appraises their own coping resources (secondary appraisal). However, research also shows that some people are simply more reactive to stress than others, regardless of appraisal. Two people may show similar psychological reactions to stress but different physiological reactions. In particular, there is some evidence for gender differences in stress reactivity, with men responding more strenuously to stressors than women and women showing smaller increases in blood pressure during stressful tasks than men (Stoney et al. 1987, 1990). This indicates that gender may determine the stress response to a stressful event and consequently the effect of this response on the illness or health status of the individual. Stress reactivity is thought to be dispositional and may either be genetic or a result of prenatal or childhood experiences.

Stress recovery

After reacting to stress, the body then recovers and levels of sympathetic and HPA activation return to baseline. However, there is great variability in the rate of recovery both between

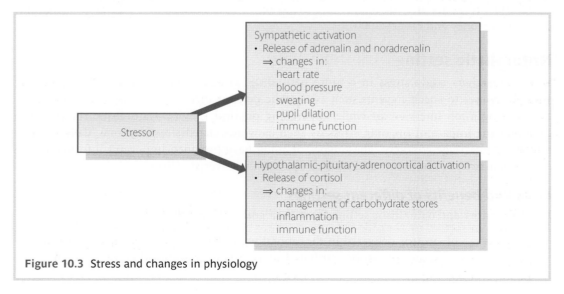

Figure 10.3 Stress and changes in physiology

individuals, as some people recover more quickly than others, and within the same individual across the lifespan.

Allostatic load

Stress recovery is linked with allostatic load which was described by McEwan and Stellar (1993). They argued that the body's physiological systems constantly fluctuate as the individual responds and recovers from stress – a state of allostasis – and that, as time progresses, recovery is less and less complete and the body is left increasingly depleted.

Stress resistance

To reflect the observation that not all individuals react to stressors in the same way, researchers developed the concept of stress resistance to emphasize how some people remain healthy even when stressors occur (e.g. Holahan and Moos 1990). Stress resistance includes adaptive coping strategies, certain personality characteristic and social support.

Stress reactivity, stress recovery, allostatic load and stress resistance all influence an individual's reaction to a stressor. They also all affect the stress–illness link. This is described in Chapter 11.

Measuring stress

Stress has been measured both in the laboratory and in a naturalistic setting and using both physiological measures and those involving self-report.

Laboratory setting

Many stress researchers use the acute stress paradigm to assess stress reactivity and the stress response. This involves taking people into the laboratory and asking them either to complete a stressful task such as an intelligence test, a mathematical task, giving a public talk or watching a horror film, or exposing them to an unpleasant event such as a loud noise, white light or a puff of air in the eye. The acute stress paradigm has enabled researchers to study gender differences in stress reactivity, the interrelationship between acute and chronic stress, the role of personality in the stress response and the impact of exercise on mediating stress-related changes (e.g. Pike et al. 1997; Stoney and Finney 2000).

Naturalistic setting

Some researchers study stress in a more naturalistic environment. This includes measuring stress responses to specific events such as a public performance, before and after an examination, during a job interview or while undergoing physical activity. Naturalistic research also examines the impact of ongoing stressors such as work-related stress, normal 'daily hassles', poverty or marriage conflicts. These types of study have provided important information on how people react to both acute and chronic stress in their everyday lives.

Costs and benefits of different settings

Both laboratory and naturalistic settings have their costs and benefits:

1 The degree of stressor delivered in the laboratory setting can be controlled so that differences in stress response can be attributed to aspects of the individual rather than to the stressor itself.

2 Researchers can artificially manipulate aspects of the stressor in the laboratory to examine corresponding changes in physiological and psychological measures.

3 Laboratory researchers can artificially manipulate mediating variables such as control and the presence or absence of social support to assess their impact on the stress response.

4 The laboratory is an artificial environment which may produce a stress response that does not reflect that triggered by a more natural environment. It may also produce associations between variables (i.e. control and stress) which might be an artefact of the laboratory.

5 Naturalistic settings allow researchers to study real stress and how people really cope with it.

6 However, there are many other uncontrolled variables which the researcher needs to measure in order to control for it in the analysis.

Physiological measures

Physiological measures are mostly used in the laboratory as they involve participants being attached to monitors or having fluid samples taken. However, some ambulatory machines have been developed which can be attached to people as they carry on with their normal activities. To assess stress reactivity from a physiological perspective, researchers can use a polygraph to measure heart rate, respiration rate, blood pressure and the galvanic skin response (GSR), which is effected by sweating. They can also take blood, urine or saliva samples to test for changes in catecholamine and cortisol production.

Self-report measures

Researchers use a range of self-report measures to assess both chronic and acute stress. Some of these focus on life events and include the original social readjustment rating scale (SRRS) (Holmes and Rahe 1967) which asks about events such as 'death of a spouse', 'changing to a different line of work' and 'change of residence'. Other measures focus more on an individual's own perception of stress. The perceived stress scale (PSS) (Cohen et al. 1983) is the most commonly used scale to assess self-perceived stress and asks questions such as 'In the last month how often have you been upset because of something that happened unexpectedly?', and 'In the last month how often have you felt nervous or stressed?' Some researchers also assess minor stressors in the form of 'daily hassles'. Kanner et al. (1981) developed the hassles scale which asks participants to rate how severe a range of hassles have been over the past month including 'misplacing or losing things', 'health of a family member' and 'concerns about owing money'. Johnston, Beedie et al. (2006) used a small hand-held computer called a personal digital assistant (PDA) which participants carry around with them and which prompts them at pre-set intervals to complete a diary entry describing their level of stress. Self-report measures have been used to describe the impact of environmental factors on stress whereby stress is seen as the outcome variable (i.e. 'a poor working environment causes high stress'). They have also been used to explore the impact of stress on the individual's health status whereby stress in seen as the input variable (i.e. 'high stress causes poor health').

Costs and benefits of different measures

Physiological and self-report measures of stress are used in the main to complement each other. The former reflect a more physiological emphasis and the latter a more psychological perspective. A researcher who has a greater interest in physiology might argue that physiological measures are more central to stress research, while another researcher who believes that experience is more important might favour self-report. Most stress researchers measure both physiological and psychological aspects of stress and study how these two components interact. However, in general the different types of measures have the following costs and benefits:

1 Physiological measures are more objective and less affected by the participant's wish to give a desirable response or the researcher's wish to see a particular result.

2 Self-report measures reflect the individual's experience of stress rather than just what their body is doing.

3 Self-report measures can be influenced by problems with recall, social desirability, and different participants interpreting the questions in different ways.

4 Self-report measures are based upon the life events or hassles that have been chosen by the author of the questionnaire. One person's hassle, such as 'troublesome neighbours' which appears on the hassles scale, may not be a hassle for another, whereas worries about a child's school might be, which doesn't appear on this scale.

Associations between research in different settings using different measures

Given that stress research takes place in both the laboratory and in more naturalistic setting and uses both physiological and self-report measures it is important to know how these different studies relate to each other. This is illustrated in **Focus on Research 10.1** on the next page.

Laboratory versus naturalistic research

Laboratory research is artificial whereas real-life research is uncontrolled. Some studies, however, illustrate high levels of congruence between physiological responses in the laboratory and those assessed using ambulatory machines in real life. For example, Matthews et al. (1986) reported similarity between reactivity following laboratory tasks and public speaking and Turner and Carroll (1985) reported a correlation between the response to video games and real-life stress identified from diaries. However, other studies have found no relationship or only some relationship with some measures (e.g. Johnston et al. 1990). Johnston and colleagues (Anastasiades et al. 1990; Johnston et al. 1990, 1994) designed a series of studies to try to explain this variability. Using a battery of tasks to elicit stress in the laboratory and ambulatory machines to assess stress reactivity in real life, they concluded that physiological measures taken in the laboratory concord if the following conditions are met: the field measure is taken continuously; the analysis takes into account physical activity levels (as this produces a similar response to the stressor); and when the laboratory task involves active coping such as a video game rather than a passive coping task such as the cold pressor task (i.e. placing the hand in icy water). In addition, they argued that appraisal is central to the congruence between laboratory and naturalistic measures and that higher congruence is particularly apparent when the stressors selected are appraised as stressful by the individual rather than identified as stressful by the researcher. This indicates that laboratory assessments may be artificial but do bear some resemblance to real-life stress.

Putting theory into practice

Psychophysiological effects of relaxation training in children (Lohaus et al. 2001).

Background

Stress is conceptualized as involving both physiological and subjective changes that can be assessed using laboratory and self-report procedures. This study assessed the impact of two types of relaxation training on different aspects of the stress response. It is interesting as it allows an insight into how these different aspects of stress may interrelate. It also illustrates the impact of relaxation training on children who are a rarely studied subject group.

Aims

The study aimed to explore the relative impact of two types of relaxation training on children's physiological and self-report responses. The training types were progressive muscle relaxation and imagery-based relaxation.

Participants

The study involved 64 children from a school in Germany who were aged between 10 and 12 years.

Design

The study used a randomized control trial design and participants were randomly allocated to one of three arms of the trial: progressive muscle relaxation, imagery-based relaxation or the control group.

The interventions

Each intervention involved five training sessions. Each session lasted about 30 minutes. The children were asked to sit quietly for five minutes (baseline period), then they took part in the intervention, and the children were then asked to sit quietly again for five minutes (follow-up).

- *Progressive muscle relaxation.* Children were asked to tense and relax specific muscle groups for a period of 7 minutes. These were hand muscles, arms, forehead, cheeks, chest, shoulders, stomach and thighs.
- *Imagery-based relaxation.* Children in this group were asked to imagine that they were a butterfly going on a fantasy journey such as to a meadow, a tree or a boat.
- *Control group.* Children in this group listened to audiotapes of neutral stories which were designed not to elicit any feeling of either tension or relaxation.

Measures

The study involved physiological and self-report measures. Subjective measurements were taken before and after the baseline period, after the intervention and after the follow-up period. Physiological measurements were taken continuously throughout.

- *Physiological measures.* Measures were taken of heart rate, skin temperature and skin conductance level.

■ *Self-report measures.* Measures were also taken of the children's mood (e.g. sensation of perceived calmness, subjective feeling of wellness, feeling of perceived attentiveness) and their physical well-being (e.g. calmness of their heart beats, subjective body warmth, perceived dampness of the hands).

Results

The results were assessed to examine the impact of relaxation training regardless of type of relaxation and also to explore whether one form of relaxation training was more effective.

■ *Physiological changes.* The results showed that imagery relaxation was related to a decrease in heart rate and skin conductance but did not result in changes in skin temperature. In contrast, progressive muscle relaxation resulted in an increase in heart rate during the training session.

■ *Self-report changes.* The results showed increased ratings of mood and physical well-being during baseline and training sessions for all interventions.

Conclusions

The authors conclude that relaxation training can result in psychophysiological changes but that these vary according to type of training. What is also interesting, however, is the degree of variability between the different measures of change. In particular, differences were found in the changes between different aspects of the children's physiology – a change in heart rate did not always correspond to a change in skin temperature. Further, changes in physiology did not always correspond to changes in self-reported mood or physical well-being. Therefore a measure indicating that heart rate had gone down did not always correspond with a self-report that the individual's heart was more calm.

Physiological versus self-report measures

Stress is considered to reflect both the experience of 'I feel stress' and the underlying physiological changes in factors such as heart rate and cortisol levels. But do these two sets of measures relate to each other? This question is central not only to stress research but also to an understanding of mind–body interactions. Research has addressed this association and has consistently found no or only poor relationships between physiological and perceived measures of stress (see **Focus on Research 10.1**, p. 233). This is surprising given the central place that perception is given in the stress response. It is possible, however, that this lack of congruence between these two types of measure reflects a role for other mediating variables. For example, it might be that physiological measures only reflect self-report measures when the stressor is controllable by the individual, when it is considered a threat rather than a challenge or when the individual draws upon particular coping strategies.

The interaction between psychological and physiological aspects of stress

Stress is generally considered to illustrate the interaction between psychological and physiological factors. The psychological appraisal of a stressor is central to the stress response and without

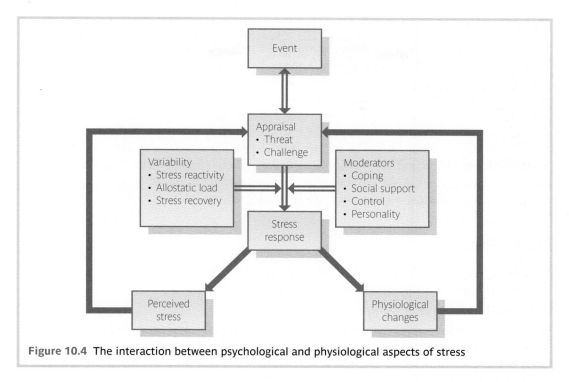

Figure 10.4 The interaction between psychological and physiological aspects of stress

appraisal physiological changes are absent or minimal. Further, the degree of appraisal also influences the extent of the physiological response. However, there is little research illustrating a link between how stressed people say they are feeling (perceived stress) and how their body is reacting (physiological stress). It is likely that the mind–body interactions illustrated by stress are dynamic and ongoing. Therefore, rather than appraisal causing a change in physiology which constitutes the response, appraisal probably triggers a change in physiology which is then detected and appraised causing a further response and so on. In addition, psychological factors such as control, personality, coping and social support will impact upon this ongoing process. This psychophysiological model of the stress response is described in Figure 10.4.

To conclude

This chapter has examined the different models of stress, the psychological and physiological responses to stress and the way in which stress has been measured. Early models of stress regarded stress as an automatic response to an external stressor. However, the introduction of the concept of appraisal suggested that stress was best understood as an interaction between the individual and the outside world. Accordingly, a stress response would be elicited if an event were appraised as stressful. Once appraised as a stressor, the individual then shows a stress response involving both a sense of being stressed and physiological changes including both sympathetic activation and activation of the hypothalamus pituitary axis. The stress response can be measured either in the laboratory or in a more naturalistic setting and can be assessed using either physiological measures or those involving self-report.

? Questions

1 Stress is an automatic response to external stressors. Discuss.

2 Discuss the role of appraisal in the stress response.

3 How does stress cause changes in physiology?

4 How and where can stress be measured and what are the costs and benefits of each measurement approach?

5 Design a study to show whether or not appraisal is necessary for the stress response to occur.

For discussion

Consider the last time you felt stressed. What were the characteristics of the stressful event that made it feel stressful?

Assumptions in health psychology

The stress research highlights some of the assumptions in health psychology.

1 *Dividing up the soup.* Stress research defines appraisal as central to eliciting stress as a means to progress beyond the more simplistic stimulus response theories of Cannon and Selye. Therefore it states that appraisal ('is it stressful?', 'can I cope?') is necessary for a stressor to elicit stress. However, research then explores whether coping reduces the stress response. Coping and stress are sometimes one construct and sometimes two constructs which can be associated.

2 *The problem of mind–body split.* Although much of the stress research examines how the mind may influence the body (e.g. appraisal relates to the release of stress hormones, social support relates to resulting stress-related illnesses), how this process occurs is unclear. In addition, although these relationships suggest an interaction between the mind and the body, they still define them as separate entities which influence each other, not as the same entity.

3 *The problem of progress.* It is often assumed that the most recent theories are better than earlier theories. Therefore models including appraisal, social support and so on are better than those describing stress as a knee-jerk reaction to a stressor. Perhaps these different theories are not necessarily better than each other, but are simply different ways of describing the stress process.

Further reading

Cohen, S., Kessler, R.C. and Gordon, L.U. (eds) (1995) *Measuring Stress: A Guide for Health and Social Scientists.* New York: Oxford University Press.
This is a comprehensive edited collection for anyone interested in the details of stress measurement using physiological and self-report approaches.

Jones, F. and Bright, J. (2001) *Stress: Myth, Theory and Research.* Harlow: Prentice Hall.
This is a highly accessible book that describes and analyses the research and theories of stress and particularly addresses the methodological problems with this area.

Lazarus, R.S. (2000) Toward better research on stress and coping, *American Psychologist,* 55: 665–73.
This paper is part of a special issue on stress and coping, and reflects Lazarus's own comments on recent developments and critiques of the stress literature.

11

Stress and illness

Chapter overview

This chapter first assesses whether stress causes illness and then explores a chronic and acute model of the mechanisms behind this association. The chapter next explores the relationship between stress and illness in terms of behavioural and physiological pathways. It then outlines the approach of psychoneuroimmunology (PNI) and explores the impact of psychological factors such as mood, beliefs, emotional expression and stress on immunity. Finally, it highlights the role of coping, social support, personality and control as moderators of the stress–illness link.

This chapter covers

- Does stress cause illness?
- How does stress cause illness?
- Stress and changes in behaviour
- Stress and changes in physiology
- Psychoneuroimmunology (PNI)
- Which factors moderate the stress–illness link?
- The role of coping, social support, personality and control

Does stress cause illness?

One of the reasons that stress has been studied so consistently is because of its potential effect on the health of the individual. Research shows that hypertension rates are more common in those with high-stress jobs such as air traffic controllers (Cobb and Rose 1973) than in less stressed occupations such as nuns (Timio et al. 1988) and that higher life stress is associated with greater reporting of physical symptoms (Cropley and Steptoe 2005). Further, both cross-sectional and longitudinal studies show that stressful occupations are associated with an increased risk of coronary heart disease (Karasek et al. 1981; Lynch et al. 1997; Kivimaki et al. 2002). In addition, Appels and Mulder (1989) and Appels et al. (2002) indicated that 'vital exhaustion' is common in the year preceding a heart attack. In one study people were given nasal drops either containing viruses responsible for the common cold or placebo saline drops. Their level of stress was then assessed in terms of life events during the past year (Cohen et al. 1991). The results showed that not everyone who was given the virus contracted the virus and not everyone who did contract the virus actually exhibited cold symptoms and became ill. Stress was shown to predict, first, who contracted the virus, and second, who developed symptoms. However, these studies involved a cross-sectional, prospective or retrospective design which raises the problem of causality as it is unclear whether stress causes illness or illness causes stress (or stress ratings). To solve this problem some research has used an experimental design which involves inducing stress and assessing subsequent changes in health. Because of the ethical problems with such a design most experimental work has been done using animals. A classic series of animal studies by Manuck, Kaplan and colleagues (e.g. Kaplan et al. 1983; Manuck et al. 1986) experimentally manipulated the social groupings of Bowman Gray monkeys who have a strong social hierarchy. The results showed that the monkeys illustrated not only behavioural signs of stress but also a marked increase in the disease of their coronary arteries. In addition, stress management, which involves experimentally reducing stress, has had some success in reducing coronary heart disease (Johnston 1989, 1992) and in reducing recurrent cold and flu in children (Hewson-Bower and Drummond 2001).

How does stress cause illness?

Johnston (2002) argued that stress can cause illness through two interrelated mechanisms and developed his model of the stress–illness link which involves chronic and acute processes (see Figure 11.1).

The chronic process

The most commonly held view of the link between stress and illness suggests that stress leads to disease due to a prolonged interaction of physiological, behavioural and psychological factors. For example, chronic work stress may cause changes in physiology and changes in behaviour which over time lead to damage to the cardiovascular system. In particular, chronic stress is associated with atherosclerosis which is a slow process of arterial damage that limits the supply of blood to the heart. Further, this damage might be greater in those individuals with a particular genetic tendency. This chronic process is supported by research indicating links between job stress and cardiovascular disease (Karasek et al. 1981; Lynch et al. 1997; Kivimaki et al. 2002). Such an approach is parallel to Levi's (1974) 'stress-diathesis' model of illness which is illustrated in Figure 11.2.

However, there are several problems with a purely chronic model of the stress–illness link:

1 Exercise protects against the wear and tear of stress with more active individuals being less likely to die from cardiovascular disease than more sedentary individuals (Kivimaki et al. 2002). However, exercise can also immediately precede a heart attack.

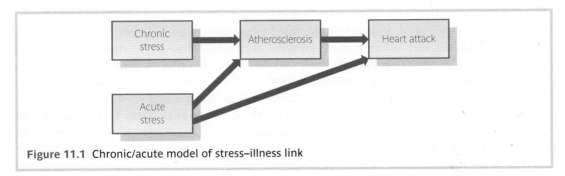

Figure 11.1 Chronic/acute model of stress–illness link

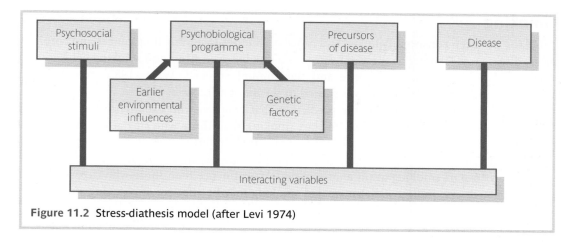

Figure 11.2 Stress-diathesis model (after Levi 1974)

2 The wear and tear caused by stress can explain the accumulative damage to the cardiovascular system. But this chronic model does not explain why coronary events occur when they do.

In the light of these problems, Johnston (2002) argues for an acute model.

The acute process

Heart attacks are more likely to occur following exercise, following anger, upon wakening, during changes in heart rate and during changes in blood pressure (e.g. Muller et al. 1994, 1985; Moller et al. 1999). They are acute events and involve a sudden rupture and thrombogenesis. Johnston (2002) argues that this reflects an acute model of the link between stress and illness with acute stress triggering a sudden cardiac problem. This explains how exercise can be protective in the longer term but a danger for an at-risk individual. It also explains why and when a heart attack occurs.

Links between the acute and chronic processes

The acute and chronic processes are intrinsically interlinked. Chronic stress may simply be the frequent occurrence of acute stress; acute stress may be more likely to trigger a cardiac event in someone who has experienced chronic stress; and acute stress may also contribute to the wear and tear on the cardiovascular system. Furthermore, both the chronic and acute processes highlight the central role for stress-induced changes in behaviour and changes in physiology. These will now be considered.

Stress and changes in behaviour

Stress has been mostly studied in the context of coronary heart disease (CHD). However, there are also studies exploring links between illnesses such as cancer, diabetes and recovery from surgery. Research exploring the links between stress and CHD highlight the impact of stress on the classic risk factors for CHD, namely raised blood cholesterol, raised blood pressure and smoking. These risk factors are strongly influenced by behaviour and reflect the behavioural pathway between stress and illness (Krantz et al. 1981). In line with this, some research has examined the effect of stress on specific health-related behaviours.

Smoking

Smoking has been consistently linked to a range of illnesses including lung cancer and coronary heart disease (see Chapter 5). Research suggests a link between stress and smoking behaviour in terms of smoking initiation, relapse and the amount smoked. Wills (1985) reported that smoking initiation in adolescents was related to the amount of stress in their lives. In addition, there has been some support for the prediction that children who experience the stressor of changing schools may be more likely to start smoking than those who stay at the same school throughout their secondary education (Santi et al. 1991). In terms of relapse, Lichtenstein et al. (1986) and Carey et al. (1993) reported that people who experience high levels of stress are more likely to start smoking again after a period of abstinence than those who experience less stress. Research also indicates that increased smoking may be effective at reducing stress. In an experimental study, Perkins et al. (1992) exposed smokers to either a stressful or a non-stressful computer task and asked the subjects to smoke a cigarette or sham smoke an unlit cigarette. The results showed that, regardless of whether the smokers smoked or not, all subjects reported an increased desire to smoke in the stressful condition. However, this desire was less in those smokers who were actually allowed to smoke. This suggests that stress causes an increased urge for a cigarette, which can be modified by smoking. In a more naturalistic study, smokers were asked to attend a stressful social situation and were instructed either to smoke or not to smoke. Those who could not smoke reported the occasion as more socially stressful than those who could smoke (Gilbert and Spielberger 1987). Similarly, Metcalfe et al. (2003) used the Reeder stress inventory to relate stress to health behaviours and concluded that higher levels of stress were associated with smoking more cigarettes. This association was also found in one large-scale study of over 6000 Scottish men and women which showed that higher levels of perceived stress were linked to smoking more (Heslop et al. 2001).

Alcohol

High alcohol intake has been linked to illnesses such as CHD, cancer and liver disease (see Chapter 5). Research has also examined the relationship between stress and alcohol consumption. Many authors have suggested that work stress, in particular, may promote alcohol use (e.g. Herold and Conlon 1981; Gupta and Jenkins 1984). The tension-reduction theory suggests that people drink alcohol for its tension-reducing properties (Cappell and Greeley 1987). Tension refers to states such as fear, anxiety, depression and distress. Therefore according to this model, negative moods are the internal stressors, or the consequence of an external stressor, which cause alcohol consumption due to the expected outcome of the alcohol. For example, if an individual feels tense or anxious (their internal state) as a result of an exam (the external stressor) and believes that alcohol will reduce this tension (the expected outcome), they may drink alcohol to improve their mood. This theory has been supported by some evidence of the relationship between negative mood and drinking behaviour (Violanti et al. 1983), suggesting that people are more likely to drink when they are feeling depressed or anxious. Similarly, both Metcalfe et al. (2003) and Heslop et al. (2001) reported an association between perceived stress and drinking more alcohol (if a drinker). Furthermore, it has been suggested that medical students' lifestyle and the occurrence of problem drinking may be related to the stress they experience (Wolf and Kissling 1984). In one study, this theory was tested experimentally and the health-related behaviours of medical students were evaluated both before and during a stressful examination period. The results showed that the students reported a deterioration in mood in terms of anxiety and depression and changes in their behaviour in terms of decreases in exercise and food intake

(Ogden and Mtandabari 1997). However, alcohol consumption also went down. The authors concluded that acute exposure to stress resulted in negative changes in those behaviours that had only a minimal influence on the students' ability to perform satisfactorily. Obviously chronic stress may have more damaging effects on longer-term changes in behaviour.

Eating

Diet can influence health either through changes in body weight or via the over- or underconsumption of specific dietary components (see Chapter 6). Greeno and Wing (1994) proposed two hypotheses concerning the link between stress and eating: (1) the general effect model, which predicts that stress changes food intake generally; and (2) the individual difference model, which predicts that stress only causes changes in eating in vulnerable groups of individuals. Most research has focused on the individual difference model and has examined whether either naturally occurring stress or laboratory-induced stress causes changes in eating in specific individuals. For example, Michaud et al. (1990) reported that exam stress was related to an increase in eating in girls but not in boys; Baucom and Aiken (1981) reported that stress increased eating in both the overweight and dieters; and Cools et al. (1992) reported that stress was related to eating in dieters only. Therefore gender, weight and levels of dieting (see Chapter 6) seem to be important predictors of a link between stress and eating. However, the research is not always consistent with this suggestion. For example, Conner et al. (1999) examined the link between daily hassles and snacking in 60 students who completed diaries of their snacking and hassles for seven consecutive days. Their results showed a direct association between increased daily hassles and increased snacking but showed no differences according to either gender or dieting. Such inconsistencies in the literature have been described by Stone and Brownell (1994) as the 'stress eating paradox' to explain how at times stress causes overeating and at others it causes undereating without any clear pattern emerging.

Exercise

Exercise has been linked to health in term of its impact on body weight and via its beneficial effects on CHD (see Chapter 7). Research indicates that stress may reduce exercise (e.g. Heslop et al. 2001; Metcalfe et al. 2003) whereas stress management, which focuses on increasing exercise, has been shown to result in some improvements on coronary health.

Accidents

Accidents are a very common and rarely studied cause of injury or mortality. Research has also examined the effects of stress on accidents and correlational research suggests that individuals who experience high levels of stress show a greater tendency to perform behaviours that increase their chances of becoming injured (Wiebe and McCallum 1986). Further, Johnson (1986) has also suggested that stress increases accidents at home, at work and in the car.

Illness as a stressor

Being ill itself could be a stressful event. If this is the case then the stress following illness also has implications for the health of individuals. Such stress may influence individuals' behaviour in terms of their likelihood to seek help, their compliance with interventions and medical recommendations, and also adopting healthy lifestyles (see later for a discussion of stress management and the progression of HIV). Therefore stress may cause behaviour changes, which are related to the health status of the individual.

Stress and changes in physiology

The physiological consequences of stress and their effect on health have been studied extensively. Research indicates that stress causes physiological changes that have implications for promoting both the onset of illness and its progression.

Stress and illness onset and progression

Stress causes changes in both sympathetic activation (e.g. heart rate, sweating, blood pressure) via the production of catecholamines and the hypothalamic-pituitary-adrenocortical activation via the production of cortisol. These changes can directly impact upon health and illness onset.

Sympathetic activation

The prolonged production of adrenalin and noradrenalin can result in the following:

- blood clot formation
- increased blood pressure
- increased heart rate
- irregular heart beats
- fat deposits
- plaque formation
- immunosuppression.

These changes may increase the chances of heart disease and kidney disease and leave the body open to infection.

HPA activation

The prolonged production of cortisol can result in the following:

- decreased immune function
- damage to neurons in the hippocampus.

These changes may increase the chances of infection, psychiatric problems and losses in memory and concentration.

These physiological changes can be further understood in terms of Johnston's (2002) chronic and acute model of the stress–illness link. Chronic stress is more likely to involve HPA activation and the release of cortisol. This results in ongoing wear and tear and the slower process of atherosclerosis and damage to the cardiovascular system. Acute stress operates primarily through changes in sympathetic activation with changes in heart rate and blood pressure. This can contribute to atherosclerosis and kidney disease but is also related to sudden changes such as heart attacks.

Interaction between the behavioural and physiological pathways

Stress can therefore influence health and illness by changing behaviour or by directly impacting upon an individual's physiology. So far the behavioural and physiological pathways have been presented as separate and discrete. However, this is very much an oversimplification. Stress may cause changes in behaviours such as smoking and diet which impact upon health by changing the individual's physiology. Likewise, stress may cause physiological changes such as raised blood pressure but this is often most apparent in those that also exhibit particularly unhealthy behaviours (Johnston 1989). Therefore, in reality, stress is linked to illness via a complex interaction between behavioural and physiological factors. Further, Johnston (1989) argued that these factors are multiplicative, indicating that the more factors that are changed by stress, the greater the chance that stress will lead to illness.

Individual variability in the stress–illness link

Not everyone who experiences stress becomes ill. To some extent this is due to the role of variables such as coping, control, personality and social support which are described in detail later on. However, research indicates that this variability is also due to individual differences in stress reactivity, stress recovery, the allostatic load and stress resistance.

Stress reactivity

Some individuals show a stronger physiological response to stress than others which is known as their level of 'cardiovascular reactivity' or 'stress reactivity'. This means that when given the same level of stressor and regardless of their self-perceived stress, some people show greater sympathetic activation than others (e.g. Vitaliano et al. 1993). Research suggests that greater stress reactivity may make people more susceptible to stress-related illnesses. For example, individuals with both hypertension and heart disease have higher levels of stress reactivity (e.g. Frederickson and Matthews 1990; Frederickson et al. 1991, 2000). However, these studies used a cross-sectional design which raises the problem of causality. Some research has therefore used a prospective design. For example, in an early study Keys et al. (1971) assessed baseline blood pressure reaction to a cold pressor test and found that higher reactivity predicted heart disease at follow-up 23 years later. Similarly, Boyce et al. (1995) measured baseline levels of stress reactivity in children following a stressful task and then rated the number of family stressors and illness rates over the subsequent 12 weeks. The results showed that stress and illness were not linked in the children with low reactivity but that those with higher reactivity showed more illness if they had experienced more stress. Everson and colleagues (1997) also assessed baseline stress reactivity and explored cardiac health using echo cardiography at follow-up. The results showed that higher stress reactivity at baseline was predictive of arterial deterioration after four years. In addition, stress reactivity has been suggested as the physiological mechanism behind the impact of coronary-prone behaviours on the heart (Harbin 1989; Suarez et al. 1991). This doesn't mean that individuals who show greater responses to stress are more likely to become ill. It means that they are more likely to become ill if subjected to stress (see Figure 11.3).

Stress recovery

After reacting to stress the body then recovers and levels of sympathetic and HPA activation return to baseline. However, some people recover more quickly than others and some research indicates that this rate of recovery may relate to a susceptibility to stress-related illness. This is reflected in Selye's (1956) notion of 'exhaustion' and the general wear and tear caused by stress. Some research has focused particularly on changes in cortisol production, suggesting that slower recovery from raised cortisol levels could be related to immune function and a susceptibility to infection and illness (e.g. Perna and McDowell 1995).

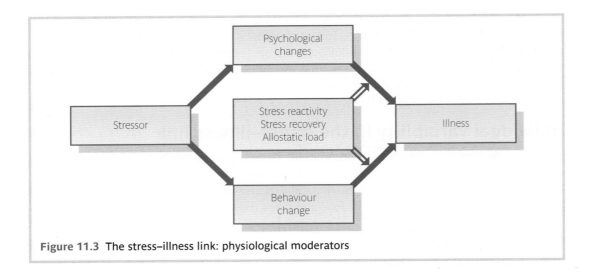

Figure 11.3 The stress–illness link: physiological moderators

Allostatic load

McEwan and Stellar (1993) described the concept of 'allostatic load' to reflect the wear and tear on the body which accumulates over time after exposure to repeated or chronic stress. They argued that the body's physiological systems constantly fluctuate as the individual responds and recovers from stress, a state of allostasis, and that as time progresses recovery is less and less complete and the body is left increasingly depleted. Therefore, if exposed to a new stressor the person is more likely to become ill if their allostatic load is quite high.

Stress resistance

To reflect the observation that not all individuals react to stressors in the same way, researchers developed the concept of stress resistance to emphasize how some people remain healthy even when stressors occur (e.g. Holahan and Moos 1990). Stress resistance includes adaptive coping strategies, certain personality characteristics and social support. These factors are dealt with in detail later on.

Stress has therefore been linked to a range of illnesses and research highlights the role of both a behavioural and physiological pathway. One area of research that emphasizes the physiological pathway and has received much interest over recent years is psychoneuroimmunology (PNI).

Psychoneuroimmunology

PNI is based on the prediction that an individual's psychological state can influence their immune system via the nervous system. This perspective provides a scientific basis for the 'mind over matter', 'think yourself well' and 'positive thinking, positive health' approaches to life. PNI can be understood in terms of: (1) what is the immune system; (2) conditioning the immune system; (3) measuring immune changes; and (4) psychological state and immunity.

The immune system

The role of the immune system is to distinguish between the body and its invaders and to attack and protect the body from anything that is considered foreign. These invaders are called 'antigens'. When the immune system works well the body is protected and infections and illnesses are kept at bay. If the immune system overreacts then this can lead to allergies. If the immune system mistakes the body itself for an invader then this can form the basis of autoimmune disorders. The main organs of the immune system are the lymphoid organs which are distributed throughout the body and include the bone marrow, lymph nodes and vessels, the spleen and thymus. These organs produce a range of 'soldiers' which are involved in identifying foreign bodies and disabling them. There are three levels of immune system activity. The first two are called specific immune processes and are 'cell mediated immunity' and 'humoral mediated immunity'. Cell mediated immunity involves a set of lymphocytes called T cells (killer T cells, memory T cells, delayed hypersensitivity T cells, helper T cells and suppressor T cells). These operate within the cells of the body and are made within the thymus (hence 'T'). Humoral mediated immunity involves B cells and antibodies and takes place in the body's fluids before the antigens have entered any cells. Third, there is non-specific immunity which involves phagocytes which are involved in non-specifically attacking any kind of antigen. Immunocompetence is when the immune system is working well. Immunocompromise is when the immune system is failing in some way.

Conditioning the immune system

Originally it was believed that the immune system was autonomous and did not interact with any other bodily systems. However, research indicates that this is not the case and that not only does the immune system interact with other systems, but it can be conditioned to respond in a particular way using the basic rules of classical and operant conditioning. The early work in this area was carried out by Ader and Cohen (1975, 1981) and showed that changes in the immune system brought about by an immunosuppressive drug could be paired with a sweet taste. This meant that after several pairings, the sweet taste itself began to bring about immunosuppression. These results were important for two reasons. First, they confirmed that the immune system could be manipulated. Second, the results opened up the area for PNI and the possibility that psychological factors could change an individual's immune response.

Measuring immune changes

Although it is accepted that the immune system can be changed, measuring such changes has proved to be problematic. The four main markers of immune function used to date have been as follows: (1) tumour growth, which is mainly used in animal research; (2) wound healing, which can be used in human research by way of a removal of a small section of the skin and can be monitored to follow the healing process; (3) secretory immunoglobulin A (sIgA), which is found in saliva and can be accessed easily and without pain or discomfort to the subject; and (4) natural killer cell cytoxicity (NKCC), T lymphocytes and T helper lymphocytes, which are found in the blood.

All these markers have been shown to be useful in the study of immune functioning (see Chapter 14 for a discussion of immunity and longevity). However, each approach to measurement has its problems. For example, both wound healing and tumour growth present problems of researcher accuracy. But both these measures are actual rather than only proxy measures of outcome (i.e. a healed wound is healthier than an open one). In contrast, whereas measures of sIgA, NKCC, T lymphocytes and T helper cells are more accurate, their link to actual health status is more problematic. In addition, the measurement of immune function raises questions such as 'How long after an event should the immune system marker be assessed?' (i.e. is the effect immediate or delayed?), 'How can baseline measures of the immune system be taken?' (i.e. does actually taking blood/saliva, etc., cause changes in immune functioning?) and 'Are changes in immune functioning predictive of changes in health?' (i.e. if we measure changes in a marker do we really know that this will impact on health in the long term?).

Psychological state and immunity

Research has focused on the capacity of psychological factors to change immune functioning. In particular, it has examined the role of mood, beliefs, emotional expression and stress.

Mood

Studies indicate that positive mood is associated with better immune functioning (as measured by sIgA), that negative mood is associated with poorer functioning (Stone et al. 1987) and that humour appears to be specifically beneficial (Dillon et al. 1985–1986; Newman and Stone 1996). Johnston, Earll et al. (1999) explored the impact of mood on the progression of the disease, disability and survival in patients with amyotrophic lateral sclerosis/motor neurone disease. The study used a prospective design with 38 consecutive patients completing measures of mood (anxiety and depression), self-esteem, well-being and disability at time of diagnosis and after six weeks. Survival and disability were also measured after six months. Ten patients had died by six months. Controlling for disease severity, the results showed that those who died reported lower mood at the six-week interview and that low mood at six weeks was also predictive of greater disability in the survivors.

Beliefs

It has also been suggested that beliefs may themselves have a direct effect on the immune system. Kamen and Seligman (1987) reported that an internal, stable, global attributional style (i.e. a pessimist approach to life whereby the individual blames themselves when things go wrong) predicted poor health in later life. This was supported by Seligman et al. (1988) who argued that pessimism may be related to health through a decrease in T-cells and immunosuppression. The authors argued that this was not mediated through behavioural change but was indicative of a direct effect of attributional style and beliefs on physiology. In a further study, Greer et al. (1979) suggested that denial and a fighting spirit, not hopelessness, predicted survival for breast cancer, suggesting again that beliefs might have a direct effect on illness and recovery. Similarly, Gidron et al. (2001) measured hopelessness (defined as pessimism and helplessness) at baseline and assessed change in a serological marker for breast cancer in women with breast cancer after four months. The results showed that helplessness but not pessimism was related to poorer outcome (see Chapter 14 for a discussion of cancer).

Emotional expression

There is evidence that certain coping styles linked to emotional expression may relate to illness onset and progression. For example, some studies have studied suppression and denial and have reported associations with poorer health outcomes (e.g. Kune et al. 1991; Gross and Levenson 1997). Other studies have focused on emotional (non-) expression and an emotionally inexpressive coping style known as 'type C' and have described a link with illness (e.g. Solano et al. 2001, 2002; Nyklíček et al. 2002), while other researchers have highlighted the importance of a repressive coping style (e.g. Myers 2000). This research consistently indicates that non-expression of emotions, particularly negative emotions in stressful situations, can be harmful for health. There is also evidence that encouraging emotional expression through writing or disclosure groups may be beneficial. This work has been particularly pioneered by Pennebaker (e.g. 1993, 1997) using his basic writing paradigm. This has involved randomly allocating participants to either the experimental or control group with both groups being asked to write for three to five consecutive days for 15 to 30 minutes each day. The experimental group is asked to 'write about your very deepest thoughts and feelings about an extremely emotional issue that has affected you and your life. In your writing I'd really like you to let go and explore your very deepest emotions and thoughts . . .'. The control group is asked to write about more superficial topics such as how they spend their time. This intervention has been used with a range of people including adults, children, students, patients, maximum-security prisoners and survivors of the holocaust who disclose a range of traumatic experiences including relationship break-ups, deaths and abuse. The writing paradigm has been shown to impact upon a range of outcome measures. Some research has shown a reduction in subsequent visits to the doctor (e.g. Pennebaker and Beall 1986; Greenberg and Stone 1992), re-employment following job loss (e.g. Spera et al. 1994), absenteeism from work (Francis and Pennebaker 1992), self-reported physical symptoms (Greenberg and Stone 1992; Petrie et al. 1995) and changes in negative mood (Petrie et al. 1995). In terms of PNI, emotional expression through writing has also been shown to affect the immune system. For example, it has resulted in changes in T helper cell responses (Pennebaker et al. 1988; Petrie et al. 1998), natural killer cell activity (Futterman et al. 1992; Christensen et al. 1996) and CD4 (T lymphocyte) levels (Booth et al. 1997). Therefore this simple intervention provides support for the PNI model, suggesting a link between an individual's psychological state and their immune system. However, as with all associations, research indicates that the impact of emotional expression might vary according to aspects of the task and aspects of the individual.

Aspects of the task
Writing versus talking
Some research has compared the effectiveness of writing versus talking either into a tape recorder or to a therapist (e.g. Donnelly and Murray 1991; Esterling et al. 1994). The results showed that both writing and talking about emotional topics were more effective than writing about superficial topics.

Type of topic
Some research has shown that changes in outcome only occur after writing about particularly traumatic experiences (e.g. Greenberg and Stone 1992). Others have found that it is the relevance of the topic to the outcome variable that is important. For example, Pennebaker and Beall (1986) found that writing about the experience of coming to college had a greater impact upon college grades than writing about 'irrelevant' traumatic experiences.

Amount of writing
Research using the writing paradigm has varied the stipulated time of writing both in terms of the length of sessions (from 15 to 30 mins) and the spread of sessions (over a few days to over a month). Smyth (1998) carried out a meta analysis and concluded that writing over a longer period might be the most effective approach.

Aspects of the individual
Demographics

Pennebaker (1997) concludes that the effectiveness of emotional expression does not seem to vary according to age, level of education, language or culture. However, a meta-analysis of writing studies by Smyth (1998) indicated that men may benefit more from writing than women and those who do not naturally talk openly about their emotion may benefit more than those who do.

Personality and mood

Pennebaker (1997) also concludes that anxiety, inhibition or constraint do not influence the effectiveness of writing. However, Christensen et al. (1996) concluded that individuals high on hostility scores benefited more from writing than those low on hostility.

Use of language

To explain the effectiveness of writing Pennebaker et al. (2001) developed a computer programme to analyse the content of what people were writing during the task. They coded the transcripts in terms of the types of words used: negative emotion words (sad, angry), positive emotion words (happy, laugh), causal words (because, reason) and insight words (understand, realize). The results from this analysis showed that greater improvement in health was associated with a high number of positive emotion words and a moderate number of negative emotion words. More interestingly, they also found that those who showed a shift towards more causal and insight words also showed greater improvement (Pennebaker et al. 1997). They concluded from this that this shift in language use reflected a shift from poorly organized descriptions towards a coherent story and that a coherent story was associated with better health status. However, in contrast to this Graybeal et al. (2002) directly assessed story making and found no relationship with health outcomes.

Stress and immunity

Stress can cause illness through physiological changes such as raised heart rate, blood pressure, heart beat irregularities and an increase in fatty deposits (see earlier). It can also result in changes in immune function. Research on rats showed that stressors such as tail pinching, a loud noise and electric shocks could produce immunosuppression (Moynihan and Ader 1996). Research in humans shows a similar picture. One area of research which has received much attention relates to the impact of caregiver stress. In an early study, Kiecolt-Glaser et al. (1995) explored differences in wound healing between people who were caring for a person with Alzheimer's and a control group. Using a punch biopsy, which involves removing a small area of skin and tissue they explored the relationship between caregiver stress and the wound healing process. The results showed that wound healing was slower in the caregivers than the control group. The wound healing paradigm has also been used to show links between stress and slower healing in students during an exam period (Marucha et al. 1998) and slower healing using high resolution ultrasound scanning which is more accurate than the more traditional measurement strategies involving photography (Ebrecht et al. 2004). Herbert and Cohen (1993) carried out a meta-analysis of 38 studies which had explored the stress–immune system link. They concluded that stress consistently resulted in changes in immune function in terms of proliferative response to mitogens and NK cell activity, and was related to greater numbers of circulating white blood cells, immunoglobulin levels and antibody titers to herpes viruses. They also concluded that greater changes in immune response were found following objective rather than subjectively rated stressful events and that immune response varied according to the duration of the stressor and whether the stressor involved interpersonal or non-social events. Given that stress can change health behaviours (see earlier), it is possible that stress causes changes in the immune system by changing behaviour. Ebrecht et al. (2004) examined this possibility, by assessing the link between perceived stress and wound healing and controlling for alcohol consumption, smoking, sleeping, exercise and diet. The results showed that stress was related to wound healing regardless of changes in behaviour, indicating that the stress–immunity link may not be explained by an unhealthy lifestyle. In contrast, however, a review of 12 studies exploring the impact of smoking and smoking cessation on recovery following surgery concluded that a longer period of smoking cessation prior to surgery was related to fewer post-operative complications. Health behaviours may not have an association with wound healing when measured following a punch biopsy and when smoking is measured at the same time, but in real life and when smoking changes are assessed then there may well be a link.

Research also indicates that stress may relate to illness progression. Kiecolt-Glaser and Glaser (1986) argue that stress causes a decrease in the hormones produced to fight carcinogens and repair DNA. In particular, cortisol decreases the number of active T cells, which could increase the rate of tumour development. This suggests that stress while ill could exacerbate the illness through physiological changes. Such stress may occur independently of the illness. However, stress may also be a result of the illness itself such as relationship breakdown, changes in occupation or simply the distress from a diagnosis. Therefore, if the illness is appraised as being stressful, this itself may be damaging to the chances of recovery. The relationship between stress and illness progression has particularly been explored in the context of HIV. For example, Pereira et al. (2003) explored the progression of cervical problems in women with HIV. Women who are HIV positive are more at risk from cervical intraepithelial neoplasia (CIN) and cervical cancer. Pereira et al. explored the relationship between the likelihood of developing the lesions associated with CIN and life stress. The results showed that higher life stress increased the odds of developing lesions by sevenfold over a one-year period. Life stress therefore seemed to link with illness progression. Some research has also addressed the stress–illness link with a focus on stress management interventions. For example, Antoni et al. (2006) randomized 130 gay men who were HIV positive to receive either a cognitive behavioural stress management intervention (CBSM) and anti-retroviral medication adherence training (MAT), or to receive MAT alone. The men were then followed up after 9 and 15 months in terms of viral load. The results showed no differences overall between the two groups. When only those men who already showed detectable viral loads at baseline were included (i.e. those with a lot of virus in the blood already), differences were found. In particular, for these men, those who received the stress management showed a reduction in their viral load over the 15-month period even when medication adherence was controlled for. The authors conclude that for HIV-positive men who already show a detectable viral load, stress management may enhance the beneficial effects of their anti-retroviral treatment. In a similar study, the mechanisms behind the impact of stress management were explored (Antoni et al. 2005). For this study 25 HIV-positive men were randomized to receive stress management or a waiting list control. Urine samples were taken before and after the intervention period. The results again showed that stress management was effective and that this effect was related to reduction in cortisol and depressed mood. The authors conclude that stress management works by reducing the stress induced by being ill with a disease such as HIV. Therefore from these studies, whereas stress can exacerbate illness, stress management can aid the effectiveness of treatment and reduce the consequences of the stress resulting from being ill.

> ## Box 11.1 **Some problems with . . . stress and illness research**
>
> Below are some problems with research in this area that you may wish to consider.
>
> 1 Research indicates that stress is linked to illness. However, without some degree of stress we probably wouldn't get many of the pleasures from life (e.g. rewards from hard work, satisfaction of small children, etc.). What differentiates stress that produces illness and that which produces a sense of worth is unclear.
>
> 2 Stress is seen to cause illness through either a direct route via physiological shifts or an indirect route via behaviour. Much research considers these two pathways as separate. However, it is likely that they constantly interact and that behaviour and physiology exist in a dynamic relationship. This has implications for both measuring and predicting the stress–illness link.
>
> 3 Factors such as coping, social support and control are considered to mediate the stress–illness link. From this perspective the stress–illness link is seen as occurring first, which in turn can then be influenced by these factors. It is likely, however, that the very identification of a stressor in the first place which may or may not then lead to illness is determined by the degree of coping, social support or control.

The impact of chronic stress

Most research described to date has explored the impact of acute stress induced in the laboratory or individual stressors such as life events. However, many people exist in a life of ongoing chronic stressors including poverty, unemployment, job stress and marital conflict. There is much research linking these social factors to health inequalities with research consistently showing that psychological distress, coronary heart disease and most cancers are more prevalent among lower-class individuals who have more chronic stress in their lives (e.g. Adler et al. 1993, 1994; Marmot 1998). However, untangling this relationship is difficult: although chronic stressors such as poverty may cause heart disease, they are also linked to a range of other factors such as nutrition, hygiene, smoking and social support which are also linked to health status. Furthermore, whereas lower socioeconomic position is linked to chronic stressors such as poverty, higher socioeconomic position is linked to higher perceived stress (Heslop et al. 2001). As a result of these methodological problems many researchers have focused on specific areas of chronic stress including job stress and relationship stress.

Job stress

Occupational stress has been studied primarily as a means to minimize work-related illness but also as it provides a forum to clarify the relationship between stress and illness. Early work on occupational stress highlighted the importance of a range of job-related factors including work overload, poor work relationships, poor control over work and role ambiguity. Karasek and colleagues integrated many of these factors into their job demand–job control model of stress, central to which is the notion of job strain (Karasek et al. 1981; Karasek and Theorell 1990). According to the model, there are two aspects of job strain: *job demands*, which reflect conditions that affect performance, and *job autonomy*, which reflects the control over the speed or the nature of decisions made within the job. Karasek's job demand and control model suggests that high job demands and low job autonomy (control) predict coronary heart disease. Karasek and co-workers have since developed the job demand–control hypothesis to include social support. Within this context, social support is defined as either *emotional support*, involving trust between colleagues and social cohesion, or *instrumental social support*, involving the provision of extra resources and assistance. It is argued that high social support mediates and moderates the effects of low control and high job demand. Karasek and Theorell (1990) report a study in which subjects were divided into low social support and high social support groups, and their decisional control and the demands of their job were measured. The results indicated that subjects in the high social support group showed fewer symptoms of CHD than those subjects in the low social support group. In addition, within those groups high job control and low job demands predicted fewer CHD symptoms. A series of studies have tested and applied Karasek's model of job strain and associations have been reported between job strain and risk factors for heart disease and heart disease itself (Pickering et al. 1996; Schnall et al. 1998; Marmot 1998; Tsutsumi et al. 1998) as well as psychiatric morbidity (Cropley et al. 1999). For example, Kivimaki et al. (2002) used a prospective design to explore the links between job strain and subsequent death from cardiovascular disease. A total of 812 employees from a metal factory in Finland that manufactures paper machines, tractors and firearms along with other equipment completed a baseline assessment in 1973 including measures of their behavioural and biological risks and their work stress. Those with cardiovascular disease at baseline were excluded. Cardiovascular mortality was then recorded between 1973 and 2001 using the national mortality register. The results showed that 73 people had died from cardiovascular disease since the study onset, who were more likely to be older, male, have low worker status, to smoke, have a sedentary lifestyle, high blood pressure, high cholesterol and higher body mass index. Further, when age and sex were controlled for, death was predicted by high job strain and low job control. However, after occupational group was also controlled for (i.e. a measure of class), high job strain remained the best predictor.

In line with the emphasis on job strain some research has also explored the impact of changing work and domestic patterns on women's health. Whereas as 50 years ago women may have worked until they had children, and then given up work to be at home with the children nowadays an increasing number of women take on multiple roles and balance working with being a parent and a partner. There are two contrasting models of the impact of such multiple roles. The first is the enhancement model which suggests that multiple roles have a positive effect on health as they bring benefits such as economic independence, social contact and self-esteem (Collijn et al. 1996; Moen 1998). In contrast the role strain model suggests that multiple roles can be detrimental to health as people only have limited resources and can experience role overload and role conflict (Weatherall et al. 1994). Steptoe et al. (2000) explored the effect of multiple roles on cardiovascular activity throughout the day. They monitored the blood pressure and heart rate throughout the working day and evening in 162 full-time teachers and explored the impact of whether the teacher was also married and/or a parent with a child at home. The results showed that marital status or parenthood had no effect on cardiovascular changes throughout the working day. However, these factors did affect the day–evening drop in blood pressure. In particular, parents who reported good social support showed the greatest drop in blood pressure between the end of the working day and evening. The authors conclude that this supports the enhancement model of job strain as those who worked and were parents with support (i.e. had multiple roles) showed a lower allostatic load. This may have been because they found it easier to switch off from their work stress at the end of the day. To explain the possible effects of multiple roles recent research has focused on the impact of rumination. Rumination is defined as 'unintentional preservative thoughts in the absence of obvious external cues' (Cropley and Millward Purvis 2003) and has been linked with anxiety, physical symptoms and depression. Rumination about work is essentially thinking about work out of work hours when the individual no longer wants to think about work. In terms of its relationship with job strain, research shows that higher job strain is associated with more rumination. Further, research indicates that people report more ruminative thoughts about work when alone than with family or friends (Cropley and Millward Purvis 2003). Job strain would seem to be damaging to health and may also result in rumination. If people go home at the end of a busy day to partners or children they are less likely to ruminate and thus continue feeling the stress of work than if they go home to be on their own.

Relationship stress

There is much evidence indicating an association between relationship status, psychological distress and health status. For example, separated and divorced people have the highest rates of both acute and chronic medical problems even when many demographic factors are controlled for (Verbrugge 1979). In addition, these people also have higher rates of mortality from infectious diseases such as pneumonia (Lynch 1977). They are also over-represented in both inpatient and outpatient psychiatric populations (Crago 1972; Bachrach 1975). However, it is not just the presence or absence or a relationship that is important. The quality is also linked to health. For example, whereas marital happiness is one of the best predictors of global happiness (Glenn and Weaver 1981), those in troubled marriages show more distress than those who are unmarried (Glenn and Weaver 1981). These links between relationship status and quality have been understood using a range of literatures including attachment theory, life events theory and self-identity theory. Kiecolt-Glaser et al. (1987, 2003) have explored these links within the context of stress and the role of immune function. In one study they assessed the associations between marital status and marital quality and markers of immune function. Their results showed that poor marital quality was associated with both depression and a poorer immune response. In addition, they reported that women who had been recently separated showed poorer immune response than matched married women and that time since separation and attachment to the ex-husband predicted variability in this response (Kiecolt-Glaser et al. 1987). In another study they explored the relationship between measures of stress hormones during the first year of marriage and marital status and satisfaction ten years later. The results showed that those who were divorced at follow-up had shown higher levels of stress hormones during conflict, throughout the day and during the night than those who were still married. Further, those whose marriages were troubled at follow-up also showed higher levels of stress hormones at baseline than those whose marriages were untroubled. This suggests that stress responses during the first year of marriage are predictive of marital dissatisfaction and divorce ten years later (Kiecolt-Glaser et al. 2003).

Research therefore shows a link between stress and illness. For many, this stress takes the form of discrete events. However, many people also experience chronic stress caused by factors such as poverty, unemployment or work load. Much research has focused on two aspects of chronic stress, namely job stress and relationship stress. This research indicates an association between chronic stress and illness, with a role for changes in immune function. However, there exists much variability in the stress–illness link. In part this can be explained by factors such as stress reactivity and stress recovery which have already been described. However, research also highlights a role for other moderating variables which will now be considered.

Which factors moderate the stress–illness link?

The relationship between stress and illness is not straightforward, and there is much evidence to suggest that several factors may moderate the stress–illness link. These factors are as follows:

- *Exercise.* This can cause a decrease in stress (see Chapter 7).
- *Coping styles.* The individual's type of coping style may well mediate the stress–illness link and determine the extent of the effect of the stressful event on their health status (see Chapter 3 for a discussion of coping with illness).
- *Social support.* Increased social support has been related to a decreased stress response and a subsequent reduction in illness.
- *Personality.* It has been suggested that personality may influence the individual's response to a stressful situation and the effect of this response on health. This has been studied with a focus on type A behaviour and personality and the role of hostility (see Chapter 15 for details in the context of CHD).
- *Actual or perceived control.* Control over the stressor may decrease the effects of stress on the individual's health status.

Coping with stress, social support, personality and control will now be examined in greater detail (see Figure 11.4).

Coping

Over the past few years the literature on coping has grown enormously and has explored different types of coping styles, the links between coping and a range of health outcomes and the nature of coping itself. How individuals cope with illness was described in Chapter 3 with a focus on coping with a diagnosis, crisis theory and cognitive adaptation theory. This chapter will describe how coping relates to stress and the stress–illness link.

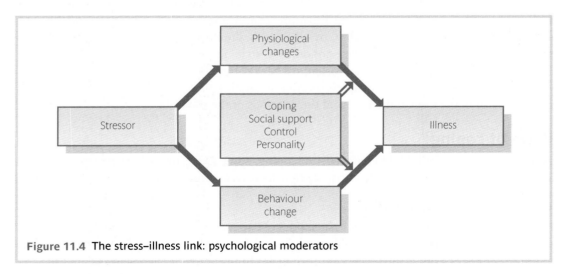

Figure 11.4 The stress–illness link: psychological moderators

What is coping?

Coping has been defined by Lazarus and colleagues as the process of managing stressors that have been appraised as taxing or exceeding a person's resources and as the 'efforts to manage . . . environmental and internal demands' (Lazarus and Launier 1978). In the context of stress, coping therefore reflects the ways in which individuals interact with stressors in an attempt to return to some sort of normal functioning. This might involve correcting or removing the problem, or it might involve changing the way a person thinks about the problem or learning to tolerate and accept it. For example, coping with relationship conflict could involve leaving the relationship or developing strategies to make the relationship better. In contrast, it could involve lowering one's expectations of what a relationship should be like. Lazarus and Folkman (1987) emphasized the dynamic nature of coping which involves appraisal and reappraisal, evaluation and re-evaluation. Lazarus's model of stress emphasized the interaction between the person and their environment. Likewise, coping is also seen as a similar interaction between the person and the stressor. Further, in the same way that Lazarus and colleagues described responses to stress as involving primary appraisal of the external stressor and secondary appraisal of the person's internal resources, coping is seen to involve regulation of the external stressor and regulation of the internal emotional response. Cohen and Lazarus (1979) defined the goals of coping as the following:

1 To reduce stressful environmental conditions and maximize the chance of recovery.
2 To adjust or tolerate negative events.
3 To maintain a positive self-image.
4 To maintain emotional equilibrium.
5 To continue satisfying relationships with others.

Styles, processes and strategies

When discussing coping, some research focuses on 'styles', some on 'processes' and some on 'strategies'. At times this may just reflect a different use of terminology. However, it also reflects an ongoing debate within the coping literature concerning whether coping should be considered a 'trait' similar to personality, or whether it should be considered a 'state' which is responsive to time and situation. The notion of a 'style' tends to reflect the 'trait' perspective and suggests that people are quite consistent in the way that they cope. The notions of 'process' or 'strategy' tends to reflect a 'state' perspective suggesting that people cope in different ways depending upon the time of their life and the demands of the situation.

Ways of coping

Researchers have described different types of coping. Some differentiate between approach and avoidance coping, while others describe emotion-focused and problem-focused coping.

Approach versus avoidance

Roth and Cohen (1986) defined two basic modes of coping: approach and avoidance. Approach coping involves confronting the problem, gathering information and taking direct action. In contrast, avoidant coping involves minimizing the importance of the event. People tend to show one form of coping or the other, although it is possible for someone to manage one type of problem by denying it and another by making specific plans. Some researchers have argued that approach coping is consistently more adaptive than avoidant coping. However, research indicates that the effectiveness of the coping style depends upon the nature of the stressor. For example, avoidant coping might be more effective for short-term stressors (Wong and Kaloupek 1986), but less effective for longer-term stressors (Holahan and Moos 1986). Therefore it might be best to avoid thinking about a one-off stressor such as going to the dentist but make plans and attend to a longer-term stressor such as marital conflict. Some researchers have also explored repressive coping (Myers 2000) and emotional (non-) expression (Solano et al. 2001) which are similar to avoidance coping.

Problem focused versus emotion focused (also known as instrumentality–emotionality)

In contrast to the dichotomy between approach and avoidant coping, the problem- and emotion-focused dimensions reflect types of coping strategies rather than opposing styles. People can show both problem-focused coping and emotional-focused coping when facing a stressful event. For example, Tennen et al. (2000) examined daily coping in people with rheumatoid arthritis and showed that problem-focused and emotion-focused coping usually occurred together and that emotion-focused coping was 4.4 times more likely to occur on a day when problem-focused coping had occurred than when it had not.

Problem-focused coping

This involves attempts to take action to either reduce the demands of the stressor or to increase the resources available to manage it. Examples of problem-focused coping include devising a revision plan and sticking to it, setting an agenda for a busy day, studying for extra qualifications to enable a career change and organizing counselling for a failing relationship.

Emotion-focused coping

This involves attempts to manage the emotions evoked by the stressful event. People use both behavioural and cognitive strategies to regulate their emotions. Examples of behavioural strategies include talking to friends about a problem, turning to drink or smoking more or getting distracted by shopping or watching a film. Examples of cognitive strategies include denying the importance of the problem and trying to think about the problem in a positive way.

Several factors have been shown to influence which coping strategy is used:

- *Type of problem.* Work problems seem to evoke more problem-focused coping whereas health and relationship problems tend to evoke emotion-focused coping (Vitaliano et al. 1990).

- *Age.* Children tend to use more problem-focused coping strategies whereas emotion-focused strategies seem to develop in adolescence (Compas et al. 1991, 1996). Folkman et al. (1987) reported that middle-aged men and women tended to use problem-focused coping whereas the elderly used emotion-focused coping.

- *Gender.* It is generally believed that women use more emotion-focused coping and that men are more problem focused. Some research supports this belief. For example, Stone and Neale (1984) considered coping with daily events and reported that men were more likely to use direct action than women. However, Folkman and Lazarus (1980) and Hamilton and Fagot (1988) found no gender differences.

- *Controllability.* People tend to use problem-focused coping if they believe that the problem itself can be changed. In contrast they use more emotion-focused coping if the problem is perceived as being out of their control (Lazarus and Folkman 1987).

■ *Available resources.* Coping is influenced by external resources such as time, money, children, family and education (Terry 1994). Poor resources may make people feel that the stressor is less controllable by them, resulting in a tendency not to use problem-focused coping.

Measuring coping

The different styles of coping have been operationalized in several measures which have described a range of specific coping strategies. The most commonly used measures are the 'ways of coping' checklist (Folkman and Lazarus 1988) and Cope (Carver et al. 1989). The coping strategies described by these measures include the following:

■ active coping (e.g. 'I've been taking action to try to make the situation better')
■ planning (e.g. 'I've been trying to come up with a strategy about what to do')
■ positive reframing (e.g. 'I've been looking for something good in what is happening')
■ self-distraction (e.g. 'I've been turning to work or other activities to take my mind off things')
■ using emotional support (e.g. 'I've been getting emotional support from others')
■ substance use (e.g. 'I've been using alcohol or other drugs to help me get through it')
■ behavioural disengagement (e.g. 'I've been giving up trying to deal with it')
■ denial (e.g. 'I've been saying to myself, "this isn't real"')
■ self-control (e.g. 'I tried to keep my feelings to myself')
■ distancing (e.g. 'I didn't let it get to me. I refused to think about it too much')
■ escape/avoidance (e.g. 'I wished that the situation would go away').

Some of these strategies are clearly problem-focused coping such as active coping and planning. Others are more emotion focused such as self-control and distancing. Some strategies, however, are a mix of both problem and emotion focused. For example, positive reframing involves thinking about the problem in a different way as a means to alter the emotional response to it. Some strategies can also be considered approach coping such as using emotional support and planning, whereas others reflect a more avoidance coping style such as denial and substance use.

According to models of stress and illness, coping should have two effects. First, it should reduce the intensity and duration of the stressor itself. Second, it should reduce the likelihood that stress will lead to illness. Therefore effective coping can be classified as that which reduces the stressor and minimizes the negative outcomes. Some research has addressed these associations. In addition, recent research has shifted the emphasis away from just the absence of illness towards positive outcomes.

Coping and the stressor

According to Lazarus and colleagues, one of the goals of coping is to minimize the stressor. Much research has addressed the impact of coping on the physiological and self-report dimensions of the stress response. For example, Harnish et al. (2000) argued that effective coping terminates, minimizes or shortens the stressor.

Coping and the stress–illness link

Some research indicates that coping styles may moderate the association between stress and illness. For some studies the outcome variable has been more psychological in its emphasis and has taken the form of well-being, psychological distress or adjustment. For example, Kneebone and Martin (2003) critically reviewed the research exploring coping in carers of persons with dementia. They examined both cross-sectional and longitudinal studies and concluded that problem-solving and acceptance styles of coping seemed to be more effective at reducing stress and distress. In a similar vein, research exploring coping with rheumatoid arthritis suggests that active and problem-solving coping are associated with better outcomes whereas passive avoidant coping is associated with poorer outcomes (Manne and Zautra 1992; Young 1992; Newman et al. 1996). For patients with chronic obstructive pulmonary disease (COPD), wishful thinking and emotion-focused coping were least effective (Buchi et al. 1997). Similarly, research exploring stress and psoriasis shows that avoidant coping is least useful (e.g. Leary et al. 1998). Other studies have focused on more illness-associated variables. For example, Holahan and Moos (1986) examined the relationship between the use of avoidance coping, stress and symptoms such as stomach-ache and headaches. The results after one year showed that, of those who had experienced stress, those who used avoidance coping had more symptoms than those who used more approach coping strategies.

Coping and positive outcomes

Over recent years there has been an increasing recognition that stressful events such as life events and illness may not only result in negative outcomes but may also lead to some positive changes in people lives. This phenomenon has been given a range of names including stress-related growth (Park et al. 1996), benefit finding (Tennen and Affleck 1999), meaning making (Park and Folkman 1997), and growth-orientated functioning and crisis growth (Holahan et al. 1996). This finds reflection in Taylor's (1983) cognitive adaptation theory and is in line with a new movement called 'positive psychology' (Seligman and Csikszentmihalyi 2000). Though a new field of study, research indicates that coping processes that involve finding meaning in the stressful event, positive reappraisal and problem-focused coping are more associated with positive outcomes (Folkman and Moskowitz 2000). See Chapter 3 for further discussion.

Coping is considered to moderate the stress–illness link and to impact upon the extent of the stressor. Much research has involved the description of the kinds of coping styles and strategies used by people and a few studies suggest that some styles might be more effective than others.

Social support

What is social support?

Social support has been defined in a number of ways. Initially, it was defined according to the number of friends that were available to the individual. However, this has been developed to include not only the number of friends supplying social support, but the satisfaction with this support (Sarason et al. 1983). Wills (1985) has defined several types of social support:

- esteem support, whereby other people increase one's own self-esteem
- support, whereby other people are available to offer advice
- companionship, which involves support through activities
- instrumental support, which involves physical help.

The term 'social support' is generally used to refer to the perceived comfort, caring, esteem or help one individual receives from others (e.g. Wallston et al. 1983).

Does social support affect health?

A number of studies have examined whether social support influences the health status of the individual. Lynch (1977) reported that widowed, divorced or single individuals have higher mortality rates from heart disease than married people and suggested that heart disease and mortality are related to lower levels of social support. However, problems with this study include the absence of a direct measure of social support and the implicit assumption that marriage is an effective source of social support.

Berkman and Syme (1979) reported the results of a prospective study whereby they measured social support in 4700 men and women aged 30–69, whom they followed up for nine years. They found that increased social support predicted a decrease in mortality rate. This indicates a role for social support in health. Research has also indicated that birth complications are lower in women who have high levels of social support, again suggesting a link between social support and health status (Oakley 1992). Research has also examined the effects of social support on immune functioning and consequently health. For example, Arnetz et al. (1987) examined the immune function of 25 women who were either employed ($n = 8$) or unemployed ($n = 17$). The unemployed group received either standard economic benefits only or received benefits as well as a psychosocial support programme. The results showed that those unemployed subjects who received the psychosocial support showed better immune functioning than the subjects who received benefits only. It would seem that social support reduced immunosuppression, thus promoting health.

How does social support influence health?

If social support does influence or mediate the stress–illness link, then what are the possible mechanisms? Two theories have been developed to explain the role of social support in health status:

1 The *main effect hypothesis* suggests that social support itself is beneficial and that the absence of social support is itself stressful. This suggests that social support mediates the stress–illness link, with its very presence reducing the effect of the stressor and its absence itself acting as a stressor.

2 The *stress buffering hypothesis* suggests that social support helps individuals to cope with stress, therefore mediating the stress–illness link by buffering the individual from the stressor; social support influences the individual's appraisal of the potential stressor. This process, which has been described using *social comparison theory*, suggests that the existence of other people enables individuals exposed to a stressor to select an appropriate coping strategy by comparing themselves with others. For example, if an individual was going through a stressful life event, such as divorce, and existed in a social group where other people had dealt with divorces, the experiences of others would help them to choose a suitable coping strategy. The stress buffering hypothesis has also been described using role theory. This suggests that social support enables individuals to change their role or identity according to the demands of the stressor. Role theory emphasizes an individual's role and suggests that the existence of other people offers choices as to which role or identity to adopt as a result of the stressful event.

Testing a theory – social support and health

A study to examine the effects of a stressor (unemployment) and social support on health among East German refugees (Schwarzer et al. 1994).

This study examined the relationship between social support and health. It is interesting because it accessed a naturally occurring stressor.

Background

Research suggests that stress may influence health either via changes in health-related behaviour and/or via a physiological pathway. However, the relationship between stress and illness is not automatic, and appears to be mediated by factors such as coping style, perceived control over the stressor and social support. This study examined the effects of stress on health in East German refugees and evaluated which factors were related to their health complaints. In particular, the study focused on employment status and social support.

Methodology

Subjects

In 1989, prior to the fall of the Berlin Wall, the authors launched the study to examine the experiences of being a refugee/migrant in West Berlin. The authors recruited East German migrants who were living in temporary accommodation in West Berlin. The subjects were asked to take part in three waves of data collection: autumn/winter 1989, summer 1990, summer 1991. A total of 235 migrants took part in all three stages of data collection. Of these, 62 per cent were defined as refugees (arrived before the fall of the wall) and 38 per cent were legal immigrants (arrived after the fall of the wall).

Design

The study involved a longitudinal design and data were collected at three time points.

Measures

The subjects completed the following measures:

- *Employment status.* This was recorded at the three time points and subjects were coded as 'always jobless' (jobless throughout the study), 'job hunt successful' (jobless at the beginning but employed by the end) and 'never jobless' (employed throughout the study). Seven subjects who were employed at the beginning and lost their jobs were excluded from the analysis as their numbers were too small.

- *Social support.* The subjects were asked to rate statements on a four-point Likert scale relating to: (1) 'received social support', which referred to their retrospective assessment of actual behaviours, such as 'Friends and relatives have helped me look for a job'; and (2) 'perceived social support', which referred to their anticipation of social support in the future when in times of need, such as 'There are people on whom I can rely when I need help'.

- *Ill health.* The subjects were asked to rate a series of physical symptoms relating to: (1) heart complaints; (2) pains in the limbs; (3) stomach complaints; and (4) exhaustion.

Results

The effect of employment on ill health

The results were analysed to examine overall differences between the groups (always jobless/job hunt successful/never jobless) and showed that at all three time points the subjects who remained unemployed reported a greater number of physical symptoms than the other subject groups. This difference was also related to gender, with men who were always jobless reporting more ill health than other individuals.

The effects of employment and social support on ill health

The results were also analysed to examine the effect of social support on ill health. The results showed that social support had only a small effect on ill health in those subjects who were employed but had a much larger effect on those who had always been jobless. Within the 'always jobless' group, those who reported higher levels of social support reported far fewer physical symptoms than those who reported lower social support. In addition, subjects who were both unemployed and reported low social support reported more ill health than all the other subjects.

The effects of employment on social support

The results were also analysed to examine the long-term effects of employment on both social support and ill health. The results suggest that employment is related to both ill health and social support and that the relationship between employment and social support is reciprocal over time (i.e. employment influences social support, and social support influences employment).

Conclusion

The results from this study provide support for the relationship between stress (unemployment) and health and suggest that this relationship is mediated by social support. Therefore ill health was greatest in those subjects who were both unemployed and who reported low social support. In addition, the results suggest that, although social support may act as a mediating factor, it is itself related to employment status, with individuals gaining social support from work colleagues.

Personality

Early research exploring the role of personality as a moderator of the stress–illness link focused on type A behaviour. For example, Friedman and Rosenman (1959) initially defined type A behaviour in terms of excessive competitiveness, impatience, hostility and vigorous speech. Using a semi-structured interview, three types of type A behaviour were identified. Type A1 reflected vigour, energy, alertness, confidence, loud speaking, rapid speaking, tense clipped speech, impatience, hostility, interrupting, frequent use of the word 'never' and frequent use of the word 'absolutely'. Type A2 was defined as being similar to type A1, but not as extreme, and type B was regarded as relaxed, showing no interruptions and quieter (e.g. Rosenman 1978). The *Jenkins Activity Survey* was developed in 1971 to further define type A behaviour. Support for a relationship between type A behaviour and coronary heart disease using the Jenkins Activity Survey has been reported by a number of studies (Rosenman et al. 1975; Jenkins et al. 1979; Haynes et al. 1980). However, research has also reported no relationship between type A behaviour and CHD. For example, Johnston et al. (1987) used Bortner's (1969) questionnaire to predict heart attacks in 5936 men aged 40–59 years, who were randomly selected from British general practice lists. All subjects were examined at the start of the study for the presence of heart disease and completed the Bortner questionnaire. They were then followed up for morbidity and mortality from heart attack and for sudden cardiac death for an average of 6.2 years. The results showed that non-manual workers had higher type A scores than manual workers and that type A score decreased with age. However, at follow-up the results showed no relationship between type A behaviour and heart disease. More recently, however, much research has focused on hostility and aspects of anger expression as the most important personality types to be linked to stress and illness. Hostility has most frequently been measured using the Cook Medley hostility scale (Cook and Medley 1954) which asks people to rate statements such as 'I have often met people who were supposed to be experts who were no better than I', 'It is safer to trust nobody', and 'My way of doing things is apt to be misunderstood by others'. Agreement with such statements is an indication of high hostility. Hostility has also been classified according to cynical hostility and neurotic hostility. Research has asked 'Who is hostile?', 'How does hostility link to stress?' and 'How does hostility link to illness?'

Who is hostile?

Hostility is higher in men than women (Matthews et al. 1992), higher in those of lower socio-economic status (e.g. Siegman et al. 2000) and seems to run in families (Weidner et al. 2000). It seems to be more common in people whose parents were punitive, abusive or interfering and where there was a lot of conflict (Matthews et al. 1996), and Houston and Vavak (1991) have argued that it relates to feelings of insecurity and negative feelings about others.

How does hostility link to stress?

As described earlier, individuals vary in their physiological reactions to stress, with some showing greater stress reactivity than others. Researchers have argued that hostility may be the social manifestation of this heightened reactivity. To assess this, Guyll and Contrada (1998) explored the relationship between hostility and stress reactivity and reported that chronically hostile people showed greater reactivity to stressors involving interpersonal interactions than non-hostile people. In addition, Fredrickson et al. (2000) indicated that hostile people show larger and longer-lasting changes in blood pressure when made to feel angry. Therefore hostility and stress reactivity seem to be closely linked. What are the implications of this for the stress–illness link?

How does hostility link to illness?

Much research has shown an association between hostility and CHD. In particular, researchers have argued that hostility is not only an important risk factor for the development of heart disease (e.g. Williams and Barefoot 1988; Houston 1994; Miller et al. 1996) but also as a trigger for heart attack (Moller et al. 1999). However, it may not be hostility *per se* that predicts heart disease but how this hostility is expressed. Ramsay et al. (2001) and McDermott et al. (2001) explored associations between a range of components of hostility and symptoms of coronary artery disease (CAD) in men with CAD versus a control group of men attending a fracture clinic. Results at baseline and at two-year follow-up showed that the best predictor of CAD symptoms was not hostility but anger expression. Similarly, Siegman and Snow (1997) argued that the expression of anger and hostility might be a better predictor of stress reactivity and subsequent health outcomes than the state of either anger or hostility on their own. So how might hostility and the expression of hostility cause illness? The link between hostility and heart disease illustrates a role for a physiological pathway with the associated heightened stress reactivity leading to cardiac damage. However, research also suggests that hostility may also impact upon health through two other pathways. First, hostility is linked to unhealthy behaviours such as smoking, alcohol intake, caffeine consumption and poorer diet (e.g. Lipkus et al. 1994; Greene et al. 1995). Second, hostility may be associated with other moderating factors. For example, hostile individuals may avoid social support and refuse to draw upon any help when under stress. In fact, this is implicit within some of the measures of hostility with responses to statements such as 'No one cares much what happens to me'. Hostility may also relate to coping as believing that 'It is safer to trust nobody' could be seen to reflect an avoidant coping style.

Control

The effect of control on the stress–illness link has also been extensively studied.

What is control?

Control has been studied within a variety of different psychological theories.

1 *Attributions and control.* Kelley's (1967, 1971) attributional theory examines control in terms of attributions for causality (see Chapter 2 for a discussion of attribution theory). If applied to a stressor, the cause of a stressful event would be understood in terms of whether the cause was controllable by the individual or not. For example, failure to get a job could be understood in terms of a controllable cause (e.g. 'I didn't perform as well as I could in the interview', 'I should have prepared better') or an uncontrollable cause (e.g. 'I am stupid', 'The interviewer was biased').

2 *Self-efficacy and control.* Control has also been discussed by Bandura (1977) in his self-efficacy theory. Self-efficacy refers to an individual's confidence to carry out a particular behaviour. Control is implicit in this concept.

3 *Categories of control.* Five different types of control have been defined by Thompson (1986): behavioural control (e.g. avoidance), cognitive control (e.g. reappraisal of coping strategies), decisional control (e.g. choice over possible outcome), informational control (e.g. the ability to access information about the stressor) and retrospective control (e.g. 'Could I have prevented that event from happening?').

4 *The reality of control.* Control has also been subdivided into perceived control (e.g. 'I believe that I can control the outcome of a job interview') and actual control (e.g. 'I can control the outcome of a job interview'). The discrepancy between these two factors has been referred to as illusory control (e.g. 'I control whether the plane crashes by counting throughout the journey'). However, within psychological theory, most control relates to perceived control.

Does control affect the stress response?

Research has examined the extent to which the controllability of the stressor influences the stress response to this stressor, both in terms of the subjective experience of stress and the accompanying physiological changes.

1 *Subjective experience.* Corah and Boffa (1970) examined the relationship between the controllability of the stressor and the subjective experience of stress. Subjects were exposed to a loud noise (the experimental stressor) and were either told about the noise (the stressor was predictable) or not (an unpredictable stressor). The results indicated that if the noise was predictable, there was a decrease in subjective experiences of stress. The author argued that the predictability enables the subject to feel that they have control over the stressor, and that this perceived control reduces the stress response. Baum et al. (1981) further suggested that if a stressor is predicted, there is a decrease in the stress response, and reported that predictability or an expectation of the stress enables the individual to prepare their coping strategies.

2 *Physiological changes.* Research has also examined the effect of control on the physiological response to stress. For example, Meyer et al. (1985) reported that if a stressor is regarded as uncontrollable, the release of corticosteroids is increased.

Does control affect health?

If control influences the stress response, does control also influence the effect of stress on health and illness? This question has been examined by looking at both animal and human models.

Animal research

Seligman and Visintainer (1985) reported the results of a study whereby rats were injected with live tumour cells and exposed to either controllable or uncontrollable shocks. The results indicated that the uncontrollable shocks resulted in promotion of the tumour growth. This suggests that controllability may influence the stress response, which may then promote illness. In a further study, the relationship between control and CHD was studied in monkeys (Manuck et al. 1986). Some breeds of monkey exist in social hierarchies with clearly delineated roles. The monkeys are categorized as either dominant or submissive. Usually this hierarchy is stable. However, the authors introduced new members to the groups to create an unstable environment. They argued that the dominant monkeys show higher rates of CHD in the unstable condition than the dominant monkeys in the stable condition, or the submissive monkeys in the stable condition. It is suggested that the dominant monkeys have high expectations of control, and are used to experiencing high levels of control. However, in the unstable condition, there is a conflict between their expectations of control and the reality which, the authors argued, results in an increase in CHD. These animal models are obviously problematic in that many assumptions are made about the similarities between the animals' experience of control and that of humans. However, the results indicate an association between control and health in the predicted direction.

Human research

Human models have also been used to examine the effect of control on the stress–illness link. For example, the job strain model was developed to examine the effects of control on coronary heart disease (e.g. Karasek and Theorell 1990). The three factors involved in the model are (1) psychological demands of the job in terms of workload; (2) the autonomy of the job, reflecting control; and (3) the satisfaction with the job. This model has been used to predict coronary heart disease in the USA (Karasek et al. 1988), and in Sweden (Karasek et al. 1981). The results of these studies suggest that a combination of high workload (i.e. high demand), low satisfaction and low control are the best predictors of coronary heart disease.

How does control mediate the stress–illness link?

A number of theories have been developed to explain how control influences health and mediates the stress–illness link:

- *Control and preventive behaviour.* It has been suggested that high control enables the individual to maintain a healthy lifestyle by believing that 'I can do something to prevent illness'.

- *Control and behaviour following illness.* It has also been suggested that high control enables the individual to change behaviour after illness. For example, even though the individual may have low health status following an illness, if they believe there is something they can do about their health they will change their behaviour.

- *Control and physiology.* It has been suggested that control directly influences health via physiological changes.

- *Control and personal responsibility.* It is possible that high control can lead to a feeling of personal responsibility and consequently personal blame and learned helplessness. These feelings could lead either to no behaviour change or to unhealthy behaviours resulting in illness.

The possible benefits of low control

Most theories of the relationship between control and stress suggest that high control (such as predictability, responsibility, etc.) relates to a reduction in stress and is therefore beneficial to health. However, in certain situations a perception of low control may result in lowered stress. For example, flying in a plane can be made less stressful by acknowledging that there is nothing one can do about the possibility of crashing. To an extent this perception of helplessness may be less stressful than attempting to control an uncontrollable situation.

Control and social support in stress and illness

Haynes et al. (1980) carried out a study to examine the interrelationship between perceived control and social support and their effects on the stress–illness link. They examined the preva-

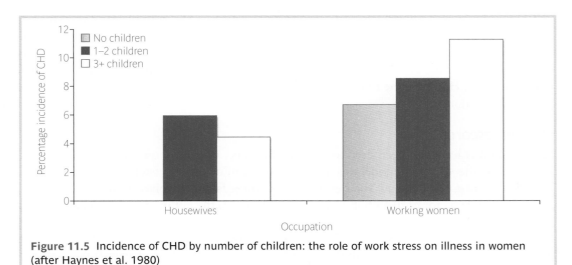

Figure 11.5 Incidence of CHD by number of children: the role of work stress on illness in women (after Haynes et al. 1980)

lence of CHD in women and compared this prevalence between working and non-working women. In addition, they measured aspects of work such as job demand, social support and perceived control over work. The results showed that the working women were not more likely to have CHD than the non-working women, suggesting that job demand is not simply a predictor of CHD. However, within the working women, those women who reported low perceived control over their work were more likely to have CHD than those who reported high perceived control, suggesting that within that group of people with high job demand, low control was a predictor of illness, supporting the predicted association between social support and health. In addition, within the group of working women, those who showed low work support were also more likely to have CHD, supporting the research on social support and its relationship to illness. The study also looked at how many children both the working and the non-working women had and related this to CHD. The results showed that a higher number of children increased the risk of CHD in the working women, but not in the non-working women. The authors argued that the number of children may be a contributor to job demand, but that this increased CHD in working women but not in the non-working women. The results for this study are shown in Figure 11.5.

To conclude

Cross-sectional research suggests an association between stress and illness and some experimental studies indicate that stress can cause illness. Theories of the stress–illness link suggest that stress may cause illness through chronic and acute processes involving chronic and acute stress. Both these pathways involve changes in behaviour and changes in physiology. The behavioural pathway involves changes in health behaviours such as smoking, alcohol consumption, eating and exercise, whereas the physiological pathway involves changes in sympathetic activation or hypothalamic-pituitary-adrenocortical activation. This chapter has also explored research in the area of PNI which provides some insights into how psychological factors such as emotional expression, mood, belief and stress might directly influence health. However, there is much variability in the link between stress and illness and this chapter has also examined coping, social support, personality and control as possible moderators of this association.

Questions

1 Stress causes illness. Critically analyse the evidence to support this statement.

2 To what extent might the acute and chronic pathways of stress interact?

3 Describe the mechanisms behind the stress–illness association.

4 How might the behavioural and physiological pathways interact?

5 Discuss the role of PNI in explaining the stress–illness link.

6 Discuss the possible factors that moderate the stress–illness link.

7 Describe a study designed to assess the potential effect of perceived control on the development of illness.

For discussion

Consider the ways you cope with stress and discuss the extent to which these are either beneficial or detrimental to your health.

Assumptions in health psychology

The stress research highlights some of the assumptions in health psychology.

1 *The problem of mind–body split.* Although much of the stress research examines how the mind may influence the body (e.g. appraisal relates to the release of stress hormones, social support relates to resulting stress-related illnesses), how this process occurs is unclear. In addition, although these relationships suggest an interaction between the mind and the body, they still define them as separate entities which influence each other, not as the same entity.

2 *The problem of progress.* It is often assumed that the most recent theories are better than earlier theories. Therefore models including appraisal, social support and so on, are better than those describing stress as a knee-jerk reaction to a stressor. Perhaps these different theories are not necessarily better than each other, but are simply different ways of describing the stress process.

3 *The problem of methodology.* It is assumed that methodology is neutral and separate to the data collected. For example, factors such as hardiness, self-efficacy and control exist before they are measured. Perhaps, however, methodology is not so neutral, and asking subjects questions relating to these factors actually encourages them to see themselves/the world in terms of hardiness, self-efficacy and control.

Further reading

Evans, P., Hucklebridge, F. and Clow, A. (2000) *Mind, Immunity and Health: The Science of Psychoimmunology.* London: Free Association Books.
    This book provides a good introduction to the area of PNI and explains how factors such as stress, depression and conditioning can affect the immune system.

Johnston, D. (1992) The management of stress in the prevention of coronary heart disease, in S. Maes, H. Leventhal and M. Johnston (eds), *International Review of Health Psychology.* London: Wiley.
    This chapter reviews the literature relating to the role of stress on CHD and evaluates the effectiveness of interventions aimed at reducing stress in individuals.

Jones, F., Burke, R.J. and Westmen, M. (eds) (2006) *Work–Life Balance: A Psychological Perspective.* East Sussex: Psychology Press.
    This book is an edited collection of chapters which describe and explore different aspects of the work–life balance including the changing nature of work, the legal and policy context of work, managing home and work, managing family and work and recovery after work.

Vedhara, K. and Irwin, M. (eds) (2005) *Human Psychoneuroimmunology.* Oxford: Oxford University Press.
    This book provides an excellent up-to-date overview of the research on PNI and covers key concepts, research and methods.

12

Pain

Chapter overview

This chapter examines early models of pain and their description of pain as a sensation. It then examines the increasing emphasis on a role for psychology in pain, the shift towards the notion of pain perception and the development of the gate control theory. The chapter then describes the three process models of pain with a focus on how cognitive, affective and behavioural factors can either exacerbate or reduce pain perception. Next, the role of psychology in treating and managing pain is discussed. Finally, the chapter examines the problems with pain measurement and the ways in which pain can be assessed.

This chapter covers

- What is pain?
- Early pain theories – pain as a sensation
- The gate control theory of pain – pain as a perception
- The role of psychosocial factors in pain perception
- The role of psychology in pain treatment
- Measuring pain

What is pain?

Pain seems to have an obvious function. Pain provides constant feedback about the body, enabling us to make adjustments to how we sit or sleep. Pain is often a warning sign that something is wrong and results in protective behaviour such as avoiding moving in a particular way or lifting heavy objects. Pain also triggers help-seeking behaviour and is a common reason for patients visiting their doctor. Pain also has psychological consequences and can generate fear and anxiety. From an evolutionary perspective therefore, pain is a sign that action is needed. It functions to generate change either in the form of seeking help or avoiding activity. However, pain is not that simple. Some pain seems to have no underlying cause and functions to hinder rather than to help a person carry on with their lives. Such pain has a strong psychological component. Researchers differentiate between acute pain and chronic pain. Acute pain is defined as pain that lasts for six months or less. It usually has a definable cause and is mostly treated with painkillers. A broken leg or a surgical wound is an example of acute pain. In contrast, chronic pain lasts for longer than six months and can be either benign in that it varies in severity or progressive in that it gets gradually worse. Chronic low back pain is often described as chronic benign pain whereas illnesses such as rheumatoid arthritis result in chronic progressive pain. Most of the research described in this chapter is concerned with chronic pain which shows an important role for psychological factors.

Early pain theories – pain as a sensation

Early models of pain described pain within a biomedical framework as an automatic response to an external factor. Descartes, perhaps the earliest writer on pain, regarded pain as a response to a painful stimulus. He described a direct pathway from the source of pain (e.g. a burnt finger) to an area of the brain that detected the painful sensation. Von Frey (1895) developed the *specificity theory of pain*, which again reflected this very simple stimulus–response model. He suggested that there were specific sensory receptors which transmit touch, warmth and pain, and that each receptor was sensitive to specific stimulation. This model was similar to that described by Descartes in that the link between the cause of pain and the brain was seen as direct and automatic. In a similar vein, Goldschneider (1920) developed a further model of pain called the *pattern theory*. He suggested that nerve impulse patterns determined the degree of pain and that messages from the damaged area were sent directly to the brain via these nerve impulses. Therefore these three models of pain describe pain in the following ways:

- Tissue damage causes the sensation of pain.
- Psychology is involved in these models of pain only as a consequence of pain (e.g. anxiety, fear, depression). Psychology has no causal influence.
- Pain is an automatic response to an external stimulus. There is no place for interpretation or moderation.
- The pain sensation has a single cause.
- Pain was categorized into being either psychogenic pain or organic pain. Psychogenic pain was considered to be 'all in the patient's mind' and was a label given to pain when no organic basis could be found. Organic pain was regarded as being 'real pain' and was the label given to pain when some clear injury could be seen.

Including psychology in theories of pain

The early simple models of pain had no role for psychology. However, psychology came to play an important part in understanding pain through the twentieth century. This was based on several observations.

First, it was observed that medical treatments for pain (e.g. drugs, surgery) were, in the main, only useful for treating acute pain (i.e. pain with a short duration). Such treatments were fairly ineffective for treating chronic pain (i.e. pain that lasts for a long time). This suggested that there must be something else involved in the pain sensation which was not included in the simple stimulus–response models.

It was also observed that individuals with the same degree of tissue damage differed in their reports of the painful sensation and/or painful responses. Beecher (1956) observed soldiers' and civilians' requests for pain relief in a hospital during the Second World War. He reported that although soldiers and civilians often showed the same degree of injury, 80 per cent of the civilians requested medication, whereas only 25 per cent of the soldiers did. He suggested that this reflected a role for the meaning of the injury in the experience of pain; for the soldiers, the injury had a positive meaning as it indicated that their war was over. This meaning mediated the pain experience.

The third observation was phantom limb pain. The majority of amputees tend to feel pain in an absent limb. This pain can actually get worse after the amputation, and continues even after complete healing. Sometimes the pain can feel as if it is spreading and is often described as a hand being clenched with the nails digging into the palm (when the hand is missing) or the bottom of the foot being forced into the ankle (when the foot is missing). Phantom limb pain has no peripheral physical basis because the limb is obviously missing. In addition, not everybody feels phantom limb pain and those who do, do not experience it to the same extent. Further, even individuals who are born with missing limbs sometimes report phantom limb pain.

These observations, therefore, suggest variation between individuals. Perhaps this variation indicates a role for psychology.

The gate control theory of pain

Melzack and Wall (1965, 1982; Melzack 1979), developed the gate control theory of pain (GCT), which represented an attempt to introduce psychology into the understanding of pain. This model is illustrated in Figure 12.1. It suggested that, although pain could still be understood in terms of a stimulus–response pathway, this pathway was complex and mediated by a network of interacting processes. Therefore the GCT integrated psychology into the traditional biomedical model of pain and not only described a role for physiological causes and interventions, but also allowed for psychological causes and interventions.

Input to the gate

Melzack and Wall suggested that a gate existed at the spinal cord level, which received input from the following sources:

- *Peripheral nerve fibres.* The site of injury (e.g. the hand) sends information about pain, pressure or heat to the gate.

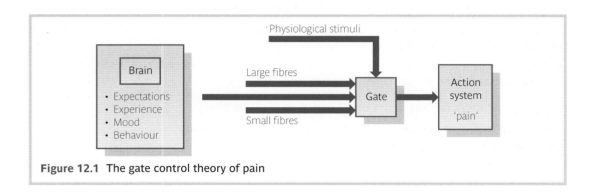

Figure 12.1 The gate control theory of pain

- *Descending central influences from the brain.* The brain sends information related to the psychological state of the individual to the gate. This may reflect the individual's behavioural state (e.g. attention, focus on the source of the pain); emotional state (e.g. anxiety, fear, depression); and previous experiences or self-efficacy (e.g. I have experienced this pain before and know that it will go away) in terms of dealing with the pain.
- *Large and small fibres.* These fibres constitute part of the physiological input to pain perception.

Output from the gate

The gate integrates all of the information from these different sources and produces an output. This output from the gate sends information to an action system, which results in the perception of pain.

How does the GCT differ from earlier models of pain?

The GCT differs from earlier models in a number of fundamental ways:

- *Pain as a perception.* According to the GCT, pain is a perception and an experience rather than a sensation. This change in terminology reflects the role of the individual in the degree of pain experienced. In the same way that psychologists regard vision as a perception, rather than a direct mirror image, pain is described as involving an active interpretation of the painful stimuli.
- *The individual as active, not passive.* According to the GCT, pain is determined by central and peripheral fibres. Pain is seen as an active process as opposed to a passive one. The individual no longer just responds passively to painful stimuli, but actively interprets and appraises this painful stimuli.
- *The role of individual variability.* Individual variability is no longer a problem in understanding pain but central to the GCT. Variation in pain perception is understood in terms of the degree of opening or closing of the gate.
- *The role for multiple causes.* The GCT suggests that many factors are involved in pain perception, not just a singular physical cause.
- *Is pain ever organic?* The GCT describes most pain as a combination of physical and psychological. It could, therefore, be argued that within this model, pain is never totally either organic or psychogenic.
- *Pain and dualism.* The GCT attempts to depart from traditional dualistic models of the body and suggests an interaction between the mind and body.

What opens the gate?

The more the gate is opened, the greater the perception of pain. Melzack and Wall (1965, 1982) suggest that several factors can open the gate:

- *physical factors,* such as injury or activation of the large fibres
- *emotional factors,* such as anxiety, worry, tension and depression
- *behavioural factors,* such as focusing on the pain or boredom.

What closes the gate?

Closing the gate reduces pain perception. The gate control theory also suggests that certain factors close the gate:

- *physical factors*, such as medication, stimulation of the small fibres
- *emotional factors*, such as happiness, optimism or relaxation
- *behavioural factors*, such as concentration, distraction or involvement in other activities.

Problems with the GCT

The gate control theory represented an important advancement on previous simple stimulus–response theories of pain. It introduced a role for psychology and described a multidimensional process rather than a simple linear one. However, there are several problems with the theory.

First, although there is plenty of evidence illustrating the mechanisms to increase and decrease pain perception, no one has yet actually located the gate itself. Second, although the input from the site of physical injury is mediated and moderated by experience and other psychological factors, the model still assumes an organic basis for pain. This integration of physiological and psychological factors can explain individual variability and phantom limb pain to an extent, but because the model still assumes some organic basis, it is still based around a simple stimulus–response process.

Third, the GCT attempted to depart from traditional dualistic models of health by its integration of the mind and the body. However, although the GCT suggests some integration or interaction between mind and body, it still sees them as separate processes. The model suggests that physical processes are influenced by the psychological processes, but that these two sets of processes are distinct.

Box 12.1 Some problems with . . . pain research

Below are some problems with research in this area that you may wish to consider.

1 Pain cannot be observed and is a subjective experience. Therefore measuring pain is problematic. Self-report measures are reliant upon the individual attempting to give an accurate description of how they feel which may well be influenced by how they want other people to believe that they feel and the ability of the existing measures to describe their experience. More objective measures such as the observation of pain behaviour or medication use may miss the subjective nature of the pain experience.

2 Pain research highlights the interaction between biological and psychological processes. This is particularly apparent in the gate control theory of pain and the role of affect and cognitions in mediating the pain experience. However, how these different processes actually interact remains unclear. Why is it that focusing on pain actually makes it hurt more?

3 Pain research emphasizes the role of psychological factors in promoting chronic pain and exacerbating acute pain. Little, however, is known about pain onset. Why do some people get headaches while others do not? Why is there such cultural variation in where and when people experience pain?

The role of psychosocial factors in pain perception

The GCT was a development from previous theories in that it allowed for the existence of mediating variables, and emphasized active perception rather than passive sensation. The GCT and the subsequent attempts at evaluating the different components of pain perception reflect a *three-process model* of pain. The components of this model are: physiological processes, subjective–affective–cognitive processes and behavioural processes. Physiological processes involve factors such as tissue damage, the release of endorphins and changes in heart rate. The subjective–affective–cognitive and behavioural processes are illustrated in Figure 12.2 and described in more detail below.

Subjective–affective–cognitive processes
The role of learning
Classical conditioning

Research suggests that classical conditioning may have an effect on the perception of pain. As described by theories of associative learning, an individual may associate a particular environment with the experience of pain. For example, if an individual associates the dentist with pain due to past experience, the pain perception may be enhanced when attending the dentist due to this expectation. In addition, because of the association between these two factors, the individual may experience increased anxiety when attending the dentist, which may also increase pain. Jamner and Tursky (1987) examined the effect of presenting migraine sufferers with words associated with pain. They found that this presentation increased both anxiety and pain perception and concluded that the words caused a change in mood, which caused a change in the subject's perception of pain. This is further discussed in terms of the impact of anxiety.

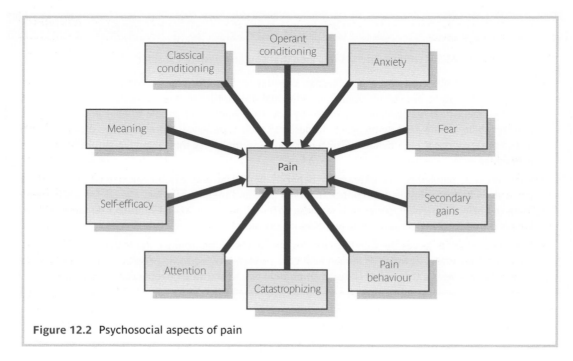

Figure 12.2 Psychosocial aspects of pain

Operant conditioning

Research suggests that there is also a role for operant conditioning in pain perception. Individuals may respond to pain by showing pain behaviour (e.g. resting, grimacing, limping, staying off work). Such pain behaviour may be positively reinforced (e.g. sympathy, attention, time off work), which may itself increase pain perception (see below).

The role of affect

Anxiety

Some research has explored how patients worry about their pain. For example, Eccleston et al. (2001) asked 34 male and female chronic pain patients to describe their experience of pain over a seven-day period. The results showed that the patients reported both pain-related and non-pain-related worry and that these two forms of worry were qualitatively different. In particular, worry about chronic pain was seen as more difficult to dismiss, more distracting, more attention grabbing, more intrusive, more distressing and less pleasant than non-pain-related worry. Other research has explored how worry and anxiety relate to pain perception. Fordyce and Steger (1979) examined the relationship between anxiety and acute and chronic pain. They reported that anxiety has a different relationship to these two types of pain. In terms of acute pain, pain increases anxiety; the successful treatment for the pain then decreases the pain which subsequently decreases the anxiety. This can then cause a further decrease in the pain. Therefore, because of the relative ease with which acute pain can be treated, anxiety relates to this pain perception in terms of a cycle of pain reduction. However, the pattern is different for chronic pain. Because treatment has very little effect on chronic pain, this increases anxiety, which can further increase pain. Therefore, in terms of the relationship between anxiety and chronic pain, there is a cycle of pain increase. Research has also shown a direct correlation between high anxiety levels and increased pain perception in children with migraines and sufferers of back pain and pelvic pain (Feuerstein et al. 1987; McGowan et al. 1998). In a recent experimental study, participants took part in the cold pressor test which involves placing the hand and arm in icy water as a means to induce pain. Their trait anxiety was assessed and some were actively distracted from thinking about their pain (James and Hardardottir 2002). The results showed that both distraction and low anxiety reduced the pain experience.

Fear

Many patients with an experience of pain can have extensive fear of increased pain or of the pain reoccurring which can result in them avoiding a whole range of activities that they perceive to be high risk. For example, patients can avoid moving in particular ways and exerting themselves to any extent. However, these patients often do not describe their experiences in terms of fear but rather in terms of what they can and cannot do. Therefore they do not report being frightened of making the pain worse by lifting a heavy object, but they state that they can no longer lift heavy objects. Fear of pain and fear avoidance beliefs have been shown to be linked with the pain experience in terms of triggering pain in the first place. For example, Linton et al. (2000) measured fear avoidance beliefs in a large community sample of people who reported no spinal pain in the preceding year. The participants were then followed up after one year and the occurrence of a pain episode and their physical functioning was assessed. The results showed that 19 per cent of the sample reported an episode of back pain at follow-up and that those with higher baseline scores of fear avoidance were twice as likely to report back pain and had a 1.7 times higher risk of lowered physical functioning. The authors argue that fear avoidance may relate to the early onset of pain. Some research also suggests that fear may also be involved in exacerbating existing pain and turning acute pain into chronic pain. For example, Crombez et al. (1999) explored the interrelationship between attention to pain and fear. They argued that pain functions by demanding attention which results in a lowered ability to focus on other activities. Their results indicated that pain-related fear increased this attentional interference suggesting that fear about pain increased the amount of attention demanded by the pain. They concluded that pain-related fear can create a hyper-vigilance towards pain which could contribute to the progression from acute to chronic pain. These conclusions were further supported by a comprehensive review of the recent research. This indicates that treatment that exposes patients to the very situations that they are afraid of, such as going out and being in crowds, can reduce fear avoidance beliefs and modify their pain experience (Vlaeyen and Linton 2000).

The role of cognition
Catastrophizing

Patients with pain, particularly chronic pain, in line with many other patients often show catastrophizing. Keefe et al. (2000) described catastrophizing as involving three components: (1) rumination – a focus on threatening information, both internal and external ('I can feel my neck click whenever I move'); (2) magnification – overestimating the extent of the threat ('The bones are crumbling and I will become paralysed'); and (3) helplessness – underestimating personal and broader resources that might mitigate the danger and disastrous consequences ('Nobody understands how to fix the problem and I just can't bear any more pain'). Catastrophizing has been linked to both the onset of pain and the development of longer-term pain problems (Sullivan et al. 2001). For example, in the prospective study described earlier by Linton et al. (2000), the authors measured baseline levels of pain catastrophizing. The results showed some small associations between this and the onset of back pain by follow-up. Crombez et al. (2003) developed a new measure of catastrophizing to assess this aspect of pain in children. Their new measure consisted of three subscales reflecting the dimensions of catastrophizing, namely rumination, magnification and helplessness. They then used this measure to explore the relationship between catastrophizing and pain intensity in a clinical sample of 43 boys and girls aged between 8 and 16. The results indicated that catastrophizing independently predicted both pain intensity and disability regardless of age and gender. The authors argued that catastrophizing functions by facilitating the escape from pain and by communicating distress to others.

Meaning

Although at first glance any pain would seem to be only negative in its meaning, research indicates that pain can have a range of meanings to different people. For example, the pain experienced during childbirth, although intense, has a very clear cause and consequence. If the same kind of pain were to happen outside childbirth then it would have a totally different meaning and would probably be experienced in a very different way. Beecher (1956), in his study of soldiers' and civilians' requests for medication, was one of the first people to examine this and asked the question, 'What does pain mean to the individual?' Beecher argued that differences in pain perception were related to the meaning of pain for the individual. In Beecher's study, the soldiers benefited from their pain. This has also been described in terms of secondary gains whereby the pain may have a positive reward for the individual.

Self-efficacy

Some research has emphasized the role of self-efficacy in pain perception and reduction. Turk et al. (1983) suggest that increased pain self-efficacy may be an important factor in determining the degree of pain perception. In addition, the concept of pain locus of control has been developed to emphasize the role of individual cognitions in pain perception (Manning and Wright 1983; Dolce 1987; Litt 1988).

Attention

There has also been research exploring the impact of attention on pain. Much work shows that attention to the pain can exacerbate pain whereas distraction can reduce the pain experience. For example, in the experimental study described earlier, James and Hardardottir (2002) illustrated this association using the cold pressor task. Eccleston and Crombez have carried out much work in this area which they review in Eccleston and Crombez (1999). They illustrate that patients who attend to their pain experience more pain than those who are distracted. This association explains why patients suffering from back pain who take to their beds and therefore focus on their pain take longer to recover than those who carry on working and engaging with their lives. This association is also reflected in relatively recent changes in the general management approach to back pain problems – bed rest is no longer the main treatment option. In addition, Eccleston and Crombez provide a model of how pain and attention are related (Eccleston 1994; Eccleston and Crombez 1999). They argue that pain interrupts and demands attention and that this interruption depends upon pain-related characteristics such as the threat value of the pain and environmental demands such as emotional arousal. They argue that pain causes a shift in attention towards the pain as a way to encourage escape and action. The result of this shift in attention towards the pain is a reduced ability to focus on other tasks, resulting in attentional interference and disruption. This disruption has been shown in a series of experimental studies indicating that patients with high pain perform less well on difficult tasks that involve the greatest demand of their limited resources (e.g. Eccleston 1994; Crombez et al. 1998a, 1999).

Behavioural processes

Pain behaviour and secondary gains

The way in which an individual responds to pain can itself increase or decrease the pain perception. In particular, research has looked at pain behaviours which have been defined by Turk et al. (1985) as facial or audible expression (e.g. clenched teeth and moaning), distorted posture or movement (e.g. limping, protecting the pain area), negative affect (e.g. irritability, depression) or avoidance of activity (e.g. not going to work, lying down). It has been suggested that pain behaviours are reinforced through attention, the acknowledgement they receive, and through secondary gains, such as not having to go to work. Positively reinforcing pain behaviour may increase pain perception. Pain behaviour can also cause a lack of activity and muscle wastage, no social contact and no distraction leading to a sick role, which can also increase pain perception. Williams (2002) provides an evolutionary analysis of facial expressions of pain and argues that if the function of pain is to prioritize escape, recovery and healing, facial expressions are a means to communicate pain and to elicit help from others to achieve these goals. Further, she argues that people often assume that individuals have more control over the extent of their pain-induced facial expressions than they actually do and are more likely to offer help or sympathy when expressions are mild. Stronger forms of expressions are interpreted as amplified and as indications of malingering.

The interaction between these different processes

The three-process model describes the separate components that influence pain perception. However, these three processes are not discrete but interact and are at times interchangeable. For example, emotional factors may influence an individual's physiology and cognitive factors may influence an individual's behaviour. Further, the different components within each process also interact. For example, association may increase pain in terms of learning. However, it is likely that this process can be explained by changes in anxiety and focus with places and experiences that have previously been associated with pain resulting in increased anxiety and increased attention to pain, therefore increasing the pain experience. Likewise, pain behaviours may exacerbate pain by limiting physical movement. But it is also likely that they operate by increasing focus and anxiety – staying in bed leaves the individual with nothing to do other than think and worry about their pain. Research also indicates that fear influences attention, that fear interacts with catastrophizing and that catastrophizing influences attentional interference (Crombez et al. 1998a, 1998b, 1999; Van Damme et al. 2002). The three-process model offers a framework for mapping out the different factors that influence pain. However, this categorization is probably best seen as a framework only with the different components being interrelated rather than discrete categories of discrete factors.

The experience of pain

To date, this chapter has explored the kinds of factors that contribute to why people feel pain and theories that can explain pain onset, maintenance and the translation of acute pain into chronic pain. What is missing in all this research, however, is how pain is experienced. Some of the measures of pain capture these experiences by asking people whether their pain can be described by words such as flickering, punishing, cruel, killing or annoying (see later for discussion of pain measures). Qualitative research has further explored the pain experience. For example, Osborn and Smith (1998) interviewed nine women who experienced chronic back pain and analysed the transcripts using interpretative phenomenological analysis (IPA) (Smith and Osborn 2003). The results showed that the patients experienced their pain in a range of ways which were conceptualized into four main themes. First, they showed a strong motivation to understand and explain their situation and to know why they had developed chronic pain. They also described how they could not believe that nothing else could be done for their condition, they felt poorly informed about their pain and often described their pain as acting of its own volition. Their need to make sense of their pain was therefore frustrated, leaving them with feelings of uncertainty and ambiguity about their experience. Second, they showed a process of social comparison and compared themselves with others and with themselves in the past and future. In general they saw their pain as denying them the chance to be who they once were and who they wanted to be in the future and attempts to boost their self-esteem by making comparisons with those more unfortunate seemed to fail as they only acted as reminders of their gloomy prognosis. Third, they described how they were often not believed by others as they had no visible signs to support their suffering or disability. Finally, they described how their pain had resulted in them withdrawing from public view as they felt a burden to others and felt that when in public they had to hide their pain and appear healthy and mobile. For these sufferers, chronic back pain seemed to have a profound effect on their lives, affecting how they felt about themselves and how they interacted with others. The experience of pain is further discussed in **Focus on Research 12.1** on the next page.

The experience of pain

A study to examine how people experience chronic benign back pain (Smith 2007).

Background

Chronic benign pain is any pain that lasts longer than six months and is unrelated to any ongoing disease. It does not seem to have any biological function and is generally experienced as acute pain that simply does not go away. Chronic benign low back pain is most often a mid-life condition and is the single largest cause of disability and time lost at work in the western world. This study aimed to explore participants' experiences of their chronic benign back pain in the context of their sense of self with a focus on their subjective experience. It is an interesting study as it presents a clear picture of what it is like to suffer chronic pain and illustrates how this ongoing problem challenges people's sense of who they are.

Methodology

The study used a qualitative method using semi-structured interviews which included questions such as 'How did your pain start?', 'Has your pain changed things for you at all?', 'How would you describe yourself as a person?' and 'Has having pain changed the way you think or feel about yourself?'.

Sample

Six people were interviewed who had all been recently referred to a pain clinic in the UK. They were a reasonably homogenous sample being European, Caucasian, from a working-class background and in middle adulthood and had been in pain for between 5 and 15 years. None was taking major opiates or waiting for any medical interventions and none had any prior experience of a pain clinic.

Data analysis

The data were analysed using IPA (Smith and Osborn 2003).

Results

The results showed that pain had a powerful negative impact upon the sufferers' self and identity. In particular, the interviewees described how their pain resulted in them often experiencing themselves as two separate identities; the 'nice person' and the 'mean me' and that these two selves created a struggle for the individual as they attempted to retain the good self. In addition, they described how they moved between these two selves and employed coping strategies in an attempt to prevent the pain eroding the good self. Further, they described how this struggle over self was exacerbated by the public arena as they were concerned about how others would see them. This often led to the pain sufferers becoming socially isolated or consciously acting when with others. They also described how they sometimes directed the 'mean me' at others by stopping caring and taking pleasure in the suffering of others. Finally, some also described how they felt they may be punished in some way for being so negative towards others.

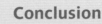

Conclusion

Smith concludes from his analysis that the pain experience generates a cycle of negative thoughts, with the sufferer having negative thoughts which get internalized, which are then discharged onto others which in turn lead to further negative thoughts. Further, he suggests that this has a serious debilitating impact on the person's sense of self which is further exacerbated by the public arena. This study therefore offers an insight into chronic benign back pain and illustrates how an ongoing problem can change how an individual feels about themselves and in addition influence how they react to the world around them.

The role of psychology in pain treatment

Acute pain is mostly treated with pharmacological interventions. However, chronic pain has proved to be more resistant to such approaches and recently multidisciplinary pain clinics have been set up that adopt a multidisciplinary approach to pain treatment. The goals set by such clinics include the following:

- *Improving physical and lifestyle functioning.* This involves improving muscle tone, improving self-esteem, improving self-efficacy, improving distraction and decreasing boredom, pain behaviour and secondary gains.

- *Decreasing reliance on drugs and medical services.* This involves improving personal control, decreasing the sick role and increasing self-efficacy.

- *Increasing social support and family life.* This aims to increase optimism and distraction and decrease boredom, anxiety, sick role behaviour and secondary gains.

In addition, current treatment philosophy emphasizes early intervention to prevent the transition of acute pain to chronic pain.

Research shows that psychology is involved in the perception of pain in terms of factors such as learning, anxiety, worry, fear, catastrophizing, meaning and attention. Multidisciplinary pain clinics increasingly place psychological interventions at their core. There are several methods of pain treatment, which reflect an interaction between psychology and physiological factors. These methods can be categorized as respondent, cognitive and behavioural methods and are illustrated in Figure 12.3.

- *Respondent methods.* Respondent methods are designed to modify the physiological system directly by reducing muscular tension. Examples are relaxation methods which aim to decrease anxiety and stress and consequently to decrease pain and biofeedback which is used to enable the individual to exert voluntary control over their bodily functions. Biofeedback aims to decrease anxiety and tension and therefore to decrease pain. However, some research indicates that it adds nothing to relaxation methods. Hypnosis is also used as a means to relax the individual. It seems to be of most use for acute pain and for repeated painful procedures such as burn dressing.

- *Cognitive methods.* A cognitive approach to pain treatment focuses on the individuals' thoughts about pain and aims to modify cognitions that may be exacerbating their pain experience. Techniques used include attention diversion (i.e. encouraging the individual not to focus on the pain), imagery (i.e. encouraging the individual to have positive, pleas-

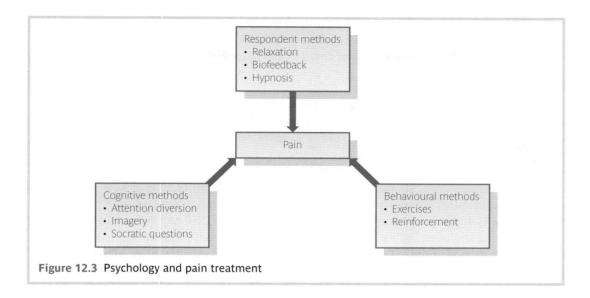

Figure 12.3 Psychology and pain treatment

ant thoughts) and the modification of maladaptive thoughts by the use of Socratic questions. Socratic questions challenge the individual to try to understand their automatic thoughts and involve questions such as 'What evidence do you have to support your thoughts?' and 'How would someone else view this situation?' The therapist can use role play and role reversal.

■ *Behavioural methods.* Some treatment approaches draw upon the basic principles of operant conditioning and use reinforcement to encourage the individual to change their behaviour. For example, if a chronic pain patient has stopped activities that they believe may exacerbate their pain, the therapist will incrementally encourage them to become increasingly more active. Each change in behaviour will be rewarded by the therapist and new exercises will be developed and agreed to encourage the patient to move towards their pre-set goal.

The three components of psychological therapy are often integrated into a cognitive behavioural treatment package.

Cognitive behavioural therapy

Cognitive behavioural therapy (CBT) is increasingly used with chronic pain patients. CBT is based upon the premise that pain is influenced by four sources of information: cognitive sources such as the meaning of the pain ('it will prevent me from working'); emotional sources such as the emotions associated with the pain ('I am anxious that it will never go away'); physiological sources such as the impulses sent from the site of physical damage and behavioural sources such as pain behaviour that may either increase the pain (such as not doing any exercise) or decrease the pain (such as doing sufficient exercise). CBT focuses on these aspects of pain perception and uses a range of psychological strategies to enable people to unlearn unhelpful practices and learn new ways of thinking and behaviours. CBT draws upon the three treatment approaches described earlier, namely respondent methods such as relaxation and biofeedback, cognitive methods such as attention diversion and Socratic questioning, and behavioural methods involving graded exercises and reinforcement. Several individual studies have been carried out to explore the relative effectiveness of CBT compared to other forms of intervention and/or waiting list controls. Recently systematic reviews have been published which have synthesized these studies in terms of CBT for adults and for children and adolescents.

CBT and adults

Van Tulder et al. (2000) carried out a systematic review of randomized controlled trials which had used behavioural therapy for chronic non-specific low back pain in adults. Their extensive search of the databases produced six studies of sufficient quality for inclusion and involved methodological practices such as blinding of outcome assessment, adequate length of follow-up and a high quality randomization procedure. The analysis showed that behavioural treatments effectively reduced pain intensity, increased functional status (e.g. return to work) and improved behavioural outcomes (e.g. activity level). In a similar vein, Morley et al. (1999) carried out a systematic review and meta-analysis of trials of CBT and behaviour therapy for chronic pain in adults excluding headache. Their database search produced 25 trials for inclusion. The analysis showed that CBT was more effective than alternative active treatment approaches such as relaxation, exercise and education in terms of pain experience, positive coping, and the behavioural expression of pain. In addition, the results showed that CBT was more effective than waiting-list controls on all these outcome measures and also for mood, negative coping such as catastrophizing and social functioning. Overall, therefore, psychological therapies that include CBT seem to be an effective way to reduce aspects of chronic pain.

CBT and children and adolescents

Due the success of psychological therapies with adults, children with chronic and or recurrent pain are also increasingly offered some form of psychological intervention. At times this takes the form of CBT. However, it also takes the form of individual components such as relaxation and reinforcement. Eccleston et al. (2002, 2003a) searched a range of databases and located 18 trials that included some form of psychological therapy and sufficient information to be entered into the analysis. These trials were for chronic or recurrent headache, abdominal pain and sickle-cell pain and involved over 800 patients with about half receiving the psychological treatment which was mostly relaxation or CBT. The control groups received standard medical care, placebo or were waiting-list controls. The results of their analysis showed that psychological therapies were very effective at reducing headache in children and adolescents. However, the authors concluded that there was no evidence to date for their effectiveness for other pain-related problems or for outcomes other than pain severity and frequency.

Psychological factors can therefore exacerbate pain perception. Research also indicates that they are also important in the treatment and management of pain.

Placebos and pain reduction

Placebos have been defined as inert substances that cause symptom relief (see Chapter 13). Traditionally, placebos were used in randomized control trials to compare an active drug with the effects of simply taking something. However, placebos have been shown to have an effect on pain relief. Beecher (1955) suggested that 30 per cent of chronic pain sufferers experience pain relief after taking placebos. In the 1960s Diamond et al. (1960) carried out several sham operations to examine the effect of placebos on pain relief. A sham heart bypass operation involved the individual believing that they were going to have a proper operation, being prepared for surgery, being given a general anaesthetic, cut open and then sewed up again without any actual bypass being carried out. The individual therefore believed that they had had an operation and had the

Putting theory into practice – treating chronic pain

A study to examine the effectiveness of cognitive behavioural treatment for chronic pain (Basler and Rehfisch 1990).

This is an interesting paper, as it illustrates how a theoretical approach can be used as a basis for clinical practice. The paper emphasizes pain as a perception and suggests that treatment interventions can focus on the different factors that contribute to this perception. In addition, the paper highlights the role of adherence in treatment success, which has implications for understanding placebos and compliance with medical/clinical recommendations.

Background
What is the cognitive behavioural approach to pain?

A cognitive behavioural approach to pain regards pain as a perception that involves an integration of four sources of pain-related information:

1 *Cognitive*, or the meaning of the pain ('it will prevent me from working').
2 *Emotional*, or the emotions associated with the pain ('I am anxious that it will never go away').
3 *Physiological*, or the impulses sent from the site of physical damage.
4 *Behavioural*, or pain behaviour that may increase the pain (such as not doing any exercise) and pain behaviour that may decrease the pain (such as doing sufficient exercise).

The cognitive behavioural approach to pain therefore aims to reduce pain by focusing on these different sources of pain-related information.

The central role of self-control

In particular, the cognitive behavioural approach to pain aims to improve the individual's self-control over the pain. Turk and Rudy (1986) summarize the objectives of interventions to improve self-control as follows:

- *Combat demoralization.* Chronic pain sufferers may become demoralized and feel helpless. They are taught to reconceptualize their problems so that they can be seen as manageable.
- *Enhance outcome efficacy.* If patients have previously received several forms of pain treatment, they may believe that nothing works. They are taught to believe in the cognitive behavioural approach to pain treatment and that with their cooperation the treatment will improve their condition.
- *Foster self-efficacy.* Chronic pain sufferers may see themselves as passive and helpless. They are taught to believe that they can be resourceful and competent.
- *Break up automatic maladaptive coping patterns.* Chronic pain sufferers may have learnt emotional and behavioural coping strategies that may be increasing their pain, such as feeling consistently anxious, limping or avoiding exercise. They are taught to monitor these feelings and behaviours.
- *Skills training.* Once aware of the automatic emotions and behaviours that increase their pain, pain sufferers are taught a range of adaptive coping responses.

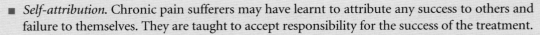

- *Self-attribution.* Chronic pain sufferers may have learnt to attribute any success to others and failure to themselves. They are taught to accept responsibility for the success of the treatment.

- *Facilitate maintenance.* Any effectiveness of the cognitive behavioural treatment should persist beyond the actual treatment intervention. Therefore pain sufferers are taught how to anticipate any problems and to consider ways of dealing with these problems.

Within this model of pain treatment, Basler and Rehfisch (1990) set out to examine the effectiveness of a cognitive behavioural approach to pain. In addition, they aimed to examine whether such an approach could be used within general practice.

Methodology
Subjects
Sixty chronic pain sufferers, who had experienced chronic pain in the head, shoulder, arm or spine for at least six months, were recruited for the study from general practice lists in West Germany. Subjects were allocated to either: (1) the immediate treatment group (33 subjects started the treatment and 25 completed it); or (2) the waiting-list control group (27 subjects were allocated to this group and 13 completed all measures).

Design
All subjects completed measures at baseline (time 1), after the 12-week treatment intervention (time 2) and at six-month follow-up (time 3). Subjects in the control group completed the same measures at comparable time intervals.

Measures
At times 1, 2 and 3, all subjects completed a 14-day pain diary, which included measures of the following:

- *Intensity of pain:* the subjects rated the intensity of their pain from 'no pain' to 'very intense pain' every day.

- *Mood:* for the same 14 days, subjects also included in the diary measures of their mood three times a day.

- *Functional limitation:* the subjects also included measures of things they could not do within the 14 days.

- *Pain medication:* the subjects also recorded the kind and quantity of pain medication.

The subjects also completed the following measures:

- *The state–trait anxiety inventory,* which consists of 20 items and asks subjects to rate how frequently each of the items occurs.

- *The Von Zerssen depression scale* (Von Zerssen 1976), which consists of 16 items describing depressive symptoms (e.g. 'I can't help crying').

- *General bodily symptoms:* the subjects completed a checklist of 57 symptoms, such as 'nausea' and 'trembling'.

- *Sleep disorders due to pain:* the subjects were asked to rate problems they experienced in sleep onset, sleep maintenance and sleep quality.

- *Bodily symptoms due to pain attacks*: the subjects rated 13 symptoms for their severity during pain attacks (e.g. heart rate increase, sweating).
- *Pain intensity* over the last week was also measured.

In addition, at six-month follow-up (time 2), subjects who had received the treatment were asked which of the recommended exercises they still carried out and the physicians rated the treatment outcome on a scale from 'extreme deterioration' to 'extreme improvement'.

The treatment intervention

The treatment programme consisted of 12 weekly 90-minute sessions, which were carried out in a group with up to 12 patients. All subjects in the treatment group received a treatment manual. The following components were included in the sessions:

- *Education.* This component aimed to educate the subjects about the rationale of cognitive behaviour treatment. The subjects were encouraged to take an active part in the programme; they received information about the vicious circle of pain, muscular tension and demoralization and about how the programme would improve their sense of self-control over their thoughts, feelings and behaviour.
- *Relaxation.* The subjects were taught how to control their responses to pain using progressive muscle relaxation. They were given a home relaxation tape, and were also taught to use imagery techniques and visualization to distract themselves from pain and to further improve their relaxation skills.
- *Modifying thoughts and feelings.* The subjects were asked to complete coping cards to describe their maladaptive thoughts and adaptive coping thoughts. The groups were used to explain the role of fear, depression, anger and irrational thoughts in pain.
- *Pleasant activity scheduling.* The subjects were encouraged to use distraction techniques to reduce depression and pain perception. They were encouraged to shift their focus from those activities they could no longer perform to those that they could enjoy. Activity goals were scheduled and pleasant activities were reinforced at subsequent groups.

Results

The results were analysed to examine differences between the two groups (treatment versus control) and to examine differences in changes in the measures (from time 1 to time 2 and at follow-up) between the two groups.

Time 1 to time 2

The results showed significantly different changes between the two groups in all their ratings. Compared with the control group, the subjects who had received cognitive behavioural treatment reported lower pain intensity, lower functional impairment, better daily mood, fewer bodily symptoms, less anxiety, less depression, fewer pain-related bodily symptoms and fewer pain-related sleep disorders.

Time 1 to time 2 to time 3

When the results at six-month follow-up were included, again the results showed significant differences between the two groups on all variables except daily mood and sleep disorders.

The role of adherence

The subjects in the treatment condition were then divided into those who adhered to the recommended exercise regimen at follow-up (adherers) and those who did not (non-adherers). The results from this analysis indicate that the adherers showed an improvement in pain intensity at follow-up compared with their ratings immediately after the treatment intervention, while the non-adherers' ratings at follow-up were the same as immediately after the treatment.

Conclusion

The authors conclude that the study provides support for the use of cognitive behavioural treatment for chronic pain. The authors also point to the central role of treatment adherence in predicting improvement. They suggest that this effect of adherence indicates that the improvement in pain was a result of the specific treatment factors (i.e. the exercises), not the non-specific treatment factors (contact with professionals, a feeling of doing something). However, it is possible that the central role for adherence in the present study is similar to that discussed in Chapter 13 in the context of placebos, with treatment adherence itself being a placebo effect.

scars to prove it. This procedure obviously has serious ethical problems. However, the results suggested that angina pain can actually be reduced by a sham operation by comparable levels to an actual operation for angina. This suggests that the expectations of the individual changes their perception of pain, again providing evidence for the role of psychology in pain perception.

The outcome of pain treatment and management: a role for pain acceptance?

The psychological treatment of pain includes respondent, cognitive and behavioural methods. These are mostly used in conjunction with pharmacological treatments involving analgesics or anaesthetics. The outcome of such interventions has traditionally been assessed in terms of a reduction in pain intensity and pain perception. Recently, however, some researchers have been calling for a shift in focus towards pain acceptance. Risdon et al. (2003) asked 30 participants to describe their pain using a Q factor analysis. This methodology encourages the participant to describe their experiences in a way that enables the researcher to derive a factor structure. From their analysis the authors argued that the acceptance of pain involves eight factors. These were: taking control, living day-by-day, acknowledging limitations, empowerment, accepting loss of self, a belief that there's more to life than pain, a philosophy of not fighting battles that can't be won and spiritual strength. In addition, the authors suggest that these factors reflect three underlying beliefs: (1) the acknowledgement that a cure for pain is unlikely; (2) a shift of focus away from pain to non-pain aspects of life; and (3) a resistance to any suggestion that pain is a sign of personal weakness. In a further study McCracken and Eccleston (2003) explored the relationship between pain acceptance, coping with pain and a range of pain-related outcomes in 230 chronic pain patients. The results showed that pain acceptance was a better predictor than coping with pain adjustment variables such as pain intensity, disability, depression and anxiety and better work status. The authors of these studies suggest that the extent of pain acceptance may relate to changes in an individual's sense of self and how their pain has been incorporated into their self-identity. In addition, they argue that the concept of pain acceptance may be an important way forward for pain research, particularly given the nature of chronic pain.

Measuring pain

Whether it is to examine the causes or consequences of pain or to evaluate the effectiveness of a treatment for pain, pain needs to be measured. This has raised several questions and problems. For example, 'Are we interested in the individual's own experience of the pain?' (i.e. what someone says is all important), 'What about denial or self-image?' (i.e. someone might be in agony but deny it to themselves and to others), 'Are we interested in a more objective assessment?' (i.e. can we get over the problem of denial by asking someone else to rate their pain?) and 'Do we need to assess a physiological basis to pain?' These questions have resulted in three different perspectives on pain measurement: self-reports, observational assessments and physiological assessments, which are very similar to the different ways of measuring health status (see Chapter 16). In addition, these different perspectives reflect the different theories of pain.

Self-reports

Self-report scales of pain rely on the individuals' own subjective view of their pain level. They take the form of visual analogue scales (e.g. 'How severe is your pain?' Rated from 'not at all' (0) to 'extremely' (100)), verbal scales (e.g. 'Describe your pain: no pain, mild pain, moderate pain, severe pain, worst pain') and descriptive questionnaires (e.g. the McGill pain questionnaire (MPQ); Melzack 1975). The MPQ attempts to access the more complex nature of pain and asks individuals to rate their pain in terms of three dimensions: sensory (e.g. flickering, pulsing, beating), affective (e.g. punishing, cruel, killing) and evaluative (e.g. annoying, miserable, intense). Some self-report measures also attempt to access the impact that the pain is having upon the individuals' level of functioning and ask whether the pain influences the individuals' ability to do daily tasks such as walking, sitting and climbing stairs. Similarly, pain is often assessed within the context of quality-of-life scales which include a pain component (e.g. Skevington 1998; Skevington et al. 2001).

Observational assessment

Observational assessments attempt to make a more objective assessment of pain and are used when the patients' own self-reports are considered unreliable or when they are unable to provide them. For example, observational measures would be used for children, some stroke sufferers and some terminally ill patients. In addition, they can provide an objective validation of self-report measures. Observational measures include an assessment of the pain relief requested and used, pain behaviours (such as limping, grimacing and muscle tension) and time spent sleeping and/or resting.

Physiological measures

Both self-report measures and observational measures are sometimes regarded as unreliable if a supposedly 'objective' measure of pain is required. In particular, self-report measures are open to the bias of the individual in pain and observational measures are open to errors made by the observer. Therefore physiological measures are sometimes used as an index of pain intensity. Such measures include an assessment of inflammation and measures of sweating, heart rate and skin temperature. However, the relationship between physiological measures and both observational and self-report measures is often contradictory, raising the question 'Are the individual and the rater mistaken or are the physiological measurements not measuring pain?'

To conclude

Early biomedical models of pain suggested that pain was a simple response to external stimuli and within this model categorized the individual as a passive responder to external factors. Such models had no causal role for psychology. However, the gate control theory, developed in the 1960s and 1970s by Melzack and Wall, included psychological factors. As a result, pain was no longer understood as a sensation but as an active perception. Due to this inclusion of psychological factors into pain perception, research has examined the role of factors such as learning, anxiety, fear, catastrophizing, meaning, attention and pain behaviour in either decreasing or exacerbating pain. As psychological factors appeared to have a role to play in eliciting pain perception, multidisciplinary pain clinics have been set up to use psychological factors in its treatment. These often use psychological therapies, particularly CBT, which have been shown to be effective for adults, children and adolescents. Recently researchers have suggested a role for pain acceptance as a useful outcome measure and some research indicates that acceptance rather than coping might be a better predictor of adjustment to pain and changes following treatment.

❓ Questions

1 Pain is a response to painful stimuli. Discuss.
2 To what extent does the gate control theory of pain depart from biomedical models of pain?
3 What are the implications of the GCT of pain for the mind–body debate?
4 Pain is a perception. Discuss.
5 How might psychological factors exacerbate pain perception?
6 To what extent can psychological factors be used to reduce pain perception?
7 Self-report is the only true way of measuring pain. Discuss.
8 Develop a research protocol to examine the role of secondary gains in pain perception.

For discussion

Consider the last time you experienced pain (e.g. period pain, headache, sports injury) and discuss the potential cognitive, emotional and behavioural factors that may have exacerbated the pain.

Assumptions in health psychology

The research into pain highlights some of the assumptions underlying health psychology.

1 *The mind–body split.* Early models of pain regarded the physical aspects of pain as 'real' and categorized pain as either 'organic' or 'psychogenic'. Such models conceptualized the mind and body as separate and conform to a dualistic model of individuals. Recent models of pain have attempted to integrate the mind and the body by examining pain as a perception that is influenced by a multitude of different factors. However, even within these models the mind and the body are still regarded as separate.

2 *The problem of progression.* Over the last 100 years, different theories have been developed to explain pain. It is often assumed that changes in theoretical perspective over time represents improvement, with the recent theories reflecting a better approximation to the truth of 'what pain really is'. However, perhaps these different theories can also be used themselves as data to show how psychologists have thought in the past and how they now think about individuals. For example, in the past pain was seen as a passive response to external stimuli; therefore individuals were seen as passive responders. However, today pain is increasingly seen as a response to the individual's self-control – pain is a sign of either successful or failed self-control. Therefore contemporary individuals are seen as having self-control, self-management and self-mastery. Perhaps the different theories over time reflect different (not necessarily better) versions of individuality.

Further reading

Dekker, J., Lundberg, U. and Williams, A. (eds) (2001) *Behavioural Factors and Interventions in Pain and Musculoskeletal Disorders: A Special Issue of the International Journal of Behavioural Medicine.* Mahawah, NJ: Lawrence Erlbaum Associates.
This provides a detailed analysis of the psychosocial factors involved in the development of chronic pain.

Horn, S. and Munafo, M. (1997) *Pain: Theory, Research and Intervention.* Buckingham: Open University Press.
This book provides a more detailed overview of the pain literature.

Karoly, P. and Jensen, M.P. (1987) *Multimethod Assessment of Chronic Pain.* New York: Pergamon Press.
This book provides a comprehensive and critical overview of the complex area of pain assessment.

Main C.J. and Spanswick C.C. (eds) (2000) *Pain Management: An Interdisciplinary Approach.* Edinburgh: Churchill Livingstone.
This edited collection provides a detailed account of contemporary approaches to treating pain.

Turk, D.C. and Melzack, R. (eds) (2001) *Handbook of Pain Assessment,* 2nd edn. New York: Guilford Press.
This edited collection provides an excellent overview of how pain can be measured and the problems inherent within pain assessment.

Placebos and the interrelationship among beliefs, behaviour and health

Chapter overview

The study of placebos is a good illustration of many of the issues central to health psychology. This chapter examines problems with defining placebos and then assesses the different theories concerning how they work, highlighting the central role for patient expectations. It then outlines the implications of placebos for the different areas of health psychology discussed in the rest of this book, such as health beliefs and illness cognitions, health behaviours, stress, pain and illness and places this within a discussion of the relationship between the mind and body and the interrelationship between beliefs, behaviour and health and illness.

This chapter covers

- What is a placebo?
- How do placebos work?
- The central role of patient expectations
- Cognitive dissonance theory
- The role of placebo effects in health psychology

What is a placebo?

Placebos have been defined as follows:

- Inert substances that cause symptom relief (e.g. 'My headache went away after having a sugar pill').
- Substances that cause changes in a symptom not directly attributable to specific or real pharmacological actions of a drug or operation (e.g. 'After I had my hip operation I stopped getting headaches').
- Any therapy that is deliberately used for its non-specific psychological or physiological effects (e.g. 'I had a bath and my headache went away').

These definitions illustrate some of the problems with understanding placebos. For example:

- What are specific/real versus non-specific/unreal effects? For example, 'My headaches went after the operation': is this an unreal effect (it was not predicted) or a real effect (it definitely happened)?
- Why are psychological effects non-specific? (e.g. 'I feel more relaxed after my operation': is this a non-specific effect?).
- Are there placebo effects in psychological treatments? For example, 'I specifically went for cognitive restructuring therapy and ended up simply feeling less tired': is this a placebo effect or a real effect?

The problems inherent in the distinctions between specific versus non-specific effects and physiological versus psychological effects are illustrated by examining the history of apparently medically inert treatments.

A history of inert treatments

For centuries, individuals (including doctors and psychologists) from many different cultural backgrounds have used (and still use) apparently inert treatments for various different conditions. For example, medicines such as wild animal faeces and the blood of a gladiator were supposed to increase strength, and part of a dolphin's penis was supposed to increase virility. These so-called 'medicines' have been used at different times in different cultures but have no apparent medical (active) properties. In addition, treatments such as bleeding by leeches to decrease fever or travelling to religious sites such as Lourdes in order to alleviate symptoms have also continued across the years without any obvious understanding of the processes involved. Faith healers are another example of inert treatments, including Jesus Christ, Buddha and Krishna. The tradition of faith healers has persisted, although our understanding of the processes involved is very poor.

Such apparently inert interventions, and the traditions involved with these practices, have lasted over many centuries. In addition, the people involved in these practices have become famous and have gained a degree of credibility. Furthermore, many of the treatments are still believed in. Perhaps the maintenance of faith both in these interventions and in the people carrying out the treatments suggests that they were actually successful, giving the treatments themselves some validity. Why were they successful? It is possible that there are medically active substances in some of these traditional treatments that were not understood in the past and are still not understood now (e.g. gladiators' blood may actually contain some still unknown active chemical). It is also possible that the effectiveness of some of these treatments can be understood in terms of modern-day placebo effects.

Modern-day placebos

Recently placebos have been studied more specifically and have been found to have a multitude of effects. For example, placebos have been found to increase performance on a cognitive task (Ross and Buckalew 1983), to be effective in reducing anxiety (Downing and Rickels 1983), and Haas et al. (1959) listed a whole series of areas where placebos have been shown to have some effect, such as allergies, asthma, cancer, diabetes, enuresis, epilepsy, multiple sclerosis, insomnia, ulcers, obesity, acne, smoking and dementia.

Perhaps one of the most studied areas in relation to placebo effects is pain. Beecher (1955), in an early study of the specific effects of placebos in pain reduction, suggested that 30 per cent of chronic pain sufferers show relief from a placebo when using both subjective (e.g. 'I feel less pain') and objective (e.g. 'You are more mobile') measures of pain. In addition, Diamond et al. (1960) reported a sham operation for patients suffering from angina pain. They reported that half the subjects with angina pain were given a sham operation, and half of the subjects were given a real heart bypass operation. The results indicated that pain reduction in both groups was equal, and the authors concluded that the belief that the individual had had an operation was sufficient to cause pain reduction and alleviation of the angina.

Placebos: to be taken out of an understanding of health?

Since the 1940s, research into the effectiveness of drugs has used randomized controlled trials and placebos to assess the real effects of a drug versus the unreal effects. Placebos have been seen as something to take out of the health equation. However, if placebos have a multitude of effects as already discussed, perhaps, rather than being taken out, they should be seen as central to health status. For this reason it is interesting to examine how placebos work.

How do placebos work?

If placebos have a multiple number of possible effects, what factors actually mediate these changes? Several theories have been developed to try to understand the process of placebo effects. These theories can be described as *non-interactive* theories in that they examine individual characteristics, characteristics of the treatment and characteristics of the health professional, or *interactive* theories in that they involve an examination of the processes involved in the interactions between patients, the treatment and the health professionals.

Non-interactive theories
Characteristics of the individual

Individual trait theories suggest that certain individuals have characteristics that make them susceptible to placebo effects. Such characteristics have been described as emotional dependency, extroversion, neurosis and being highly suggestible. Research has also suggested that individuals who respond to placebos are introverted. However, many of the characteristics described are conflicting and there is little evidence to support consistent traits as predictive of placebo responsiveness.

Characteristics of the treatment

Other researchers have focused on treatment characteristics and have suggested that the characteristics of the actual process involved in the placebo treatment relate to the effectiveness or degree of the placebo effect. For example, if a treatment is perceived by the individual as being serious, the placebo effect will be greater. Accordingly, surgery, which is likely to be perceived as very serious, has the greatest placebo effect, followed by an injection, followed by having two pills versus one pill. Research has also looked at the size of the pill and suggests that larger pills are more effective than small pills in eliciting a change.

Characteristics of the health professional

Research has also looked at the characteristics of the health professional, suggesting that the kind of professional administering the placebo treatment may determine the degree of the placebo effect. For example, higher professional status and higher concern have been shown to increase the placebo effect.

Problems with the non-interactive theories

Theories that examine only the patient, only the treatment or only the professional ignore the interaction between patient and health professional that occurs when a placebo effect has taken place. They assume that these factors exist in isolation and can be examined independently of each other. However, if we are to understand placebo effects then perhaps theories of the interaction between health professionals and patients described within the literature (see Chapter 4) can be applied to understanding placebos.

Interactive theories

It is therefore necessary to understand the process of placebo effects as an active process, which involves patient, treatment and health professional variables. Placebo effects should be conceptualized as a multidimensional process that depends on an interaction between a multitude of different factors. To understand this multidimensional process, research has looked at possible mechanisms of the placebo effect.

Experimenter bias

Experimenter bias refers to the impact that the experimenter's expectations can have on the outcome of a study. For example, if an experimenter was carrying out a study to examine the effect of seeing an aggressive film on a child's aggressive behaviour (a classic social psychology study), the experimenter's expectations may themselves be responsible for changing the child's behaviour (by their own interaction with the child), not the film.

This phenomenon has been used to explain placebo effects. For example, Gracely et al. (1985) examined the impact of doctors' beliefs about the treatment on the patients' experience of placebo-induced pain reduction. Subjects were allocated to one of three conditions and were given either an analgesic (a painkiller), a placebo or naloxone (an opiate antagonist, which increases the pain experience). The patients were therefore told that this treatment would either reduce, have no effect or increase their pain. The doctors giving the drugs were themselves allocated to one of two conditions. They believed that either the patients would receive one of three of these substances (a chance of receiving a painkiller), or that the patient would receive either a placebo or naloxone (no chance of receiving a pain killer). Therefore one group of doctors believed that there was a chance that the patient would be given an analgesic and would show pain reduction, and the other group of doctors believed that there was no chance that the patient would receive some form of analgesia. In fact, all subjects were given a placebo. This study, therefore, manipulated both the patients' beliefs about the kind of treatment they had received and the doctors' beliefs about the kind of treatment they were administering. The results showed that the subjects who were given the drug treatment by the doctor who believed they had a chance to receive the analgesic, showed a decrease in pain whereas the patients whose doctor believed that they had no chance of receiving the painkiller showed no effect. This suggests that if the doctors believed that the subjects may show pain reduction, this belief was communicated to the subjects who actually reported pain reduction. However, if the doctors believed that the subjects would not show pain reduction, this belief was also communicated to the subjects who accordingly reported no change in their pain experience. This study highlights a role for an interaction between the doctor and the patient and is similar to the effect described as experimenter bias described within social psychology. Experimenter bias suggests that the experimenter is capable of communicating their expectations to the subjects who respond in accordance with these expectations. Therefore, if applied to placebo effects, subjects show improvement because the health professionals expect them to.

Patient expectations

Research has also looked at the expectations of the patient. Ross and Olson (1981) examined the effects of patients' expectations on recovery following a placebo. They suggested that most patients experience spontaneous recovery following illness as most illnesses go through periods of spontaneous change and that patients attribute these changes to the treatment. Therefore, even if the treatment is a placebo, any change will be understood in terms of the effectiveness of this treatment. This suggests that because patients want to get better and expect to get better, any changes that they experience are attributed to the drugs they have taken. However, Park and Covi (1965) gave sugar pills to a group of neurotic patients and actually told the patients that the pills were sugar pills and would therefore have no effect. The results showed that the patients still showed some reduction in their neuroticism. It could be argued that in this case, even though the patients did not expect the treatment to work, they still responded to the placebo. However, it could also be argued that these patients would still have some expectations that they would get better otherwise they would not have bothered to take the pills. Jensen and Karoly (1991) also argue that patient motivation plays an important role in placebo effects, and differentiate between patient motivation (the desire to experience a symptom change) and patient expectation (a belief that a symptom change would occur). In a laboratory study, they examined the relative effects of patient motivation and patient expectation of placebo-induced changes in symptom perception following a 'sedative pill'. The results suggested a role for patient expectation but also suggested that higher motivation was related to a greater placebo effect.

Reporting error

Reporting error has also been suggested as an explanation of placebo effects. In support of previous theories that emphasize patient expectations, it has been argued that patients expect to show improvement following medical intervention, want to please the doctor and therefore show inaccurate reporting by suggesting that they are getting better, even when their symptoms remain unchanged. (In fact the term 'placebo' is derived from the Latin meaning 'I will please'.) It has also been suggested that placebos are a result of reporting error by the doctor. Doctors also wish to see an improvement following their intervention, and may also show inaccurate measurement. The theory of reporting error therefore explains placebo effects in terms of error, misrepresentation or misattributions of symptom changes to placebo. However, there are problems with the reporting error theory in that not all symptom changes reported by the patients or reported by the doctor are positive. Several studies show that patients report negative side effects to placebos, both in terms of subjective changes, such as drowsiness, nausea, lack of concentration, and also objective changes such as sweating, vomiting and skin rashes. All these factors would not be pleasing to the doctor and therefore do not support the theory of reporting error as one of demand effects. In addition, there are also objective changes to placebos in terms of heart rate and blood pressure, which cannot be understood either in terms of the patient's desire to please the doctor, or the doctor's desire to see a change.

Conditioning effects

Traditional conditioning theories have also been used to explain placebo effects (Wickramasekera 1980). It is suggested that patients associate certain factors with recovery and an improvement in their symptoms. For example, the presence of doctors, white coats, pills, injections and surgery are associated with improvement, recovery and effective treatment. According to conditioning theory, the unconditioned stimulus (treatment) would usually be associated with an unconditioned response (recovery). However, if this unconditioned stimulus (treatment) is paired with a conditioned stimulus (e.g. hospital, a white coat), the conditioned stimulus can itself elicit a conditioned response (recovery, the placebo effect). The conditioned stimulus might be comprised of a number of factors, including the appearance of the doctor, the environment, the actual site of the treatment or simply taking a pill. This stimulus may then elicit placebo recovery. For example, people often comment that they feel better as soon as they get into a doctor's waiting room, that their headache gets better before they have had time to digest a pill and that symptoms disappear when a doctor appears. According to conditioning theory, these changes would be examples of placebo recovery. Several reports provide support for conditioning theory. For example, research suggests that taking a placebo drug is more effective in a hospital setting when given by a doctor, than if taken at home given by someone who is not associated with the medical profession. This suggests that placebo effects require an interaction between the patient and their environment. In addition, placebo pain reduction is more effective with clinical and real pain than with experimentally created pain. This suggests that experimentally created pain does not elicit the association with the treatment environment, whereas the real pain has the effect of eliciting memories of previous experiences of treatment, making it more responsive to placebo intervention.

Anxiety reduction

Placebos have also been explained in terms of anxiety reduction. Downing and Rickels (1983) argued that placebos decrease anxiety, thus helping the patient to recover. In particular, such a decrease in anxiety is effective in causing pain reduction (Sternbach 1978). For example, according to the gate control theory, anxiety reduction may close the gate and reduce pain, whereas increased anxiety may open the gate and increase pain (see Chapter 12). Placebos may decrease anxiety by empowering the individual and encouraging them to feel that they are in control of their pain. This improved sense of control may lead to decreased anxiety, which itself reduces the pain experience. Placebos may be particularly effective in chronic pain by breaking the anxiety–pain cycle (see Chapter 12). The role of anxiety reduction is supported by reports that placebos are more effective in reducing real pain than reducing experimental pain, perhaps because real pain elicits a greater degree of anxiety, which can be alleviated by the placebo, whereas experimentally induced pain does not make the individual anxious. However, there are problems with the anxiety-reducing theory of placebos. Primarily, there are many other effects of placebos besides pain reduction. In addition, Butler and Steptoe (1986) reported that although placebos increased lung function in asthmatics, this increase was not related to anxiety.

Physiological theories

Physiologists have also developed theories to explain placebo effects, with specific focus on pain reduction. Levine et al. (1978) have argued that placebos increase endorphin (opiate) release – the brain's natural painkillers – which therefore decreases pain. Evidence for this comes in several forms. Placebos have been shown to create dependence, withdrawal and tolerance, all factors that are similar to those found in abstinent heroin addicts, suggesting that placebos may well increase opiate release. In addition, results suggest that placebo effects can be blocked by giving naloxone, which is an opiate antagonist. This indicates that placebos may increase the opiate release, but that this opiate release is blocked by naloxone, supporting the physiological theory of placebos. However, the physiological theories are limited as pain reduction is not the only consequence of placebos.

Box 13.1 Some problems with . . . placebo research

Below are some problems with research in this area that you may wish to pause to consider.

1 Central to understanding the placebo effect is the role of expectations, with people seeming to feel pain or get better if they expect to do so. But how can the role of expectations be tested as taking part in any study or being offered any medication that will ultimately change an individual's expectations? It is not really possible therefore to 'placebo' the placebo effect.

2 Placebo research suggests that expecting to get better, even just in the form of adhering to medication, seems to make people better. However, it is not clear how this process actually works. How does a placebo effect make a wound heal faster, a pain go away or lungs function better?

3 Placebos illustrate a direct relationship between a person's mind and their body. This is central to health psychology. We still, however, do not know how this works – it seems to have a magical feel to it which remains unexplained.

The central role of patient expectations

Galen is reported to have said about the physician, 'He cures most in whom most are confident' (quoted by Evans 1974). In accordance with this, all theories of placebo effects described so far involve the patient expecting to get better. Experimenter bias theory describes the expectation of the doctor, which is communicated to the patient, changing the patient's expectation. Expectancy effects theory describes directly the patients' expectations derived from previous experience of successful treatment. Reporting error theory suggests that patients expect to show recovery and therefore inaccurately report recovery, and theories of misattribution argue that patients' expectations of improvement are translated into understanding spontaneous changes in terms of the expected changes. In addition, conditioning theory requires the individual to expect the conditioned stimuli to be associated with successful intervention, and anxiety-reduction theory describes the individual as feeling less anxious after a placebo treatment because of the belief that the treatment will be effective. Finally, even the physiological theory assumes that the individual will expect to get better. The central role of patient expectations is illustrated in Figure 13.1.

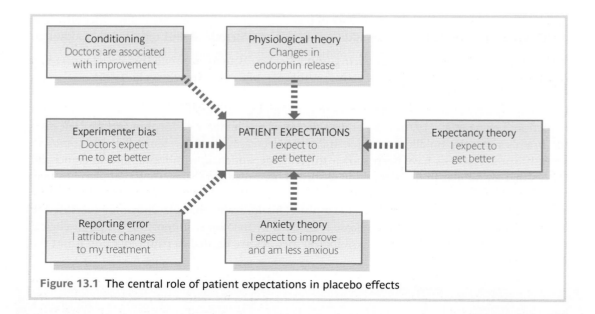

Figure 13.1 The central role of patient expectations in placebo effects

Ross and Olson (1981) summarize the placebo effects as follows:

- the direction of placebo effects parallels the effects of the drug under study
- the strength of the placebo effect is proportional to that of the active drug
- the reported side effects of the placebo drug and the active drug are often similar
- the time needed for both the placebo and the active drug to become active are often similar.

As a result, they conclude that 'most studies find that an administered placebo will alter the recipient's condition (or in some instances self-report of the condition) in accordance with the placebo's expected effects' (1981: 419). Therefore, according to the above theories, placebos work because the patient and the health professionals expect them to work. This emphasizes the role of expectations and regards placebo effects as an interaction between individuals and between individuals and their environment.

Cognitive dissonance theory

Theories of placebos described so far emphasize patient expectations. The cognitive dissonance theory of placebos developed by Totman (1976, 1987) attempted to remove patient expectations from the placebo equation and emphasized justification and dissonance. Totman (1976, 1987) placed his cognitive dissonance theory of placebos in the following context: 'Why did faith healing last for such a long time?' and 'Why are many of the homeopathic medicines, which have no medically active content, still used?' He argued that faith healing has lasted and homeopathic medicines are still used because they work. In answer to his question why this might be, Totman suggested that the one factor that all of these medically inert treatments have in common, is that they required an investment by the individual in terms of money, dedication, pain, time or inconvenience. He argued that if medically inactive drugs were freely available they would not be effective and that if an individual lived around the corner to Lourdes then a trip to Lourdes would have no effect on their health status.

Testing a theory – 'doing as you're told' as a placebo

A study to examine the role of adhering to medical treatment in predicting recovery from a heart attack – taking pills (whether active or not) as a placebo (Horwitz et al. 1990).

For a long time, medicine has regarded adherence (compliance) with medical recommendations to be important for recovery: 'take these drugs and you will get better'. However, this study suggests that simply adhering to medical recommendations to take pills may be beneficial to recovery following a heart attack, regardless of whether the pills taken are active pills or placebo pills. This has implications for understanding the relationship between the mind and body ('I believe that I have taken my medication' is related to actually getting better) and for understanding the central role of beliefs and expectations in health and illness.

Background

Randomized controlled trials (RCTs) have been used since the 1940s to assess the effectiveness of drugs compared with placebos. For these trials, subjects are randomly allocated to either the experimental condition (and receive the real drug) or the control condition (and receive the placebo drug). Placebo drugs are used as a comparison point in order to distinguish the 'real' effects of the chemically active drug from both the 'placebo effects' and changes that may spontaneously happen over time. The RCT methodology acknowledges that changes in symptoms may occur following a placebo drug, but regards these as less important than the real changes that occur following the real drug. However, in 1982, data from the Coronary Drug Project were published which suggested that the best predictor of mortality in men who had survived a heart attack was not taking the lipid-lowering drug compared with taking the placebo drug, but adherence to taking any drug at all (whether an active drug or a placebo drug). The results indicated that adherers had lower mortality at five years than the non-adherers in both the experimental and the placebo groups. Horwitz et al. (1990) set out to examine whether adherence was a good predictor of risk of death in a large beta-blocker heart attack trial (Beta-blocker Heart Attack Trial Research Group 1982) and to evaluate whether any effects of adherence could be explained by social and behavioural characteristics (e.g. were the non-adherers also the smokers with stressful lives?).

Methodology

Horwitz et al. reported a reanalysis of the data collected as part of the beta-blocker heart attack trial, which was a multicentre, randomized, double-blind trial comparing proprandol (a beta-blocker) with a placebo drug in patients who had survived an acute heart attack (this is known as secondary data analysis).

Subjects

The original study included 3837 men and women aged 30–69 years who were reassessed every three months for an average of 25 months. The data from 1082 men in the experimental condition (who had received the beta-blocker) and 1094 men in the placebo condition were analysed (all women and those men who had not completed the psychosocial measures were excluded from the analysis). Follow-up data were analysed for 12 months.

focus on research 13.1

Design

The study was prospective, with subjects completing initial measures six weeks after hospital discharge and completing subsequent follow-up measures every three months.

Measures

Measures were taken of psychosocial factors, adherence and clinical characteristics:

- *Psychosocial factors.* The subjects completed a structured interview six weeks after discharge. The answers to this were grouped to form four psychosocial variables: levels of life stress, social isolation, depression and type A behaviour pattern. In addition, data were collected concerning their health practices both at baseline and at follow-up (e.g. smoking, alcohol use, diet, physical activity other than work).
- *Adherence.* For each follow-up interval (three months), adherence was calculated as the amount of medication divided by the amount prescribed. The subjects were divided into poor adherers (taking less than or equal to 75 per cent of prescribed medication) and good adherers (taking more than 75 per cent of prescribed medication).
- *Clinical characteristics.* Measures were also taken of the clinical severity of the heart attack (congestive heart failure, severity of heart attack, age) and sociodemographic features (ethnicity, marital status, education).
- *Mortality.* Mortality was measured after 12 months.

Results

Adherence and mortality

The results were analysed to examine the relationship between adherence and mortality, and showed that, compared with patients with good adherence, those with poor adherence were twice as likely to have died at one-year follow-up. This association was also present when the data were analysed according to treatment category (i.e. for both the experimental group and the control group). Therefore, regardless of what the drug was (whether a beta-blocker or a placebo), taking it as recommended halved the subjects' chances of dying.

The role of psychosocial and clinical factors

The results showed that death after one year was higher for those subjects who had a history of congestive heart failure, were not married, and had high social isolation and high life stress. In addition, those who had died after one year were more likely to have been smokers at baseline and less likely to have given up smoking during the follow-up. However, even when the data were analysed to take into account these psychosocial and clinical factors, adherence was still strongly associated with mortality at one year.

Conclusion

These results therefore indicate a strong link between adherence to medical recommendations and mortality, regardless of the type of drug taken. This effect does not appear to be due to psychosocial or clinical factors (the non-adherers did not simply smoke more than the adherers). Therefore 'doing as the doctor suggests' appears to be beneficial to health, but not for the traditional reasons ('the drugs are good for you') but perhaps because by taking medication, the patient expects to get better. The authors concluded in a review article that 'perhaps the most provocative explanation for the good effect of good adherence on health is the one most perplexing to clinicians: the role of patient expectancies or self-efficacy'. They suggested that 'patients who expect treatment to be effective engage in other health practices that lead to improved clinical outcomes' (Horwitz and Horwitz 1993). In addition, they suggested that the power of adherence may not be limited to taking drugs but may also occur with adherence to recommendations of behaviour change. Adherence may be a measure of patient expectation, with these expectations influencing the individual's health status – adherence is an illustration of the placebo effect and a reflection of the complex interrelationship between beliefs, behaviour and health.

The effect of investment

Totman suggested that this investment results in the individual having to go through two processes: (1) the individual needs to justify their behaviour; and (2) the individual needs to see themselves as rational and in control. If these two factors are in line with each other (e.g. 'I spent money on a treatment and it worked'), then the individual experiences low dissonance. If, however, there is a conflict between these two factors (e.g. 'I spent money on a treatment and I do not feel any better'), the individual experiences a state of high dissonance. Totman argued that high justification (it worked) results in low guilt and low dissonance (e.g. 'I can justify my behaviour, I am rational and in control'). However, low justification (e.g. 'it didn't work') results in high guilt and high dissonance (e.g. 'I cannot justify my behaviour, I am not rational or in control'). How does this relate to placebo effects and changes in symptoms?

Justification and changes in symptoms

If an individual travels far and pays a lot of money to see a faith healer then they need to justify this behaviour. Also they need to see themselves as being rational and in control. If they have put a lot of investment into seeing a faith healer and the faith healer has no effect on their health status, then they will not be able to see themselves as being rational and in control, and will therefore be in a state of high dissonance. The best way to resolve this dissonance, according to Totman, is for there to be an outcome that enables the individual to be able to justify their behaviour and to see themselves as rational and in control. In terms of the faith healer, the best outcome would be an improvement in health status. This would enable the individual to justify their behaviour and maintain a sense of self as one who is rational and sensible. Totman argued that when in a state of high dissonance, unconscious regulating mechanisms are activated, which may cause physical changes that improve the health of the individual, which enables the individual to justify their behaviour, and this resolves the dissonance. Totman therefore suggested that for a placebo effect to occur, the individual does not require an expectation that they will get better, but a need to find justification for their behaviour and a state of cognitive dissonance to set this up. Totman's model is illustrated in Figure 13.2.

Evidence for the role of justification

Research has examined whether a need for justification does in fact relate to symptom perception. Zimbardo (1969) evaluated the effects of *post hoc* justification on hunger and thirst. Subjects were asked not to eat or drink for a length of time, and were divided into two groups.

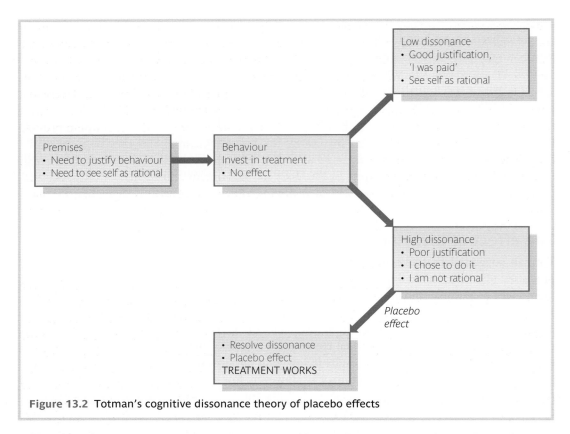

Figure 13.2 Totman's cognitive dissonance theory of placebo effects

Group 1 were offered money if they managed to abstain from eating and drinking, providing these subjects with good justification for their behaviour. Group 2 were simply asked not to eat or drink for a length of time, but were given no reason or incentive, and therefore had no justification. Having good justification for their behaviour, group 1 were not in a state of dissonance; they were able to justify not eating and still maintain a sense of being rational and in control. Group 2 had no justification for their behaviour and were therefore in a state of high dissonance, as they were performing a behaviour for very little reason. Therefore in order to resolve this dissonance it was argued that group 2 needed to find a justification for their behaviour. At the end of the period of abstinence all subjects were allowed to eat and drink as much as they wished. The results showed that group 2 (those in high dissonance) ate and drank less when free food was available to them than group 1 (those in low dissonance).

The results were interpreted as follows. The subjects in group 2, being in a state of high dissonance, needed to find a justification for their behaviour and justified their behaviour by believing 'I didn't eat because I was not hungry'. They therefore ate and drank less when food was available. The subjects in group 1, being in a state of low dissonance, had no need to find a justification for their behaviour as they had a good justification: 'I didn't eat because I was paid not to'. They therefore ate more when the food was offered. The results of this study have been used to suggest that high dissonance influenced the subject's physiological state, and the physiological state changed in order to resolve the problem of dissonance.

Research has also examined the effects of justification on placebo-induced pain reduction. Totman (1987) induced pain in a group of subjects using heat stimulation. Subjects were then offered the choice of a drug in order to reduce pain. In fact this drug was a placebo. Half of the subjects were offered money to take part in the study, and half were offered no money. Totman argued that because one group were offered an incentive to carry out the study and to experience the pain, they therefore had high justification for their behaviour and were in a state of low dissonance. The other group, however, were offered no money and therefore had low justification for subjecting themselves to a painful situation; they therefore had low justification and were in a state of high dissonance. Totman argued that this group needed to find some kind of justification to resolve this state of dissonance. If the drug worked, the author argued that this would provide them with justification for subjecting themselves to the experiment and for choosing to take the drug. The results showed that the group in a state of high dissonance experienced less pain following the placebo than the group in low dissonance. Totman argued that this suggests that being in a state of low justification activated the individual's unconscious regulating mechanisms, which caused physiological changes to reduce the pain, providing the group with justification for their behaviour, which therefore eradicated their state of dissonance.

An example of Totman's theory

The following example illustrates the relationship between justification and the need to see oneself as rational and in control, and the problem of dissonance between these two factors.

Visiting Lourdes in order to improve one's health status involves a degree of investment in that behaviour in terms of time, money and so on. If the visit to Lourdes has no effect, then the behaviour begins to appear irrational and unjustified. If the individual can provide justification for their behaviour, for example 'I was paid to go to Lourdes', then they will experience low dissonance. If, however, the individual can find no justification for their visit to Lourdes and therefore believes 'I chose to do it and it didn't work', they remain in a state of high dissonance. Dissonance is an uncomfortable state to be in and the individual is motivated to remove this state. Changing the outcome (e.g. 'I feel better following my visit to Lourdes') removes this dissonance and the individual can believe 'I chose to do it and it worked'. Therefore, according to cognitive dissonance theory, dissonance can be resolved by the placebo having an effect on the individual's health status by activating unconscious regulating mechanisms.

Support for cognitive dissonance theory

The following factors provide support and evidence for cognitive dissonance theory:

- The theory can explain all placebo effects, not just pain.
- The theory does not require patient expectations, but choice. This helps to explain those reported instances where the individual does not appear to expect to get better.
- The theory suggests that the individual needs commitment to the medical procedure, which explains why the individual may need to show some investment (e.g. pain, time, money) in order to get better. This can explain some of the proposed effects of treatment characteristics, individual characteristics and therapist characteristics.

Problems with cognitive dissonance theory

However, there are several problems with cognitive dissonance theory:

- Much of the research examining the effects of justification has involved giving money to subjects to enable them to provide justification for their behaviour. It is possible that providing subjects with money increases their anxiety and therefore increases pain perception.

- It is also possible that the experimenter's attempt to persuade the individual to participate, itself also increases anxiety.

- Cognitive dissonance theory has mainly been tested using acute pain, which has been elicited in a laboratory setting. Whether the results are transferable to 'real life' is questionable.

- Totman argues that patient expectations are not necessary. However, an individual must expect some changes following the intervention otherwise they would not make the original investment. It is also possible that paying subjects to participate changes their expectations of a successful outcome.

- Totman does not explain what these unconscious regulating mechanisms may be.

The role of placebo effects in health psychology

Placebos have implications for many areas of health psychology and illustrate how these different areas may interact. These are outlined in terms of the areas of health psychology described in this book, which provides additional insights into possible mechanisms of the placebo effect. The interactions between these different areas are illustrated in Figure 13.3.

Health beliefs

For a placebo to have an effect, the individual needs to have a belief that the intervention will be effective. For example, a placebo in the form of a pill will work if the individual subscribes to a medical model of health and illness and believes that traditional medical interventions are

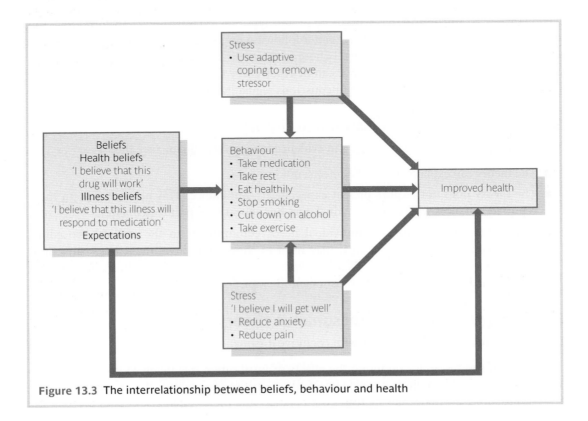

Figure 13.3 The interrelationship between beliefs, behaviour and health

effective. A placebo in the form of herbal tea may only be effective if the individual believes in alternative medicines and is open to non-traditional forms of intervention. Furthermore, the conditioning effects, reporting error and misattribution process may only occur if the individual believes that health professionals in white coats can treat illness, that hospitals are where people get better and that medical interventions should produce positive results. Patients' beliefs may themselves be a mechanism for explaining placebo effects. Perhaps the belief about a treatment has either a direct effect on health through physiological changes, or an indirect effect via behavioural change. For example, the belief that a treatment intervention will work may directly influence the individual's immune system or alternatively may promote a change in lifestyle.

Illness cognitions

For a placebo to have an effect, the individual needs to hold particular beliefs about their illness. For example, if an illness is seen as long lasting without episodes of remission, times of spontaneous recovery may not happen, which therefore cannot be explained in terms of the effectiveness of the treatment. Likewise, if an individual believes that their illness has a medical cause then a placebo in the form of a pill would be effective. However, if the individual believes that their illness is caused by their lifestyle, a pill placebo may not be effective.

Health professionals' health beliefs

Placebos may also be related to the beliefs of the health professionals. For example, a doctor may need to believe in the intervention for it to have an effect. If the doctor believes that an illness is the result of lifestyle, and can be cured by changes in that lifestyle, then a placebo in the form of a medical intervention may not work, as the doctor's expectation of failure may be communicated to the patient. Furthermore, theories of health professionals' health beliefs and their role in doctor–patient communication illustrate a useful emphasis on interaction rather than individual characteristics.

Health-related behaviours

A placebo may function via changes in health-related behaviour. If an individual believes that they have taken something or behaved in a way that may promote good health, they may also change other health-related behaviours (e.g. smoking, drinking, exercise), which may also improve their health. Furthermore, the choice to take a medication may itself be seen as a health-related behaviour, and may be predicted by theories of behaviour and behaviour change.

Stress

Placebos also have implications for understanding responses to stress. If placebos have an effect either directly (physiological change) or indirectly (behaviour change) then this is in parallel with theories of stress. In addition, placebos may function by reducing any stress caused by illness. The belief that an individual has taken control of their illness (perceived control) may reduce the stress response, reducing any effects this stress may have on the illness.

Pain

Placebo-induced pain reduction may be mediated either by physiological changes, such as opiate release, or by anxiety reduction. Both of these changes can be explained in terms of the gate control theory of pain, which suggests that the experience of pain is a result of an inter-action between psychological (beliefs, anxiety) and physiological (opiates) processes. Previous experience and expectation are also implicated in pain reduction. Perhaps placebo-induced pain reduction may also be mediated by patient expectations and previous experience about the efficacy of the treatment intervention.

Implications for dualism

Placebos indicate that an individual's symptoms and health status may be influenced by their expectations, beliefs and previous experience. These factors are central to health psychology in its attempt to challenge the traditional biomedical approach to health and illness. If an indi-vidual's psychological state can influence their health, then perhaps the mind and body should not be seen as separate entities but as interacting. This is, in part, in contradiction to dualistic models of the individual. However, this interaction still assumes that the mind and body are distinct; to interact with each other, they still need to be defined as being separate.

To conclude

Placebos have been shown to have a multitude of effects ranging from pain relief to changing cognitive state. Many theories have been developed in an attempt to explain how placebos work, and these can be categorized as non-interactive theories, which focus on the characteristics of either the patient, the health professional or the treatment, and interactive theories, which regard placebo effects as arising from interaction between these different variables. In particular, most explanations of placebos point to a central role for expectations both of the patient and the health professional. These theories suggest that if a patient expects to get better, then this expectation will influence their health. Therefore, through expectancies, it is possible that patient and doctor expectations, anxiety, conditioning, opiates and cognitive dissonance, could interact with each other. However, how this interaction would actually influence health remains unclear. Finally, placebos have many implications for the areas of health psychology examined in this book. They indicate that beliefs, behaviours, stress, pain and illness may not be separate areas, requiring separate theories and research, but may be interrelated, and that rather than being a factor to be taken out of an understanding of health the placebo effect may itself play a central role in determining health status.

Questions

1 Discuss the evidence for the possible theories of the placebo effect.
2 Placebos are all in the mind. Discuss.
3 Placebos are a useful treatment for pain. Discuss.
4 Discuss the role of patient expectations in improvements in health.
5 How might patient adherence be a placebo effect?
6 Discuss the implications of theories of placebos for the interrelationship among beliefs, behaviours and health.
7 Design a research study to illustrate the role of expectations in recovery from an acute illness.

For discussion

Consider the last time you took any medication (e.g. painkiller, antibiotics, etc.). To what extent were any subsequent changes due to the placebo effect?

Assumptions in health psychology

The research into placebo effects highlights some of the assumptions in health psychology:

1 *The mind–body split.* Placebos suggest an interaction between the mind and the body – expecting to get better may produce both subjective ('I feel better') and objective ('You did not have another heart attack') changes in the individual's physical well-being. This is in line with health psychology's aim of challenging traditional dualistic models. However, implicit in the interaction between the mind and body is a definition of these two factors being separate in order to interact.

2 *Dividing up the soup.* Health psychology discusses variables such as beliefs, expectations, anxiety, behaviour and health as separate facets of individuals. It then examines how these factors interact and emphasizes the complex interrelationships between them all (e.g. beliefs create changes in behaviour, behaviours cause changes in health, emotions cause changes in behaviours). However, perhaps individuals are not made up of these separate factors but are a blurred 'soup' of undefined and unseparated 'everything'. Within this soup all the factors are one as they are not undifferentiated. Health psychology takes the soup and divides it up into different separate factors as if these different factors exist. It then discusses how they relate to each other. However, the discussion of how they interrelate can only occur because health psychology has separated them in the first place. Perhaps psychological theory creates separate 'things' in order to look at the relationship between these 'things'. Without the original separation there would be no need for a discussion of interaction – it would be obvious that 'things' were related as they would be as one!

Further reading

Critelli, J.W. and Neumann, K.F. (1984) The placebo: conceptual analysis of a construct in transition, *American Psychologist*, 39: 32–9.
    This paper provides a theoretical discussion on placebos and analyses the role of placebos in health and illness.

Simpson, S.H., Eurich, D.T., Majumdar, S.R., Padwal, R.S., Tsuyuki, R.T., Varney, J. and Johnson, J.A. (2006) A meta-analysis of the association between adherence to drug therapy and mortality, *British Medical Journal*, 333: 15.
    This is an excellent review of the literature exploring how simply adhering to medication has a powerful placebo effect which is linked with improved mortality.

Totman, R.G. (1987) *The Social Causes of Illness*. London: Souvenir Press.
    This book provides an interesting perspective on placebos and the interrelationship among beliefs, behaviours and health.

14

HIV and cancer
Psychology throughout the course of illness (1)

Chapter overview

The next two chapters (14 and 15) examine the role that psychology plays at each stage of an illness, from illness onset, to its progression, to the psychological consequences and longevity. They do not aim to be comprehensive overviews of the immense literature on illness, but to illustrate the possible varied role of psychology in illness. This chapter uses the examples of HIV and cancer and the next chapter focuses on obesity and coronary heart disease. However, these psychological factors are relevant to a multitude of other chronic and acute illnesses. It suggests that, rather than being seen as a passive response to biomedical factors, such chronic illnesses are better understood in terms of a complex interplay of physiological and psychological processes.

This chapter covers

- What is HIV?
- The role of psychology in the study of HIV
- Attitudes to AIDS
- Psychology and susceptibility to HIV
- Psychology and the progression to AIDS
- Psychology and longevity
- What is cancer?
- The role of psychology in cancer initiation
- Psychological consequences of cancer
- Psychology and the alleviation of symptoms
- Psychology and promoting longevity and the disease-free interval

HIV and AIDS

This section examines the history of HIV, what HIV is and how it is transmitted. It then evaluates the role of psychology in understanding HIV in terms of attitudes to HIV and AIDS, susceptibility to HIV and AIDS, progression from HIV to AIDS and longevity. A detailed discussion of condom use in the context of HIV and AIDS can be found in Chapter 8 and a detailed description of psychoneuroimmunology (PNI) can be found in Chapter 11.

The history of HIV

AIDS (acquired immune deficiency syndrome) was identified as a new syndrome in 1981. At that time, it was regarded as specific to homosexuality and was known as GRIDS (gay-related immune deficiency syndrome). As a result of this belief a number of theories were developed to try to explain the occurrence of this new illness among homosexuals. These ranged from the suggestion that AIDS may be a response to the over-use of recreational drugs such as 'poppers' or to over-exposure to semen, and they focused on the perceived lifestyles of the homosexual population. In 1982, however, AIDS occurred in haemophiliacs. As haemophiliacs were seen not to have lifestyles comparable with the homosexual population, scientists started to reform their theories about AIDS and suggested, for the first time, that perhaps AIDS was caused by a virus. Such a virus could reach haemophiliacs through their use of Factor VIII, a donated blood-clotting agent.

The HIV virus was first isolated in 1983. However, there is debate as to whether this was achieved by Gallo in the USA or/and Montagnier in France. Both these researchers were looking for a retrovirus, having examined a cat retrovirus that caused leukaemia and appeared to be very similar to what they thought was causing this new illness. In 1984, the human immunodeficiency virus type 1 (HIV 1) was identified, and in 1985 HIV 2 was identified in Africa.

What is HIV?
The structure of HIV

The HIV virus is a retrovirus, a type of virus containing RNA. There are three types of retrovirus: oncogenic retroviruses which cause cancer, foamy retroviruses which have no effect at all on the health status of the individual, and lentiviruses, or slow viruses, which have slow long-term effects. HIV is a lentivirus.

The HIV virus is structured with an outer coat and an inner core. The RNA is situated in the core and contains eight viral genes, which encode the proteins of the envelope and the core, and also contains enzymes, which are essential for replication.

The transmission of HIV

In order to be transmitted from one individual to the next, the HIV virus generally needs to come into contact with cells that have CD4 molecules on their surface. Such cells are found within the immune system and are called T-helper cells. The process of transmission of the HIV virus involves the following stages:

1 HIV binds to the CD4 molecule of T-helper cell.
2 HIV virus is internalized into the cytoplasm of the cell.
3 The cell itself generates a pro-viral DNA, which is a copy of the host cell.
4 This pro-virus enters the nucleus of the host cell.
5 The host cell produces new viral particles, which it reads off from the viral code of the viral DNA.
6 These viral particles bud off and infect new cells.
7 Eventually, after much replication, the host T-helper cell dies.

The progression from HIV to AIDS

The progression from HIV to HIV disease and AIDS varies in time. AIDS reflects a reduction in T-helper cells and specifically those that are CD4-positive T-cells. This causes immune deficiency and the appearance of opportunistic infections. The progression from initial HIV sero-conversion through to AIDS tends to go through the following stages:

1 The initial viral seroconversion illness.
2 An asymptomatic stage.
3 Enlargement of the lymph nodes, onset of opportunistic infections.
4 AIDS-related complex (ARC).
5 AIDS.

The prevalence of HIV and AIDS

At the end of 2005 there were 38.6 million people living with HIV and in 2005 4.1 million became newly infected and 2.8 million died from HIV. Generally, the incidence of HIV peaked in the late 1990s and has now mostly stabilized. However, the numbers of people living with HIV has increased due to population growth and the numbers of people now taking anti-retroviral therapy which has significantly improved the life expectancy of those infected with the HIV virus. Although much western interest has been on the incidence of HIV within the gay populations of the western world, the epicentre of the global epidemic is in Sub-Saharan Africa. Rates are also very high in parts of Asia, particularly India and China. At the end of 2005 there were 5.5 million people in Sub-Saharan Africa who were living with HIV. This includes about 18.8 per cent of adults, and about 1 in 3 pregnant women attending antenatal care in 2004 were found to be HIV positive. In Asia about 8.3 million people were living with HIV at the end of 2005 and most of these were in India. In China, about 650,000 were living with HIV in 2005 and of these 44 per cent are injecting drug users. In Europe the highest incident rate is in the Russian Federation. Overall, the prevalence of HIV is very low in the Middle East and North Africa (except the Sudan). In terms of changing rates of HIV, there was a decline in new cases across the USA and Europe in the 1990s although there is some evidence of a resurgent epidemic in men who have sex with men in the USA and some European countries. There has also been a recent increase in the UK, mostly due to heterosexual transmission with an increasing number of women accounting for the rise in numbers. It is estimated that about 80 per cent of these cases are due to the virus being contracted in countries where there are much higher rates. There have been declines in rates in some parts of Sub-Saharan Africa (Kenya and Zimbabwe), declines in some parts of India (Tamil Nadu) but no signs of decline in most of Southern Africa, and increases in China, Indonesia, Papua New Guinea, Bangladesh and Pakistan. Across Europe the highest rates of people living with HIV per million people are Portugal (79.6), Spain (43.0), Switzerland (42.8) and Italy (29.2). By the end of 2004 about 300,000 people across Europe were living with HIV and about 170,000 had died. In the UK, by the end of 2004, 58,000 people were living with HIV. In 2005 there were 7205 new diagnoses and of the 22,281 diagnoses ever, 17,014 people had died.

The role of psychology in the study of HIV

HIV is transmitted mostly because of people's behaviour (e.g. sexual intercourse, needle use). Health psychology has studied HIV in terms of attitudes to HIV, changing these attitudes, and examining predictors of behaviour. The following observations suggest that psychology has an additional role to play in HIV:

■ Not everyone exposed to HIV virus becomes HIV positive. This suggests that psychological factors may influence an individual's susceptibility to the HIV virus.

■ The time for progression from HIV to AIDS is variable. Psychological factors may have a role in promoting the replication of the HIV virus and the progression from being HIV positive to having AIDS.

■ Perhaps not everyone with HIV dies from AIDS. Psychological factors may have a role to play in determining the longevity of the individual.

The potential role of psychological factors in understanding HIV and AIDS is shown in Figure 14.1.

The role of psychology in AIDS in terms of attitudes to AIDS, susceptibility to AIDS, progression from HIV to AIDS, and longevity will now be examined.

Attitudes to AIDS

Research has examined attitudes to HIV and the relationship between these attitudes and behaviour. As AIDS is a new disease, the research into attitudes reflects not only differences in these attitudes between individuals but also changes in attitude across time.

Research has asked the question, 'Do people feel vulnerable to the HIV virus?' Temoshok et al. (1987) carried out a survey of people living in a number of different cities in the USA and asked these people whether AIDS was seen as a personal health concern. The proportions responding 'yes' were as follows: San Francisco, 33 per cent; New York, 57 per cent; Miami, 50 per cent; and Los Angeles, 47 per cent.

It is interesting to note that subjects in San Francisco, which had the highest incidence of HIV-positive individuals in the USA, reported seeing HIV as less of a personal health concern than those living in other cities. There are two possible explanations for this, which raise

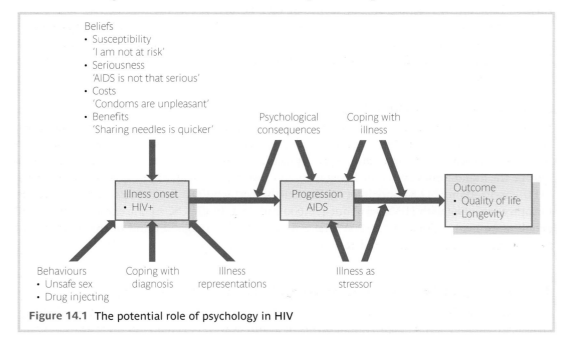

Figure 14.1 The potential role of psychology in HIV

questions about the complex interrelationship between knowledge, education, personal experience and attitudes. First, by living in a city with high levels of HIV and high exposure to health education on information around HIV and AIDS, knowledge of the disease is increased. This knowledge makes people feel less vulnerable because they believe they can do something about it. Alternatively, however, perhaps being exposed to AIDS and HIV, and death following AIDS, increases the sense of fear and denial in individuals living in cities where there is a high prevalence of the illness. Feeling less vulnerable may reflect this denial.

Many studies in the UK have also examined individuals' perception of risk and its relationship to knowledge. Research in the late 1980s and early 1990s indicated that although knowledge about transmission of HIV was high, many college students reported being relatively invulnerable to HIV. Abrams et al. (1990: 49) reported that 'young people have a strong sense of AIDS invulnerability which seems to involve a perception that they have control over the risk at which they place themselves'. Woodcock et al. (1992) examined young people's interpretations of their personal risk of infection and suggested that although some subjects acknowledged that they were at risk, this was often dismissed because it was in the past and 'it would show by now'. However, many subjects in this study denied that they were at risk and justified this in terms of beliefs such as 'it's been blown out of proportion', 'AIDS is a risk you take in living', 'partners were (or are) not promiscuous', or partners came from geographical areas that were not regarded as high risk (e.g. the New Forest in southern England was considered a low-risk area and Glasgow a high-risk area) (see Chapter 8 for a discussion of risk perception and condom use).

Another question that has been asked about HIV is, 'Does the sexuality and sexual behaviour of individuals influence their beliefs about HIV?' Temoshok et al. (1987) examined gay, bisexual and heterosexual men's beliefs about HIV. The results suggested that gay and bisexual men believe that AIDS was more important than heterosexual men. This group showed higher levels of knowledge about HIV, reported having been concerned about HIV for a longer period of time, reported feeling more susceptible to HIV, and reported feeling that their chances of getting HIV were higher than the heterosexual population.

Some researchers have also looked at how teenagers and students view HIV, as they tend to be particularly sexually active. Price et al. (1985) found that this group of individuals, despite being high risk and sexually active, reported low levels of knowledge and said that they were less likely to get AIDS.

Attitudes and behaviour change

Research has specifically examined the relationship between beliefs about HIV and behaviour change. Temoshok et al. (1987) reported that perceived risk of AIDS was not related to changes in sexual behaviour. However, they reported that anti-gay attitudes and fear were related to a change in sexual behaviour. Several studies have also looked at the change in risky sexual behaviour in gay men. Curran et al. (1985), McKusick et al. (1990) and Martin (1987) suggested that there has been a reduction in such behaviour in gay men, reflecting their attitudes and beliefs about HIV. Likewise Simkins and Ebenhage (1984) examined the sexual behaviour of heterosexual college students and reported no changes in their behaviour. This again reflects their attitudes towards HIV with their reports of being at low risk.

The interrelationship among knowledge, attitudes and behaviour

The relationship between knowledge and beliefs about HIV is a complex one. Health education campaigns assume that improving knowledge will change attitudes and therefore change behaviour. In terms of HIV, one behaviour that is targeted by health educational campaigns is safer sex (see Chapter 8 for a discussion of condom use). However, whether increasing knowledge actually increases the practice of safer sex is questionable. There are several possible consequences of knowledge:

■ It is possible that increasing knowledge increases fear in the individual, which may then cause denial, resulting in no effect on behaviour or even a detrimental effect on behaviour.

■ Alternatively, improved knowledge may improve the individual's perception of reality and their perception of risk, which could therefore cause a change in behaviour as the individual is not experiencing fear.

■ It is also possible that improving knowledge may increase the awareness of the seriousness of the illness, which could cause individuals who actually contract the illness to be blamed for this (victim blaming). Fear and victim blaming can also have a complicated interaction with other beliefs and also on the safer sex practices of individuals. Fear and victim blaming may be related to denial, or behavioural change, or prejudice, or helplessness, or a feeling of lack of control.

Therefore promoting safer sex may be more complicated than simply increasing knowledge (see Chapter 8 for a discussion of sex education influences).

Psychology and susceptibility to the HIV virus

Psychology may also have a role to play in an individual's susceptibility to the HIV virus once exposed to it. Several studies have examined the possibility that not all those individuals who come into contact with HIV become HIV positive, and have suggested several reasons for this. One train of thought argues that the lifestyle of an individual may increase their chances of contracting HIV once exposed to the virus. Van Griensven et al. (1986) suggested that the use of other drugs, such as nitrates and cannabis, increases the chance of contracting HIV once exposed the virus. Lifson et al. (1989) also argued that the existence of other viruses, such as herpes simplex and cytomegalovirus (CMV), in the bloodstream may increase the chances of contracting HIV. These viruses are also thought to be associated with unsafe sex and injecting drugs. Therefore unhealthy behaviours may not only be related to exposure to the HIV virus but also the likelihood that an individual will become HIV positive. However, much of the lifestyle literature surrounding susceptibility to HIV virus was based on the beliefs about HIV that existed during the 1980s, when HIV was still regarded as a homosexual illness. It therefore focused on the lifestyles of homosexuals and made generalizations about this lifestyle in order to explain susceptibility to the virus.

Psychology and the progression from HIV to AIDS

Research has also examined the role of psychology in the progression from HIV to AIDS. It has been argued that HIV provides a useful basis for such research for the following reasons: (1) there are large numbers of individuals who can be identified at the asymptomatic stage of their illness, allowing an analysis of disease progression from a symptom-free stage; (2) as people with HIV tend to be young, the problem of other coexisting diseases can be avoided; and (3) the measurement of disease progression using numbers of CD4 T-helper cells is accurate (Taylor et al. 1998).

This research points to roles for lifestyle, adherence to medication, stress, cognitive adjustment and type C coping style in the progression of the illness.

Lifestyle

It has been suggested that injecting drugs further stimulates the immune system, which may well influence replication, and thereby points to a role for drug use not only in contracting the virus but also for its replication. In addition, research has also indicated that replication of the HIV virus may be influenced by further exposure to the HIV virus, suggesting a role for unsafe sex and drug use in its progression. Furthermore, it has been suggested that contact with drugs, which may have an immunosuppressive effect, or other viruses, such as herpes complex and CMV, may also be related to an increase in replication.

Adherence to medication

Over recent years the life expectancy and quality of life of those with HIV has improved dramatically (e.g. Mocroft et al. 1998). Much of this has been attributed to the success of highly active anti-retroviral therapy (HAART) and HIV is often now described as a chronic illness rather than a terminal illness. Many people who are offered HAART, however, do not take the treatment. For example, Steinberg (2001) reported that only 75 per cent of those eligible for treatment received treatment. Of those who did not receive treatment, 58 per cent had declined the offer. Research has therefore explored the reasons behind adherence and non-adherence to medication. Before HAART the most common medication was AZT monotherapy. Siegel et al. (1992) reported that reasons for non-adherence included lack of trust in doctors, feelings of well-being, negative beliefs about medical treatments, the belief that AZT would make the person worse and the belief that taking AZT would reduce treatment options in future. In a similar vein, Cooper et al. (2002b) explored people's beliefs about HAART. They interviewed 26 gay men about their views about HAART shortly after it had been recommended by their doctor. The results showed that the men held beliefs about the necessity of their medication in terms of whether they felt it could control their HIV or whether they were inclined to let their condition take its natural course; they described their concerns about taking the drugs in terms of side effects, the difficulties of the drug regimen and its effectiveness; and they described feelings about their control over the decision to take the medication. In an associated study, Gellaitry et al. (2005) further examined beliefs about HAART and linked them with adherence. These results showed that concerns about the adverse effects of HAART were related to declining treatment.

Stress

Sodroski et al. (1984) suggested that stress or distress may well increase the replication of the HIV virus, causing a quicker progression to AIDS. Women who are HIV positive are more at risk from cervical intraepithelial neoplasia (CIN) and cervical cancer. Pereira et al. (2003) explored the relationship between the likelihood of developing the lesions associated with CIN and life stress. The results showed that higher life stress increased the odds of developing lesions by sevenfold over a one-year period. Life stress therefore seemed to link with illness progression. Some research has also addressed the effectiveness of stress management in slowing down the progression of HIV. Antoni et al. (2006) randomized 130 gay men who were HIV positive to receive either a cognitive behavioural stress management intervention (CBSM) and anti-retroviral medication adherence training (MAT), or to receive MAT alone. The men were then followed up after 9 and 15 months in terms of viral load. The results showed that men who already showed a detectable viral load at baseline (i.e. those with a lot of virus in the blood already) who received the stress management showed a reduction in their viral load over the 15-month period even when medication adherence was controlled for. The authors conclude that for HIV-positive men who already show a detectable viral load, stress management may enhance the beneficial effects of their anti-retroviral treatment. In a similar study, the mechanisms behind the impact of stress management were explored (Antoni et al. 2005). For this study 25 HIV-positive men were randomized to receive stress management or a waiting-list control. Urine samples were taken before and after the intervention period. The results again showed that stress management was effective and that this effect was related to reduction in cortisol and depressed mood. The authors conclude that stress management works by reducing the stress induced by being ill with a disease such as HIV. This supports the early work of Solomon and Temoshok (Solomon and Temoshok 1987; see also Solomon et al. 1987), who argued that social homophobia may well cause stress in individuals who have contracted HIV, which could exacerbate their illness.

Cognitive adjustment

Research from the Multi Center AIDS Cohort Study (MACS) in the USA has suggested a role for forms of cognitive adjustment to bereavement and illness progression (Reed et al. 1994, 1999; Bower et al. 1998). In the first part of this study, 72 men who were HIV positive, asymptomatic and half of whom had recently experienced the death of a close friend or primary partner, completed measures of their psychosocial state (HIV-specific expectancies, mood state and hopelessness) and had the number of their CD4 T-helper cells recorded. They were then followed up over a six-year period. The results showed that about half of the sample showed symptoms over the follow-up period. However, the rate and extent of the disease progression were not consistent for everyone. In particular, the results showed that symptom development was predicted by baseline HIV-specific expectancies, particularly in those who had been bereaved. Therefore it would seem that having more negative expectancies of HIV progression is predictive of actual progression (Reed et al. 1999). In the second part of this study, 40 HIV-positive men who had recently lost a close friend or partner to AIDS were interviewed about how they made sense of this death. These interviews were then classified according to whether the individual had managed to find meaning in the death in line with Taylor's cognitive adaptation theory of coping (Taylor 1983) (see Chapter 3). An example of meaning would be: 'What his death did was snap a certain value into my behaviour, which is "Listen, you don't know how long you've got. You've just lost another one. Spend more time with the people that mean something to you"'. The results showed that those who had managed to find meaning maintained their levels of CD4 T-helper cells at follow-up, whereas those who did not find meaning showed a decline.

Type C coping style

Research has also explored the link between how people cope with HIV and the progression of their disease with a focus on type C coping style which reflects emotional inexpression and a decreased recognition of needs and feelings. For example, Solano et al. (2001, 2002) used CD4 cells as a measure of disease status, assessed baseline coping and followed 200 patients up after 6 and 12 months. The results showed that type C coping style predicted progression at follow-up, suggesting that a form of coping that relies upon a lack of emotional expression may exacerbate the course of HIV disease. However, the results also showed that very high levels of emotional expression were also detrimental. The authors conclude that working through emotions rather than just releasing them may be the most protective coping strategy for people diagnosed as HIV positive.

Psychology and longevity

Research has also examined the role of psychological factors in longevity following infection with HIV. In particular, this has looked at the direct effects of beliefs and behaviour on the state of immunosuppression of the individual (see Chapter 11 for a discussion of PNI). In 1987, Solomon et al. studied 21 AIDS patients and examined their health status and the relationship of this health status to predictive baseline psychological variables. At follow-up, they found that survival was predicted by their general health status at baseline, their health behaviours, hardiness, social support, type C behaviour (self-sacrificing, self-blaming, not emotionally expressive) and coping strategies. In a further study, Solomon and Temoshok (1987) reported an additional follow-up of AIDS patients. They argued that a positive outcome was predicted by perceived control over illness at baseline, social support, problem solving, help-seeking behaviour, low social desirability and the expression of anger and hostility. This study indicated that type C behaviour was not related to longevity.

Reed et al. (1994) also examined the psychological state of 78 gay men who had been diagnosed with AIDS in terms of their self-reported health status, psychological adjustment and psychological responses to HIV, well-being, self-esteem and levels of hopelessness. In addition, they completed measures of 'realistic acceptance', which reflected statements such as 'I tried to accept what might happen', 'I prepare for the worst' and 'I go over in my mind what I say or do about this problem'. At follow-up, the results showed that two-thirds of the men had died. However, survival was predicted by 'realistic acceptance' at baseline with those who showed greater acceptance of their own death dying earlier. Therefore psychological state may also relate to longevity.

Conclusion

The study of HIV and AIDS illustrates the role of psychology at different stages of an illness. Psychological factors are important not only for attitudes and beliefs about HIV and the resulting behaviour, but may also be involved in an individual's susceptibility to contracting the virus, the replication of the virus once it has been contracted and their subsequent longevity.

Box 14.1 Some problems with . . . HIV and cancer research

Below are some problems with research in this area that you may wish to consider.

1 Much psychological research explores the predictors of becoming HIV positive in terms of safer sex behaviour and needle sharing. HIV, however, is a worldwide problem which affects people from all religions and cultural backgrounds. The reasons that people do or do not engage in risky behaviours are highly linked to their specific cultures. It is therefore very difficult to generalize from one study to populations outside the study group.

2 The management of HIV and AIDS has changed enormously over the past 20 years, resulting in an increase in longevity due to combination therapies. HIV is now seen as a chronic illness rather than a terminal illness. This means that combining research on longevity across the years is difficult as people at different times have been managed in very different ways.

3 Research on cancer shows some commonalities across different types of cancers. However, there are also vast differences in ways in which different cancers impact upon people's lives and are and should be managed. Generalizations across cancers should therefore be limited to those areas where there is consistent cross-cancer variation. For example, while screening and early detection for breast cancer can result in improved management and health outcomes, screening for prostate cancer may result in anxiety, a painful procedure and a recommendation of watchful waiting which can make people regret knowing about their condition in the first place.

Testing a theory – psychology and immune functioning

A study to examine the role of psychosocial factors such as coping style, life stress and social support on immune functioning in HIV-positive homosexual men (Goodkin et al. 1992).

This study examined the relationship between psychosocial factors and the physical health of HIV-positive men. Models of the relationship between psychological factors and physical health suggest that the link between psychology and health may be via behaviour change (e.g. feeling stressed increases smoking behaviour) and/or via direct physiological changes (e.g. feeling stressed causes a release of stress hormones). This study is based on the belief that psychological variables such as coping style, stress and social support may influence health and illness directly through changes in the individual's physiology (their immune system) regardless of behaviour.

Background

Research has suggested that psychosocial factors may be associated with changes in natural killer cell cytotoxicity (NKCC), which is an important defence against infections and cancer growth. For example, lowered NKCC has been shown in medical students under stress, bereaved individuals, and those with major depressive disorder. In addition, research has suggested that social support, active coping style and joy may be related to changes in NKCC in patients with breast cancer. Although the research into NKCC in still in its early stages and is somewhat controversial, Goodkin et al. (1992) aimed to examine the relationship between psychosocial factors and NKCC in HIV-positive men.

Methodology
Subjects

Sixty-two asymptomatic HIV-positive homosexual men from Miami volunteered for the study. They were recruited from the University of Miami School of Medicine Clinical Research Unit, community-based HIV-related service agencies, community physicians, advertisements in magazines and referrals from other studies. Subjects were excluded from the study if they were taking anti-viral medication, had a history of alcohol/substance abuse, a history of psychiatric disorder, or a severe head trauma. All subjects were aware of their HIV-positive status and either had no symptoms or a sign of physical infection of no more than three months. Their average age was 33.8 years; 72.6 per cent were native English speakers; nearly half had a first degree; the majority were in full-time employment; 66.1 per cent described themselves as exclusively homosexual; 51.6 per cent were single; 30.6 per cent were in a monogamous relationship and the remainder were either in an open relationship, divorced or widowed.

Design

The study was cross-sectional with all subjects completing all measures once.

Measures

The subjects completed the following psychosocial, behavioural control and physiological measures:

1 *Psychosocial measures*
   ■ Life experience survey: this assesses the count and impact of life events over the previous six months. For the present study, the authors focused on the number of life events and categorized subjects as either mild (0–5), moderate (6–10), high (11–15) or very high (>15).

- Social provisions scale: this measures the individual's perception of available social support. The authors used a shortened 20-item version and computed a total 'perceived social support' score.

- The coping orientations to problems experienced scale: this is a 57-item scale, which measures coping strategies. The present study examined these items in terms of: (i) active coping (made up of all the problem-focused strategies, such as planning, suppression of competing activities, restraint coping, seeking instrumental support, active coping, and three of the emotion-focused scales, such as seeking emotional support, positive reinterpretation, acceptance); (ii) disengagement/denial (which is made up of behavioural and mental disengagement items and denial); (iii) focus on and venting emotions; and (iv) turning to religion (see Chapter 3 for a discussion of coping).

- *Profile of mood states*: this is a 65-item scale of mood-related items. The present study computed a composite 'emotional distress score' composed of items relating to anxiety, depression, fatigue and confusion.

2 *Measures to control for behaviour.* Subjects completed measures of diet (using a food frequency questionnaire), alcohol and substance use (e.g. marijuana, cocaine, LSD, nitrate inhalants, amphetamines and opioids), smoking behaviour and prescribed medication. These were included in order to determine whether any differences in immune status were due to the psychosocial or behavioural factors. Measures of blood proteins, vitamins and minerals were also taken.

3 *Physiological measures.* Measurements were taken of anti-HIV-1 antibody, to confirm the subjects' HIV-positive status, and NKCC.

Results

Individual variables and NKCC

The results were first analysed to examine how individual variables were related to NKCC. The results showed that active coping and retinol A (a dietary source of vitamin A) were associated with improved NKCC and that alcohol use was associated with decreased NKCC. There was a trend for a relationship between focus on and venting emotions and improved NKCC, but no effect for social support, life stressors and emotional distress.

Predicting NKCC

All variables were then entered into the analysis to examine the best predictors of NKCC. The results showed that although the control behaviour variables (diet and alcohol) accounted for most of the variance in NKCC, active coping remained predictive of improved NKCC.

Conclusion

The authors conclude that active coping is related to improved immune functioning in terms of NKCC in HIV-positive men. In addition, immune functioning was also related to diet (vitamin A) and alcohol use. This supports the prediction that psychosocial variables may influence health and illness. However, the results indicate that the link between psychological variables and health status is probably via both a behavioural pathway (i.e. changes in health-related behaviours) *and* a direct physiological pathway (i.e. changes in immune functioning).

Cancer

This section examines what cancer is, looks at its prevalence and then assesses the role of psychology in understanding cancer in terms of the initiation and promotion of cancer, the psychological consequences of cancer, dealing with the symptoms of cancer, longevity and the promotion of a disease-free interval.

What is cancer?

Cancer is defined as an uncontrolled growth of abnormal cells, which produces tumours called neoplasms. There are two types of tumour: *benign* tumours, which do not spread throughout the body, and *malignant* tumours, which show metastasis (the process of cells breaking off from the tumour and moving elsewhere). There are three types of cancer cell: *carcinomas*, which constitute 90 per cent of all cancer cells and which originate in tissue cells; *sarcomas*, which originate in connective tissue; and *leukaemias*, which originate in the blood.

The prevalence of cancer

In 1991, it was reported that there were 6 million new cases of cancer in the world every year, and that one-tenth of all deaths in the world are caused by cancer. In 1989, it was reported that cancers are the second leading cause of death in the UK and accounted for 24 per cent of all deaths in England and Wales in 1984 (Smith and Jacobson 1989). The main causes of cancer mortality among men in England and Wales are lung cancer (36 per cent), colorectal cancer (11 per cent) and prostate cancer (9 per cent); and, among women, breast cancer (20 per cent), lung cancer (15 per cent), colorectal cancer (14 per cent), ovarian cancer (6 per cent) and cervical cancer (3 per cent). While the overall number of cancer deaths does not appear to be rising, the incidence of lung cancer deaths in women has risen over the past few years.

The role of psychology in cancer

A role for psychology in cancer was first suggested by Galen in AD 200–300, who argued for an association between melancholia and cancer, and also by Gedman in 1701, who suggested that cancer might be related to life disasters. Eighty-five per cent of cancers are thought to be potentially avoidable. Psychology therefore plays a role in terms of attitudes and beliefs about cancer and predicting behaviours, such as smoking, diet and screening which are implicated in its initiation (details of these behaviours can be found in Chapters 2, 5, 6, 7, 8 and 9). In addition, sufferers of cancer report psychological consequences, which have implications for their quality of life. The role of psychology in cancer is also illustrated by the following observations:

- Cancer cells are present in most people but not everybody gets cancer; in addition, although research suggests a link between smoking and lung cancer, not all heavy smokers get lung cancer. Perhaps psychology is involved in the susceptibility to cancer.
- All those who have cancer do not always show progression towards death at the same rate. Perhaps psychology has a role to play in the progression of cancer.
- Not all cancer sufferers die of cancer. Perhaps psychology has a role to play in longevity.

The potential role of psychology in understanding cancer is shown in Figure 14.2.

The role of psychology in cancer will now be examined in terms of: (1) the initiation and promotion of cancer; (2) the psychological consequences of cancer; (3) dealing with the symptoms of cancer; and (4) longevity and promoting a disease-free interval.

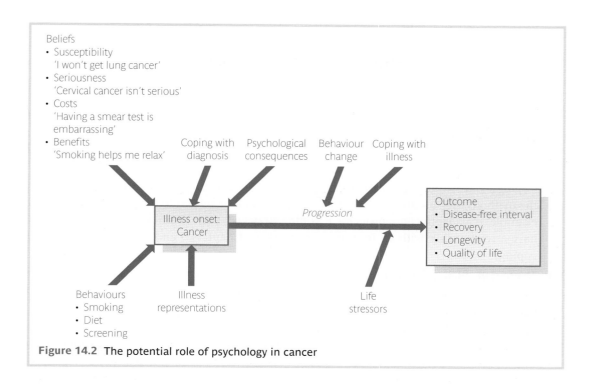

Beliefs
• Susceptibility
  'I won't get lung cancer'
• Seriousness
  'Cervical cancer isn't serious'
• Costs
  'Having a smear test is
  embarrassing'
• Benefits
  'Smoking helps me relax'

Coping with
diagnosis

Psychological
consequences

Behaviour
change

Coping with
illness

Illness onset:
Cancer

Progression

Outcome
• Disease-free interval
• Recovery
• Longevity
• Quality of life

Behaviours
• Smoking
• Diet
• Screening

Illness
representations

Life
stressors

Figure 14.2 The potential role of psychology in cancer

The psychosocial factors in the initiation and promotion of cancer

1 *Behavioural factors.* Behavioural factors have been shown to play a role in the initiation and promotion of cancer. Smith and Jacobson (1989) reported that 30 per cent of cancers are related to tobacco use, 35 per cent are related to diet, 7 per cent are due to reproductive and sexual behaviour and 3 per cent are due to alcohol. These behaviours can be predicted by examining individual health beliefs (see Chapters 2, 5, 6 and 9).

2 *Stress.* Stress has also been shown to have a role to play in cancer. Laudenslager et al. (1983) reported a study that involved exposing cancer-prone mice to stress (shaking the cage). They found that if this stressor could be controlled, there was a decrease in the rate of tumour development. However, if the stressor was perceived as uncontrollable, this resulted in an increase in the development. This suggests a role for stress in the initiation of cancer. However, Sklar and Anisman (1981) argued that an increase in stress increased the promotion of cancer, not its initiation (see Chapter 11 for a discussion of the relationship between stress and illness).

3 *Life events.* It has also been suggested that life events play a role in cancer (see Chapter 10 for a discussion of life events). A study by Jacobs and Charles (1980) examined the differences in life events between families who had a cancer victim and families who did not. They reported that in families who had a cancer victim there were higher numbers who had moved house, higher numbers who had changed some form of their behaviour, higher numbers who had had a change in health status other than the cancer person, and higher numbers of divorces, indicating that life events may well be a factor contributing to the onset of cancer. However, the results from a meta-analysis by Petticrew et al. (1999) do not support this suggestion. They identified 29 studies, from 1966 to 1997, which met their

inclusion criteria (adult women with breast cancer, group of cancer-free controls, measure of stressful life events) and concluded that although several individual studies report a relationship between life events and breast cancer, when methodological problems are taken into account and when the data across the different studies are merged, 'the research shows no good evidence of a relationship between stressful life events and breast cancer'.

4 *Control.* Control also seems to play a role in the initiation and promotion of cancer and it has been argued that control over stressors and control over environmental factors may be related to an increase in the onset of cancer (see Chapter 11 for a discussion of control and the stress–illness link).

5 *Coping styles.* Coping styles are also important. If an individual is subjected to stress, then the methods they use to cope with this stress may well be related to the onset of cancer. For example, maladaptive, disengagement coping strategies, such as smoking and alcohol, may have a relationship with an increase in cancer (see Chapters 3 and 11 for a discussion of coping).

6 *Depression.* Bieliauskas (1980) highlighted a relationship between depression and cancer and suggests that chronic mild depression, but not clinical depression, may be related to cancer.

7 *Personality.* Over the past few years there has been some interest in the relationship between personality and cancer. Temoshok and Fox (1984) argued that individuals who develop cancer have a 'type C personality'. A type C personality is described as passive, appeasing, helpless, other focused and unexpressive of emotion. Eysenck (1990) described 'a cancer-prone personality', and suggests that this is characteristic of individuals who react to stress with helplessness and hopelessness, and individuals who repress emotional reactions to life events. An early study by Kissen (1966) supported this relationship between personality and cancer and reported that heavy smokers who develop lung cancer have a poorly developed outlet for their emotions, perhaps suggesting type C personality. In 1987, Shaffer et al. carried out a prospective study to examine the predictive capacity of personality and its relationship to developing cancer in medical students over 30 years. At follow-up they described the type of individual who was more likely to develop cancer as having impaired self-awareness, being self-sacrificing and self-blaming, and not being emotionally expressive. The results from this study suggest that those individuals who had this type of personality were 16 times more likely to develop cancer than those individuals who did not. However, the relationship between cancer and personality is not a straightforward one. It has been argued that the different personality types predicted to relate to illness are not distinct from each other and also that people with cancer do not consistently differ from either healthy people or people with heart disease in the predicted direction (Amelang and Schmidt-Rathjens 1996).

8 *Hardiness.* Kobasa et al. (1982) described a coping style called 'hardiness', which has three components: control, commitment and challenge. Low control suggests a tendency to show feelings of helplessness in the face of stress. Commitment is defined as the opposite of alienation: individuals high in commitment find meaning in their work, values and personal relationships. Individuals high in challenge regard potentially stressful events as a challenge to be met with expected success. Hardiness may be protective in developing cancer.

Psychological consequences of cancer

Emotional responses

Up to 20 per cent of cancer patients may show severe depression, grief, lack of control, personality change, anger and anxiety. Pinder et al. (1993) examined the emotional responses of women with operable breast cancer and reported that these can differ widely from little disruption of mood to clinical states of depression and anxiety. The emotional state of breast cancer sufferers appears to be unrelated to the type of surgery they have (Kiebert et al. 1991), whether or not they have radiotherapy (Hughson et al. 1987) and is only affected by chemotherapy in the medium term (Hughson et al. 1986). However, persistent deterioration in mood does seem to be related to previous psychiatric history (Dean 1987), lack of social support (Bloom 1983), age, and lack of an intimate relationship (Pinder et al. 1993). Pinder et al. (1993) also reported that in sufferers with advanced cancer, psychological morbidity was related to functional status (how well the patient functioned physically) and suggested that lowered functional status was associated with higher levels of depression, which was also related to lower social class. However, lowered mood is not the only emotional consequence of cancer. Women with breast cancer often report changes in their sense of femininity, attractiveness and body image. This has been shown to be greater in women who have radical mastectomies rather than lumpectomies (e.g. Moyer 1997) and to occur across a range of ethnic groups (e.g. Petronis et al. 2003).

Cognitive responses

Research has also examined cognitive responses to cancer and suggests that a 'fighting spirit' is negatively correlated with anxiety and depression while 'fatalism', 'helplessness' and 'anxious preoccupation' are related to lowered mood (Watson et al. 1991). Taylor (1983) examined the cognitive adaptation of 78 women with breast cancer. She reported that these women responded to their cancer in three ways. First, they made a search for meaning, whereby the cancer patients attempted to understand why they had developed cancer. Meanings that were reported included stress, hereditary factors, ingested carcinogens such as birth control pills, environmental carcinogens such as chemical waste, diet, and a blow to the breast. Second, they also attempted to gain a sense of mastery by believing that they could control their cancer and any relapses. Such attempts at control included meditation, positive thinking, and a belief that the original cause is no longer in effect. Third, the women began a process of self-enhancement. This involved social comparison, whereby the women tended to analyse their condition in terms of others they knew. Taylor argued that they showed 'downward comparison', which involved comparing themselves to others worse off, thus improving their beliefs about their own situation. According to Taylor's theory of cognitive adaptation, the combination of meaning, mastery and self-enhancement creates illusions which are a central component of attempts to cope. This theory is discussed in more detail in Chapter 3.

Psychology and the alleviation of symptoms

Psychology also has a role to play in the alleviation of symptoms of cancer, and in promoting quality of life (see Chapter 16 for a discussion of quality-of-life theory and measurement). Cartwright et al. (1973) described the experiences of cancer sufferers, which included very distressing pain, breathing difficulties, vomiting, sleeplessness, loss of bowel and bladder control, loss of appetite, and mental confusion. Psychosocial interventions have therefore been used to attempt to alleviate some of the symptoms of the cancer sufferer and to improve their quality of life:

1   *Pain management.* One of the main roles of psychology is in terms of pain management, and this has taken place through a variety of different pain management techniques (see Chapter 12). For example, biofeedback and hypnosis have been shown to decrease pain. Turk and Rennert (1981) encouraged patients with cancer to describe and monitor their pain, encouraged them to develop coping skills, taught them relaxation skills, encouraged them to do positive imagery and to focus on other things. They reported that these techniques were successful in reducing the pain experience.

2   *Social support interventions.* Social support interventions have also been used through the provision of support groups, which emphasize control and meaningful activities and aim to reduce denial and promote hope. It has been suggested that although this intervention may not have any effect on longevity, it may improve the meaningfulness of the cancer patient's life. In line with this, Holland and Holahan (2003) explored the relationship between social support, coping and positive adaptation to breast cancer in 56 women. The results showed that higher levels of perceived social support and approach coping strategies were related to positive adjustment.

3   *Treating nausea and vomiting.* Psychology has also been involved in treating the nausea and vomiting experienced by cancer patients. Cancer patients are often offered chemotherapy as a treatment for their cancer, which can cause anticipatory nausea, vomiting and anxiety. Respondent conditioning and visual imagery, relaxation, hypnosis and desensitization have been shown to decrease nausea and anxiety in cancer patients. Redd (1982) and Burish et al. (1987) suggested that 25–33 per cent of cancer patients show conditioned vomiting and 60 per cent show anticipatory anxiety. It is reported that relaxation and guided imagery may decrease these problems.

4   *Body image counselling.* The quality of life of cancer patients may also be improved through altered body image counselling, particularly following the loss of a breast and, more generally, in dealing with the grief at loss of various parts of the body.

5   *Cognitive adaptation strategies.* Research also suggests that quality of life may also be improved using cognitive adaptation strategies. Taylor (1983) used such strategies to improve patients' self-worth, their ability to be close to others, and improvement in the meaningfulness of their lives. Such methods have been suggested to involve self-transcendence and this has again been related to improvement in well-being and decrease in illness-related distresses.

6   *The work of the Simontons.* Simonton and Simonton (1975) are well known for applying psychosocial factors and interventions for improving the quality of life of cancer patients using a whole-person approach. This involves the following processes: (1) relaxation, which aims to decrease muscle tension and therefore decrease pain; (2) mental imagery, whereby cancer patients are encouraged to focus on something positive (this aims to develop a belief in the ability to recover, therefore decreasing pain, tension and fear); and (3) exercise programmes, which aim to increase the sense of well-being. In 1975, Simonton and Simonton encouraged a positive attitude towards treatment using whole-person approach among 152 cancer patients for 18 months, and argued that this intervention predicted a good response to treatment and reduced side effects. These methods are also currently being used at Penny Brohn Cancer Care in the UK.

Adjuvant psychological therapy

Greer et al. (1992) suggested that, in addition to physical interventions, patients with breast cancer should be offered adjuvant psychological therapy. This involves encouraging cancer patients to examine the personal meaning of their cancer and what they can do to cope with it (see **Focus on Research 14.2** on p. 328).

Psychological factors in longevity

The final question about the role of psychology in cancer is its relationship to longevity: do psychosocial factors influence longevity?

Cognitive responses and longevity

Greer et al. (1979) carried out a prospective study in which they examined the relationship between cognitive responses to a breast cancer diagnosis and disease-free intervals. Using semi-structured interviews, they defined three types of responders: those with 'fighting spirit', those who showed denial of the implications of their disease and those who showed a hopeless/helpless response. The authors reported that the groups who showed either 'fighting spirit' or 'denial' had a longer disease-free interval than the other group. In addition, at a further 15-year follow-up, both a fighting spirit and denial approach also predicted longevity. However, there were problems with this study. At baseline the authors did not measure several important physiological prognostic indicators, such as lymph node involvement, as these measures were not available at the time. These physiological factors may have contributed to both the disease-free interval and the survival of the patients. More recently, Gidron et al. (2001) examined the role of hopelessness defined as helplessness and pessimism in predicting changes in breast cancer. Clinical data, measures of hopelessness, life changes and measures of affect were collected at baseline from 49 Israeli women diagnosed with breast cancer. Follow-up data were collected over a four-month period. The results showed that hopelessness was related to aspects of mood. In addition, helplessness (not pessimism) predicted changes in CA15–3, which was used as the marker for breast cancer development.

Life stress and disease-free interval

In a case control study, Ramirez et al. (1989) examined the relationship between life stress and relapse in operable breast cancer. The life events and difficulties occurring during the disease-free interval were recorded in 50 women who had developed their first recurrence of breast cancer and 50 women who were in remission. The two subject groups were matched for the main physical and pathological factors believed to be associated with prognosis and for the sociodemographic variables believed to be related to life events and difficulties. The results showed that life events rated as severe were related to first recurrence of breast cancer. However, the study was cross-sectional in nature, which has implications for determining causality.

Personality/coping style and longevity

In 1991, Eysenck and Grossarth-Maticek reported a study whereby they selected 'at risk' individuals who were healthy (the controls) and another group of individuals (the experimental group) who showed conflict-avoiding and emotion-suppression type personality (a type C/cancer-prone personality). The experimental group received cognitive behavioural therapy in an attempt to change how they dealt with stress. At follow-up, the authors reported that this group showed a decrease in mortality rate compared with the controls who did not receive the

Putting theory into practice – treating cancer symptoms

A randomized controlled trial to examine the effects of adjuvant psychological therapy on the psychological sequelae of cancer (Greer et al. 1992).

Research has examined the psychological consequences of having cancer. This study examined changes in cancer patients' psychological state as a result of adjuvant psychological therapy (APT). The study used a randomized controlled trial design in order to compare changes in measures of quality of life in patients receiving APT with those receiving no therapy.

Background

Evidence suggests that a substantial minority of cancer patients show psychological ill health, particularly in terms of depression and anxiety. As a result, a number of psychotherapeutic procedures have been developed to improve cancer patients' emotional well-being. However, evaluating the effectiveness of such procedures raises several ethical and methodological problems, and these are addressed by Greer et al. (1992). These are: (1) the ethical considerations of having a control group (can patients suffering from psychological distress not be given therapy?); (2) the specificity of any psychological intervention (terms such as counselling and psychotherapy are vague and any procedure being evaluated should be clarified); and (3) the outcome measures chosen (many measures of psychological state include items that are not appropriate for cancer patients, such as weight loss and fatigue, which may change as a result of the cancer, not the individual's psychological state). The authors of this study aimed to examine the effects of APT on the psychological state of cancer patients in the light of these problems.

Methodology

Subjects

A total of 174 patients attending the Royal Marsden Hospital in the UK were recruited for the study using the following criteria: (1) any form of cancer except cerebral tumours and benign skin cancers; (2) a life expectancy of at least 12 months; (3) aged 18–74 years; (4) no obvious intellectual impairments, psychotic illness or suicide risk; (5) residence within 65 km of the hospital; and (6) psychological morbidity defined above a set of cut-off points for anxiety, depression and helplessness, and below a cut-off point for fighting spirit. Altogether, 153 subjects completed the baseline and eight-week measures and 137 completed all measures.

Design

All subjects completed measures of their psychological state at baseline. They were then allocated to either the experimental group (and received eight weeks of APT) or the control group. The subjects then completed follow-up measures at eight weeks and four months.

Measures

Subjects completed the following measures at baseline (before randomization), at eight weeks' and four months' follow-up:

- *The hospital anxiety and depression scale.*
- *The mental adjustment to cancer scale*: this measures four dimensions of adjustment – fighting spirit, helplessness, anxious preoccupation and fatalism.

- *The psychosocial adjustment to illness scale*: this measures health-care orientation, work adjustment, domestic environment, sexual relationships, extended family relationships, the social environment, psychological distress.
- *Rotterdam symptom checklist*: this measures quality of life in terms of both physical and psychological symptoms.

The intervention

The subjects were randomly allocated to either the experimental (APT) or the control group. ATP is a cognitive behavioural treatment developed specifically for cancer patients. Therapy involved approximately eight one-hour weekly sessions with individual patients and their spouses (if appropriate). However, many patients in the present study did not attend all these sessions and several received additional sessions throughout the four months. The therapy focused on the personal meaning of the cancer for the patient, examined their coping strategies and emphasized the current problems defined jointly by the therapist and the patient. APT uses the following cognitive behavioural techniques:

- Identifying the patient's strengths and using these to develop self-esteem, overcome feelings of helplessness and promote fighting spirit.
- Teaching patients to identify any automatic thoughts underlying their anxiety and depression and developing means to challenge these thoughts.
- Teaching patients how to use imagination and role play as a means of coping with stressors.
- Encouraging patients to carry out activities that give them a sense of pleasure and achievement in order to promote a sense of control.
- Encouraging expression of emotions and open communication.
- Teaching relaxation to control anxiety.

Results

The results showed that at eight weeks the patients receiving the APT had significantly higher scores on fighting spirit and significantly lower scores on helplessness, anxious preoccupation, fatalism, anxiety, psychological symptoms and orientation towards health care than the control patients. At four months, patients receiving the APT had significantly lower scores than the controls on anxiety, psychological symptoms and psychological distress.

Conclusion

The authors concluded that APT improves the psychological well-being of cancer patients who show increased psychological problems and that some of these improvements persist for up to four months. They suggest that APT relates to 'improvement in the psychological dimension of the quality of life of cancer patients'.

cognitive behavioural therapy. In a further study by Temoshok and Fox (1984), the results from a 15-year follow-up of women with breast cancer indicated that poor outcome was associated with a passive, helpless coping style. However, it has been questioned as to whether the personality styles predicted to be associated with different illnesses are distinct (Amelang and Schmidt-Rathjens 1996).

There is no relationship between psychological factors and longevity

However, not all research has pointed to an association between psychological factors and longevity. Barraclough et al. (1992) measured severe life events, social difficulties and depression at baseline in a group of breast cancer patients, and followed them up after 42 months. Of a total of 204 subjects, 26 died and 23 per cent relapsed. However, the results showed no relationship between these outcomes and the psychosocial factors measured at baseline. These results caused debate in the light of earlier studies and it has been suggested that the absence of a relationship between life events and outcome may be due to the older age of the women in Barraclough and co-workers' study, the short follow-up period used, and the unreported use of chemotherapy (Ramirez et al. 1992).

To conclude

Psychology appears to have a role to play in understanding cancer, not only in terms of beliefs and behaviours, which may be related to the onset of cancer, but also in terms of psychological consequences, the treatment of symptoms, improving quality of life, disease-free intervals and longevity.

❓ Questions

1 Discuss the role of psychological factors in the progression to full-blown AIDS.

2 To what extent is the transmission of the HIV virus due to a lack of knowledge?

3 AIDS kills. Discuss.

4 Discuss the factors that may explain why patients do not take their medication for AIDS.

5 Describe the role of psychology in cancer onset.

6 Discuss the role of psychological factors in a disease-free interval following a diagnosis of breast cancer.

7 To what extent do psychological factors relate to the recovery from cancer?

For discussion

Do you know anyone who has had either HIV or cancer? Think about how psychological factors such as behaviour, beliefs and coping influenced their state of health.

Assumptions in health psychology

An examination of the role of psychological factors in illness highlights some of the assumptions in health psychology:

1 *The mind–body split.* By examining the role of psychology in illness, it is implicitly assumed that psychology and illness (the body) are separate. This promotes a model of an individual who has a physical and a mental world which interact but are separate. Although this interaction is an attempt at a holistic approach to health and illness, it is still intrinsically dualistic.

2 *Correlational studies.* Many of the research studies carried out in health psychology are cross-sectional (i.e. they examine the relationship between variables measured at the same time). For example, 'What is the relationship between coping style and immune status?', and 'What is the relationship between life stressors and illness?' Studies using cross-sectional designs often make statements about causality (e.g. 'coping style causes changes in immune status', 'stressors cause illness'). However, it is quite possible that the relationship between these variables is either causal in the opposite direction (e.g. illness causes high reports of stressors, 'I am now ill and remember the last six months differently'), or non-existent (e.g. 'I am ill and I have had lots of stressful events in my life recently but they are unrelated' (the third variable problem)). Prospective studies are used as an attempt to solve this problem, but even prospective studies only examine the correlation between variables – it is still difficult to talk about causality.

Further reading

Barraclough, J. (2000) *Cancer and Emotion: A Practical Guide To Psycho-oncology*. Chichester: Wiley.
This book provides a thorough and accessible review of the research and theories exploring links between psychological factors and cancer in terms of cancer onset, progression and recovery.

Mulder, C.L. and Antoni, M.H. (1992) Psychosocial correlates of immune status and disease progression in HIV-1 infected homosexual men: review of preliminary findings and commentary, *Psychology and Health*, 6: 175–92.
This paper reviews the literature on the role of behavioural and psychological factors in the course of HIV infection. It is also a good introduction to psychoneuroimmunology.

Vedhara, K. and Irwin, M. (eds) (2005) *Human Psychoneuroimmunology*. Oxford: Oxford University Press.
This book provides an excellent up-to-date overview of the research on PNI and covers key concepts, research and methods.

Obesity and coronary heart disease

Psychology throughout the course of illness (2)

Chapter overview

This chapter illustrates the role of psychology throughout the course of illness with a focus on obesity and coronary heart disease. It first examines the definitions of obesity, its prevalence and potential consequences. It then examines the role of physiological factors and behaviour in causing obesity. The chapter then explores obesity treatment, raising the question 'should obesity be treated at all?' Next, the chapter looks at coronary heart disease. It describes what it is and how it is defined and then looks at the role of psychology in its aetiology. Finally, it explores the role of psychology in treatment and rehabilitation.

This chapter covers

- What is obesity?
- What causes obesity?
- Obesity treatment
- Should obesity be treated at all?
- What is coronary heart disease?
- The role of psychology in coronary heart disease onset
- Predicting and changing behavioural risk factors
- Psychology and the rehabilitation of patients

Obesity

The role of psychological factors in obesity

This section explores what obesity is and then examines the role of psychology in understanding obesity in terms of its consequences, causes and treatment. The potential role of psychological factors in obesity is illustrated in Figure 15.1.

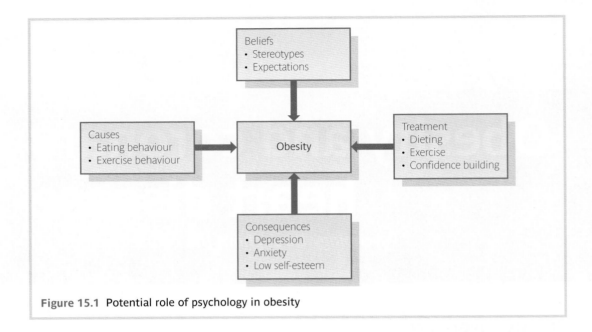

Figure 15.1 Potential role of psychology in obesity

What is obesity?

Obesity can be defined in a number of ways:

- *Population means.* Population means involves exploring mean weights, given a specific population, and deciding whether someone is below average weight, average or above average in terms of percentage overweight. Stunkard (1984) suggested that obesity should be categorized as either mild (20–40 per cent overweight), moderate (41–100 per cent overweight) or severe (100 per cent overweight) obesity. This approach is problematic as it depends on which population is being considered – someone could be obese in India but not in the USA.

- *BMI.* Body mass index (BMI) is calculated using the equation weight (kg)/height (m²). This produces a figure that has been categorized as normal weight (20–24.9) overweight (grade 1, 25–29.9); clinical obesity (grade 2, 30–39.9); and severe obesity (grade 3, 40) (see Figure 15.2). This is the most frequently used definition of obesity. However, it does not allow for differences in weight between muscle and fat – a bodybuilder would be considered obese.

- *Waist circumference.* BMI is the most frequently used measure of obesity but it does not allow for an analysis of the location of fat. This is important as some problems such as diabetes are predicted by abdominal fat rather than lower body fat. Researchers originally used waist:hip ratios to assess obesity but recently waist circumference on its own has become the preferred approach. Weight reduction is recommended when waist circumference is greater than 102 cm in men and greater than 88 cm in women (Lean et al. 1995, 1998). A reduction in waist circumference is associated with a reduction in cardiovascular risk factors and abdominal obesity is associated with insulin resistance and the development of type 2 diabetes (Chan et al. 1994; Han et al. 1997). Waist circumference has been suggested as the basis for routine screening in primary care (Despres et al. 2001) although Little and Byrne (2001) have argued that more evidence is needed before such a programme should be implemented.

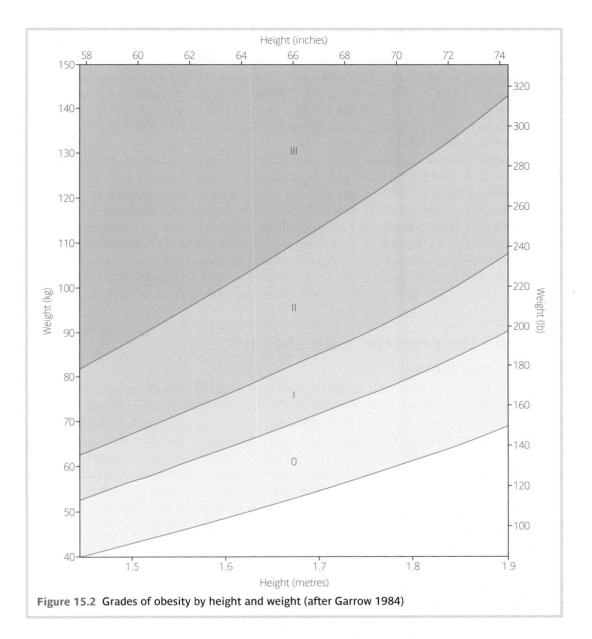

Figure 15.2 Grades of obesity by height and weight (after Garrow 1984)

■ *Percentage body fat.* As health is mostly associated with fat rather than weight *per se*, researchers and clinicians have also developed methods of measuring percentage body fat directly. At its most basic this involves assessing skinfold thickness using callipers normally around the upper arm and upper and lower back. This is not suitable for those individuals who are severely obese and misses abdominal fat. At a more advanced level, body fat can be measured using bioelectrical impedence which involves passing an electrical current between a person's hand and foot. As water conducts electricity and fat is an insulator, the impedence of the current can be used to calculate the ratio between water and fat and therefore an overall estimate of percentage body fat can be made.

How common is obesity?

In the UK the rates of obesity are on the increase. If obesity is defined as a BMI greater than 30, reports show that in 1980, 6 per cent of men and 8 per cent of women were obese and that this had increased to 13 per cent and 16 per cent in 1994 and to 18 per cent and 24 per cent respectively by 2005. For children in England, Chinn and Rona (2001) reported that in 1994, 9 per cent of boys and 13.5 per cent girls were overweight, that 1.7 per cent of boys and 2.6 per cent of girls were obese and that these figures were more than 50 per cent higher than ten years earlier. Estimates for the USA suggest that roughly half of American adults are overweight, that a third are obese, that women have grown particularly heavier in recent years and that the prevalence of overweight children has doubled in the past 20 years (Ogden et al. 1997d; National Institutes of Health 1998). Across the world, the highest rates of obesity are found in Tunisia, the USA, Saudi Arabia and Canada, and the lowest are found in China, Mali, Japan, Sweden and Brazil; the UK, Australia and New Zealand are all placed in the middle of the range. Across Europe the highest rates are in Lithuania, Malta, Russia and Serbia and the lowest are in Sweden, Ireland, Denmark and the UK. Overall, people in Northern and Western Europe are thinner than Eastern and Southern Europe and women are more likely to be obese than men.

What are the problems with obesity?

Physical problems

Obesity has been associated with cardiovascular disease, diabetes, joint trauma, back pain, cancer, hypertension and mortality. The effects of obesity are related to where the excess weight is carried; weight stored in the upper body, particularly in the abdomen, is more detrimental to health than weight carried on the lower body. It is interesting to note that although men are more likely than women to store fat on their upper bodies, and are therefore more at risk if obese, women are more concerned about weight than men and most treatment studies examine women. The relationship between BMI and mortality is shown in Figure 15.3. It has been suggested that most problems seem to be associated with severe obesity and weights in the top 10 per cent (Wooley and Wooley 1984); however, a study of 14,077 women indicated a direct linear relationship between BMI and risk factors for heart disease including blood pressure, cholesterol and blood glucose (Ashton et al. 2001). Similar studies have also reported a relationship between BMI increases in the lower range of the spectrum and hypertension (National Institutes of Health 1998), diabetes (Ford et al. 1997) and heart attack (Willett et al. 1995) (see Romero-Corral et al. 2006 for a systematic review of the literature).

Psychological problems

Research has examined the relationship between psychological problems and obesity. The contemporary cultural obsession with thinness, the aversion to fat found in both adults and children and the attribution of blame to the obese may promote low self-esteem and poor self-image in those individuals who do not conform to the stereotypically attractive thin image. Some studies have explored levels of depression in those waiting for surgical treatment for their obesity and consistently show that such patients report more depressive symptoms than average-weight individuals (e.g. Bull et al. 1983; Wadden et al. 1986). In addition, Rand and MacGregor (1991) concluded that individuals who had lost weight following gastric bypass surgery stated that they would rather be deaf, dyslexic, diabetic, or have heart disease or acne

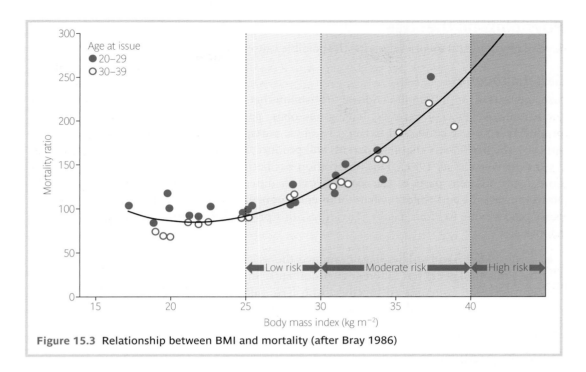

Figure 15.3 Relationship between BMI and mortality (after Bray 1986)

than return to their former weight. More recently, Simon et al. (2006) carried out a large survey on over 9000 adults in the USA and concluded that obesity was associated with increased life-time diagnosis of major depression, bipolar disorder, panic disorder or agoraphobia. In line with this, Ogden and Clementi (in press) carried out a qualitative study of the experience of being obese and reported that the obese describe a multitude of negative ways in which their weight impacts upon their self-identity which is exacerbated by living in a society that stigma-tizes their condition. However, it is possible that depressed obese individuals are more likely to seek treatment for their obesity than the ones who are not depressed and that there may be many obese individuals who are quite happy and therefore do not come into contact with health professionals. Ross (1994) addressed this possibility and interviewed a random sample of more than 2000 adults by telephone. These were individuals who varied in weight and were not necessarily in the process of seeking help for any weight-related issues. The results from this large-scale study showed that overweight was unrelated to depression. There was a small sub-group in Ross's study who were both overweight and depressed who tended to be the most edu-cated. Ross argued that these individuals were also dieting to lose weight and that it was the attempt to lose weight rather than the weight *per se* that was distressing. Therefore, although many obese people may experience their obesity in negative ways, there is no consistent support for a simple relationship between body size and psychological problems.

What causes obesity?

The theories relating to the causes of obesity include both physiological theories and behav-ioural theories.

Physiological theories

Several physiological theories describe the possible causes of obesity.

Genetic theories

Size appears to run in families and the probability that a child will be overweight is related to the parents' weight. For example, having one obese parent results in a 40 per cent chance of producing an obese child, and having two obese parents results in an 80 per cent chance. In contrast, the probability that thin parents will produce overweight children is very small, about 7 per cent (Garn et al. 1981). This observation has been repeated in studies exploring populations from different parts of the world living in different environments (Maes et al. 1997). However, parents and children share both environment and genetic constitution, so this likeness could be due to either factor. To address this problem, research has examined twins and adoptees.

- *Twin studies.* Twin studies have examined the weight of identical twins reared apart, who have identical genes but different environments. Studies have also examined the weights of non-identical twins reared together, who have different genes but similar environments. The results show that the identical twins reared apart are more similar in weight than non-identical twins reared together. For example, Stunkard et al. (1990) examined the BMI in 93 pairs of identical twins reared apart and reported that genetic factors accounted for 66–70 per cent in the variance in their body weight, suggesting a strong genetic component in determining obesity. However, the role of genetics appears to be greater in lighter twin pairs than in heavier pairs.

- *Adoptee studies.* Research has also examined the role of genetics in obesity using adoptees. Such studies compare the adoptees' weight with both their adoptive parents and their biological parents. Stunkard, Sorensen et al. (1986) gathered information about 540 adult adoptees in Denmark, their adopted parents and their biological parents. The results showed a strong relationship between the weight class of the adoptee (thin, median weight, overweight, obese) and their biological parents' weight class but no relationship with their adoptee parents' weight class. This relationship suggests a major role for genetics and was also found across the whole range of body weight. Interestingly, the relationship to biological mother's weight was greater than the relationship with the biological father's weight.

Research therefore suggests a strong role for genetics in predicting obesity. Research also suggests that the primary distribution of this weight (upper versus lower body) is also inherited (Bouchard et al. 1990). However, how this genetic predisposition expresses itself is unclear. *Metabolic rate*, the *number of fat cells* and *appetite regulation* may be three factors influenced by genetics.

Metabolic rate theory

The body uses energy for exercise and physical activity and to carry out all the chemical and biological processes that are essential to being alive (e.g. respiration, heart rate, blood pressure). The rate of this energy use is called the 'resting metabolic rate', which has been found to be highly heritable (Bouchard et al. 1990). It has been argued that lower metabolic rates may be associated with obesity as people with lower metabolic rates burn up less calories when they are resting and therefore require less food intake to carry on living.

Research in the USA has evaluated the relationship between metabolic rate and weight gain. A group in Phoenix assessed the metabolic rates of 126 Pima Indians by monitoring their breathing for a 40-minute period. The study was carried out using Pima Indians because they have an abnormally high rate of obesity (about 80–85 per cent) and were considered an interesting population. The subjects remained still and the levels of oxygen consumed and carbon dioxide produced was measured. The researchers then followed any changes in weight and metabolic rate for a four-year period and found that the people who gained a substantial amount of weight were the ones with the lowest metabolic rates at the beginning of the study. In a further study, 95 subjects spent 24 hours in a respiratory chamber and the amount of energy used was measured. The subjects were followed up two years later and the researchers found that those who had originally shown a low level of energy use were four times more likely to also show a substantial weight increase (cited in Brownell 1989).

These results suggest a relationship between metabolic rate and the tendency for weight gain. If this is the case, then it is possible that some individuals are predisposed to become obese because they require fewer calories to survive than thinner individuals. Therefore a genetic tendency to be obese may express itself in lowered metabolic rates. However, in apparent contrast to this prediction, there is no evidence to suggest that obese people generally have lower metabolic rates than thin people. In fact, research suggests that overweight people tend to have slightly higher metabolic rates than thin people of similar height. To explain these apparently contradictory findings it has been suggested that obese people may have lower metabolic rates to start with, which results in weight gain and this weight gain itself results in an increase in metabolic rate (Ravussin and Bogardus 1989).

Fat cell theory

A genetic tendency to be obese may also express itself in terms of the number of fat cells. People of average weight usually have about 25–35 billion fat cells, which are designed for the storage of fat in periods of energy surplus and the mobilization of fat in periods of energy deficit. Mildly obese individuals usually have the same number of fat cells but they are enlarged in size and weight. Severely obese individuals, however, have more fat cells – up to 100–125 billion (Sjostrom 1980). Cell number is mainly determined by genetics; however, when the existing number of cells have been used up, new fat cells are formed from pre-existing preadipocytes. Most of this growth in the number of cells occurs during gestation and early childhood and remains stable once adulthood has been reached. Although the results from studies in this area are unclear, it would seem that if an individual is born with more fat cells, then there are more cells immediately available to fill up. In addition, research suggests that, once fat cells have been made, they can never be lost (Sjostrom 1980). An obese person with a large number of fat cells may be able to empty these cells but will never be able to get rid of them.

Appetite regulation

A genetic predisposition may also be related to appetite control. Over recent years researchers have attempted to identify the gene, or collection of genes, responsible for obesity. Although some work using small animals has identified a single gene that is associated with profound obesity, for humans the work is still unclear. Two children have, however, been identified with a defect in the 'ob gene', which produces leptin which is responsible for telling the brain to stop eating (Montague et al. 1997). It has been argued that the obese may not produce leptin and therefore overeat. To support this, researchers have given these two children daily injections of leptin, which has resulted in a decrease in food intake and weight loss at a rate of 1–2 kg per month (Farooqi et al. 1999). Despite this, the research exploring the role of genetics on appetite control is still in the very early stages.

Behavioural theories

Behavioural theories of obesity have examined both physical activity and eating behaviour.

Physical activity

Increases in the prevalence of obesity coincide with decreases in daily energy expenditure due to improvements in transport systems, and a shift from an agricultural society to an industrial and increasingly information-based society. As a simple example, a telephone company in the USA has suggested that in the course of one year an extension phone saves an individual approximately one mile of walking, which could be the equivalent of 2–3 lb of fat or up to 10,500 kcals (Stern 1984). Further, at present only 20 per cent of men and 10 per cent of women are employed in active occupations (Allied Dunbar National Fitness Survey 1992) and for many people leisure times are dominated by inactivity (Central Statistical Office 1994). Although data on changes in activity levels are problematic, there exists a useful database on television viewing which shows that, whereas the average viewer in the 1960s watched 13 hours of television per week, in England this has now doubled to 26 hours per week (*General Household Survey* 1994). This is further exacerbated by the increased use of videos and computer games by both children and adults. It has therefore been suggested that obesity may be caused by inactivity. In a survey of adolescent boys in Glasgow in 1964 and 1971, whereas daily food diaries indicated a decrease in daily energy intake from 2795 kcals to 2610 kcals, the boys in 1971 showed an increase in body fat from 16.3 per cent to 18.4 per cent. This suggests that decreased physical activity was related to increased body fat (Durnin et al. 1974). To examine the role of physical activity in obesity, research has asked, 'Are changes in obesity related to changes in activity?', 'Do the obese exercise less?', 'What effect does exercise have on food intake?' and 'What effect does exercise have on energy expenditure?' These questions will now be examined.

Are changes in obesity related to changes in activity?

This question can be answered in two ways, first using epidemiological data on a population; and second, using prospective data on individuals.

In 1995, Prentice and Jebb presented epidemiological data on changes in physical activity from 1950 to 1990, as measured by car ownership and television viewing, and compared these with changes in the prevalence of obesity. The results from this study suggested a strong association between an increase in both car ownership and television viewing and an increase in obesity (see Figure 15.4). They commented that 'it seems reasonable to conclude that the low levels of physical activity now prevalent in Britain must play an important, perhaps dominant role in the development of obesity by greatly reducing energy needs' (Prentice and Jebb 1995). However, their data were only correlational. Therefore it remains unclear whether obesity and physical activity are related (the third factor problem – some other variable may be determining both obesity and activity) and whether decreases in activity cause increases in obesity or whether, in fact, increases in obesity actually cause decreases in activity. In addition, the data are at the population level and therefore could miss important individual differences (i.e. some people who become obese could be active and those who are thin could be inactive).

In an alternative approach to assessing the relationship between activity and obesity a large Finnish study of 12,000 adults examined the association between levels of physical activity and excess weight gain over a five-year follow-up period (Rissanen et al. 1991). The results showed that lower levels of activity were a greater risk factor for weight gain than any other baseline measures. However, although these data were prospective, it is still possible that a third factor may explain the relationship (i.e. those with lower levels of activity at baseline were women, the

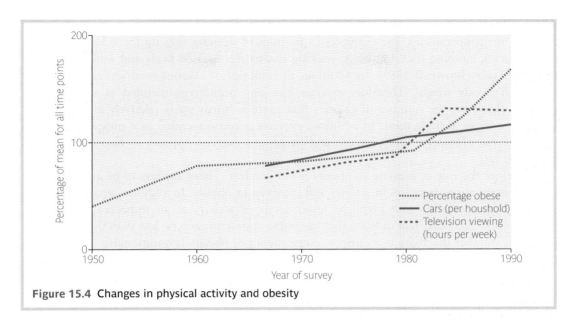

Figure 15.4 Changes in physical activity and obesity

women had children and therefore put on more weight). Unless experimental data are collected, conclusions about causality remain problematic.

Do the obese exercise less?

Research has also examined the relationship between activity and obesity using a cross-sectional design to examine differences between the obese and non-obese. In particular, several studies in the 1960s and 1970s examined whether the obese exercised less than the non-obese. Using time-lapse photography, Bullen et al. (1964) observed girls considered obese and those of normal weight on a summer camp. They reported that during swimming the obese girls spent less time swimming and more time floating, and while playing tennis the obese girls were inactive for 77 per cent of the time compared with the girls of normal weight, who were inactive for only 56 per cent of the time. In addition, research indicates that the obese walk less on a daily basis than the non-obese and are less likely to use stairs or walk up escalators. However, whether reduced exercise is a cause or a consequence of obesity is unclear. It is possible that the obese take less exercise due to factors such as embarrassment and stigma and that exercise plays a part in the maintenance of obesity but not in its cause.

What effect does exercise have on food intake?

The relationship between exercise and food intake is complex, with research suggesting that exercise may increase, decrease or have no effect on eating behaviour. For example, a study of middle-aged male joggers who ran approximately 65 km per week suggested that increased calorie intake was related to increased exercise with the joggers eating more than the sedentary control group (Blair et al. 1981). However, another study of military cadets reported that decreased food intake was related to increased exercise (Edholm et al. 1955). Much research has also been carried out on rats, which shows a more consistent relationship between increased exercise and decreased food intake. However, the extent to which such results can be generalized to humans is questionable.

What effect does exercise have on energy expenditure?

Exercise burns up calories. For example, 10 minutes of sleeping uses up to 16 kcals, standing uses 19 kcals, running uses 142 kcals, walking downstairs uses 88 kcals and walking upstairs uses 229 kcals (Brownell 1989). In addition, the amount of calories used increases with the individual's body weight. Therefore exercise has long been recommended as a weight loss method. However, the number of calories that exercise burns up is relatively few compared with those in an average meal. In addition, exercise is recommended as a means to increase metabolic rate. However, only intense and prolonged exercise appears to have an effect on metabolic rate.

Therefore the role of exercise in obesity is still unclear. There appears to be an association between population decreases in activity and increases in obesity. In addition, prospective data support this association and highlight lower levels of activity as an important risk factor. Further, cross-sectional data indicate that the obese appear to exercise less than the non-obese. However, whether inactivity is a cause or consequence of obesity is questionable. It is possible that an unidentified third factor may be creating this association, and it is also debatable whether exercise has a role in reducing food intake and promoting energy expenditure. However, exercise may have psychological and general health effects, which could benefit the obese either in terms of promoting weight loss or simply by making them feel better about themselves (see Chapter 7 for the effects of exercise on mood and health).

Eating behaviour

In an alternative approach to understanding the causes of obesity, research has examined eating behaviour. Research has asked, 'Are changes in food intake associated with changes in obesity?', 'Do the obese eat for different reasons than the non-obese?' and 'Do the obese eat more than the non-obese?' These questions will now be examined.

Are changes in food intake associated with changes in obesity?

The UK National Food Survey collects data on food intake in the home, which can be analysed to assess changes in food intake over the past 50 years. The results from this database illustrate that, although overall calorie consumption increased between 1950 and 1970, since 1970 there has been a distinct decrease in the amount we eat (see Figure 15.5).

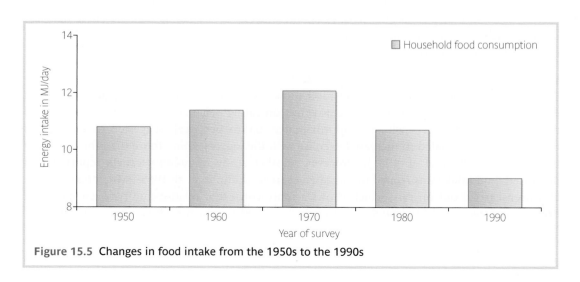

Figure 15.5 Changes in food intake from the 1950s to the 1990s

Prentice and Jebb (1995) examined the association between changes in food intake in terms of energy intake and fat intake and changes in obesity. Their results indicated no obvious association between the increase in obesity and the changes in food intake (see Figure 15.6).

Therefore, using population data, there appears to be no relationship between changes in food intake and changes in obesity.

Do the obese eat for different reasons than the non-obese?

Throughout the 1960s and 1970s theories of eating behaviour emphasized the role of food intake in predicting weight. Original studies of obesity were based on the assumption that the obese ate for different reasons than people of normal weight (Ferster et al. 1962). Schachter's externality theory suggested that, although all people were responsive to environmental stimuli such as the sight, taste and smell of food, and that such stimuli might cause overeating, the obese were highly and sometimes uncontrollably responsive to external cues. It was argued that normal-weight individuals mainly ate as a response to internal cues (e.g. hunger, satiety) and obese individuals tended to be underresponsive to their internal cues and overresponsive to external cues. Within this perspective, research examined the eating behaviour and eating style of the obese and non-obese in response to external cues such as the time of day, the sight of food, the taste of food and the number and salience of food cues (e.g. Schachter 1968; Schachter and Gross 1968; Schachter and Rodin 1974). The results from these studies produced fairly inconsistent results. Therefore research also examined whether the obese ate more than the non-obese.

Do the obese eat more than the non-obese?

Research exploring the amount eaten by the obese has either focused on the amount consumed *per se* or on the type of food consumed.

Because it was believed that the obese ate for different reasons than the non-obese, it was also believed that they ate more. Research therefore explored the food intake of the obese in restaurants and at home, and examined what food they bought. For example, Coates et al. (1978) suggested that perhaps the obese were overeating at home and went into the homes of

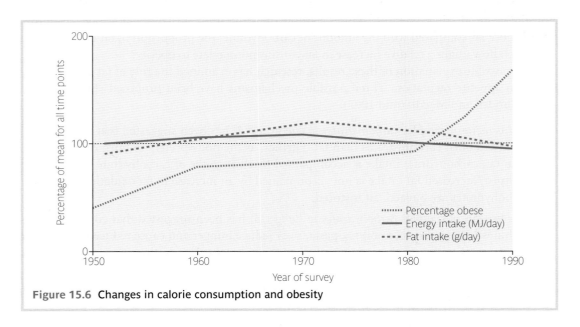

Figure 15.6 Changes in calorie consumption and obesity

60 middle-class families to examine what was stored in their cupboards. They weighed all members of the families and found no relationship between body size and the mass and type of food they consumed at home. In an attempt to clarify the problem of whether the obese eat more than the non-obese, Spitzer and Rodin (1981) examined the research into eating behaviour and suggested that 'of twenty-nine studies examining the effects of body weight on amount eaten in laboratory studies . . . only nine reported that overweight subjects ate significantly more than their lean counterparts'. Therefore the answer to the question 'Do the obese eat more/ differently to the non-obese?' appears to be 'no'; the obese do not necessarily overeat (compared with others). If overeating is defined as 'compared with what the body needs', it could be argued that the obese overeat because they have excess body fat. Over recent years, research has focused on the eating behaviour of the obese not in terms of calories consumed, or in terms of amount eaten, but more specifically in terms of the type of food eaten.

Population data indicate that calorie consumption has decreased since the 1970s and that this decrease is unrelated to the increase in obesity (see Figures 15.5 and 15.6). However, these data also show that the ratio between carbohydrate consumption and fat consumption has changed; whereas we now eat less carbohydrate, we eat proportionally more fat (Prentice and Jebb 1995). One theory that has been developed is that, although the obese may not eat more than the non-obese overall, they may eat proportionally more fat. Further, it has been argued that not all calories are equal (Prentice 1995) and that calories from fat may lead to greater weight gain than calories from carbohydrates. To support this theory, one study of 11,500 people in Scotland showed that men consuming the lowest proportion of carbohydrate in their diets were four times more likely to be obese than those consuming the highest proportion of carbohydrate. A similar relationship was also found for women, although the difference was only two- to three-fold. Therefore it was concluded that relatively lower carbohydrate consumption is related to lower levels of obesity (Bolton-Smith and Woodward 1994). A similar study in Leeds also provided support for the fat proportion theory of obesity (Blundell and Macdiarmid 1997). This study reported that high fat eaters who derived more than 45 per cent of their energy from fat were 19 times more likely to be obese than those who derived less than 35 per cent of their energy from fat. Therefore these studies suggest that the obese do not eat more overall than the non-obese, nor do they eat more calories, carbohydrate or fat *per se* than the non-obese. But they do eat more fat compared with the amount of carbohydrate; the proportion of fat in their diet is higher. So how might a relative increase in fat consumption relate to obesity?

As a possible explanation of these results, research has examined the role of fat and carbohydrates in appetite regulation. Three possible mechanisms have been proposed (Blundell et al. 1996; Blundell and Macdiarmid 1997):

1 *The benefits of complex carbohydrates to energy use.* It has been suggested that it takes more energy to burn carbohydrates than fat. Further, as the body prefers to burn carbohydrates than fat, carbohydrate intake is accompanied by an increase of carbohydrate oxidation. In contrast, increased fat intake is not accompanied by an increase in fat oxidation. Therefore carbohydrates are burned, fat is stored.

2 *The benefits of complex carbohydrates to hunger.* It has been suggested that complex carbohydrates (such as bread, potatoes, pasta, rice) reduce hunger and cause reduced food intake due to their bulk and the amount of fibre they contain. In addition, they switch off the desire to eat. Therefore carbohydrates make you feel fuller faster.

3 *The costs of fat to hunger.* It has been suggested that fat does not switch off the desire to eat, making it easier to eat more and more fat without feeling full.

What does all this research mean?

The evidence for the causes of obesity is therefore complex and can be summarized as follows:

- There is good evidence for a genetic basis to obesity. The evidence for how this is expressed is weak.
- The prevalence of obesity has increased at a similar rate to decreases in physical activity.
- There is some evidence that the obese exercise less than the non-obese.
- The prevalence of obesity has increased at a rate unrelated to the overall decrease in calorie consumption.
- There is no evidence that the obese eat more calories than the non-obese.
- The relative increase in fat is parallel to the increase in obesity.
- The obese may eat proportionally more fat than the non-obese.

Therefore the following points would seem likely:

- Some individuals have a genetic tendency to be obese.
- Obesity is related to underexercise.
- Obesity is related to consuming relatively more fat and relatively less carbohydrates.

Therefore the causes of obesity remain complex and unclear. Perhaps an integration of all theories is needed before proper conclusions can be drawn.

Box 15.1 Some problems with . . . obesity and CHD research

Below are some problems with research in this area that you may wish to consider.

1 Measuring and defining obesity is problematic as it relies upon assessments of body weight and body size, whereas the factor that is most linked to health status is probably body fat. Therefore research can show contradictory evidence for the consequences of obesity which probably illustrate the drawbacks of using proxy measures (i.e. BMI and waist circumference) for what the real measurement should be (i.e. body fat).

2 Obesity is a product of biological factors (e.g. genetics), social factors (e.g. the food industry, town planning) and psychological factors (e.g. diet, exercise, beliefs). Research tends to focus on the contribution of one set of these factors. How they all interact remains unclear. This means that most research misses the complexity of the obesity problem. However, if research were to try to address all these factors the studies would become unwieldy and the conclusions would be too complex to put into practice.

3 CHD illustrates the impact of stress and behaviour on illness. Research focuses on how these factors can predict CHD and how they can be changed to prevent the development of CHD or prevent the reoccurrence of a myocardial infarction in the future. Central to this is the measurement of stress and behaviour which are problematic due to the reliance upon self-report. This may be particularly biased if a person has been identified as having CHD and wishes to seem to be compliant with any recommendations they have been given by their health professional.

Obesity treatment

Traditional treatment approaches

The traditional treatment approach to obesity was a corrective one, the assumption being that obesity was a product of overeating and underactivity. Treatment approaches therefore focused on encouraging the obese to eat 'normally' and this consistently involved putting them on a diet. Stuart (1967) and Stuart and Davis (1972) developed a behavioural programme for obesity involving monitoring food intake, modifying cues for inappropriate eating and encouraging self-reward for appropriate behaviour, which was widely adopted by hospitals and clinics. The programme aimed to encourage eating in response to physiological hunger and not in response to mood cues such as boredom or depression, or in response to external cues such as the sight and smell of food or the sight of other people eating. In 1958, Stunkard concluded his review of the past 30 years' attempts to promote weight loss in the obese with the statement, 'Most obese persons will not stay in treatment for obesity. Of those who stay in treatment, most will not lose weight, and of those who do lose weight, most will regain it' (Stunkard 1958). More recent evaluations of their effectiveness indicate that although traditional behavioural therapies may lead to initial weight losses of, on average, 0.5 kg per week (Brownell and Wadden 1992), 'weight losses achieved by behavioural treatments for obesity are not well maintained'.

However, it is now generally accepted that obesity is not simply a behavioural problem and, as Brownell and Steen said somewhat optimistically in 1987, 'psychological problems are no longer inferred simply because an individual is overweight'. Therefore traditional behavioural programmes make some unsubstantiated assumptions about the causes of obesity by encouraging the obese to eat 'normally' like individuals of normal weight.

Multidimensional behavioural programmes

The failure of traditional treatment packages for obesity resulted in longer periods of treatment, an emphasis on follow-up and the introduction of a multidimensional perspective to obesity treatment. Recent comprehensive, multidimensional cognitive behavioural packages aim to broaden the perspective for obesity treatment and combine traditional self-monitoring methods with information, exercise, cognitive restructuring, attitude change and relapse prevention (e.g. Brownell 1990). Brownell and Wadden (1991) emphasized the need for a multidimensional approach, the importance of screening patients for entry onto a treatment programme and the need to match the individual with the most appropriate package. State-of-the-art behavioural treatment programmes aim to encourage the obese to eat less than they do usually rather than encouraging them to eat less than the non-obese. Analysis of the effectiveness of this treatment approach suggests that average weight loss during the treatment programme is 0.5 kg per week, that approximately 60–70 per cent of the weight loss is maintained during the first year but that follow-up at three and five years tends to show weight gains back to baseline weight (Brownell and Wadden 1992). In a comprehensive review of the treatment interventions for obesity, Wilson (1994) suggested that although there has been an improvement in the effectiveness of obesity treatment since the 1970s, success rates are still poor.

Wadden (1993) examined both the short- and long-term effectiveness of both moderate and severe caloric restriction on weight loss. He reviewed all the studies involving randomized control trials in four behavioural journals and compared his findings with those of Stunkard (1958). Wadden concluded that 'Investigators have made significant progress in inducing weight loss in the 35 years since Stunkard's review.' He states that 80 per cent of patients will now stay in treatment for 20 weeks and that 50 per cent will achieve a weight loss of 20 lb or more. Therefore modern methods of weight loss produce improved results in the short term. However, Wadden also concludes that 'most obese patients treated in research trials still regain their lost weight'. This conclusion has been further supported by a systematic review of interventions for the treatment and prevention of obesity, which identified 92 studies that fitted the authors' inclusion criteria (NHS Centre for Reviews and Dissemination 1997). The review examined the effectiveness of dietary, exercise, behavioural, pharmacological and surgical interventions for obesity and concluded that 'the majority of the studies included in the present review demonstrate weight regain either during treatment or post intervention'. Accordingly, the picture for long-term weight loss is still fairly pessimistic.

The role of dieting in treating obesity

With the exception of the surgical interventions now available (see later), all obesity treatment programmes involve recommending dieting in one form or another. Traditional treatment programmes aimed to correct the obese individual's abnormal behaviour, and recent packages suggest that the obese need to readjust their energy balance by eating less than they usually do. But both styles of treatment suggest that to lose weight the individual must impose cognitive restraint upon their eating behaviour. They recommend that the obese deny food and set cognitive limits to override physiological limits of satiety. And this brings with it all the problematic consequences of restrained eating (see Chapter 6).

Psychological problems and obesity treatment

Wadden et al. (1986) reported that dieting resulted in increased depression in a group of obese patients, and McReynolds (1982) reported an association between ongoing obesity treatment and psychological disturbance. In addition, results from a study by Loro and Orleans (1981) indicated that obese dieters report episodes of bingeing precipitated by 'anxiety, frustration, depression and other unpleasant emotions'. This suggests that the obese respond to dieting in the same way as the non-obese, with lowered mood and episodes of overeating, both of which are detrimental to attempts at weight loss. The obese are encouraged to impose a cognitive limit on their food intake, which introduces a sense of denial, guilt and the inevitable response of overeating. Consequently any weight loss is precluded by episodes of overeating, which are a response to the many cognitive and emotional changes that occur during dieting.

Physiological problems and obesity treatment

In addition to the psychological consequences of imposing a dieting structure on the obese, there are physiological changes which accompany attempts at food restriction. Heatherton et al. (1991) reported that restraint in the non-obese predicts weight fluctuation, which parallels the process of weight cycling or 'yo-yo' dieting in the obese. Research on rats suggests that repeated attempts at weight loss followed by weight regain result in further weight loss becoming increasingly difficult due to a decreased metabolic rate and an increase in the percentage of body fat (Brownell et al. 1986a). Human research has found similar results in dieters and athletes who show yo-yo dieting (Brownell et al. 1989). Research has also found that weight fluctuation may have negative effects on health, with reports suggesting an association between weight fluctuation and mortality and morbidity from CHD (Hamm et al. 1989) and all-cause mortality (Lissner et al. 1991). Repeated failed attempts at dieting, therefore, may be more detrimental to physical health than remaining statically obese.

Dieting, obesity and health

Restraint theory (see Chapter 6) suggests that dieting has negative consequences, and yet the treatment of obesity recommends dieting as a solution. This paradox can be summarized as follows:

- Obesity is a physical health risk, but restrained eating may promote weight cycling, which is also detrimental to health.

- Obesity treatment aims to reduce food intake, but restrained eating can promote overeating.

- The obese may suffer psychologically from the social pressures to be thin (although evidence of psychological problems in the non-dieting obese is scarce), but failed attempts to diet may leave them depressed, feeling a failure and out of control. For those few who do succeed in their attempts at weight loss, Wooley and Wooley (1984: 187) suggest that they 'are in fact condemned to a life of weight obsession, semi-starvation and all the symptoms produced by chronic hunger . . . and seem precariously close to developing a frank eating disorder'.

If restraint theory is applied to obesity, the obese should not be encouraged to restrain their food intake. Obesity may not be caused by overeating but overeating may be a consequence of obesity if restrained eating is recommended as a cure.

Should obesity be treated at all?

The problems with treating obesity raise the question of whether it should be treated at all. In order to answer this it is necessary to examine the benefits of treatment, the treatment alternatives and the role of individual responsibility.

The benefits of treatment

Although failed obesity treatment may be related to negative mood, actual weight loss has been found to be associated with positive changes such as elation, self-confidence and increased feelings of well-being (Stunkard 1984). This suggests that, whereas failed dieting attempts are detrimental, successful treatment may bring with it psychological rewards. The physical effects of obesity treatment also show a similar pattern of results. Yo-yo dieting and weight fluctuation may increase chances of CHD and death, but actual weight loss of only 10 per cent may result in improved blood pressure and benefits for type II diabetes (Blackburn and Kanders 1987; Wing et al. 1987). These results again suggest that actual weight loss can be beneficial. Halmi et al. (1980) reported significant psychological and physical benefits of weight loss in the severely obese. They compared a group of severely obese subjects who received surgery with a comparison group who received a behavioural diet programme. The results indicated that the surgery group showed higher rates of both weight loss and weight maintenance. In addition, the diet group reported significantly higher changes in psychological characteristics, such as preoccupation with food and depression, than the surgery group (Halmi et al. 1980). Thus permanent weight loss through surgery brought both physical and psychological benefits. Weight loss therefore can be beneficial in the obese, but only if treatment is successful and the results are permanent. Therefore dieting may be rejected as a treatment but weight loss may still be seen as beneficial.

An argument for treating severe obesity can be made, but only if a positive outcome can be guaranteed, as failed treatment may be more detrimental than no treatment attempts at all.

The treatment alternatives
The problems with dieting

The implications of restraint theory suggest that the obese should avoid restrained eating. Dieting offers a small chance of weight loss and a high chance of both negative physical and psychological consequences. Taking dieting out of the treatment equation leaves us primarily with drug treatment and surgery.

Drug treatments of obesity

Drug therapy is only legally available to patients in the UK with a BMI of 30 or more and government bodies have become increasingly restrictive on the use of anti-obesity drugs. For example, both fenfluramine and dexfenfluramine were recently withdrawn from the market because of their association with heart disease even though they were both quite effective at bringing about weight loss. Current recommendations state that drugs should be used only when other approaches have failed, that they should not be prescribed for longer than three months in the first instance and should be stopped if a 10 per cent reduction in weight has not been achieved (Kopelman 1999). There are currently two groups of anti-obesity drugs available which are offered in conjunction with dietary and exercise programmes. The first group of drugs work on the central nervous system and suppress appetite. The most commonly used of these are phentermine, which acts on the catecholamine pathway, and sibutramine, which acts on the noradronergic and serotonergic pathways. There is some evidence for the effectiveness of these drugs although they can be accompanied by side effects such as nausea, dry mouth and constipation (Lean 1997). The second group of drugs act on the gastrointestinal system and the more successful of these reduce fat absorption. Orlistat is one of these and has been shown to cause substantial weight loss in obese subjects (James et al. 1997; Sjostrom et al. 1998; Rossner et al. 2000). It can be, however, accompanied by a range of unpleasant side effects including liquid stools, an urgency to go to the toilet and anal leakage which are particularly apparent following a high fat meal. Although Orlistat is designed to work by reducing fat absorption, it probably also has a deterrent effect as eating fat causes unpleasant consequences. Ogden and Sidhu (2006) carried out a qualitative study exploring patients' experiences of taking Orlistat and concluded that, although it constitutes a medical approach to obesity, it provides a window into the processes of adherence to medication and behaviour change and also has some interesting effects on the individual's psychological state. The results from this study suggest that adherence to the drug was related to being motivated to lose weight by a life event rather than just the daily hassles of being obese. Further, if the unpleasant, highly visual side effects were regarded as an education into the relationship between fat eaten and body fat, then they helped to change the patient's model of their problem by encouraging a model that emphasized behaviour. Such a behavioural model of obesity was then related to behaviour change. This is similar to the importance of matched models described in Chapter 3.

Surgical treatments of obesity

Although there are 21 different surgical procedures for obesity (Kral 1983, 1995), the two most popular are the gastric bypass and gastric banding. Halmi et al. (1980) reported high levels of weight loss and maintenance following surgery, with accompanying changes in satiety, body image and eating behaviour. Stunkard, Stinnett et al. (1986) suggested that after one year weight losses average at 50 per cent of excess weight. In fact, Stunkard (1984: 171) stated that 'Severe obesity . . . is most effectively treated by surgical measures, particularly ones that reduce the size of the stomach and of its opening into the large gastrointestinal tract'. More recently researchers in Sweden have carried out the large-scale Swedish Obese Subjects (SOS) study which explored nearly 1000 matched pairs of patients who received either surgery or conventional treatment for their obesity (Torgerson and Sjostrom 2001). The results showed an average weight loss of 28 kg in the surgical group after two years compared to only 0.5 kg in the conventional group. After eight years the weight loss in the surgical group remained high (average of 20 kg) while the control group had gained an average of 0.7 kg. The weight loss in the surgical group was associated with a reduction in diabetes and hypertension at two years and diabetes at eight years. This study indicated that surgery can be effective for both weight loss and maintenance and brings with it a reduction in the risk factors for cardiovascular disease. The surgical management of obesity has been endorsed by expert committees in the USA (Institute of Medicine 1995) and the UK (Garrow 1997) and is recommended for those with a BMI over $40 \, kg/m^2$ (or > 35 with complications of obesity), who have not lost weight with dietary or pharmacological interventions, as long as they made aware of the possible side effects. Obesity surgery, however, does not only affect weight. Some research has also explored post-operative changes in aspects of the individual's psychological state such as health status and psychological morbidity and a series of studies have shown significant improvements, particularly in those patients who show sustained weight loss. For example, cross-sectional research has illustrated improved quality of life in surgical patients compared to control subjects (De Zwann et al. 2002; Ogden et al. 2005) which has been supported by studies using either retrospective or longitudinal designs. In particular, in a large-scale follow-up of the SOS patients, Karlsson et al. (1998) reported an improvement in health-related quality of life operationalized in terms of mood disorders, mental well-being, health perceptions and social interaction. Bocchieri et al. (2002) carried out a comprehensive review of much of the literature examining the impact of obesity surgery on psychosocial outcomes and concluded that in general 'the empirical evidence ... seems to be pointing in a positive direction' (p. 164). Ogden et al. (2006a) carried out a qualitative study to explore patients' experiences of obesity surgery. In line with patient experiences of taking medication (see previous section), although surgery is considered a form of medical management the results from this study suggest that it also has some profound effects upon the individual's psychological state. In particular, as well as resulting in all the improvements associated with weight loss as described by the quantitative studies on health status and quality of life, the patients also described some changes in their cognitive state which were specific to the process of surgery. Specifically the patients described how, by imposing control and limited choice upon how much and what they could eat, surgery and the process of making their stomach much smaller paradoxically made them feel more in control of their weight and eating behaviour. Handing over control to their stomach size made them feel more in control of their behaviour. This is in contrast to much of the literature on communication and choice discussed in Chapter 4.

The success stories

Randomized control trials examining the effectiveness of interventions indicate that, although the majority of individuals may lose weight initially, the large majority eventually return to their baseline weight. Within each trial, however, a small minority not only lose weight initially but successfully maintain this loss. Klem et al. (1997) examined the psychological states of 784 men and women who had both lost weight and maintained their weight loss and concluded that weight suppression was not associated with psychological distress. In contrast, Wooley and

Wooley (1984: 187) suggested that the minority of 'success stories' are 'in fact condemned to a life of weight obsession, semi-starvation and all the symptoms produced by chronic hunger . . . and seem precariously close to developing a frank eating disorder'.

What factors distinguish between the majority of failures and the minority of long-term successes? To date, some studies have specifically examined this minority group. This research together with data from the trials of obesity treatment provide some preliminary insights into the factors that predict and/or correlate with successful weight loss and maintenance. In particular, the literature highlights a role for a range of variables which can be conceptualized as profile characteristics, historical factors, help-seeking behaviours and psychological factors.

- *Profile characteristics.* Research suggests that baseline BMI predicts weight loss and maintenance; however, while some studies indicate that lower baseline weight is predictive of greater success (Stuart and Guire 1978; Neumark-Sztainer et al. 1995; Ogden 2000), other studies show the reverse effect (Wadden et al. 1992). Research also suggests that employment outside the home, higher income and being older are predictive of weight loss and maintenance (Neumark-Sztainer et al. 1995; Wong et al. 1997; Ogden 2000). Some research has also looked at gender although the data remain contradictory (e.g. Colvin and Olson 1983).

- *Historical factors.* Some research points to an individual's previous dieting attempts and their weight history as important for successful weight loss and maintenance. In particular, studies indicate that a history of dieting for longer and a higher number of dieting attempts predict success (Hoiberg et al. 1994; Ogden 2000). In contrast, Kiernan et al. (1998) concluded from their study that success was greater in those who did not have a history of repeated weight loss. Whether the 'try, try and try again' ethos holds for dieting therefore remains unclear. It is also possible that changes in smoking behaviour (e.g. Klesges and Klesges 1988) and an individual's reproductive history may be contributory factors to success as weight gain and maintenance often follow smoking cessation and childbirth (e.g. Ohlin and Rossner 1990).

- *Help-seeking behaviours.* There appear to be several help-seeking factors which are predictive of success. Primarily research highlights a role for the types and intensity of weight loss methods used. For example, many studies have emphasized the importance of dietary changes (e.g. Kayman et al. 1990; McGuire et al. 1999) although Ogden (2000) reported that calorie-controlled diets were associated with weight loss and regain rather than maintenance. Many studies have also highlighted the role of exercise and general increases in physical activity (Haus et al. 1994; Hoiberg et al. 1994; French and Jeffrey 1997; Klem et al. 1997; Wong et al. 1997). Furthermore, research has highlighted the relative effectiveness of different interventions involving contact with a range of health professionals. These include psychological interventions such as CBT, counselling, self-help groups and medical interventions involving drug therapy and surgery (see NHS Centre for Reviews and Dissemination 1997 for review). The general conclusion from this research is that the more intense the intervention, the longer the follow-up period and the greater the professional contact, the higher the probability of successful weight loss and maintenance.

- *Psychological factors.* Rodin et al. (1977) reported the results from a study designed to assess the baseline psychological predictors of successful weight loss. Their results indicated a role for the individual's beliefs about the causes of obesity and their motivations for weight loss. A similar focus on motivations was also reported by Williams et al. (1996) whose results indicated that motivational style was predictive of weight loss and maintenance. Likewise, Kiernan et al. (1998) indicated that individuals who were more dissatisfied with their body shape at baseline were more successful, suggesting that motivations for weight loss guided by a high value placed on attractiveness may also be important. Ogden (2000) examined differences in psychological factors between weight loss regainers, stable obese and weight loss maintainers who were classified as those individuals who had been obese (BMI > 29.9), lost sufficient weight to be considered non-obese (BMI < 29.9) and maintained this weight loss for a minimum of three years. The results showed that the weight loss maintainers were more likely to endorse a psychological model of obesity in terms of its consequences such as depression and low self-esteem and to have been motivated to lose weight for psychological reasons such as wanting to increase their self-esteem and feel better about themselves. Further, they showed less endorsement of a medical model of causality including genetics and hormone imbalance. These results suggested that it is not only what an individual does that is predictive of success, but also what they believe. Accordingly, for an obese person to lose weight and keep this weight off it would seem that they need both to change their behaviour and believe that their own behaviour is important. Further, they need to perceive the consequences of their behaviour change as valuable. This supports the research exploring the psychological effects of taking obesity medication (Ogden and Sidhu 2006) and reflects the role of matched models described in Chapter 3.

In summary, a small minority of individuals show successful weight loss and maintenance which relates to their profile characteristics, dieting history, help-seeking behaviours and their beliefs about obesity.

To answer the question 'Should obesity be treated at all?' it is necessary to consider the following points:

■ Obesity is a health risk.

■ Obesity is caused by a combination of physiological and behavioural factors – it is not simply a product of overeating.

■ Treating obesity with dieting emphasizes personal responsibility ('you can make yourself well'), but may result in overeating, which could exacerbate the weight problem.

■ Treating obesity with drugs and/or surgery emphasizes the physiological causes and places the obese in the hands of the medical profession ('we can make you well'). This can result in weight loss but has side effects and can result in medical complications and weight regain. These medical approaches to obesity also have an impact upon the individual's psychological state.

■ Any treatment intervention should therefore weigh up the potential benefits of any weight loss (e.g. improved self-esteem, reduced risk of CHD, etc.) against the potential costs of intervention (e.g. overeating, weight fluctuations).

Conclusion

Obesity is related to several health problems and a number of theories have been developed in an attempt to understand its aetiology. In particular, research has suggested that there may be a strong genetic predisposition to obesity, which is reflected in underactivity and the relative overconsumption of fat. However, the research examining the causes of obesity is often contradictory, suggesting that the story is not yet complete. This chapter has also explored obesity treatment in terms of behavioural interventions, surgery and drugs. Research indicates that all forms of intervention are effective at promoting weight loss but weight maintenance is particularly poor for dieting-based treatments. Given that all treatments have side effects raises the question 'Should obesity be treated at all?' The answer seems to be that it should be treated as long as the costs and benefits of any intervention are assessed and both physical and psychological consequences are taken into account.

Coronary heart disease (CHD)

This section examines what coronary heart disease is and the role of psychology in understanding CHD in terms of beliefs about CHD, the psychological impact of CHD, predicting and changing behavioural risk factors and patient rehabilitation (see Figure 15.7).

What is CHD?

The term 'coronary heart disease' (CHD) refers to a disease of the heart involving coronary arteries which are not functioning properly. The most important diseases are angina, acute myocardial infarction (MI – heart attack) and sudden cardiac death. All these forms of CHD are caused by atherosclerosis which involves a narrowing of the arteries due to fatty deposits which obstruct the flow of blood. Angina is a powerful pain in the chest, which sometimes radiates down the left arm. It develops when blood flow to the coronary arteries is restricted to such an extent that the heart muscle is starved of oxygen. An acute MI occurs when blood flow is restricted below a threshold level and some heart tissue is destroyed. It also seems to happen when a blood clot has further restricted blood flow to the heart. Sudden cardiac death typically occurs in patients who have already suffered damage to the heart through previous MIs although it can occur in patients who previously seemed to have healthy arteries.

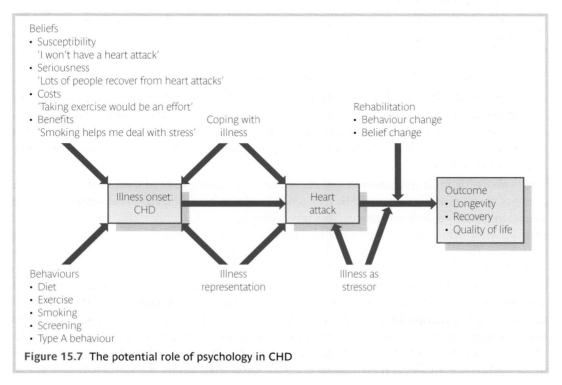

Figure 15.7 The potential role of psychology in CHD

The prevalence of CHD

CHD is responsible for 33 per cent of deaths in men under 65 and 28 per cent of all deaths. It is the leading cause of death in the UK and accounted for 4300 deaths in men and 2721 deaths in women per million in 1992. It has been estimated that CHD cost the UK National Health Service (NHS) about £390 million in 1985–86. The highest death rates from CHD are found in men and women in the manual classes, and men and women of Asian origin. In middle age, the death rate is up to five times higher for men than for women; this evens out, however, in old age when CHD is the leading cause of death for both men and women. Interestingly, women show poorer recovery from MI than men in terms of both mood and activity limitations.

Risk factors for CHD

Many risk factors for CHD have been identified. Some of these are regarded as: (1) *non-modifiable*, such as educational status, social mobility, social class, age, gender, stress reactivity, family history and ethnicity; or (2) *modifiable*, such as smoking behaviour, obesity, sedentary lifestyle, perceived work stress and personality. However, whether some of the latter can be changed is debatable.

The role of psychology in CHD

The role of psychology in CHD will now be examined in terms of: (1) beliefs about CHD; (2) the psychological impact of MI; (3) predicting and changing risk factors; and (4) patient rehabilitation.

Beliefs about CHD

Chapter 3 described the kinds of beliefs that people have about their illness and explored how these beliefs may influence the development and progression of the disease. Some research has specifically examined the beliefs that people have about CHD with a particular focus on beliefs about causes. For example, French, Marteau et al. (2002) explored how members of the general public understand MI and differentiated between beliefs about proximal causes that directly cause MI and distal causes that are mediated by other causal factors. The results showed that even though the respondents did not have CHD they still had quite complex beliefs about its causes. In particular, type of work was seen as a distal cause of MI which operated through stress and high blood pressure: stress was seen to operate via raised blood pressure rather than behaviour and genes were seen to have a direct effect on CHD which was not mediated by any behavioural or physiological processes. French, Maissi et al. (2005) further explored people's beliefs about MI in 12 patients who had had an MI. The results showed that, while people were aware of many possible causes of MI, they tended to focus on a single cause for their MI which was often related to their symptoms. This was driven by a need to understand why they had had their MI 'now' which was further motivated by a desire not to blame themselves or others while at the same time trying to assert control over having another MI in the future. Gudmundsdottir et al. (2001) also explored people's beliefs about CHD but examined the beliefs of people who had had an MI in the past year. Using a longitudinal design they assessed the patients' beliefs within 72 hours of admission into hospital and interviewed the patients about the causes of their MI. They were then followed up three times over the next year. In addition, the study used four different types of method to explore causal attributions. These were spontaneous attributions (i.e. responses to an open question about the illness), elicited attributions (i.e. responses to an open question about the cause of the MI), cued attributions (i.e. responses to a list of possible causes) and most important attribution (i.e. selected cause from the given list). The results showed that the most common causes derived from all methods were 'smoking', 'stress', 'it's in the family', 'working' and 'eating fatty foods'. The results also showed some changes over time, with patients being less likely to blame their behaviour and/or personality as time went on. Therefore both sufferers and non-sufferers of CHD seem to hold beliefs about the cause of an MI which might influence their subsequent risky behaviour and reflect a process of adjustment once they have become ill.

The psychological impact of CHD

Research has addressed the psychological impact of having an MI in terms of psychological morbidity and measures of anxiety and depression. For example, Lane et al. (2002) used a longitudinal design to assess changes in depression and anxiety immediately post MI, 2–15 days post MI and after 4 and 12 months. The results showed that during hospitalization 30.9 per cent of patients reported elevated depression scores and 26.1 per cent reported elevated anxiety scores. The results also indicated that this increase in psychological morbidity persisted over the year of study. Some research has also explored whether such changes in psychological morbidity can be modified. For example, Johnston, Foulkes et al. (1999) evaluated the impact of nurse counsellor-led cardiac counselling compared to normal care. The study used an RCT design with a one-year follow-up and patients and their partners were recruited within 72 hours of the patients' first MI. The results showed that although patients did not show particularly raised levels of anxiety and depression while still in hospital, those who did not receive counselling showed an increase in these factors following discharge. Counselling seemed to minimize this increase. In contrast to the patients, the partners did show very high levels of anxiety and depression while the patients were still in hospital. This dropped to normal levels in those that received counselling. However, depression and anxiety might not be the only consequences of CHD. Bury (1982) argued that illness can be seen as a form of biographical disruption which requires people to question 'what is going on here?' and results in a sense of uncertainty. Radley (1984, 1989) has drawn upon this perspective to explore how people adjust and respond to CHD. In particular, Radley argues that patients diagnosed with CHD try to resolve the dual demands of symptoms and society. He suggests that people with a chronic illness such as CHD need to establish a new identity as someone who has been ill but can be well again. This need occurs against a backdrop of a family and friends who are worried about their health and often results in the ill person persistently acting in a 'healthy way' as a means to communicate that things are 'back to normal'. This approach finds reflection in theories of coping and the re-establishment of equilibrium described in Chapter 3. The consequences of disease have also been explored in the context of impairment, disability and handicap which is discussed in **Focus on Research 15.1**, on the next page.

Predicting and changing behavioural risk factors for CHD

CHD is strongly linked with a range of risk factors. Some research has addressed whether these risk factors can be changed:

1 *Smoking.* One in four deaths from CHD is thought to be caused by smoking. Smoking more than 20 cigarettes a day increases the risk of CHD in middle age threefold. In addition, stopping smoking can halve the risk of another heart attack in those who have already had one. Smoking cessation is discussed in Chapter 5.

Testing a theory – the consequences of disease

To explore the impact of disease on the constructs defined by the WHO (Johnston and Pollard 2001).

Background

In 1980 the World Health Organization (WHO 1980) proposed a model to describe the consequences of disease. The aim of the model was to clarify terminology and to present a structure for understanding disease that went beyond a simple medical perspective. The model proposed a sequence of consequences of disease which suggested that disease resulted either in impairment, then disability, then handicap, or in a direct path from impairment to handicap. These constructs are defined as follows. Impairment is the loss or abnormality of structure or function and often operates at the level of the organ rather than the individual. Lung cancer may cause impairment to the lungs and heart disease results in impairment of the cardiovascular system. Disability refers to the restriction or lack of ability to perform activities and operates at the level of the individual. For example, lung cancer and heart disease may both result in the inability to climb stairs. Finally, handicap refers to disadvantage and role limitation and operates at the level of the individual as they exist within their social context. Lung cancer and heart disease may prevent an individual from bringing in an income and being financially independent. The WHO model treats these concepts as separate and suggests some degree of causal link between them.

Aims

In this paper, Johnston and Pollard aimed to empirically test the WHO model of the consequences of disease, first, to see whether existing measurements allow separation of the three main concepts, and second, to assess whether there was any support for the causal link between them.

Methodology
Design

The study used cross-sectional and longitudinal designs with three patients groups. Disabled adults were examined using a cross-sectional design, and MI and stroke patients were explored using a longitudinal design.

Participants

- *MI patients:* 108 male and female patients were recruited within 72 hours of admission to a coronary care unit following an MI. They were interviewed on admission and 1 week, 2 months, 6 months and 12 months after discharge.
- *Stroke patients:* 68 men and women were recruited within 20 days of admission for stroke. They were interviewed in hospital and then 1 and 6 months after discharge.
- *Disabled patients:* 101 male and female disabled adults were selected from a primary care database. They were interviewed once.

Measurements

- *Impairment:* MI and stroke patients completed condition-specific measures of impairment. These were the Orgogozo neurological index for the stroke patients (Orgogozo et al. 1983) and the Norris index of hospital mortality (Norris et al. 1969). For the disabled patients, impairment was assessed by the patient's GP using existing criteria of impairment.

- *Disability and handicap:* all patients completed the sickness impact profile (Bergner et al. 1981) and the functional limitations profile (Patrick and Peach 1989). Stroke patients also completed the Barthel index (Mahoney and Barthel 1965) which was complemented with the observer assessed disability scale (Partridge et al. 1987).

Using expert judges

In order to develop separate measures of impairment, disability and handicap, independent expert judges were asked to rate the measures as either disability or handicap according to WHO definitions. The psychometric properties of these new scales were then assessed for reliability and validity.

Data analysis

Data were analysed to assess whether the three concepts could be considered separate and then to examine any causal relationships between them.

Results

The results showed that the three constructs of impairment, disability and handicap could be considered separate constructs for stroke patients but not for MI patients or disabled adults. For the analysis of causality the focus was therefore on stroke patients. This analysis showed that impairment did not predict disability and handicap, suggesting that there is not a simple causal progression between the different consequences of disease. However, disability did consistently predict handicap.

Conclusions

The authors suggest that there are three possible explanations for their lack of support for the WHO model. First, the results may relate to the measurement tools used. Second and relatedly, the results may reflect the conceptualization of impairment. Third (and the explanation preferred by the authors) the WHO model is too simplistic. The authors argue that the transition between impairment, disability and handicap may involve a multitude of other variables not described by the model. In particular, they suggest that the transition from initial impairment through to being limited in social functioning may relate to psychological factors. Healthy people behave in particular ways as a result of their beliefs and mood. The authors argue that this is also the case for people with some form of impairment – it is just that their impairment may influence these psychological factors. There is much variability in the ways in which people experience and manage their illness. Psychological factors may be a better explanation of this variation than a simple transition through a series of stages.

2 *Diet.* Diet, in particular cholesterol levels, has also been implicated in CHD. It has been suggested that the 20 per cent of a population with the highest cholesterol levels are three times more likely to die of heart disease than the 20 per cent with the lowest levels. Cholesterol levels may be determined by the amount of saturated fat consumed (derived mainly from animal fats). Cholesterol reduction can be achieved through a reduction in total fats and saturated fats, an increase in polyunsaturated fats and an increase in dietary fibre. Dietary change is discussed in Chapter 6 and under the dietary section.

3 *High blood pressure.* High blood pressure is also a risk factor for CHD – the higher the blood pressure, the greater the risk. It has been suggested that a 10 mmHg decrease in a population's average blood pressure could reduce the mortality attributable to heart disease by 30 per cent. Blood pressure appears to be related to a multitude of factors such as genetics, obesity, alcohol intake and salt consumption.

Other possible behavioural risk factors include exercise and coffee, alcohol and soft water consumption. The risk factors for CHD can be understood and possibly changed by examining and modifying an individual's health beliefs (see Chapters 2, 6, 7 and 9).

4 *Type A behaviour and hostility.* Type A behaviour and its associated characteristic, hostility, is probably the most extensively studied risk factor for CHD (see Chapter 11 for details). Support for a relationship between type A behaviour and CHD has been reported by a number of studies (Rosenman et al. 1975; Jenkins et al. 1979; Haynes et al. 1980). However, research has also reported no relationship between type A behaviour and CHD (e.g. Johnston et al. 1987). Recent research has focused more on hostility which has been shown to predict stress reactivity and to be linked to the development of CHD (e.g. Williams and Barefoot 1988; Houston 1994; Miller et al. 1996).

5 *Stress.* Stress has also been studied extensively as a predictor of CHD and research has shown links between stress reactivity and CHD, life events and CHD, and job stress and CHD (see Chapters 10 and 11). Stress management is used to reduce stress in people already diagnosed with CHD (see p. 361). However, interventions have also been developed to reduce stress in non-patient samples. For example, Jones and Johnston (2000) developed and evaluated a stress management intervention to reduce distress in 79 student nurses who had previously reported significant distress. Subsequent changes were compared to a waiting-list control group. The results showed that the intervention produced significant reductions in anxiety, depression and domestic satisfaction. In addition, the nurses showed an increase in direct coping. In line with this latter finding, some interventions have directly challenged how people cope with stressful situations. Kaluza (2000) evaluated an intervention designed to change the coping profiles of 82 healthy working men and women. The intervention lasted for 12 weeks and focused on assertiveness, cognitive restructuring, time management, relaxation, physical activities and the scheduling of pleasant activities. Changes were compared to a control group who received no intervention. The results showed significant improvements in emotion-focused coping and problem-focused coping which were related to the individual's original coping profiles. In particular, those who were originally more problem focused became more emotion focused and those who were more avoidant copers became more problem focused. The authors suggest that the intervention changed unbalanced coping profiles. In addition, these changes were related to improvements in aspects of well-being.

Psychology and rehabilitation of patients with CHD

Psychology also plays a role in the rehabilitation of individuals who have been diagnosed with CHD in terms of angina, atherosclerosis or heart attack. Rehabilitation programmes use a range of techniques including health education, relaxation training and counselling, and have been developed to encourage CHD sufferers to modify their risk factors. Research has explored predictors of uptake of rehabilitation programmes and whether they can modify factors such as exercise, type A behaviour, general lifestyle factors, illness cognitions and stress.

Predicting uptake of rehabilitation

Although heart attack (MI) is the primary cause of premature mortality in many western countries, over 60 per cent of patients will survive their MI. Furthermore, if risk factors can be modified then the likelihood of a further MI is greatly reduced. Rehabilitation programmes are therefore designed to reduce these risk factors. Despite the benefits of rehabilitation, however, many patients fail to attend either some or all of the classes. For example, in a systematic review of the literature, attendance rates across 15 studies varied from 13 to 74 per cent although what constituted attendance also varied from missing a few sessions to missing all sessions (Cooper et al. 2002a). So why do people not turn up if rehabilitation can be effective? Cooper et al. (2002a) explored the factors that predicted non-attendance in 15 studies of cardiac rehabilitation involving patients from Europe, the USA, Canada and New Zealand, and concluded that non-attenders were more likely to be older, to have lower income and greater deprivation, to deny the severity of their illness, to be less likely to believe that they can influence the outcome of their illness and to be less likely to perceive that their doctor recommends rehabilitation. Further, women are less likely to be referred for rehabilitation than men, as are the elderly.

Modifying exercise

Most rehabilitation programmes emphasize the restoration of physical functioning through exercise with the assumption that physical recovery will in turn promote psychological and social recovery. Meta-analyses of these exercise-based programmes have suggested that they may have favourable effects on cardiovascular mortality (e.g. Oldridge et al. 1988). However, such meta-analyses are problematic as there is a trend towards publishing positive results, thereby influencing the overall picture. In addition, whether these exercise-based programmes influence risk factors other than exercise, such as smoking, diet and type A behaviour, is questionable.

Modifying type A behaviour

The recurrent coronary prevention project was developed by Friedman et al. (1986) in an attempt to modify type A behaviour. This programme was based on the following questions: can type A behaviour be modified? If so, can such modification reduce the chances of a recurrence of a heart attack? The study involved 1000 subjects and a five-year intervention. Subjects had all suffered a heart attack and were allocated to one of three groups: cardiology counselling, type A behaviour modification or no treatment. Type A behaviour modification involved discussions of the beliefs and values of type A, discussing methods of reducing work demands, relaxation and education about changing the cognitive framework of the individuals. At five years, the results showed that the type A modification group showed a reduced recurrence of heart attacks, suggesting that not only can type A behaviour be modified but that, when modified, there may be a reduction of reinfarction. However, the relationship between type A behaviour and CHD is still controversial, with recent discussions suggesting that type A may at times be protective against CHD.

Modifying general lifestyle factors

In addition, rehabilitation programmes have been developed which focus on modifying other risk factors such as smoking and diet. For example, van Elderen et al. (1994) developed a health education and counselling programme for patients with cardiovascular disease after hospitalization, with weekly follow-ups by telephone. Thirty CHD sufferers and their partners were offered the intervention and were compared with a group of 30 control patients who received standard medical care only. The results showed that after two months, the patients who had received health education and counselling reported a greater increase in physical activity and a greater decrease in unhealthy eating habits. In addition, within those subjects in the experimental condition (receiving health education and counselling), those whose partners had also participated in the programme showed greater improvements in their activity and diet and, in addition, showed a decrease in their smoking behaviour. At 12 months, subjects who had participated in the health education and counselling programme maintained their improvement in their eating behaviour. The authors concluded that, although this study involved only a small number of patients, the results provide some support for including health education and counselling in rehabilitation programmes. More recently, however, van Elderen and Dusseldorp (2001) reported results from a similar study which produced more contradictory results. They explored the relative impact of providing health education, psychological input, standard medical care and physical training to patients with CHD and their partners after discharge from hospital. Overall, all patients improved their lifestyle during the first three months and showed extra improvement in their eating habits over the next nine months. However, by one-year follow-up many patients had increased their smoking again and returned to their sedentary lifestyles. In terms of the relative effects of the different forms of interventions the results were more complex than the authors' earlier work. Although health education and the psychological intervention had an improved impact on eating habits over standard medical care and physical training, some changes in lifestyle were more pronounced in the patients who had only received the latter. For example, receiving health education and psychological intervention seemed to make it more difficult to quit a sedentary lifestyle, and receiving health education seemed to make it more difficult to stop smoking. Therefore, although some work supports the addition of health education and counselling to rehabilitation programmes, at times this may have a cost.

Modifying illness cognitions

Research illustrates that patients' beliefs about their MI may relate to health outcomes in terms of attendance at rehabilitation, return to work and adjustment (see Chapter 3 for illness cognitions and outcomes). In line with this, Petrie et al. (2002) developed an intervention designed to change illness cognitions and explored the subsequent impact upon a range of patient outcomes. In particular the intervention consisted of three sessions of about 40 minutes with a psychologist and was designed to address and change patients' beliefs about their MI. For session 1 the psychologist gave an explanation about the nature of an MI in terms of its symptoms and explored patients' beliefs about the causes of the MI. In session 2 the psychologist further explored beliefs about causes, helped the patient to develop a plan to minimize the future risk of a further MI and tried to increase patient control beliefs about their condition. In the final session, this action plan was reviewed, concerns about medication were explored and symptoms that were part of the recovery process such as breathlessness upon exercise were distinguished from those that were indicative of further pathology such as severe chest pain. Throughout the intervention the information and discussion were targeted to the specific beliefs and concerns of the patient. The results showed that patients who had received the intervention reported more positive views about their MI at follow-up in terms of beliefs about consequences, time line, control/cure and symptom distress (see Chapter 3 for a description of these dimensions). In addition, they reported that they were better prepared to leave hospital, returned to work at a faster rate and reported a lower rate of angina symptoms. No differences were found in rehabilitation attendance. The intervention therefore seemed to change cognitions and improve patients' functional outcome after MI.

Modifying stress

Stress management involves teaching individuals about the theories of stress, encouraging them to be aware of the factors that can trigger stress, and teaching them a range of strategies to reduce stress, such as 'self-talk', relaxation techniques and general life management approaches, such as time management and problem solving. Stress management has been used successfully to reduce some of the risk factors for CHD, including raised blood pressure (Johnston et al. 1993), blood cholesterol (Gill et al. 1985) and type A behaviour (Roskies et al. 1986). Further, some studies also indicate that it can reduce angina, which is highly predictive of heart attack and/or death. For example, Gallacher et al. (1997) randomly allocated 452 male angina patients to receive either stress management or no intervention at all. The results showed that at six months' follow-up, those who had received stress management reported a reduced frequency of chest pain when resting. In a similar trial, Bundy et al. (1998) examined both the independent and the combined effect of stress management and exercise on angina compared with a control group taken from a waiting list. The results indicated that those who undertook both stress management and exercise reported fewer angina attacks and reduced reliance on medication. Therefore stress management appears to reduce angina, which in turn could reduce the occurrence of myocardial infarctions.

Conclusion

CHD is a common cause of death in the western world. It illustrates the role of psychology in illness in terms of the beliefs people have about CHD, the psychological consequences of a diagnosis, identifying and changing risk factors (e.g. smoking, diet, exercise, type A behaviour and stress) and the development and evaluation of programmes designed to modify risk factors in individuals who already have the disease.

To conclude

Illnesses such as obesity and CHD illustrate the role of psychology throughout the course of an illness. For example, psychological factors play a role in illness onset (e.g. health beliefs, health behaviours, personality, coping mechanisms), illness progression (e.g. psychological consequences, adaptation, health behaviours) and longevity (e.g. health behaviours, coping mechanisms, quality of life). These psychological factors are also relevant to a multitude of other chronic and acute illnesses, such as diabetes, asthma, chronic fatigue syndrome and multiple sclerosis. This suggests that illness is best conceptualized not as a biomedical problem, but as a complex interplay of physiological and psychological factors.

❓ Questions

1 To what extent can obesity be explained by physiological factors?

2 Discuss the role of psychological factors in explaining the recent increase on the prevalence of obesity.

3 Obesity is an eating disorder. Discuss.

4 Treating obesity causes more problems than it solves. Discuss.

5 CHD is an inevitable product of lifestyle. Discuss.

6 Discuss the role of psychological factors in the onset and progression of CHD.

7 To what extent can a reinfarction be prevented?

For discussion

In the light of the literature on obesity and CHD, discuss the possible role of psychological factors throughout the course of an alternative chronic illness (e.g. diabetes, multiple sclerosis).

Assumptions in health psychology

The research into obesity and CHD highlights some of the assumptions in health psychology:

1 *The role of behaviour in illness.* Throughout the twentieth century there was an increasing emphasis on behavioural factors in health and illness. Research examined the problem of obesity from the same perspective and evaluated the role of overeating as a causal factor. However, perhaps not all problems are products of behaviour.

2 *Treatment as beneficial.* Drug and surgical interventions are stopped if they are found to be either ineffective or to have negative consequences. However, behavioural interventions to promote behaviour change, such as smoking cessation, exercise and weight loss programmes, are developed and promoted even when the evidence for their success is poor. Within health psychology, behavioural programmes are considered neutral enough to be better than nothing. However, obesity treatment using dieting is an example of the potential negative side effects of encouraging individual responsibility for health and attempting to change behaviour. Perhaps behavioural interventions can have as many negative consequences as other medical treatments.

3 *The mind–body problem.* Research into obesity and CHD raises the problem of the relationship between the mind and the body. Theories are considered either physiological or psychological and treatment perspectives are divided in a similar fashion, therefore maintaining a dualistic model of individuals.

Further reading

Brownell, K.D. (1991) Personal responsibility and control over our health: when expectation exceeds reality, *Health Psychology*, 10: 303–10.

This paper discusses the emphasis on patient responsibility for health and suggests that encouraging the obese to diet may be an example of attempting to control the uncontrollable.

Ogden, J. (2003) *The Psychology of Eating: From Health to Disordered Behaviour.* Oxford: Blackwell.

This book provides an account of the continuum of eating behaviour from healthy eating, through dieting and body dissatisfaction, to obesity and eating disorders. In particular, it provides a detailed analysis of obesity and its treatment.

Romero-Corral, A., Montori, V.M., Somers, V.K., Korinek, J., Thomas, R.J., Allison, T.G., Mookadam, F. and Lopez-Jimenez, F. (2006) Association of bodyweight with total mortality and with cardiovascular events in coronary artery disease: a systematic review of cohort studies, *Lancet*, 368: 666–78.

This paper provides an up-to-date analysis of research exploring the links between body weight and CHD.

16

Women's health issues

Chapter overview

There are many areas of health specific to women. This chapter does not aim to cover all of them but will describe four key health issues. First, it will examine the psychological impact of having a miscarriage. Next, it will describe issues relating to having a termination of pregnancy in terms of contact with the health care systems and the short- and longer-term psychological consequences. It will then focus on pregnancy, the transition into motherhood and the birth experience. Finally, it will explore women's experiences of the menopause. Many of these women's health issues are managed in different ways. Central to this chapter will also be a description of how the mode of treatment or intervention used can impact upon women's experiences.

> **This chapter covers**
>
> - Miscarriage
> - Termination of pregnancy
> - Pregnancy and birth
> - The menopause

Miscarriage

Miscarriage is a relatively common phenomenon occurring in 15–20 per cent of known pregnancies, with 80 per cent of these occurring within the first trimester (Broquet 1999). Miscarriage or 'spontaneous abortion' has been defined as the unintended end of a pregnancy before a foetus can survive outside the mother, which is recognized as being before the twentieth week of gestation (Borg and Lasker 1982). Despite the frequency with which miscarriage occurs, it has only been in the last 10 to 15 years that research has begun to identify and explore the consequences of early pregnancy loss. This chapter will explore the psychological consequences of miscarriage in terms of the quantitative and qualitative research and then examine the impact of how miscarriage is managed on women's experiences.

Quantitative research

Quantitative research has tended to conceptualize women's reactions to miscarriage in terms of grief, depression and anxiety or coping.

■ *Grief.* One main area of research has conceptualized miscarriage as a loss event, assuming that after miscarriage women experience stages of grief parallel to that of the death of a loved one (Herz 1984). The main symptoms identified are sadness, yearning for the lost child, a desire to talk to others about the loss and a search for meaningful explanations (Herz 1984; Beutel et al. 1995; Athey and Spielvogel 2000). In addition, research has highlighted grief reactions that are unique to the miscarriage experience. For example, women often perceive themselves as failures for not being able to have a healthy pregnancy and this loss is often not acknowledged by the community because there are no rituals that can be performed (Herz 1984).

■ *Depression and anxiety.* Other research has focused on depression and anxiety following miscarriage. Friedman and Gath (1989) used the present state examination (PSE) to assess psychiatric 'caseness' in women four weeks post-miscarriage. They found that 48 per cent of the sample had sufficiently high scores on the scale to qualify as 'cases' patients, which is over four times higher than that in women in the general population. When analysed, these women were all classified as having depressive disorders. Klier et al. (2000) similarly found that women who had miscarried had a significantly increased risk of developing a minor depressive disorder in the six months following their loss, compared to a cohort drawn from the community. Thapar and Thapar (1992) also found that women who had miscarried experienced a significant degree of anxiety and depression at both the initial interview and at the six weeks' follow-up compared to that of the control group. In contrast, Prettyman et al. (1993) used the hospital anxiety and depression scale (HADS) and found that anxiety rather than depression was the predominant response at 1, 6 and 12 weeks after miscarriage. Further, Beutel et al. (1995) reported that immediately after the miscarriage the majority of the sample experienced elevated levels of psychological morbidity compared to a community cohort and a pregnant control group, much of which persisted up until the 12-month follow-up. The authors concluded that depression and grief should be considered as two distinct reactions to pregnancy loss, with grief being the normal reaction and depression only developing when certain circumstances are met. This study also showed that a large minority reported no negative emotional reaction post-miscarriage, suggesting that a focus on anxiety, depression and grief may only tap into a part of the miscarriage experience.

■ *Coping.* A small number of studies have considered the experience of miscarriage from a coping viewpoint. For example, Madden (1988) completed 65 structured interviews with women two weeks post-miscarriage and concluded that, rather than self-blame, external blame for the miscarriage and the ability to be able to control the outcome of future pregnancies are predictive of depressive symptoms post-miscarriage. Tunaley et al. (1993) drew upon the theory of cognitive adaptation (Taylor 1983) which focuses on meaning, self-enhancement and mastery to explore the miscarriage experience (see Chapter 3). They found that 86 per cent of the sample had established their own set of reasons as to why the miscarriage had occurred, ranging from medical explanations to feelings of punishment and judgement which finds reflection in work on attributions for heart disease (e.g. French et al. 2001) and breast cancer (Taylor 1983). In terms of self-enhancement, 50 per cent of the sample made downward social comparisons with women who had reproductive problems. By comparing themselves with women who were worse off than themselves they were able to increase their own self-esteem. The search for mastery was less visible. There was little evidence that the women in the sample tried to gain control over their lives in general. Although 81 per cent of the sample believed that they could make changes to prevent future miscarriage, they had little or no confidence in the difference these changes would make to future outcomes (Tunaley et al. 1993).

The quantitative research has therefore explored the reaction to miscarriage in terms of grief, anxiety and depression and coping. Other research has used a qualitative method to assess women's broader experience of having a miscarriage.

Qualitative research

In an early study Hutti (1986) conducted in-depth interviews at two time points with two women. The results showed that although both women referred to a similar inventory of events, the significance that they attached to these events was different and dependent upon their previous experience. For example, one woman had had a previous miscarriage and was described as taking more control over her medical treatment; she found her grief to be less severe than with her first miscarriage. In contrast, the woman who had experienced her first miscarriage represented the miscarriage as a 'severe threat to her perception of herself as a childbearing woman' (p. 383). On a larger scale, Bansen and Stevens (1992) focused on 10 women who had experienced their first pregnancy loss of a wanted pregnancy. The authors concluded that miscarriage was a 'silent event' which was not discussed within the wider community. The women were described as being unable to share their experiences and felt isolated as a result. When they did get the opportunity to talk about their loss, they realized how common miscarriage is and that was a source of comfort to them. The authors concluded that miscarriage constituted a major life event that changed the way in which women viewed their lives in the present and affected the way in which they planned for the future (Bansen and Stevens 1992). Maker and Ogden (2003) carried out in-depth interviews with a heterogenous sample of 13 women who had experienced a miscarriage up to five weeks previously. The women described their experiences using a range of themes which were conceptualized into three stages: turmoil, adjustment and resolution. For the majority, the turmoil stage was characterized by feelings of being unprepared and negative emotions. Some women who had had an unwanted pregnancy described their shock at the physical trauma of miscarriage but described the experience as a relief. The women then described a period of adjustment involving social comparisons, sharing and a search for meaning. The latter included a focus on causality which left a minority, particularly those who had had previous miscarriages, feeling frustrated with the absence of a satisfactory medical explanation. The final resolution stage was characterized by a decline in negative emotions, a belief by some that the miscarriage was a learning experience and the integration of the experience into their lives. This resolution seemed more positive for those with children and more negative if the miscarriage was not their first. The authors argued that, rather than being a trigger to psychological morbidity, a miscarriage should be conceptualized as a process involving the stages of turmoil, adjustment and resolution.

Impact of mode of treatment

Miscarriages can occur throughout a pregnancy but most occur during the first trimester (Steer et al. 1989). Until recently, the standard management of first trimester miscarriages involved the evacuation of the retained products of conception (ERPC), also sometimes known as a D&C (dilatation and curettage). This uses either a general or local anaesthetic and surgically removes the lining of the womb and the foetus if it is still there. This occasionally causes infection, uterine perforation and bowel damage and brings with it all the associated risks of an anaesthetic. It also constitutes a large proportion of the surgical work load for gynaecology in the UK (MacKensie and Bibby 1978). Expectant management is a possible alternative and has been adopted by several clinics across the UK. This involves letting the miscarriage take its natural course and enables the woman to be at home as the miscarriage occurs. Trials suggest that expectant management might produce less infection (Neilson and Hahlin 1995) and observational studies show that it usually results in complete evacuation of the products of conception (Sairam et al. 2001; Luise et al. 2002). It would seem to be feasible, effective and safe and may be preferred treatment by many women (Luise et al. 2002). Rates of surgical management of miscarriage vary by age and are shown in Figure 16.1.

Little is known about what women expect, or about their subsequent experiences of each management approach. Ogden and Maker (2004) assessed women's reasons for deciding upon a given treatment and the impact of treatment type upon their subsequent experiences. The choice of expectant management was motivated by desire for a natural solution and a fear of operation. Women described how pain and bleeding had made them anxious that something was wrong and how they felt unprepared for how gruelling the experience would be. Some also described how their support had dwindled as the miscarriage progressed. In contrast, women who chose surgery valued a quick resolution and focused on the support from hospital staff, although some commented that their emotional needs had not always been met. The mode of treatment therefore seemed to influence how the miscarriage was experienced. Furthermore, even though expectant management is becoming increasingly common, women feel unprepared for how this will make them feel.

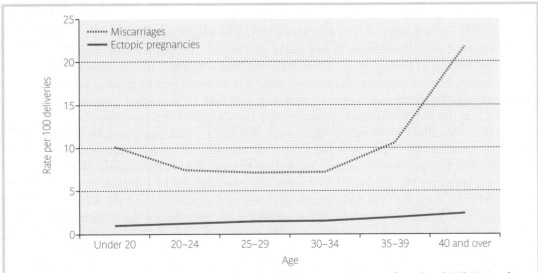

Figure 16.1 Rates of miscarriage that require a hospital stay vary by age of mother (NHS Maternity Statistics, DOH, 2003–2004)

Problems with miscarriage research

Research into miscarriage is problematic in the following ways:

1 Miscarriage is very common. Many women come into contact with health professionals as they visit their GP or are referred to a hospital clinic. Some, however, have early miscarriages that are considered to be late periods or miscarriages that will resolve themselves without medical intervention. To date, most research focuses on those who seek help. This offers an unrepresentative sample and means that very little is known about those women who experience miscarriage but never seek help.

2 Research exploring miscarriage tends to use either quantitative or qualitative methods. To date, there has been no use of mixed methods or any real integration of the two literatures. Future research needs to take the findings from the qualitative approaches and test them quantitatively.

3 The use of expectant management is relatively new. Women's experiences of this approach are coloured by the lack of familiarity in recommending this approach by the professionals. Research is needed to explore how women experience expectant management as it becomes the more 'normal' approach used.

4 Research to date has focused on women's experiences of miscarriage. Future research could explore how men feel about this form of pregnancy loss.

Conclusion

Research exploring the psychological impact of having a miscarriage has used both quantitative and qualitative research methods. The results indicate that miscarriage can result in feelings of grief, anxiety and depression. In addition, women experience their miscarriage as a process involving a series of stages which can result in women reassessing both their past and future experiences. Furthermore, research indicates that a woman's experience is clearly influenced by how it is managed, and that, although the medical management of miscarriage brings with it the risks associated with surgery, a more 'natural' approach can leave women feeling misinformed and unprepared.

Termination of pregnancy

In 1967 the Abortion Act was passed in the UK and abortions (also known as termination of pregnancy – TOP) were made legal. Although this did not mean that abortions were available simply 'on demand', the Act was welcomed by many women who could subsequently gain access to a legal abortion on the grounds that it was considered to be less physically and mentally harmful than childbirth. Nowadays, abortions can be obtained through the National Health Service, through private for-profit services or alternatively through the specialist non-profit services set up by charitable organizations shortly after the introduction of the Act. The latter of these continue to lead the way in developing and implementing improved provision both within their own organizations and within the NHS including such practices as day care, the use of local anaesthetics and, more recently, the introduction of medical abortions. Further, with the introduction of agency contracts such specialist services have enabled health authorities and general practitioners to deal with inadequate abortion provision within the NHS (Munday 1994). Although the law places the abortion decision in the hands of doctors (Greenwood 2001), in practice women make this decision and their choice is respected (Lee 2003).

Abortion is also legal in the USA and most European countries. In England and Wales one in three women is likely to have an abortion in their lifetime (calculated from The Abortion Statistics England and Wales 2001); however, debate continues over the moral status of a human foetus and consequently also over that of abortions (Gillon 2001). The abortion rate by age is shown in Figure 16.2.

Up until recently all abortions involved the surgical removal of the foetus using a D&C and a general anaesthetic. Nowadays, however, women can chose to have their abortion using either the D&C with a general or local anaesthetic, a suction technique which can involve general or local anaesthetic or no anaesthetic, or the abortion pill which induces a miscarriage (later miscarriages may be managed through inducing labour). The type of abortion procedure depends upon the gestation of the pregnancy, the preference of the woman and the methods preferred by the clinic involved. In the UK an abortion is legal up until the 24th week of gestation although abortions occur within the first trimester. Abortion is illegal in a number of countries in all circumstances except to save a woman's life. These include Brazil, Chile, Mexico, Venezuela, Angola, Congo, Mali, Niger, Nigeria, Uganda, Afghanistan, Iran, Egypt, Libya, Syria Bangladesh, Ireland and Malta. In addition, many countries only allow abortion to protect a woman's health. These include Argentina, Peru, Cameroon, Ethiopia, Malawi, Zimbabwe, Kuwait, Saudi Arabia, Pakistan, Thailand, Poland and Portugal. Rates of abortions across the world are shown in Figure 16.3 and the rates of unsafe abortions are shown in Figure 16.4.

Research focusing on abortions has addressed a range of issues including deciding to have an abortion, the provision of services, women's experiences of such services, their experiences of having an abortion, the longer-term consequences of having an abortion and the impact of the mode of intervention used. This research will now be described.

Deciding to have an abortion

Research has explored how women decide whether or not to have an abortion and what factors influence this decision. Freeman and Rickels (1993) report the results from the Penn State study in the USA which followed over 300 black teenagers aged 13–17 for two years who were either

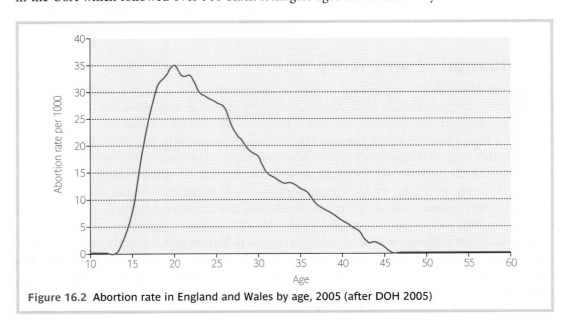

Figure 16.2 Abortion rate in England and Wales by age, 2005 (after DOH 2005)

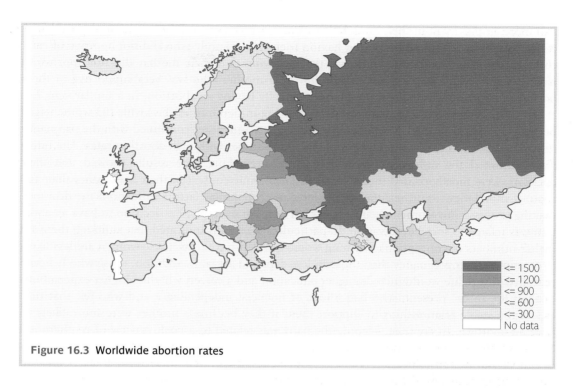

Figure 16.3 Worldwide abortion rates

Figure 16.4 Worldwide rates of unsafe abortions

pregnant and intending to keep the baby ($n = 137$), had terminated their first pregnancy ($n = 94$) or who had never been pregnant ($n = 110$). The results were analysed to explore a range of factors including contraception use and the meaning of pregnancy. The study also examined what factors related to whether or not the teenager decided to continue with their pregnancy. Using quantitative data, the results illustrated that those who opted for an abortion had more employment in their households, were more likely to still be in school, showed better course grades at school and reported having friends and family who did not approve of early childbearing. The results also indicated that believing that their mother did not approve of having a child while still a teenager and having a mother who was very supportive of them having an abortion was the best predictor of actually having an abortion. In a similar vein, Lee et al. (2004) carried out a qualitative study involving in-depth interviews with 103 women aged between 15 and 17 in the UK who had been pregnant and either continued with the pregnancy or had an abortion and with older people in communities with high abortion rates. The interviews explored the influences upon their decision making. The results showed that their decisions were mostly related to the social and economic context of their lives rather than any abstract moral views. Further, the results indicate that similar factors influenced the decision-making processes for women regardless of their age. For example, the decision to have an abortion was related to social deprivation. In particular, the results indicated that although there are higher numbers of conceptions in young women in deprived areas, these women are less likely to terminate their pregnancy than those in less deprived areas. In addition, those who believed that their future life would include higher education and a career, who had higher expectations of their life in the present, who had a lack of financial independence and who felt that they lacked the stable relationships to support them if they became a mother were more likely to have an abortion. In contrast, keeping the baby was related to a positive view of motherhood that was not associated with lack or loss and those who viewed motherhood as rewarding, associating it with responsibility and seeing it as an achievement, were more likely to carry on with the pregnancy. Further, the decision-making process seemed to be highly related to the views of the women's family and community. For example, some women described how having children early was considered by their world to be acceptable and normal and these tended to have the baby. In contrast, those who went on to have an abortion described how their parents saw abortion in a pragmatic way, regarding young motherhood as a more negative event. Finally, although most women had made up their minds whether or not to have an abortion before they had any contact with a health professional, the results also showed an association between the abortion rate and provision of local family planning provision, higher proportions of female GPs and a greater independent section providing abortion services. This suggests that, although much of the decision-making process is influenced by social and economic factors prior to professional contact, structural factors such as service provision also have a role to play. Deciding to have an abortion seems to relate to the context of the woman's life and the beliefs and support offered by those important to her.

The provision of services

In line with the role of structural factors already described, some research has examined the changes in both the provision and accessibility of services. For example, research has highlighted that, despite increasing provision for abortion in the UK within the NHS, there remains wide variation in the level of NHS provision in different health authorities (Clarke et al. 1983; Paintin 1994; Abortion Law Reform Association 1997). In particular, figures revealed that, while on average 70.5 per cent of abortions are funded by the NHS in England and Wales, this figure ranges from 28 to 96 per cent across regional and district health authorities (Office for National Statistics Population and Health Monitors 1995). A report by the Abortion Law Reform Association examined the reasons for this variation and found that informal means testing is applied by many health authorities and general practitioners resulting in targets for abortion services being set below the local known need (Abortion Law Reform Association 1997). Other studies from this perspective have mapped the stages involved in accessing and using the abortion services. For example, Clarke et al. (1983) examined why half the women in their study had their abortion within a private or charitable clinic despite generous provision of NHS abortion services. The study showed that an important reason for women bypassing the NHS was that women either thought or had been actually told by their own GP or another doctor that it was difficult to get an abortion on the NHS. Other reasons for not having an abortion on the NHS included not wanting to delay the abortion, expectation of better personal treatment within a private clinic and wanting to ensure anonymity. The results also indicated that women feared insensitive treatment from local NHS hospitals which resonates with a survey of abortion patients carried out in the UK (Pro-choice Alliance 1993). This is supported by studies of women's experiences of having an abortion which suggests that women may have a more positive experience if they are managed through specialist independent clinics (Lee et al. 2004).

Women's experiences of services

Sociological research has emphasized the importance of women's experiences of having an abortion. For some, this has involved a study of the factors that are likely to impinge upon a woman's experience. For example, reports indicate that decisions about the provision of services are often based upon moral judgements (MacIntyre 1977). In addition, it has been shown that referrals to services and therefore service access are also influenced by judgements and assumptions concerning a woman's circumstances (e.g. marital status) rather than health need (MacIntyre 1977). Accordingly, several authors have noted that such a judgemental context is likely to impact negatively upon women's experiences of such services (Doyal 1985; Simms 1985; Stacey 1988; Hadley 1996). In contrast, some psychological research has examined women's experiences directly. In terms of surgical abortion, a recent analysis of women's experiences of seeking an abortion in Australia (Ryan et al. 1994) found that limitations in current service provision and the legal and health contexts in which women sought abortion had an impact on women's experience and treatment. In particular, they reported that confusion in the laws surrounding abortion could lead to women facing long drawn-out referral procedures as a result of the idiosyncratic eligibility criteria that a particular GP or gynaecologist applied in a given case. Furthermore they found that the women had many ideas about how abortion services could be improved. These ranged from specific issues such as the importance of accessibility of information and recommendations that abortion be treated as an urgent rather than elective procedure, to the wider social context of abortion regarding women's ownership and respect for their decisions and the removal of the stigma that surrounds abortion. Harden and Ogden (1999a) interviewed 54 women aged between 16 and 24 up to three hours after their abortion about their experiences. They reported that, overall, having an unwanted pregnancy was experienced as a rare event which was accompanied by feelings of lack of control and loss of status. Further, the process of arranging and having an abortion led to a reinstatement of status, control and normality. However, this process was sometimes hindered by inaccessible information, judgemental health professionals and the wider social context of abortion in which abortion is seen as a generally negative experience. In the main, however, most of these negative experiences were associated with accessing the abortion service and the professionals who act as gatekeepers to the service rather than those who work within the service itself. Therefore, although young women's experiences were wide ranging and varied, most were positive and at times even negative expectations were compensated by supportive staff, indicating that abortion services may not be as judgemental in the late twentieth century as suggested in previous decades.

Psychological impact of an abortion

Much research has addressed the psychological consequences of abortion (see Coleman et al. 2005 for a comprehensive review). Some of this has explored the extent of emotional reactions post-abortion. For example, Zolese and Blacker (1992) argue that approximately 10 per cent of women experience depression or anxiety that is severe or persistent after an abortion. Other authors have used case studies of women who are distressed to suggest that this may be more widespread (Butler and Llanedeyrn 1996). In contrast, although Major et al. (2000) found that 20 per cent of their sample experienced clinical depression within two years of an abortion, they argue that this is equivalent to population rates. Adler et al. (1990) reviewed the most methodologically sound US studies and concluded that incidence of severe negative responses is low, that distress is greatest before an abortion and reactions are often positive. They argue that abortion can be considered within a stress and coping framework and that the small numbers of women who experience distress are insignificant from a public health perspective. Some research has also considered what type of psychological reactions occur after an abortion. Söderberg et al. (1998) conducted interviews with a large sample of Swedish women ($n = 845$) a year after their abortion and found that 55 per cent experienced some form of emotional distress. In contrast, however, Kero et al. (2004) interviewed 58 women in Sweden a year after their abortion and concluded that most reported no distress following their abortion and that more than half reported only positive experiences. Other researchers have found that relief is commonly expressed after an abortion (Rosenfeld 1992) and Major et al. (2000) found that 72 per cent of their sample was satisfied with their decision two years after. Similarly, Alex and Hammarström (2004) conducted a study in Sweden of five women's experiences and concluded that the women reported gaining a sense of maturity and experience.

The longer-term impact of having an abortion

It would therefore seem that, although some women experience emotional distress post-abortion, others experience more positive reactions such as relief, a return to normality and satisfaction. But do these emotional states persist over time? Russo and Zierk (1992) followed up women eight years after their abortion and compared them to those who had kept the child. They found that having an abortion was related to higher global self-esteem than having an unwanted birth, suggesting that any initial negative reactions decay over time. In a similar vein, Major et al. (2000) explored the variation in emotional reactions over time and reported that negative emotions increased between the time of the abortion and two years, and satisfaction with the decision decreased. These results also suggest a linear pattern of change but one towards worse rather than better adaptation. In contrast, however, some researchers have argued that emotional responses do not always alter in a linear way. For example, Kumar and Robson (1987) found that neurotic disturbances during pregnancy were significantly higher in those who had had a previous termination than those who had not and suggest that this is due to unresolved feelings about the abortion that had been reawakened by the pregnancy. In contrast, however, Adler et al. (1990) argued that research from other life stressors has found that if no severe negative responses are present from a few months to a year after the event, it is unlikely that they will develop later.

The research therefore illustrates variability both in terms of the initial emotional reactions to an abortion and how these reactions change over time. Some research has addressed what factors may explain variability in the initial response. For example, immediate distress has been reported as being higher in those that belong to a society that is antagonistic towards abortion (Major and Gramzow 1999), in those who experienced difficulty making the decision (Lyndon et al. 1996), and in those who are younger, unmarried, have the abortion later in pregnancy (which may be due to the features of women who delay), show low self-esteem or an external locus of control, have had multiple abortions, and self-blame for the pregnancy or abortion (Harris 2004). Further, believing in the human qualities of the foetus has also been associated with higher levels of distress (Conklin and O'Connor 1995). Goodwin and Ogden (2006) explored women's reactions to their abortion up to nine years later and examined how they believed their feelings about the abortion had changed over time. The results showed that, although a few women reported a linear pattern of change in their emotions, some also described different patterns including persistent upset that remained ongoing many years after the event, negative reappraisal some time after the event and a positive appraisal at the time of the event with no subsequent negative emotions. The results also provide some insights into this variability. Those who described how they had never been upset or experienced a linear recovery also tended to conceptualize the foetus as less human, reported having had more social support and described either a belief that abortions are supported by society or an ability to defend against a belief that society is judgemental. In contrast, patterns of emotional change involving persistent upset or negative appraisal were entwined with a more human view of the foetus, a lack of social support and a belief that society is either overly judgemental or negates the impact that an abortion can have on a woman.

The impact of mode of intervention

An abortion can be carried out using a D&C (surgical), vacuum aspiration (suction) or the abortion pill (medical) and may or may not involve a general or local anaesthetic. Some research has explored the relative impact of type of procedure on women's experiences. For example, Slade et al. (1998) examined the impact of having either a medical or surgical abortion. The results showed that those opting for surgical procedure had to wait longer and were more advanced by the time of the abortion but that the two groups showed similar emotional responses prior to having the abortion. After the abortion, however, the medical procedure was seen as more stressful and was associated with more post-termination problems and was seen as more disruptive to their life. Further, seeing the foetus was associated with more intrusive events such as nightmares, flashbacks and unwanted thoughts. Fifty-three per cent of the medical group said they would have the same procedure again whereas 77 per cent of the surgical group felt this. Similarly, Goodwin and Ogden (2006) suggest from their study that the abortion pill technique may result in a more negative experience for several women than other methods as some women described seeing the foetus as it was expelled from their bodies. In contrast, Lowenstein et al. (2006) compared surgical and medical management of abortion and reported no differences in anxiety by two weeks following the abortion. In line with this, Howie et al. (1997) reported no differences in emotional change two years after having either a medical abortion or vacuum aspiration. Perhaps the mode of intervention does result in short-term differences in the women's experiences but after a while the differences begin to disappear. Given the increasing use of these newer modes of intervention, research is required to assess their relative impact on women's short- and longer-term adjustment.

Problems with termination research

People have extremely strong views about terminations which are reflected in alliances such as 'pro-choice' and 'pro-life'. However hard they try, researchers are not immune to their own political or moral positions. Research exploring the impact of termination is therefore problematic because the researcher's own views and experiences are highly likely to influence the research process. For example, an ideological position either for or against termination could affect the choice of research design, the selection of participants, the ways the data are analysed or the ways the data are interpreted and the results presented. Furthermore, the existence of such views may also promote a more black and white view of women's experiences. For example, a researcher who is pro-life may encounter women's experiences which illustrate the times when termination is acceptable (against the researcher's own beliefs) but she may be reluctant to report this. Similarly, a researcher who is pro-choice may encounter data that suggest that abortion is not always a 'good thing' but may be similarly reluctant to add such accounts to the literature. Therefore the highly moral nature of terminations makes the research open to bias. Furthermore, even the existence of an understanding of the moral nature of the subject matter may encourage researchers to be more polarized in their positions.

Conclusion

Research exploring abortions has focused on women's experiences of access to services, the short- and longer-term impact of having a termination of pregnancy and the impact of the mode of treatment on women's experiences. In general the research indicates that access to services varies according to locality but that private specialized services are experienced in a more positive way than state-run services. Further, the results indicate that, although some women report negative mood changes following an abortion, many describe a return to normality and relief although this varies according to a range of individual and social factors as well as the type of intervention used.

Box 16.1 **Some problems with . . . women's health research**

Below are some problems with research in this area that you may wish to consider.

1 Much women's health research generates political and ideological perspectives. For example, termination and menopause management can create a strong sense of what is right or wrong. Research in these areas may therefore be biased in terms of what questions are asked, how data are collected and how the results are interpreted and presented.

2 Many areas of women's health are constantly changing. For example, the use of HRT for the menopause, the management of miscarriages and terminations and the social context of giving birth change from year to year. Summarizing results within these areas across time is therefore difficult.

3 Research in women's health is often addressed from many different theoretical perspectives of which psychology is only one. Integrating research and theories from sociology, gender studies, medicine and anthropology can either produce conflicting conclusions or ones that are so complex and multifactorial that they become difficult to summarize or put into any useful practice.

Pregnancy and birth

Improved access to contraception has resulted in an increasing number of women being able to choose whether and when to have children, and although fertility rates in many developed countries are now below replacement rates, the majority of women do make the choice to become mothers. Motherhood is generally regarded as central to a woman's life and identity, and Oakley (1974) has described the 'motherhood mystique' to reflect the belief that ultimate fulfilment for a woman can only be achieved through having children. Nicolson (1999b) also argues that the 'maternal instinct' is used by evolutionary psychology to present motherhood as normal and Nicolson (1990) describes how media images consistently portray happy mothers, with helpful partners and contented babies. In contrast, much psychological research has explored the problems with pregnancy and motherhood. For example, research has examined anxiety during pregnancy, complications during labour, maladaption to mothering and the onset of motherhood as a life crisis. This chapter will focus on two aspects of pregnancy and birth: the birth experience and how women experience the transition into motherhood.

The birth experience

Much research exploring childbirth focuses on women's experiences of pain and the effectiveness of pain management. This section will focus on women's experiences of the birth process in a broader sense and the impact of the place of birth on these experiences.

The place of birth

In the late nineteenth century, it was the prerogative of the wealthy woman to have her baby at home (Foster 1995). A home birth supported by private health care providers was viewed as the safe and preferable alternative to hospital births with their high rates of maternal mortality and unsanitary conditions. However, throughout most of the twentieth century the medical profession were determined to reverse this position. Hospital births have been recommended increasingly as the safest place of birth and the wide range of possible medical interventions such as Caesareans, forceps and induced births have been presented as central components in the safety debate. However, the 1990s saw a shift in perspective and since this time home births have begun to make a reappearance. Following a thorough examination of the research into birth safety, Tew (1990) argued that changes in infant and maternal morbidity and mortality were in response to nutrition and general health rather than the use of medical interventions. Furthermore, the Winterton Report (Department of Health 1992) argued that the 'policy of encouraging all women to give birth in hospitals cannot be justified on the grounds of safety'. In addition, in response to the recommendations from this report the Expert Maternity Group was established by the government in 1992 and produced the Cumberledge Report *Changing Childbirth* (Department of Health 1993). This report also questioned the policy of systematically recommending hospital births and included a separate section on the place of birth. In particular, the *Changing Childbirth* document called for the development of a woman-centred service which met the needs of the individual and proposed that women should 'be able to choose where they would like their baby to be born'. Therefore the potential benefits of having a home birth are now being given serious consideration although they remain in the minority (see Figure 16.5).

Research to date has explored women's experiences of having either a hospital birth or a home birth and has drawn conclusions about the impact of the place of birth on women's experiences.

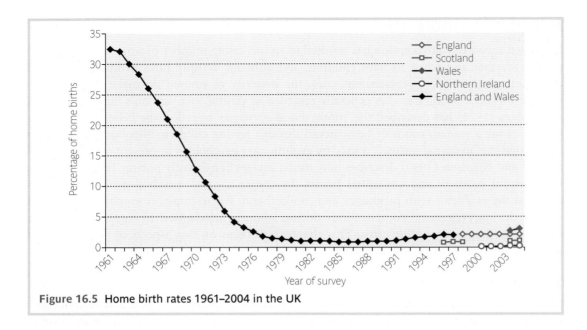

Figure 16.5 Home birth rates 1961–2004 in the UK

Having a hospital birth

Some research has explored women's experiences of having a hospital birth (Oakley 1980; Green et al. 1988; Ogden et al. 1998; Weaver 1998). In general, although research indicates that every pregnant woman wants her child to be healthy and that the birth experience is ultimately seen as a means to an end (Martin 1989; Walton and Hamilton 1995), research indicates that women are often dissatisfied with aspects of their hospital birth experience. For example, research indicates that women feel that they lacked privacy and that the machinery made their environment feel impersonal. Further, they describe how the many professionals around them can feel intrusive, resulting in a sense of anonymity; how they were left in the dark; and how medical interventions can be seen as unnecessary or intrusive (Ogden et al. 1998). Further, much research indicates that a hospital birth can result in a woman feeling out of control of the birth experience, making her feel vulnerable and powerless (Oakley 1980; Weaver 1998). In contrast, however, research also indicates that some women are impressed by the hospital's attempts to make them feel comfortable, how the medical staff are seen as a source of support and how medical interventions are considered a welcome chance for pain relief (Ogden et al. 1998). Although no research to date has explored the reasons behind this variability in experience, likely explanatory factors must include the women's prior expectations and experiences, the quality of care provided in the hospital and the medical requirements of the birth itself.

Having a home birth

Research has also explored women's experiences of having a home birth in terms of their decision making, the experience of the actual birth and the longer-term impact.

Decision making

In terms of the processes involved in choosing to have a home birth, research shows that, while some women are clear from the beginning of their pregnancy that they want a home birth and are determined to stand by their choice whatever the obstacles, for the majority, the decision to have a home birth involves balancing up a range of sometimes conflicting factors (Wesson 1990; Mosse 1993; Ogden et al. 1997a). The factors that women consider include the benefits of being in their own home, the perceived negative aspects of being in a hospital, and the relative safety of their home environment. In particular, although hospitals are regarded as safer in the case of an emergency, women who chose a home birth believe that hospitals are associated with illness and disease and therefore in certain ways more dangerous than their own home. Women also report being exposed to a range of both professional and lay views which had supported their decision and indicated that the views of their GP, midwives, partners, friends and families had helped them to decide on a home birth and carry this decision through to fruition. Women, however, also report several obstacles that hinder having a home birth. For example, some GPs and midwives are described as being obstructive, and partners, families and friends are sometimes seen as unenthusiastic, worried and concerned for the woman's health or anxious about their own potential involvement (Wesson 1990; Mosse 1993; Ogden et al. 1997a).

The home-birth experience

Research has also explored how women experience having a home birth. In particular, women seem to emphasize a sense of normality, the peaceful atmosphere and the role of other people around them. In addition, women describe how these aspects of the environment influenced their experience in terms of feeling in control, their pain and being able to share their experiences with others important to them. For example, the familiarity of the environment helped them to integrate the time leading up to the birth into their normal life with other family members. It increased their sense of control as they felt a sense of ownership over the birth and it also provided a role for the partner. Further, it appeared to influence how they experienced pain. Generally, therefore, women express beliefs that being at home improves the birth experience for them (Oakley 1986; Drew et al. 1989; Seguin et al. 1989; Ogden et al. 1997b, 1997c). The research therefore indicates that home births are generally regarded in a positive way.

The longer-term effect of having a home birth

Some research has also explored the longer-term impact of having a home birth and describes how women feel that their ability to have a baby at home can make them feel more confident about themselves and subsequently better equipped to deal with their children. Further, women describe how the home birth reassured them that their bodies functioned properly. Women also describe the impact of the home birth in terms of their reappraisal of past events and their interpretation of future ones. The home birth appears to help some women put negative past events such as death and difficult births into a more positive framework. Further, a home birth appeared to have a lasting positive influence on their interpretation of future relationships with a range of individuals (Wesson 1990; Mosse 1993; Ogden et al. 1997a, 1997b, 1997c).

The impact of the place of birth

The research therefore indicates that home births are mainly regarded in a more positive way than hospital births. Research on the birth experience in general illustrates that a better experience is related to feelings of control and support from partners (Oakley 1986). A home birth may be experienced in such a positive way because these very factors which are associated with a positive birth experience are more likely to occur if the birth happens at home (Oakley 1986; Drew et al. 1989; Seguin et al. 1989; Ogden et al. 1997b, 1997c; Weaver 1998). However, there are several problems with directly comparing the experiences of hospital and home births. In particular, no research to date has carried out a randomized control trial to explore the impact of place of birth and the woman's experiences. This is primarily due to the different medical requirements of different births and the ultimate need to protect the safety of the baby and mother but results in a multitude of differences between births other than just whether they occur in a hospital or at home. For example, the mothers who chose a home birth may be different to those who chose a hospital birth in terms of a wide range of factors such as physical health, social class, expectations, beliefs about the birth, support from partners, previous birth experiences, their own place of birth, their ability to manage pain and their ability to negotiate a home birth if confronted with obstacles. Further, the births may differ in terms of factors such as size of the baby, gestation of the baby and health of the baby during pregnancy. In addition, many structural factors determine the place of birth including access to home support and community midwives, medical support for home births and general cultural differences in beliefs about where babies should be born. Therefore evidence indicates that home births are associated with a more positive birth experience which seems to have a longer-term impact upon the woman. However, such conclusions need to be drawn in the context of an understanding of the vast methodological problems with research in this area.

The transition into motherhood

Research has also explored how women feel when they become mothers and how motherhood impacts upon a range of factors including self-esteem, identity, marital quality, well-being and quality of life. This chapter will explore research that emphasizes the negative impact of motherhood and a more positive view, and research that has taken a broader perspective.

The negative impact of motherhood

In the main most research indicates that motherhood has a negative impact upon most of the psychological factors measured. For example, Feldman and Nash (1984) reported that, while expectant parents are optimistic and excited about the birth of their first child, parenthood itself is associated with unexpected upheaval and distress. Similarly, Elliott and Huppert (1991) reported that women with children aged under 5 had lower well-being and that those with several children under 5 reported even lower well-being, and Willen and Montgomery (1993) concluded that having a child was associated with a sense of emotional separation, alienation and disappointment. Furthermore, Belsky and Rovine (1990) concluded from a longitudinal study that, while marital quality decreases after the birth of a child, those relationships already under strain will deteriorate the most following parenthood.

As a means to explore why motherhood can have such detrimental effects, Oakley (1980) carried out 66 interviews with women while pregnant and shortly after childbirth. She presents a detailed analysis of their experiences and argues that pregnancy results in an overwhelming loss of identity for women due to four major changes: becoming a patient, stopping paid work, becoming a housewife and becoming a mother. Further, she argues that these changes are all experienced as loss by the woman as they are all considered to result in lowered status by society. Other research has explored what factors are related to changes in psychological state following motherhood. Much of this has addressed the issue of partners' roles and the division of labour. For example, research indicates that perceived inequity in household tasks between partners following the birth of a child relates to decreased marital quality (Terry et al. 1991) and that is particularly the case if women have high expectations that are not met (Nicolson 1990a; Hackel and Ruble 1992).

A more positive view

Not all research indicates that pregnancy and motherhood are systematically negative events. For example, Moss et al. (1987) explored British couples' experiences of becoming parents and reported that 90 per cent reported no significant deterioration in the marriages. Similarly, Palkovitz and Copes (1988) contacted new parents within a month of the birth of their first child and reported increases in self-esteem for both parents. Furthermore, research shows more positive reactions to motherhood in older mothers who have delayed childbearing, older fathers who can be more involved with their children and couples who have been together for longer (Robinson et al. 1988; Dion 1995; Cooney et al. 1993). It has been suggested that such parents are more likely to have less traditional approaches to role division of labour and to believe in the importance of the achievement of life goals before embarking upon parenthood (Robinson et al. 1988; Cooney et al. 1993; Dion 1995).

A broader perspective

Much psychological research has assessed the impact of motherhood using pre-existing measures with a focus upon aspects of psychological morbidity. In contrast, some qualitative research has taken a broader perspective. Smith (1994a, 1994b, 1999) carried out an in-depth idiographic case study analysis of four women's experiences of pregnancy and early motherhood which involved interviews at four time points: three, six and nine months' pregnant and then five months after the birth of the child. The women also kept a diary throughout the pregnancy and at five months they were asked to write a retrospective account of the pregnancy to enable a comparison with the real-time accounts obtained through the interviews. Over the course of the study women expressed a range of experiences including feeling more self-contained and less concerned about external events, feeling more self-confident, seeing birth as a primeval experience, wondering about the birth process and feeling fear and anxiety about pain, realizing that the baby is becoming an independent being, building connections with important other people such as their partner and mother, and coming to terms with their future selves. Three key themes emerged from the analysis which illustrate women's experiences of pregnancy and mothering and how their reflections upon their experiences change over time. First, the narratives illustrate how the women saw the process of pregnancy as preparation for giving birth and becoming a mother. Second, the results showed a gradual movement inwards which was reflected in a shift in attention from the women's outside world towards their inner pregnant world whereby external factors such as work seem trivial compared to the internal world of containment and a sense of self-confidence. Third, the results illustrated a shift towards becoming a more relational self as women conceptualized themselves as part of a unit including the baby, their partner and other key people. Overall, Smith (1994a, 1994b, 1999) concludes that pregnancy is a time when women become both more autonomous and more affiliated at the same time and that these factors are not mutually exclusive. Further, he concludes that pregnancy offers a metaphor for motherhood, enabling mothers to rehearse and come to terms with their new future role. In a similar vein, Millward (2006) explored women's experiences of pregnancy and returning to work and concluded that women who chose to work after they have children struggle to maintain their identity within their workplace while simultaneously managing their needs and concerns as mothers. This is discussed in depth in **Focus on Research 16.1**.

Exploring experience – the transition into motherhood

A study to explore women's experience of returning to work after childbirth (Millward 2006).

Background

Women make up about 45 per cent of the workforce in the UK and, as most women have children at some time, every organization will at some time employ mothers. Further, the proportion of women returning to work soon after childbirth has doubled since 1983 with about two-thirds of women who have children being economically active again within nine months. This study used a qualitative design to explore women's experience of returning to work after childbirth. This is an interesting paper as it offers a balanced insight into the complexities of the transition into motherhood for those mothers who choose to continue to work.

Methodology
Design

The study used a qualitative design with in-depth interviews.

Sample

Ten women were interviewed during pregnancy and eight of these were reinterviewed after they had returned to work.

Data analysis

The transcripts were analysed using interpretative phenomenological analysis (Smith 2003).

Results

Two master themes emerged from the analysis. These were changes in identity and changed psychological contracts:

- *Changes in identity.* The transcripts illustrated identity changes arising out of a dynamic between the woman and the perceived reactions of others. These were described across three stages of transition: pre-leave, maternity leave, post-leave. At pre-leave the women described how, though becoming physically more visible, they felt that they were becoming invisible to the company as an employee. They described being excluded from the prospect of the future of the company, resulting in a sense of insecurity, confusion and concern and alienation. This was contrasted in many cases with a feeling that motherhood would bring with it a sense of validation. During the maternity-leave period the women experienced a series of dilemmas about whether returning to work would be good for the baby, and whether they could justify returning to work to themselves. They seemed to draw upon the 'good mother stays at home' benchmark. At this time some described being fearful of losing their work identity and some felt guilty about wanting to return to work. During the post-leave period all women described finding it difficult to reintegrate and some found it difficult to revalidate themselves as both a worker and a mother. In part this was due to the practicalities of managing two life roles but also to the need to be seen as a valued employee rather than a working mother. All women described achieving validation if they could share their experiences with others at work, make social comparisons and draw upon role models.

■ *Changed psychological contracts.* A psychological contract describes a process of exchange between employer and employee which comprises a set of terms and conditions about the exchange. In this study nearly all women described an awareness of a set of performance expectations and a fear that they would no longer be able to meet them. In the pre-leave time all women said that they felt guilty that they would not be able to fulfil performance expectations because of tiredness and the need to take time out which came from the internal pressures that they placed upon themselves. On returning to work they felt that their commitment and aspirations were under question and either felt patronized by comments about their new motherhood status or were relieved to have changes in their status acknowledged. In addition, many had returned to part-time posts with different responsibilities. Some felt that they were still expected to do their old jobs and resented this, while some felt that they wanted their old jobs back with the status associated with them.

Conclusion

The results therefore suggest that returning to work after childbirth brings with it issues of changes of identity and psychological contracts. In particular the author concludes that women struggle with their needs, concerns and rights as mothers while trying to maintain their identity as a valued member of the organization. This is an interesting paper as it explores the complexity of becoming a mother and provides an antidote to much of the literature which tends to highlight either the pros or the cons of having a child.

Problems with research exploring pregnancy and birth

Some problems with research in this area are as follows:

1 Exploring the impact of place of birth upon the birth experience is hampered by the absence of randomized studies and the vast differences between women who have their children at home and those who have them in hospital.

2 Women's experience of hospital births are very dependent upon the attitude of the hospital staff which will vary enormously. Negative experiences may be due to the specific hospital or the specific staff members rather than hospitals in general.

3 Studies exploring women's experiences of motherhood generally seem to suggest that becoming a parent has many negative consequences. This may be the case. But it may also reflect psychologists' tendency to focus on negative constructs and negative outcomes. It may be the case that, although women do show deterioration in the areas measured, they simultaneously show improvements in areas that have yet to be assessed.

Conclusion

Although more women can now choose whether to have children, the majority still do and pregnancy and becoming a mother remain a central part of the lives of many women. This section has explored women's experiences of childbirth and the impact of the transition into motherhood. Research exploring women's experiences of birth illustrates how varied these experiences can be and that, while some women find hospitals lacking in privacy and feel out of control, some enjoy the independence and control they feel from a home birth, and others welcome the medical support and opportunities for pain relief they can get in a hospital setting. Research exploring the transition into motherhood indicates that motherhood can have several detrimental effects on aspects of a woman's health and well-being but that these are not the case for all women and are lessened in those who delay having children.

The menopause

The word 'menopause' means the end of monthly menstruation and for the average woman occurs at the age of 51 years with 80 per cent of women reaching the menopause by age 54. In general the menopause is considered to be a transition which has been classified according to three stages (World Health Organization 1996). The pre-menopause refers to the whole of the women's reproductive life up until the end of the last menstrual period. The peri-menopause is the time prior to the final menstrual period when hormonal changes are taking place and continues until a year after the last menstrual period. The post-menopause stage refers to any time after the last menstrual period but has to be defined retrospectively after 12 months of no menstruation. Therefore the menopause reflects the end point of a gradual change in biological function which is finally lost as the woman stops producing eggs and the level of oestrogen produced is reduced as it is no longer required to stimulate the lining of the womb in preparation for fertilization. The cessation of menstruation for 12 consecutive months is the required period of time for a doctor to define a woman as menopausal, with research showing that around 75 per cent of women present to their doctor about the menopause (Hope et al. 1998). Although there is a strong genetic determinant of the time of the menopause, with mothers and daughters tending to become menopausal at a similar age, smoking can result in an earlier menopause and being heavier can result in a later menopause. In addition to the cessation of periods, the menopause brings with it other symptoms while it is happening and results in longer-term physical changes due to the reduction in female hormones.

Symptoms

During the menopause women report a range of symptoms, some of which are clearly linked to a reduction in oestrogen while others have unclear origins. These illustrate the complex nature of symptoms and the role of social and psychological factors in influencing symptom perception. The most common symptoms are the following:

- change in pattern and heaviness of periods
- hot flushes
- night sweats
- tiredness
- poor concentration
- aches and pains in joints
- vaginal dryness
- changes in the frequency of passing urine.

As part of a large-scale survey, 413 women completed a questionnaire about their experiences of menopausal symptoms and their perceptions of severity, and the results showed that the most common symptoms were hot flushes, night sweats and tiredness, and of these, night sweats seemed to cause the most distress with over a third describing their night sweats as severe (Ballard 2003). The results from this study are illustrated in Figure 16.6.

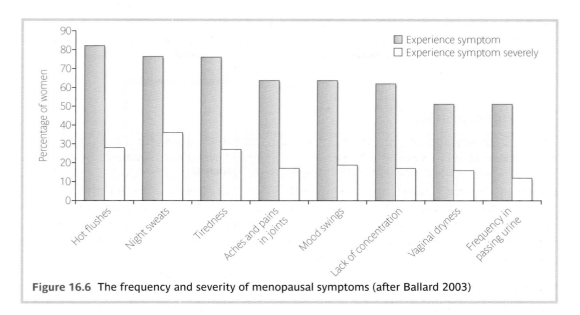

Figure 16.6 The frequency and severity of menopausal symptoms (after Ballard 2003)

Physical changes

Women also experience a range of physical changes which persist after the menopause has passed. In particular they show changes in their breasts and it is suggested that older women should have regular mammograms to check for breast cancer. There is a post-menopausal increase in cholesterol in the blood which places women more at risk of heart disease; bone loss becomes more rapid, increasing the chance of osteoporosis; the urinary organs can become less elastic and pliable, resulting in many women suffering from incontinence, and finally women experience vaginal dryness, making sexual intercourse uncomfortable.

The menopause therefore signifies the end of a woman's reproductive capacity and brings with it a wide range of symptoms and physical changes. Ballard (2003) describes how the menopause experience is influence by a range of social, cultural and biological factors which in turn have a psychological impact upon the individual. This reflects why the menopause is also referred to as 'the change of life'. This is illustrated in Figure 16.7.

Research exploring the impact of the menopause has highlighted the experience of the menopause as a life transition and the social and psychological factors that affect this transition. This chapter will now explore these different areas.

The menopause as a transition

As part of a larger-scale cohort study which has collected data regularly from people born during the first week of March 1946 (see Wadsworth 1991; Wadsworth and Kuh 1997; Ballard et al. 2001), 1572 women described their menopausal years. The women completed questions about their symptoms and health in general and then 65 per cent also completed a 'free comments' section. These data were then analysed using both quantitative and qualitative methods. From this study the authors conclude that women experience the menopause as a status passage which involves five stages. These are as follows:

1 *Expectations of symptoms.* The results illustrate that, prior to the menopause onset, women are searching for symptoms and looking for signs of any biological changes. At this point some women seek help from the doctor and start to find further information.

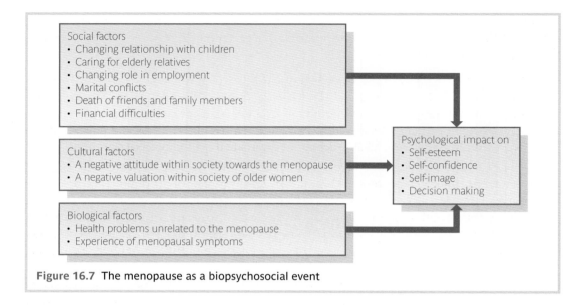

Figure 16.7 The menopause as a biopsychosocial event

2 *Experience of symptoms and loss of control.* Women then start to experience symptoms such as night sweats, hot flushes and mood swings, which for some interfere with their sense of well-being and can make them feel out of control.

3 *Confirmation of the menopause.* Once women sense a loss of control, they then try to confirm the onset of the menopause by visiting their doctor as a means to regain control. The doctor can use blood tests to measure hormone levels to confirm the onset of the menopause and at this stage many women are offered hormone replacement therapy (HRT).

4 *Regaining control.* Women try to regain control in several ways. Some try to minimize the impact of their symptoms by taking HRT while others try a range of methods such as wearing different clothes to cope with hot flushes or taking alternative medicines.

5 *Freedom from menstruation.* The end of menstruation is often welcomed by women as, for the majority, decisions about family size have been made long ago. Women therefore feel relieved that they do not have to experience the pain and bleeding from periods any more and the inconvenience that this can cause.

The menopause is therefore seen as a process through which women go, which starts with a sense of expectation and loss of control and finishes with a sense of freedom and regained control. For many women and doctors this transition is managed through the use of HRT as the symptoms and changes associated with the menopause are attributed to changes in hormone levels. For some researchers, however, this perspective has been seen as over medicalizing the menopause which provides a platform for medicine to take control of women's bodies (Oakley 1984; Doyal 1994). The results from the large-scale women's health study (Ballard et al. 2001) suggest that, although many women conceptualize the menopause as a medical event, they also locate it within the complex social and psychological changes that also occur at this time.

Social factors and the menopause

The menopause happens at a time in a woman's life when she is probably also experiencing a range of other changes. Whether or not such changes have a direct or indirect effect upon the menopausal experience, research indicates that the menopause needs to be understood in the context of these changes and describes these changes and their effect upon the menopause as follows (Ballard et al. 2001; Ballard 2003):

1 *Elderly relatives.* At the time of the menopause women often find that they are also increasingly responsible for caring for elderly relatives. Further, this may come at a time when women are just starting to enjoy a newfound freedom from the children leaving home. The added pressure of elderly relatives can make women feel under stress and guilty and can affect their physical health, all of which may exacerbate their menopausal symptoms.

2 *Changes in employment and finance.* In middle life many women increase their hours of work as the children leave home. This may bring with it new opportunities and a sense of rebirth. However, it can also be an extra stressor, particularly if women still have the primary responsibility for the home. In contrast, some women retire in middle life which brings with it its own sets of stresses in terms of readjustment and a need to develop a new self-image. Both these types of changes in employment can influence the menopause and its associated symptoms.

3 *Changing relationships.* At the time of the menopause women often experience changes in their role as a mother as this is the time when children leave home, and a change in their relationships with their partners as they renegotiate a new life without children. Such changes can make the menopause seem more pertinent as it reflects the end of an era.

4 *Death of family or friends.* As women reach their fifties they may experience the death of similar-age family or friends. The menopause may represent a sense of mortality which can be exacerbated by a sense of loss.

According to Ballard et al. (2001) these social factors coexist alongside the time of the menopause and can influence the ways in which the menopause is experienced. In turn they result in subsequent changes in the individual's psychological state.

Psychological effects of the menopause

Psychological factors influence the menopause in terms of symptom perception as symptoms such as hot flushes, night sweats, lack of concentration and tiredness are all influenced by processes such as distraction, focus, mood, meaning and the environment (see Chapter 3). In addition, the menopause has more direct effects upon the individual's psychological state. Ballard (2003) describes these as the following:

1 *Changes in body image.* The menopause brings with it physical changes such as dryer skin, changing fat distribution and softer breasts, which can all impact upon a woman's body image. In addition, becoming 50 is also seen as a milestone, particularly within a society that associates getting older with being less attractive. Ballard (2003) provides interesting descriptions of how women can suddenly catch themselves in a mirror and think 'it's my mum' or 'you are getting old'. Such changes in body image and body dissatisfaction are in line with those described in Chapter 5.

2 *Mood changes.* Some women report experiencing moods such as anxiety and depression and some report having panic attacks. Given the many life changes that co-occur with the menopause, it is not surprising that women experience changes in their mood. However, many women view their emotional shifts as directly linked to their changing hormone levels. This therefore raises the problem of attribution as there is a danger of all

menopausal women's emotional shifts being attributed to their biological state which make them seem 'unstable'. However, there is also the converse problem that 'real' biological mechanisms are ignored and that emotions are inappropriately attributed to more social reasons.

3 *Self-esteem and self-confidence.* Some women also report decreases in their self-esteem and self-confidence. They describe not feeling confident in everyday tasks such as cooking or work, and feeling less able to manage relationships.

4 *Lack of concentration.* Several surveys report that women describe how the menopause disrupts their cognitive function in terms of concentration and memory (Rubin and Quine 1995; Ballard et al. 2001). Experimental studies in controlled conditions, however, show no evidence for any cognitive decline that could be attributed to the menopause above and beyond standard age effects (Herlitz et al. 1997).

The research exploring women's experiences of the menopause therefore shows that it is experienced as a transition which is accompanied by symptoms and longer-term physical changes. Although many of these factors may be related to underlying shifts in a woman's biology, the research also indicates that the experience of the menopause needs to be understood in the context of other social changes which in turn influence a woman's psychological state. The menopause can therefore be conceptualized as one part of a series of changes that happen to a woman during her midlife.

The impact of mode of management

The menopause can be managed in a range of ways. Some women simply carry on with their lives and wait for the symptoms to pass. They may manage these symptoms using 'tricks of the trade' such as wearing layered clothes rather than thick jumpers to make removing clothes easier should they have a hot flush, sleeping with the window open to cope with night sweats and buying lubricants to manage vaginal dryness, but they do not necessarily present their symptoms to the doctor. Others may try alternative medicines for symptom relief including herbal remedies, homeopathy and acupuncture, preferring a more natural approach. Many, however, do visit their doctor and are prescribed HRT. Further, the numbers of women taking HRT increased threefold between 1981 and 1990 up to 19 per cent and increased to a rate of 60 per cent by 2000 (Moorhead et al. 1997; Kuh et al. 2000; Ballard 2002b). HRT was originally developed to reduce menopausal symptoms but has subsequently been shown to treat and prevent osteoporosis, Alzheimer's disease, cardiovascular disease and depression. It also has its own risks, however, and has been associated with breast and endometrial cancer, heart attack, cerebrovascular disease and thromboembolic disease (see Writing Group for the Women's Health Initiative Investigators 2002; Beral et al. 2005 for a comprehensive review). Research has explored how women decide whether or not to take HRT and the impact of taking HRT upon symptoms.

Deciding how to manage the menopause

HRT may help to alleviate menopausal symptoms and can protect against menopause-related diseases. But at the same time evidence indicates that it can increase the risk of longer-term health problems. Women therefore have to weigh up the pros and cons of HRT if they are to decide how to manage their menopause. Ballard (2002b) analysed questionnaire data from 413 women of menopausal age to explore why women take HRT. The results showed that the main reason women took HRT was for the relief of symptoms, particularly hot flushes, tiredness and irritability. Similarly, Welton et al. (2004) carried out eight focus groups with 82 women aged between 50 and 69. The results showed that, for those women taking HRT, the main reason was perceived improvement in quality of life regardless of either the costs or benefits in the longer term. In addition, however, Ballard (2002b) also reported that 58 per cent also took HRT to prevent osteoporosis. Symptom relief would therefore be the main factor influencing the decision-making process. Protection from illness, however, also seems to have a role to play. As a means to further understand the decision-making process, Buick et al. (2005) carried out a systematic review of the literature between 1980 and 2002 to explore women's beliefs about HRT. The results from their analysis support the results described earlier and indicate that use and discontinuation of HRT are more related to symptom relief than considerations of long-term benefits. Further, the results indicate that those women who refuse HRT often believe that the menopause is a natural event that does not require chemical intervention and that women's beliefs about the benefits of HRT are often countered by their concerns about potential adverse events (see Chapter 3 for a discussion of beliefs about medicines). Not all women, however, take HRT and Wathen (2006) explored women's use of complementary and alternative medicines (CAM). This study used a mixed method approach and reported that 57 per cent of the Canadian sample had either considered or used CAM as an alternative to HRT and that these women tended to be younger and had experienced worse symptoms than those who had not tried CAM.

The impact of HRT on symptoms

Women report a wide range of menopausal symptoms which vary in their severity and the impact they have on their quality of life. HRT was invented as a means to relieve these symptoms and, as described earlier, those who take HRT do so mostly for symptom relief. Much research has explored the extent to which HRT does actually relieve menopausal symptoms. From the perspective of the patient, research indicates that women feel better when taking HRT and report improvements in their symptoms and quality of life. For example, Abraham et al. (1995) explored 60 women's beliefs about HRT when they were pre-menopausal and then 10 years later when they were post-menopausal. Thirty-eight of these had taken HRT. The results showed that the majority of the women believed that HRT helped hot flushes, non-specific emotional changes, vaginal dryness, insomnia and loss of muscle tone. In contrast, however, a large randomized trial, which explored the effectiveness of HRT compared to a placebo, suggested that HRT may not be as effective as believed (Utian et al. 1999). In particular this double-blind placebo-controlled study showed that HRT was only effective at relieving vasomotor symptoms such as hot flushes and night sweats. Similarly, another placebo-controlled trial showed that HRT only improved vaginal dryness, increased frequency of passing urine and the tendency to get urinary infections (Eriksen and Rasmussen 1992). These data suggest no effect for insomnia and mood. Further, they were placebo controlled, suggesting that such changes cannot simply be attributed to women wanting to feel better. Rymer et al. (2003) explored the effectiveness of HRT and suggest that this discrepancy between perceived effectiveness and actual effectiveness may illustrate a domino effect. In particular, while HRT may only relieve hot flushes and vaginal dryness, which can be directly explained by oestrogen deficiency, such changes may in turn improve mood, sleep and general quality of life.

Problems with research on the menopause

Problems with research on the menopause include the following:

1   The menopause happens to all women regardless of class, culture or time. Most research to date, however, has explored the experiences of western women for whom the menopause is often seen as an event that needs to be managed medically. It is likely that other cultures have very different beliefs and experiences of the menopause and that this would influence their management strategies. More cross-cultural research is needed to explore how cultural factors impact upon the menopause experience.

2   New research is constantly being published about the risks and benefits of HRT. Studies exploring women's beliefs and use of HRT must therefore be located within the time that the data were collected and the current state of evidence at this time. This means that aggregating studies is problematic and drawing conclusions across time is difficult.

3   The menopause and HRT generate strong beliefs in researchers, clinicians and patients according to the need for any medical intervention, the dangers of HRT and the dangers of menopause-related disease. Interpreting research is therefore problematic as results and the ways in which results are presented may well reflect the beliefs of the people involved.

4   Research on the menopause and HRT illustrates the complex problem of risk analysis and risk communication as symptoms, side effects and longer-term costs and benefits will have different meanings to all the parties involved. There is a tendency within the literature to attempt to find the state of 'truth' within all these risks and probabilities. Future psychological research could focus on how different risks are managed and communicated without attempting to synthesize them.

Conclusion

The menopause reflects the end of a woman's reproductive life and brings with it a range of symptoms and longer-term physical changes. Research has explored how women experience the menopause and suggests that it is considered a life transition which results in a range of psychological shifts and changes. However, the research also suggests that, although some of these changes may be directly related to the biological nature of the menopause, they are also created or exacerbated by the multitude of social changes that occur in a women's life at the same time. The menopause is therefore best understood as a time where biological, social and psychological factors come together. Research has also explored how women choose to manage their menopause and the impact of HRT on menopausal symptoms. The results indicate that many women choose HRT primarily for symptom relief but that its effect on symptoms may not be as straightforward as once believed.

To conclude

There are many areas of health that are specific to women. This chapter has explored four of these areas which were chosen because they seemed to have generated the most research and to most closely reflect the interests of the health psychology community. Miscarriage, termination, childbirth and the menopause are generally regarded as negative events that women often have to endure. The results from the studies described in this chapter indicate that, although these are difficult and often unpleasant times for women, many women report how they can also see the benefit in these experiences. In particular, miscarriage is sometimes seen as a pivotal point in a woman's life, enabling her to re-evaluate her past and future self; termination is often accompanied by feelings of relief and a return to normality; childbirth brings with it a new identity and sense of self; and the menopause introduces a new period of life and a sense of liberation. Furthermore the research illustrates how women's experiences of these events are influenced by the mode of management as all can be managed either medically or in a more natural way.

❓ Questions

1 To what extent are women's responses to miscarriage similar to those following bereavement?

2 Discuss the problems inherent in carrying out research into the experience of having an abortion.

3 To what extent is the experience of having an abortion influenced by the social context?

4 'Motherhood is a natural state which brings ultimate satisfaction'. Discuss.

5 To what extent are women's experiences of the menopause a response to the biological changes that occur at this time?

6 How are women's experiences of their health problems influenced by the mode of management chosen?

For discussion

Consider how someone you know (your mother, friend, etc.) experienced the menopause. Reflect upon how this experience may have been affected by other factors that were changing at the same time.

Assumptions in health psychology

1 *The mind–body split.* Research often assumes that the mind and the body are separate. Women's health issues illustrate how the physical changes caused by factors such as miscarriage, termination, pregnancy and the menopause have a direct influence upon the individual's psychological state. From this perspective the body influences the mind. It is also likely, however, that the actual physical changes themselves are also affected by the individual's psychology.

▶

2 *Progression.* It is often assumed that research and technology result in improvements. In terms of women's health issues there have been many developments that have resulted in changes in how these issues are managed, such as the invention of HRT and the development of new procedures to management termination and miscarriage. Whether such developments are of benefit, however, is unclear as they often illustrate the issue of iatrogenesis; although they are new solutions they can end up causing harm.

3 *Research as theory generating.* Research aims to be objective and explore and generate ideas. Much research in the area of women's health is very contentious and touches upon highly politicized and ideological areas. The research is therefore likely to be open to researcher bias and the desired objectivity will be undermined by the researcher's own perspective.

Further reading

Clements, S. (1998) *Psychological Perspectives on Pregnancy and Childbirth.* Edinburgh: Churchill Livingstone.
This is an edited collection of chapters describing a range of aspects of childbirth and pregnancy including women's experiences of antenatal care, PTSD following childbirth and men becoming fathers. It is written from a psychological perspective and provides good coverage of some of the areas not addressed in the current chapter.

Freeman, E.W. and Rickels, K. (1993) *Early Childbearing: Perspectives of Black Adolescents on Pregnancy, Abortion and Childbearing.* Thousand Oaks, CA: Sage.
This book is based upon the Penn study of black teenagers' experiences and provides detailed descriptions of their beliefs about pregnancy, abortion and childbearing. It also explores the longer-term impact of their decisions and behaviour and locates them within the literature. Although focusing on a very specific sample, the results resonate with the wider literature.

Lee, C. (1998) *Women's Health: Psychological and Social Perspectives.* London: Sage.
This book covers a wide range of issues relating to women's health not covered by the present chapter, including pre-menstrual syndrome, post-partum depression and fertility control. It therefore offers a useful background into the areas not addressed by this book.

Moulder, C. (1998) *Understanding Pregnancy Loss: Perspectives and Issues in Care.* London: Macmillan.
This is an excellent book that draws upon the experiences of women who have had either a miscarriage, termination or still birth and locates their experiences within the existing literature. It explores a range of factors including health care prior to admission, experiences of being in hospital, health professionals' views and care after discharge.

Chapter 17

Measuring health status

From mortality rates to quality of life

Chapter overview

This chapter examines the different ways in which health status has been measured from mortality rates to quality of life. In addition, it describes the ways in which quality of life has been used in research both in terms of the factors that predict quality of life (quality of life as an outcome variable) and the association between quality of life and longevity (quality of life as a predictor).

This chapter covers

- Mortality rates
- Morbidity rates
- Measures of functioning
- Subjective health status
- Quality of life measures
- Predicting quality of life
- Quality of life and longevity

Mortality rates

At its most basic, a measure of health status takes the form of a very crude mortality rate, which is calculated by simply counting the number of deaths in one year compared with either previous or subsequent years. The question asked is, 'Has the number of people who have died this year gone up, gone down or stayed the same?' An increase in mortality rate can be seen as a decrease in health status and a decrease as an increase in health status. This approach, however, requires a denominator: a measure of who is at risk. The next most basic form of mortality rate therefore includes a denominator reflecting the size of the population being studied. Such a measure allows for comparisons to be made between different populations: more people may die in a given year in London when compared with Bournemouth, but London is simply bigger. In order to provide any meaningful measure of health status, mortality rates are corrected for age (Bournemouth has an older population and therefore we would predict that more people would die each year) and sex (men generally die younger than women and this needs to be taken into account). Furthermore, mortality rates can be produced to be either age specific, such as infant mortality rates, or illness specific, such as sudden death rates. As long as the population being studied is accurately specified, corrected and specific, mortality rates provide an easily available and simple measure: death is a good reliable outcome.

Morbidity rates

Laboratory and clinical researchers and epidemiologists may accept mortality rates as the perfect measure of health status. However, the juxtaposition of social scientists to the medical world has challenged this position to raise the now seemingly obvious question, 'Is health really only the absence of death?' In response to this, there has been an increasing focus upon morbidity. However, in line with the emphasis upon simplicity inherent within the focus on mortality rates, many morbidity measures still use methods of counting and recording. For example, the expensive and time-consuming production of morbidity prevalence rates involves large surveys of 'caseness' to simply count how many people within a given population suffer from a particular problem. Likewise, sickness absence rates simply count days lost due to illness and caseload assessments count the number of people who visit their general practitioner or hospital within a given time frame. Such morbidity rates provide details at the level of the population in general. However, morbidity is also measured for each individual using measures of functioning.

Measures of functioning

Measures of functioning ask the question, 'To what extent can you do the following tasks?' and are generally called activity-of-daily-living scales (ADLs). For example, Katz et al. (1970) designed the index of activities of daily living to assess levels of functioning in the elderly. This was developed for the therapist and/or carer to complete and asked the rater to evaluate the individual on a range of dimensions including bathing, dressing, continence and feeding. ADLs have also been developed for individuals themselves to complete and include questions such as, 'Do you or would you have any difficulty: washing down/cutting toenails/running to catch a bus/going up/down stairs?' Measures of functioning can either be administered on their own or as part of a more complex assessment involving measures of subjective health status.

Subjective health status

Over recent years, measures of health status have increasingly opted for measures of subjective health status, which all have one thing in common: they ask the individuals themselves to rate their health. Some of these are referred to as subjective health measures, while others are referred to as either quality-of-life scales or health-related quality-of-life scales. However, the literature in the area of subjective health status and quality of life is plagued by two main questions: 'What is quality of life?' and 'How should it be measured?'

What is quality of life?

Reports of a Medline search on the term 'quality of life' indicate a surge in its use from 40 citations (1966–74), to 1907 citations (1981–85), to 5078 citations (1986–90) (Albrecht 1994). Quality of life is obviously in vogue. However, to date there exists no consensus as to what it actually is. For example, it has been defined as 'the value assigned to duration of life as modified by the impairments, functional states, perceptions and social opportunities that are influenced by disease, injury, treatment or policy' (Patrick and Ericson 1993), 'a personal statement of the positivity or negativity of attributes that characterise one's life' (Grant et al. 1990) and by the World Health Organization as 'a broad ranging concept affected in a complex way by the person's physical health, psychological state, level of independence, social relationships and their relationship to the salient features in their environment' (WHOQoL Group 1993). Further, while some researchers treat the concepts of quality of life as interchangeable, others argue that they are separate (Bradley 2001).

Such problems with definition have resulted in a range of ways of operationalizing quality of life. For example, following the discussions about an acceptable definition of quality of life, the European Organization for Research on Treatment of Cancer operationalized quality of life in terms of 'functional status, cancer and treatment specific symptoms, psychological distress, social interaction, financial/economic impact, perceived health status and overall quality of life' (Aaronson et al. 1993). In line with this, their measure consisted of items that reflected these different dimensions. Likewise, the researchers who worked on the Rand Corporation health batteries operationalized quality of life in terms of 'physical functioning, social functioning, role limitations due to physical problems, role limitations due to emotional problems, mental health, energy/vitality, pain and general health perception', which formed the basic dimensions of their scale (e.g. Stewart and Ware 1992). Furthermore, Fallowfield (1990) defined the four main dimensions of quality of life as psychological (mood, emotional distress, adjustment to illness), social (relationships, social and leisure activities), occupational (paid and unpaid work) and physical (mobility, pain, sleep and appetite).

Creating a conceptual framework

In response to the problems of defining quality of life, researchers have recently attempted to create a clearer conceptual framework for this construct. In particular, researchers have divided quality-of-life measures either according to who devises the measure or in terms of whether the measure is considered objective or subjective.

Who devises the measure?

Browne et al. (1997) differentiated between the standard-needs approach and the psychological processes perspective. The first of these is described as being based on the assumption that 'a consensus about what constitutes a good or poor quality of life exists or at least can be discovered through investigation' (Browne et al. 1997: 738). In addition, the standard-needs approach assumes that needs rather than wants are central to quality of life and that these needs are common to all, including the researchers. In contrast, the psychological-processes approach considers quality of life to be 'constructed from individual evaluations of personally salient aspects of life' (Browne et al. 1997: 737). Therefore Browne et al. conceptualized measures of quality of life as being devised either by researchers or by the individuals themselves.

Is the measure objective or subjective?

Muldoon et al. (1998) provided an alternative conceptual framework for quality of life based on the degree to which the domains being rated can be objectively validated. They argued that quality of life measures should be divided into those that assess objective functioning and those that assess subjective well-being. The first of these reflects those measures that describe an individual's level of functioning, which they argue must be validated against directly observed behavioural performance, and the second describes the individual's own appraisal of their well-being.

Therefore some progress has been made to clarify the problems surrounding measures of quality of life. However, until a consensus among researchers and clinicians exists, it remains unclear what quality of life is, and whether quality of life is different to subjective health status and health-related quality of life. In fact, Annas (1990) argued that we should stop using the term altogether. However, 'quality of life', 'subjective health status' and 'health-related quality of life' continue to be used and their measurement continues to be taken. The range of measures developed will now be considered in terms of (1) unidimensional measures and (2) multidimensional measures.

How should it be measured?

Unidimensional measures

Many measures focus on one particular aspect of health. For example, Goldberg (1978) developed the general health questionnaire (GHQ), which assesses mood by asking questions such as 'Have you recently: been able to concentrate on whatever you're doing/spent much time chatting to people/been feeling happy or depressed?' The GHQ is available as long forms, consisting of 30, 28 or 20 items, and a short form, which consists of 12 items. While the short form is mainly used to explore mood in general and provides results as to an individual's relative mood (i.e. is the person better or worse than usual?), the longer forms have been used to detect 'caseness' (i.e. is the person depressed or not?). Other unidimensional measures include the following: the hospital anxiety and depression scale (HADS) (Zigmond and Snaith 1983) and the Beck depression inventory (BDI) (Beck et al. 1961), both of which focus on mood; the McGill pain questionnaire, which assesses pain levels (Melzack 1975); measures of self-esteem, such as the self-esteem scale (Rosenberg 1965) and the self-esteem inventory (Coopersmith 1967); measures of social support (e.g. Sarason et al. 1983, 1987); measures of satisfaction with life (e.g. Diner et al. 1985); and measures of symptoms (e.g. deHaes et al. 1990). Therefore these unidimensional measures assess health in terms of one specific aspect of health and can be used on their own or in conjunction with other measures.

Multidimensional measures

Multidimensional measures assess health in the broadest sense. However, this does not mean that such measures are always long and complicated. For example, researchers often use a single item such as, 'Would you say your health is: excellent/good/fair/poor?' or 'Rate your current state of health' on a scale ranging from 'poor' to 'perfect'. Further, some researchers simply ask respondents to make a relative judgement about their health on a scale from 'best possible' to 'worst possible'. Although these simple measures do not provide as much detail as longer measures, they have been shown to correlate highly with other more complex measures and to be useful as an outcome measure (Idler and Kasl 1995).

In the main, researchers have tended to use composite scales. Because of the many ways of defining quality of life, many different measures have been developed. Some focus on particular populations, such as the elderly (Lawton 1972, 1975; McKee et al. 2002), children (Maylath 1990; Jirojanakul and Skevington 2000), or those in the last year of life (Lawton et al. 1990). Others focus on specific illnesses, such as diabetes (Brook et al. 1981; Bradley 1996; Bradley et al. 1999), arthritis (Meenan et al. 1980), heart disease (Rector et al. 1993), HIV (Skevington and O'Connell 2003) and renal disease (Bradley 1997). In addition, generic measures of quality of life have also been developed, which can be applied to all individuals. These include: the Nottingham health profile (NHP) (Hunt et al. 1986), the short form 36 (SF36) (Ware and Sherbourne 1992), the sickness impact profile (SIP) (Bergner et al. 1981) and the WHOQoL-100 (Skevington 1999; Skevington et al. 2004a, 2004b). Research using these generic measures has explored quality of life in people from different cultures, with different levels of health and different levels of economic security (e.g. Skevington et al. 2004a, 2004b). All of these measures have been criticized for being too broad and therefore resulting in a definition of quality of life that is all-encompassing, vague and unfocused. In contrast, they have also been criticized for being too focused and for potentially missing out aspects of quality of life that may be of specific importance to the individual concerned. In particular, it has been suggested that by asking individuals to answer a pre-defined set of questions and to rate statements that have been developed by researchers, the individual's own concerns may be missed. This has led to the development of individual quality-of-life measures.

Individual quality-of-life measures

Measures of subjective health status ask the individual to rate their own health. This is in contrast to measures of mortality, morbidity and most measures of functioning, which are completed by carers, researchers or an observer. However, although such measures enable individuals to rate their own health, they do not allow them to select the dimensions along which to rate it. For example, a measure that asks about an individual's work life assumes that work is important to this person, but they might not want to work. Furthermore, one that asks about family life might be addressing the question to someone who is glad not to see their family. How can one set of individuals who happen to be researchers know what is important to the quality of life of another set of individuals? In line with this perspective, researchers have developed individual quality-of-life measures, which not only ask the subjects to rate their own health status but also to define the dimensions along which it should be rated. One such measure, the schedule for evaluating individual quality of life (SEIQoL) (McGee et al. 1991; O'Boyle et al. 1992), asks subjects to select five areas of their lives that are important to them, to weight them in terms of their importance and then to rate how satisfied they currently are with each dimension (see **Focus on Research 17.1** on the next page).

Health status can be assessed in terms of mortality rates, morbidity, levels of functioning and subjective health measures. Subjective health measures overlap significantly with measures of quality of life and health-related quality of life. These different measures illustrate a shift among a number of perspectives (see Figure 17.1).

Putting theory into practice – evaluating hip replacement surgery

Individual quality of life in patients undergoing hip replacement (O'Boyle et al. 1992).

This is an interesting paper as it illustrates how a measurement tool, developed within a psychological framework, can be used to evaluate the impact of a surgical intervention. In addition, it compared the use of composite scales with an individual quality-of-life scale.

Background

There are a multitude of measures of quality of life available, most of which ask patients to rate a set of statements that a group of researchers consider to reflect quality of life. However, whether this approach actually accesses what the patient thinks is unclear. Therefore O'Boyle et al. (1992) devised their own measure of quality of life and this asks the patients themselves to decide what is important to them. It is called the schedule for the evaluation of individual quality of life (SEIQoL). In addition, the authors wanted to compare the results using SEIQoL with those of more traditional assessment tools: 'We wanted to know whether SEIQoL could answer the question "What does the patient think?"'.

Methodology

Subjects

Consecutive patients attending a hospital in Dublin for osteoarthritis of the hip were asked to participate. These were matched to control subjects from local general practices in terms of age, sex and class. The study consisted of 20 subjects, who underwent hip replacement operations, and 20 controls.

Design

The study used a repeated-measures design with measures completed before (baseline) and after (six-month follow-up) unilateral total hip replacement surgery.

Measures

The subjects completed the following measures at baseline and follow-up:

- *Individual quality of life.* This involved the following stages. First, the subjects were asked to list the five areas of life that they considered to be most important to their quality of life. Second, the subjects were then asked to rate each area for their status at the present time, ranging from 'as good as could possibly be' to 'as bad as could possibly be'. Finally, in order to weight each area of life, the subjects were presented with 30 randomly generated profiles of hypothetical people labelled with the five chosen areas and were asked to rate the quality of life of each of these people. These three ratings were then used to compute total quality-of-life score (i.e. adding up each current rating and multiplied by weighting per area).

- *Global health status.* The subjects completed the McMaster health index questionnaire, which assesses physical, social and emotional functioning (Chambers et al. 1982).

- *Disease-specific health status.* Subjects completed the arthritis impact scale which assesses nine aspects of functioning: mobility, physical activity, dexterity, household activities, social activity, activities of daily living, pain, anxiety and depression (Meenan et al. 1980).

Results

The results were analysed in terms of the areas of life selected as part of the individual quality-of-life scale and to assess the impact of the hip replacement operation in terms of changes in all measures from baseline to follow-up and differences in these changes between the patients and the controls.

- *Areas of life selected.* Social/leisure activities and family were nominated most frequently by both groups. Happiness, intellectual function and living conditions were nominated least frequently. Health was nominated more frequently by the control than the patients who rated independence and finance more frequently.
- *The impact of the hip replacement operation.* The results showed that all measures of quality of life improved following the hip replacement operation.

Conclusion

The authors concluded that their individual quality-of-life measure can be used to elicit the views of patients and in addition can detect changes in quality of life over time. Further, they argued that 'a major advantage of a patient centred measure such as SEIQoL especially with elicited cues is that it is applicable across all patients, illnesses and diseases and is not specific to any one culture'. Therefore this study illustrates the usefulness of an individual quality-of-life measure in evaluating the effectiveness of a surgical procedure.

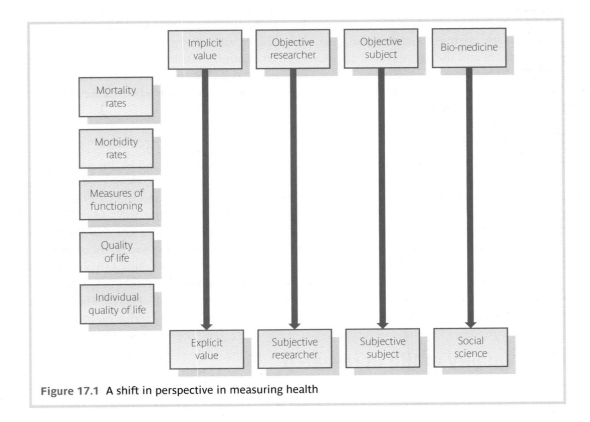

Figure 17.1 A shift in perspective in measuring health

A shift in perspective
Value

The shift from mortality rates to subjective health measures represents a shift from implicit value to attempts to make this value explicit. For example, mortality and morbidity measures assume that what they are measuring is an absolute index of health. The subjects being studied are not asked, 'Is it a bad thing that you cannot walk upstairs?' or the relatives asked, 'Did they want to die?' Subjective health measures attempt to make the value within the constructs being studied explicit by asking, 'To what extent are you prevented from doing the things you would like to do?'

Subjectivity of the subject

Mortality and morbidity measures are assumed to be objective scientific measures that access a reality that is uncontaminated by bias. In contrast, the subjective measures make this bias the essence of what they are interested in. For example, mortality data are taken from hospital records or death certificates, and morbidity ratings are often made by the health professionals rather than the individuals being studied. However, subjective health measures ask the individual for their own experiences and beliefs in terms of 'How do you rate your health?' or 'How do you feel?' They make no pretence to be objective and, rather than attempting to exclude the individuals' beliefs, they make them their focus.

Subjectivity of the researcher

In addition, there is also a shift in the ways in which measures of health status conceptualize the researcher. For example, mortality and morbidity rates are assumed to be consistent regardless of who collected them; the researcher is assumed to be an objective person. Subjective measures, however, attempt to address the issue of researcher subjectivity. For example, self-report questionnaires and the use of closed questions aim to minimize researcher input. However, the questions being asked and the response frames given are still chosen by the researcher. In contrast, the SEIQoL (O'Boyle et al. 1992) in effect presents the subject with a blank sheet and asks them to devise their own scale.

Definition of health

Finally, such shifts epitomize the different perspectives of biomedicine and health psychology. Therefore, if health status is regarded as the presence or absence of death, then mortality rates provide a suitable assessment tool. Death is a reliable outcome variable and mortality is appropriately simple. If, however, health status is regarded as more complex than this, more complex measures are needed. Morbidity rates account for a continuum model of health and illness and facilitate the assessment of the greyer areas, and even some morbidity measures accept the subjective nature of health. However, if health psychology regards health status as made up of a complex range of factors that can only be both chosen and evaluated by the individuals themselves, then it could be argued that it is only measures that ask the individuals themselves to rate their own health that are fully in line with a health psychology model of what health means.

Using quality of life in research

Quality-of-life measures, in the form of subjective health measures and both simple and composite scales, play a central role in many debates within health psychology, medical sociology,

> Box 17.1 **Some problems with . . . health status research**
>
> Below are some problems with research in this area that you may wish to consider.
>
> 1 Health status can be measured using either tools that include predefined domains or those that rely on the individual themselves to generate the domains. Both are problematic.
>
> 2 Quality-of-life measures are sometimes criticized for missing important domains and for being too simple. Sometimes they are criticized for being overinclusive, unwieldy and difficult to use. The choice of measure therefore has to be pragmatic and based upon what a particular person is deemed able to complete at any particular time rather than perfect theoretical principles.
>
> 3 Research measuring health outcomes often includes a range of health status, quality-of-life and physiological measures. Often these measures contradict each other. For example, while an intervention may improve longevity, it may be detrimental to quality of life. How these different outcomes are combined is unclear and can cause conflict or confusion for health professionals.

primary care and clinical medicine. Most funded trials are now required to include a measure of quality of life among their outcome variables, and interventions that only focus on mortality are generally regarded as narrow and old-fashioned. However, a recent analysis of the literature suggested that the vast majority of published trials still do not report data on quality of life (Sanders et al. 1998). For example, following an assessment of the Cochrane Controlled Trials Register from 1980 to 1997, Sanders et al. (1998) reported that, although the frequency of reporting quality-of-life data had increased from 0.63 to 4.2 per cent for trials from all disciplines, from 1.5 to 8.2 per cent for cancer trials and from 0.34 to 3.6 per cent for cardiovascular trials, less than 5 per cent of all trials reported data on quality of life. Furthermore, they showed that this proportion was below 10 per cent even for cancer trials. In addition, they indicated that, while 72 per cent of the trials used established measures of quality of life, 22 per cent used measures developed by the authors themselves. Therefore it would seem that, although quality of life is in vogue and is a required part of outcome research, it still remains underused. For those trials that do include a measure of quality of life, it is used mainly as an outcome variable and the data are analysed to assess whether the intervention has an impact on the individual's health status, including their quality of life.

Quality of life as an outcome measure

Research has examined how a range of interventions influence an individual's quality of life using a repeated-measures design. For example, a trial of breast reduction surgery compared women's quality of life before and after the operation (Klassen et al. 1996). The study involved 166 women who were referred for plastic surgery, mainly for physical reasons, and their health status was assessed using the SF36 to assess general quality of life, the 28-item GHQ to assess mood and Rosenberg's self-esteem scale. The results showed that the women reported significantly better quality of life both before and after the operation than a control group of women in the general population and, further, that the operation resulted in an improvement in the women's physical, social and psychological functioning, including their levels of 'caseness' for psychiatric morbidity. Accordingly, the authors concluded that breast reduction surgery is beneficial for quality of life and should be included in NHS purchasing contracts.

Quality of life has also been included as an outcome variable for disease-specific randomized controlled trials. For example, Grunfeld et al. (1996) examined the relative impact of providing either hospital (routine care) or primary care follow-ups for women with breast cancer. The study included 296 women with breast cancer who were in remission and randomly allocated them to receive follow-up care either in hospital or by their general practitioner. Quality of life was assessed using some of the dimensions from the SF36 and the HADS. The results showed that general practice care was not associated with any deterioration in quality of life. In addition, it was not related to an increased time to diagnose any recurrence of the cancer. Therefore the authors concluded that general practice care of women in remission from breast cancer is as good as hospital care.

Other studies have explored the impact of an intervention for a range of illnesses. For example, the DAFNE study group (2002) explored the impact of teaching diabetic patients flexible intensive treatment which combines dietary freedom and insulin adjustment (dose adjustment for normal eating – DAFNE). The results showed that this approach to self-management improved both the patients' glycaemic control and their quality of life at follow-up. Shepperd et al. (1998) also used quality of life as an outcome measure. They examined the relative effectiveness of home versus hospital care for patients with a range of problems, including hip replacement, knee replacement and hysterectomy. Quality of life was assessed using tools such as the SF36 and disease-specific measures, and the results showed no differences between the two groups at a three-month follow-up. Therefore the authors concluded that if there are no significant differences between home and hospital care in terms of quality of life, then the cost of these different forms of care becomes an important factor.

Problems with using quality of life as an outcome measure

Research uses quality of life as an outcome measure for trials that have different designs and are either focused on specific illnesses or involve a range of problems. However, there are the following problems with such studies:

- Different studies use different ways of measuring quality of life: generalizing across studies is difficult.

- Some studies use the term 'quality of life' while others use the term 'subjective health status': generalizing across studies is difficult.

- Some studies report results from the different measures of quality of life, which are in the opposite direction to each other: drawing conclusions is difficult.

- Some studies report the results from quality-of-life measures, which are in the opposite direction to mortality or morbidity data: deciding whether an intervention is good or bad is difficult.

Quality of life as a predictor of longevity

Most research using quality of life explores its predictors and therefore places this variable as the end-point. However, it is possible that quality of life may also be a predictor of future events. In particular, quality of life could be seen as a predictor of longevity. To date, there are no studies that have directly addressed this possibility, although there are some studies that indirectly suggest an association between quality of life and longevity. For example, several studies indicate that mortality is higher in the first six months after the death of a spouse, particularly from heart disease or suicide (e.g. Kaprio et al. 1987; Schaefer et al. 1995; Martikainen and Valkonen 1996). It is possible that this could relate to a lowering of quality of life. Further, some studies suggest a link between life events and longevity (see Chapters 11 and 14). Perhaps these links could also be explained by quality of life. Therefore quality of life may not only be an outcome variable in itself but a predictor of further outcomes in the future.

To conclude

This chapter has explored the different ways of measuring health status. In particular, it has examined the use of mortality rates, morbidity rates, measures of functioning, measures of subjective health status and quality of life. It has then described how the shift from mortality rates to quality of life reflects a shift from implicit to explicit value, an increasing subjectivity on behalf of both the subject being studied and the researcher, and a change in the definition of health from a biomedical dichotomous model to a more complex psychological one. Further, it has explored definitions of quality of life and the vast range of scales that have been developed to assess this complex construct and their use in research.

? Questions

1 Mortality rates are the most accurate measure of health status. Discuss.
2 The views of the subject get in the way of measuring health. Discuss.
3 The views of the researcher get in the way of measuring health. Discuss.
4 To what extent is quality of life a useful construct?
5 Should all outcome research include an assessment of quality of life?

For discussion

Consider the last time you felt that your quality of life was reduced. What did this mean to you and would this be addressed by the available measures?

Assumptions in health psychology

The measurement of health status highlights some of the assumptions in health psychology:

1 *The problem of methodology.* It is assumed that methodology is separate to the data being collected. Accordingly, it is assumed that subjects experience factors as important to their quality of life even before they have been asked about them. It is possible that items relating to family life, physical fitness and work may only become important once the individual has been asked to rate them.

2 *The problem of the mind–body split.* Although much outcome research examines both mortality and quality of life, it is often assumed that these two factors are separate. Therefore research explores the impact of an intervention either on an individual's quality of life or on their longevity. Very little relationship assesses the impact of quality of life itself on longevity. Therefore factors influencing the mind are deemed to be separate to those influencing the body.

3 *The problem of progress.* Mortality rates were very much in vogue at the beginning of the last century whereas quality-of-life measures are in vogue at the end of the century. This shift is mainly regarded as an improvement in the way in which we understand health status. However, rather than being an improvement, perhaps it simply reflects a change of the way in which we make sense of what health is.

Further reading

Bowling, A. (2005) *Measuring Health: A Review of Quality of Life Measurement Scales*, 3rd edn. Maidenhead: Open University Press.

This is an extremely comprehensive overview of the different scales that have been developed to assess quality of life. It also includes two interesting chapters on what quality of life is and theories of measurement.

Browne, J., McGee, H.M. and O'Boyle, C.A. (1997) Conceptual approaches to the assessment of quality of life, *Psychology and Health*, 12: 737–51.

This paper explores a possible way of conceptualizing quality of life and presents a way forward for future research.

Joyce, C.R.B., O'Boyle, C.A. and McGee, H.M. (eds) (1999) *Individual Quality of Life*. London: Harwood.

This edited book provides details on the conceptual and methodological principles of quality of life and focuses on individual measures. It then provides some examples of using these measures, together with some ideas for future directions.

Chapter 18

The assumptions of health psychology

Chapter overview

This book has highlighted a range of assumptions within health psychology. This chapter outlines these assumptions and points towards the possibility of studying a discipline as a means to understanding the changing nature of the individual.

The assumptions of health psychology

Throughout this book, several assumptions central to health psychology have been highlighted. These include the following.

The mind–body split

Health psychology sets out to provide an integrated model of the individual by establishing a holistic approach to health. Therefore it challenges the traditional medical model of the mind–body split and provides theories and research to support the notion of a mind and body that are one. For example, it suggests that beliefs influence behaviour, which in turn influences health; that stress can cause illness and that pain is a perception rather than a sensation. In addition, it argues that illness cognitions relate to recovery from illness and coping relates to longevity. However, does this approach really represent an integrated individual? Although all these perspectives and the research that has been carried out in their support indicate that the mind and the body interact, they are still defined as separate. The mind reflects the individuals' psychological states (i.e. their beliefs, cognitions, perceptions), which influence but are separate to their bodies (i.e. the illness, the body, the body's systems).

Dividing up the soup

Health psychology describes variables such as beliefs (risk perception, outcome expectancies, costs and benefits, intentions, implementation intentions), emotions (fear, depression, anxiety) and behaviours (smoking, drinking, eating, screening) as separate and discrete. It then develops models and theories to examine how these variables interrelate. For example, it asks, 'What beliefs predict smoking?', 'What emotions relate to screening?' Therefore it separates out 'the soup' into discrete entities and then tries to put them back together. However, perhaps these different beliefs, emotions and behaviours were not separate until psychology came along. Is there really a difference between all the different beliefs? Is the thought 'I am depressed' a cognition or an emotion? When I am sitting quietly thinking, am I behaving? Health psychology assumes differences and then looks for association. However, perhaps without the original separation there would be nothing to associate!

The problem of progression

This book has illustrated how theories, such as those relating to addictions, stress and screening, have changed over time. In addition, it presents new developments in the areas of social cognition models and PNI. For example, early models of stress focused on a simple stimulus–response approach. Nowadays we focus on appraisal. Furthermore, nineteenth-century models of addiction believed that it was the fault of the drug. In the early twenty-first century, we see addiction as being a product of learning. Health psychology assumes that these shifts in theory represent improvement in our knowledge about the world. We know more than we did a hundred years ago and our theories are more accurate. However, perhaps such changes indicate different, not better, ways of viewing the world. Perhaps these theories tell us more about how we see the world now compared with then, rather than simply that we have got better at seeing the world.

The problem of methodology

In health psychology we carry out research to collect data about the world. We then analyse these data to find out how the world is, and we assume that our methodologies are separate to the data we are collecting. In line with this, if we ask someone about their implementation intentions it is assumed that they have such intentions before we ask them. Further, if we ask someone about their anxieties we assume that they have an emotion called anxiety, regardless of whether or not they are talking to us or answering our questionnaire. However, how do we know that our methods are separate from the data we collect? How do we know that these objects of research (beliefs, emotions and behaviours) exist prior to when we study them? Perhaps by studying the world we are not objectively examining what is really going on but are actually changing and possibly even creating it.

The problem of measurement

In line with the problem of methodology is the problem of measurement. Throughout the different areas of health psychology, researchers develop research tools to assess quality of life, pain, stress, beliefs and behaviours. These tools are then used by the researchers to examine how the subjects in the research feel/think/behave. However, this process involves an enormous leap of faith – that our measurement tool actually measures something out there. How do we know this? Perhaps what the tool measures is simply what the tool measures. A depression scale may not assess 'depression' but only the score on the scale. Likewise, a quality-of-life scale may not assess quality of life but simply how someone completes the questionnaire.

Integrating the individual with their social context

Psychology is traditionally the study of the individual. Sociology is traditionally the study of the social context. Recently, however, health psychologists have made moves to integrate this individual with their social world. To do this they turn to social epidemiology (i.e. explore class, gender and ethnicity), social psychology (i.e. turn to subjective norms) or social constructionism (i.e. turn to qualitative methods). Therefore health psychologists access either the individuals' location within their social world via their demographic factors or ask the individuals for their beliefs about the social world. However, does this really integrate the individual with the social world? A belief about the social context is still an individual's belief. Can psychology really succeed with this integration? Would it still be psychology if it did?

Data are collected in order to develop theories; these theories are not data

Health psychologists collect data and develop theories about the individual, for example theories about smoking, eating, stress and pain. These theories are then used to tell us something about the world. However, these theories could also be used as data, and in the same way that we study the world, we could study our theories about the world. Perhaps this would not tell us about the world *per se* but about how we see it. Furthermore, changes in theories could also tell us about the way in which we see the world has changed. Likewise we could study our methods and our measurement tools. Do these also tell us something about the changing psychology of the past hundred years?

Theories concerning different areas of health psychology are distinct from each other

This book has outlined many theories relating to stress, pain and health behaviours, but has not examined parallels within these theories. Perhaps there are patterns within these different theories that reflect 'umbrella' changes within health psychology. Perhaps also these changes indicate consistent shifts in the way psychological theory describes the individual.

Studying a discipline

Therefore there are many assumptions underlying the discipline of health psychology. Acknowledging and understanding these assumptions provides the basis of a more critical perspective on research. Findings from research are not taken for granted and theories can be seen within their inherent limitations. However, these assumptions themselves provide a basis for research – research into how a discipline has changed. In addition, this kind of research can provide insights into how the focus of that discipline (the individual) has also changed. This approach provides a basis for a social study of a discipline. In the same way that sociologists study scientists, biographers study authors and literary theorists study literature, a discipline can also be studied.

A critical health psychology

Over the past few years a subsection of health psychology has developed which has become known as 'critical health psychology'. Researchers within this area emphasize the qualitative, critical and alternative approaches to understanding health and illness. Further, they highlight the role of the social context and the political dimensions to health. Some of the assumptions addressed in this chapter are also addressed within the domain of critical health psychology.

Further reading

Ogden, J. (1995a) Changing the subject of health psychology, *Psychology and Health*, 10: 257–65.
This paper addresses some of the assumptions in health psychology and discusses the interrelationship between theory, methodology and the psychological individual.

Ogden, J. (1995b) Psychosocial theory and the creation of the risky self, *Social Science and Medicine*, 40: 409–15.
This paper examines the changes in psychological theory during the twentieth century and relates them to discussions about risk and responsibility for health and illness.

Ogden, J. (1997) The rhetoric and reality of psychosocial theories: a challenge to biomedicine? *Journal of Health Psychology*, 2: 21–9.
This paper explores health psychology's apparent challenge to biomedicine.

Ogden, J. (2002) *Health and the Construction of the Individual.* London: Routledge.
This book explores how both psychological and sociological theories construct the individual through an exploration of methodology, measurement, theory and the construction of boundaries.

For critical health psychology read:

Crossley, M. (2000) *Rethinking Health Psychology*. Buckingham: Open University Press.
This book argues that 'mainstream' health psychology neglects some of the contextual factors that impact upon health and is over-reliant upon quantitative methodologies.

Hardey, M. (1998) *The Social Context of Health*. Buckingham: Open University Press.
This books explores the role of a range of social factors that contribute both to our understanding of health and to the decisions we make about how to behave.

Marks, D.F. (2002) Freedom, responsibility and power: contrasting approaches to health psychology, *Journal of Health Psychology*, 7, 5–14.

B

Between-subjects design: this involves making comparisons between different groups of subjects; for example, males versus females, those who have been offered a health-related intervention versus those who have not.

C

Case-control design: this involves taking a group of subjects who show a particular characteristic (e.g. lung cancer – the dependent variable), selecting a control group without the characteristic (e.g. no lung cancer) and retrospectively examining these two groups for the factors that may have caused this characteristic (e.g. did those with lung cancer smoke more than those without?).

Condition: experimental studies often involve allocating subjects to different conditions; for example, information versus no information, relaxation versus no relaxation, active drug versus placebo versus control condition.

Cross-sectional design: a study is described as being cross-sectional if the different variables are measured at the same time as each other.

D

Dependent variable: the characteristic that appears to change as a result of the independent variable; for example, changing behavioural intentions (the independent variable) causes a change in behaviour (the dependent variable).

E

Experimental design: this involves a controlled study in which variables are manipulated in order to specifically examine the relationship between the independent variable (the cause) and the dependent variable (the effect); for example, does experimentally induced anxiety change pain perception?

I

Independent variable: the characteristic that appears to cause a change in the dependent variable; for example, smoking (the independent variable) causes lung cancer (the dependent variable).

L

Likert scale: variables can be measured on a scale marked by numbers (e.g. 1 to 5) or terms (e.g. never/seldom/sometimes/often/very often). The subject is asked to mark the appropriate point.

Longitudinal design: this involves measuring variables at a baseline and then following up the subjects at a later point in time (sometimes called prospective or cohort design).

P

Prospective design: this involves following up subjects over a period of time (sometimes called longitudinal or cohort design).

Q

Qualitative study: this involves methodologies such as interviews in order to collect data from subjects. Qualitative data is a way of describing the variety of beliefs, interpretations and behaviours from a heterogenous subject group without making generalizations to the population as a whole. It is believed that qualitative studies are more able to access the subjects' beliefs without contaminating the data with the researcher's own expectations. Qualitative data are described in terms of themes and categories.

Quantitative study: this involves collecting data in the form of numbers using methodologies such as questionnaires and experiments. Quantitative data are a way of describing the beliefs, interpretations and behaviours of a large population and generalizations are made about the population as a whole. Quantitative data are described in terms of frequencies, means and statistically significant differences and correlations.

R

Randomly allocated: subjects are randomly allocated to different conditions in order to minimize the effects of any individual differences; for example, to ensure that subjects who receive the drug versus the placebo versus nothing are equivalent in age and sex. If all the subjects who received the placebo happened to be female, this would obviously influence the results.

Repeated-measures design: this involves asking subjects to complete the same set of measures more than once; for example, before and after reading a health information leaflet.

S

Subjects: these are the individuals who are involved in the study. They may also be referred to as participants, clients, respondents or cases.

V

Variable: a characteristic that can be measured (e.g. age, beliefs, fitness).

Visual analogue scale: variables such as beliefs are sometimes measured using a 100mm line with anchor points at each end (such as not at all confident/extremely confident). The subject is asked to place a cross on the line in the appropriate point.

W

Within-subjects design: this involves making comparisons within the same group of subjects. How do subjects respond to receiving an invitation to attend a screening programme? How does a belief about smoking relate to the subjects' smoking behaviour?

Aaronson, N.K., Ahmedzai, S., Bergman, B. et al. (1993) The European Organisation for research and treatment of cancer QLQ-C30: a quality of life instrument for use in international clinical trials in oncology, *Journal for the National Cancer Institute*, 85: 365–76.

Aarts, H., Verplanken, B. and van Knippenberg, A. (1998) Predicting behaviour from actions in the past: repeated decision making or matter of habit? *Journal of Applied Social Psychology*, 28: 1355–74.

Abortion Law Reform Association (1997) *A Report on NHS Abortion Services*. London: ALRA.

Abraham, C., Krahé, B., Dominic, R. and Fritsche, I. (2002) Do health promotion messages target cognitive and behavioural correlates of condom use? A content analysis of safer sex promotion leaflets in two countries, *British Journal of Health Psychology*, 7: 227–46.

Abraham, C. and Sheeran, P. (1993) In search of a psychology of safer-sex promotion: beyond beliefs and text, *Health Education Research: Theory and Practice*, 8: 245–54.

Abraham, C. and Sheeran, P. (1994) Modelling and modifying young heterosexuals' HIV preventive behaviour: a review of theories, findings and educational implications, *Patient Education and Counselling*, 23: 173–86.

Abraham, C., Sheeran, P., Abrams, D., Spears, R. and Marks, D. (1991) Young people learning about AIDS: a study of beliefs and information sources, *Health Education Research: Theory and Practice*, 6: 19–29.

Abraham, S., Perz, J., Clarkson, R. and Llewellyn-Jones, D. (1995) Australian women's perceptions of hormone replacement therapy over 10 years, *Maturitas*, 21: 91–5.

Abraham, S.C.S., Sheeran, P., Abrams, D. and Spears, R. (1994) Exploring teenagers' adaptive and maladaptive thinking in relation to the threat of HIV infection, *Psychology and Health*, 7: 253–72.

Abraham, S.C.S., Sheeran, P., Abrams, D. and Spears, R. (1996) Health beliefs and teenage condom use: a prospective study, *Psychology and Health*, 11: 641–55.

Abrams, D., Abraham, C., Spears, R. and Marks, D. (1990) AIDS invulnerability: relationships, sexual behaviour and attitudes among 16–19-year-olds, in P. Aggleton, P. Davies and G. Hart (eds), *AIDS: Individual, Cultural and Policy Dimensions*, pp. 35–52. London: Falmer Press.

Abrams, K., Allen, L. and Gray, J. (1992) Disordered eating attitudes and behaviours, psychological adjustment and ethnic identity: a comparison of black and white female college students, *International Journal of Eating Disorders*, 14: 49–57.

Ader, R. and Cohen, N. (1975) Behaviourally conditioned immuno suppression, *Psychosomatic Medicine*, 37: 333–40.

Ader, R. and Cohen, N. (1981) Conditioned immunopharmacologic responses, in R. Ader (ed.), *Psychoneuroimmunology*. New York: Academic Press.

Adler, N.E., Boyce, T., Chesney, M.A. et al. (1994) Socio-economic status and health: the challenge of the gradient, *American Psychologist*, 49: 15–24.

Adler, N.E., Boyce, T., Chesney, M.A., Folkman, S. and Syme, L. (1993) Socio-economic inequalities in health: no easy solution, *Journal of the American Medical Association*, 269: 3140–5.

Aggleton, P. (1989) HIV/AIDS education in schools: constraints and possibilities, *Health Education Journal*, 48: 167–71.

Aggleton, P. and Homans, H. (1988) *Social Aspects of AIDS*. London: Falmer Press.

Ahmed, S., Waller, G. and Verduyn, C. (1994) Eating attitudes among Asian school girls: the role of perceived parental control, *International Journal of Eating Disorders*, 15: 91–7.

Ajzen, I. (1985) From intention to actions: a theory of planned behavior, in J. Kuhl and J. Beckman (eds), *Action-control: From Cognition to Behavior*, pp. 11–39. Heidelberg: Springer.

Ajzen, I. (1988) *Attitudes, Personality and Behavior*. Chicago, IL: Dorsey Press.

Ajzen, I. and Fishbein, M. (1970) The prediction of behaviour from attitudinal and normative beliefs, *Journal of Personality and Social Psychology*, 6: 466–87.

Ajzen, I. and Madden, T.J. (1986) Prediction of goal-directed behavior: attitudes, intentions, and perceived behavioral control, *Journal of Experimental Social Psychology*, 22: 453–74.

Akan, G.E. and Grilo, C.M. (1995) Sociocultural influences on eating attitudes and behaviors, body image, and psychological functioning: a comparison of African-American, Asian-American and Caucasian college women, *International Journal of Eating Disorders*, 18: 181–7.

Alagna, S.W. and Reddy, D.M. (1984) Predictors of proficient technique and successful lesion detection in breast self-examination, *Health Psychology*, 3: 113–27.

Albrecht, G.L. (1994) Subjective health status, in C. Jenkinson (ed.), *Measuring Health and Medical Outcomes*, pp. 7–26. London: UCL Press.

Alder, N., David, H., Major, B.N., Roth, S.H. et al. (1990) Psychological responses after abortion, *Science*, 248: 41–4.

Alderson, T. and Ogden, J. (1999) What mothers feed their children and why, *Health Education Research: Theory and Practice*, 14: 717–27.

Alex, L. and Hammarström, A. (2004) Women's experiences in connection with induced abortion: a feminist perspective, *Scandinavian Journal of Caring Sciences*, 18: 160–8.

Allen, I. (1991) *Family Planning and Pregnancy Counseling Projects for Young People*. London: Policy Studies Institute.

Allied Dunbar National Fitness Survey (1992) *A Report on Activity Patterns and Fitness Levels*. London: Sports Council and Health Education Authority.

Almqvist, E.W., Brinkman, R.R., Wiggins, S. et al. (2003) Psychological consequences and predictors of adverse events in the first 5 years after predictive testing for Huntington disease, *Clinical Genetics*, 64: 300–9.

Alonso, J., Black, C., Norregaard, J.C., Dunn, E., Andersen, T.F., Esallargues, M., Bernth-Petersen, P. and Andersen, G.F. (1998) Cross-cultural differences in the reporting of global functional capacity: an example in cataract patients, *Medical Care*, 36: 868–78.

Amelang, M. and Schmidt-Rathjens, C. (1996) Personality, cancer and coronary heart disease: further evidence on a controversial issue, *British Journal of Health Psychology*, 1: 191–205.

Anastasiades, P., Clark, D.M., Salkovskis, P.M. et al. (1990) Psychophysiological responses in panic and stress, *Journal of Psychophysiology*, 27: 34–44.

Andersen, R.E., Franckowiak, S.C., Snyder, J., Barlett, S.J. and Fontaine, K.R. (1998) Physical activity promotion by the encouraged use of stairs, *Annals of Internal Medicine*, 129: 363–9.

Anderson, H.R., Freeling, P. and Patel, S.P. (1983) Decision making in acute asthma, *Journal of the Royal College of General Practitioners*, 33: 105–8.

Annas, G.J. (1990) Quality of life in the courts: early spring in fantasyland, in J.J. Walter and T.A. Shannon (eds), *Quality of Life: The New Medical Dilemma*. New York: Paulist Press.

Antoni, M.H., Carrico, A.W., Duran, R.E., Spitzer, S., Penedo, F., Ironson, G., Fletcher, M.A., Klimas, N. and Schneiderman, N. (2006) Randomized clinical trial of cognitive behavioral stress management on human immunodeficiency virus viral load in gay men treated with highly active antiretroviral therapy, *Psychosomatic Medicine*, 68: 143–51.

Antoni, M.H., Cruess, D.G., Klimas, N., Carrico, A.W., Maher, K., Cruess, S., Lechner, S.C., Kumar, M., Lutgendorf, S., Ironson, G., Fletcher, M.A. and Scheiderman, N. (2005) Increases in marker of immune system reconstitution are predated by decreases in 24-h urinary cortisol output and depressed mood during a 10-week stress management intervention in symptomatic HIV-infected men, *Journal of Psychosomatic Research*, 58(1): 3–13.

Appels, A. and Mulder, P. (1989) Fatigue and heart disease: the association between vital exhaustion and past, present and future coronary heart disease, *Journal of Psychosomatic Research*, 33: 727–38.

Appels, A., Golombeck, B., Gorgels, A., De Vreede, J. and Van Breukelen, G. (2002) Psychological risk factors of sudden cardiac arrest, *Psychology and Health*, 17: 773–81.

Appleton, P.L. and Pharoah, P.O.D. (1998) Partner smoking behaviour change is associated with women's smoking reduction and cessation during pregnancy, *British Journal of Health Psychology*, 3: 361–74.

Armitage, C.J. (2004) Evidence that implementation intentions reduce dietary fat intake: a randomized trial, *Health Psychology*, 23(3): 319–23.

Armitage, C.J. (2005) Can the theory of planned behaviour predict the maintenance of physical activity? *Health Psychology*, 24(3): 235–45.

Armitage, C.J. and Conner, M. (2000) Social cognition models and health behaviour: a structured review, *Psychology and Health*, 15: 173–89.

Armitage, C.J. and Conner, M. (2001) Efficacy of the theory of planned behaviour: a meta-analytic review, *British Journal of Social Psychology*, 40: 471–99.

Armstrong, D. (1995) The rise of surveillance medicine, *Sociology of Health and Illness*, 17: 393–404.

Arnetz, B.B., Wasserman, J., Petrini, B. et al. (1987) Immune function in unemployed women, *Psychosomatic Medicine*, 49: 3–12.

Ashton, W., Nanchahal, K. and Wood, D. (2001) Body mass index and metabolic risk factors for coronary heart disease in women, *European Heart Journal*, 22: 46–55.

Ashworth, H.W. (1963) An experiment in presymptomatic diagnosis, *Journal of the Royal College of General Practice*, 6: 71.

Athey, J. and Spielvogel, A. (2000) Risk factors and interventions for psychological sequelae in women after miscarriage, *Primary Care Update for Obstetrics and Gynaecology*, 7: 64–9.

Attie, I. and Brooks-Gunn, J. (1989) Development of eating problems in adolescent girls: a longitudinal study, *Developmental Psychology*, 25: 70–9.

Autorengruppe Nationales Forschungsprogramm (1984) *Wirksamkeit der Gemeindeorientierten Pravention Kardiovascularer Krankheiten (Effectiveness of community-orientated prevention of cardiovascular diseases)*. Bern: Hans Huber.

Axelson, M.L., Brinberg, D. and Durand, J.H. (1983) Eating at a fast-food restaurant: a social psychological analysis, *Journal of Nutrition Education*, 15: 94–8.

Bachrach, L.L. (1975) *Marital Status and Mental Disorder: An Analytic Review*. Washington, DC: US Printing Office.

Bagozzi, R.P. (1993) On the neglect of volition in consumer research: a critique and proposal, *Psychology and Marketing*, 10: 215–37.

Bagozzi, R.P. and Warshaw, P.R. (1990) Trying to consume, *Journal of Consumer Research*, 17: 127–40.

Baillie, C., Smith, J., Hewison, J. and Mason, G. (2000) Ultrasound screening for chromosomal abnormality: women's reactions to false positive results, *British Journal of Health Psychology*, 5: 377–94.

Bain, D.J.G. (1977) Patient knowledge and the content of the consultation in general practice, *Medical Education*, 11: 347–50.

Ballard, K. (2002a) Understanding risk: women's perceived risk of menopause-related disease and the value they place on preventive hormone replacement therapy, *Family Practice*, 19(6): 591–5.

Ballard, K. (2002b) Women's use of hormone replacement therapy for disease prevention: results of a community survey, *British Journal of General Practice*, 52: 835–7.

Ballard, K. (2003) *Understanding Menopause*. West Sussex: John Wiley.

Ballard, K., Kuh, D.J. and Wadsworth, M.E.J. (2001) The role of the menopause in women's experiences of the 'changes of life', *Sociology of Health and Illness*, 23(4): 397–424.

Ballenger, J.C., Davidson, J.R., Lecrubier, Y., Nutt, D.J., Kirmayer, L.J., Lepine, J.P., Lin, K.M., Tajima, O. and Ono, Y. (2001) Consensus statement on transcultural issues in depression and anxiety from the International Consensus Group on Depression and Anxiety, *Journal of Clinical Psychiatry*, 62(Suppl. 13): 47–55.

Bandura, A. (1977) Self efficacy: toward a unifying theory of behavior change, *Psychological Review*, 84: 191–215.

Bandura, A. (1986) *Social Foundations of Thought and Action*. Englewood Cliffs, NJ: Prentice Hall.

Bandura, A. (1997) *Self-efficacy: The Exercise Control*. New York: Freeman.

Bandura, A., Cio, D., Taylor, C.B. and Brouillard, M.E. (1988) Perceived self-efficacy in coping with cognitive stressors and opioid activation, *Journal of Personality and Social Psychology*, 55: 479–88.

Bandura, A., Reese, L. and Adams, N.E. (1982) Micro-analysis of action and fear arousal as a function of differential levels of perceived self efficacy, *Journal of Personality and Social Psychology*, 43: 5–21.

Bansen, S. and Stevens, H.A. (1992) Women's experiences of miscarriage in early pregnancy, *Journal of Nurse-Midwifery*, 37: 84–90.

Barraclough, J., Pinder, P., Cruddas, M. et al. (1992) Life events and breast cancer prognosis, *British Medical Journal*, 304: 1078–81.

Basler, H.D. and Rehfisch, H.P. (1990) Follow up results of a cognitive behavioural treatment for chronic pain in a primary care setting, *Psychology and Health*, 4: 293–304.

Baucom, D.H. and Aiken, P.A. (1981) Effect of depressed mood on eating among obese and nonobese dieting and nondieting persons, *Journal of Personality and Social Psychology*, 41: 577–85.

Baum, A., Fisher, J.D. and Solomon, S. (1981) Type of information, familiarity and the reduction of crowding stress, *Journal of Personality and Social Psychology*, 40: 11–23.

Beck, A.T., Mendelson, M., Mock, J. et al. (1961) Inventory for measuring depression, *Archives of General Psychiatry*, 4: 561–71.

Beck, K.H. and Lund, A.K. (1981) The effects of health threat seriousness and personal efficacy upon intentions and behaviour, *Journal of Applied Social Psychology*, 11: 401–15.

Becker, M.H. (ed.) (1974) The health belief model and personal health behavior, *Health Education Monographs*, 2: 324–508.

Becker, M.H. and Rosenstock, I.M. (1984) Compliance with medical advice, in A. Steptoe and A. Mathews (eds), *Health Care and Human Behaviour*. London: Academic Press.

Becker, M.H. and Rosenstock, I.M. (1987) Comparing social learning theory and the health belief model, in W.B. Ward (ed.), *Advances in Health Education and Promotion*, pp. 245–9. Greenwich, CT: JAI Press.

Becker, M.H., Kaback, M., Rosenstock, I. and Ruth, M. (1975) Some influences on public participation in a genetic screening program, *Journal of Community Health*, 1: 3–14.

Becker, M.H., Maiman, L.A., Kirscht, J.P., Haefner, D.P. and Drachman, R.H. (1977) The health belief model and prediction of dietary compliance: a field experiment, *Journal of Health and Social Behaviour*, 18: 348–66.

Beecher, H.K. (1955) The powerful placebo, *Journal of the American Medical Association*, 159: 1602–6.

Beecher, H.K. (1956) Relationship of significance of wound to the pain experienced, *Journal of the American Medical Association*, 161: 1609–13.

Bekker, H. (2003) Genetic testing: facilitating informed choices, *Encyclopedia of the Human Genome*. London: Macmillan www.ehgonline.net.

Bekker, H., Modell, M., Dennis, G. et al. (1993) Uptake of cystic fibrosis carrier testing in primary care: supply push or demand pull? *British Medical Journal*, 306: 1584–6.

Belar, C.D. and Deardorff, W.W. (1995) *Clinical Health Psychology in Medical Settings: A Practitioner's Guidebook*. Hyattsville, MD: APA.

Belloc, N.B. (1973) Relationship of health practices and mortality, *Preventative Medicine*, 2: 67–81.

Belloc, N.B. and Breslow, L. (1972) Relationship of physical health status and health practices, *Preventative Medicine*, 1: 409–21.

Belsky, J. and Rovine, M. (1990) Patterns of marital change across the transition to parenthood: pregnancy to three years postpartum, *Journal of Marriage and the Family*, 52: 5–19.

Bennett, P., Moore, L., Smith, A., Murphy, S. and Smith, C. (1995) Health locus of control and value for health as predictors of dietary behaviour, *Psychology and Health*, 10: 41–54.

Benwell, M.E., Balfour, D.J. and Anderson, J.M. (1988) Evidence that nicotine increases the density of (-)-[$_3$H] nicotine binding sites in human brain, *Journal of Neurochemistry*, 50: 1243–7.

Beral, V., Reeves, G. and Banks, E. (2005) Current evidence about the effect of hormone replacement therapy on the incidence of major conditions in postmenopausal women, *BJOG: An International Journal of Obstetrics and Gynaecology*, 112(6): 692–5.

Bergner, M., Bobbitt, R.A., Carter, W.B. and Gilson, D. (1981) The sickness impact profile: development and final revision of a health status measure, *Medical Care*, 19: 787–805.

Berkman, L.F. and Syme, S.L. (1979) Social networks, lost resistance and mortality: a nine year follow up study of Alameda County residents, *American Journal of Epidemiology*, 109: 186–204.

Berry, D.C. (2004) *Risk Communication and Health Psychology*. New York: Open University Press.

Berry, D.C., Michas, I.C. and Bersellini, E. (2003) Communicating information about medication: the benefits of making it personal, *Psychology and Health*, 18(1): 127–39.

Berry, D.C., Michas, I.C., Gillie, T. and Forster, M. (1997) What do patients want to know about their medicines, and what do doctors want to tell them? A comparative study, *Psychology and Health*, 12: 467–80.

Beta-blocker Heart Attack Trial Research Group (BHAT) (1982) A randomized trial of propranolol in patients with acute myocardial infarction. I. Mortality results, *Journal of the American Medical Association*, 247: 1707–14.

Beutel, M., Deckhardt, R., von Rad, M. and Weiner, H. (1995) Grief and depression after miscarriage: their separation, antecedents and course, *Psychosomatic Medicine*, 57: 517–26.

Bieliauskas, L.A. (1980) Life stress and aid seeking, *Journal of Human Stress*, 6: 28–36.

Biener, L., Abrams, D.B., Follick, M.J. and Dean, L. (1989) A comparative evaluation of a restrictive smoking policy in a general hospital, *American Journal of Public Health*, 79: 192–5.

Birch, L.L. (1980) Effects of peer models' food choices and eating behaviors on preschoolers' food preferences, *Child Development*, 51: 489–96.

Birch, L.L. (1989) Developmental aspects of eating, in R. Shepherd (ed.) *Handbook of the Psychophysiology of Human Eating*, pp. 179–203. Chichester: Wiley.

Birch, L.L. (1999) Development of food preferences, *Annual Review of Nutrition*, 19: 41–62.

Birch, L.L. and Deysher, M. (1986) Caloric compensation and sensory specific satiety: evidence for self-regulation of food intake by young children, *Appetite*, 7: 323–31.

Birch, L.L. and Fisher, J.O. (2000) Mothers' child-feeding practices influence daughters' eating and weight, *American Journal of Clinical Nutrition*, 71: 1054–61.

Birch, L.L. and Marlin, D.W. (1982) I don't like it; I never tried it: effects of exposure on two-year-old children's food preferences, *Appetite*, 23: 353–60.

Birch, L.L., Birch, D., Marlin, D. and Kramer, L. (1982) Effects of instrumental eating on children's food preferences, *Appetite*, 3: 125–34.

Birch, L.L., Fisher, J.O., Grimm-Thomas, K., Markey, C.N., Sawyer, R. and Johnson, S.L. (2001) Confirmatory factor analysis of the Child Feeding Questionnaire: a measure of parental attitudes, beliefs and practices about child feeding and obesity proneness, *Appetite*, 36: 201–10.

Birch, L.L., Gunder, L., Grimm-Thomas, K. and Laing, D.G. (1998) Infant's consumption of a new food enhances acceptance of similar foods, *Appetite*, 30: 283–95.

Birch, L.L., McPhee, L., Shoba, B.C., Pirok, E. and Steinberg, L. (1987) What kind of exposure reduces children's food neophobia? Looking vs tasting, *Appetite*, 9: 171–8.

Birch, L.L., Marlin, D. and Rotter, J. (1984) Eating as the 'means' activity in a contingency: effects on young children's food preference, *Child Development*, 55: 431–9.

Birch, L.L., Zimmerman, S. and Hind, H. (1980) The influence of social affective context on pre-school children's food preferences, *Child Development*, 51: 856–61.

Bish, A., Sutton, S. and Golombok, S. (2000) Predicting uptake of a routine cervical smear test: a comparison of the health belief model and the theory of planned behaviour, *Psychology and Health*, 15: 35–50.

Bishop, G.D. and Converse, S.A. (1986) Illness representations: a prototype approach, *Health Psychology*, 5: 95–114.

Black, R.B. (1989) A 1 and 16 month follow up of prenatal diagnosis patients who lost pregnancies, *Prenatal Diagnosis*, 9: 795–804.

Blackburn, G.L. and Kanders, B.S. (1987) Medical evaluation and treatment of the obese patient with cardiovascular disease, *American Journal of Cardiology*, 60: 55–8.

Blair, S.N. (1993) Evidence for success of exercise in weight loss and control, *Annals of Internal Medicine*, 199: 702–6.

Blair, S.N., Ellsworth, N.M., Haskell, W.L. et al. (1981) Comparison of nutrient intake in middle aged men and women runners and controls, *Medicine, Science and Sports and Exercise*, 13: 310–15.

Blair, S.N., Kampert, J.B., Kohl, H.W. et al. (1996) Influences of cardiorespiratory fitness and other precursors on cardiovascular disease and all-cause mortality in men and women, *Journal of the American Medical Association*, 276: 205–10.

Blair, S.N., Kohl, H.W., Barlow, C.E., Paffenbarger, R.S. Jr, Gibbons, L.W. and Macera, C.A. (1995) Changes in physical fitness and all-cause mortality: a prospective study of health and unhealthy men, *Journal of the American Medical Association*, 273: 1093–8.

Blair, S.N., Kohl, H.W., Gordon, N.F. and Paffenbarger, R.S. (1992) How much physical activity is good for health? *Annual Review of Public Health*, 13: 99–126.

Blair, S.N., Kohl, H.W., Paffenbarger, R.S. et al. (1989) Physical fitness and all-cause mortality: a prospective study of healthy men and women, *Journal of the American Medical Association*, 262: 2395–401.

Blaxter, M. (1990) *Health and Lifestyles*. London: Routledge.

Bloom, J.R. (1983) Social support, accommodation to stress and adjustment to breast cancer, *Social Science and Medicine*, 16: 1329–38.

Bloom, J.R. and Monterossa, S. (1981) Hypertension labelling and sense of well-being, *American Journal of Public Health*, 71: 1228–32.

Blundell, J. and Macdiarmid, J. (1997) Fat as a risk factor for over consumption: satiation, satiety and patterns of eating, *Journal of the American Dietetic Association*, 97: S63–S69.

Blundell, J.E., Lawton, C.L., Cotton, J.R. and Macdiarmid, J.I. (1996) Control of human appetite: implications for the intake of dietary fat, *Annual Review of Nutrition*, 16: 285–319.

Bocchieri, L.E., Meana, M. and Fisher, B.L. (2002) A review of psychosocial outcomes of surgery for morbid obesity, *Journal of Psychosomatic Research*, 52: 155–65.

Bogg, T. and Roberts, B.W. (2004) Conscientiousness and health-related behaviours: a meta-analysis of the leading behavioural contributors to mortality, *Psychological Bulletin*, 130: 887–919.

Boldero, J., Moore, S. and Rosenthal, D. (1992) Intention, context, and safe sex: Australian adolescents' responses to AIDS, *Journal of Applied Social Psychology*, 22: 1374–98.

Bolton-Smith, C. and Woodward, M. (1994) Dietary composition and fat to sugar ratios in relation to obesity, *International Journal of Obesity*, 18: 820–8.

Boon, B., Stroebe, W., Schut, H. and Ijntema, R. (2002) Ironic processes in eating behaviour of restrained eaters, *British Journal of Health Psychology*, 7: 1–10.

Booth, R.J., Petrie, K.J. and Pennebaker, J.W. (1997) Changes in circulating lymphocyte numbers following emotional disclosure: evidence of buffering? *Stress Medicine*, 13: 23–9.

Boreham, C.A., Wallace, W.F. and Nevill, A. (2000) Training effects of accumulated daily stairclimbing exercise in previously sedentary young women, *Preventive Medicine*, 30: 277–81.

Borg, S. and Lasker, J. (1982) *When Pregnancy Fails: Coping with Miscarriage, Stillbirth and Infant Death*. London: Routledge & Kegan Paul.

Borland, R., Owens, N., Hill, D. and Chapman, S. (1990) Changes in acceptance of workplace smoking bans following their implementation: a prospective study, *Preventative Medicine*, 19: 314–22.

Borland, R., Owens, N. and Hocking, B. (1991) Changes in smoking behaviour after a total work place ban, *Australian Journal of Public Health*, 15: 130–4.

Borrayo, E. and Jenkins, S. (2001) Feeling indecent: breast cancer-screening resistance of Mexican-descent women, *Journal of Health Psychology*, 6(5): 537–49.

Bortner, R.W. (1969) A short rating scale as a potential measure of pattern A behaviour, *Journal of Chronic Disease*, 22: 87–91.

Bouchard, C., Trembley, A., Despres, J.P. et al. (1990) The response to long term overfeeding in identical twins, *New England Journal of Medicine*, 322: 1477–82.

Boulton, M., Schramm Evans, Z., Fitzpatrick, R. and Hart, G. (1991) Bisexual men: women, safer sex, and HIV infection, in P. Aggleton, P.M. Davies and G. Hart (eds), *AIDS: Responses, Policy and Care*. London: Falmer Press.

Bower, J.E., Kemeny, M.E., Taylor, S.E., Visscher, B.R. and Fahey, J.L. (1998) Cognitive processing, discovery of meaning, CD 4 decline, and AIDS-related mortality among bereaved HIV seropositive men, *Journal of Consulting and Clinical Psychology*, 66: 979–86.

Boyce, W.T., Alkon, A., Tschann, J.M., Chesney, M.A. and Alpert, B.S. (1995) Dimensions of psychobiologic reactivity: cardiovascular responses to laboratory stressors in preschool children, *Annals of Behavioural Medicine*, 17: 315–23.

Boyd, B. and Wandersman, A. (1991) Predicting undergraduate condom use with the Fishbein and Ajzen and the Triandis attitude-behaviour models: implications for public health interventions, *Journal of Applied Social Psychology*, 21: 1810–30.

Boyer, C.B. and Kegles, S.M. (1991) AIDS risk and prevention among adolescents, *Social Science and Medicine*, 33: 11–23.

Boyle, C.M. (1970) Differences between patients' and doctors' interpretations of common medical terms, *British Medical Journal*, 2: 286–9.

Bradley, C. (1985) Psychological aspects of diabetes, in D.G.M.M. Alberti and L.P. Drall (eds), *Diabetes Annual*. Amsterdam: Elsevier.

Bradley, C. (1996) Measuring quality of life in diabetes, in S.M. Marshall, P.D. Home and R.A. Rizza (eds), *The Diabetes Annual/10*, pp. 207–24. Amsterdam: Elsevier.

Bradley, C. (1997) Design of renal-dependent individualized quality of life questionnaire, *Advances in Peritoneal Dialysis*, 13: 116–20.

Bradley, C. (2001) Importance of differentiating health status from quality of life, *Lancet*, 357(9249): 7–8.

Bradley, C., Todd, C., Symonds, E., Martin, A. and Plowright, R. (1999) The development of an individualized questionnaire measure of perceived impact of diabetes on quality of life: the ADDQoL, *Quality of Life Research*, 8: 79–91.

Bray, G.A. (1986) Effects of obesity on health and happiness, in K.D. Brownell and J.P. Foreyt (eds), *Handbook of Eating Disorders: Physiology, Psychology and Treatment of Obesity, Anorexia and Bulimia*. New York: Basic Books.

Breckler, S.J. (1994) A comparison of numerical indexes for measuring attitude ambivalence, *Educational and Psychological Measurement*, 54: 350–65.

Breslow, L. and Enstrom, J. (1980) Persistence of health habits and their relationship to mortality, *Preventive Medicine*, 9: 469–83.

Brewer, N.T., Chapman, G.B., Brownlee, S. and Leventhal, E.A. (2002) Cholesterol control, medication adherence and illness cognition, *British Journal of Health Psychology*, 7: 433–47.

Brewin, C.R. (1984) Perceived controllability of life events and willingness to prescribe psychotropic drugs, *British Journal of Social Psychology*, 23: 285–7.

Brickman, P., Rabinowitz, V.C., Karuza, J. et al. (1982) Models of helping and coping, *American Psychologist*, 37: 368–84.

Broadbent, E., Ellis, C.J., Gamble, G. and Petrie, K.J. (in press) Changes in patient drawings of the heart identity slow recovery following myocardial infarction, *Psychosomatic Medicine*, 68: 910–13.

Broadstock, M., Michie, S. and Marteau, T.M. (2000) Psychological consequences of predictive genetic testing: a systematic review, *European Journal of Human Genetics*, 8: 731–8.

Brodie, D.A., Slade, P.D. and Rose, H. (1989) Reliability measures in disturbing body image, *Perceptual and Motor Skills*, 69: 723–32.

Brook Advisory Centres (1991) *Annual Report 1990–91*. London: Brook Advisory Centres.

Brook, R.H., Berman, D.M., Lohr, K.N. et al. (1981) *Conceptualisation and Measurement of Health for Adults, Vol. 7, Diabetes Mellitus*. Santa Monica, CA: Rand Corporation.

Broquet, K. (1999) Psychological reactions to pregnancy loss, *Primary Care Update for Obstetrics and Gynecology*, 6: 12–16.

Brown, R. and Ogden, J. (2004) Children's eating attitudes and behaviour: a study of the modelling and control theories of parental influence, *Health Education and Research*, 19(3): 261–71.

Brown, R.A., Lichtenstein, E., McIntyre, K. and Harrington-Kostur, J. (1984) Effects of nicotine fading and relapse prevention on smoking cessation, *Journal of Consulting and Clinical Psychology*, 52: 307–8.

Brown, T.A., Cash, T.F. and Mikulka, P.J. (1990) Attitudinal body-image assessment: factor analysis of the body self relations questionnaire, *Journal of Personality Assessment*, 55: 135–44.

Browne, J.P., McGee, H.M. and O'Boyle, C.A. (1997) Conceptual approaches to the assessment of quality of life, *Psychology and Health*, 12: 737–51.

Brownell, K.D. (1989) Weight control and your health, in *World Book Encyclopedia*.

Brownell, K.D. (1990) *The LEARN Programme for Weight Control*. Dallas, TX: American HealthPub.

Brownell, K.D., Greenwood, M.R.C., Stellar, E. and Shrager, E.E. (1986a) The effects of repeated cycles of weight loss and regain in rats, *Physiology and Behaviour*, 38: 459–64.

Brownell, K.D. and Steen, S.N. (1987) Modern methods for weight control: the physiology and psychology of dieting, *The Physician and Sports Medicine*, 15: 122–37.

Brownell, K.D. and Wadden, T.A. (1991) The heterogeneity of obesity: fitting treatments to individuals, *Behaviour Therapy*, 22: 153–77.

Brownell, K.D. and Wadden, T.A. (1992) Etiology and treatment of obesity: understanding a serious, prevalent and refractory disorder, *Journal of Consulting and Clinical Psychology*, 60: 435–42.

Brownell, K.D., Marlatt, G.A., Lichtenstein, E. and Wilson, G.T. (1986b) Understanding and preventing relapse, *American Psychologist*, 41: 765–82.

Brownell, K.D., Steen, S.N. and Wilmore, J.H. (1989) Weight regulation practices in athletes: analysis of metabolic and health effects, *Medical Science and Sports Exercise*, 7: 125–32.

Brownell, K.D., Stunkard, A.J. and Albaum, J.M. (1980) Evaluation and modification of exercise pattern in natural environment, *American Journal of Psychiatry*, 137: 1540–5.

Brubaker, C. and Wickersham, D. (1990) Encouraging the practice of testicular self-examination: a field application of the theory of reasoned action, *Health Psychology*, 9: 154–63.

Bruch, H. (1974) *Eating Disorders: Obesity, Anorexia and the Person Within*. New York: Basic Books.

Buchi, S.T., Villiger, B., Sensky, T., Schwarz, F., Wolf, C.H. and Buddenberg, C. (1997) Psychosocial predictors of long term success in patient pulmonary rehabilitation of patients with COPD, *European Respiratory Journal*, 10: 1272–7.

Bucknall, C.A., Morris, G.K. and Mitchell, J.R.A. (1986) Physicians' attitudes to four common problems: hypertension, atrial fibrillation, transient ischaemic attacks, and angina pectoris, *British Medical Journal*, 293: 739–42.

Buick, D.L., Crook, D. and Horne, R. (2005) Women's perceptions of hormone replacement therapy: risks and benefits (1980–2002) – a literature review, *Climacteric*, 8(1): 24–35.

Bull, R.H., Engels, W.D., Engelsmann, F. and Bloom, L. (1983) Behavioural changes following gastric surgery for morbid obesity: a prospective, controlled study, *Journal of Psychosomatic Research*, 27: 457–67.

Bullen, B.A., Reed, R.B. and Mayer, J. (1964) Physical activity of obese and non-obese adolescent girls appraised by motion picture sampling, *American Journal of Clinical Nutrition*, 4: 211–33.

Bundy, C., Carroll, D., Wallace, L. and Nagle, R. (1998) Stress management and exercise training in chronic stable angina pectoris, *Psychology and Health*, 13: 147–55.

Burish, T.G., Carey, M.P., Krozely, M.G. and Greco, F.F. (1987) Conditioned side-effects induced by cancer chemotherapy: prevention through behavioral treatment, *Journal of Consulting and Clinical Psychology*, 55: 42–8.

Burke, P. (1992) The ethics of screening, in C.R. Hart and P. Burke (eds), *Screening and Surveillance in General Practice*. London: Churchill Livingstone.

Burnett, J. (1989) *Plenty and Want: A Social History of Food in England from 1815 to the Present Day*, 3rd edn. London: Routledge.

Bury, M. (1982) Chronic illness as biographical disruption, *Sociology of Health and Illness*, 4: 167–82.

Butler, C. and Llanedeyrn, M. (1996) Late psychological sequelae of abortion: questions from a primary care perspective, *The Journal of Family Practice*, 43: 396–401.

Butler, C. and Steptoe, A. (1986) Placebo responses: an experimental study of psychophysiological processes in asthmatic volunteers, *British Journal of Clinical Psychology*, 25: 173–83.

Butterfield, W.J.H. (1968) *Priorities in Medicine*. London: Nufield.

Byrne, D., Jazwinski, C., DeNinno, J.A. and Fisher, W.A. (1977) Negative sexual attitudes and contraception, in D. Byrne and L.A. Byrne (eds), *Exploring Human Sexuality*. New York: Crowell.

Byrne, P.S. and Long, B.E.L. (1976) *Doctor Talking to Patient*. London: HMSO.

Calnan, M. (1987) *Health and Illness: The Lay Perspective*. London: Tavistock.

Campion, M.J., Brown, J.R., McCance, D.J. et al. (1988) Psychosexual trauma of an abnormal cervical smear, *British Journal of Obstetrics and Gynaecology*, 95: 175–81.

Cancer Research Campaign (1991) *Smoking Policy and Prevalence Among 16–19 Year Olds*. London: HMSO.

Cannon, W.B. (1932) *The Wisdom of the Body*. New York: Norton.

Cappell, H. and Greeley, J. (1987) Alcohol and tension reduction: an update on research and theory, in H.T. Blane and K.E. Leonard (eds), *Psychological Theories of Drinking and Alcoholism*, pp. 15–54. New York: Guilford Press.

Carey, M.P., Kalra, D.L., Carey, K.B., Halperin, S. and Richard, C.S. (1993) Stress and unaided smoking cessation: a prospective investigation, *Journal of Consulting and Clinical Psychology*, 61: 831–8.

Cartwright, A., Hockey, L. and Anderson, J.L. (1973) *Life Before Death*. London: Routledge.

Carver, C.S., Scheier, M.F. and Weintraub, J.K. (1989) Assessing coping strategies: a theoretically based approach, *Journal of Personality and Social Psychology*, 56: 267–83.

Casey, R. and Rozin, P. (1989) Changing children's food preferences: parents' opinions, *Appetite*, 12P: 171–82.

Caspersen, C.J., Powell, K.E. and Christenson, G.M. (1985) Physical activity, exercise, and physical fitness: definitions and distinctions for health-related research, *Public Health Reports*, 100: 126–31.

Castle, C.M., Skinner, T.C. and Hampson, S. (1999). Young women and suntanning: an evaluation of a health education leaflet, *Psychology and Health*, 14, 517–27.

Catania, J.A., Coates, T.J., Kegeles, S.M. et al. (1989) Implications of the AIDS risk-reduction model for the gay community: the importance of perceived sexual enjoyment and help seeking behaviors, in V.M. Mays, G.W. Albee and S.F. Schneider (eds), *Primary Prevention of AIDS*, pp. 242–61. Newbury Park, CA: Sage.

Central Statistical Office (1994) *Social Trends 24*. London: HMSO.

Chambers, L.W., McDonald, L.A., Tugwell, P. et al. (1982) The McMaster health index questionnaire as a measure of quality of life for patients with rheumatoid arthritis, *Journal of Rheumatology*, 9: 780–4.

Champion, V.L. (1990) Breast self-examination in women 35 and older: a prospective study, *Journal of Behavioural Medicine*, 13: 523–38.

Chan, J.M., Rimm, E.B., Colditz, G.A., Stampfer, M.J. and Willett, W.C. (1994) Obesity, fat distribution and weight gain as risk factors for clinical diabetes in men, *Diabetes Care*, 17: 961–9.

Charles, N. and Kerr, M. (1986) Eating properly: the family and state benefit, *Sociology*, 20(3): 412–29.

Charlton, A. (1984) Children's opinion about smoking, *Journal of the Royal College of General Practitioners*, 34: 483–7.

Charlton, A. (1992) Children and tobacco, *British Journal of Cancer*, 66: 1–4.

Charlton, A. and Blair, V. (1989) Predicting the onset of smoking in boys and girls, *Social Science and Medicine*, 29: 813–18.

Chinn, S. and Rona, R.J. (2001) Prevalence and trends in overweight and obesity in three cross-sectional studies of British children, 1974–94, *British Medical Journal*, 322: 24–6.

Christensen, A.J., Edwards, D.L., Wiebe, J.S. et al. (1996) Effect of verbal self-disclosure on natural killer cell activity: moderation influence on cynical hostility, *Psychosomatic Medicine*, 58: 150–5.

Clarke, L., Farrell, C. and Beaumont, B. (1983) *Camden Abortion Study*. London: BPAS.

Clement, S. (1998) *Psychological Perspectives on Pregnancy & Childbirth*. Edinburgh: Churchill Livingstone.

Coates, T.J., Jeffrey, R.W. and Wing, R.R. (1978) The relationship between a person's relative body weight and the quality and quantity of food stored in their homes, *Addictive Behaviours*, 3: 179–84.

Cobb, S. and Rose, R. (1973) Hypertension, peptic ulcer and diabetes in air traffic controllers, *Journal of the American Medical Association*, 224: 489–92.

Cockburn, J., Staples, M., Hurley, S.F. and DeLuise, T. (1994) Psychological consequences of screening mammography, *Journal of Medical Screening*, 1: 7–12.

Cohen, F. and Lazarus, R.S. (1979) Coping with the stresses of illness, in G.C. Stone, F. Cohen and N.E. Adler (eds), *Health Psychology: A Handbook*, pp. 217–54. San Francisco, CA: Jossey-Bass.

Cohen, J.B., Severy, L.J. and Ahtola, O.T. (1978) An extended expectancy value approach to contraceptive alternatives, *Journal of Population Studies*, 1: 22–41.

Cohen, S. and Lichtenstein, E. (1990) Partner behaviours that support quitting smoking, *Journal of Consulting and Clinical Psychology*, 58: 304–9.

Cohen, S., Kamarck, T. and Mermelstein, R. (1983) A global measure of perceived stress, *Journal of Health and Social Behaviour*, 24: 385–96.

Cohen, S., Mermelstein, R., Kamarck, T. and Hoberman, N.H. (1985) Measuring the functional components of social support, in I. Sarason and B. Sarason (eds), *Social Support: Theory, Research, and Applications*, pp. 73–94. Dordrecht: Martinus Nijhoff.

Cohen, S., Tyrell, A.J. and Smith, A.P. (1991) Psychological stress and susceptibility to the common cold, *New England Journal of Medicine*, 325: 606–12.

Cole, S. and Edelmann, R. (1988) Restraint, eating disorders and the need to achieve in state and public school subjects, *Personality and Individual Differences*, 8: 475–82.

Coleman, P.K., Reardon, D.C., Strahan, T. and Cougle, J.R. (2005) The psychology of abortion: a review and suggestions for future research, *Psychology and Health*, 20: 237–71.

Collijn, D.H., Appels, A.D. and Nijhuis, F. (1996) Are multiple roles a risk factor for myocardial infarction in women? *Journal of Psychosomatic Research*, 40: 271–9.

Collins, M.E. (1991) Body figure perceptions and preferences among preadolescent children, *International Journal of Eating Disorders*, 10: 199–208.

Collins, R.L., Taylor, S.E. and Skokan, L.A. (1990). A better world or a shattered vision? Changes in life perspective following victimization, *Social Cognition*, 8, 263–85.

Colvin, R.H. and Olson, S.B. (1983) A descriptive analysis of men and women who have lost significant weight and are highly successful at maintaining the loss, *Addictive Behaviours*, 8: 287–95.

Compas, B.E., Barnez, G.A., Malcarne, V. and Worshame, N. (1991) Perceived control and coping with stress: a developmental perspective, *Journal of Social Issue*, 47: 23–34.

Compas, B.E., Worshame, N., Ey, S. and Howell, D.C. (1996) When mom or dad has a cancer: II. Coping, cognitive appraisals and psychological distress in children of cancer patients, *Health Psychology*, 15: 167–75.

Conklin, M.P. and O'Connor, B.P. (1995) Beliefs about the foetus as a moderator of post-abortion psychological well-being, *Journal of Social and Clinical Psychology*, 14: 76–95.

Conner, M. and Godin, G. (2006) Temporal stability of behavioural intention as a moderator of intention-health behaviour relationships, *Psychology & Health* (in press).

Conner, M., Fitter, M. and Fletcher, W. (1999) Stress and snacking: a diary study of daily hassles and between-meal snacking, *Psychology and Health*, 14: 51–63.

Conner, M., Graham, S. and Moore, B. (1999b) Alcohol and intentions to use condoms: applying the theory of planned behaviour, *Psychology and Health*, 14: 795–812.

Conner, M., Lawton, R., Parker, D., Chorlton, K., Manstead, A.S.R. and Stradling, S. (2006) Application of the theory of planned behaviour to the prediction of objectively assessed breaking of posted speed limits, *British Journal of Psychology* (in press).

Conner, M., Sandberg, T., McMillan, B. and Higgins, A. (2006) Role of anticipated regret, intentions and intention stability in adolescent smoking initiation, *British Journal of Health Psychology*, 11: 85–101.

Constanzo, P.R. and Woody, E.Z. (1985) Domain specific parenting styles and their impact on the child's development of particular deviance: the example of obesity proneness, *Journal of Social and Clinical Psychology*, 4: 425–45.

Contento, I.R., Basch, C., Shea, S. et al. (1993) Relationship of mothers' food choice criteria to food intake of pre-school children: identification of family subgroups, *Health Education Quarterly*, 20: 243–59.

Cook, W.W. and Medley, D.M. (1954) Proposed hostility and pharasaic virtue scales for the MMPI, *Journal of Applied Psychology*, 38: 414–18.

Cools, J., Schotte, D.E. and McNally, R.J. (1992) Emotional arousal and overeating in restrained eaters, *Journal of Abnormal Psychology*, 101: 348–51.

Cooney, T.M., Pedersen, F.A., Indelicato, S. and Palkovitz, R. (1993) Timing of fatherhood: is 'on-time' optimal? *Journal of Marriage and the Family*, 55: 205–15.

Cooper, A.F., Jackson, G., Weinman, J. and Horne, R. (2002a) Factors associated with cardiac reha-bilitation attendance: a systematic review of the literature, *Clinical Rehabilitation*, 16: 541–52.

Cooper, P.J., Taylor, M.J., Cooper, Z. and Fairburn, C.G. (1987) The development and validation of the body shape questionnaire, *International Journal of Eating Disorders*, 6: 485–94.

Cooper, V., Buick, D., Horne, R., Lambert, N., Gellaitry, G., Leake, H. and Fisher, M. (2002b) Per-ceptions of HAART among gay men who declined a treatment offer: preliminary results from an interview-based study, *AIDS Care*, 14: 319–28.

Coopersmith, S. (1967) *The Antecedents of Self-esteem.* San Francisco, CA: WH Freeman. Reprinted in 1981.

Corah, W.L. and Boffa, J. (1970) Perceived control, self-observation and responses to aversive stimu-lation, *Journal of Personality and Social Psychology*, 16: 1–4.

Coulter, A. (1999) Paternalism or partnership? Patients have grown up and there's no going back, *British Medical Journal*, 319: 719–20.

Counts, C.R. and Adams, H.E. (1985) Body image in bulimia, dieting and normal females, *Journal of Psychopathology and Behavioral Assessment*, 7: 289–300.

Courneya, K.S., Plotnikoff, R.C., Hotz, S.B and Birkett, N.J. (2001) Predicting exercise stage trans-ition over two consecutive 6-month periods: a test of the theory of planned behaviour in a popu-lation-based sample, *British Journal of Health Psychology*, 6: 135–50.

Crago, M.A. (1972) Psychopathology in marital couples, *Psychological Bulletin*, 77: 114–28.

Crichton, E.F., Smith, D.L. and Demanuele, F. (1978) Patients' recall of medication information, *Drug Intelligence and Clinical Pharmacy*, 12: 591–9.

Crisp, A., Palmer, R. and Kalucy, R. (1976) How common is anorexia nervosa? A prevalence study, *British Journal of Psychiatry*, 128: 549–54.

Crisp, A.H., Hsu, L., Harding, B. and Hartshorn, J. (1980) Clinical features of anorexia: a study of consecutive series of 102 female patients, *Journal of Psychosomatic Research*, 24: 179–91.

Crombez, G., Bijttebier, P., Eccleston, C. et al. (2003) The child version of the pain catastrophizing scale (PCS-C): a preliminary validation, *Pain*, 104(3): 639–46.

Crombez, G., Eccleston, C., Baeyens, F. and Eelen, P. (1998a) Attentional disruption is enhanced by threat of pain, *Behaviour Research and Therapy*, 36: 195–204.

Crombez, G., Eccleston, C., Baeyens, F. and Eelen, P. (1998b) When somatic information threatens, catastrophic thinking enhances attentional interference, *Pain*, 75(2–3): 187–98.

Crombez, G., Eccleston, C., Baeyens, F., Van Houdenhover, B. and Van de Broeck, A. (1999) Atten-tion to chronic pain is dependent upon pain-related fear, *Journal of Psychosomatic Research*, 47(5): 403–10.

Cropley, M. and Millward Purvis, L.J. (2003) Job strain and rumination about work issues during leisure time: a diary study, *European Journal of Work and Organizational Psychology*, 12(3): 195–207.

Cropley, M. and Steptoe, A. (2005) Social support, life events and physical symptoms: a prospective study of chronic and recent life stress in men and women, *Psychology, Health & Medicine*, 10(4): 317–25.

Cropley, M., Ayers, S. and Nokes, L. (2003) People don't exercise because they can't think of reasons to exercise: an examination of causal reasoning within the transtheoretical model, *Psychology, Health & Medicine*, 8(4): 409–14.

Cropley, M., Dijk, D.J. and Stanley, N. (2006) Job strain, work rumination, and sleep in school teachers, *European Journal of Work and Organizational Psychology*, 15(2): 181–96.

Cropley, M., Steptoe, A. and Joekes, K. (1999) Job strain and psychiatric morbidity, *Psychological Medicine*, 29: 1411–16.

Cummings, K., Hellmann, R. and Emont, S.L. (1988) Correlates of participation in a worksite stop-smoking contest, *Journal of Behavioral Medicine*, 11: 267–77.

Curran, J.W., Morgan, W.M., Hardy, A.M. et al. (1985) The epidemiology of AIDS: current status and future prospects, *Science*, 229: 1352–7.

Cvetkovich, G. and Grote, B. (1981) Psychosocial maturity and teenage contraceptive use: an investigation of decision-making and communication skills, *Population and Environment*, 4: 211–26.

DAFNE study group (2002) Training in flexible, intensive insulin management to enable dietary freedom in people with type I diabetes: dose adjustment for normal eating (DAFNE) randomised controlled trial, *British Medical Journal*, 325: 1–6.

Danaher, B.G. (1977) Rapid smoking and self-control in the modification of smoking behaviour, *Journal of Consulting and Clinical Psychology*, 45: 1068–75.

Daniel, J.Z., Cropley, M. and Fife-Schaw, C. (2006) The effect of exercise in reducing desire to smoke and cigarette withdrawal symptoms is not caused by distraction, *Addiction*, 101(8): 1187–92.

Daniel, J.Z., Cropley, M., Ussher, M. and West, R. (2004) Acute effects of a short bout of moderate versus light intensity exercise versus inactivity on tobacco withdrawal symptoms in sedentary smokers, *Psychopharmacology*, 174: 320–6.

Davies, D.L. (1962) Normal drinking in recovered alcohol addicts, *Quarterly Journal of Studies on Alcohol*, 23: 94–104.

Davis, C. (1928) Self-selection of diets by newly weaned infants, *American Journal of Disease of Children*, 36: 651–79.

Davis, C. (1939) Results of the self selection of diets by young children, *The Canadian Medical Association Journal*, 41: 257–61.

De Zwann, M., Lancaster, K.L., Mitchell, J.E., Howell, L.M., Monson, N. and Roerig, J.L. (2002) Health related quality of life in morbidly obese patients: effect of gastric bypass surgery, *Obesity Surgery*, 12: 773–80.

Dean, C. (1987) Psychiatric morbidity following mastectomy: preoperative predictors and types of illness, *Journal of Psychosomatic Research*, 31: 385–92.

Dean, C., Roberts, M.M., French, K. and Robinson, S. (1984) Psychiatric morbidity after screening for breast cancer, *Journal of Epidemiology and Community Health*, 40: 71–5.

Debro, S.C., Campbell, S.M. and Peplau, L.A. (1994) Influencing a partner to use a condom: characteristics of the situation are more important than characteristics of the individual, *Psychology, Health and Medicine*, 4: 265–79.

deHaes, J.C.J.M., van Knippenberg, F.C. and Neigt, J.P. (1990) Measuring psychological and physical distress in cancer patients: structure and application of the Rotterdam symptom checklist, *British Journal of Cancer*, 62: 1034–8.

Dekker, F.W., Kaptein, A.A., van der Waart, M.A.C. and Gill, K. (1992) Quality of self-care of patients with asthma, *Journal of Asthma*, 29: 203–8.

DeLamater, J. and MacCorquodale, P. (1978) Premarital contraceptive use: a test of two models, *Journal of Marriage and the Family*, 40: 235–47.

DeLamater, J. and MacCorquodale, P. (1979) *Premarital Sexuality: Attitudes, Relationships, Behavior.* Madison, WI: University of Wisconsin Press.

Department of Health (DoH) (1991a) *Dietary Reference Values for Food Energy and Nutrients for the United Kingdom*, Report on Health and Social Subjects No. 41. London: HMSO.

Department of Health (DoH) (1991b) *The Health of the Nation*. London: HMSO.

Department of Health (DoH) (1992) Winterton Report. *Second Report on the Maternity Services*, London: HMSO.

Department of Health (DoH) (1993) *Cumberlege Report: Changing Childbirth*. London: HMSO.

Department of Health (DoH) (1995) *Obesity: Reversing the Increasing Problem of Obesity in England – A Report from the Nutrition and Physical Activity Task Forces*. London: HMSO.

Department of Health (DoH) (2005) *Maternity Statistics 2003–2004*. London: OPCS.

Department of Health and Welsh Office (1989) *General Practice in the National Health Service: A New Contract*. London: HMSO.

Despres, J-P., Lemieux, I. and Prudhomme, D. (2001) Treatment of obesity: need to focus on high risk abdominally obese patients, *British Medical Journal*, 322: 716–20.

Diamond, E.G., Kittle, C.F. and Crockett, J.F. (1960) Comparison of internal mammary artery ligation and sham operation for angina pectoris, *American Journal of Cardiology*, 5: 483–6.

DiClemente, C.C. (1986) Self-efficacy and the addictive behaviors, *Journal of Social and Clinical Psychology*, 4: 303–15.

DiClemente, C.C. and Hughes, S.O. (1990) Stages of change profiles in outpatient alcoholism treatment, *Journal of Substance Abuse*, 2: 217–35.

DiClemente, C.C. and Prochaska, J.O. (1982) Self-change and therapy change of smoking behavior: a comparison of processes of change in cessation and maintenance, *Addictive Behaviours*, 7: 133–42.

DiClemente, C.C. and Prochaska, J.O. (1985) Processes and stages of change: coping and competence in smoking behavior change, in F. Shiffman and T.A. Wills (eds), *Coping and Substance Abuse*, pp. 319–43. New York: Academic Press.

DiClemente, C.C., Prochaska, J.O., Fairhurst, S.K. et al. (1991) The process of smoking cessation: An analysis of precontemplation, contemplation, and preparation stages of change, *Journal of Consulting and Clinical Psychology*, 59: 295–304.

DiClemente, C.C., Prochaska, J.O. and Gilbertini, M. (1985) Self-efficacy and the stages of self-change of smoking, *Cognitive Therapy and Research*, 9: 181–200.

Diederiks, J.P., Bar, F.W., Hopponer, P. et al. (1991) Predictors of return to former leisure and social activities in MI patients, *Journal of Psychosomatic Research*, 35: 687–96.

Dillon, K.M., Mincho., B. and Baker, K.H. (1985–1986) Positive emotional states and enhancement of the immune system, *International Journal of Psychiatry in Medicine*, 15: 13–17.

Diner, E., Emmons, R.A., Larson, R.J. and Griffen, S. (1985) The satisfaction with life scale, *Journal of Personality Assessment*, 49: 71–6.

Dion, K.K. (1995) Delayed parenthood and women's expectations about the transition to parenthood, *International Journal of Behavioural Development*, 18: 315–33.

Dishman, R.K. (1982) Compliance/adherence in health-related exercise, *Health Psychology*, 1: 237–67.

Dishman, R.K. and Gettman, L.R. (1980) Psychobiologic influences on exercise adherence, *Journal of Sport Psychology*, 2: 295–310.

Dishman, R.K., Sallis, J.F. and Orenstein, D.M. (1985) The determinants of physical activity and exercise, *Public Health Reports*, 100: 158–72.

Dolan, B., Lacey, J. and Evans, C. (1990) Eating behaviour and attitudes to weight and shape in British women from three ethnic groups, *British Journal of Psychiatry*, 157: 523–8.

Dolce, J.J. (1987) Self-efficacy and disability beliefs in the behavioral treatment of pain, *Behavior Research and Therapy*, 25: 289–96.

Doll, R. and Hill, A.B. (1954) The mortality of doctors in relation to their smoking habits: a preliminary report, *British Medical Journal*, 1: 1451–5.

Doll, R. and Peto, R. (1981) *The Causes of Cancer*. New York: Oxford University Press.

Donnelly, D.A. and Murray, E.J. (1991) Cognitive and emotional changes in written essays and therapy interviews, *Journal of Social and Clinical Psychology*, 10: 334–50.

Dornbusch, S., Carlsmith, J., Duncan, P. et al. (1984) Sexual maturation, social class and the desire to be thin among adolescent females, *Developmental and Behavioural Paediatrics*, 5: 475–82.

Dowey, A.J. (1996) Psychological determinants of children's food preferences. Unpublished doctoral dissertation, University of Wales, Bangor.

Downing, R.W. and Rickels, K. (1983) Physician prognosis in relation to drug and placebo response in anxious and depressed psychiatric outpatients, *The Journal of Nervous and Mental Disease*, 171: 182–5.

Doyal, L. (1985) Women and the National Health Service: the carers and the careless, in E. Lewin and V. Olesen (eds) *Women, Health and Healing: Toward a New Perspective*. London: Tavistock.

Doyal, L. (1994) Changing medicine? Gender and the politics of health care, in J. Gabe, D. Kelleher and G. Williams (eds) *Challenging Medicine*. London: Routledge.

Doyal, L. (2001) Informed consent: moral necessity or illusion? *Quality in Health Care*, 10: 29i–33i.

Drenowski, A., Kurt, C. and Krahn, D. (1994) Body weight and dieting in adolescence: impact of socioeconomic status, *International Journal of Eating Disorders*, 16: 61–5.

Drew, N.C. Salmon, P. and Webb, L. (1989) Mothers, midwives and obstetricians' views on the features of obstetric care which influence satisfaction with childbirth, *British Journal of Obstetrics and Gynaecology*, 96: 1084–8.

Duncan, I. (ed.) (1992) *Guidelines for Clinical Practice and Programme Management*. Oxford: NHS Cervical Screening Programme.

Duncker, K. (1938) Experimental modification of children's food preferences through social suggestion, *Journal of Abnormal Social Psychology*, 33: 489–507.

Dunn, A.L., Andersen, R.E. and Jakicic, J.M. (1998) Lifestyle physical activity interventions: history, short and long-term effects and recommendation, *American Journal of Preventive Medicine*, 15: 398–412.

Durnin, J.V.G.A., Lonergan, M.E., Good, J. and Ewan, A. (1974) A cross-sectional nutritional and anthropometric study with an interval of 7 years on 611 young adolescent school children, *British Journal of Nutrition*, 32: 169–79.

Ebrecht, M., Hextall, J., Kirtley, L.G., Taylor, A., Dyson, M. and Weinman, J. (2004) Perceived stress and cortisol levels predict speed of wound healing in healthy male adults, *Psychoneuroendocrinology*, 29: 798–809.

Eccleston, C. (1994) Chronic pain and attention: a cognitive approach, *British Journal of Clinical Psychology*, 33(Pt 4): 535–47.

Eccleston, C. and Crombez, G. (1999) Pain demands attention: a cognitive-affective model of the interruptive function of pain, *Psychological Bulletin*, 125(3): 356–66.

Eccleston, C., Crombez, G., Aldrich, S. and Stannard, C. (2001) Worry and chronic pain patients: a description and analysis of individual differences, *European Journal of Pain*, 5(3): 309–18.

Eccleston, C., Malleson, P.N., Clinch, J., Connell, H. and Sourbut, C. (2003) Chronic pain in adolescents: evaluation of a programme of interdisciplinary cognitive behavioural therapy, *Archives of Disease in Childhood*, 88(10): 881–5.

Eccleston, C., Morley, S., Williams, A., Yorke, L. and Mastroyannopoulou, K. (2002) Systematic review of randomised controlled trials of psychological therapy for chronic pain in children and adolescents with a subset meta-analysis of pain relief, *Pain*, 99(1–2): 157–65.

Eccleston, C., Yorke, L., Morley, S., Williams, A.C. and Mastroyannopoulou, K. (2003) Psychological therapies for management of chronic and recurrent pain in children and adolescents, *Cochrane Database of Systematic Reviews*, 1: CD003968.

Edholm, O.G., Fletcher, J.G., Widdowson, E.M. and McCance, R.A. (1955) The food intake and individual expenditure of individual men, *British Journal of Nutrition*, 9: 286–300.

Edwards, G. and Gross, M. (1976) Alcohol dependence: provisional description of a clinical syndrome, *British Medical Journal*, i: 1058–61.

Edwards, N. (1954) The theory of decision making, *Psychological Bulletin*, 51: 380–417.

Egbert, L.D., Battit, G.E., Welch, C.E. and Bartlett, M.K. (1964) Reduction of postoperative pain by encouragement and instruction of patients, *The New England Journal of Medicine*, 270: 825–7.

Egger, G., Fitzgerald, W., Frape, G. et al. (1983) Result of a large scale media antismoking campaign in Australia: North Coast 'Quit For Life' Programme, *British Medical Journal*, 286: 1125–8.

Eiser, J.R. (2000) The influence of question framing on symptom report and perceived health status, *Psychology and Health*, 15: 13–20.

Eiser, J.R. and Cole, N. (2002) Participation in cervical screening as a function of perceived risk, barriers and need for cognitive closure, *Journal of Health Psychology*, 7(1): 99–105.

Eisler, I. and Szmukler, G. (1985) Social class as a confounding variable in the eating attitudes test, *Journal of Psychiatric Research*, 19: 171–6.

Elliott, B.J. and Huppert, F.A. (1991) In sickness and in health: associations between physical and mental well-being, employment and parental status in a British nationwide sample of married women, *Psychological Medicine*, 21: 515–24.

Elwyn, G., Edwards, A. and Kinnersley, P. (1999) Shared decision making: the neglected second half of the consultation, *British Journal of General Practice*, 49: 477–82.

Emmons, R.A. (1996) Strivings and feeling: personal goals and subjective well-being, in P.M. Gollwitzer and J.A. Bargh (eds), *The Psychology of Action: Linking Cognition and Motivation to Behavior*, pp. 313–37. New York: Guilford.

Engel, G.L. (1977) The need for a new medical model: A challenge for biomedicine, *Science*, 196: 129–35.

Engel, G.L. (1980) The clinical application of the biopsychosocial model, *American Journal of Psychiatry*, 137: 535–44.

Entwistle, V.A., Sheldon, T.A., Sowden, A. and Watt, I.S. (1998) Evidence-informed patient choice: practical issues of involving patients in decisions about health-care technologies, *International Journal of Technological Assessment in Health-care*, 14: 212–25.

Eriksen, P.S. and Rasmussen, H. (1992) Low dose 17-β oestradiol vaginal tablets in the treatment of atrophic vaginitis: a double-blind placebo controlled study, *European Journal of Obstetrics & Gynaecology and Reproductive Biology*, 44: 137–44.

Esterling, B.A., Kiecolt-Glaser, J.K., Bodnar, J.C. and Glaser, R. (1994) Chronic stress, social support and persistent alterations in the natural killer cell response to cytokines in older adults, *Health Psychology*, 13: 291–8.

Etzwiler, D.D. (1967) Who's teaching the diabetic? *Diabetes*, 16: 111–17.

Evans, F.J. (1974) The power of the sugar pill, *Psychology Today*, April: 55–9.

Everson, S.A., Lynch, J.W., Chesney, M.A. et al. (1997) Interaction of workplace demands and cardiovascular reactivity in progression of carotid atherosclerosis: population based study, *British Medical Journal*, 314: 553–8.

Eysenck, H.J. (1990) The prediction of death from cancer by means of personality/stress questionnaire: too good to be true? *Perceptual Motor Skills*, 71: 216–18.

Eysenck, H.J. and Grossarth-Maticek, R. (1991) Creative novation behaviour therapy as a prophylactic treatment for cancer and coronary heart disease. Part II – effects of treatment, *Behaviour Research and Therapy*, 29: 17–31.

Fallowfield, L. (1990) *The Quality of Life: The Missing Measurement in Health Care*. London: Souvenir Press.

Fallowfield, L.J., Rodway, A. and Baum, M. (1990) What are the psychological factors influencing attendance, non-attendance and re-attendance at a breast screening centre? *Journal of the Royal Society of Medicine*, 83: 547–51.

Farooqi, I.S., Jebb, S.A., Cook, G. et al. (1999) Effects of recombinant leptin therapy in a child with leptin deficiency, *New England Journal of Medicine*, 16: 879–84.

Farquhar, J.W., Fortmann, S.P., Flora, J.A. et al. (1990) Effects of communitywide education on cardiovascular disease risk factors: the Stanford Five-City Project, *Journal of the American Medical Association*, 264: 359–65.

Feldman, S.S. and Nash, S.C. (1984) The transition from expectancy to parenthood: impact of the firstborn child on men and women, *Sex Roles*, 11: 61–78.

Fernbach, M. (2002) The impact of a media campaign on cervical screening knowledge and self-efficacy, *Journal of Health Psychology*, 7(1): 85–97.

Ferster, C.B., Nurnberger, J.I. and Levitt, E.B. (1962) The control of eating, *Journal of Mathetics*, 1: 87–109.

Festinger, L. (1957) *A Theory of Cognitive Dissonance*. Evanston, IL: Row, Peterson.

Feuerstein, M., Carter, R.L. and Papciak, A.S. (1987) A prospective analysis of stress and fatigue in recurrent low back pain, *Pain*, 31: 333–44.

Fife-Schaw, C.R. and Breakwell, G.M. (1992) Estimating sexual behaviour parameters in the light of AIDS: a review of recent UK studies of young people, *Aids Care*, 4: 187–201.

Figueiras, M.J. and Weinman, J. (2003) Do similar patient and spouse perceptions of myocardial infarction predict recovery? *Psychology and Health*, 18(2): 201–16.

Fiore, M.C., Novotny, T.F., Pierce, J.P. et al. (1990) Methods used to quit smoking in the United States: do cessation programs help? *Journal of the American Medical Association*, 263: 2760–5.

Fishbein, M. (ed.) (1967) *Readings in Attitude Theory and Measurement*. New York: Wiley.

Fishbein, M. and Ajzen, I. (1975) *Belief, Attitude, Intention, and Behavior: An Introduction to Theory and Research*. Reading, MA: Addison-Wesley.

Fishbein, M. and Middlestadt, S.E. (1989) Using theory of reasoned action as a framework for understanding and changing AIDS-related behaviours, in V.M. Mays, J. Albee and S.F. Schneider (eds), *Primary Prevention for AIDS: Psychological Approaches*. Newbury Park, CA: Sage.

Fisher, J.D. and Fisher, W.A. (1992) Changing AIDS-risk behaviour, *Psychological Bulletin*, 111: 455–74.

Fisher, J.O. and Birch, L.L. (1999) Restricting access to a palatable food affects children's behavioral response, food selection and intake, *American Journal of Clinical Nutrition*, 69: 1264–72.

Fisher, J.O., Birch, L.L., Smiciklas-Wright, H. and Piocciano, M.F. (2000) Breastfeeding through the first year predicts maternal control in feeding and subsequent toddler energy intakes, *Journal of the American Dietician Association*, 100: 641–6.

Fisher, W.A. (1984) Predicting contraceptive behavior among university men: the role of emotions and behavioral intentions, *Journal of Applied Social Psychology*, 14: 104–23.

Fitzpatrick, R. (1993) Scope and measurement of patient satisfaction, in R. Fitzpatrick and A. Hopkins (eds), *Measurement of Patients' Satisfaction with Their Care*. London: Royal College of Physicians of London.

Flannelly, G., Anderson, D., Kitchener, H.C. et al. (1994) Management of women with mild and moderate cervical dyskaryosis, *British Medical Journal*, 308: 1399–403.

Flay, B.R. (1985) Psychosocial approaches to smoking prevention: a review of findings, *Health Psychology*, 4: 449–88.

Flegal, K.M., Harlan, W.R. and Landis, J.R. (1988) Secular trends in body mass index and skinfold thickness with socioeconomic factors in young adult women, *American Journal of Clinical Nutrition*, 48: 535–43.

Flowers, P., Smith, J.A., Sheeran, P. and Beail, N. (1997) Health and romance: understanding unprotected sex in relationships between gay men, *British Journal of Health Psychology*, 2: 73–86.

Flowers, P., Smith, J.A., Sheeran, P. and Beail, N. (1998) 'Coming out' and sexual debut: understanding the social context of HIV risk-related behaviour, *Journal of Community & Applied Social Psychology*, 8: 409–21.

Folkman, S. and Lazarus, R.S. (1980) An analysis of coping in a middle-aged community sample, *Journal of Health and Social Behaviour*, 21: 219–39.

Folkman, S. and Lazarus, R.S. (1988) *Manual for the Ways of Coping Questionnaire*. Palo Alto, CA: Consulting Psychologist Press.

Folkman, S. and Moskowitz, J.T. (2000) Positive affect and the other side of coping, *American Psychologist*, 55: 647–54.

Folkman, S., Lazarus, R.S., Dunkel-Schetter, C., DeLongis, A. and Gruen, R.J. (1986) Dynamics of a stressful encounter: cognitive appraisal, coping and encounter outcomes, *Journal of Personality and Social Psychology*, 50: 992–1003.

Folkman, S., Lazarus, R.S., Pimley, S. and Novacek, J. (1987) Age differences in stress and coping processes, *Psychology and Ageing*, 2: 171–84.

Ford, E., Williamson, D. and Liu, S. (1997) Weight change and diabetes incidence: findings from a national cohort of US adults, *American Journal of Epidemiology*, 146: 214–22.

Fordyce, W.E. and Steger, J.C. (1979) Chronic pain, in O.F. Pomerleau and J.P. Brady (eds), *Behavioral Medicine: Theory and Practice*, pp. 125–53. Baltimore, MD: Williams & Wilkins.

Formon, S.J. (1974) *Infant Nutrition*, 2nd edn. Philadelphia, PA: WB Saunders.

Forrest, A.P.M. (1986) *Breast Cancer Screening. Report to the Health Ministers of England, Wales, Scotland and Northern Ireland*. London: HMSO.

Foster, P. (1995) *Women and the Health Care Industry: An Unhealthy Relationships?* Buckingham: Open University Press.

Foucault, M. (1979) *The History of Sexuality, Vol. 1: An Introduction*. London: Allen & Lane.

Francis, M.E and Pennebaker, J.W. (1992) Putting stress into words: writing about personal upheavals and health, *American Journal of Health Promotion*, 6: 280–7.

Fredrickson, B.L. and Matthews, K.A. (1990) Cardiovascular responses to behavioural stress and hypertension: a meta-analytic review, *Annals of Behavioural Medicine*, 12: 30–9.

Fredrickson, B.L., Maynard, K.E., Helms, M.J. et al. (2000) Hostility predicts magnitude and duration of blood pressure response to anger, *Journal of Behavioural Medicine*, 23: 229–43.

Fredrickson, B.L., Robson, A. and Ljungdell, T. (1991) Ambulatory and laboratory blood pressure in individuals with negative and positive family history of hypertension, *Health Psychology*, 10: 371–7.

Freeling, P. (1965) Candidates for exfoliative cytology of the cervix, *Journal of the Royal College of General Practitioners*, 10: 261.

Freeman, E.W. and Rickels, K. (1993) *Early Childbearing: Perspectives of Black Adolescents on Pregnancy, Abortion, and Contraception*. Newbury Park, CA: Sage.

Freeman, R.F., Thomas, C.D., Solyom, L. and Hunter, M.A. (1984) A modified video camera for measuring body image distortion: technical description and reliability, *Psychological Medicine*, 14: 411–16.

Freidson, E. (1970) *Profession of Medicine*. New York: Dodds Mead.

French, D.P. and Hankins, M. (2003) The expectancy-value muddle in the theory of planned behaviour and some proposed solutions, *British Journal of Health Psychology*, 8: 37–55.

French, D.P., Maissi, E. and Marteau, T.M. (2004) Psychological costs of inadequate cervical smear test results, *British Journal of Cancer*, 91: 1887–92.

French, D.P., Maissi, E. and Marteau, T.M. (2005) The purpose of attributing cause: beliefs about the causes of myocardial infarction, *Social Science & Medicine*, 60: 1411–21.

French, D.P., Maissi, E. and Marteau, T.M. (2006) The psychological costs of inadequate cervical smear test results: three-month follow-up, *Psycho-oncology*, 15: 498–508.

French, D.P., Marteau, T., Senior, V. and Weinman, J. (2002) The structure of belief about the causes of heart attacks: a network analysis, *British Journal of Health Psychology*, 7: 463–79.

French, D.P., Marteau, T.M., Senior, V. and Weinman, J. (2005) How valid are measures of beliefs about the causes of illness? The example of myocardial infarction, *Psychology and Health*, 20(5): 615–35.

French, D.P., Senior, V., Weinman, J. and Marteau, T.M. (2001) Causal attributions for heart disease: a systematic review, *Psychology and Health*, 16: 77–98.

French, D.P, Senior, V., Weinman, J. and Marteau, T.M. (2002) Elicit causal beliefs about heart attacks: a comparison of implicit and explicit methods, *Journal of Health Psychology*, 7(4): 433–44.

French, S.A. and Jeffrey, R.W. (1997) Current dieting, weight loss history and weight suppression: behavioural correlates of three dimensions of dieting, *Addictive Behaviours*, 22: 31–44.

Friedman, L.A. and Kimball, A.W. (1986) Coronary heart disease mortality and alcohol consumption in Framingham, *American Journal of Epidemiology*, 124: 481–9.

Friedman, M. and Rosenman, R.H. (1959) Association of specific overt behavior pattern with blood and cardiovascular findings, *Journal of the American Medical Association*, 169: 1286–97.

Friedman, M., Thoresen, C., Gill, J. et al. (1986) Alteration of Type A behavior and its effects on cardiac recurrences in post myocardial infarction patients: summary results of the recurrent coronary prevention project, *American Heart Journal*, 112: 653–65.

Friedman, T. and Gath, D. (1989) The psychiatric consequences of spontaneous abortion, *British Journal of Psychiatry*, 155: 810–13.

Frostholm, L., Fink, P., Christensen, K.S., Toft, T., Oernbel, E., Olesen, F. and Weinman, J. (2005) The patients' illness perceptions and the use of primary health care, *Psychosomatic Medicine*, 7(6): 997–1005.

Furstenberg, F., Shea, J., Allison, P., Herceg-Baron, R. and Webb, D. (1983) Contraceptive continuation among adolescents attending family planning clinics, *Family Planning Perspectives*, 15: 211–17.

Futterman, A.D., Kemeny, M.E., Shapiro, D., Polonsky, W. and Fahey, J.L. (1992) Immunological variability associated with experimentally-induced positive and negative affective states, *Psychological Medicine*, 22: 231–8.

Gallacher, J.E.J., Hopkinson, C.A., Bennett, P., Burr, M.L. and Elwood, P.C. (1997) Effect of stress management on angina, *Psychology and Health*, 12: 523–32.

Garcia, J., Hankins, W.G. and Rusiniak, K. (1974) Behavioral regulation of the milieu intern in man and rat, *Science*, 185: 824–31.

Gardner, R.M., Martinez, R. and Sandoval, Y. (1987) Obesity and body image: an evaluation of sensory and non-sensory components, *Psychological Medicine*, 17: 927–32.

Garn, S.M., Bailey, S.M., Solomon, M.A. and Hopkins, P.J. (1981) Effects of remaining family members on fatness prediction, *American Journal of Clinical Nutrition*, 34: 148–53.

Garner, D.M. (1991) *EDI-2: Professional Manual*. Odessa, FL: Psychological Assessment Resources Inc.

Garrow, J. (1984) *Energy Balance and Obesity in Man*. New York: Elsevier.

Garrow, J. (1997) Treatment of obesity IV: Surgical treatments, in Garrow, J. (1997) *Obesity*. Blackwell: British Nutrition Foundation.

Geis, B.D. and Gerrard, M. (1984) Predicting male and female contraceptive behaviour: a discriminant analysis of groups in high, moderate, and low in contraceptive effectiveness, *Journal of Personality and Social Psychology*, 46: 669–80.

Gellaitry, G., Cooper, V., Davis, C., Fisher, M., Date, H.L. and Horne, R. (2005) Patients' perception of information about HAART: impact on treatment decisions, *AIDS Care*, 7(3): 367–76.

General Household Survey (GHS) (1992) London: OPCS.

General Household Survey (GHS) (1993) London: OPCS.

General Household Survey (GHS) (1994) London: OPCS.

General Household Survey (GHS) (2004) London: OPCS.

George, W.H. and Marlatt, G.A. (1983) Alcoholism: the evolution of a behavioral perspective, in M. Galanter (ed.), *Recent Developments in Alcoholism, 1*, pp. 105–38. New York: Plenum Press.

Gerrard, M., Gibbons, F.X., Benthin, A.C. and Hessling, R.M. (1996) A longitudinal study of the reciprocal nature of risk behaviors and cognitions in adolescents: what you do shapes what you think and vice versa, *Health Psychology*, 15: 344–54.

Giannetti, V.J., Reynolds, J. and Rihen, T. (1985) Factors which differentiate smokers from ex-smokers among cardiovascular patients: a discriminant analysis, *Social Science and Medicine*, 20: 241–5.

Gibbons, F.X., Gerrard, M., Ouelette, J. and Burzette, R. (1998) Cognitive antecedents to adolescent health risk: discriminating between behavioural intention and behavioural willingness, *Psychology and Health*, 13: 319–39.

Gidron, Y., Magen, R. and Ariad, S. (2001) The relation between hopelessness and psychological and serological outcomes in Israeli women with breast-cancer, *Psychology and Health*, 16: 289–96.

Gilbert, D.G. and Spielberger, C.D. (1987) Effects of smoking on heart rate, anxiety, and feelings of success during social interaction, *Journal of Behavioral Medicine*, 10: 629–38.

Gill, J.J., Price, V.A. and Friedman, M. (1985) Reduction of type A behavior in healthy middle-aged American military officers, *American Heart Journal*, 110: 503–14.

Gillies, P.A. and Galt, M. (1990) Teenage smoking – fun or coping? in J.A.M. Wimbust and S. Maes (eds), *Lifestyles and Health: New Developments in Health Psychology*. Netherlands: DSWO/Leiden University Press.

Gillon, R. (2001) Is there a 'new ethics of abortion'? *Journal of Medical Ethics*, 27(suppl. II): ii5–ii9.

Glass, D.C. and Singer, J.E. (1972) *Urban Stress*. New York: Academic Press.

Gleghorn, A.A., Penner, L.A., Powers, P.S. and Schulman, R. (1987) The psychometric properties of several measures of body image, *Journal of Psychopathology and Behavioral Assessment*, 9: 203–18.

Glenn, N.D. and Weaver, C.N. (1981) The contribution of marital happiness to global happiness, *Journal of Marriage and the Family*, 43: 161–8.

Glynn, S.M. and Ruderman, A.J. (1986) The development and validation of an Eating Self-efficacy Scale, *Cognitive Therapy and Research*, 10: 403–20.

Goddard, E. (1990) *Why Children Start Smoking*. London: HMSO.

Godin, G., Conner, M. and Sheeran, P. (2005) Bridging the intention–behaviour 'gap': the role of moral norm, *British Journal of Social Psychology*, 44: 497–512.

Godin, G., Valois, P., Lepage, L. and Desharnais, R. (1992) Predictors of smoking behaviour: an application of Ajzen's theory of planned behaviour, *British Journal of Addiction*, 87: 1335–43.

Gold, R.S., Skinner, M.J., Grant, P.J. and Plummer, D.C. (1991) Situational factors and thought processes associated with unprotected intercourse in gay men, *Psychology and Health*, 5: 259–78.

Goldberg, D.P. (1978) *Manual of the General Health Questionnaire*. Windsor: NFER-Nelson.

Goldberg, I.R. (1999) A broad-bandwidth, public-domain, personality inventory measuring the lower-level facets of several five-factor models, in I. Merveilde, I. Deary, F. De Fryt and F. Ostendorf (eds) *Personality Psychology in Europe: Vol. 7*, pp. 7–28. Tilburg: Tilburg University Press.

Goldschneider, A. (1920) *Das Schmerz Problem*. Berlin: Springer.

Gollwitzer, P.M. (1993) Goal achievement: the role of intentions, *European Review of Social Psychology*, 4: 141–85.

Gollwitzer, P.M. and Brandstatter, V. (1997) Implementation intentions and effective goal pursuit, *Journal of Personality and Social Psychology*, 73: 186–99.

Gollwitzer, P.M. and Sheeran, P. (2006) Implementation intentions and goal achievement: a meta-analysis of effects and processes, *Advances in Experimental Social Psychology*, 38: 69–119.

Gomel, M., Oldenburg, B., Lemon, J., Owen, N. and Westbrook, F. (1993) Pilot study of the effects of a workplace smoking ban on indices of smoking, cigarette craving, stress and other health behaviours, *Psychology and Health*, 8: 223–9.

Gooding, H.C., Organista, K., Burack, J. et al. (2006) Genetic susceptibility testing from a stress and coping perspective. *Social Science and Medicine*, 62: 1880–90.

Goodkin, K., Blaney, T., Feaster, D. et al. (1992) Active coping style is associated with natural killer cell cytotoxicity in asymptomatic HIV-I seropositive homosexual men, *Journal of Psychosomatic Research*, 36: 635–50.

Goodwin, P. and Ogden, J. (2006) Women's reflections about their past abortions: an exploration of how emotional reactions change over time, *Psychology and Health* (in press).

Gould, G.M. (1900) A system of personal biologic examination: the condition of adequate medical and scientific conduct of life, *Journal of the American Medical Association*, 35: 134.

Gracely, R.H., Dubner, R., Deeter, W.R. and Wolskee, P.J. (1985) Clinical expectations influence placebo analgesia, *Lancet*, i: 43.

Graham, H. (1987) Women's smoking and family health, *Social Science and Medicine*, 25: 47–56.

Grant, A. and Elbourne, D. (1989) Fetal movement counting to assess fetal well-being, in I. Chalmers, M. Enkin and M.J.N.C. Keirse (eds), *Effective Care in Pregnancy and Childbirth*, pp. 440–54. Oxford: Oxford University Press.

Grant, M., Padilla, G.V., Ferrell, B.R. and Rhiner, M. (1990) Assessment of quality of life with a single instrument, *Seminars in Oncology Nursing*, 6: 260–70.

Gray, J., Ford, K. and Kelly, L. (1987) The prevalence of bulimia in a black college population, *International Journal of Eating Disorders*, 6: 733–40.

Graybeal, A., Sexton, J.D. and Pennebaker, J.W. (2002) The role of story making in disclosure writing: the psychometrics of narrative, *Psychology and Health*, 17: 571–81.

Green, J.M., Coupland, V.A. and Kitzinger, J.V. (1988) *Great Expectation: A Prospective Study of Women's Expectations and Experiences of Childbirth*. Childcare and Development Group. Cambridge: University of Cambridge.

Greenberg, M.A. and Stone, A.A. (1992) Writing about disclosed versus undisclosed traumas: immediate and long term effects on mood and health, *Journal of Personality and Social Psychology*, 63: 75–84.

Greene, R.E., Houston, B.K. and Holleran, S.A. (1995). Aggressiveness, dominance, developmental factors and serum cholesterol level in college males, *Journal of Behavioural Medicine*, 18, 569–80.

Greeno, C.G. and Wing, R.R. (1994) Stress-induced eating, *Psychological Bulletin*, 115: 444–64.

Greenwood, J. (2001) The new ethics of abortion, *Journal of Medical Ethics*, 27(suppl. II): ii2–ii4.

Greer, S., Moorey, S., Baruch, J.D.R. et al. (1992) Adjuvant psychological therapy for patients with cancer: a prospective randomised trial, *British Medical Journal*, 304: 675–80.

Greer, S., Morris, T.E. and Pettingale, K.W. (1979) Psychological responses to breast cancer: effect on outcome, *Lancet*, 2: 785–7.

Gregg, I. (1966) The recognition of early chronic bronchitis, *Journal of the American Medical Association*, 176: 1114–16.

Grilo, C.M., Shiffman, S. and Wing, R.R. (1989) Relapse crisis and coping among dieters, *Journal of Consulting and Clinical Psychology*, 57: 488–95.

Grimes, D.S. (1988) Value of a negative cervical smear, *British Medical Journal*, 296: 1363.

Gross, J. and Levenson, R.W. (1997) Hiding feelings: the acute effects of inhibiting negative and positive emotion, *Journal of Abnormal Psychology*, 106: 95–103.

Grunberg, N.E. (1986) Nicotine as a psychoactive drug: appetite regulation, *Psychopharmacology Bulletin*, 22: 875–81.

Grunberg, N.E., Winders, S.E. and Wewers, M.E. (1991) Gender differences in tobacco use, *Health Psychology*, 10: 143–53.

Grunfeld, E., Mant, D., Yudkin, P. et al. (1996) Routine follow up of breast cancer in primary care: randomised trial, *British Medical Journal*, 313: 665–9.

Guadagnoli, E. and Ward, P. (1998) Patient participation on decision making, *Social Science and Medicine*, 47: 329–39.

Gudmundsdottir, H., Johnston, M., Johnston, D. and Foulkes, J. (2001) Spontaneous, elicited and cued casual attribution in the year following a first myocardial infarction, *British Journal of Health Psychology*, 6: 81–96.

Gupta, N. and Jenkins, D.G. Jr (1984) Substance use as an employee response to the work environment, *Journal of Vocational Behaviour*, 24: 84–93.

Gureje, O., Simon, G.E., Ustun, T.B. and Goldberg, D.P. (1997) Somatisation in cross-cultural perspective: a World Health Organization study in primary care, *American Journal of Psychiatry*, 154: 989–95.

Guyll, M. and Contrada, R.J. (1998) Trait hostility and ambulatory cardiovascular activity: response to social interaction, *Health Psychology*, 17: 30–9.

Haas, H., Fink, H. and Hartfelder, G. (1959) Das placeboproblem, *Fortschritte der Arzneimittelforschung*, 1: 279–354.

Hackel, L.S. and Ruble, D.N. (1992) Changes in the marital relationship after the first baby is born: predicting the impact of expectancy disconfirmation, *Journal of Personality and Social Psychology*, 62: 944–57.

Hadley, J. (1996) *Abortion: Between Freedom and Necessity*. London: Virago.

Hagger, M.S. and Orbell, S. (2003) A meta-analytic review of the common-sense model of illness representations, *Psychology and Health*, 18(2): 141–84.

Hagger, M.S., Chatzisarantiz, N., Biddle, S.J.H. and Orbell, S. (2001) Antecedents of children's physical activity intentions and behaviour: predictive validity and longitudinal effects, *Psychology and Health*, 16: 391–407.

Hall, A. and Brown, L.B. (1982) A comparison of the attitudes of young anorexia nervosa patients and non patients with those of their mothers, *British Journal of Psychology*, 56: 39–48.

Hall, E.E., Ekkekakis, P. and Petruzzello, S.J. (2002) The affective beneficence of vigorous exercise, *British Journal of Health Psychology*, 7: 47–66.

Hall, J.A., Epstein, A.M. and McNeil, B.J. (1989) Multidimensionality of health status in an elderly population: construct validity of a measurement battery, *Medical Care*, 27: 168–77.

Hall, S., Weinman, J. and Marteau, T.M. (2004) The motivating impact of informing women smokers of a link between smoking and cervical cancer: the role of coherence, *Health Psychology*, 23(4): 419–24.

Hall, S.M., Hall, R.G. and Ginsberg, D. (1990) Cigarette dependence, in A.S. Bellack, M. Hersen and

A.E. Kazdin (eds), *International Handbook of Behavior Modification and Therapy*, 2nd edn, pp. 437–47. New York: Plenum Press.

Halm, E.A., Mora, P. and Leventhal, H. (2006) No symptoms, no asthma: the acute episodic disease belief is associated with poor self-management among inner-city adults with persistent asthma, *Chest*, 129: 573–80.

Halmi, K.A., Stunkard, A.J. and Mason, E.E. (1980) Emotional responses to weight reduction by three methods: diet, jejunoileal bypass, and gastric, *American Journal of Clinical Nutrition*, 33: 446–51.

Hamilton, K. and Waller, G. (1993) Media influences on body size estimation in anorexia and bulimia: an experimental study, *British Journal of Psychiatry*, 162: 837–40.

Hamilton, S. and Fagot, B.I. (1988) Chronic stress and coping style: a comparison of male and female undergraduates, *Journal of Personality and Social Psychology*, 55(5): 819–23.

Hamm, P.B., Shekelle, R.B. and Stamler, J. (1989) Large fluctuations in body weight during young adulthood and twenty five year risk of coronary death in men, *American Journal of Epidemiology*, 129: 312–18.

Han, T.S., Richmond, P., Avenell, A. and Lean, M.E.J. (1997) Waist circumference reduction and cardiovascular benefits during weight loss in women, *International Journal of Obesity*, 21: 127–34.

Hankins, M., French, D. and Horne, R. (2000) Statistical guidelines for studies of theory of reasoned action and the theory of planned behaviour, *Psychology and Health*, 15: 151–61.

Hannah, M.C., Happer, J.L. and Mathews, J.D. (1985) Twin concordance for a binary trait. Nested analysis of never smoking and ex smoking traits and unnested analysis of a committed smoking trait, *American Journal of Human Genetics*, 37: 153–65.

Harbin, T.J. (1989) The relationship between Type A behaviour and physiological responsivity: a quantitative view, *Psychophysiology*, 26: 110–19.

Hardeman, W., Johnston, M., Johnston, D.W. et al. (2002) Application of the theory of planned behaviour in behaviour change interventions: a systematic review, *Psychology and Health*, 17(2): 123–58.

Hardeman, W., Sutton, S., Griffin, S., Johnston, M., White, A., Wareham, N.J. and Kinmonth, A.L. (2005) A causal modeling approach to the development of theory-based behavior change programmes for trial evaluation, *Health Education Research Theory and Practice*, 20(6): 676–87.

Harden, A. and Ogden, J. (1999a) Young women's experiences of arranging and having abortions, *Sociology of Health and Illness*, 21: 426–44.

Harden, A., and Ogden, J. (1999b) 16–19 year olds' beliefs about contraceptive services and the intentions to use contraception, *British Journal of Family Planning*, 24: 135–41.

Harnish, J.D., Aseltine, R.H. and Gore, S. (2000) Resolution of stressful experiences as an indicator of coping effectiveness in young adults: an event history analysis, *Journal of Health and Social Behaviour*, 41: 121–36.

Harris, A.A. (2004) Supportive counselling before and after elective pregnancy termination, *Journal of Midwifery and Women's Health*, 49: 105–12.

Harris, P.R. and Napper, L. (2005) Self-affirmation and the biased processing of threatening health risk information, *Personality and Social Psychology Bulletin*, 31(9): 1250–63.

Harris, P.R. and Smith, V. (2005) When the risks are low: the impact of absolute and comparative information on disturbance and understanding in US and UK samples, *Psychology and Health*, 20(3): 319–30.

Harris, P.R., Mayle, K., Mabbott, L. and Napper, L. (2006) Self-affirmation and graphic warning labels, *Health Psychology* (in press).

Hart, J.T. (1971) The inverse care law, *Lancet*, i: 405–12.

Hart, J.T. (1987) *Hypertension*, 2nd edn. Edinburgh: Churchill Livingstone.

Hatherall, B., Ingham, R., Stone, N. and McEachran, J. (2006) How, not just if, condoms are used:

the timing of condom application and removal during vaginal sex among young people in England, *Sexually Transmitted Infections* (in press).

Haus, G., Hoerr, S.L., Mavis, B. and Robison, J. (1994) Key modifiable factors in weight maintenance: fat intake, exercise and weight cycling, *Journal of the American Dietetic Association*, 94: 409–13.

Hausenblas, H.A., Nigg, C.R., Dannecker, E.A. et al. (2001) A missing piece of transtheoretical model applied to exercise: development and validation of the temptation to not exercise scale, *Psychology and Health*, 16: 381–90.

Havelock, C., Edwards, R., Cuzlick, J. and Chamberlain, J. (1988) The organisation of cervical screening in general practice, *Journal of the Royal College of General Practitioners*, 38: 207–11.

Haynes, R.B. (1982) Improving patient compliance: an empirical review, in R.B. Stuart (ed.), *Adherence, Compliance and Generalisation in Behavioral Medicine*. New York: Brunner/Mazel.

Haynes, R.B., Sackett, D.L. and Taylor, D.W. (1978) Increased absenteeism from work after detection and labeling of hypertension patients, *New England Journal of Medicine*, 299: 741.

Haynes, R.B., Sackett, D.L. and Taylor, D.W. (eds) (1979) *Compliance in Health Care*. Baltimore, MD: Johns Hopkins University Press.

Haynes, S.G., Feinleib, M. and Kannel, W.B. (1980) The relationship of psychosocial factors to coronary heart disease in the Framingham study. III: eight year incidence of coronary heart disease, *American Journal of Epidemiology*, 111: 37–58.

Hays, R.D. and Stewart, A.L. (1990) The structure of self-reported health in chronic disease patients, *Psychological Assessment*, 2: 22–30.

He, Y., Lam, T.H., Li, L.S. et al. (1994) Passive smoking at work as a risk factor for coronary heart disease in Chinese women who have never smoked, *British Medical Journal*, 308: 380–4.

Healy, J. (1991) *The Grass Arena*. London: Faber & Faber.

Heatherton, T.F. and Baumeister, R.F. (1991) Binge eating as an escape from self-awareness, *Psychological Bulletin*, 110: 86–108.

Heatherton, T.F., Herman, C.P., Polivy, J.A., King, G.A. and McGree, S.T. (1988) The (mis)measurement of restraint: an analysis of conceptual and psychometric issues, *Journal of Abnormal Psychology*, 97: 19–28.

Heatherton, T.F., Polivy, J. and Herman, C.P. (1991) Restraint, weight loss and variability of body weight, *Journal of Abnormal Psychology*, 100: 78–83.

Heatherton, T.F., Polivy, J., Herman, C.P. and Baumeister, R.F. (1993) Self-awareness, task failure, and disinhibition: how attentional focus affects eating, *Journal of Personality and Social Psychology*, 61(1): 49–61.

Heider, F. (1944) Social perception and phenomenal causality, *Psychological Review*, 51: 358–74.

Heider, F. (1958) *The Psychology of Interpersonal Relations*. New York: John Wiley.

Heijmans, M., Foets, M. and Rijken, M. (2001) Stress in chronic disease: do the perceptions of patients and their general practitioners match? *British Journal of Health Psychology*, 6: 229–42.

Helman, C. (1978) Feed a cold, starve a fever: folk models of infection in an English suburban community and their relation to medical treatment, *Culture Medicine and Psychiatry*, 2: 107–37.

Henbest, R.J. and Stewart, M. (1990) Patient centredness in consultation. Part 2. Does it really make a difference? *Family Practice*, 7: 28–33.

Herbert, T.B. and Cohen, S. (1993) Stress and immunity in humans: a meta-analytic review. *Psychosomatic Medicine*, 55(4): 364–79.

Herlitz, A., Nilsson, L.-G. and Backman, L. (1997) Gender differences in episodic memory, *Memory and Cognition*, 25: 801–11.

Herman, P. and Mack, D. (1975) Restrained and unrestrained eating, *Journal of Personality*, 43: 646–60.

Herman, C.P. and Polivy, J. (1980). Restrained eating, in A.J. Stunkard (ed.), *Obesity*, pp. 208–25. Philadelphia, PA: WB Saunders.

Herman, C.P. and Polivy, J.A. (1984) A boundary model for the regulation of eating, in A.J. Stunkard and E. Stellar (eds), *Eating and Its Disorders*, pp. 141–56. New York: Raven Press.

Herman C.P. and Polivy, J.A. (1988) Restraint and excess in dieters and bulimics, in K.M. Pirke, W. Vandereycken and D. Ploog (eds), *The Psychobiology of Bulimia Nervosa*. Berlin: Springer Verlag.

Herman, C.P., Polivy, J.A. and Esses, V.M. (1987) The illusion of counterregulation, *Appetite*, 9: 161–9.

Herold, D.M. and Conlon, E.J. (1981) Work factors as potential causal agents of alcohol abuse, *Journal of Drug Issues*, 11: 337–56.

Herold, E.S. (1981) Contraceptive embarrassment and contraceptive behaviour among young single women, *Journal of Youth and Adolescence*, 10: 233–42.

Herold, E.S. and McNamee, J.E. (1982) An explanatory model of contraceptive use among young women, *Journal of Sex Research*, 18: 289–304.

Herold, E.S. and Samson, M. (1980) Differences between women who begin pill use before and after first intercourse: Ontario, Canada, *Family Planning Perspectives*, 12: 304–5.

Herz, E. (1984) Psychological repercussions of pregnancy loss, *Psychiatric Annals*, 14: 454–7.

Herzlich, C. (1973) *Health and Illness*. London: Academic Press.

Heslop, P., Smith, G.D., Carroll, D. et al. (2001) Perceived stress and coronary heart disease risk factors: the contribution of socio-economic position, *British Journal of Health Psychology*, 6: 167–78.

Hewson-Bower, B. and Drummond, P.D. (2001) Psychological treatment for recurrent symptoms of colds and flu in children, *Journal of Psychosomatic Research*, 51(1): 369–77.

Hill, A.J. and Bhatti, R. (1995) Body shape perception and dieting in preadolescent British Asian girls: links with eating disorders, *International Journal of Eating Disorders*, 17: 175–83.

Hill, A.J., Weaver, C. and Blundell, J.E. (1990) Dieting concerns of 10 year old girls and their mothers, *British Journal of Clinical Psychology*, 29: 346–8.

Hill, D., Gardner, G. and Rassaby, J. (1985) Factors predisposing women to take precautions against breast and cervix cancer, *Journal of Applied Social Psychology*, 15(1): 59–79.

Hingson, R.W., Strunin, L., Berlin, M. and Heeren, T. (1990) Beliefs about AIDS, use of alcohol and drugs and unprotected sex among Massachusetts adolescents, *American Journal of Public Health*, 80: 295–9.

Hinton, C. (1992) Breast cancer, in C.R. Hart and P. Burke (eds), *Screening and Surveillance in General Practice*. London: Churchill Livingstone.

Hite, S. (1976) *The Hite Report*. New York: Macmillan.

Hite, S. (1981) *The Hite Report on Male Sexuality*. New York: A.A. Knopf.

Hite, S. (1987) *The Hite Report on Women and Love*. London: Penguin.

Hodgkins, S. and Orbell, S. (1998) Can protection motivation theory predict behaviour? A longitudinal study exploring the role of previous behaviour, *Psychology and Health*, 13: 237–50.

Hoiberg, A., Berard, S., Watten, R.H. and Caine, C. (1994) Correlates of weight loss in treatment and at follow up, *International Journal of Obesity*, 8: 457–65.

Holahan, C.J. and Moos, R.H. (1986) Personality, coping, and family resources in stress resistance: a longitudinal analysis, *Journal of Personality and Social Psychology*, 51(2): 389–95.

Holahan, C.J. and Moos, R.H. (1990) Life stressors, resistance factors and improved psychological functioning: an extension of the stress resistance paradigm, *Journal of Personality and Social Psychology*, 58: 909–17.

Holahan, C.J., Moos, R.H. and Schaefer, J.A. (1996) Coping, stress resistance and growth: conceptualising adaptive functioning, in M. Zeidner and N.S. Endler (eds), *Handbook of Coping*, pp. 24–43. New York: Wiley.

Holland, J., Ramazanoglu, C. and Scott, S. (1990a) Managing risk and experiencing danger: tensions between government AIDS health education policy and young women's sexuality, *Gender and Education*, 2: 125–46.

Holland, J., Ramazanoglu, C., Scott, S., Sharpe, S. and Thompson, R. (1990b) Sex, gender and power: young women's sexuality in the shadow of AIDS, *Sociology of Health and Illness*, 12: 336–50.

Holland, K.D. and Holahan, C.K. (2003) The relation of social support and coping to positive adaptation to breast cancer, *Psychology and Health*, 18(1): 15–29.

Holleb, A.I., Venet, L., Day, E. and Hayt, S. (1960) Breast cancer detection by routine physical examinations, *New York Journal of Medicine*, 60: 823–7.

Holmes, T.H. and Rahe, R.H. (1967) The social readjustment rating scale, *Journal of Psychosomatic Research*, 11: 213–18.

Hooykaas, C., van der Linden, M.M.D., van Doornum, G.J.J. et al. (1991) Limited changes in sexual behaviour of heterosexual men and women with multiple partners in the Netherlands, *AIDS Care*, 3: 21–30.

Hope, S., Wager, E. and Rees, M. (1998) Survey of British women's views on the menopause and HRT, *Journal of the British Menopause Society*, 4(1): 33–6.

Hopkinson, G. and Bland, R.C. (1982) Depressive syndromes in grossly obese women, *Canadian Journal of Psychiatry*, 27: 213–15.

Hoppe, R. and Ogden, J. (1996) The effect of selectively reviewing behavioural risk factors on HIV risk perception, *Psychology and Health*, 11: 757–64.

Hoppe, R. and Ogden, J. (1997) Practice nurses' beliefs about obesity and weight related interventions in primary care, *International Journal of Obesity*, 21: 141–6.

Horne, R. (1997) Representations of medication and treatment: advances in theory and measurement, in K.J. Petrie and J. Weinman (eds), *Perceptions of Health and Illness: Current Research and Applications*. London: Harwood Academic Press.

Horne, R. and Weinman, J. (1999) Patients' beliefs about prescribed medicines and their role in adherence to treatment in chronic physical illness, *Journal of Psychosomatic Research*, 47(6): 555–67.

Horne, R. and Weinman, J. (2002) Self-regulation and self-management in asthma: exploring the role of illness perceptions and treatment beliefs in explaining non-adherence to preventer medication, *Psychology and Health*, 17(1): 17–32.

Horne, R., Buick, D., Fisher, M., Leake, H., Cooper, V. and Weinman, J. (2004a) Doubts about necessity and concerns about adverse effects: identifying the types of beliefs that are associated with non-adherence to HAART, *International Journal of STD & AIDS*, 15(1): 38–44.

Horne, R., Graupner, L., Frost, S., Weinman, J., Wright, S.M. and Hankins, M. (2004b) Medicine in a multi-cultural society: the effect of cultural background on beliefs about medications, *Social Science and Medicine*, 59: 1307–13.

Horne, R., Weinman, J. and Hankins, M. (1999) The beliefs about medicines questionnaire: the development and evaluation of a new method for assessing the cognitive representation of medication, *Psychology and Health*, 14: 1–24.

Hornick, J.P., Doran, L. and Crawford, S.H. (1979) Premarital contraceptive usage among male and female adolescents, *Family Coordinator*, 28: 181–90.

Horwitz, R.I. and Horwitz, S.M. (1993) Adherence to treatment and health outcome, *Archives of International Medicine*, 153: 1863–8.

Horwitz, R.I., Viscoli, C.M., Berkman, L. et al. (1990) Treatment adherence and risk of death after a myocardial infarction, *Lancet*, 336(8714): 542–5.

Houston, B.H. and Vavak, C.R. (1991) Cynical hostility: developmental factors, psychosocial correlates and health behaviours, *Health Psychology*, 10: 9–17.

Houston, B.K. (1994) Anger, hostility and psychophysiological reactivity, in A.W. Siegman and T.W. Smith (eds), *Anger, Hostility and the Heart*, pp. 97–115. Hillsdale, NJ: Erlbaum.

Howie, F.L., Henshaw, R.C., Naji, S.A., Russell, I.T. and Templeton, A.A. (1997) Medical abortion or vacuum aspiration? Two year follow up of a patient preference trial, *British Journal of Obstetrics and Gynaecology*, 104(7): 829–33.

Hughson, A., Cooper, A., McArdle, C. and Smith, D. (1986) Psychological impact of adjuvant chemotherapy in the first two years after mastectomy, *British Medical Journal*, 293: 1268–72.

Hughson, A., Cooper, A., McArdle, C. and Smith, D. (1987) Psychosocial effects of radiotherapy after mastectomy, *British Medical Journal*, 294: 1515–16.

Hunt, S.M., McEwen, J. and McKenna, S.P. (1986) *Measuring Health Status*. Beckenham: Croom Helm.

Hursti, U.K.K. and Sjoden, P.O. (1997) Food and general neophobia and their relationship with self-reported food choice: familial resemblance in Swedish families with children of ages 7–17 years, *Appetite*, 29: 89–103.

Hutti, M.H. (1986) An exploratory study of the miscarriage experience, *Health Care for Women International*, 7: 371–89.

Idler, E.L. and Kasl, S.V. (1995) Self-ratings of health: do they predict change in function as ability? *Journal of Gerontology Series B – Psychological Sciences and Social Sciences*, 50B: S344–S53.

Illich, I. (1974) *Medical Nemesis*. London: Caldar Boyars.

Ingham, R. (2005) 'We didn't cover that at school': education *against* pleasure or education *for* pleasure? *Sex Education*, 5(4): 375–88.

Ingham, R., Woodcock, A. and Stenner, K. (1991) Getting to know you . . . young people's knowledge of their partners at first intercourse, *Journal of Community and Applied Social Psychology*, 1: 117–32.

Ingledew, D.K. and Ferguson, E. (2006) Personality and riskier sexual behaviour: motivational mediators, *Psychology & Health* (in press).

Ingledew, D.K., Markland, D. and Medley, A.R. (1998) Exercise motives and stages of change, *Journal of Health Psychology*, 3(4): 477–89.

Institute of Medicine (1995) Committee to develop criteria for evaluating the outcomes of approaches to prevent and treat obesity. In *Weighing the Options: Criteria for Evaluating Weight-management Programs*. Available: www.iom.edu.

Isen, A.M., Rosenzweig, A.S. and Young, M.J. (1991) The influence of positive affect on clinical problem solving, *Medical Decision Making*, 11: 221–7.

Jacobs, T.J. and Charles, E. (1980) Life events and the occurrence of cancer in children, *Psychosomatic Medicine*, 42: 11–24.

James, J.E. and Hardardottir, D. (2002) Influence of attention focus and trait anxiety on tolerance of acute pain, *British Journal of Health Psychology*, 7: 149–62.

James, W.P.T., Avenell, A., Broom, J. and Whitehead, J. (1997) A one year trial to assess the value of orlistat in the management of obesity, *International Journal of Obesity*, 21(Supp. 3): S24–S30.

Jamner, L.D. and Tursky, B. (1987) Syndrome-specific descriptor profiling: a psychophysiological and psychophysical approach, *Health Psychology*, 6: 417–30.

Janis, I. (1958) *Psychological Stress*. New York: Wiley.

Janis, I. and Mann, L. (1977) *Decision Making: A Psychological Analysis of Conflict, Choice, and Commitment*. New York: Free Press.

Janz, N.K. and Becker, M.H. (1984) The health belief model: a decade later, *Health Education Quarterly*, 11: 1–47.

Jeffery, R.W., Drewnowski, A., Epstein, L.H., Stunkard, A.J. and Wilson, G.T. (2000) Long-term maintenance of weight loss: current status, *Health Psychology*, 19: 5–16.

Jellinek, E.M. (1960) *The Disease Concept in Alcoholism*. New Brunswick, NJ: Hill House Press.

Jenkins, C.D., Zyzanski, S.J. and Rosenman, R.H. (1979) *The Jenkins Activity Survey for Health Prediction*. New York: The Psychological Corporation.

Jensen, M.P. and Karoly, P. (1991) Motivation and expectancy factors in symptom perception: a laboratory study of the placebo effect, *Psychosomatic Medicine*, 53: 144–52.

Jirojanakul, P. and Skevington, S. (2000) Developing a quality of life measure for children aged 5–8 years, *British Journal of Health Psychology*, 5: 299–321.

Johnson, J.E. and Leventhal, H. (1974) Effects of accurate expectations and behavioural instructions on reactions during a noxious medical examination, *Journal of Personality and Social Psychology*, 29: 710–18.

Johnson, J.H. (1986) *Life Events as Stressors in Childhood and Adolescence*. Newbury Park, CA: Sage.

Johnston, D.W. (1989) Will stress management prevent coronary heart disease? *The Psychologist: Bulletin of British Psychological Society*, 7: 275–8.

Johnston, D.W. (1992) The management of stress in the prevention of coronary heart disease, in S. Maes, H. Leventhal and M. Johnston (eds), *International Review of Health Psychology*. Chichester: Wiley.

Johnston, D.W. (2002) Acute and chronic psychological processes in cardiovascular disease, in K.W. Schaie, H. Leventhal and S.L. Willis (eds), *Effective Health Behaviour in Older Adults*, pp. 55–64. New York: Springer.

Johnston, K.L. and White, K.M. (2003) Binge-drinking: a test of the role of group norms in the theory of planned behaviour, *Psychology and Health*, 18(1): 63–77.

Johnston, D.W., Anastasiades, P. and Wood, C. (1990) The relationship between cardiovascular responses in a laboratory and in the field, *Psychophysiology*, 4: 331–9.

Johnston, D.W., Beedie, A. and Jones, M.C. (2006) Using computerized ambulatory diaries for the assessment of job characteristics and work-related stress in nurses, *Work & Stress*, 20(2): 163–72.

Johnston, D.W., Cook, D.G. and Shaper, A.G. (1987) Type A behaviour and ischaemic heart disease in middle aged British men, *British Medical Journal*, 295: 86–9.

Johnston, D.W., Gold, A., Kentish, J. et al. (1993) Effect of stress management on blood pressure in mild primary hypertension, *British Medical Journal*, 306: 963–6.

Johnston, D.W., Schmidt, T.F.H., Albus, C. et al. (1994) The relationship between cardiovascular reactivity in the laboratory and heart rate response in real life: active coping and beta blockade, *Psychosomatic Medicine*, 56: 369–76.

Johnston, M. (1980) Anxiety in surgical patients, *Psychological Medicine*, 10: 145–52.

Johnston, M. and Kennedy, P. (1998) Editorial: Special issue on clinical health psychology in chronic conditions, *Clinical Psychology and Psychotherapy*, 5: 59–61.

Johnston, M. and Pollard, B. (2001) Consequences of disease: testing the WHO International Classi-Johnston, M., Bonetti, D., Joice, S., Pollard, B., Morrison, V., Francis, J.J. and Macwalter, R. (2006) Recovery from disability after stroke as a target behavioural intervention: results of a randomized controlled trial, *Disability & Rehabilitation* (in press).

Johnston, M., Earll, L., Giles, M. et al. (1999) Mood as a predictor of disability and survival in patients newly diagnosed with ALS/MND, *British Journal of Health Psychology*, 4: 127–36.

Johnston, M., Foulkes, J., Johnston, D.W., Pollard, B. and Gudmundsdottir, H. (1999) Impact on patient and partners of impatient and extended cardiac counselling and rehabilitation: a controlled trial, *Psychosomatic Medicine*, 61: 225–33.

Johnston, M., Morrison, V., MacWalter, R. and Partridge, C. (1999) Perceived control, coping and recovery from stroke, *Psychology and Health*, 14: 181–92.

Johnston, M. and Pollard, B. (2001) Consequences of disease: testing the WHO International Classification of Impairments, Disabilities and Handicaps (ICIDH) model, *Social Science and Medicine*, 53: 1261–73.

Johnston, M., Pollard, B., Morrison, V and Macwalter, R. (2004) Functional limitations of survival following stroke: psychological and clinical predictors of 3-year outcome, *International Journal of Behavioral Medicine*, 11(4): 187–96.

Johnston, M. and Vogele, C. (1993) Benefits of psychological preparation for surgery: a meta analysis, *Annals of Behavioural Medicine*, 15: 245–56.

Jonas, K., Stroebe, W. and Eagly, A. (1993) Adherence to an exercise program. Unpublished manuscript, University of Tübingen.

Jones, F., Harris, P. and Waller, H. (1998) Expectations of an exercise prescription scheme: an exploratory study using repertory grids, *British Journal of Health Psychology*, 3: 277–89.

Jones, M.C. and Johnston, D.W. (2000) Evaluating the impact of a worksite stress management programme for distressed student nurses: a randomised controlled trial, *Psychology and Health*, 15: 689–706.

Jones, R. (1992) Gastrointestinal disorders, in C.R. Hart and P. Burke (eds), *Screening and Surveillance in General Practice*, pp. 283–90. London: Churchill Livingstone.

Joseph, J.G., Montgomery, S.B., Emmons, C.A. et al. (1987) Magnitude and determinants of behaviour risk reduction: longitudinal analysis of a cohort at risk for AIDS, *Psychological Health*, 1: 73–96.

Kalat, J.W. and Rozin, P. (1973) 'Learned safety' as a mechanism in long-delay taste-aversion learning in rats, *Journal of Comparative and Physiological Psychology*, 83(2): 198–207.

Kalucy, R.S., Crisp, A.H. and Harding, B. (1977) A study of 56 families with anorexia nervosa, *British Journal of Medical Psychology*, 50: 381–95.

Kaluza, G. (2000) Changing unbalanced coping profiles: a prospective controlled intervention trial in worksite health promotion, *Psychology and Health*, 15: 423–33.

Kamen, L.P. and Seligman, M.E.P. (1987) Explanatory style and health, *Current Psychological Research and Reviews*, 6: 207–18.

Kanner, A.D., Coyne, J.C., Schaeffer, C. and Lazarus, R.S. (1981) Comparison of two modes of stress measurement: daily hassles and uplifts versus major life events, *Journal of Behavioural Medicine*, 4: 1–39.

Kaplan, J.R., Manuck, S.B., Clarkson, T.B. et al. (1983) Social stress and atherosclerosis in normocholesterolemic monkeys, *Science*, 220: 733–5.

Kaprio, J., Koskenvuo, M. and Rita, H. (1987) Mortality after bereavement: a prospective study of 95,647 widowed persons, *American Journal of Public Health*, 77: 283–7.

Karasek, R. and Theorell, T. (1990) *Healthy Work: Stress, Productivity and the Reconstruction of Working Life*. New York: Basic Books.

Karasek, R.A., Baker, D., Marxer, F., Ahlbom, A. and Theorell, T. (1981) Job decision latitude, job demands and cardiovascular disease: A prospective study of Swedish men, *American Journal of Public Health*, 71: 694–705.

Karasek, R.A., Theorell, T., Schwartz, J. et al. (1988) Job characteristics in relation to the prevalence of myocardial infarction in the U.S. HES and HANES, *American Journal of Public Health*, 78: 910–18.

Karlsson, J., Sjostrom, L. and Sullivan, M. (1998) Swedish Obesity Study (SOS) – an intervention study of obesity: two year follow up of health related quality of life (HRQL) and eating behaviour after gastric surgery for severe obesity, *International Journal of Obesity*, 22: 113–26.

Kasl, S.V. and Cobb, S. (1966) Health behaviour, illness behaviour, and sick role behaviour: II. Sick role behaviour, *Archives of Environmental Health*, 12: 531–41.

Katz, M.H. (1997) AIDS epidemic in San Francisco among men who report sex with men: successes and challenges of HIV prevention, *Journal of Acquired Immune Deficiency Syndrome and Human Retrovirology*, 14: S38–S46.

Katz, S., Downs, T.D., Cash, H.R. and Grotz, R.C. (1970) Progress in development of the index of ADL, *Gerontology*, 10: 20–30.

Keefe, F.J., Lefebvre, J.C., Egert, J.R. et al. (2000) The relationship of gender to pain, pain behaviour and disability in osteoarthritis patients: the role of catastrophizing, *Pain*, 87: 325–34.

Kelleher, D., Gabe, J. and Williams, G. (eds) (1994) *Challenging Medicine*. London: Routledge.

Kelley, H.H. (1967) Attribution theory in social psychology, in D. Levine (ed.), *Nebraska Symposium on Motivation*, pp. 192–238. Lincoln, NE: University of Nebraska Press.

Kelley, H.H. (1971) *Attribution: Perceiving the Causes of Behaviour*. New York: General Learning Press.

Kero, A., Högberg, U. and Lalos, A. (2004) Wellbeing and mental growth: long-term effects of legal abortion, *Social Science and Medicine*, 58: 2559–69.

Kerr, J., Eves, F.F. and Carroll, D. (2001) The influence of poster prompts on stair use: the effects of setting, poster size and content, *British Journal of Health Psychology*, 6: 397–405.

Keys, A., Brozek, J., Henscel, A., Mickelson, O. and Taylor, H.L. (1950) *The Biology of Human Starvation*. Minneapolis, MN: University of Minnesota Press.

Keys, A., Taylor, H.L., Blackburn, H. et al. (1971) Mortality and coronary heart disease among men studied for 23 years. *Archives of Internal Medicine*, 128: 201–14.

Kiebert, G., de Haes, J. and van der Velde, C. (1991) The impact of breast conserving treatment and mastectomy on the quality of life of early stage breast cancer patients: a review, *Journal of Clinical Oncology*, 9: 1059–70.

Kiecolt-Glaser, J.K., Bane, C., Glaser, R. and Malarkey, W.B. (2003) Love, marriage, and divorce: newlyweds' stress hormones foreshadow relationship changes, *Journal of Consulting and Clinical Psychology*, 71: 176–88.

Kiecolt-Glaser, J.K. and Glaser, R. (1986) Psychological influences on immunity, *Psychosomatics*, 27: 621–4.

Kiecolt-Glaser, J.K., Fisher, L.D., Ogrocki, P. et al. (1987) Marital quality, marital disruption and immune function, *Psychosomatic Medicine*, 49(1): 13–34.

Kiecolt-Glaser, J.K., Marucha, P.T., Malarkey, W.B., Mercado, A.M. and Glaser, R. (1995) Slowing wound healing by psychosocial stress, *Lancet*, 4: 1194–6.

Kiernan, M., King, A.C., Kraemer, H.C., Stefanick, M.L. and Killen, I.D. (1998) Characteristics of successful and unsuccessful dieters: an application of signal detection methodology, *Annals of Behavioral Medicine*, 20: 1–6.

Killen, J.D., Fortmenn, S.P., Newman, B. and Vardy, A. (1990) Evaluation of a treatment approach combining nicotine gum with self-guided behavioral treatments for smoking relapse prevention, *Journal of Consulting and Clinical Psychology*, 58: 85–92.

Killen, J.D., Maccoby, N. and Taylor, C.B. (1984) Nicotine gum and self-regulation training in smoking relapse prevention, *Behaviour Therapy*, 15: 234–8.

King, A.C., Blair, S.N., Bild, D.E. et al. (1992) Determinants of physical activity and interventions in adults, *Medicine and Science in Sports and Exercise*, 24: S221–S37.

King, A.C., Haskell, W.L., Taylor, C.B., Kraemer, H.C. and DeBusk, R.F. (1991) Group- *vs* home-based exercise training in healthy older men and women: a community-based clinical trial, *Journal of the American Medical Association*, 266: 1535–42.

King, G.A., Herman, C.P. and Polivy, J. (1987) Food perception in dieters and non-dieters, *Appetite*, 8: 147–58.

King, J.B. (1982) The impact of patients' perceptions of high blood pressure on attendance at screening: an attributional extension of the health belief model, *Social Science and Medicine*, 16: 1079–92.

Kinlay, S. (1988) High cholesterol levels: is screening the best option? *Medical Journal of Australia*, 148: 635–7.

Kinsey, A., Pomeroy, W. and Martin, C. (1948) *Sexual Behaviour in the Human Male*. London: Saunders.

Kirkley, B.G., Burge, J.C. and Ammerman, M.P.H. (1988) Dietary restraint, binge eating and dietary behaviour patterns, *International Journal of Eating Disorders*, 7: 771–8.

Kissen, D.M. (1966) The significance of personality in lung cancer in men, *Annals of the New York Academy of Sciences*, 125: 820–6.

Kivimaki, M., Leino-Arjas, P., Luukkonem, R. et al. (2002) Work stress and risk of cardiovascular mortality: prospective cohort study of industrial employees, *British Medical Journal*, 325: 857–60.

Klassen, A., Fitzpatrick, R., Jenkinson, C. and Goodacre, T. (1996) Should breast reduction surgery be rationed? A comparison of the health status of patients before and after treatment: postal questionnaire survey, *British Medical Journal*, 313: 454–7.

Klem, M.L., Wing, R.R., McGuire, M.T., Seagle, H.M. and Hill, J.O. (1997) A descriptive study of individuals successful at long term maintenance of substantial weight loss, *American Journal of Clinical Nutrition*, 66: 239–46.

Klesges, R.C. and Klesges, L. (1988) Cigarette smoking as a dieting strategy in a university population, *International Journal of Eating Disorders*, 7: 413–19.

Klesges, R.C., Stein, R.J., Eck, L.H., Isbell, T.R. and Klesges, L.M. (1991) Parental influences on food selection in young children and its relationships to childhood obesity, *American Journal of Clinical Nutrition*, 53: 859–64.

Klier, C.M., Geller, P.A. and Neugebauer, R. (2000) Minor depressive disorder in the context of miscarriage, *Journal of Affective Disorders*, 59: 13–21.

Kneebone, I.I. and Martin, P.R. (2003) Coping and caregivers of people with dementia, *British Journal of Health Psychology*, 8: 1–17.

Kobasa, S.C., Maddi, S.R. and Puccetti, M.C. (1982) Personality and exercise as buffers in the stress–illness relationship, *Journal of Behavioral Medicine*, 5: 391–404.

Kohlmann, C.W., Ring, C., Carroll, D., Mohiyeddini, C. and Bennet, P. (2001) Cardiac coping style, heartbeat detection, and the interpretation of cardiac events, *British Journal of Health Psychology*, 6: 285–301.

Kopelman, P. (1999) Treatment of obesity V: Pharmacotherapy for obesity, in *Obesity: The Report of the British Nutrition Foundation Task Force*. Oxford: Blackwell Science.

Kral, J.G. (1983) Surgical therapy: contemporary issues in clinical nutrition, *Obesity*, 4: 25–38.

Kral, J.G. (1995) Surgical interventions for obesity, in K.D. Brownell and C.G. Fairburn (eds), *Eating Disorders and Obesity*, pp. 510–15. New York: Guilford Press.

Krantz, D.S., Glass, D.C., Contrada, R. and Miller, N.E. (1981) *Behavior and Health: National Science Foundation's Second Five Year Outlook on Science and Technology*. Washington, DC: US Government Printing Office.

Kristiansen, C.M. (1985) Value correlates of preventive health behaviour, *Journal of Personality and Social Psychology*, 49: 748–58.

Kuczmarski, R.J. (1992) Prevalence of overweight and weight gain in the United States, *American Journal of Clinical Nutrition*, 55: 495–502.

Kuh, D.J., Hardy, R. and Wadsworth, M.E.J. (2000) Social and behavioural influences on the uptake of hormone replacement therapy among younger women, *BJOG: An International Journal of Obstetrics and Gynaecology*, 107(6): 731–9.

Kuh, D.J., Wadsworth, M.E.J. and Hardy, R. (1997) Women's health in midlife: the influence of the menopause, social factors and health in earlier life, *British Journal of Obstetrics and Gynaecology*, 104: 923–33.

Kumar, R. and Robson, K. (1987) Previous induced abortion and ante-natal depression in primiparae: preliminary report of a survey of mental health in pregnancy, *Psychological Medicine*, 8: 711–15.

Kune, G.A., Kune, S., Watson, L.F. and Bahnson, C.B. (1991) Personality as a risk factor in large bowel cancer: data from the Melbourne Colorectal Cancer Study, *Psychological Medicine*, 21: 29–41.

Lader, D. and Matheson, J. (1991) *Smoking among Secondary School Children in England (1990): An Enquiry Carried out by the Social Survey Division of OPCS.* London: HMSO.

Laerum, E., Johnsen, N., Smith, P. and Larsen, S. (1988) Myocardial infarction can induce positive changes in life style and in the quality of life, *Scandinavian Journal of Primary Health Care*, 6: 67–71.

Laessle, R.G., Tuschl, R.J., Kotthaus, B.C. and Pirke, K.M. (1989) Behavioural and biological correlates of dietary restraint in normal life, *Appetite*, 12: 83–94.

Lancet (1985) Cancer of the cervix – death by incompetence (Editorial), *Lancet*, ii: 363–4.

Lando, H.A. (1977) Successful treatment of smokers with a broad-spectrum behavioral approach, *Journal of Consulting and Clinical Psychology*, 45: 361–6.

Lando, H.A. and McGovern, P.G. (1982) Three-year data on a behavioural treatment for smoking: a follow-up note, *Addictive Behaviours*, 7: 177–81.

Lane, D., Carroll, D., Ring, C., Beeveres, D.G. and Lip, G.Y.H. (2002) The prevalence and persistence of depression and anxiety following myocardial infarction, *British Journal of Health Psychology*, 7: 11–21.

Lang, A.R. and Marlatt, G.A. (1982) Problem drinking: a social learning perspective, in R.J. Gatchel, A. Baum and J.E. Singer (eds), *Handbook of Psychology and Health. Vol. 1. Clinical Psychology and Behavioral Medicine: Overlapping Disciplines*, pp. 121–69. Hillsdale, NJ: Erlbaum.

Langlie, J.K. (1977) Social networks, health beliefs, and preventative health behaviour, *Journal of Health and Social Behaviour*, 18: 244–60.

Larsson, G., Spangberg, L., Lindgren, S. and Bohlin, A.B. (1990) Screening for HIV in pregnant women: a study of maternal opinion, *AIDS Care*, 2: 223–8.

Lashley, M.E. (1987) Predictors of breast self-examination practice among elderly women, *Advances in Nursing Science*, 9: 25–34.

Last, J.M. (1963) The clinical iceberg in England and Wales, *Lancet*, 2: 28–31.

Lau, R. (1995) Cognitive representations of health and illness, in D. Gochman (ed.), *Handbook of Health Behavior Research, Vol. I.* New York: Plenum.

Lau, R., Bernard, J.M. and Hartman, K.A. (1989) Further explanations of common sense representations of common illnesses, *Health Psychology*, 8: 195–219.

Laudenslager, M.L., Ryan, S.M., Drugan, R.C., Hyson, R.L. and Maier, S.F. (1983) Coping and immunosuppression: inescapable but not escapable shock suppresses lymphocyte proliferation, *Science*, 221: 568–70.

Lawton, M.P. (1972) The dimensions of morale, in D. Kent, R. Kastenbaum and S. Sherwood (eds), *Research, Planning and Action for the Elderly.* New York: Behavioral Publications.

Lawton, M.P. (1975) The Philadelphia Geriatric Center Moral Scale: a revision, *Journal of Gerontology*, 30: 85–9.

Lawton, M.P., Moss, M. and Glicksman, A. (1990) The quality of life in the last year of life of older persons, *The Millbank Quarterly*, 68: 1–28.

Lawton, R., Conner, M. and Parker, D. (2006) Beyond cognition: predicting health risk behaviours from instrumental and affective beliefs, *Health Psychology* (in press).

Lazarus, R.S. (1975) A cognitively oriented psychologist looks at biofeedback, *American Psychologist*, 30: 553–61.

Lazarus, R.S. (2000) Toward better research on stress and coping, *American Psychologist*, 55(6): 665–73.

Lazarus, R.S. and Cohen, F. (1973) Active coping processes, coping dispositions, and recovery from surgery, *Psychosomatic Medicine*, 35: 375–89.

Lazarus, R.S. and Cohen, J.B. (1977) Environmental stress, in L. Altman and J.F. Wohlwill (eds), *Human Behavior and the Environment: Current Theory and Research*, Vol. 2, pp. 89–127. New York: Plenum.

Lazarus, R.S. and Folkman, S. (1987) Transactional theory and research on emotions and coping, *European Journal of Personality*, 1: 141–70.

Lazarus, R.S. and Launier, R. (1978) Stress related transactions between person and environment, in L.A. Pervin and M. Lewis (eds), *Perspectives in International Psychology*, pp. 287–327. New York: Plenum.

Lean, M. (1997) Sibutramine: a review of clinical efficacy, *International Journal of Obesity*, 21(Supp. 1): S30–S36.

Lean, M.E.J., Han, T.S. and Morrison, C.E. (1995) Waist circumference as a measure for indicating need for weight management, *British Medical Journal*, 311: 158–61.

Lean, M.E.J., Han, T.S. and Seidall, J.C. (1998) Impairment of health and quality of life in people with large waist circumference, *Lancet*, 351: 853–6.

Leary, M.R., Rapp, S.R., Herbst, K.C., Lyn Exum, M. and Feldman, S.R. (1998) Interpersonal concerns and psychological difficulties of psoriasis patients: effects of disease severity and fear of negative evaluation, *Health Psychology*, 17: 530–6.

Leck, I. (1986) An epidemiological assessment of neonatal screening for the dislocation of the hip, *Journal of the Royal College of Physicians*, 20: 56–62.

Lee, C. (1998) *Women's Health: Psychological and Social Perspectives*. London: Sage.

Lee, E. (2003) Tensions in the regulation of abortion in Britain, *Journal of Law and Society*, 30: 532–53.

Lee, E., Clements, S., Ingham, R. and Stone, N. (2004) *A Matter of Choice? Explaining National Variations in Teenage Abortion and Motherhood*. York: Joseph Rowntree Foundation.

Légaré, F., Godin, G., Dodin, S., Turcot, L. and Lapèrriere, L. (2003) Adherence to hormone replacement therapy: a longitudinal study using the theory of planned behaviour, *Psychology and Health*, 18(3): 351–71.

Lepper, M., Sagotsky, G., Dafoe, J.L. and Greene, D. (1982) Consequences of superfluous social constraints: effects on young children's social inferences and subsequent intrinsic interest, *Journal of Personality and Social Psychology*, 42: 51–65.

Lerman, C., Hughes, C., Croyle, R.T. et al. (2000) Prophylactic surgery and surveillance practices one year following BRCA1/2 genetic testing, *Preventative Medicine*, 1: 75–80.

Lerman, C., Schwartz, M.D., Narod, S. et al. (1997) The influence of psychological distress on use of genetic testing for cancer risk, *Journal of Consulting and Clinical Psychology*, 65: 414–20.

Levenstein, J.H., McCracken, E.C., McWhinney, I.R., Stewart, M.A. and Brown, J.B. (1986) The patient centred clinical method. Part 1. A model for the doctor–patient interaction in family medicine, *Family Practice*, 3: 24–30.

Leventhal, H. and Nerenz, D. (1985) The assessment of illness cognition, in P. Karoly (ed.), *Measurement Strategies in Health Psychology*, pp. 517–54. New York: Wiley.

Leventhal, H., Benyamini, Y., Brownlee, S. et al. (1997) Illness representations: theoretical foundations, in K.J. Petrie and J.A. Weinman (eds), *Perceptions of Health and Illness*, pp. 1–18. Amsterdam: Harwood.

Leventhal, H., Meyer, D. and Nerenz, D. (1980) The common sense representation of illness danger, *Medical Psychology*, 2: 7–30.

Leventhal, H., Prohaska, T.R. and Hirschman, R.S. (1985) Preventive health behavior across the life span, in J.C. Rosen and L.J. Solomon (eds), *Prevention in Health Psychology*. Hanover, NH: University Press of New England.

Levi, L. (1974) Psychosocial stress and disease: a conceptual model, in E.K. Gunderson and R.H. Rahe (eds), *Life Stress and Illness*. Springfield, IL: Thomas.

Levine, J.D., Gordon, N.C. and Fields, H.L. (1978) The mechanism of placebo analgesia, *Lancet*, 2: 654–7.

Ley, P. (1981) Professional non-compliance: a neglected problem, *British Journal of Clinical Psychology*, 20: 151–4.

Ley, P. (1988) *Communicating with Patients*. London: Croom Helm.

Ley, P. (1989) Improving patients' understanding, recall, satisfaction and compliance, in A. Broome (ed.), *Health Psychology*. London: Chapman & Hall.

Ley, P. and Morris, L.A. (1984) Psychological aspects of written information for patients, in S. Rachman (ed.), *Contributions to Medical Psychology*, pp. 117–49. Oxford: Pergamon Press.

Lichtenstein, E. and Brown, R.A. (1983) Current trends in the modification of cigarette dependence, in A.S. Bellack, M. Hersen and A.E. Kazdin (eds), *International Handbook of Behavior Modification and Therapy*. New York: Plenum.

Lichtenstein, E. and Glasgow, R. (1992) Smoking cessation: what have we learnt over the past decade? *Journal of Consulting and Clinical Psychology*, 60: 518–27.

Lichtenstein, E., Weiss, S.M., Hitchcock, J.L. et al. (1986) Task force 3: patterns of smoking relapse, *Health Psychology*, 5(supp.): 29–40.

Lifson, A., Hessol, N., Rutherford, G.W. et al. (1989) The natural history of HIV infection in a cohort of homosexual and bisexual men: clinical manifestations, 1978–1989. Paper presented to the 5th International Conference on AIDS, Montreal, September.

Lindemann, C. (1977) Factors affecting the use of contraception in the nonmarital context, in R. Gemme and C.C. Wheeler (eds), *Progress in Sexology*. New York: Plenum.

Linton, S.J., Buer, N., Vlaeyen, J. and Hellising, A. (2000) Are fear-avoidance beliefs related to the inception of an episode of back pain? A prospective study, *Psychology and Health*, 14: 1051–9.

Lipkus, I.M., Barefoot, J.C., Williams, R.B. and Siegler, I.C. (1994) Personality measures as predictors of smoking initiation and cessation in the UNC Alumni Heart study, *Health Psychology*, 13: 149–55.

Lissner, L., Odell, P.M., D'Agostino, R.B. et al. (1991) Variability of body weight and health outcomes in the Framingham population, *New England Journal of Medicine*, 324: 1839–44.

Litt, M.D. (1988) Self-efficacy and perceived control: cognitive mediators of pain tolerance, *Journal of Personality and Social Psychology*, 54: 149–60.

Little, P. and Byrne, C.D. (2001) Abdominal obesity and the hypertriglyceridaemic waist phenotype, *British Medical Journal*, 322: 687–9.

Llewellyn, C.D., Miners, A.H., Lee, C.A., Harrington, C. and Weinman, J. (2003) The illness perceptions and treatment beliefs of individuals with severe haemophilia and their role in adherence to home treatment, *Psychology and Health*, 18, 185–200.

Lohaus, A., Klein-Hebling, J., Vogele, C. and Kuhn-Hennighausen, C. (2001) Psychophysiological effects of relaxation training in children, *Psychology and Health*, 6: 197–206.

Loro, A.D. and Orleans, C.S. (1981) Binge eating in obesity: preliminary findings and guidelines for behavioural analysis and treatment, *Addictive Behaviours*, 7: 155–66.

Lowe, C.F., Dowey, A. and Horne, P. (1998) Changing what children eat, in A. Murcott (ed.),

The Nation's Diet: The Social Science of Food Choice, pp. 57–80. Harlow: Addison Wesley Longman.

Lowe, C.S. and Radius, S.M. (1982) Young adults' contraceptive practices: an investigation of influences, *Adolescence*, 22: 291–304.

Lowenstein, L., Deutsch, M., Gruberg, R., Solt, I., Yagil, Y., Nevo, O. and Bloch, M. (2006) Psychological distress symptoms in women undergoing medical vs. surgical termination of pregnancy, *General Hospital Psychiatry*, 28(1): 43–7.

Ludwig, A.M. and Stark, L.H. (1974) Alcohol craving: subjective and situational aspects, *Quarterly Journal of Studies on Alcohol*, 35: 899–905.

Luise, C., Jermy, K., May, C., Costello, G., Collins, W.P. and Bourne, T.H. (2002) Outcomes of expectant management of spontaneous first trimester miscarriage: observational study, *British Medical Journal*, 324: 873–5.

Luker, K. (1975) *Taking Chances: Abortion and the Decision Not to Contracept.* Berkeley, CA: University of California Press.

Lundgren, B. (1981) Breast cancer in Sweden by single oblique-view mammography, *Reviews of Endocrine-related Cancer*, 10(supp.): 67–70.

Luszczynska, A. and Schwarzer, R. (2003) Planning and self-efficacy in the adoption and maintenance of breast self-examination: a longitudinal study on self-regulatory cognitions, *Psychology and Health*, 18(1): 93–108.

Lynch, J. (1977) *The Broken Heart: The Medical Consequences of Loneliness.* New York: Basic Books.

Lynch, J., Krause, N., Kaplan, G.A., Salonen, R. and Salonen, J.T. (1987) Workplace demands, economic reward and progression of carotid atherosclerosis, *Circulation*, 96: 302–7.

Lynch, J., Krause, N., Kaplan, G.A., Tuomilehto, J. and Salonen, J.T. (1997) Workplace conditions, socioeconomic status and the risk of mortality and acute myocardial infarction: the Kuopio ischemic heart disease risk factor study, *American Journal of Public Health*, 87: 617–22.

Lyndon, J., Dunkel-Schetter, C., Cohan, C.L. and Pierce, T. (1996) Pregnancy decision making as a significant life event: a commitment approach, *Journal of Personality and Social Psychology*, 71: 141–51.

MacDonald, D., Grant, A., Sheridan-Pereira, M. et al. (1985) The Dublin randomised trial of intrapartum fetal heart rate monitoring, *American Journal of Obstetrics and Gynaecology*, 25: 33–8.

MacIntyre, S. (1977) *Single and Pregnant.* London: Croom Helm.

MacIntyre, S., Reilly, J., Miller, D. and Eldridge, J. (1998) Food choice, food scares and health: the role of the media, in A. Murcott (ed.), *The Social Science of Food Choice.* London: Longman.

MacKensie, J. and Bibby, J. (1978) Critical assessment of dilatation and curettage in 1029 women, *Lancet*, ii: 566–8.

MacKenzie, I. (1965) Breast cancer following multiple fluoroscopies, *British Journal of Cancer*, 19: 1–18.

MacLean, U., Sinfield, D., Klein, S. and Harnden, B. (1984) Women who decline breast screening, *Journal of Epidemiology and Community Health*, 24: 278–83.

MacWhinney, D.R. (1973) Problem solving and decision making in primary medical practice, *Proceeds of the Royal Society of Medicine*, 65: 934–8.

Madden, M.E. (1988) Internal and external attributions following miscarriage, *Journal of Social and Clinical Psychology*, 7: 113–21.

Maddi, S. and Kobasa, S.G. (1984) *The Hardy Executive: Health Under Stress.* Homewood, IL: Dow Jones-Irwin.

Maeland, J.G. and Havik, O.E. (1987) Psychological predictors for return for work after a myocardial infarction, *Journal of Psychosomatic Research*, 31: 471–81.

Maes, H.H., Neale, M.C. and Eaves, L.J. (1997) Genetic and environmental factors in relative body weight and human adiposity, *Behavior Genetics*, 27(4): 325–51.

Mahoney, F.I. and Barthel, D.W. (1965) Functional evaluation: the Barthel Index, *Maryland State Medical Journal*, 14: 61–5.

Main, C.J. and Spanswick, C.C. (eds) (2000) *Pain Management: An Interdisciplinary Approach*. Edinburgh: Churchill Livingstone.

Major, B., Cozzarelli, C., Cooper, M.L., Zubeck, J., Richards, C., Wilhite, M. and Gramzow, R.H. (2000) Psychological responses of women after first-trimester abortion, *Archives of General Psychiatry*, 57: 777–84.

Major, B. and Gramzow, R.H. (1999) Abortion as stigma: cognitive and emotional implications of concealment, *Journal of Personality and Social Psychology*, 77: 735–45.

Maker, C. and Ogden, J. (2003) The miscarriage experience: more than just a trigger to psychological morbidity, *Psychology and Health*, 18(3): 403–25.

Mann, J.M., Chin, J., Piot, P. and Quinn, T. (1988) The international epidemiology of AIDS, in *The Science of AIDS*, pp. 51–61. New York: W.H. Freeman.

Manne, S.L. and Zautra, A.J. (1992) Coping with arthritis: current status and critique, *Arthritis & Rheumatism*, 35: 1273–80.

Manning, M.M. and Wright, T.L. (1983) Self-efficacy expectancies, outcome expectancies and the persistence of pain control in child birth, *Journal of Personality and Social Psychology*, 45: 421–31.

Manstead, A.S.R. and Parker, D. (1995) Evaluating and extending the theory of planned behaviour, *European Review of Social Psychology*, 6: 69–95.

Manuck, S.B., Kaplan, J.R. and Matthews, K.A. (1986) Behavioural antecedents of coronary heart disease and atherosclerosis, *Arteriosclerosis*, 6: 1–14.

Mapes, R. (ed.) (1980) *Prescribing Practice and Drug Usage*. London: Croom Helm.

Marcus, B.H., Rakowski, W. and Rossi, J.S. (1992) Assessing motivational readiness and decision-making for exercise, *Health Psychology*, 22: 3–16.

Marks, D.F., Brucher-Albers, N.C., Donker, F.J.S. et al. (1998) Health psychology 2000: the development of professional health psychology, *Journal of Health Psychology*, 3: 149–60.

Marlatt, G.A. (1978) Craving for alcohol, loss of control and relapse: a cognitive behavioral analysis, in P.E. Nathan, G.A. Marlatt and T. Loberg (eds), *Alcoholism: New Directions in Behavioral Research and Treatment*. New York: Plenum.

Marlatt, G.A. and Gordon, J.R. (1985) *Relapse Prevention*. New York: Guilford Press.

Marmot, M.G. (1998) Improvement of social environment to improve health, *Lancet*, 331: 57–60.

Marteau, T.M. (1989) Psychological costs of screening, *British Medical Journal*, 291: 97.

Marteau, T.M. (1993) Health related screening: psychological predictors of uptake and impact, in S. Maes, H. Leventhal and M. Johnston (eds), *International Review of Health Psychology*, 2, pp. 149–74. Chichester: Wiley.

Marteau, T.M. and Baum, J.D. (1984) Doctors' views on diabetes, *Archives of Disease in Childhood*, 56: 566–70.

Marteau, T.M. and Johnston, M. (1990) Health professionals: a source of variance in health outcomes, *Psychology and Health*, 5: 47–58.

Marteau, T.M. and Riordan, D.C. (1992) Staff attitudes to patients: the influence of causal attributions for illness, *British Journal of Clinical Psychology*, 31: 107–10.

Marteau, T.M. and Weinman, J. (2006) Self-regulation and the behavioural response to DNA risk information: a theoretical analysis and framework for future research, *Social Science and Medicine*, 62: 1360–8.

Marteau, T.M., Dormandy, E. and Michie, S. (2001) A measure of informed choice, *Health Expectations*, 4: 99–108.

Marteau, T.M., Senior, V., Humphries, S.E., Bobrow, M., Cranston, T., Crook, M.A., Day, L. et al. (2004) Psychological impact of genetic testing for familial hypercholesterolemia within a previously aware population: a randomized controlled trial, *American Journal of Medical Genetics*, 128A: 285–93.

Marteau, T.M., Senior, V. and Sasieni, P. (2006) Women's understanding of a 'normal smear test result': experimental questionnaire based study, *British Medical Journal*, 322(7285): 526–8.

Marteau, T.M., van Duijn, M. and Ellis, I. (1992) Effects of genetic screening on perceptions of health: a pilot study, *Journal of Medicine and Genetics*, 24: 24–6.

Martikainen, P. and Valkonen, T. (1996) Mortality after death of spouse in relation to duration of bereavement in Finland, *Journal of Epidemiology Community Health*, 50(3): 264–8.

Martin, E. (1989) *The Woman in the Body*. Oxford: Oxford University Press.

Martin, J.E., Dubbert, P.M., Kattell, A.D. et al. (1984) Behavioral control of exercise in sedentary adults: studies 1 through 6, *Journal of Consulting and Clinical Psychology*, 52: 795–811.

Martin, J.L. (1987) The impact of AIDS on the gay male sexual behavior patterns in New York City, *American Journal of Public Health*, 77: 578–81.

Marucha, P.T., Kiecolt-Glaser, J.K. and Favagehi, M. (1998) Mucosal wound healing is impaired by examination stress, *Psychosomatic Medicine*, 60: 362–5.

Mason, E.E. (1987) Morbid obesity: use of vertical banded gastroplasty, *Surgical Clinics of North America*, 67: 521–37.

Mason, J.W. (1975) A historical view of the stress field, *Journal of Human Stress*, 1: 22–36.

Masters, W. and Johnson, V. (1966) *Human Sexual Response*. Boston, MA: Little Brown.

Matarazzo, J.D. (1980) Behavioral health and behavioral medicine: frontiers for a new health psychology, *American Psychologist*, 35: 807–17.

Matarazzo, J.D. (1984) Behavioral health: a 1990 challenge for the health sciences professions, in J.D. Matarazzo, N.E. Miller, S.M. Weiss, J.A. Herd and S.M. Weiss (eds), *Behavioral Health: A Handbook of Health Enhancement and Disease Prevention*, pp. 3–40. New York: Wiley.

Matthews, K.A., Manuck, S.B. and Saab, P.G. (1986) Cardiovascular responses of adolescents during a naturally occurring stressor and their behavioural and psychophysiological predictors, *Psychophysiology*, 23: 198–209.

Matthews, K.A., Owens, J.F., Allen, M.T. and Stoney, C.M. (1992) Do cardiovascular responses to laboratory stress relate to ambulatory blood pressure levels? Yes in some of the people some of the time, *Psychosomatic Medicine*, 54, 686–97.

Matthews, K.A., Woodall, K.L., Kenyon, K. and Jacob, T. (1996) Negative family environment as a predictor of boys' future status on measures of hostile attitudes, interview behaviour and anger expression, *Health Psychology*, 15: 30–7.

Maylath, N.S. (1990) Development of the children's Health Rating Scale, *Health Education Quarterly*, 17: 89–97.

McCann, I.L. and Holmes, D.S. (1984) Influence of aerobics on depression, *Journal of Personality and Social Psychology*, 46: 1142–7.

McClelland, D., Davis, W., Kalin, R. and Wanner, E. (1972) *The Drinking Man*. New York: Free Press.

McClendon, B.T. and Prentice-Dunn, S. (2001) Reducing skin cancer risk: an intervention based on protection motivation theory, *Journal of Health Psychology*, 6(3): 321–8.

McCormick, J. (1989) Cervical smears: a questionable practice? *Lancet*, 2: 207–9.

McCormick, N., Izzo, A. and Folcik, J. (1985) Adolescents' values, sexuality, and contraception in a rural New York county, *Adolescence*, 20: 385–95.

McCracken, L.M. and Eccleston, C. (2003) Coping or acceptance: what to do about chronic pain? *Pain*, 105(1–2): 197–204.

McCusker, J., Stoddard, J.G., Zapka, M.Z. and Meyer, K.H. (1989) Predictors of AIDS preventive behaviour among homosexually active men: a longitudinal study, *AIDS*, 3: 443–6.

McDermott, M.R., Ramsay, J.M. and Bray, C. (2001) Components of the anger-hostility complex as a risk factor for coronary artery disease severity: a multi-measure study, *Journal of Health Psychology*, 6, (3): 309–19.

McDonald, D.G. and Hodgdon, J.A. (1991) *Psychological Effects of Aerobic Fitness Training: Research and Theory*. New York: Springer.

McEwan, B.S. and Stellar, E. (1993) Stress and the individual: mechanisms leading to disease. *Archives of Internal Medicine*, 153: 2093–101.

McGee, H.M., O'Boyle, C.A., Hickey, A., O'Malley, K. and Joyce, C.R. (1991) Assessing the quality of life of the individual: the SEIQoL with a healthy and a gastroenterology unit population, *Psychological Medicine*, 21: 749–59.

McGowan, L.P.A., Clarke-Carter, D.D. and Pitts, M.K. (1998) Chronic pelvic pain: a meta-analytic review, *Psychology and Health*, 13: 937–51.

McGuire, M.T., Wing, R.R., Klem, M.L. and Hill, J.O. (1999) Behavioral strategies of individuals who have maintained long term weight losses, *Obesity Research*, 7: 334–41.

McIntosh, P. and Charlton, V. (1985) *The Impact of the Sport for All Policy 1966–1984 and a Way Forward*. London: The Sports Council.

McKee, K.J., Houston, D.M. and Barnes, S. (2002) Methods for assessing quality of life and wellbeing in frail older people, *Psychology and Health*, 17(6): 737–51.

McKeown, T. (1979) *The Role of Medicine*. Oxford: Blackwell.

McKusick, L., Coates, T.J., Morin, S.F., Pollack, L. and Ho., C. (1990) Longitudinal predictors of reduction in unprotected anal intercourse among gay men in San Francisco: the AIDS behavioral research project, *American Journal of Public Health*, 80: 978–83.

McNair, D., Lorr, M. and Droppleman, L. (1971) *Manual for the Profile of Mood States*. San Diego, CA: Educational and Industrial Testing Service.

McNeil, A.D., Jarvis, M.J., Stapleton, J.A. et al. (1988) Prospective study of factors predicting uptake of smoking in adolescents, *Journal of Epidemiology and Community Health*, 43: 72–8.

McNeil, B.J., Pauker, S.G., Sox, H.C. and Tversky, A. (1982) On the elicitation of preferences for alternative therapies, *New England Journal of Medicine*, 306: 1259–62.

McReynolds, W.T. (1982) Towards a psychology of obesity: review of research on the role of personality and level of adjustment, *International Journal of Eating Disorders*, 2: 37–57.

McWhinney, I.R. (1995) Why we need a new clinical method, in M. Stewart, B.B. Brown, W.W. Weston et al. (eds), *Patient Centred Medicine: Transforming the Clinical Method*, pp. 1–20. London: Sage.

Mead, N. and Bower, P. (2000) Patient centredness: a conceptual framework and review of empirical literature, *Social Science and Medicine*, 51: 1087–110.

Meadows, J., Jenkinson, S., Catalan, J. and Gazzard, B. (1990) Voluntary HIV testing in the antenatal clinic: differing uptake rates for individual counselling midwives, *AIDS Care*, 2: 229–33.

Mechanic, D. (1962) *Students under Stress: A Study in the Social Psychology of Adaptation*. Glencoe, IL: Free Press of Glencoe.

Meenan, R.F., Gertman, P.M. and Mason, J.H. (1980) Measuring health status in arthritis: the arthritis impact measurement scales, *Arthritis & Rheumatology*, 23: 146–52.

Melzack, R. (1975) The McGill pain questionnaire: major properties and scoring methods, *Pain*, 1: 277–99.

Melzack, R. (1979) *The Puzzle of Pain*. New York: Basic Books.

Melzack, R. and Wall, P.D. (1965) Pain mechanisms: a new theory, *Science*, 150: 971–9.

Melzack, R. and Wall, P.D. (1982) *The Challenge of Pain*. New York: Basic Books.

Metcalfe, C., Smith, G.D, Wadsworth, E. et al. (2003) A contemporary validation of the Reeder Stress Inventory, *British Journal of Health Psychology*, 8: 83–94.

Metler, F.A., Hempelmann, L.H. and Dutton, A.M. (1969) Breast neoplasias in women treated with X-rays for acute postpartum mastitis, *Journal of the National Cancer Institute*, 43: 803–22.

Meyer, D., Leventhal, H. and Guttman, M. (1985) Common-sense models of illness: the example of hypertension, *Health Psychology*, 4: 115–35.

Michaud, C., Kahn, J.P., Musse, N. et al. (1990) Relationships between a critical life event and eating behaviour in high school students, *Stress Medicine*, 6: 57–64.

Michie, S., Smith, J.A., Heaversedge, J. and Read, S. (1999) Genetic counselling: clinical genetics views, *Journal of Genetic Counselling*, 8(5): 275–87.

Michie, S., Smith, J.A., Senior, V. and Marteau, T.M. (2003) Understanding why negative genetic test results sometimes fail to reassure, *American Journal of Medical Genetics*, 119(A): 340–7.

Michie, S., Weinman, J., Miller, J. et al. (2002) Predictive genetic testing: high risk expectations in the face of low risk information, *Journal of Behavioural Medicine*, 25: 33–50.

Miller, P. (1975) A behavioral intervention program for chronic public drunkenness offenders, *Archives of General Psychiatry*, 32: 915–18.

Miller, S.M., Brody, D.S. and Summerton, J. (1987) Styles of coping with threat: implications for health, *Journal of Personality and Social Psychology*, 54: 142–8.

Miller, T.Q., Smith, T.W., Turner, C.W., Guijarro, M.L. and Hallet, A.J. (1996) A meta-analytic review of research on hostility and physical health, *Psychological Bulletin*, 119: 322–48.

Millward, L. (2006) The transition to motherhood in an organizational context: an interpretative phenomenological analysis, *Journal of Occupational and Organizational Psychology*, 79(3): 315–33.

Milne, S.E., Orbell, S. and Sheeran, P. (2002) Combining motivational and volitional interventions to promote exercise participation: protection motivation theory and implementations intentions: *British Journal of Social Psychology*, 7: 163–84.

Minsky, S., Vega, W., Miskimen, T., Gara, M. and Escobar, J. (2003) Diagnostic patterns in Latino, African American and European American psychiatric patients, *Archives of General Psychiatry*, 60: 637–44.

Mintel (1990) *Eggs. Market Intelligence*. London: Mintel.

Minuchin, S., Rosman, B.L. and Baker, L. (1978) *The Anorectic Family in Psychosomatic Families: Anorexia Nervosa in Context*. London: Harvard University Press.

Misselbrook, D. and Armstrong, D. (2000) How do patients respond to presentation of risk information? A survey in general practice of willingness to accept treatment for hypertension, *British Journal of General Practice*, 51, 276–9.

Moatti, J.-P., Le Gales, C., Seror, J., Papiernik, E. and Henrion, R. (1990) Social acceptability of HIV screening among pregnant women, *AIDS Care*, 2: 213–22.

Mocroft, A., Vella, S., Benfield, T.L., Chiesi, A. et al. (1998) Changing patterns of mortality across Europe inpatients infected with HIV-1. EuroSIDA Study Group, *Lancet*, 352(9142): 1725–30.

Moen, P. (1998) Women's roles and health: a life-course approach, in K. Orth-Gomér, M. Chesney and N.K. Wenger (eds), *Women, Stress, and Heart Disease*. Mahwah, NJ: Erlbaum.

Mokdad, A.H., Marks, J.S., Stroup, D.F. and Gerberding, J.L. (2004) Actual causes of death in the United States, 200, *JAMA*, 10(29): 1238–45.

Moller, J., Hallqvist, J., Diderichensen, F. et al. (1999) Do episodes of anger trigger myocardial infarction? A case-crossover analysis in the Stockholm heart epidemiology program (SHEEP), *Psychosomatic Medicine*, 61: 842–9.

Montague, C.T., Farooqi, I.S., Whitehead, J.P. et al. (1997) Congenital leptin deficiency is associated with severe early onset obesity in humans, *Nature*, 387: 903–8.

Moorhead, J. (1997) *New Generations: 40 Years of Birth in Britain*, (National Childbirth Trust Guides). London: The Stationery Office.

Moos, R.H. and Schaefer, J.A. (1984) The crisis of physical illness: an overview and conceptual approach, in R.H. Moos (ed.), *Coping with Physical Illness: New Perspectives*, 2, pp. 3–25. New York: Plenum.

Moos, R.H. and Swindle, R.W. Jr (1990) Stressful life circumstances: concepts and measures, *Stress Medicine*, 6: 171–8.

Mora, P.A., Halm, E., Leventhal, H. and Ceric, F. (in press) Elucidating the relationship between negative affectivity and symptoms: the role of illness specific affective responses, *Annals of Behavioural Medicine*.

Morgan, W.P. and O'Connor, P.J. (1988) Exercise and mental health, in R.K. Dishman (ed.), *Exercise Adherence: Its Impact on Public Health*, pp. 91–121. Champaign, IL: Human Kinetics.

MORI (1984) *Public Attitudes Towards Fitness: Research Study Conducted for Fitness Magazine.* London: MORI.

Morley, S., Eccleston, C. and Williams, A. (1999) Systematic review and meta-analysis of randomised controlled trials of cognitive behavioural therapy and behavioural therapy for chronic pain in adults, excluding headache, *Pain*, 80: 1–13.

Morris, J.N. (1964) *Uses of Epidemiology*, 2nd edn. Edinburgh: Churchill Livingstone.

Morris, J.N., Pollard, R., Everitt, M.G. and Chave, S.P.W. (1980) Vigorous exercise in leisure-time protection against coronary heart disease, *Lancet*, 2: 1207–10.

Morrison, D.M. (1985) Adolescent contraceptive behaviour: a review, *Psychological Bulletin*, 98: 538–68.

Mosbach, P. and Leventhal, H. (1988) Peer group identification and smoking: implications for intervention, *Journal of Abnormal Psychology*, 97: 238–45.

Moss, P., Bolland, G., Foxman, R. and Owen, C. (1987) The division of household work during the transition to parenthood, *Journal of Reproductive and Infant Psychology*, 5: 71–86.

Moss-Morris, R., Petrie, K.J. and Weinman, J. (1996) Functioning in chronic fatigue syndrome: do illness perceptions play a regulatory role? *British Journal of Health Psychology*, 1: 15–26.

Moss-Morris, R., Weinman, J., Petrie, K.J., Horne, R., Cameron, L.D. and Buick, D. (2002) The revised illness perception questionnaire (IPQ-R), *Psychology and Health*, 17: 1–16.

Mosse, K. (1993) *Becoming a Mother.* London: Virago.

Moulder, C. (1998) *Understanding Pregnancy Loss: Perspectives and Issues in Care.* London: Macmillan.

Moyer, A. (1997) Psychosocial outcomes of breast conserving surgery versus mastectomy: a meta analytic review, *Health Pyschology*, 16: 284–98.

Moynihan, J.A. and Ader, R. (1996) Psychoneuroimmunology: animal models of disease, *Psychosomatic Medicine*, 58: 546–58.

Muir, J., Mant, D., Jones, L. and Yudkin, P. (1994) Effectiveness of health checks conducted by nurses in primary care: results of the OXCHECK study after one year, *British Medical Journal*, 308: 308–12.

Muldoon, M.F., Barger, S.D., Flory, J.D. and Manuck, S.B. (1998) What are quality of life measurements measuring? *British Medical Journal*, 316: 542–5.

Mullen, P.D., Green, L.W. and Persinger, G.S. (1985) Clinical trials of patient education for chronic conditions: a comparative meta analysis of intervention types, *Preventive Medicine*, 14: 753–81.

Muller, J.E., Abela, G.S., Nesto, R.W. and Tofler, G.H. (1994) Triggers, acute risk factors and vulnerable plaques: the lexicon of a new frontier, *Journal of American College of Cardiology*, 23: 809–13.

Muller, J.E., Stone, P.H. and Turi, Z.G. (1985) Circadian variation in the frequency of onset of acute myocardial infarction, *New England Journal of Medicine*, 313: 1315–22.

Mumford, D.B., Whitehouse, A.M. and Platts, M. (1991) Sociocultural correlates of eating disorders among Asian school girls in Bradford, *British Journal of Psychiatry*, 158: 222–8.

Munday, D. (1994) The development of abortion services since 1968, in D. Paintin (ed.), *Abortion Services in England and Wales*. London: Pregnancy Advisory Service and Birth Control Trust.

Murray, M. and McMillan, C. (1993) Health beliefs, locus of control, emotional control and women's cancer screening behaviour, *British Journal of Clinical Psychology*, 32: 87–100.

Murray, M., Swan, A.V., Bewley, B.R. and Johnson, M.R.D. (1984) The development of smoking during adolescence: the MRC/Derbyshire smoking study, *International Journal of Epidemiology*, 12: 185–92.

Murray, S., Narayan, V., Mitchell, M. and Witte, H. (1993) Study of dietetic knowledge among members of the primary health care team, *British Journal of General Practice*, 43: 229–31.

Myers, L.B. (2000) Identifying repressors: a methodological issue for health psychology, *Psychology and Health*, 15: 205–14.

Nathoo, V. (1988) Investigation of non-responders at a cervical screening clinic in Manchester, *British Medical Journal*, 296: 1041–2.

National Institutes of Health (1998) Clinical guidelines on the identification, evaluation, and treatment of overweight and obesity in adults: the evidence report [published correction appears in *Obesity Research*, 6: 464] *Obesity Research*, 6(suppl. 2): 51–209S.

National Statistics 2005 [online] Available: www.statistics.gov.uk [10.09.05].

Neighbour, R. (1987) *The Inner Consultation*. London: Petroc Press.

Neilson, S. and Hahlin, M. (1985) Expectant management of first trimester miscarriage, *Lancet*, 345: 84–6.

Neumark-Sztainer, D., Kaufmann, N.A. and Berry, E.M. (1995) Physical activity within community based weight control programme: programme evaluation and predictors of stress, *Public Health Review*, 23: 237–51.

Newell, A. and Simon, H.A. (1972) *Human Problem Solving*. Englewood Cliffs, NJ: Prentice Hall.

Newman, J. and Taylor, A. (1992) Effect of a means–end contingency on young children's food preferences, *Journal of Experimental Psychology*, 64: 200–16.

Newman, M.G. and Stone, A.A. (1996) Does humour moderate the effects of experimentally induced stress? *Annals of Behavioural Medicine*, 18: 101–9.

Newman, S., Fitzpatrick, R., Revenson, T.A., Skevington, S. and Williams, G. (1996) *Understanding Rheumatoid Arthritis*. London: Routledge.

NHS Centre for Reviews and Dissemination (1997) *Systematic Review of Interventions in the Treatment and Prevention of Obesity*. York: University of York.

Nicolson, P. (1986) Developing a feminist approach to depression following childbirth, in S. Wilkinson (ed.), *Feminist Social Psychology: Developing Theory and Practice*. Milton Keynes: Open University Press.

Nicolson, P. (1990a) A brief report of women's expectations of men's behaviour in the transition to parenthood: contradictions and conflicts for counselling psychology practice, *Counselling Psychology Quarterly*, 3(4): 353–61.

Nicolson, P. (1990b) Understanding postnatal depression: a mother-centred approach, *Journal of Advanced Nursing*, 15: 689–95.

Nicolson, P. (1999a) Loss, happiness and postpartum depression: the ultimate paradox, *Canadian Psychology*, 40(2): 162–78.

Nicolson, P. (1999b) The myth of maternal instinct, *Psychology, Evolution & Gender*, 1(2): 161–81.

Noar, S.M., Moroko., P.J. and Harlow, L.L. (2002) Condom negotiation in heterosexually active men and women: development and validation of a condom influence strategy questionnaire, *Psychology and Health*, 17(6): 711–35.

Norman, P. and Conner, M. (1993) The role of social cognition models in predicting attendance at health checks, *Psychology and Health*, 8: 447–62.

Norman, P. and Conner, M. (1996) The role of social cognition models in predicting health behaviours: future directions, in M. Conner and P. Norman (eds), *Predicting Health Behaviour: Research and Practice with Social Cognition Models*, pp. 197–225. Buckingham: Open University Press.

Norman, P. and Fitter, M. (1989) Intention to attend a health screening appointment: some implications for general practice, *Counselling Psychology Quarterly*, 2: 261–72.

Norman, P., Conner, M. and Bell, R. (1999) The theory of planned behavior and smoking cessation, *Health Psychology*, 18: 89–94.

Norman, P. and Smith, L. (1995) The theory of planned behaviour and exercise: an investigation into the role of prior behaviour, behavioural intentions and attitude variability, *European Journal of Social Psychology*, 25: 403–15.

Norman, P., Searle, A., Harrad, R. and Vedhara, K. (2003) Predicting adherence to eye patching in children with amblyopia: an application of protection motivation theory, *British Journal of Health Psychology*, 8: 67–82.

Normandeau, S., Kalinins, I., Jutras, S. and Hanigan, D. (1998) A description of 5 to 12 year old children's conception of health within the context of their daily life, *Psychology and Health*, 13: 883–96.

Norris, R.M., Brandt, P.W.T., Caughey, D.E., Lee, A.J. and Scott, P.J. (1969) A new coronary prognostic index, *Lancet*, 1: 274–8.

Nyklíček, I., Vingerhoets, A.D. and Denollett, J. (2002) Emotional (non-)expression and health: data, questions and challenges, *Psychology and Health*, 17(5): 517–28.

O'Boyle, C., McGee, H., Hickey, A., O'Malley, K. and Joyce, C.R.B. (1992) Individual quality of life in patients undergoing hip replacements, *Lancet*, 339: 1088–91.

O'Brien, S. and Lee, L. (1990) Effects of videotape intervention on Pap smear knowledge, attitudes and behavior. Special issue: Behavioural research in cancer, *Behaviour Changes*, 7: 143–50.

O'Connor, A. and O'Brien-Pallas L.L. (1989) Decisional conflict, in G.K. Mcfarlane and E.A. Mcfarlane (eds), *Nursing Diagnosis and Intervention*, pp. 486–96. Toronto: Mosby.

O'Connor, R.C., Armitage, C.J. and Gray, L. (2006) The role of clinical and social cognitive variables in parasuicide, *British Journal of Clinical Psychology* (in press).

Oakley, A. (1974) *The Sociology of Housework*. New York: Pantheon Books.

Oakley, A. (1979) *Becoming a Mother*. Oxford: Martin Robertson.

Oakley, A. (1980) *Women Confined: Towards a Sociology of Childbirth*. Oxford: Martin Robertson.

Oakley, A. (1984) *The Captured Womb*. Oxford: Blackwell.

Oakley, A. (1986) *From Here to Maternity*. Harmondsworth: Pelican.

Oakley, A. (1992) *Social Support and Motherhood*. Oxford: Blackwell.

Oakley, A., Fullerton, D., Holland, J. et al. (1995) Sexual health education interventions for young people: a methodological review, *British Medical Journal*, 310: 158–62.

Obesity in the United Kingdom 2005 [online] Available: www.weightconcern.org.uk [15.10.05].

Office for National Statistics Population and Health Monitors (1995) Available: www.statistics.gov.uk.

Ogden, C.L., Carroll, M.D., Curtin, L.R., McDowell, M.A., Tabak, C.J. and Flegal, K.M. (2006) Prevalence of overweight and obesity in the United States, 1999–2004, *JAMA*, 295: 1549–55.

Ogden, C.L., Troiano, R.P., Briefel, R.R., Kuczmarski, R.J., Flegal, K.M. and Johnson, C.L. (1997) Prevalence of overweight among preschool children in the United States, 1971 through 1994, *Pediatrics*, 99: E11–17.

Ogden, J. (1992) *Fat Choice: The Myth of Dieting Explained.* London: Routledge.

Ogden, J. (1993) The measurement of restraint: confounding success and failure? *International Journal of Eating Disorders*, 13: 69–76.

Ogden, J. (1994) The effects of smoking cessation, restrained eating, and motivational states on food intake in the laboratory, *Health Psychology*, 13: 114–21.

Ogden, J. (1995a) Cognitive and motivational consequence of dieting, *European Eating Disorders Review*, 24: 228–41.

Ogden, J. (1995b) Changing the subject of health psychology, *Psychology and Health*, 10: 257–65.

Ogden, J. (1995c) Psychosocial theory and the creation of the risky self, *Social Science and Medicine*, 40: 409–15.

Ogden, J. (1999) Body dissatisfaction, *Counselling News*, January: 20–1.

Ogden, J. (2000) The correlates of long-term weight loss: a group comparison study of obesity, *International Journal of Obesity*, 24: 1018–25.

Ogden, J. (2003) Some problems with social cognition models: a pragmatic and conceptual analysis, *Health Psychology*, 22(4): 424–8.

Ogden, J. and Chanana, A. (1998) Explaining the effect of ethnicity in body dissatisfaction and dieting: finding a role for values, *International Journal of Obesity*, 22: 641–7.

Ogden, J. and Clementi, C. (in press) The experience of being obese and the many consequences of stigma. Submitted to *Psychology and Health.*

Ogden, J. and Elder, C. (1998) The role of family status and ethnic group on body image and eating behaviour, *International Journal of Eating Disorders*, 23: 309–15.

Ogden, J. and Fox, P. (1994) An examination of the use of smoking for weight control in restrained and unrestrained eaters, *International Journal of Eating Disorders*, 16: 177–86.

Ogden, J. and Greville, L. (1993) Cognitive changes to preloading in restrained and unrestrained eaters as measured by the Stroop task, *International Journal of Eating Disorders*, 14: 185–95.

Ogden, J. and Knight, D. (1995) Attributions for illness and treatment interventions in community nurses, *Journal of Advanced Nursing*, 22: 290–3.

Ogden, J. and Maker, C. (2004) Expectant or surgical management: a qualitative study of miscarriage, *British Journal of Obstetrics and Gynaecology*, 111: 463–7.

Ogden, J. and Mtandabari, T. (1997) Examination stress and changes in mood and health related behaviours, *Psychology and Health*, 12: 289–99.

Ogden, J. and Mundray, K. (1996) The effect of the media on body satisfaction: the role of gender and size, *European Eating Disorders Review*, 4: 171–82.

Ogden, J. and Sidhu, S. (2006) Adherence, behaviour change and visualisation: a qualitative study of patients' experiences of obesity medication, *The Journal of Psychosomatic Research*, 62: 545–52.

Ogden, J. and Steward, J. (2000) The role of the mother–daughter relationship in explaining weight concern, *International Journal of Eating Disorders*, 28: 78–83.

Ogden, J. and Thomas, D. (1999) The role of familial values in understanding the impact of social class on weight concern, *International Journal of Eating Disorders*, 25: 273–9.

Ogden, J. and Wardle, J. (1990) Control of eating and attributional style, *British Journal of Clinical Psychology*, 29: 445–6.

Ogden, J. and Wardle, J. (1991) Cognitive and emotional responses to food, *International Journal of Eating Disorders*, 10: 297–311.

Ogden, J., Ambrose, L., Khadra, A. et al. (2002) A questionnaire study of GPs' and patients' belief about the different components of patient centredness, *Patient Education and Counselling*, 47: 223–7.

Ogden, J., Andrade, J., Eisner, M. et al. (1997) To treat? To befriend? To prevent? Patients' and GPs' views of the doctor's role, *Scandinavian Journal of Primary Health Care*, 15: 114–17.

Ogden, J., Baig, S., Earnshaw, G. et al. (2001) What is health? Where GPs' and patients' worlds collide, *Patient Education and Counselling*, 45: 265–9.

Ogden, J., Bandara, I., Cohen, H. et al. (2001) GPs' and patients' models of obesity: whose problem is it anyway? *Patient Education and Counselling*, 40: 227–33.

Ogden, J., Boden, J., Caird, R. et al. (1999) You're depressed; no I'm not: GPs' and patients' different models of depression, *British Journal of General Practice*, 49: 123–4.

Ogden, J., Branson, R., Bryett, A. et al. (2003) What's in a name? An experimental study of patients' views of the impact and function of a diagnosis, *Family Practice*, 20(3): 248–53.

Ogden, J., Branson, R., Bryett, A., Campbell, A., Febles, A., Ferguson, I., Lavender, H., Mizan, J., Simpson, R. and Tayler, M. (2003) What's in a name? An experimental study of patients' view of the impact and function of a diagnosis, *Family Practice*, 20(3): 248–53.

Ogden, J., Clementi, C. and Aylwin, S. (2006a) The impact of obesity surgery and the paradox of control: a qualitative study, *Psychology and Health*, 21(2): 273–93.

Ogden, J., Clementi, C., and Aylwin, S. (2006b) Having obesity surgery: a qualitative study and the paradox of control, *Psychology and Health*, 21: 273–93.

Ogden, J., Clementi, C., Aylwin, S. and Patel, A. (2005) Exploring the impact of obesity surgery on patient's health status: a quantitative and qualitative study, *Obesity Surgery*, 15: 266–72.

Ogden, J., Karim, L., Choudry, A. and Brown, K. (2006) Understanding successful behaviour change: the role of intentions, attitudes to the target and motivations and the example of diet, *Health Education Research Advance Access*, published September 13, 2006, doi:10.1093/her/cy1090.

Ogden, J., Reynolds, R. and Smith, A. (2006) Expanding the concept of parental control: a role for overt and covert control in children's snacking behaviour? *Appetite*, 47: 100–6.

Ogden, J., Shaw, A. and Zander, L. (1997a) Women's homebirth memories: a decision with a lasting effect? *British Journal of Midwifery*, 5: 216–18.

Ogden, J., Shaw, A. and Zander, L. (1997b) The homebirth experience: women's memories 3–5 years on, *British Journal of Midwifery*, 5: 208–11.

Ogden, J., Shaw, A. and Zander, L. (1997c) Deciding to have a homebirth: womens' memories of help and hindrances 3–5 years on, *British Journal of Midwifery*, 5: 212–15.

Ogden, J., Shaw, A. and Zander, L. (1998) Women's experiences of having a hospital birth, *British Journal of Midwifery*, 6: 339–45.

Ohlin, A. and Rossner, S. (1990) Maternal body weight development after pregnancy, *International Journal of Obesity*, 14: 159–73.

Oldridge, N.B. and Jones, N.L. (1983) Improving patient compliance in cardiac exercise rehabilitation: effects of written agreement and self-monitoring, *Journal of Cardiac Rehabilitation*, 3: 257–62.

Oldridge, N.B., Guyatt, G.H., Fischer, M.E. and Rimm, A.A. (1988) Cardiac rehabilitation after myocardial infarction: Combined experience of randomised clinical trials, *Journal of the American Medical Association*, 260(7): 945–50.

Olivera, S.A., Ellison, R.C., Moore, L.L. et al. (1992) Parent–child relationships in nutrient intake: the Framingham Children's Study, *American Journal of Clinical Nutrition*, 56: 593–8.

Orbach, S. (1978) *Fat Is a Feminist Issue: The Anti-diet Guide to Weight Loss.* New York: Paddington Press.

Orbell, S., Hodgkins, S. and Sheeran, P. (1997) Implementation intentions and the theory of planned behaviour, *Personality and Social Psychology Bulletin*, 23: 945–54.

Orford, J. (1985) *Excessive Appetites: A Psychological View of Addictions.* Chichester: Wiley.

Orford, J. and Velleman, R. (1991) The environmental intergenerational transmission of alcohol problems: a comparison of two hypotheses, *British Journal of Medical Psychology*, 64: 189–200.

Orgogozo, J.M., Capildeo, R., Anagnostou, C.N. et al. (1983) Development of neurological scale for clinical evaluation of middle cerebral artery (MCA) infarction (translation), *La Presse Médicale*, 48: 3039–44.

Orton, M., Fitzpatrick, R., Fuller, A. et al. (1991) Factors affecting women's responses to an invitation to attend for a second breast cancer screening examination, *British Journal of General Practice*, 41: 320–3.

Osborn, M. and Smith, J.A. (1998) The professional experience of chronic benign lower back pain: an interpretative phenomenological analysis, *Journal of Health Psychology*, 3: 65–83.

Owens, R.G., Daly, J., Heron, K. and Leinster, S.J. (1987) Psychological and social characteristics of attenders for breast screening, *Psychology and Health*, 1: 320–3.

Paffenbarger, R.S. and Hale, W.E. (1975) Work activity and coronary heart mortality, *New England Journal of Medicine*, 292: 545–50.

Paffenbarger, R.S., Hyde, R.T., Wing, A.L. and Hsieh, C.C. (1986) Physical activity, all-cause mortality, and longevity of college alumni, *New England Journal of Medicine*, 314: 605–13.

Paffenbarger, R.S., Wing, A.L. and Hyde, R.T. (1978) Physical activity as an index of heart attack risk in college alumni, *American Journal of Epidemiology*, 108: 161–75.

Paffenbarger, R.S., Wing, A.L., Hyde, R.T. and Jung, D.L. (1983) Physical activity and incidence of hypertension in college alumni, *American Journal of Epidemiology*, 117: 245–57.

Paintin, D. (ed.) (1994) *Abortion Services in England and Wales*. London: Pregnancy Advisory Service and Birth Control Trust.

Paisley, C.M. and Sparks, P. (1998) Expectations of reducing fat intake: the role of perceived need within the theory of planned behaviour, *Psychology and Health*, 13: 341–53.

Pakenham, K., Pruss, M. and Clutton, S. (2000) The utility of socio-demographics, knowledge and health belief model variables in predicting reattendance for mammography screening: a brief report, *Psychology and Health*, 15: 585–91.

Palkovitz, R. and Copes, M. (1988) Changes in attitudes, beliefs and expectations associated with the transition to parenthood, *Marriage and Family Review*, 12: 183–99.

Palmer, A.G., Tucker, S., Warren, R. and Adams, M. (1993) Understanding women's responses for cervical intra-epithelial neoplasia, *British Journal of Clinical Psychology*, 32: 101–12.

Park, C.L. and Folkman, S. (1997) The role of meaning in the context of stress and coping, *General Review of Psychology*, 2: 115–44.

Park, C.L., Cohen, L.H. and Murch, R.L. (1996) Assessment and prediction of stress-related growth, *Journal of Personality*, 64: 71–105.

Park, L.C. and Covi, L. (1965) Non blind placebo trial: an exploration of neurotic patients' responses to placebo when its inert content is disclosed, *Archives of General Psychiatry*, 12: 336–45.

Parker, D., Manstead, A.S. and Stradling, S.G. (1995) Extending the theory of planned behaviour: the role of personal norm, *British Journal of Social Psychology*, 34: 127–37.

Partridge, C., Johnston, M. and Edwards, S. (1987) Recovery from physical disability after stroke: normal pattern as a basis for evaluation, *Lancet*, 1: 373–5.

Partridge, C.J. and Johnston, M. (1989) Perceived control and recovery from physical disability, *British Journal of Clinical Psychology*, 28: 53–60.

Patrick, D.L. and Ericson, P.E. (1993) *Health Status and Health Policy: Allocating Resources to Health Care*. Oxford: Oxford University Press.

Patrick, D.L. and Peach, H. (1989) *Disablement in a Community*. Oxford: Oxford University Press.

Patterson, K.R. (1993) Population screening for diabetes, report from the professional Advisory Committee of the British Diabetic Association, *Diabetic Medicine*, 10: 777–81.

Paxton, S.J., Browning, C.J. and O'Connell, G. (1997) Predictors of exercise program participation in older women, *Psychology and Health*, 12: 543–52.

Pearse, I.H. and Crocker, L. (1943) *The Peckham Experiment*. London: Allen & Unwin.

Peele, S. (1984) The cultural context of psychological approaches to alcoholism: can we control the effects of alcohol? *American Psychologist*, 39: 1337–51.

Pendleton, D., Schofield, T., Tate, P. and Havelock, P. (1984) *The Consultation: An Approach to Learning and Teaching*. Oxford: Oxford Medical Publications.

Pennebaker, J.W. (1983) Accuracy of symptom perception, in A. Baum, S.E. Taylor and J. Singer (eds), *Handbook of Psychology and Health*, Vol. 4. Hillsdale, NJ: Erlbaum.

Pennebaker, J.W. (1993) Social mechanisms of constraint, in D.M. Wegner and J.W. Pennebaker (eds), *Handbook of Mental Control*, pp. 200–19. Englewood Cliffs, NJ: Prentice Hall.

Pennebaker, J.W. (1997) Writing about emotional experiences as a therapeutic process, *Psychological Science*, 8(3): 162–6.

Pennebaker, J.W. and Beall, S.K. (1986) Confronting a traumatic event: toward an understanding of inhibition and disease, *Journal of Abnormal Psychology*, 95: 274–82.

Pennebaker, J.W., Francis, M.E. and Booth, R.J. (2001) *Linguistic Inquiry and Word Count: LIWC 2001*. Mahwah, NJ: Erlbaum.

Pennebaker, J.W., Kiecolt-Glasser, J.K. and Glaser, R. (1988) Disclosure of trauma and immune function: health implications for psychotherapy, *Journal of Consulting and Clinical Psychology*, 56: 239–45.

Pennebaker, J.W., Mayne, T.J. and Francis, M.E. (1997) Linguistic predictors of adaptive bereavement, *Journal of Personality and Social Psychology*, 72: 863–71.

Pereira, D.B., Antoni, M.H., Danielson, A., Simon, T., Efantis-Potter, J., Carver, C.S., Durán, R.E.F., Ironson, G., Klimas, N. and O'Sullivan, M.J. (2003) Life stress and cervical squamous intraepithelial lesions in women with human papillomavirus and human immunodeficiency virus, *Psychosomatic Medicine*, 65(1): 1–8.

Perkins, K.A., Grobe, J.E., Stiller, R.L., Fonte, C. and Goettler, J.E. (1992) Nasal spray nicotine replacement suppresses cigarette smoking desire and behaviour, *Clinical Pharmacology and Therapeutics*, 52: 627–34.

Perna, F.M. and McDowell, S.L. (1995) Role of psychological stress in cortisol recovery from exhaustive exercise among elite athletes, *International Journal of Behavioural Medicine*, 2: 13–26.

Perquin, B., Baillet, F. and Wilson, J.F. (1976) Radiation therapy in the management of primary breast cancer, *American Journal of Roentgenology*, 127: 645–8.

Peto, R., Lopez, A.D., Boreham, J. et al. (1994) *Mortality from Smoking in Developed Countries 1950–2000*. Oxford: Oxford University Press.

Petrie, K.J., Booth, R.J. and Pennebaker, J.W. (1998) The immunological effects of thought suppression, *Journal of Personality and Social Psychology*, 75: 1264–72.

Petrie, K.J., Booth, R.J., Pennebaker, J.W., Davison, K.P. and Thomas, M.G. (1995) Disclosure of trauma and immune response to a hepatitis B vaccination program, *Journal of Consulting and Clinical Psychology*, 63: 787–92.

Petrie, K.J., Cameron, L.D., Ellis, C.J., Buick, D. and Weinman, J. (2002) Changing illness perceptions after myocardial infarction: an early intervention randomized controlled trial, *Psychosomatic Medicine*, 64: 580–6.

Petrie, K.J., Weinman, J.A., Sharpe, N. and Buckley, J. (1996) Role of patients' view of their illness in predicting return to work and functioning after myocardial infarction: longitudinal study, *British Medical Journal*, 312: 1191–4.

Petronis, V.M., Carver, C.S., Antoni, M.H. and Weiss, S. (2003) Investment in body image and psychosocial well-being among women treated for early stage breast cancer: partial replication and extension, *Psychology and Health*, 18(1): 1–13.

Petticrew, M., Fraser, J.M. and Regan, M. (1999) Adverse life-events and risk of breast cancer: a meta-analysis, *British Journal of Health Psychology*, 4: 1–17.

Petty, R.E. and Cacioppo, J.T. (1986) The elaboration likelihood model of persuasion, in L. Berkowitz (ed.), *Advances in Experimental Social Psychology*, Vol. 19, pp. 123–205. New York: Academic Press.

Piccinelli, M. and Simon, G. (1997) Gender and cross-cultural differences in somatic symptoms associated with emotion distress: an international study in primary care, *Psychological Medicine*, 27(2): 433–44.

Pickering, T.G., Devereux, R.B., James, G.D. et al. (1996) Environmental influences on blood pressure and the role of job strain, *Journal of Hypertension*, 14(suppl.): S179–S85.

Pike, J., Smith, T., Hauger, R. et al. (1997) Chronic life stress alters sympathetic, neuroendocrine and immune responsivity to an acute psychological stressor in humans, *Psychosomatic Medicine*, 59: 447–57.

Pilkonis, P.A., Imler, S.D. and Rubinsky, P. (1985) Dimensions of life stress in psychiatric patients, *Journal of Human Stress*, 11: 5–10.

Pill, R. and Stott, N.C.H. (1982) Concepts of illness causation and responsibility: some preliminary data from a sample of working class mothers, *Social Science and Medicine*, 16: 315–22.

Pinder, K.L., Ramierz, A.J., Black, M.E. et al. (1993) Psychiatric disorder in patients with advanced breast cancer: prevalence and associated factors, *European Journal of Cancer*, 29A: 524–7.

Pliner, P. and Loewen, E.R. (1997) Temperament and food neophobia in children and their mothers, *Appetite*, 28: 239–54.

Polivy, J. and Herman, C.P. (1983) *Breaking the Diet Habit*. New York: Basic Books.

Polivy, J. and Herman, C.P. (1985) Dieting and bingeing: a causal analysis, *American Psychologist*, 40: 193–201.

Polivy, J. and Herman, C.P. (1999) Distress and eating: why do dieters overeat? *International Journal of Eating Disorders*, 26(2): 153–64.

Polivy, J., Herman, C.P. and McFarlane, T. (1994) Effects of anxiety on eating: does palatability moderate distress-induced overeating in dieters? *Journal of Abnormal Psychology*, 103(3): 505–10.

Pomerleau, O.F. and Brady, J.P. (1979) *Behavioral Medicine: Theory and Practice*. Baltimore, MD: Williams & Wilkins.

Povey, R., Conner, M., Sparks, P., James, R. and Shepherd, R. (2000) The theory of planned behaviour and healthy eating: examining additive and moderating effects of social influence variables, *Psychology and Health*, 14: 991–1006.

Powell, D. and Khan, S. (1995) Racial differences in women's desire to be thin, *International Journal of Eating Disorders*, 17: 191–5.

Prentice, A.M. (1995) Are all calories equal? in R. Cottrell (ed.), *Weight Control: The Current Perspective*. London: Chapman & Hall.

Prentice, A.M. and Jebb, S.A. (1995) Obesity in Britain: gluttony or sloth? *British Medical Journal*, 311: 437–9.

Prettyman, R.J., Cordle, C.J. and Cook, G.D. (1993) A three-month follow-up of psychological morbidity after early miscarriage, *British Journal of Medical Psychology*, 66: 363–72.

Price, J.H., Desmond, S. and Kukulka, G. (1985) High school students' perceptions and misperceptions of AIDS, *Journal of School Health*, 55: 107–9.

Pro-choice Alliance (1993) *A Survey of Abortion Patients*. London: Pro-choice Alliance.

Prochaska, J.O. and DiClemente, C.C. (1982) Transtheoretical therapy: toward a more integrative model of change, *Psychotherapy: Theory Research and Practice*, 19: 276–88.

Prochaska, J.O. and DiClemente, C.C. (1984) *The Transtheoretical Approach: Crossing Traditional Boundaries of Therapy.* Homewood, IL: Dow Jones Irwin.

Prochaska, J.O. and Velicer, W.F. (1997) The transtheoretical model of health behaviour change, *American Journal of Health Promotion*, 12: 38–48.

Puska, P., Nissinen, A., Tuomilehto, J. et al. (1985) The community-based strategy to prevent coronary heart disease: conclusions from ten years of the North Karelia Project, in L. Breslow, J.E. Fielding and L.B. Lave (eds), *Annual Review of Public Health*, Vol. 6, pp. 147–94. Palo Alto, CA: Annual Reviews Inc.

Quine, L. and Rubin, R. (1997) Attitude, subjective norm and perceived behavioural control as predictors of women's intentions to take hormone replacement therapy, *British Journal of Health Psychology*, 2: 199–216.

Quine, L., Rutter, D.R. and Arnold, L. (1998) Predicting safety helmet use among schoolboy cyclists: a comparison of the theory of planned behaviour and the health belief model, *Psychology and Health*, 13: 251–69.

Quine, L., Rutter, D.R. and Arnold, L. (2001) Persuading school-age cyclists to use safety helmets: effectiveness of an intervention based on the theory of planned behaviour, *British Journal of Health Psychology*, 6: 327–45.

Raats, M.M., Shepherd, R. and Sparks, P. (1995) Including moral dimensions of choice within the structure of the theory of planned behavior, *Journal of Applied Social Psychology*, 25: 484–94.

Radley, A. (1984) The embodiment of social relation in coronary heart disease, *Social Science and Medicine*, 19: 1227–34.

Radley, A. (1989) *Prospects of Heart Surgery: Psychological Adjustment to Coronary Bypass Grafting.* New York: Springer Verlag.

Radley, A. (1990) Style, discourse and constraint in adjustment to chronic illness, *Sociology of Health and Illness*, 11: 230–52.

Rains, P. (1971) *Becoming an Unwed Mother.* Chicago: Aldine.

Ramirez, A.J., Craig, T.J.K., Watson, J.P. et al. (1989) Stress and relapse of breast cancer, *British Medical Journal*, 298: 291–3.

Ramirez, A.J., Watson, J.P., Richards, M.A. et al. (1992) Life events and breast cancer prognosis: letter to the editor, *British Medical Journal*, 304: 1632.

Ramsay, J.M., McDermott, M.R. and Bray, C. (2001) Components of anger-hostility complex and symptom reporting in patient with coronary artery disease: a multi-measure study, *Journal of Health Psychology*, 6(6): 713–29.

Rand, C.S.W. and MacGregor, A.M.C. (1991) Successful weight loss following obesity surgery and the perceived liability of morbid obesity, *International Journal of Obesity*, 15: 577–9.

Ravussin, E. and Bogardus, C. (1989) Relationship of genetics, age and physical activity to daily energy expenditure and fuel utilisation, *American Journal of Clinical Nutrition*, 49: 968–75.

Rector, T.S., Kubo, S.H. and Cohn, J.N. (1993) Validity of the Minnesota Living with Heart Failure Questionnaire as a measure of therapeutic response: effects of enalapril and placebo, *American Journal of Cardiology*, 71: 1006–7.

Redd, W.H. (1982) Behavioural analysis and control of psychosomatic symptoms in patients receiving intensive cancer treatment, *British Journal of Clinical Psychology*, 21: 351–8.

Redhead, I.H. (1960) The incidence of glycosuria and diabetes mellitus in general practice, *British Medical Journal*, 1: 695.

Reed, G.M., Kemeny, M.E., Taylor, S.E. and Visscher, B.R. (1999) Negative HIV-specific expectancies and AIDS-related bereavement as predictors of symptom onset in asymptomatic HIV-positive gay men, *Health Psychology*, 18: 354–63.

Reed, G.M., Kemeny, M.E., Taylor, S.E., Wang, H.-Y.J. and Visscher, B.R. (1994) Realistic acceptance as a predictor of decreased survival time in gay men with AIDS, *Health Psychology*, 13: 299–307.

Reelick, N.F., DeHaes, W.F.M. and Schuurman, J.H. (1984) Psychological side effects of the mass screening on cervical cancer, *Social Science and Medicine*, 18: 1089–93.

Reiss, I.L., Banwart, A. and Foreman, H. (1975) Premarital contraceptive usage: a study and some theoretical explorations, *Journal of Marriage and the Family*, 37: 619–30.

Reiss, I.L. and Leik, R.K. (1989) Evaluating strategies to avoid AIDS: numbers of partners versus use of condoms, *Journal of Sex Research*, 26: 411–33.

Repetti, R.L. (1993) Short-term effects of occupational stressors on daily mood and health complaints, *Health Psychology*, 12: 125–31.

Resnicow, K., Davis-Hearn, M., Smith, M. et al. (1997) Social cognitive predictors of fruit and vegetable intake in children, *Health Psychology*, 16: 272–6.

Reynolds, B.D., Puck, M.H. and Robertson, A. (1974) Genetic counselling: an appraisal, *Clinical Genetics*, 5: 177–87.

Richard, R. and van der Pligt, J. (1991) Factors affecting condom use among adolescents, *Journal of Community and Applied Social Psychology*, 1: 105–16.

Riddle, P.K. (1980) Attitudes, beliefs, intentions, and behaviours of men and women toward regular jogging, *Research Quarterly for Exercise and Sport*, 51: 663–74.

Riegel, B.J. (1993) Contributions to cardiac invalidism after acute myocardial infarction, *Coronary Artery Disease*, 4: 569–78.

Rimer, B.K., Trock, B., Lermon, C. et al. (1991) Why do some women get regular mammograms? *American Journal of Preventative Medicine*, 7: 69–74.

Rippetoe, P.A. and Rogers, R.W. (1987) Effects of components of protection-motivation theory on adaptive and maladaptive coping with a health threat, *Journal of Personality and Social Psychology*, 52: 596–604.

Risdon, A., Eccleston, C., Crombez, G. and McCracken, L. (2003) How can we learn to live with pain? A Q-methodological analysis of the diverse understandings of acceptance of chronic pain, *Social Science and Medicine*, 56(2): 375–86.

Rissanen, A.M., Heliovaara, M., Knekt, P., Reunanen, A. and Aromaa, A. (1991) Determinants of weight gain and overweight in adult Finns, *European Journal of Clinical Nutrition*, 45: 419–30.

Robinson, G.E., Olmsted, M.P., Garner, D.M. and Gare, D.J. (1988) Transition to parenthood in elderly primiparas, *Journal of Psychosomatic Obstetrics and Gynaecology*, 9: 89–101.

Rodgers, W.M., Hall, C.R., Blanchard, C.M, McAuley, E. and Munroe, C. (2002) Task and scheduling self-efficacy as predictors of exercise behaviour, *Psychology and Health*, 17(4): 405–16.

Rodin, J., Bray, G.A., Atkinson, R.L., Dahms, W.T., Greenway, F.L., Hamilton, K. and Molitch, M. (1977) Predictors of successful weight loss in an outpatient obesity clinic, *International Journal of Obesity*, 1: 79–87.

Rogers, R.W. (1975) A protection motivation theory of fear appeals and attitude change, *Journal of Psychology*, 91: 93–114.

Rogers, R.W. (1983) Cognitive and physiological processes in fear appeals and attitude change: a revised theory of protection motivation, in J.R. Cacioppo and R.E. Petty (eds), *Social Psychology: A Source Book*, pp. 153–76. New York: Guilford Press.

Rogers, R.W. (1985) Attitude change and information integration in fear appeals, *Psychological Reports*, 56: 179–82.

Romero-Corral, A.R., Montori, V.M., Somers, V.K., Korinek, J., Thomas, R.J., Allison, T.G., Mookadam, F. and Jimenez, F.L. (2006) Association of body weight with total mortality and with cardiovascular events in coronary artery disease: a systematic review of cohort studies, *Lancet*, 368: 666–78.

Rosenberg, M. (1965) *Society and the Adolescent Self-image.* Princeton, NJ: Princeton University Press.

Rosenfeld, J.A. (1992) Emotional responses to therapeutic abortion, *American Family Physician*, 45: 137–40.

Rosenman, R.H. (1978) Role of type A pattern in the pathogenesis of ischaemic heart disease and modification for prevention, *Advances in Cardiology*, 25: 34–46.

Rosenman, R.H., Brand, R.J., Jenkins, C.D. et al. (1975) Coronary heart disease in the western collaborative heart study: final follow-up experience of $8\frac{1}{2}$ years, *Journal of the American Medical Association*, 233: 872–7.

Rosenstock, I.M. (1966) Why people use health services, *Millbank Memorial Fund Quarterly*, 44: 94–124.

Roskies, E., Seraganian, P., Oseasohn, R. et al. (1986) The Montreal type A intervention project: major findings, *Health Psychology*, 5: 45–69.

Ross, C.E. (1994) Overweight and depression, *Journal of Health and Social Behaviour*, 35: 63–78.

Ross, M. and Olson, J.M. (1981) An expectancy attribution model of the effects of placebos, *Psychological Review*, 88: 408–37.

Ross, S. and Buckalew, L.W. (1983) The placebo as an agent in behavioural manipulation: a review of the problems, issues and affected measures, *Clinical Psychology Review*, 3: 457–71.

Rossner, S., Sjostrom, L., Noak, R., Meinders, A.E. and Noseda, G. (2000) Weight loss, weight maintenance and improved cardiovascular risk factors after 2 years' treatment with Orlistat for obesity, *Obesity Research*, 8: 49–61.

Roter, D.L., Steward, M., Putnam, S.M. et al. (1997) Communication pattern of primary care physicians, *Journal of the American Medical Association*, 277: 350–6.

Roth, H.P. (1979) Problems in conducting a study of the effects of patient compliance of teaching the rationale for antacid therapy, in S.J. Cohen (ed.), *New Directions in Patient Compliance*, pp. 111–26. Lexington, MA: Lexington Books.

Roth, S. and Cohen, L.J. (1986) Approach avoidance and coping with stress, *American Psychologist*, 41: 813–19.

Rozin, P. (1976) *The Selection of Foods by Rats, Humans, and Other Animal: Advances in the Study of Behavior.* New York: Academic Press.

Rubin, R. and Quine, L. (1995) Women's attitudes to the menopause and the use of Hormone Replacement Therapy. Paper presented at the conference of the British Psychological Society, London.

Ruble, D.N. (1977) Premenstrual symptoms: a reinterpretation, *Science*, 197: 291–2.

Rucker, C.E. and Cash, T. (1992) Body images, body size perceptions and eating behaviors among African-American and white college women, *International Journal of Eating Disorders*, 12: 291–9.

Ruderman, A.J. and Wilson, G.T. (1979) Weight, restraint, cognitions and counterregulation, *Behaviour Research and Therapy*, 17: 581–90.

Russell, M.A.H., Wilson, C., Taylor, C. and Baker, C.D. (1979) Effect of general practitioners' advice against smoking, *British Medical Journal*, 2: 231–5.

Russell, W.D., Dzewaltowski, D.A. and Ryan, G.J. (1999) The effectiveness of a point-of-decision prompt in deterring sedentary behaviour, *American Journal of Health Promotion*, 13: 257–9.

Russo, N.F. and Zierk, K.I. (1992) Abortion, childbearing, and women's well-being, *Professional Psychology: Research and Practice*, 23: 269–80.

Rutter, D.R. and Quine, L. (2002) *Changing Health Behaviour: Intervention and Research with Social Cognition Models.* Buckingham: Open University Press.

Ryan, L., Ripper, M. and Buttfield, B. (1994) *We Women Decide: Women's Experience of Seeking Abortion in Queensland, South Australia and Tasmania 1985–1992.* Adelaide: Flinders University.

Rymer, J. and Morris, E.P. (2002) Extracts from clinical evidence: menopausal symptoms, *British Medical Journal,* 321(15): 16–19.

Rymer, J., Wilson, R. and Ballard, K. (2003) Making decisions about hormone replacement therapy, *British Medical Journal,* 326(7384): 322–6.

Sackett, D.L. and Holland, W.W. (1975) Controversy in the detection of disease, *Lancet,* ii: 357–9.

Sairam, S., Khare, M., Michailidis, G. and Thilaganathan, B. (2001) The role of ultrasound in the expectant management of early pregnancy loss, *Ultrasound in Obstetrics and Gynecology,* 17: 506–9.

Sala, F., Krupat, E. and Rother, D. (2002) Satisfaction and the use of humour by physicians and patients, *Psychology and Health,* 17: 269–80.

Sallis, J.F., Haskell, W.L., Fortmann, S.P. et al. (1986) Predictors of adoption and maintenance of physical activity in a community sample, *Preventive Medicine,* 15: 331–41.

Salonen, J.T., Puska, P. and Tuomilehto, J. (1982) Physical activity and risk of myocardial infarction, cerebral stroke and death: a longitudinal study in eastern Finland, *American Journal of Epidemiology,* 115: 526–37.

Sanders, C., Egger, M., Donovan, J., Tallon, D. and Frankel, S. (1998) Reporting on quality of life in randomised controlled trials: bibliographic study, *British Medical Journal,* 317: 1191–4.

Santi, S., Best, J.A., Brown, K.S. and Cargo, M. (1991) Social environment and smoking initiation, *International Journal of the Addictions,* 25: 881–903.

Sarason, I.G., Levine, H.M., Basham, R.B. et al. (1983) Assessing social support: the social support questionnaire, *Journal of Personality and Social Psychology,* 44: 127–39.

Sarason, I.G., Sarason, B.R., Shearin, E.N. and Pierce, G.R. (1987) A brief measure of social support: practical and theoretical implications, *Journal of Social and Personal Relationships,* 4: 497–510.

Savage, R. and Armstrong, D. (1990) Effect of a general practitioner's consulting style on patients' satisfaction: a controlled study, *British Medical Journal,* 301: 968–70.

Scalley, G. and Hadley, A. (1995) Accessibility of sexual health services for young people: survey of clinics in a region, *Journal of Management in Medicine,* 9(4): 51–2.

Scambler, A., Scambler, G. and Craig, D. (1981) Kinship and friendship networks and women's demands for primary care, *Journal of the Royal College of General Practice,* 26: 746–50.

Schachter, S. (1968) Obesity and eating, *Science,* 161: 751–6.

Schachter, S. and Gross, L. (1968) Manipulated time and eating behaviour, *Journal of Personality and Social Psychology,* 10: 98–106.

Schachter, S. and Rodin, J. (1974) *Obese Humans and Rats.* Potomac, MD: Erlbaum.

Schaefer, C., Quesenberry, C.P. Jr and Wi, S. (1995) Mortality following conjugal bereavement and the effects of a shared environment, *American Journal of Epidemiology,* 141: 1142–52.

Scheiderich, S.D., Freidbaum, D.M. and Peterson, L.M. (1983) Registered nurses' knowledge about diabetes mellitus, *Diabetes Care,* 6: 57–61.

Schifter, D.A. and Ajzen, I. (1985) Intention, perceived control, and weight loss: an application of the theory of planned behavior, *Journal of Personality and Social Psychology,* 49: 843–51.

Schmidt, L.R. and Frohling, H. (2000) Lay concepts of health and illness from a developmental perspective, *Psychology and Health,* 15: 229–38.

Schnall, P.L., Schwartz, J.E., Landsbergis, P.A., Warren, K. and Pickering, T.G. (1998) A longitudinal study of job strain and ambulatory blood pressure: results from a three-year follow-up, *Psychosomatic Medicine,* 60: 697–706.

Schuckit, M.A. (1985) Genetics and the risk for alcoholism, *Journal of the American Medical Association,* 254: 2614–17.

Schwarcz, S., Kellogg, T., McFarland, W., Louie, B., Kohn, R., Busch, M., Katz, M., Bolan, G., Klausner, J. and Weinstock, H. (2001) Differences in the temporal trends of HIV seroincidence and seroprevalence among sexually transmitted disease clinic patients, 1989–1998: application of the serologic testing algorithm for recent HIV seroconversion, *American Journal of Epidemiology*, 153(10): 925–34.

Schwartz, G.E. and Weiss, S.M. (1977) *Yale Conference on Behavioral Medicine*. Washington, DC: Department of Health, Education and Welfare; National Heart, Lung, and Blood Institute.

Schwartz, J.L. (1987) *Review and Evaluation of Smoking Cessation Methods: The United States and Canada, 1978–1985*, NIH Pub. No. 87–2940. Washington, DC: National Cancer Institute.

Schwarzer, R. (ed.) (1992) *Self Efficacy: Thought Control of Action*. Washington, DC: Hemisphere.

Schwarzer, R., Jerusalem, M. and Hahn, A. (1994) Unemployment, social support and health complaints: a longitudinal study of stress in East German refugees, *Journal of Community and Applied Social Psychology*, 4: 31–45.

Segal, L. (1994) *Straight Sex: The Politics of Pleasure*. London: Virago.

Seguin, L., Therrien, R., Champagne, F. and Larouche, D. (1989) The components of women's satisfaction with maternity care, *Birth*, 16: 109–13.

Seligman, M.E.P. and Csikszentmihalyi, M. (2000) Positive psychology: an introduction, *American Psychology*, 55: 5–14.

Seligman, M.E.P. and Visintainer, M.A. (1985) Turnout rejection and early experience of uncontrollable shock in the rat, in F.R. Brush and J.B. Overmier (eds), *Affect Conditioning and Cognition: Essays on the Determinants of Behavior*. Hillstate, NJ: Erlbaum.

Seligman, M.E.P., Peterson, C. and Vaillant, G.E. (1988) Pessimistic explanatory style is a risk factor for illness: a 35 year longitudinal study, *Journal of Personality and Social Psychology*, 55: 23–7.

Selvini, M. (1988) Self-starvation: the last synthesis on anorexia nervosa, in M. Selvini and M. Selvini Palazzoli (eds), *The Work of Mara Selvini Palazzoli*, pp. 147–50. New Jersey: Jason Aronson.

Selye, H. (1956) *The Stress of Life*. New York: McGraw-Hill.

Senior, V. and Marteau, T.M. (2006) Causal attributions for raised cholesterol and perceptions of effective risk-reduction: self-regulation strategies for an increased risk of coronary heart disease, *Psychology & Health* (in press).

Senior, V., Marteau, T.M. and Weinman, J. (2000) Impact of genetic testing on causal models of heart disease and arthritis: an analogue study, *Psychology and Health*, 14: 1077–88.

Seydel, E., Taal, E. and Wiegman, O. (1990) Risk appraisal, outcome and self efficacy expectancies: cognitive factors in preventative behaviour related to cancer, *Psychology and Health*, 4: 99–109.

Shaffer, J.W., Graves, P.L., Swank, R.T. and Pearson, T.A. (1987) Clustering of personality traits in youth and the subsequent development of cancer among physicians, *Journal of Behavioural Medicine*, 10: 441–7.

Shafi, M.I. (1994) Management of women with mild dyskaryosis: cytological surveillance avoids overtreatment, *British Medical Journal*, 309: 590–2.

Shapiro, S. (1977) Evidence on screening for breast cancer from a randomised trial, *Cancer*, 39: 2772–82.

Shapiro, S., Strax, P., Venet, L. and Venet, W. (1972) Changes in 5-year breast cancer mortality in a breast cancer screening programme, in *Seventh National Cancer Conference Proceedings*. New York: American Cancer Society.

Shapiro, S., Venet, W., Strax, P. et al. (1982) Ten to fourteen year effects of breast cancer screening on mortality, *Journal of the National Cancer Institute*, 62: 340–54.

Shaw, C., Abrams, K. and Marteau, T.M. (1999) Psychological impact of predicting individuals' risk of illness: a systematic review, *Social Science and Medicine*, 49: 1571–98.

Shea, S., Basch, C.E., Lantigua, R. and Wechsler, H. (1992) The Washington Heights-Inwood

Healthy Heart Program: a third generation community-based cardiovascular disease prevention program in a disadvantaged urban setting, *Preventive Medicine*, 21: 201–17.

Sheeran, P., Abraham, C. and Orbell, S. (1999) Psychosocial correlates of heterosexual condom use: a meta-analysis, *Psychological Bulletin*, 125: 90–132.

Sheeran, P. and Orbell, S. (1998) Implementation intentions and repeated behaviour: augmenting the predictive validity of the theory of planned behaviour, *European Journal of Social Psychology*, 28: 1–21.

Sheeran, P. and Orbell, S. (2000) Using implementation intentions to increase attendance for cervical cancer screening, *Health Psychology*, 19: 283–9.

Sheeran, P. and Taylor, S. (1999) Predicting intentions to use condoms: a meta-analysis and comparison of the theories of reasoned action and planned behaviour, *Journal of Applied Social Psychology*, 29: 1624–75.

Sheeran, P., White, D. and Phillips, K. (1991) Premarital contraceptive use: a review of the psychological literature, *Journal of Reproductive and Infant Psychology*, 9: 253–69.

Sheilds, J.S. (1962) *Monozygotic Twins: Brought up Apart and Brought up Together*. London: Oxford University Press.

Shepherd, R. (1988) Belief structure in relation to low-fat milk consumption, *Journal of Human Nutrition and Dietetics*, 1: 421–8.

Shepherd, R. (ed.) (1989) *Handbook of the Psychophysiology of Human Eating*. Chichester: Wiley.

Shepherd, R. and Farleigh, C.A. (1986) Attitudes and personality related to salt intake, *Appetite*, 7: 343–54.

Shepherd, R. and Stockley, L. (1985) Fat consumption and attitudes towards food with a high fat content, *Human Nutrition: Applied Nutrition*, 39A: 431–42.

Shepherd, R. and Stockley, L. (1987) Nutrition knowledge, attitudes, and fat consumption, *Journal of the American Dietetic Association*, 87: 615–19.

Sheppard, B.H., Hartwick, J. and Warshaw, P.R. (1988) The theory of reasoned action: a meta analysis of past research with recommendations for modifications and future research, *Journal of Consumer Research*, 15: 325–43.

Shepperd, S., Harwood, D., Jenkinson, C. et al. (1998) Randomised controlled trial comparing hospital at home care with inpatient hospital care. I: Three month follow up of health outcomes, *British Medical Journal*, 316: 1786–91.

Shereshefsky, P.M. and Yarrow, L.J. (eds) (1973) *Psychological Aspects of a First Pregnancy and Early Postnatal Adaptation*. New York: Raven Press.

Sherman, D.A.K., Nelson, L.D. and Steele, C.M. (2000) Do messages about health risks threaten the self? Increasing the acceptance of threatening health messages via self-affirmation, *Personality and Social Psychology Bulletin*, 26: 1046–58.

Sherman, S.J., Barton, J., Chassin, L. and Pressin, C.C. (1982) Social image factors as motivators of smoking initiation in early and middle adolescence, *Child Development*, 53: 1499–511.

Sherr, L. (1987) An evaluation of the UK government health education campaign on AIDS, *Psychology and Health*, 1: 61–72.

Shiloh, S., Vinter, M. and Barak, A. (1997) Correlates of health screening utilisation: the roles of health beliefs and self-regulation motivation, *Psychology and Health*, 12: 301–17.

Shontz, F.C. (1975) *The Psychological Aspects of Physical Illness and Disability*. New York: Macmillan.

Shy, K.K., Luthy, D.A., Whitfield, M. et al. (1990) Effects of electronic fetal-heart-rate monitoring, as compared with periodic auscultation, on the neurologic development of premature infants, *New England Journal of Medicine*, 322: 588–93.

Sibinga, M.S. and Friedman, C.J. (1971) Complexities of parental understanding of phenylketonuria, *Paediatrics*, 48: 216–24.

Siegel, K., Raveis, V.H. and Krauss, J. et al. (1992) Factors associated with gay men's treatment initiation decisions for HIV-infection, *AIDS Education and Prevention*, 4(2): 135–42.

Siegman, A.W. and Snow, S.C. (1997) The outward expression of anger, the inward experience of anger and CVR: the role of vocal expression, *Journal of Behavioural Medicine*, 20: 29–46.

Siegman, A.W., Townsend, S.T., Civelek, A.C. and Blumenthal, R.S. (2000) Antagonistic behaviour, dominance, hostility and coronary heart disease, *Psychosomatic Medicine*, 62: 248–57.

Simkins, L. and Ebenhage, M. (1984) Attitudes towards AIDS, herpes II and toxic shock syndrome, *Psychological Reports*, 55: 779–86.

Simms, A. (1985) Legal abortion in Great Britain, in H. Homans (ed.), *The Sexual Politics of Reproduction*. Aldershot: Gower.

Simon, G.E., Von Korff, M., Saunders, K., Miglioretti, D.L., Crane, P.K., van Belle, G. and Kessler, R.C. (2006) Association between obesity and psychiatric disorders in the US adult population, *Archives of General Psychiatry*, 63: 824–30.

Simon, N. (1977) Breast cancer induced by radiation, *Journal of the American Medical Association*, 237: 789–90.

Simonton, O.C. and Simonton, S.S. (1975) Belief systems and the management of emotional aspects of malignancy, *Journal of Transpersonal Psychology*, 7: 29–47.

Simpson, W.M., Johnston, M. and McEwan, S.R. (1997) Screening for risk factors for cardiovascular disease: a psychological perspective, *Scottish Medical Journal*, 42: 178–81.

Sjostrom, L. (1980) Fat cells and body weight, in A.J. Stunkard (ed.), *Obesity*, pp. 72–100. Philadelphia, PA: Saunders.

Sjostrom, L., Rissanen, A., Andersen, T. et al. (1998) Randomised placebo controlled trial of orlistat for weight loss and prevention of weight regain in obese patients, *Lancet*, 352: 167–72.

Skelton, J.A. and Pennebaker, J.W. (1982) The psychology of physical symptoms and sensations, in G.S. Sanders and J. Suls (eds), *Social Psychology of Health and Illness*. Hillsdale, NJ: Erlbaum.

Skevington, S. (1998) Investigating the relationship between pain and discomfort and quality of life, using the WHOQoL, *Pain*, 76: 395–406.

Skevington, S. (1999) Measuring quality of life in Britain: introducing the WHOQoL-100, *Journal of Psychosomatic Research*, 47(5): 449–59.

Skevington, S. and O'Connell, K. (2003) Measuring quality of life in HIV and AIDS: a review of the recent literature, *Psychology and Health*, 18(3): 331–50.

Skevington, S., Carse, M.S. and Williams, A.C. de C. (2001) Validation of the WHOQoL-100: pain management improves quality of life in chronic pain patients, *The Clinical Journal of Pain*, 17: 264–75.

Skevington, S., O'Connell, K.A. and the WHOQoL group (2004a) Can we identify the poorest quality of life? Assessing the importance of quality of life using the WHOQoL-100, *Quality of Life Research*, 13: 23–34.

Skevington, S., Sortarius, N., Amir, M. and the WHOQoL group (2004b) Developing methods for assessing quality of life in different cultural settings, *Social Psychiatry and Psychiatric Epidemiology*, 39: 1–8.

Sklar, S.L. and Anisman, H. (1981) Stress and cancer, *Psychological Bulletin*, 89(3): 369–406.

Skrabanek, P. (1988) The physician's responsibility to the patient, *Lancet*, 1: 1155–7.

Slade, P., Heke, S., Fletcher, J. and Stewart, P. (1998) A comparison of medical and surgical termination of pregnancy: choice, emotional impact and satisfaction with care, *British Journal of Obstetrics and Gynaecology*, 105(12): 1288–95.

Slade, P. and Russell, G.F.M. (1973) Awareness of body dimensions in anorexia nervosa: cross-sectional and longitudinal studies, *Psychological Medicine*, 3: 188–99.

Slade, P., Heke, S., Fletcher, J. and Stewart, P. (2001) Termination of pregnancy: patients' perceptions of care, *The Journal of Family Planning and Reproductive Health Care*, 27: 72–7.

Smart, L. and Wegner, D.M. (1999) Covering up what can't be seen: concealable stigma and mental control, *Journal of Personality and Social Psychology*, 77: 474–86.

Smedslund, G. (2000) A pragmatic basis for judging models and theories in health psychology: the axiomatic method, *Journal of Health Psychology*, 5: 133–49.

Smith, A. and Chamberlain, J. (1987) Managing cervical screening, in *Institute of Health Service Management: Information Technology in Health Care*. London: Kluwer Academic.

Smith, A. and Jacobson, B. (1989) *The Nation's Health*. London: The King's Fund.

Smith, G.S. and Kraus, J.F. (1988) Alcohol and residential, recreational, and occupational injuries: a review of the epidemiologic evidence, in L. Breslow, J.E. Fielding and L.B. Lave (eds), *Annual Review of Public Health*, Vol. 9. Palo Alto, CA: Annual Reviews.

Smith, J.A. (1994a) Pregnancy and the transition to motherhood, in P. Nicolson and J. Ussher (eds), *The Psychology of Women's Health and Health Care*, pp. 175–99. London: Macmillan.

Smith, J.A. (1994b) Reconstructive selves: an analysis of discrepancies between women's contemporaneous and retrospective accounts of the transition to motherhood, *British Journal of Psychology*, 85: 371–92.

Smith, J.A. (1999) Towards a relational self: social engagement during pregnancy and psychological preparation for motherhood, *British Journal of Social Psychology*, 38: 409–26.

Smith, J.A. (2007) Pain as an assault on the self: an interpretative phenomenological analysis of the psychological impact of chronic benign low back pain, *Psychology and Health* (in press).

Smith, J.A. and Osborn, M. (2003) Interpretative phenomenological analysis, in J.A. Smith (ed.), *Qualitative Psychology*, pp. 51–80. London: Sage.

Smith, J.A., Michie, S., Stephenson, M. and Quarrell, O. (2002) Risk perception and decisionmaking processes in candidates for genetic testing for Huntington's disease: an interpretative phenomenological analysis, *Journal of Health Psychology*, 7(3): 131–44.

Smith, L.M., Mullis, R.L. and Hill, W.E. (1995) Identity strivings within the mother–daughter relationship, *Psychological Reports*, 76: 495–503.

Smith, R.A., Williams, D.K., Silbert, J.R. and Harper, P.S. (1990) Attitudes of mothers to neonatal screening for Duchenne muscular dystrophy, *British Medical Journal*, 300: 1112.

Smyth, J.M. (1998) Written emotional expression: effect sizes, outcome types and moderating variables, *Journal of Consulting and Clinical Psychology*, 66: 174–84.

Sobel, M.B. and Sobel, L.C. (1976) Second year treatment outcome of alcoholics treated by individualized behaviour therapy: results, *Behaviour Research and Therapy*, 14: 195–215.

Sobel, M.B. and Sobel, L.C. (1978) *Behavioral Treatment of Alcohol Problems*. New York: Plenum.

Sodegren, S.C. and Hyland, M.E. (2000) What are the positive consequences of illness? *Psychology and Health*, 15: 85–97.

Söderberg, H., Janzon, L. and Sjöberg, N.O. (1998) Emotional distress following induced abortion: a study of its incidence and determinants among abortees in Malmö, Sweden, *European Journal of Obstetrics and Gynecology, and Reproductive Biology*, 79: 173–8.

Sodergren, S.C., Hyland, M.E., Singh, S.J. and Sewell, L. (2002) The effect of rehabilitation on positive interpretations of illness, *Psychology and Health*, 17(6): 753–60.

Sodroski, J.G., Rosen, C.A. and Haseltine, W.A. (1984) Transacting transcription of the long terminal repeat of human T lymphocyte viruses in infected cells, *Science*, 225: 381–5.

Soetens, B., Braet, C., Dejonckheere, P. and Roets, A. (2006) When suppression backfires: the ironic effects of suppressing eating-related thoughts, *Journal of Health Psychology*, 11(5): 655–68.

Solano, L., Costa, M., Temoshok, L. et al. (2002) An emotionally inexpressive (Type C) coping style influences HIV disease progression at six and twelve month follow-up, *Psychology and Health*, 17(5): 641–55.

Solano, L., Montella, F., Salvati, S. et al. (2001) Expression and processing of emotions: relationship with CD4+ levels in 42 HIV-positive asymptomatic individuals, *Psychology and Health*, 16: 689–98.

Solomon, G.F. and Temoshok, L. (1987) A psychoneuroimmunologic perspective on AIDS research: questions, preliminary findings, and suggestions, *Journal of Applied Social Psychology*, 17: 286–308.

Solomon, G.F., Temoshok, L., O'Leary, A. and Zich, J.A. (1987) An intensive psychoimmunologic study of long-surviving persons with AIDS: pilot work background studies, hypotheses, and methods, *Annals of the New York Academy of Sciences*, 46: 647–55.

Sonstroem, R. (1988) Psychological models, in R.K. Dishman (ed.), *Exercise Adherence: Its Impact on Public Health*. Champaign, IL: Human Kinetics.

Sontag, S. (1988) *Illness as Metaphor*. Harmondsworth: Penguin.

Soutter, W.P. and Fletcher, A. (1994) Invasive cancer in women with mild dyskaryosis followed cytologically, *British Medical Journal*, 308: 1421–3.

Sparks, P. (1994) Food choice and health: applying, assessing, and extending the theory of planned behaviour, in D.R. Rutter and L. Quine (eds), *Social Psychology and Health: European Perspectives*, pp. 25–46. Aldershot: Avebury.

Sparks, P. and Shepherd, R. (1992) Self-identify and the theory of planned behavior: assessing the role of identification with green consumerism, *Social Psychology Quarterly*, 55: 1388–99.

Sparks, P., Conner, M., James, R., Shepherd, R. and Povey, R. (2001) Ambivalence about health-related behaviours: an exploration in the domain of food choice, *British Journal of Health Psychology*, 6: 53–68.

Sparks, P., Hedderley, D. and Shepherd, R. (1992) An investigation into the relationship between perceived control, attitude variability and the consumption of two common foods, *European Journal of Social Psychology*, 22: 55–71.

Speisman, J.C., Lazarus, R.S., Mordko, A. and Davison, L. (1964) Experimental reduction of stress based on ego defense theory, *Journal of Abnormal and Social Psychology*, 68: 367–80.

Spencer, J.A. and Fremouw, M.J. (1979) Binge eating as a function of restraint and weight classification, *Journal of Abnormal Psychology*, 88: 262–7.

Spera, S.P., Buhrfeind, E.D. and Pennebaker, J.W. (1994) Expressive writing and coping with job loss, *Academy of Management Journal*, 37: 722–33.

Spitzer, L. and Rodin, J. (1981) Human eating behaviour: a critical review of studies in normal weight and overweight individuals, *Appetite*, 2: 293–329.

Stacey, M. (1988) *The Sociology of Health and Healing*. London: Routledge.

Stanton, A.L. (1987) Determinants of adherence to medical regimens by hypertensive patients, *Journal of Behavioral Medicine*, 10: 377–94.

Steele, C.M. (1988) The psychology of self-affirmation: sustaining the integrity of the self, in L. Berkowitz (ed.), *Advances in Experimental Social Psychology*, 21, pp. 261–302. New York: Academic Press.

Steer, C., Campbell, S., Davies, M., Mason, B. and Collins, W.P. (1989) Spontaneous abortion rates after natural and assisted conception, *British Medical Journal*, 299: 1317–18.

Stegen, K., Van Diest, I., Van De Woestijne, K.P. and Van Den Berch, O. (2000) Negative affectivity and bodily sensations induced by 5.5% CO_2 enriched air inhalation: is there a bias to interpret bodily sensations negatively in persons with negative affect? *Psychology and Health*, 15: 513–25.

Steiger, H., Stotland, S., Ghadirian, A.M. and Whitehead, V. (1994) Controlled study of eating concerns and psychopathological traits in relatives of eating-disordered probands: do familial traits exist? *International Journal of Eating Disorders*, 18: 107–18.

Steinberg, H. and Sykes, E.A. (1985) Introduction to symposium on endorphins and behavioral processes: review of literature on endorphins and exercise, *Pharmacology, Biochemistry and Behaviour*, 23: 857–62.

Steinberg, J. (2001) Many undertreated HIV-infected patients decline potent antiretroviral therapy, *AIDS Patient Care*, 15: 185–91.

Steptoe, A., Kearsley, N. and Walters, N. (1993) Acute mood responses to maximal and submaximal exercise in active and inactive men, *Psychology and Health*, 8: 89–99.

Steptoe, A., Lundwall, K. and Cropley, M. (2000) Gender, family structure and cardiovascular activity during the working day and evening, *Social Science and Medicine*, 50: 531–9.

Stern, J.S. (1984) Is obesity a disease of inactivity? in A.J. Stunkard and E. Stellar (eds), *Eating and Its Disorders*. New York: Raven Press.

Sternbach, R.A. (ed.) (1978) *The Psychology of Pain*. New York: Raven Press.

Stewart, A.L. and Ware, J.E. (eds) (1992) *Measuring Functioning and Well Being: The Medical Outcomes Study Approach*. Durham, NC: Duke University Press.

Stewart, W.F., Lipton, R.B. and Liberman, J. (1996) Variation in migraine prevalence by race, *Neurology*, 47: 52–9.

Stiles, W.B. (1978) Verbal response models and dimensions of interpersonal roles: a method of discourse analysis, *Journal of Personality and Social Psychology*, 36: 693–703.

Stoate, H. (1989) Can health screening damage your health? *Journal of the Royal College of General Practitioners*, 39: 193–5.

Stokes, J. and Rigotti, N. (1988) The health consequences of cigarette smoking and the internist's role in smoking cessation, *Annals of Internal Medicine*, 33: 431–60.

Stone, A.A. and Brownell, K.D. (1994) The stress-eating paradox: multiple daily measurements in adult males and females, *Psychology and Health*, 9: 425–36.

Stone, A.A. and Neale, J.M. (1984) New measure of daily coping: development and preliminary results, *Journal of Personality and Social Psychology*, 46: 892–906.

Stone, A.A., Cox, D.S., Valdimarsdottir, H., Jandorf, L. and Neale, J.M. (1987) Evidence that secretory IgA antibody is associated with daily mood, *Journal of Personality and Social Psychology*, 52: 988–93.

Stone, N. and Ingham, R. (2000) *Young People's Sex Advice Services: Delays, Triggers and Contraceptive Use*. London: Brook Publications.

Stone, N. and Ingham, R. (2002) Factors affecting British teenagers' contraceptive use at first intercourse: the importance of partner communication, *Perspectives on Sexual and Reproductive Health*, 34(4): 191–7.

Stone, N. and Ingham, R. (2003) When and why do young people in the United Kingdom first use sexual health services? *Perspectives on Sexual and Reproductive Health*, 35(3): 114–20.

Stone, N., Hatherall, B., Ingham, R. and McEachran, J. (2006) Oral sex and condom use among young people in the United Kingdom, *Perspectives on Sexual and Reproductive Health*, 38(1): 6–12.

Stoney, C.M. and Finney, M.L. (2000) Social support and stress: influences on lipid reactivity, *International Journal of Behavioural Medicine*, 7: 111–26.

Stoney, C.M., Davis, M.C. and Mathews, K.A. (1987) Sex differences in physiological responses to stress and coronary heart disease: a causal link? *Psychophysiology*, 24: 127–31.

Stoney, C.M., Mathews, K.A., McDonald, R.H. and Johnson, C.A. (1990) Sex differences in acute stress response: lipid, lipoprotein, cardiovascular and neuroendocrine adjustments, *Psychophysiology*, 12: 52–61.

Story, M., French, S., Resnick, M. and Blum, R. (1995) Ethnic/racial and socioeconomic differences in dieting behaviours and body image perceptions in adolescents, *International Journal of Eating Disorders*, 18: 173–9.

Strax, P. (1978) Evaluation of screening programs for the early diagnosis of breast cancer, *Surgical Clinics of North America*, 58: 667–79.

Striegel-Moore, R.H., Shrieber, B., Pike, M., Wiley, E. and Rodin, J. (1995) Drive for thinness in black and white preadolescent girls, *International Journal of Eating Disorders*, 18: 59.

Striegel-Moore, R.H., Silberstein, L. and Rodin, J. (1986) Towards an understanding of risk factors for bulimia, *American Psychologist*, 41: 246–63.

Stroop, J.R. (1935) Studies of interference in serial verbal reactions, *Journal of Experimental Psychology*, 18: 643–62.

Stuart, R.B. (1967) Behavioural control of overeating, *Behaviour Research and Therapy*, 5: 357–65.

Stuart, R.B. and Davis, B. (1972) *Slim Chance in a Fat World: Behavioral Control of Obesity*. Champaign, IL: Research Press.

Stuart, R.B. and Guire, K. (1978) Some correlates of the maintenance of weight lost through behaviour modification, *International Journal of Obesity*, 2: 225–35.

Stunkard, A.J. (1958) The management of obesity, *New York State Journal of Medicine*, 58: 79–87.

Stunkard, A.J. (1984) The current status of treatment for obesity in adults, in A.J. Stunkard and E. Stellar (eds) *Eating and Its Disorders*. New York: Raven Press.

Stunkard, A.J., Harris, J.R., Pedersen, N.L. and McClearn, G.E. (1990) A separated twin study of body mass index, *New England Journal of Medicine*, 322: 1483–7.

Stunkard, A.J., Harris, J.R. and Schulsinger, F. (1983) Use of the Danish adoption register for the study of obesity and thinness, in S. Kety et al. (eds), *The Genetics of Neurological and Psychiatric Disorders*, pp. 115–20. New York: Raven Press.

Stunkard, A.J., Sorenson, T.I.A., Hanis, C. et al. (1986) An adoption study of human obesity, *New England Journal of Medicine*, 314: 193–8.

Stunkard, A.J., Stinnett, J.L. and Smoller, J.W. (1986) Psychological and social aspects of the surgical treatment of obesity, *American Journal of Psychiatry*, 143: 417–29.

Suarez, E.C, Williams, R.B., Kuhn, C.M. et al. (1991) Biobehavioural basis of coronary-prone behaviour in middle-aged man. Part II: Serum cholesterol, the Type A behaviour pattern and hostility as interactive modulators of physiological reactivity, *Psychosomatic Medicine*, 53: 528–37.

Sullivan, M.J.L., Thorn, B., Haythornthwaite, J.A. et al. (2001) Theoretical perspectives on the relation between catastrophising and pain, *Clinical Journal of Pain*, 17: 53–61.

Sumner, A., Waller, G., Killick, S. and Elstein, M. (1993) Body image distortion in pregnancy: a pilot study of the effects of media images, *Journal of Reproductive and Infant Psychology*, 11: 203–8.

Sussman, S., Dent, C., Stacy, A.W. et al. (1990) Peer group association and adolescent tobacco use, *Journal of Abnormal Psychology*, 99: 349–52.

Sutton, S. (1998a) Predicting and explaining intentions and behavior: how well are we doing? *Journal of Applied Social Psychology*, 28: 1317–38.

Sutton, S. (1998b) How ordinary people in Great Britain perceive the health risks of smoking, *Journal of Epidemiological Community Health*, 52: 338–9.

Sutton, S. (1999) The psychological costs of screening, in J.S. Tobias and I.C. Henderson (eds), *New Horizons in Breast Cancer: Current Controversies, Future Directions*. London: Chapman & Hall.

Sutton, S. (2000) Interpreting cross-sectional data on stages of change, *Psychology and Health*, 15: 163–71.

Sutton, S. (2002a) Testing attitude-behaviour theories using non-experimental data: an examination of some hidden assumptions, *European Review of Social Psychology*, 13: 293–323.

Sutton, S. (2002b) Using social cognition models to develop health behaviour interventions: problems and assumptions, in D. Rutter and L. Quine (eds), *Changing Health Behaviour: Intervention and Research with Social Cognition Models*, pp. 193–208. Buckingham: Open University Press.

Sutton, S., McVey, D. and Glanz, A. (1999) A comparative test of the theory of reasoned action and the theory of planned behaviour in the prediction of condom use intentions in a national sample of English young people, *Health Psychology*, 18: 72–81.

Sutton, S., Saidi, G., Bickler, G. and Hunter, J. (1995) Does routine screening for breast cancer raise anxiety? Results from a three wave prospective study in England, *Journal of Epidemiology and Community Health*, 49: 413–18.

Sutton, S., Wardle, J., Taylor, T. et al. (2000) Predictors of attendance in United Kingdom flexible sigmoidoscopy screening trial, *Journal of Medical Screening*, 7: 99–104.

Sutton, S.R. (1982) Fear-arousing communications: a critical examination of theory and research, in J.R. Eiser (ed.), *Social Psychology and Behavioural Medicine*, pp. 303–7. Chichester: John Wiley.

Sutton, S.R. and Hallett, R. (1989) Understanding the effect of fear-arousing communications: the role of cognitive factors and amount of fear aroused, *Journal of Behavioral Medicine*, 11: 353–60.

Swan, A.V., Murray, M. and Jarrett, L. (1991) *Smoking Behaviour from Pre-adolescence to Young Adulthood*. Aldershot: Avebury.

Swindle, R.E. Jr and Moos, R.H. (1992) Life domains in stressors, coping and adjustment, in W.B. Walsh, R. Price and K.B. Crack (eds), *Person Environment Psychology: Models and Perspectives*, pp. 1–33. Mahawah, NJ: Erlbaum.

Szasz, T. (1961) *The Myth of Mental Illness*. New York: Harper & Row.

Tayler, M. and Ogden, J. (2005) Doctors' use of euphemisms and their impact on patients' beliefs about their illness, *Patient Education and Counselling*, 57: 321–6.

Taylor, S., Kemeny, M., Reed, G. and Bower, J. (1998) Psychosocial influence on course of disease: predictors of HIV progression, *Health Psychology Update*, 34: 7–12.

Taylor, S.E. (1983) Adjustment to threatening events: a theory of cognitive adaptation, *American Psychologist*, 38: 1161–73.

Taylor, S.E., Lichtman, R.R. and Wood, J.V. (1984) Attributions, beliefs about control, and adjustment to breast cancer, *Journal of Personality and Social Psychology*, 46: 489–502.

Temoshok, L. and Fox, B.H. (1984) Coping styles and other psychosocial factors related to medical status and to prognosis in patients with cutaneous malignant melanoma, in B.H. Fox and B.H. Newberry (eds), *Impact of Psychoendocrine Systems in Cancer and Immunity*, pp. 258–87. Toronto: C.J. Hogrefe.

Temoshok, L., Sweet, D.M. and Zich, J.A. (1987) A three city comparison of the public's knowledge and attitudes about AIDS, *Psychology and Health*, 1: 43–60.

Tennen, H. and Affleck, G. (1999) Finding benefits in adversity, in C.R. Snyder (ed.), *Coping: The Psychology of What Works*, pp. 279–304. New York: Oxford University Press.

Tennen, H., Affleck, G., Armeli, S. and Carney, M.A. (2000) A daily process approach to coping: linking theory, research and practice, *American Psychologist*, 55: 626–36.

Terry, D.J. (1994) Determinants of coping: the role of stable and situational factors, *Journal of Personality and Social Psychology*, 66: 895–910.

Terry, D.J., McHugh, T.A. and Noller, P. (1991) Role dissatisfaction and the decline in marital quality across the transition to parenthood, *Australian Journal of Psychology*, 43: 129–32.

Tew, M. (1990) *Safer Childbirth? A Critical History of Maternity Care*. London: Chapman & Hall.

Thapar, A.K. and Thapar, A. (1992) Psychological sequelae of miscarriage: a controlled study using the general health questionnaire and hospital anxiety and depression scale, *British Journal of General Practice*, 42: 94–6.

Theadom, A. and Cropley, M. (2006) Effects of preoperative smoking cessation on the incidence and risk of intraoperative and postoperative complications in adult smokers: a systematic review, *Tobacco Control*, 15: 352–8.

Thompson, J.P., Palmer, R.L. and Petersen, S.A. (1988) Is there a metabolic component to counter-regulation? *International Journal of Eating Disorders*, 7: 307–19.

Thompson, M., Zanna, M. and Griffin, D. (1995) Let's not be indifferent about (attitudinal) ambivalence, in R.E. Perry and J.A. Krosnick (eds), *Attitude Strength: Antecedents and Consequences*, pp. 361–86. Hillsdale, NJ: Erlbaum.

Thompson, S.C. (1986) Will it hurt less if I can control it? A complex answer to a simple question, *Psychological Bulletin*, 90: 89–101.

Timio, M., Verdecchia, P., Venanzi, S. et al. (1988) Age and blood pressure changes: a 20-year follow-up study in nuns in a secluded order, *Hypertension*, 12: 457–61.

Torgerson, J.S. and Sjostrom, L. (2001) The Swedish Obese Subjects (SOS) study: rationale and results, *International Journal of Obesity*, May 25(Suppl. 1): S2–S4.

Totman, R.G. (1976) Cognitive dissonance and the placebo response, *European Journal of Social Psychology*, 5: 119–25.

Totman, R.G. (1987) *The Social Causes of Illness*. London: Souvenir Press.

Trafimow, D. (2000) Habit as both a direct cause of intention to use a condom and as a moderator of the attitude-intention and subjective norm intention relations, *Psychology and Health*, 15: 383–93.

Trafimow, D., Sheeran, P., Conner, M. and Finlay, K.A. (2002) Evidence that perceived behavioural control is a multidimensional construct: perceived control and perceived difficulty, *British Journal of Social Psychology*, 41: 101–21.

Trostle, J.A. (1988) Medical compliance as an ideology, *Social Science and Medicine*, 27: 1299–308.

Tsutsumi, A., Tsutsumi, K., Kayaba, K. et al. (1998) Job strain and biological coronary risk factors: a cross-sectional study of male and female workers in a Japanese rural district, *International Journal of Behavioural Medicine*, 5: 295–311.

Tuckett, D., Boulton, M., Olson, C. and Williams, A. (1985) *Meetings Between Experts*. London: Tavistock.

Tunaley, J.R., Slade, P. and Duncan, S. (1993) Cognitive processes in psychological adaptation to miscarriage: a preliminary report, *Psychology and Health*, 9: 369–81.

Tuorila, H. (1987) Selection of milks with varying fat contents and related overall liking, attitudes, norms and intentions, *Appetite*, 8: 1–14.

Tuorila-Ollikainen, H., Lahteenmaki, L. and Salovaara, H. (1986) Attitudes, norms, intentions and hedonic responses in the selection of low salt bread in a longitudinal choice experiment, *Appetite*, 7, 127–39.

Turk, D.C. and Rennert, K. (1981) Pain and the terminally ill cancer patient: a cognitive social learning perspective, in H. Sobel (ed.), *Behavior Therapy in Terminal Care*. New York: Ballinger.

Turk, D.C. and Melzack. R. (eds) (2001) *Handbook of Pain Assessment*, 2nd edn. New York: Guilford Press.

Turk, D.C. and Rudy, T.E. (1986) Assessment of cognitive factors in chronic pain: a worthwhile enterprise? *Journal of Consulting and Clinical Psychology*, 54: 760–8.

Turk, D.C., Meichenbaum, D. and Genest, M. (1983) *Pain and Behavioral Medicine*. New York: Guilford Press.

Turk, D.C., Wack, J.T. and Kerns, R.D. (1985) An empirical examination of the 'pain-behaviour' construct, *Journal of Behavioral Medicine*, 8: 119–30.

Turner, J.R. and Carroll, D. (1985) The relationship between laboratory and 'real world' heart rate reactivity: an exploratory study, in J.F. Orlebeke, G. Mulder and J.L.P. Van Doornen (eds), *Psychophysiology of Cardiovascular Control: Models, Methods and Data*, pp. 895–907. New York, Plenum.

United States National Center for Health Statistics (2006) [online] Available: www.cdc.gov/nchs.

Upton, A.L., Beebe, G.W., Brown, J.W. et al. (1977) Report of NCI ad hoc working group on the risks associated with mammography in mass screening for the detection of breast cancer, *Journal of the National Cancer Institute*, 59: 479–93.

US Department of Health and Human Services (1996) *Physical Activity and Health: A Report of the Surgeon General.* Atlanta, GA: Centres for Disease Control.

US Department of Health and Human Services (USDHHS) (1990) *The Health Benefits of Smoking Cessation: A Report of the Surgeon General.* Rockville, MD: USDHHS.

US Environmental Protection Agency (1992) *Respiratory Health Effects of Passive Smoking: Lung Cancer and Other Disorders.* Washington, DC: US Environmental Protection Agency.

USDA's Continuing Survey of Food Intakes by Individuals 1994–96 (1998), (1999). Agricultural Research Service. Available: www.ars.usda.gov.

Ussher, M., Nunziata, P. and Cropley, M. (2001) Effect of a short bout of exercise on tobacco withdrawal symptoms and desire to smoke, *Psychopharmacology*, 158: 66–72.

Utian, W.H., Burry, K.A., Archer, D.F., Gallagher, J.C., Boyett, R.L., Guy, M.P., Tachon, G.J., Chadha-Boreham, H.K. and Bouvet, A.A. (1999) Efficacy and safety of low, standard, and high dosages of an estradiol transdermal system (Esclim) compared with placebo on vasomotor symptoms in highly symptomatic menopausal patients: the Esclim study group, *American Journal of Obstetrics and Gynecology*, 181(1): 71–9.

Valois, P., Desharnais, R. and Godin, G. (1988) A comparison of the Fishbein and the Triandis attitudinal models for the prediction of exercise intention and behavior, *Journal of Behavioral Medicine*, 11: 459–72.

Van Damme, S., Crombez, G. and Eccleston, C. (2002) Retarded disengagement from pain cues: the effect of pain catastrophizing and pain expectancy, *Pain*, 100(1–2): 111–18.

Van de Pligt, J., Zeelenberg, M., van Dijk, W.W., de Vries, N.K. and Richard, R. (1998) Affect, attitudes and decisions: let's be more specific, *European Review of Social Psychology*, 8: 33–66.

Van Tulder, M.W., Ostelo, R., Vleeyen, J.W.S. et al. (2000) Behavioural treatment for chronic low back pain, *Spine*, 25(20): 2688–9.

van der Velde, F. and van der Pligt, J. (1991) AIDS related health behavior: coping, protection motivation, and previous behavior, *Behavioral Medicine*, 14: 429–52.

van der Velde, F., Hookyas, C. and van der Pligt, J. (1992) Risk perception and behavior: pessimism, realism, and optimism about AIDS-related health behavior, *Psychology and Health*, 6: 23–38.

van Elderen, T. and Dusseldorp, E. (2001) Lifestyle effects of group health education for patients with coronary heart disease, *Psychology and Health*, 16: 327–41.

van Elderen, T., Maes, S. and van den Broek, Y. (1994) Effects of a health education programme with telephone follow-up during cardiac rehabilitation, *British Journal of Clinical Psychology*, 33: 367–78.

van Griensven, G.J.P., Teilman, R.A.P., Goudsmit, J. et al. (1986) Riskofaktoren en prevalentie van LAV/HTLV III antistoffen bij homoseksuele mannen in Nederland, *Tijdschrift voor Sociale Gezondheidszorg*, 64: 100–7.

van Strien, T., Frijters, J.E., Bergers, G.P. and Defares, P.B. (1986) Dutch eating behaviour questionnaire for the assessment of restrained, emotional, and external eating behaviour, *International Journal of Eating Disorders*, 5: 295–315.

van Zuuren, F.J. (1998) The effects of information, distraction and coping style on symptom reporting during preterm labor, *Psychology and Health*, 13: 49–54.

Velicer, W.F., DiClemente, C.C., Prochaska, J.O. and Brandenberg, N. (1985) A decisional balance measure for assessing and predicting smoking status, *Journal of Personality and Social Psychology*, 48: 1279–89.

Verbrugge, L.M. (1979) Marital status and health, *Journal of Marriage and the Family*, 41: 267–85.

Violanti, J., Marshall, J. and Howe, B. (1983) Police occupational demands, psychological distress and the coping function of alcohol, *Journal of Occupational Medicine*, 25: 455–8.

Vitaliano, P.P., Maiuro, R.D., Russo, J. et al. (1990) Coping profiles associated with psychiatric, physical health, work and family problems, *Health Psychology*, 9: 348–76.

Vitaliano, P.P., Russo, J., Bailey, S.L., Young, H.M. and McCann, B.S. (1993) Psychosocial factors associated with cardiovascular reactivity in old adults, *Psychosomatic Medicine*, 55(2): 164–77.

Vlaeyen, J.W.S. and Linton, S. (2000) Fear-avoidance and its consequences in chronic muculoskeletal pain: a state of the art, *Pain*, 85: 317–32.

Vollrath, M. and Toergersen, S. (2002) Who takes health risks? A probe into eight personality types, *Personality and Individual Differences*, 32: 1185–97.

Von Frey, M. (1895) *Untersuchungen über die Sinnesfunctionen der Menschlichen Haut Erste Abhandlung: Druckempfindung und Schmerz*. Leipzig: Hirzel.

Von Zerssen, D. (1976) *Klinische Selbestbeurteilungsskalen (KSb-S) aus dem Münchener Psychiatrischen Informations System (PSYCHIS Muenchen). Die Paranoid Depressivitäts Skala*. Weinheim: Beltz.

Wadden, T.A. (1993) Treatment of obesity by moderate and severe calorie restriction: results of clinical research trials, *Annals of Internal Medicine*, 119: 688–93.

Wadden, T.A., Foster, G.D., Wang, J., Pierson, R.N., Yang, M.U., Moreland, K., Stunkard, A.J. and VanItallie, T.B. (1992) Clinical correlates of short and long term weight loss, *American Journal of Clinical Nutrition*, 56: 271S–74S.

Wadden, T.A., Stunkard, A.J. and Smoller, W.S. (1986) Dieting and depression: a methodological study, *Journal of Consulting and Clinical Psychology*, 64: 869–71.

Wadsworth, M.E.J. (1991) *The Imprint of Time: Childhood History and Adult Life*. Oxford: Oxford University Press.

Wadsworth, M.E.J. and Kuh, D.J. (1997) Childhood influences on adult health: a review of recent work from the British 1946 National Birth Cohort Study, the MRC National Survey of Health and Development, *Paediatric and Perinatal Epidemiology*, 11: 2–20.

Walker, W.B. and Franzini, L.R. (1985) Low-risk aversive group treatments, physiological feedback, and booster sessions for smoking cessation, *Behaviour Therapy*, 16: 263–74.

Waller, D., Agass, M., Mant, D. et al. (1990) Health checks in general practice: another example of inverse care? *British Medical Journal*, 300: 1115–18.

Waller, G., Hamilton, K. and Shaw, J. (1992) Media influences on body size estimation in eating disordered and comparison subjects, *British Review of Bulimia and Anorexia Nervosa*, 6: 81–7.

Wallsten, T.S. (1978) *Three biases in the cognitive processing of diagnostic information*. Unpublished paper, Psychometric Laboratory, University of North Carolina, Chapel Hill, NC.

Wallston, B.S., Alagna, S.W., Devellis, B.M. and Devellis, R.F. (1983) Social support and physical illness, *Health Psychology*, 2: 367–91.

Wallston, K.A. and Wallston, B.S. (1982) Who is responsible for your health? The construct of health locus of control, in G.S. Sanders and J. Suls (eds), *Social Psychology of Health and Illness*, pp. 65–95. Hillsdale, NJ: Erlbaum.

Wallston, K.A., Wallston, B.S. and DeVeliis, R. (1978) Development of the multidimensional health locus of control (MHLC) scales, *Health Education Monographs*, 6: 160–70.

Walton, A.J. and Eves, F. (2001) Exploring drug users' illness representations of HIV, hepatitis B and hepatitis C using repertory grids, *Psychology and Health*, 16: 489–500.

Walton, I. and Hamilton, M. (1995) *Midwives and Changing Childbirth*. Hale: Books for Midwives Press.

Wanebo, C.K., Johnson, K.G., Sato, K. and Thorslind, T.W. (1968) Breast cancer after the exposure to the atomic bombings of Hiroshima and Nagasaki, *New England Journal of Medicine*, 279: 667–71.

Wang, S.J., Liu, H.C., Fuh, J.L., Liu, C.Y., Lin, K.P., Chen, H.M., Lin, C.H., Wang, P.N., Hsu, L.C., Wang, H.C. and Lin, K.N. (1997) Prevalence of headaches in a Chinese elderly population in Kinmen: age and gender effect and cross-cultural comparisons, *Neurology*, 49: 195–200.

Wardle, J. (1980) Dietary restraint and binge eating, *Behaviour Analysis and Modification*, 4: 201–9.

Wardle, J. (1995) Parental influences on children's diets, *Proceedings of the Nutrition Society*, 54: 747–58.

Wardle, J. and Beales, S. (1988) Control and loss of control over eating: an experimental investigation, *Journal of Abnormal Psychology*, 97: 35–40.

Wardle, J. and Marsland, L. (1990) Adolescent concerns about weight and eating: a social developmental perspective, *Journal of Psychosomatic Research*, 34: 377–91.

Wardle, J., Sanderson, S., Guthrie, C.A., Rapoport, L. and Plomin, R. (2002) Parental feeding style and the intergenerational transmission of obesity risk, *Obesity Research*, 10: 453–62.

Wardle, J., Steptoe, A., Bellisle, F. et al. (1997) Health dietary practices among European students, *Health Psychology*, 16, 443–50.

Wardle, J., Volz, C. and Golding, C. (1995) Social variation in attitudes to obesity in children, *International Journal of Obesity*, 19: 562–9.

Ware, J.E. and Sherbourne, C.D. (1992) The MOS 36 item short form health survey (SF-36): conceptual framework and item selection, *Medical Care*, 30: 473–83.

Warren, C. and Cooper, P.J. (1988) Psychological effects of dieting, *British Journal of Clinical Psychology*, 27: 269–70.

Wason, P.C. (1974) The psychology of deceptive problems, *New Scientist*, 15 August: 382–5.

Wathen, C.N. (2006) Alternatives to hormone replacement therapy: a multi-method study of women's experiences, *Complementary Therapies in Medicine*, 14(3): 185–92.

Watson, M. and Greer, S. (1983) Development of a questionnaire measure of emotional control, *Journal of Psychosomatic Research*, 27: 299–305.

Watson, M., Greer, S., Rowden, L. et al. (1991) Relationships between emotional control, adjustment to cancer and depression and anxiety in breast cancer patients, *Psychological Medicine*, 21: 51–7.

Weatherall, R., Joshi, H. and Macran, S. (1994) Double burden or double blessing? Employment, motherhood and mortality in the Longitudinal Study of England and Wales, *Social Science and Medicine*, 38: 285–97.

Weatherburn, P., Hunt, A.J., Davies, P.M., Coxon, A.P.M. and McManus, T.J. (1991) Condom use in a large cohort of homosexually active men in England and Wales, *AIDS Care*, 3: 31–41.

Weaver, J. (1998) Choice control and decision making in labour, in S. Clements (ed.), *Psychological Perspectives on Pregnancy and Childbirth*. Edinburgh: Churchill Livingston.

Weeks, J. (1985) *Sexuality and Its Discontents: Meanings, Myths and Modern Sexuality*. London: Routledge & Kegan Paul.

Weg, R.B. (1983) Changing physiology of aging, in D.S. Woodruff and J.E. Birren (eds), *Ageing: Scientific Perspectives and Social Issues*, 2nd edn. Monterey, CA: Brooks/Cole.

Wegner, D.M. (1994). Ironic processes of mental control, *Psychological Review*, 101: 34–52.

Wegner, D.M., Erber, R., and Zanakos, S. (1993) Ironic processes in the mental control of mood and mood related thought, *Journal of Personality and Social Psychology*, 65, 1093–104.

Wegner, D.M., Schneider, D.J., Cater, S.R. and White, T.L. (1987) Paradoxical effects of thought suppression, *Journal of Personality and Social Psychology*, 53: 5–13.

Wegner, D.M., Shortt, J.W., Blake, A.W. and Page, M.S. (1999) The suppression of exciting thoughts, *Journal of Personality and Social Psychology*, 58: 409–18.

Weidner, G., Rice, T., Knox, S.S. et al. (2000) Familiar resemblance for hostility: the National Heart, Lung, and Blood Institute Family Heart Study, *Psychosomatic Medicine*, 62, 197–204.

Weiner, B. (1986) *An Attributional Theory of Motivation and Emotion*. New York: Springer-Verlag.

Weinman, J. (ed.) (1987) *An Outline of Psychology as Applied to Medicine*, 2nd edn. London: J. Wright.

Weinman, J. and Petrie, K.J. (1997) Illness perceptions: a new paradigm for psychosomatics? *Journal of Psychosomatic Research*, 42: 113–16.

Weinman, J., Petrie, K.J., Moss-Morris, R. and Horne, R. (1996) The illness perception questionnaire: a new method for assessing the cognitive representation of illness, *Psychology and Health*, 11: 431–46.

Weinstein, N. (1983) Reducing unrealistic optimism about illness susceptibility, *Health Psychology*, 2: 11–20.

Weinstein, N. (1984) Why it won't happen to me: perceptions of risk factors and susceptibility, *Health Psychology*, 3: 431–57.

Weinstein, N. (1987) Unrealistic optimism about illness susceptibility: conclusions from a community-wide sample, *Journal of Behavioural Medicine*, 10: 481–500.

Weinstein, N., Rothman, A.J. and Sutton, S.R. (1998) Stage theories of health behavior: conceptual and methodological issues, *Health Psychology*, 17: 290–9.

Weisman, C.S., Plichta, S., Nathanson, C.A., Ensminger, M. and Robertson, J.C. (1991) Consistency of condom use for disease prevention among adolescent users of oral contraceptives, *Family Planning Perspective*, 23: 71–4.

Weller, S.S. (1984) Cross-cultural concepts of illness: variables and validation, *American Anthropologist*, 86: 341–51.

Wellings, K., Field, J., Johnson, A.M. and Wadsworth, J. (1994) *Sexual Behaviour in Britain: The National Survey of Sexual Attitudes and Lifestyles*. Harmondsworth: Penguin.

Welton, A., Hepworth, J., Collings, N., Ford, D., Knott, C., Meredith, S., Walgrove, A., Wilkes, H., Vickers, M. (Women's International Study of long Duration Oestrogen after Menopause (WISDOM) team) (2004) Decision-making about hormone replacement therapy by women in England and Scotland, *Climacteric*, 7(1): 41–9.

Wenzlaff, R.M. and Wegner, D.M. (2000) Thought suppression, *Annual Review of Psychology*, 51: 59–91.

Werner, P.D. and Middlestadt, S.E. (1979) Factors in the use of oral contraceptives by young women, *Journal of Applied Social Psychology*, 9: 537–47.

Wesson, N. (1990) *Homebirth: A Practical Guide*. London: Optima.

West, R. (2005) Time for a change: putting the Transtheoretical (Stages of Change) Model to rest, *Addiction*, 100(8): 1036–9.

West, R. (2006) *Theory of Addiction*. Oxford: Blackwell.

West, R. and Shiffman, S. (2004) *Smoking Cessation*. Oxford: Health Press.

West, R. and Sohal, T. (2006) 'Catastrophic' pathways to smoking cessation: findings from national survey, *British Medical Journal*, 332(7539): 458–60.

Whitaker, A., Davies, M., Shaer, D. et al. (1989) The struggle to be thin: a survey of anorexic and bulimic symptoms in a non-referred adolescent population, *Psychological Medicine*, 19: 143–63.

Whitley, B.E. and Schofield, J.W. (1986) A meta-analysis of research on adolescent contraceptive use, *Population and Environment*, 8: 173–203.

WHOQoL Group (1993) *Measuring Quality of Life: The Development of a World Health Organisation Quality of Life Instrument (WHOQoL)*. Geneva: WHO.

Wickramasekera, I. (1980) A conditioned response model of the placebo effect: predictions from the model, *Biofeedback and Self Regulation*, 5: 5–18.

Wiebe, D.J. and McCallum, D.M. (1986) Health practices and hardiness as mediators in the stress–illness relationship, *Health Psychology*, 5: 425–38.

Wiedenfeld, S.A., O'Leary, A., Bandura, A. et al. (1990) Impact of perceived self-efficacy in coping with stressors on immune function, *Journal of Personality and Social Psychology*, 59: 1082–94.

Wilkinson, A.V., Holahan, C.J. and Drane-Edmundson, E.W. (2002) Predicting safer sex practices: the interactive role of partner cooperation and cognitive factors, *Psychology and Health*, 17(6): 697–709.

Wilkinson, C., Jones, J.M. and McBride, J. (1990) Anxiety caused by abnormal result of cervical smear test: a controlled trial, *British Medical Journal*, 300: 440.

Willen, H. and Montgomery, H. (1993) The impact of wish for children and having children on attainment and importance of life values, *Göteborg Psychological Reports*, 23(3): 1–18.

Willett, W.C., Manson, J.E., Stampfer, M.J., Colditz, G.A., Rosner, B. and Speizer, F.E. et al. (1995) Weight, weight change, and coronary heart disease in women: risk within the 'normal' weight range, *Journal of the American Medical Association*, 273: 461–5.

Williams, A.C. (2002) Facial expression of pain: an evolutionary account, *Behaviour and Brain Sciences*, 25(4): 439–55.

Williams, G.C., Grow, V.M., Freedman, Z.R., Ryan, R.M. and Deci, E.L. (1996) Motivational predictors of weight loss and weight loss maintenance, *Journal of Personality and Social Psychology*, 70: 115–26.

Williams, R.B. and Barefoot, J.C. (1988) Coronary prone behaviour: the emerging role of the hostility complex, in B.K. Houston and C.R. Snyder (eds), *Type A Behaviour Pattern: Research, Theory and Intervention*, pp. 189–211. New York: Wiley.

Williams, S., Weinman, J.A., Dale, J. and Newman, S. (1995) Patient expectations: what do primary care patients want from their GP and how far does meeting expectations affect patient satisfaction? *Journal of Family Practice*, 12: 193–201.

Williamson, G.S. and Pearse, I.H. (1938) *Biologists in Search of Material*. London: Faber & Faber.

Wills, T.A. (1985) Supportive functions of interpersonal relationships, in S. Cohen and S.L. Syme (eds), *Social Support and Health*. Orlando, FL: Academic Press.

Wilson, D.M., Taylor, M.A., Gilbert, J.R. et al. (1988) A randomised trial of a family physician intervention for smoking cessation, *Journal of the American Medical Association*, 260: 1570–4.

Wilson, G.T. (1978) Alcoholism and aversion therapy: issues, ethics, and evidence, in G. Marlatt and P. Nathan (eds), *Behavioral Approaches to Alcoholism*. New Brunswick, NJ: Journal of Studies on Alcohol.

Wilson, G.T. (1994) Behavioural treatment of obesity: thirty years and counting, *Advances in Behavioural Research Therapy*, 16: 31–75.

Wilson, J.M.G. (1965) Screening criteria, in G. Teeling-Smith (ed.), *Surveillance and Early Diagnosis in General Practice*. London: Office of Health Economics.

Winefield, H., Murrell, T., Clifford, J. and Farmer, E. (1996) The search for reliable and valid measures of patient centredness, *Psychology and Health*, 11: 811–24.

Wing, R.R., Koeske, R., Epstein, L.H. et al. (1987) Long term effects of modest weight loss in Type II diabetic patients, *Archives of Internal Medicine*, 147: 1749–53.

Wolf, T.M. and Kissling, G.E. (1984) Changes in life-style characteristics, health, and mood of freshman medical students, *Journal of Medical Education*, 59: 806–14.

Wong, M. and Kaloupek, D.G. (1986) Coping with dental treatment: the potential impact of situational demands, *Journal of Behavioural Medicine*, 9: 579–98.

Wong, M.L., Koh, D., Lee, M.H. and Fong, Y.T. (1997) Two year follow up of a behavioural weight control programme for adolescents in Singapore: predictors of long term weight loss, *Annals of the Academy of Medicine, Singapore*, 26: 147–53.

Wood, D.A., Kinmouth, A.L., Pyke, S.D.M. and Thompson, S.G. (1994) Randomised controlled trial evaluating cardiovascular screening and intervention in general practice: principal results of British family heart study, *British Medical Journal*, 308: 313–20.

Woodcock, A., Stenner, K. and Ingham, R. (1992) Young people talking about HIV and AIDS: interpretations of personal risk of infection, *Health Education Research: Theory and Practice*, 7: 229–47.

Wooley, S.C. and Wooley, O.W. (1984) Should obesity be treated at all? in A.J. Stunkard and E. Stellar (eds), *Eating and Its Disorders*. New York: Raven Press.

World Health Organization (WHO) (1947) *Constitution of the World Health Organization*. Geneva: WHO.

World Health Organization (WHO) (1980) *International Classification of Impairment, Disabilities and Handicaps*. Geneva: WHO.

World Health Organization (WHO) (1996) *Research on the Menopause in the 1990s*. WHO Technical Report Series. Geneva: WHO.

Wright, C.E., Ebrecht, M., Mitchell, R. Anggiansah, A. and Weinman, J. (2005) The effect of psychological stress on symptom severity and perception in patients with gastro-oesophageal reflux, *Journal of Psychosomatic Research*, 59: 415–24.

Wright, J.A., Weinman, J. and Marteau, T.M. (2003) The impact of learning of a genetic predisposition to nicotine dependence: an analogue study, *Tobacco Control*, 12: 227–30.

Writing Group for the Women's Health Initiative Investigators (2002) Risks and benefits of oestrogen plus progesterone in healthy post-menopausal women, *JAMA*, 288(3): 321–33.

Wyper, M.A. (1990) Breast self-examination and Health Belief Model, *Research in Nursing and Health*, 13: 421–8.

Young, L. (1992) Psychological factors in rheumatoid arthritis, *Journal of Consulting and Clinical Psychology*, 60: 619–27.

Young, L. and Humphrey, M. (1985) Cognitive methods of preparing women for hysterectomy: does a booklet help? *British Journal of Clinical Psychology*, 24: 303–4.

Yzer, M.C., Siero, F.W. and Buunk, B. (2001) Bringing up condom use and using condoms with new sexual partners: intentional or habitual? *Psychology and Health*, 16: 409–21.

Ziegler, D.K. (1990) Headache: public health problem, *Neurologic Clinics*, 8: 781–91.

Zigmond, A.S. and Snaith, R.P. (1983) The Hospital Anxiety and Depression Scale, *Acta Psychiatrica Scandinavica*, 67: 361–70.

Zimbardo, P.G. (1969) *The Cognitive Control of Motivation*. Illinois: Scott Foresman.

Zola, I.K. (1972) Medicine as an institution of social control, *Sociological Review*, 20: 487–504.

Zolese, G. and Blacker, C.V.R. (1992) The psychological complications of therapeutic abortion, *British Journal of Psychiatry*, 160: 742–9.

Index

Page numbers in *italics* refer to boxes, figures and theory testing studies.

A

abortion 369–76
  factors influencing decision 370–2
  intervention mode, impact of 375
  legal aspects 369–70, 372–3
  psychological impact of 374–5
  rates *370*, *371*
  research problems 376
  service provision 372–3
    women's experiences of 373–4
  spontaneous, *see* miscarriage
abstinence violation effect 121–2, 151
accidents, stress–illness relationship 243
acquired dependency 103
activities of daily living (ADL) 394
adaptive tasks, coping process 62–3, 65
addiction (drinking and smoking); *see also* alcohol; smoking
  cross-addictive behaviour perspective 122–4
  definition 100
  historical changes in attitude and theoretical approaches to 100–2
  interventions 112–17
    clinical 112–15, 119
    methodological problems in evaluating 119
    public health 116–17, 119
    self-help movements 115
  models, *see* disease model of addiction; moral model of addiction; social learning theories, of addiction
  research problems *106*
  stages 106–11
    cessation 109–12
    initiation and maintenance 107–9
    relapse 120–2
'addictive behaviour' 102
adherence, *see* compliance/adherence
adjustment; *see also* cognitive adaptation
  HIV/AIDS 318
  miscarriage 367
  social readjustment rating scale (SRRS) 231
adolescents, *see* children/adolescents
adoptee studies, causes of obesity 338
advertising
  bans 117
  and media influences 133–4, 141–2, 145
affect, *see entries beginning* emotion; mood
age factors

contraceptive use 180
  problem-focused vs emotion-focused coping strategy 257
'alarm stage', general adaptation syndrome (GAS) 222, 229
alcohol; *see also* addiction (drinking and smoking)
  craving 124
  deaths related to *99*
  initiation and maintenance 108–9
  negative effects 99
  positive effects 99
  recommended daily intake 128
  relapse 152
  statistics 96–7
  stress–illness relationship 242–3
allostatic load, stress recovery 230, 246
ambiguity/ambivalence
  meaning of illness 62
  predicting health behaviour 36
  and stress appraisal 227
anger, expression of 263–4
angina 353; *see also* coronary heart disease (CHD)
Antabuse 113
anti-obesity drugs 349
anticipated regret 36
antenatal screening 209
anxiety; *see also* stress
  associated with screening 204, 214, 215–16
  benefits of exercise 162
  contraceptive use 181
  and depression 325, 355, 366, 374
    cross-cultural differences 58–9
    hospital anxiety and depression scale (HADS) 396, 402
    rumination 253–4
    tension reduction theory of alcohol 108–9, 242–3
  and pain 277, 280, 298–9
  placebo mechanism 298–9
appetite regulation 339, 344
appraisal
  cognitive 62
  primary 225–6, 228, 229, 256
  secondary 225–6, 228, 229, 256
  self-regulatory model of illness cognitions 54
  stress 225–7, 234–5
  threat 26, 33
appraisal-focused coping skills 63–4, 65
approach vs avoidance coping strategies 256–7
arousal 222, 223, 228
associative learning, eating behaviour 134–6

atherosclerosis 353; *see also* coronary heart disease (CHD)

attention and pain perception 279, 280

attitudes; *see also* health professionals
to contraceptive use 181
to HIV/AIDS 314–16
to motherhood 372, 377
parental, to food and eating 132–3
role in predicting exercise 166–8
and theoretical approaches to addiction 100–2

attribution theory 18–19, 23; *see also* health beliefs
and control 264
illness crisis and cognitive adaptation 65
internal/self-attribution 121–2, 151

autonomy 144–5, 211, 252–3

aversion therapies 113–14

B

B cells 247

behavioural factors 14–15
cancer 323
coronary heart disease (CHD) 355–8
gate control theory (GCT) of pain 274, 275
HIV/AIDS 315–16
obesity 340–4
pain perception 279, 280

behavioural health 3

behavioural instructions 80

behavioural intentions 26, 30–1
and cognition/social cognition 35–7, 185–6
intention–behaviour gap 37–9

behavioural medicine 3

behavioural programmes
causal modelling approach 40–1
obesity 346–7
pain 283

behavioural willingness 38

beliefs; *see also* health belief model (HBM); health beliefs
predicting body dissatisfaction 144–5

Belloc and Breslow's longevity study 16–17

beneficence, ethical issue in screening 209–11

bereavement 318, 387
grief following miscarriage 366

binge drinking 109

binge eating 347

biofeedback 282, 326

biological perspectives on sex 173–5

biomedical model
of addiction 100, 101
challenges to 2–5
definition 2
outcomes 94
and theory of evolution 1

biopsychosocial model 3–4

birth, place of 377–80, 383

bisexuals 183–4

blood pressure, *see* hypertension

body dissatisfaction
causes 141–5
definition 140–1

body image
in cancer 326
during menopause 387

body mass index (BMI) 334, *335*, 336, 349, 351

body size, distorted estimation of 140

boundary model of overeating 147, *148*

breast cancer 323–4, *325*, 326, 327, 330
beliefs and immunity 248
and breast self-examination 25
causality beliefs 65
quality of life study 401–2

breast screening 200, 201, 203–4, 206–8, 209
negative aspects 210, 214, 217
post-menopausal 385

bulimia
escape theory of 150–1
ethnicity 142

C

calorie consumption 344

cancer; *see also* breast cancer
adjuvant therapy 327, *328–9*
cognitive responses 325
definition 322
emotional responses 325
initiation and promotion 323–4
longevity 327–30
prevalence 322
research problems *319*
role of psychology 322–30
screening, *see* breast screening; cervical screening; colorectal cancer/sigmoidoscopy screening
stress–illness relationship 241, 242, 251, 317
symptom alleviation 325–7

Cannons' fight or flight stress model 222–3, 228

carbohydrates 128, 344

cardiovascular disease, *see* coronary heart disease (CHD)

cardiovascular reactivity, *see* stress reactivity

caregiver stress 250, 259

carrier testing 201

catastrophizing and pain perception 278, 280

causal modelling approach to behavioural change 40–1

causality
patient understanding 76
and search for meaning 65
stress–illness link 239–40

'cell mediated immunity' 247

cervical cancer and HIV 251, 317

cervical screening 25, 200, 201, 204, 205, 206–8, 209, 211, 213–14, 215–16, 217

children/adolescents; *see also* developmental models
alcohol initiation 109
cognitive behavioural therapy (CBT) for pain 284

condom use 183
dietary recommendations 129
exercise 166
malnutrition in developing world 129
relaxation training *233–4*
smoking initiation 107, 108, 242
social cognitive approach to eating behaviour 138–9
chlamydia 183
cholesterol levels 358, 385
cholesterol screening 200, 201, 212, 213
chronic pain; *see also* pain
    and acute pain 271–2, 277, 282
    cognitive behavioural therapy (CBT) 283–4, *285–8*
    low back 280, *281–2*, 284
classical conditioning 104–5, 276
clinical decision-making 83–7
clinical geneticists 205
clinical health psychologist 7
clinical interventions for addiction 112–15, 119
cognition models 23–9; *see also* self-regulatory model
        of illness cognitions; social cognition models
    of eating behaviour 137–9
    interventions 39–41
    problems with 34–7, 139
cognition(s); *see also* illness cognitions
    in addiction 105
    in cancer 325, 327
    in dieting 149, 152–5
    and pain perception 278–9, 280
    pain treatment approaches 282–8
    and symptom perception 58, 59
cognitive adaptation theory of coping (Taylor) 65–7,
        318, 325
cognitive adjustment, *see* adjustment
cognitive appraisal 62
cognitive behavioural therapy (CBT) 283–4, *285–8*
cognitive dissonance 151
    and placebos 300–6
cognitive hypothesis of compliance (Ley) 74–6, 79,
        81–2
coherence model, illness and treatment beliefs 70
colorectal cancer/sigmoidoscopy screening 203, 204,
        209
communication
    health professional–patient 76–9, 80, 81–2, 87–91
    sexual partners 191
community-based programmes for smoking cessation
        117
complementary and alternative medicines (CAMs)
        388, 389
compliance/adherence
    coherence model 70
    communication model 82
    definitions 74, 82
    exercise treatment 67–70, 288
    HIV/AIDS treatment 317
    improving 76–9
        recommendations for 79

Ley's cognitive hypothesis of 74–6, 79, 81–2
    obesity treatment 70, 349
    placebo effect (CHD) *301–3*
    predicting 68, 74–6, 167–70
concentration, lack of 388
conditioning
    classical 104–5, 276
    operant 105, 277
    placebo mechanism 298, 299
condom machines 192
condom use 20, 182, 183–94
    changes in 184
    predicting 185–91
    social context 191–4
    by specific social categories 183–4
consultations
    patient centredness of 88–9
    patient recall 76
    patient satisfaction 75, *77–8*
    patient understanding 76
    patient–health professional agreement 89–91
contingency contracting for addiction 114
contraception 176, *177*; *see also* condom use
    accessibility 181
    decision-making models 178–80
    developmental models 177–8, 180
    integrated approach 180–2
    situational factors 181–2, *189–90*
control
    body dissatisfaction 145
    cancer initiation and promotion 324
    categories 264
    definition 264
    losing and regaining, during menopause 386
    and overeating 150, 151–2
    parental, and eating behaviour 134–6
    problem-focused vs emotion-focused coping
            strategy 257, 258
    research perspectives 265
    self- 227–8, *285–6*
    and stress response 264–5
    and stress–illness link 266
coping
    with addiction 121
    with crisis of illness 61–70
    definition 256
    with diagnosis 60–1
    measurement 258–9
    with miscarriage 366–7
    and pain acceptance 288
    and positive outcomes 259
    process 60–1, 62–6
    self-regulatory model 53–4
    strategies/styles/skills 63–5, 80, 256–8
        emotion-focused vs problem-focused 64, 257–8,
            259
        emotional expression 248–50
    and stress–illness relationship 255–9, 264–6

coping – *contd.*
  stressor minimization 258
  styles 318, 319, 324
  as 'trait' vs 'state' 256
coronary heart disease (CHD)
  beliefs about 354–5
  benefits of exercise 160–1, 243
  definition 353
  prevalence 354
  psychological impact of 355
  rehabilitation 359–61
  risk factors 354
    predicting and changing 355–8
  role of psychology *353*, 354–61
  screening 211–13, 216–17
  and social support 260
  and stress 239–41, 242, 244, 265, 266
  and stress reactivity 163–4, 229, 245, 263–4
  treatment adherence and placebo *301–3*
  and type A personality 262–3, 358, 359
  and weight fluctuations 348
cortisol 229, 244, 245, 251, 253
costs
  of cigarettes and alcohol 117
  of screening 202, 211–13
  of stress measurement 230–1, 231–2
counselling 326, 355, 359, 360
  genetic 201, 205
craving, subjective experience of 123–4
crisis of illness, coping with 61–70
crisis theory
  definition 61
  types of new equilibrium 65
critical health psychology 407
cross-cultural differences, *see* ethnicity/cross-cultural
    differences
cues
  exposure procedures 114
  obesity treatment 346
  relapse 120–1
  role in predicting health behaviours 25

D

decision-making
  abortion 370–2
  clinical 83–7
  illness as crisis 62
  models of contraceptive use 178–80
denial
  as coping strategy 54, 60, 61
  eating behaviour 150
  HIV/AIDS risk 188
  and immunity 248
depression 89–90; *see also* anxiety, and depression
  benefits of exercise 161–2, 163
  and cancer initiation and promotion 324
  and dieting 155, 347, 348
  impact of coronary heart disease (CHD) 355

and obesity 336, 337, 352
'descriptive norms' 36
developing countries 129, 313
developmental models
  contraceptive use 177–8
  eating behaviour 130–6
diabetes
  benefits of exercise 160
  benefits of weight loss 350
  dietary intervention 129
  quality of life study 402
  screening 201
diagnosis; *see also* screening
  coping with 60–1
diet; *see also* eating behaviour
  and coronary heart disease (CHD) 358
  and health relationship 129–30
  healthy, definition 127–8
  knowledge in health professional–patient
      communication 81
dieting
  and overeating 146–55
  role in mood and cognitive changes 152–5
  role in obesity treatment 347–8
  and undereating 145–6
  and weight loss 42, 152, 350, 351–2
disease model of addiction
  first disease concept 101
  problems with 103–4
  second disease concept 101, 102–3
  smoking 109, 112–13
  and social learning perspective 105, 121–3
disinhibition 146–7, 150
dissonance, *see* abstinence violation effect; cognitive
    dissonance
distress 221
doctors, *see* health professionals
drinking, *see* addiction (drinking and smoking);
    alcohol
drug use and HIV/AIDS susceptibility 316, 317
dualism, *see* mind–body dualism

E

eating behaviour; *see also* diet; dieting
  cognitive models 137–9
  developmental models 130–6
  exercise effect 341
  interventions 360
  and obesity 341, 342–4
  and smoking 123–4
  stress–illness relationship 243
  weight concern models 140–55
economic issues, *see* costs
education level, contraceptive use 180
'elaboration likelihood' model of behaviour change 41
elderly
  diet 130
  relatives 387

electronic foetal monitoring 209
emotion-focused vs problem-focused coping strategies 64, 257–8, 259
emotional expression and immunity 248–50
emotional factors; *see also* mood; *specific emotions*
  body dissatisfaction 141
  gate control theory (GCT) of pain 274, 275
  pain perception 277–8, 280
  responses to cancer 325
  screening uptake 204
  and social cognition models 37
emotional support 253
employment
  stress 252–4, 265, 266
  and unemployment 260, 261–2
  women's issues 253, 266, *267*, 382–3, 387
  worksite smoking bans 116, *118–19*
encounter reaction 60
endorphins 163, 229
energy expenditure, exercise effect 342
enkephalins 229
equal distribution of resources, ethical issue in screening 211
erotophilia 179
erotophobia 179
escape theory of eating behaviour 150–1
ethical issues in screening 209–11
ethnicity/cross-cultural differences
  body dissatisfaction 142, 144
  contraceptive use 180
  environment and symptom perception 58–9
  illness cognitions 50
  longevity 15–16
  metabolic rate and obesity 338–9
eustress 221
exercise; *see also* physical activity
  barriers to 167
  behavioural change intervention 42
  contemporary concern with 157–8
  coronary heart disease (CHD) interventions 359, 360
  definition 158
  individual vs supervised programmes 165–6
  and obesity 340–2
  participation statistics 158, *159*
  physical benefits of 159–61
  predictors of 164–8, *169–70*
  psychological benefits of 161–3, *163–4*
  relapse 170
  and smoking 124
  stress–illness relationship 243
'exhaustion', general adaptation syndrome (GAS) 222, 229, 245
expanding behavioural intentions 38
expectancies/expectations 29, 33, 35, 121, 297, 299–300
'expectancy beliefs' 35
'expectancy value' belief 35

expectant management of miscarriage 368, 369
experimenter bias, placebo mechanism 296–7, 299
externality theory of eating behaviour 343

F

facial expressions of pain 279
faith healers 294, 300, 303
false-negative results in screening 210
false-positive results in screening 210, 213–14
familial adenomatous polyposis (FAP) 214–15
family; *see also* children/adolescents; parents
  heart study 211–13
  role in predicting body dissatisfaction 143
  sex education 193–4
family planning clinics 192
fat cell theory and obesity 339
fats, dietary 128, 130, 344
  childhood diet 129
fear and pain perception 277–8
fight or flight stress model 222–3, 228
first disease concept of addiction 101
five component model of contraceptive use 178
follow-up screening 202
'food dudes' 132
'food scares' 133

G

gastric bypass/gastric banding 349–50
gate control theory (GCT) of pain 273–5
  gate closing mechanisms 275
  gate opening mechanisms 274
  input 273–4
  and other pain models 274, 276
  output 274
  problems with 275
gay men, *see* homosexuals
gender differences
  alcohol consumption 96–7
  contraceptive use 180
  power relations 194
  problem-focused vs emotion-focused coping strategies 257
  smoking 95–6, 123
  stress reactivity 229
  writing and emotional expression 250
general adaptation syndrome (GAS) (Selye) 222–3, 229, 245
general health questionnaire (GHQ) 396, 401
genetic causes of obesity 338–9
genetic counselling/counsellors 201, 205
genetic screening 200, 201, 204
  negative aspects 210–11, 214–15
genetic theories of addiction 102–3, 109
gonorrhoea 183, 184
government interventions; *see also* health education
  smoking and drinking 117
grief following miscarriage 366

guided mastery experiences 41
guilt 151, 181

H
haemophiliacs and HIV/AIDS 312
hardiness 228, 324
health
  benefits of exercise 167
  definitions 47–8, 400
  multidimensional model 47–8
health action process approach (HAPA) 32–3
health behaviours 13
  predicting 17–18
health belief model (HBM) 23–6
  components 24
  conflicting findings 25–6
  contraceptive use 179, 185–6
  problems with 26, 34, 35
  screening uptake 203–4
  support for 25
  using 24–5
health beliefs; *see also* attribution theory; cognition
    models; social cognition models; stages-of-
    change model
  coronary heart disease (CHD) 354–5, 360–1
  definition 13–14
  and exercise 166–8
  health professionals 85–7, 296–7
  and immune system 248
  lay theories 17
  locus of control 19, 23
  morality and longevity 14–17
  and placebos 296–7, 306–7
  predicting health behaviours 17–18
  research problems *23*
  self-affirmation theory 20–1
  unrealistic optimism 20, 23
health education
  coronary heart disease (CHD) 360
  HIV/AIDS 315–16
  safe sex 192–3
health professionals
  beliefs 85–7, 296–7, 307
  characteristics 296
  and patient communication 76–9, 80, 81–2,
    87–91
  screening issues 205
  smoking cessation advice 116
  variability problem 82–7, 88
health protective behaviours 14
health psychology
  aims 5–6
  background 1
  challenge to biomedical model 3–5
  future of 6–7
health status measurement 393–4; *see also* quality of
    life
  research problems *401*

shift in perspective *399*, 400
  subjective 294
health–illness relationship
  biomedical model 2
  health psychology perspective 4
  role of psychology 2, 4–5
health-impairing habits 14
heart disease, *see* coronary heart disease (CHD)
help-seeking behaviours 351
helplessness
  and cancer 324, 325
  and pain perception 278
  and stress reduction 266
  type C coping style 318, 319, 324
Herold and McNamee's model of contraceptive use
    179
highly active anti-retroviral therapy (HAART) 317
historic perspectives
  addiction models 100–2
  HIV/AIDS 312
  placebos 294–5
  problem of progression 406
  screening 200–1
  sex 173–4
Hite Reports 174–5
HIV/AIDS 182–95, 311–21
  attitudes to 314–16
  history of 312
  longevity 318–19
  prevalence 313
  prevention, condom use 184, 185–7
  progression 313, 316–18
  research problems *319*
  role of psychology 313–19, 320–1
  sex and illness discourses 195
  stress-illness relationship 251, 317–18
  susceptibility 316
  tests 203, 205
  virus structure and transmission 312
home births 377, 378–80
homosexuals
  condom use 183, 185, 189–90, 194
  and HIV/AIDS 312, 316, 319, 320–1
hormone replacement therapy (HRT) 386, 388–9,
    390
hospital anxiety and depression scale (HADS) 396, 402
hospital births 377, 378, 379–80
hostility 263–4, 358
'humoral mediated immunity' 247
humour in consultations 75
Huntington's disease screening 200, 201, 204
hyper-vigilance and pain perception 278
hypertension
  benefits of exercise 160
  and coronary heart disease (CHD) 358
  screening 201, 209, 212, 213, 215
  and stress 239, 244–5
  and weight loss 350

hypothalamic-pituitary-adrenocortical (HPA) activation 229, 244, 245
hypotheses in clinical decision-making 83–7
hypothetico-deductive model of decision-making 83
'hysterical paralysis' 2–3

I

identity change 61
illness; *see also* stress–illness relationship
  causes
    biomedical model 2
    biopsychosocial model 3–4
  and diet 129
  representations and behavioural outcomes *55–6*
  as stressor 243
  subjective definitions 49
illness behaviour 13
illness cognitions; *see also* self-regulatory model of illness cognitions
  definition 49
  measuring 51–2
  and placebos 307
  research perspectives 49–50
  research problems *52*
illness perception questionnaire (IPQ/IPQR) 51, 75
illusions 66–7, 264
immune system 246–7
  conditioning 247
  measurement 247–8
  and physiological response 250–1
  psychological state and 248–50
incentives 29
individual factors; *see also* health professionals; personality; psychological factors
  cognition and social norms 181–2, 186–7
  health professionals' clinical decision-making 87
  pain variability 272–3, 274, 275
  predictors of exercise 166
  quality of life measures 397
  screening issues 203–4, 213–17
  social world and sex education 193–4
  stress–illness variability 245–6
  trait theory and placebo mechanism 295
  weight loss 351
individual–social context integration 406–7
inductive reasoning 83
infectious diseases, decline of 14
information; *see also* knowledge
  illness as crisis 61
  oral and written 79
  patient recall 76
  patient satisfaction 75
  role in compliance 76–9
  wider role in illness 79–81
informed choice 90–1
'injunctive norms' 36
instrumental social support 253
intentions; *see also* behavioural intentions

aspect of exercise 158
interactive theories of placebo mechanism 296–9
internal locus of control 181
internal/self-attributions 121–2, 151
interpersonal perspectives
  contraceptive use 181, 185, 187, 188–91
  sex 175–6
interpretation
  positive 67
  self-regulatory model of illness cognitions 53, 54, 56–60
interventions, theory-based 39–41
intrapersonal factors, contraceptive use 180–1
'inverse care law' 211
investment effects of placebo 303, 305

J

Jenkins activity survey 262–3
job stress 252–4, 265, 266
justice, ethical issue in screening 211
justification and symptom change, placebo effect 303–5

K

Kinsey Report 174, 175
knowledge; *see also* information
  contraceptive use 180
  doctor variability problem 82–7, 88
  in health professional–patient communication 81–2
  role in exercise 166
  safe sex issues 192–3, 315–16

L

laboratory settings, stress measurement 230, 232
language
  health professionals' health beliefs 87–8
  use in emotional expression 250
lay perspectives 17
  vs medical terminology 60
  vs professional health beliefs 81–2, 88
learning; *see also* modelling; social learning
  role in pain perception 276–7, 280
leisure activity 158, 160
Leventhal, *see* self-regulatory model of illness cognitions (Leventhal)
Ley's cognitive hypothesis of compliance 74–6, 79, 81–2
life events
  and cancer 323–4, 327
  stress theory 223–5
life stressors and social resources inventory (LISRES) 225
lifestyle
  counselling 212, 360
  HIV/AIDS susceptibility 316, 317
  sedentary 164
Lindemann's three-stage theory of contraceptive use 177–8

location aspect of exercise 158
locus of control 19, 23, 181; *see also* self-efficacy
longevity; *see also* self-efficacy
   Belloc and Breslow study 16–17
   in cancer 327–30
   cross-cultural differences 15–16
   and exercise 159–60
   HIV/AIDS 318–19
   prediction and quality of life 402

M

McGill Pain Questionnaire (MPQ) 289, 396
McKeown's health beliefs thesis 14–16
magnification and pain perception 278
maladaptive response, coping process 65
mammography, *see* breast screening
marital relationships in menopause 387
marital status, stress–illness relationship 254
'masking hypothesis', mood modification model of
   overeating 149
Masters and Johnson report 174, 175
mastery
   cognitive adaptation theory 66, 67, 325
   guided mastery experiences 41
   response to cancer 325
   and stress 228
meaning
   of pain and pain perception 278
   search for 65–6, 67, 325
measurement; *see also* health status measurement;
   quality of life
   coping 258–9
   of functioning 394
   illness cognitions 51–2
   immune system 247–8
   informed choice 91
   pain 289
   problem of 406
   stress 230–4
media influences 133–4, 141–2, 145
'medical students' disease' 59
medical treatments
   for obesity 349
   for pain 272
medical vs lay terminology 60
menopause 384–90
   hormone replacement therapy (HRT) 386, 388–9,
      390
   management issues 388–9
   physical changes 385
   psychological effects 387–8
   research problems 390
   social factors 386–7
   symptoms 384, *385*
   as transition 385–6
metabolic rate and obesity 338–9
methodology 8
   glossary 409–11

problems of 34–5, 119, 406
mind–body dualism 2, 4–5, 405
   pain 274, 275
   placebo 308
miscarriage 365–9
   impact of treatment mode 367–8
   research perspectives 366–7
   research problems 369
   stages of response 367
modelling; *see also* learning; social learning
   hypothesis of eating behaviour 132, 145
   social learning process of addiction 105
mood; *see also* entries beginning emotion; *specific
   moods*
   benefits of exercise *163–4*
   changes in menopause 387–8
   and cognitive changes in dieting 152–5
   health professionals', in clinical decision-making
      87
   and immune system 248
   modification model of overeating 149
   and symptom perception 57–8, 59
   writing/emotional expression 250
moral model of addiction 100, 101
moral norms 36
morbidity rates 394, 400
mortality; *see also* entries beginning emotion; *specific
   moods*
   alcohol consumption *99*
   and behaviour 15
   rates 393–4, 400
   smoking *98*
mother–daughter relationship, body dissatisfaction
   144–5
motherhood
   attitudes to 372, 377
   negative impact of 380
   positive impact of 381
   qualitative research perspectives 381
   and returning to work *382–3*
motivation; *see also* protection motivation theory
   (PMT)
   placebo mechanism 297
   and weight loss 149, 351–2
multi-perspective cessation clinics for addiction
   114–15
multidimensional behavioural programmes for
   obesity 346–7
multidimensional measurement of quality of life
   396–7
multiphasic screening programmes 200
myocardial infarction (MI) 69–70, 353, 354–5,
   359, 360–1; *see also* coronary heart disease
   (CHD)

N

natural killer cell cytotoxicity (NKCC) 247–8, 249,
   250, 320

nausea and vomiting in cancer treatment 326
negative results in screening 214–15
    false-negative 210
negotiation of condom use 188–91, 193, 194
neophobia, childhood food exposure and preferences 131
nicotine fading 112–13
nicotine replacement 113
non-maleficence, ethical issue in screening 210–11
norepinephrine 163
norms
    expanded 35–6
    social 36, 181–2, 186–7, 194

O

'ob gene' 339
obesity 90
    benefits of exercise 160
    causes 337–45
        behavioural 340–4
        physiological 338–9
    definitions 334–5
    nurses' 87
    physical problems 336
    prevalence 336
    psychological problems 336–7
    research problems 345, 352–3
    role of psychology 334
    treatment 346–52
        benefits 348
        drug 349
        successes 350–2
        surgery 349–50
observational assessment of pain 289
occupational activity 158, 160
operant conditioning 105, 277
opportunistic screening 200
oral and written information 79
organizational factors in screening uptake 205
orgasms 174, 175
Orlistat 349
osteoporosis 385, 388, 389
    benefits of exercise 160
outcome(s)
    aspect of exercise 158
    coping 61, 65, 67, 259
    expectancies 29, 33, 35, 121
    health professional–patient agreement 90
    informed choice 91
    measurement, quality of life 401–2
    pain acceptance 288
    prediction, self-regulatory model 67–70
    smoking 55–6
overloading and stress events 227
overeating
    causes 147–52
    and dieting 146–55
    as rebellion 149, 153–4

OXCHECK study, coronary heart disease (CHD) screening 211, 213

P

pain
    acute and chronic 271–2, 277, 282
    definition 271–2
    measurement 289
    research problems 275
    theories 272–5
pain acceptance 288
pain experience 272–3, 280, 281–2
pain perception 274, 276–80
pain treatment
    cancer 326
    pain acceptance as outcome 288
    placebos 284–8, 295, 299, 304–5, 307–8
    role of psychology 282–8
parents; see also children/adolescents; family
    contraceptive use 181
    food and eating 132–3, 134–6
    sex education 193–4
partner factors in contraceptive use 181, 191, 192–3
past behaviour, role in predicting behavioural intentions 39
patient centredness 88–9
patient expectations, see expectancies/expectations
patient factors, see individual factors
patient recall 76
patient satisfaction 75, 77–8
patient understanding 76
patient–health professional communication 76–9, 80, 81–2, 87–91
peer influences
    contraceptive use 181
    sex education 193–4
    smoking 108
perceived control 264
perceived needs 38
perceived pain 274, 276–80
perceived stress scale (PSS) 231
percentage body fat 335
person–environment fit, definition of stress 221–2, 228
personal digital assistance (PDA) 231
personal harm, screening effects 210
personal responsibility, stress–illness link 266
personal susceptibility, sexual risk perception 185, 187–8
personality; see also individual factors; psychological factors
    and cancer 324, 327–30
    contraceptive use 181
    emotional expression 250
    role in predicting health behaviours 37
    and stress–illness relationship 262–4
    type A, and coronary heart disease (CHD) 262–3, 358, 359

phantom limb pain 273, 275
phentermine 349
physical abnormality, second disease concept of
    addiction 102–3
physical activity, *see* exercise
physiological factors
    causes of obesity 338–9
    consequences of foods 136
    in dieting 347
    measurement of pain 289
    placebo theories 299
placebos
    cognitive dissonance theory 300–6
    definitions 294
    and health understanding 295
    history of 294–5
    mechanisms 295–9
    modern-day 295
    and pain reduction 284–8, 295, 299, 304–5,
        307–8
    and patient expectations 297, 299–300
    research problems *299*
    role of 306–8
planned behaviour, *see* theory of planned behaviour
    (TPB)
pleasure function of sex 174–5
population screening 200
positive interpretation of illness 67
positive reframing 258
positive results of screening 215
    false-positive 210, 213–14
predictors
    of exercise 164–8, *169–70*
    of health behaviours 17–18, 35–7
    psychological, *see* psychological predictors
    social, *see* social predictors
pregnancy
    avoidance 175, 176
    and birth 377–84
    counselling services 192
    and social support 260
preload/taste test method 145–7, 149, 150, 153–4
preventative behaviour, control and stress–illness link
    266
prevention, secondary, *see* screening
primary appraisal 225–6, 228, 229, 256
problem solving
    clinical decision-making as 84–5
    model 83–4
problem-focused vs emotion-focused coping strategy
    64, 257–8, 259
procedural information 80
professional health psychologist 7
progression, problem of 406
protection motivation theory (PMT) 26–9
    anticipated regret 36
    components 26–7
    criticisms of 29, 34, 35

research focus 28–9
    using 27, 41, 107
proteins, dietary 128
psychological factors; *see also* individual factors;
    personality
    benefits of exercise 161–3, *163–4*
    causes of body dissatisfaction 143–5
    in dieting 347
    in pain theories 272–3
    pre-existing abnormality and addiction 103
    weight loss 351–2
psychological predictors
    of alcohol use 108–9
    of screening uptake 202–6, *206–8*
    of smoking 107
psychological–processes approach to quality of life
    395
psychoneuroimmunology (PNI) 246–51
psychophysiological model of stress 234–5
psychosocial factors in pain perception 276–80
psychosomatic medicine 2–3
public health interventions, addiction 116–17, 119

Q
qualitative research
    health definition 48
    illness cognitions 50
    lay theories of health 17
    miscarriage 367
quality of life
    definitions 395
    measurement 395–7, 400–2
        hip replacement surgery 398–9
        as outcome 401–2
        as predictor of longevity 402
        research issues 400–1
quantitative research
    illness cognitions 50
    miscarriage 366–7
questionnaires 51, 67, 75, 289, 396, 401

R
Rains's model of contraceptive use 178
rapid smoking 113
real vs ideal perceptions, body size 140–1
'realistic acceptance' 319
reasoned action, theory of (TRA) 30, 34, 35; *see also*
    cognitive models of eating behaviour
rebellion, overeating as 149, *153–4*
recovery
    illness cognitions and 68–70
    role of information 79–81
    stress 229–30, 245
rehabilitation (CHD) 359–61
relapse
    addiction 120–2
    alcohol 152
    exercise 170

overeating as 152
    smoking 152, 242
relationship stress 254
relaxation
    pain treatment 282, 287, 326
    training in children *233–4*
reporting error, placebo mechanism 297–8, 299
'repressors', stress 226–7
reproductive function of sex 173–4
researcher subjectivity 400
'resistance' to stress 222, 229, 230, 246
resolution stage, response to miscarriage 367
resources, problem-focused vs emotion-focused
        coping strategy 258
restraint theory of eating behaviour 145–55, 348, 349
retreat, *see* denial
reward–food relationship 134–5
risk perception 20–1
    HIV/AIDS 314–16
role theory
    enhancement and conflict, women 253
    stress buffering hypothesis of social support 260
Rosenberg's self-esteem scale 397, 401
rumination
    anxiety and depression 253–4
    and pain perception 278

S

safe sex, *see* condom use
schedule for evaluating individual quality of life
        (SEIQoL) 397, 398, 399
schedule of recent experience (SRE) 223–5
school sex-education programmes 193
screening
    definition 199–200
    early programmes 200
    guidelines 202
    history of ethos 200–1
    as problematic 208–17
        backlash 217
        cost-effectiveness 211–13
        ethical issues 209–11
        individual psychological effects 213–17
    psychological predictors of uptake 202–6, *206–8*
    recent programmes 201
    as useful tool 201–2
second disease concept of addiction 101, 102–3
secondary appraisal 225–6, 228, 229, 256
secondary gains 279
secretory immunoglobulin A (sIgA) 247–8
sedentary lifestyles 164
self-affirmation theory of health beliefs 20–1
self-attribution/internal attribution 121–2, 151
self-awareness 150–1
self-confidence
    benefits of exercise 162, 163
    menopause 388
self-control 227–8, *285–6*; *see also* control

self-efficacy 29, 33
    and cervical screening 205
    and condom use 186
    and control 264
    and pain 279, 282
    and stress 227
self-esteem
    and abortion 374, 375
    benefits of exercise 162, 163
    cognitive adaptation theory 66, 67, 325
    and menopause 388
    and parenthood 381
    Rosenberg's scale 397, 401
    and smoking initiation and maintenance 108
    and weight loss 352
self-examination/screening 200, 201
self-help 217
    addiction 114, 115
self-identity 36
self-image 166
self-predictions 38
self-regulatory model of illness cognitions
        (Leventhal) 52–4
    outcome prediction 67–70
    problems with assessment 54
    stages 53–4, 56–67
self-report
    pain measurement 289
    stress measurement 231–2
Selye's general adaptation syndrome (GAS) 222–3,
        229, 245
sensory information 80
sequence model of sexual behaviour and
        contraceptive use 179
settings
    birth 377–80, 383
    exercise 158
    stress measurement 230–1, 232
sex; *see also* condom use; contraception; HIV/AIDS
    education 192–4
    functions 173–5
    guilt and anxiety 181
    as health risk (STDs/HIV) 175, 176
    as interaction 175–6
    research perspectives 173–5
    research problems *182*
    risk perception 20
    roles 181
sexual health services 192
sexually transmitted diseases (STDs) 40, 183; *see also*
        HIV/AIDS
SF36 397, 401, 402
shock 60
sick role 14, 61, 279
sickle cell anaemia screening 201, 210–11
sigmoidoscopy screening/colorectal cancer 203, 204,
        209
silver lining questionnaire (SLQ) 67

situational factors, contraceptive use 181–2, *189–90*
smoke-holding 113–14
smoking; *see also* addiction (drinking and smoking)
  bans 116, 117, *118–19*
  cessation
    interventions 360
    and relapse 152, 242
    stages-of-change model 42, 110–11, *111–12*
    withdrawal symptoms, benefits of exercise 162
  coherence model 70
  and coronary heart disease (CHD) 212, 213, 355, 360
  deaths attributable to *98*
  doctors 87
  and eating behaviour 123–4
  gender differences 123
  illness representations and behavioural outcomes *55–6*
  initiation and maintenance 107–8
  negative effects 98
  positive effects 98
  prevalence 95–6, *97*
  stress–illness relationship 242, 251
snacking/snack foods 135–6, 243
social anthropology perspectives, health definition 48
social benefits of exercise 167
social class, *see* socio-economic status (SES)
social cognition models 29–33; *see also specific models*
  adherence to exercise 167–8
  contraceptive/condom use 182, 185–7
  interventions 39–41
  problems with 34–42, 186–7
social comparison
  coping with miscarriage 366–7
  and pain experience 280
  stress buffering hypothesis of social support 260
social context 406–7
  body dissatisfaction 141–3
  condom use 191–4
  symptom perception 58–9
social harm effects of screening 210–11
social learning models
  of addiction 100, 102, 104–5
    cessation 113–15
    and disease model 105, 121–3
  of eating behaviour 132–4
social messages 53, 59–60
social norms 36, 181–2, 186–7, 194
social predictors
  of addiction 108, 109
  of exercise 164–8
social readjustment rating scale (SRRS) 231
social support
  and cancer 326
  changes in 61
  definition 259–60
  and health 260, *261–2*
  and job stress 253

  and pain treatment 282
  and stress–illness link 260, 266
socio-economic status (SES)
  body dissatisfaction 142–3, 144
  chronic stress 252
  contraceptive use 180
  screening uptake 203
Socratic questions 282–3
spontaneous abortion, *see* miscarriage
Sports Council initiatives 157, 164
stages-of-change model 21–2, 23, 109–10
  exercise behaviour 168
  smoking cessation 42, 110–11, *111–12*
stair climbing 165
standards–needs approach to quality of life 395
stereotypes
  in decision-making 86
  genetic disorders 211
stress; *see also* anxiety; coping; stress–illness relationship
  in cancer initiation and promotion 323
  and control 227–8, 264–5
  definition 221–2
  measurement 230–4
  models, development of 222–5
  modification 361
    benefits of exercise 162
    placebos 307
    relaxation training in children *233–4*
  physiological measurement 231–2
  physiological responses 228–34, 265
  psychological factors 225–8
  psychophysiological model 234–5
  recovery 229–30, 245
    role of information 79–81
  as risk factor for CHD 358
stress buffering hypothesis of social support 260
stress reactivity 163–4, 229, 245, 263–4
stress resistance 222, 229, 230, 246
stress–illness link
  acute process 241, 244
  behaviour changes 241–3, 244–5
  causality 239–40
  chronic process 240–1, 244
    impact of 252–4
  and control 266
  and coping 259
  individual variability 245–6
  moderating factors 255–67
  and personality 262–4
  physiological responses 244–6
  psychoneuroimmunology 246–51
  research problems *252*
  and social support 260
'stress-diatheses' model of illness 240, *241*
stressors 222, 223, 224, 225, 226, 227
  and coping 258
stroke, predicting recovery from 68–9

Stroop task 149, 153–4
subjective expected utility (SEU) theory 23, 178
subjective experience of stress 265
subjective health status 394, 400
subjective vs objective measurement of quality of life 396
sudden cardiac death 353
surgery
    for obesity 349–50
    recovery from 79–80
sustained behavioural change 41–2
sympathetic activation 228, 244, 245
symptom alleviation in cancer 325–7
symptom perception 53, 54, 56–9
    and adherence 68
    and cognition 58
    individual differences in 56–7
    justification for placebo 303–5
    and mood 57–8
    social context 58–9
    social messages 59–60

T

T cells 247, 249, 251
    CD4-positive 312, 313
    immune system measurement 247–8
Taylor's cognitive adaptation theory of coping 65–7, 318, 325
temporal stability of intentions 38
tension reduction theory of alcohol 108–9, 242–3
termination of pregnancy, *see* abortion
testicular self-examination 200, 201
theoretical perspectives 7–8
'theory of ironic processes of mental control' 150
theory of planned behaviour (TPB) 30–2
    components 30–1
    and concept of ambivalence 36
    condom use 185–6
    criticisms of 32, 34, 35–6
    eating 137
    exercise 168, 169–70
    screening uptake 203
    smoking 110
    support for 31–2
    using 31, 40–1, 42
theory of reasoned action (TRA) 30, 34, 35–6, 40–1
    contraceptive use 179, 185–6
    eating 137
theory–data relationship 407
theory-based interventions 39–41
threat appraisal 26, 33
three-process model of pain perception 280

three-stage theory of contraceptive use (Lindemann) 177–8
transactional stress model 225–7
treatment
    beliefs and adherence 68, 70
    biomedical model 2
    characteristics and placebo mechanism 296
    health psychology perspectives 4
tumour growth 247, 251; *see also* cancer
turmoil stage, response to miscarriage 367
twin studies, causes of obesity 338
type A personality 262–3, 358, 359
type C coping style 318, 319, 324

U

uncontrollable stress events 227
undereating 145–6
unemployment 260, 261–2
unrealistic optimism 20, 23

V

variability 245–6, 272–3, 274, 275
    in health professionals 82–7, 88
variables and interrelationships 405–6

W

waist circumference 334
weight concern models of eating behaviour 140–55
weight loss 42, 152, 350, 351–2
well-being, benefits of exercise 162–3
whole-person approach to cancer interventions 326
women; *see also specific health issues*
    body dissatisfaction 141–3, 144–5
    control and overeating 151–2
    employment issues 253, 266, *267*, 382–3, 387
    life course perspective, health definition 48
    research problems *376*, 383
    smoking *55–6*, 108
        and dieting 123, 124
Women's Risk and AIDS Project (WRAP) 188–91
work, *see* employment
World Health Organization (WHO) 129, 384
    consequences of disease *356–7*
    definition of health 47
    definition of quality of life 395
wound healing 247, 250, 251
writing, emotional expression through 249–50
written information 79

Y

'yo-yo' dieting 347, 348

ESSENTIAL READINGS IN HEALTH PSYCHOLOGY

Clare Lee

This book examines key papers for students of health psychology and follows the structure of the same author's Health Psychology: A Textbook, which has made a major contribution to the teaching and study of this rapidly expanding discipline. Each chapter is introduced by a brief overview and reviews classic and contemporary papers which have been chosen either for their theoretical importance or as good empirical indicators of a model. Chapters include analysis of:

- The social context of health
- Behaviour and health
- Health across the lifespan

The examples use a range of methodologies – both qualitative and quantitative – with the latter including experimental and cross-sectional studies and systematic reviews.

Essential Readings in Health Psychology is interdisciplinary, drawing from a range of fields including psychology, medicine, health promotion and public health. It provides key reading for upper level and postgraduate students of psychology, nursing, medicine and related health disciplines. Professionals and researchers working in health psychology, health promotion and related medical areas will also find the book of interest.

Contents
Introduction and overview – Choosing the papers – The structure of this book – How to use this book – Section 1: The context of health psychology – Section 2: Health behaviours – Theoretical debates – Explaining behaviour – Changing behaviour – Section 3: Health care – Communication – Illness cognitions – Section 4: Stress and health – Section 5: Chronic illness – Index.

2007   400pp
978-0-335-21138-8 (Paperback)   978-0-335-21139-5 (Hardback)

INTRODUCING PSYCHOLOGY THROUGH RESEARCH

Amanda Albon

- What is psychology?
- What constitutes psychological research?
- How is psychological research reported?

This student-friendly textbook answers all these questions by clearly outlining the subject matter and research methods used in psychology for those who are new to the subject. A brief overview of the history of psychology is followed by chapters covering the core research areas defined by the British Psychological Society:

- Cognitive psychology
- Social psychology
- Developmental psychology
- Biological psychology
- Individual differences
- Clinical psychology

Each chapter provides an overview of a major sub-discipline in psychology and introduces the key concepts in that area of research. For each topic, a summary of an original research paper is presented along with a running commentary which explains and evaluates the methods used.

In order to help students, the book provides boxes, tables and glossaries of useful terms. There is also a helpful overview of the ethics of psychological research, as well as how the study of psychology might develop into a career.

Introducing Psychology Through Research is key reading for first year undergraduates in psychology, those taking an elective module in psychology and those studying psychology at AS or A2 Level and considering whether to study psychology at university.

Contents

Preface – List of tables – List of text boxes – Acknowledgements – Introduction – Part one: Introducing psychology – Introducing psychology – The method behind the psychology – How psychological research is reported – Part two: The core areas and research papers – Cognitive psychology – Social psychology – Developmental psychology – Biological psychology – Individual differences – Clinical psychology – Part three: Reviewing psychology – The ethics of psychology research – Conclusion – Glossary – References – Index.

200pp
978-0-335-22134-9 (Paperback)   978-0-335-22135-6 (Hardback)

ABNORMAL AND CLINICAL PSYCHOLOGY
An Introductory Textbook

SECOND EDITION

Paul Bennett

- What are the causes of mental health problems?
- What are the best treatments for mental health problems?
- How do the experiences of people with mental health problems compare with the academic models of disorders?

Building on the success of the first edition, this textbook has been extensively updated to include the latest research and therapeutic approaches as well as developments in clinical practice.

This book now contains:

- Expanded coverage of the aetiology of conditions
- Assessment of the DSM-IV diagnostic criteria
- Analysis of cross-cultural issues
- Case studies that include patient perspectives
- A new chapter on somatoform disorders
- Improved pedagogy such as research boxes and thinking about features that encourage readers to think critically about what they are learning

The book maintains the structure of the first edition with two main sections: the first introduces and critically evaluates the conceptual models of mental health problems and their treatment; the second contains in-depth analyses of a variety of disorders such as schizophrenia, trauma-related conditions and addictions. In the second section, chapters are now restructured to give a comprehensive aetiology of the disorder as well as analysis of treatments for the condition. Each disorder is viewed from psychological, social, and biological perspectives and different intervention types are investigated.

Abnormal and Clinical Psychology provides the most comprehensive European alternative to the long-established US texts for undergraduates in this field.

Contents

Illustrations – Acknowledgements – PART I Background and methods – Introduction – The psychological perspective – Biological explanations and treatments – Beyond the individual – PART II Specific issues – Somatoform disorders – Schizophrenia – Anxiety disorders – Mood disorders – Trauma-related conditions – Sexual disorders – Personality disorders – Eating disorders – Developmental disorders – Neurological disorders – Addictions – Glossary – References – Index.

528pp
978-0-335-21943-8 (Paperback)

HEALTH COMMUNICATION
Theory and Practice

Dianne Berry

- Why is effective communication important in health, and what does this involve?
- What issues arise when communicating with particular populations, or in difficult circumstances?
- How can the communication skills of health professionals be improved?

Effective health communication is now recognised to be a critical aspect of healthcare at both the individual and wider public level. Good communication is associated with positive health outcomes, whereas poor communication is associated with a number of negative outcomes. This book assesses current research and practice in the area and provides some practical guidance for those involved in communicating health information. It draws on material from several disciplines, including health, medicine, psychology, sociology, linguistics, pharmacy, statistics, and business and management.

The book examines:

- The importance of effective communication in health
- Basic concepts and processes in communication
- Communication theories and models
- Communicating with particular groups and in difficult circumstances
- Ethical issues
- Communicating with the wider public and health promotion
- Communication skills training

Health Communication is key reading for students and researchers who need to understand the factors that contribute to effective communication in health, as well as for health professionals who need to communicate effectively with patients and others. It provides a thorough and up to date, evidence-based overview of this important topic, examining the theoretical and practical aspects of health communication for those whose work involves communication with patients, relatives and other carers.

Contents
Preface – Introduction to health communication – Basic forms of communication – Underlying theories and models – Communication between patients and health professionals – Communicating with particular populations in healthcare – Communication of difficult information and in difficult circumstances – Health promotion and communicating with the wider public – Communication skills training – References – Index.

152pp
978-0-335-21870-7 (Paperback)   978-0-335-21871-4 (Hardback)